Peatland Restoration and Ecosystem
Science, Policy and Practice

Peatlands provide globally important ecosyste: through climate and water regulation or biodi conservation. While covering only 0.4 per cent of the Earth's surface, degrading peatlands are responsible for nearly a quarter of carbon emissions from the land-use sector. Bringing together world-class experts from science, policy and practice to highlight and debate the importance of peatlands from an ecological, social and economic perspective, this book focuses on how peatland restoration can foster climate change mitigation.

Featuring a range of global case studies, opportunities for reclamation and sustainable management are illustrated throughout against the challenges faced by conservation biologists. Written for a global audience of environmental scientists, practitioners and policy makers, as well as graduate students from natural and social sciences, this interdisciplinary book provides vital pointers towards managing peatland conservation in a changing environment.

ALETTA BONN is Professor of Ecosystem Services at the Friedrich-Schiller-University Jena and Head of the Department of Ecosystem Services at the Helmholtz Centre for Environmental Research (UFZ) within the German Centre for Integrative Biodiversity Research (iDiv) Halle-Jena-Leipzig.

TIM ALLOTT is Professor of Physical Geography and Head of the School of Environment, Education and Development at the University of Manchester.

MARTIN EVANS is Professor of Geomorphology and Head of the Department of Geography in the School of Environment, Education and Development at the University of Manchester.

HANS JOOSTEN is Professor of Peatland Studies and Palaeoecology at Ernst Moritz Arndt University Greifswald, Partner in the Greifswald Mire Centre.

ROB STONEMAN is Chief Executive of the Yorkshire Wildlife Trust.

Ecological Reviews

SERIES EDITOR
Phillip Warren *University of Sheffield*, UK

SERIES EDITORIAL BOARD
Mark Bradford *Yale University, USA*
David Burslem *University of Aberdeen, UK*
Alan Gray *CEH Wallingford, UK*
Catherine Hill *British Ecological Society, UK*
Sue Hartley *University of York, UK*
Mark Hunter *University of Michigan, USA*
Hefin Jones *Cardiff University, UK*
Heikki Setala *University of Helsinki, Finland*

Ecological Reviews publishes books at the cutting edge of modern ecology, providing a forum for volumes that discuss topics that are focal points of current activity and likely long-term importance to the progress of the field. The series is an invaluable source of ideas and inspiration for ecologists at all levels from graduate students to more-established researchers and professionals. The series has been developed jointly by the British Ecological Society and Cambridge University Press and encompasses the Society's Symposia as appropriate.

Biotic Interactions in the Tropics: Their Role in the Maintenance of Species Diversity
Edited by David F. R. P. Burslem, Michelle A. Pinard and Sue E. Hartley

Biological Diversity and Function in Soils
Edited by Richard Bardgett, Michael Usher and David Hopkins

Island Colonization: The Origin and Development of Island Communities
By Ian Thornton
Edited by Tim New

Scaling Biodiversity
Edited by David Storch, Pablo Margnet and James Brown

Body Size: The Structure and Function of Aquatic Ecosystems
Edited by Alan G. Hildrew, David G. Raffaelli and Ronni Edmonds-Brown

Speciation and Patterns of Diversity
Edited by Roger Butlin, Jon Bridle and Dolph Schluter

Ecology of Industrial Pollution
Edited by Lesley C. Batty and Kevin B. Hallberg

Ecosystem Ecology: A New Synthesis
Edited by David G. Raffaelli and Christopher L. J. Frid

Urban Ecology
Edited by Kevin J. Gaston

The Ecology of Plant Secondary Metabolites: From Genes to Global Processes
Edited by Glenn R. Iason, Marcel Dicke and Susan E. Hartley

Birds and Habitat: Relationships in Changing Landscapes
Edited by Robert J. Fuller

Trait-Mediated Indirect Interactions: Ecological and Evolutionary Perspectives
Edited by Takayuki Ohgushi, Oswald Schmitz and Robert D. Holt

Forests and Global Change
Edited by David A. Coomes, David F. R. P. Burslem and William D. Simonson

Trophic Ecology: Bottom-Up and Top-Down Interactions Across Aquatic and Terrestrial Systems
Edited by Torrance C. Hanley and Kimberly J. La Pierre

Conflicts in Conservation: Navigating Towards Solutions
Edited by Stephen M. Redpath, R. J Gutiérrez, Kevin A. Wood and Juliette C. Young

Peatland Restoration and Ecosystem Services
Science, Policy and Practice

Edited by

ALETTA BONN
Helmholtz Centre for Environmental Research (UFZ) | Friedrich-Schiller-University Jena | German Centre for Integrative Biodiversity Research (iDiv) Halle-Jena-Leipzig, Germany | IUCN UK Peatland Programme, UK

TIM ALLOTT
University of Manchester, UK

MARTIN EVANS
University of Manchester, UK

HANS JOOSTEN
Ernst Moritz Arndt University of Greifswald, Greifswald Mire Centre, Germany

ROB STONEMAN
Yorkshire Wildlife Trust and IUCN UK Peatland Programme, UK

CAMBRIDGE
UNIVERSITY PRESS

University Printing House, Cambridge CB2 8BS, United Kingdom

Cambridge University Press is part of the University of Cambridge.

It furthers the University's mission by disseminating knowledge in the pursuit of education, learning and research at the highest international levels of excellence.

www.cambridge.org
Information on this title: www.cambridge.org/9781107025189

© British Ecological Society 2016

This publication is in copyright. Subject to statutory exception and to the provisions of relevant collective licensing agreements, no reproduction of any part may take place without the written permission of Cambridge University Press.

First published 2016

Printed in the United Kingdom by TJ International Ltd. Padstow Cornwall

A catalogue record for this publication is available from the British Library

Library of Congress Cataloguing in Publication Data
Names: Bonn, Aletta, editor. | British Ecological Society.
Title: Peatland restoration and ecosystem services : science, policy, and practice / edited by Aletta Bonn, Helmholtz Centre for Environmental Research (UFZ) ... [and four others].
Description: Cambridge : Cambridge University Press, 2016. | Series: Ecological reviews | "British Ecological Society" – T.p. verso. | Includes bibliographical references and index.
Identifiers: LCCN 2015041668| ISBN 9781107025189 (hardback : alk. paper) | ISBN 9781107619708 (pbk. : alk. paper)
Subjects: LCSH: Peatland conservation. | Peatland ecology. | Peat bog ecology. | Biotic communities.
Classification: LCC QH75. P435 2016 | DDC 333.91/8–dc23
LC record available at http://lccn.loc.gov/2015041668

ISBN 978-1-107-02518-9 Hardback
ISBN 978-1-107-61970-8 Paperback

Cambridge University Press has no responsibility for the persistence or accuracy of URLs for external or third-party internet websites referred to in this publication, and does not guarantee that any content on such websites is, or will remain, accurate or appropriate.

Contents

List of contributors		page xi
Foreword by Julia Marton-Lefèvre		xix
Acknowledgements		xxi

1. Peatland restoration and ecosystem services: an introduction   1
   Aletta Bonn, Tim Allott, Martin Evans, Hans Joosten and Rob Stoneman

   Part I Peatland ecosystems services   17

2. Peatlands across the globe   19
   Hans Joosten
3. Peatland biodiversity and its restoration   44
   Tatiana Minayeva, Olivia Bragg and Andrey Sirin
4. The role of peatlands in climate regulation   63
   Hans Joosten, Andrey Sirin, John Couwenberg, Jukka Laine and Pete Smith
5. Peatland restoration and hydrology   77
   Jonathan Price, Chris Evans, Martin Evans, Tim Allott and Emma Shuttleworth
6. Peatlands as knowledge archives   95
   Benjamin Gearey and Ralph Fyfe
7. Peatlands and cultural ecosystem services   114
   Kerry A. Waylen, Robert van de Noort and Kirsty L. Blackstock
8. Peatlands and climate change   129
   Angela V. Gallego-Sala, Robert K. Booth, Dan J. Charman, I. Colin Prentice and Zicheng Yu

Part II Perspectives on peatland restoration — 151

9. Blanket mire restoration and its impact on ecosystem services — 153
   Tim Thom, Martin Evans, Chris Evans and Tim Allott
10. Restoration of temperate fens: matching strategies with site potential — 170
    Wiktor Kotowski, Michael Acreman, Ab Grootjans, Agata Klimkowska, Holger Rößling and Bryan Wheeler
11. A conceptual framework for ecosystem restoration applied to industrial peatlands — 192
    Martha D. Graf and Line Rochefort
12. Afforested and forestry-drained peatland restoration — 213
    Russell Anderson, Harri Vasander, Neville Geddes, Anna Laine, Anne Tolvanen, Aileen O'Sullivan and Kaisu Aapala
13. Restoration of high-altitude peatlands on the Ruoergai Plateau (Northeastern Tibetan Plateau, China) — 234
    Xiaohong Zhang, Martin Schumann, Yongheng Gao, J. Marc Foggin, Shengzhong Wang and Hans Joosten
14. Ecosystem services, degradation and restoration of peat swamps in the South East Asian tropics — 253
    René Dommain, Ingo Dittrich, Wim Giesen, Hans Joosten, Dipa Satriadi Rais, Marcel Silvius and Iwan Tri Cahyo Wibisono

Part III Socio-economic and political solutions to managing natural capital and peatland ecosystem services — 289

15. International carbon policies as a new driver for peatland restoration — 291
    Hans Joosten, John Couwenberg and Moritz von Unger
16. Valuing peatland ecosystem services — 314
    Sabine Wichmann, Luke Brander, Achim Schäfer, Marije Schaafsma, Pieter van Beukering, Dugald Tinch and Aletta Bonn
17. Paludiculture: sustainable productive use of wet and rewetted peatlands — 339
    Hans Joosten, Greta Gaudig, Franziska Tanneberger, Sabine Wichmann and Wendelin Wichtmann

18 Peatland conservation at the science–practice
   interface   358
   Joseph Holden, Aletta Bonn, Mark Reed, Sarah
   Buckmaster, Jonathan Walker, Martin Evans
   and Fred Worrall
19 Policy drivers for peatland conservation   375
   Rob Stoneman, Clifton Bain, David Locky, Nick
   Mawdsley, Michael McLaughlan, Shashi Kumaran-Prentice,
   Mark Reed and Vicki Swales
20 Peatland restoration and ecosystem services:
   nature-based solutions for societal goals   402
   Aletta Bonn, Tim Allott, Martin Evans, Hans Joosten
   and Rob Stoneman

References   418
Index   484

Contributors

KAISU AAPALA
Finnish Environment Institute
Helsinki
Finland
kaisu.aapala@ymparisto.fi

MICHAEL ACREMAN
Centre for Ecology and Hydrology
Wallingford
Oxfordshire
UK
man@ceh.ac.uk

TIM ALLOTT
Geography
The University of Manchester
Manchester
UK
tim.allott@manchester.ac.uk

RUSSELL ANDERSON
Forest Research
Northern Research Station
Roslin
Midlothian
UK
russell.anderson@forestry.gsi.gov.uk

CLIFTON BAIN
IUCN UK Peatland Programme
Edinburgh
UK
cbain@iucn.org.uk

KIRSTY L. BLACKSTOCK
Social, Economic and Geographical
Sciences Group
The James Hutton Institute
Craigiebuckler
Aberdeen
UK
kirsty.blackstock@hutton.ac.uk

ALETTA BONN
Helmholtz Center for
Environmental Research (UFZ)
Friedrich-Schiller-University Jena
German Centre for Integrative
Biodiversity Research (iDiv)
Halle-Jena-Leipzig
and
IUCN UK Peatland Programme
Germany
aletta.bonn@idiv.de

ROBERT K. BOOTH
Department of Earth and
Environmental Sciences
Lehigh University
Bethlehem
USA
rkb205@lehigh.edu

LIST OF CONTRIBUTORS

OLIVIA BRAGG
Geography
University of Dundee
UK
o.m.bragg@dundee.ac.uk

LUKE BRANDER
Institute for Environmental Studies
VU Amsterdam
The Netherlands
and
Division of Environment
Hong Kong University of Science and Technology
Hong Kong
lukebrander@gmail.com

SARAH BUCKMASTER
Aberdeen Centre for Environmental Sustainability
University of Aberdeen
Aberdeen
UK
s.buckmaster.08@aberdeen.ac.uk

DAN CHARMAN
Geography Department
College of Life and Environmental Sciences
University of Exeter
Exeter
UK
d.j.charman@exeter.ac.uk

JOHN COUWENBERG
Institute of Botany and Landscape Ecology
Ernst Moritz Arndt University of Greifswald, Partner in the Greifswald Mire Centre
Germany
couw@gmx.net

INGO DITTRICH
Dr. Dittrich and Partner
Hydro-Consult GmbH
Germany
dittrich@hydro-consult.de

RENÉ DOMMAIN
Institute of Botany and Landscape Ecology
Ernst Moritz Arndt University of Greifswald, Partner in the Greifswald Mire Centre
Germany
rene.dommain@gmx.de

CHRIS EVANS
Centre for Ecology and Hydrology
Environment Centre Wales
Bangor
UK
cev@ceh.ac.uk

MARTIN EVANS
Geography
The University of Manchester
Manchester
UK
martin.evans@manchester.ac.uk

J. MARC FOGGIN
Plateau Perspectives Canada
Surrey, British Columbia, Canada
and
Mountain Societies Research Institute (MSRI)
University of Central Asia
Bishkek
Kyrgyz Republic
j.m.foggin@kent.ac.uk

RALPH FYFE
Department of Geographical
Sciences
University of Plymouth
Plymouth
UK
ralph.fyfe@plymouth.ac.uk

ANGELA V. GALLEGO-SALA
College of Life and Environmental
Science
Department of Geography
University of Exeter
Exeter
UK
a.gallego-sala@exeter.ac.uk

YONGHENG GAO
Institute of Mountain Hazards and
Environment
Chinese Academy of Sciences
Chengdu
China
yhgao@imde.ac.cn

GRETA GAUDIG
Institute of Botany and Landscape
Ecology
Ernst Moritz Arndt University
of Greifswald, Partner in the
Greifswald Mire Centre
Germany
gaudig@uni-greifswald.de

BENJAMIN GEAREY
Department of Archaeology
University College Cork
Ireland
b.gearey@ucc.ie

NEVILLE GEDDES
Forestry Commission
North East England Forest District,
Eals Burn
UK
neville.geddes@forestry.gsi.gov.uk

WIM GIESEN
Euroconsult/BMB Mott MacDonald
The Netherlands
wim.giesen@mottmac.nl

MARTHA D. GRAF
Leibniz Universität Hannover
Institute for Environmental
Planning
Germany
graf@umwelt.uni-hannover.de

AB GROOTJANS
Center for Energy and
Environmental Studies
University of Groningen
The Netherlands
a.p.grootjans@rug.nl

JOSEPH HOLDEN
School of Geography
University of Leeds
UK
j.holden@leeds.ac.uk

HANS JOOSTEN
Institute of Botany and Landscape
Ecology
Ernst Moritz Arndt University
of Greifswald, Partner in the
Greifswald Mire Centre
Germany
joosten@uni-greifswald.de

AGATA KLIMKOWSKA
Eco-Recover
Ecosystem Restoration Advice
The Netherlands
agataklimkowskajobse@gmail.com

WIKTOR KOTOWSKI
Department of Plant Ecology and
Environmental Conservation
Institute of Botany, Faculty of
Biology
University of Warsaw
Centre of Biological and Chemical
Research
Poland
w.kotowski@uw.edu.pl

SHASHI KUMARAN-PRENTICE
Charles Darwin University
Darwin
Australia
shashi.kumaran@gmail.com

ANNA LAINE
Department of Forest Sciences
University of Helsinki
Finland
anna.m.laine@helsinki.fi

JUKKA LAINE
The Finnish Forest Research
Institute (METLA)
Finland
jukka.laine@metla.fi

DAVID LOCKY
MacEwan University
Department of Biological Sciences
Canada
lockyd@macewan.ca

NICK MAWDSLEY
Euroconsult Mott MacDonald
The Netherlands
nm.emrp@gmail.com

MICHAEL MCLAUGHLAN
Forest Service
Saskatchewan Ministry of
Environment
Saskatchewan
Canada
michael.mcLaughlan@gov.sk.ca

TATIANA MINAYEVA
Wetlands International
The Netherlands
and
Care for Ecosystems
Bonn
Germany
tatiana.minaeva@wetlands.org

AILEEN O'SULLIVAN
Coillte Teoranta
Newtownmountkennedy
Co. Wicklow
Ireland
aileen.osullivan@coillte.ie

IAIN COLIN PRENTICE
Imperial College London
Silwood Park Campus
London
UK
c.prentice@imperial.ac.uk

JONATHAN PRICE
University of Waterloo
Department of Geography
Ontario
Canada
jsprice@uwaterloo.ca

MARK REED
School of Agriculture, Food & Rural Development
Newcastle University
Newcastle upon Tyne
UK
mark.reed@newcastle.ac.uk

LINE ROCHEFORT
Département de Phytologie
Université Laval
Québec
Canada
line.rochefort@fsaa.ulaval.ca

HOLGER RÖßLING
Naturschutzfonds Brandenburg
LIFE Project 'Alkaline fens of Brandenburg'
Germany
holger.roessling@naturschutzfonds.de

DIPA SATRIADI RAIS
Wetlands International – Indonesia Programme
Indonesia
elitelongbowman77@yahoo.com

MARIJE SCHAAFSMA
Geography and Environment
Centre for Biological Sciences
University of Southampton
Southampton
UK
marije.schaafsma@geog.cam.ac.uk

ACHIM SCHÄFER
Institute for Sustainable Development of Landscapes of the Earth (DUENE e.V.),
Partner in the Greifswald Mire Centre
c/o Institute of Botany and Landscape Ecology
Germany
schaefea@uni-greifswald.de

MARTIN SCHUMANN
Institute of Botany and Landscape Ecology
Ernst Moritz Arndt University of Greifswald, Partner in the Greifswald Mire Centre
Germany
martinschumann@hotmail.com

EMMA SHUTTLEWORTH
Geography
The University of Manchester
UK
emma.shuttleworth@postgrad.manchester.ac.uk

MARCEL SILVIUS
Wetlands International
The Netherlands
marcel.silvius@wetlands.org

ANDREY SIRIN
Institute of Forest Science
Russian Academy of Sciences
Russia
sirin@ilan.ras.ru

PETE SMITH
Institute of Biological and Environmental Sciences
School of Biological Sciences
University of Aberdeen
UK
pete.smith@abdn.ac.uk

LIST OF CONTRIBUTORS

ROB STONEMAN
Yorkshire Wildlife Trust
UK
rob.stoneman@ywt.org.uk

VICKI SWALES
Royal Society for the Protection of Birds (RSPB)
Edinburgh
UK
vicki.swales@rspb.org.uk

FRANZISKA TANNEBERGER
Institute of Botany and Landscape Ecology
Ernst Moritz Arndt University of Greifswald
and Michael Succow Foundation, Partners in the Greifswald Mire Centre
Germany
tanne@uni-greifswald.de

TIM THOM
Yorkshire Wildlife Trust
York
UK
tim.thom@ywt.org.uk

DUGALD TINCH
University of Stirling
Stirling
UK
dugald.tinch@stir.ac.uk

ANNE TOLVANEN
Natural Resources Institute Finland
and
Department of Biology of the University of Oulu
Finland
anne.tolvanen@metla.fi

IWAN TRI CAHYO WIBISONO
Wetlands International – Indonesia Programme
Indonesia
wibisono_yoyok@wetlands.or.id

PIETER VAN BEUKERING
Institute for Environmental Studies
VU University Amsterdam
The Netherlands
pieter.van.beukering@vu.nl

ROBERT VAN DE NOORT
Vice-Chancellor's Office
University of Reading
UK
r.vandenoort@reading.ac.uk

HARRI VASANDER
Department of Forest Sciences
University of Helsinki
Finland
harri.vasander@helsinki.fi

MORITZ VON UNGER
Atlas Environmental Law Advisory
Brussels
Belgium
m.vonunger@atlasela.com

JONATHAN WALKER
The Moors for the Future Partnership
Peak District National Park Authority
The Moorland Centre
UK
jonathan.walker@peakdistrict.gov.uk

SHENGZHONG WANG
Institute for Peat and Mire Research
Northeast Normal University
China
szwang@nenu.edu.cn

KERRY A. WAYLEN
Social, Economic and Geographical Sciences Group
The James Hutton Institute
Aberdeen
UK
kerry.waylen@hutton.ac.uk

BRYAN WHEELER
Department of Animal and Plant Sciences
University of Sheffield
UK
b.d.wheeler@sheffield.ac.uk

SABINE WICHMANN
Institute of Botany and Landscape Ecology
Ernst Moritz Arndt University of Greifswald, Partner in the Greifswald Mire Centre
Germany
wichmann@uni-greifswald.de

WENDELIN WICHTMANN
Michael Succow Foundation
Partner in the Greifswald Mire Centre
Germany
wendelin.wichtmann@succow-stiftung.de

FRED WORRALL
Department of Earth Sciences
Durham University
Science Labs
UK
fred.worrall@durham.ac.uk

ZICHENG YU
Department of Earth and Environmental Sciences
Lehigh University
Bethlehem
USA
ziy2@lehigh.edu

XIAOHONG ZHANG
Wetlands International China Office
Beijing
People's Republic of China
zxh@wetwonder.org

Co-authors contributing to boxes:

RICHARD GROSSHANS
International Institute for Sustainable Development (IISD)
Canada
rgrosshans@iisd.ca

RENÉ KRAWCZYNSKI
Chair of General Ecology
Brandenburg University of Technology
Germany
rene.krawczynski@tu-cottbus.de

JAROSŁAW KROGULEC
OTOP BirdLife Poland
Poland
jaroslaw.krogulec@oto.org.pl

ULADZIMIR MALASHEVICH
APB BirdLife Belarus
Belarus
malashevich@ptushki.org

CHRISTIAN SCHRÖDER
Institute of Botany and Landscape Ecology
Ernst Moritz Arndt University of Greifswald, Partner in the Greifswald Mire Centre
Germany
christian.schroeder@uni-greifswald.de

ALIONA SHUSHKOVA
APB BirdLife Belarus
Belarus
sviatsviat@gmail.com

SVIATASLAU VALASIUK
APB BirdLife Belarus
Belarus
sviatsviat@gmail.com

Foreword
Julia Marton-Lefèvre

High on the Andean watershed, a cloud born in the Amazon billows up and over the watershed divide dumping water onto lawns of bright green *Sphagnum* moss, dotted with cushion plants and the tall stems of *Espeletia* plants. These peatlands store huge volumes of water that is filtered through to deep aquifers that daily supply water to the seasonally dry Andean cities of Quito, Bogota, Lima and Medelin. The *paramo* grasslands and wetlands are highly valued for their life-giving waters.

On the moors above Manchester, also sustained by water from upland peatlands, it is another cloudy scene. But this is a Sunday and the moors are full of walkers, enjoying the open scenery far from urban squeeze in the sprawling towns and cities now far below them.

On the other side of the globe, the 'man of the forest' – orang-utan – sits towards the top of a thin tree characteristic of this part of the peat swamp forest that stretches many tens of kilometres between the main rivers. His wide cheek flaps and the wisdom in his eyes shows that this animal is old. He shifts his weight to bend the stem of the tree down to a fruit-laden tree across the railway line, seemingly oblivious to the *orang putihs* – 'white men' – watching from the logging line that might spell his end.

Far away in Northern Canada, the carpet of *Sphagnum* dotted with shrubs and the odd tree, is unremarkable – part of a vast expanse of peatland stretching over many millions of square kilometres. The *Sphagnum* moss grows slowly in the warmth of the short summer absorbing minute quantities of carbon dioxide with an even tinier amount left in the waterlogged soil as undecayed plant matter – peat. But over time, this vast peat bog absorbs huge quantities of carbon dioxide from the atmosphere: a natural carbon capture and sequestration system that costs society nothing to build.

In 1982, an earth dam within the United States Rocky Mountain National Park collapsed, resulting in the sudden release of nearly one million cubic metres of water. A wall of water up to 10 m in height swept downstream, entering Fall River at Horseshoe Park. Fortunately, in this area, wetlands adjacent to the river – including dense stands of reed and willow – slowed the flood wave, which spread out across the wide floodplain. The disaster claimed four lives but without the Horseshoe Park wetlands the catastrophe would have been even worse.

All across the world, 365 days a year, night and day, peatlands perform manifestly important services to society. These ecosystem services are ostensibly free and certainly difficult to fully understand or monetise, until of course they are removed. Only then is the true value of these services understood – often with calamitous consequences.

If only all of Sumatra's coastal peatlands had remained intact to absorb the worst of the December 2004 tsunami, fewer lives would have been lost, both during the tsunami and after, when the peatlands provided a valuable source of freshwater to those ravaged communities. If South East Asian bogs had been exploited in a way that retained the natural vegetation, instead of making way for oil palm plantations, South East Asia would have avoided the several billion dollars of damage caused by peatland burning and perhaps one of the great apes would not now be on the verge of extinction. If upland peatlands in England were still pristine and had not been severely grazed, burnt and eroded, then water treatment costs would be minimised and money spent to treat water could be spent on reducing customer bills. If so many of the world's peatlands were not damaged through agriculture, logging and extraction, they would act as a natural carbon capture system rather than releasing carbon into the atmosphere, thus exacerbating catastrophic climate change. If only…

Yet, as this book shows, it is far from too late. By understanding the true value of peatlands as providers of essential ecosystem services and developing the policies, research and practice to conserve our remaining pristine peatlands and to restore those that have suffered damage, we can safeguard and secure those essential services for all of society.

Julia Marton-Lefèvre
Director General (2007–2014)
International Union for Conservation of Nature (IUCN)

Acknowledgements

This volume has been a very rewarding and fruitful collaboration of all authors involved. The transdisciplinary approach to this book brought together 80 experts from the natural and social sciences as well as from peatland policy and restoration practice from across 14 countries and 65 organisations. This synthesis has been an inspiring and productive journey. We sincerely thank all contributors for joining the stimulating discussion process and hope this dialogue will continue. The reviewers, both scientists and practitioners, were instrumental in constructive enhancement of all chapters of this book and we very much appreciate their contributions. We are also indebted to all practitioners and policy advisers across the globe, who have contributed to the case studies and research in this volume. Without their efforts and active collaboration this synthesis would not have been possible.

We are especially grateful to Catherine Hill from the British Ecological Society publishing team and to our editors Dominic Lewis, Ilaria Tassistro and Eleri Pipien from Cambridge University Press for their helpful advice and very encouraging guidance.

The project developed out of a productive special symposium by the British Ecological Society and the International Union for the Conservation of Nature (IUCN) UK Peatland Programme in June 2012 under the title 'Investing in Peatlands – Demonstrating Success', organised by some of the editors and authors of this volume. The IUCN UK Peatland Programme fosters a partnership embracing representatives of practitioners, conservation organisations and government authorities dedicated to strong science, sound policy and effective peatland restoration practice (www.iucn-uk-peatlandprogramme.org).

The editors have used their best endeavours to ensure URLs provided for external websites are correct and active at the time of going to press. However, the publisher has no responsibility for websites and cannot guarantee that contents will remain live or appropriate.

A special thanks goes to Karolin Tischer as editorial assistant and to Nick Scarle for redrawing some of the figures.

CHAPTER ONE

Peatland restoration and ecosystem services: an introduction

ALETTA BONN
Helmholtz Centre for Environmental Research (UFZ) | Friedrich-Schiller-University Jena | German Centre for Integrative Biodiversity Research (iDiv) Halle-Jena-Leipzig | IUCN UK Peatland Programme, UK

TIM ALLOTT
The University of Manchester, UK

MARTIN EVANS
The University of Manchester, UK

HANS JOOSTEN
Institute of Botany and Landscape Ecology, Ernst Moritz Arndt University of Greifswald, Germany

ROB STONEMAN
Yorkshire Wildlife Trust, UK

1.1 Setting the scene

In September 1997, the airports of Singapore and Kuala Lumpur shut down for several days. Fires from drained peatlands in Indonesia, over 1000 km away, were emitting vast clouds of smoke causing haze and poor visibility across large parts of South East Asia in the extremely dry El Niño year. Schools and businesses had to close, and people were admitted to hospitals with acute breathing problems. The amount of CO_2 emitted from these fires was equivalent to 13–40% of annual global emissions from fossil fuels (Page *et al.* 2002). Economic losses due to the 1997–1998 wildfires exceeded several billion US dollars (ADB 1999).

In the hot August of 2010, people in Moscow were advised to stay at home, keep their windows closed and wear gauze masks to avoid inhaling ash particles when walking on the streets. Again the cause was fires, this time raging across nearly 2000 km^2 of degraded peatlands in Russia. Carbon

Peatland Restoration and Ecosystem Services: Science, Policy and Practice, eds. A. Bonn, T. Allott, M. Evans, H. Joosten and R. Stoneman. Published by Cambridge University Press. © British Ecological Society 2016.

monoxide levels in the capital reached six times the maximum acceptable levels and death rates doubled due to heat and smog (Barriopedro et al. 2011).

These fires, resulting from peatland drainage and degradation that made them vulnerable to fire, dramatically highlight the huge liability that peatlands pose once degraded, especially in a changing climate. In sharp contrast, there is now wide recognition of the importance to human well-being of ecosystem services delivered by the peatland environment, not least the wildlife that underpins those ecosystem services. While peatlands cover not even 3% of the world's surface, they hold two times more carbon than the entire global forest biomass pool, and represent more than 30% of the total global soil carbon store (see Chapter 4). As long-term carbon sinks, they provide crucial global climate-regulating services. If not safeguarded, however, the release of this carbon could further exacerbate climate change.

The range of peatland ecosystem services is far greater than simply their role in the carbon cycle. Pivotal peatland ecosystem services further include, for example, the provision of high-quality drinking water derived from peatland catchments. Peatlands also play a role in flood-water regulation, especially in lowland or coastal settings. Importantly, peatlands constitute old and rich palaeoecological knowledge archives, as their waterlogged soils preserve both natural (pollen, macrofossils) and anthropogenic (artefacts) organic materials, and the study of peat cores has greatly contributed to our understanding of global climate change. Peatlands are often open and wild landscapes and provide a sense of place and socio-cultural connection for communities as well as important breathing spaces for millions of people to enjoy. Globally, peatlands represent some of the largest unfragmented (semi-) natural habitats, hosting nationally and internationally important biodiversity. Peatlands therefore form a globally and nationally important natural capital.

1.2 Why publish this volume now?

The current extent and rate of peatland degradation and the resulting loss of ecosystem services severely threaten the livelihoods of people and erode options to mitigate and adapt to a changing climate. With 2 Gt CO_2 emissions per year, degraded peatlands are already responsible for nearly one-quarter of the carbon emissions from the land-use sector. Globally, emissions from drained peatland have increased more than 25% since 1990, especially because of peatland drainage in the tropics (Joosten 2009c).

The scale and economic value of peatland ecosystem services are significant, yet often undervalued or taken for granted. Despite these manifest services, across the world peatlands have been and continue to be seen as worthless wastelands. Activities to 'develop' peatlands for exploitation of resources, such as livestock grazing, timber collection, plantations for pulp wood, oil palm and other crops, and peat extraction for fuel and horticultural growing media, led to widespread drainage. In Europe, the majority of peatlands have already been subject to degradation over the last century, with enhanced drainage for agricultural intensification and forestry from the 1940s onwards. In many countries, such as UK and Germany, less than 20% of peatlands remain in near-natural condition (Joosten and Clarke 2002; Bain *et al.* 2011; JNCC 2011; Bonn *et al.* 2015). Peatlands are modified or destroyed through extraction or conversion to other land uses, or are subject to severe erosion due to external pressures on the vegetation. Many peatland species are showing marked population declines. In many European countries, most socio-economic drivers for exploitation have ceased, while there are still pressures from the horticultural use of peat, peat-fired power stations and emerging energy-related developments, such as biofuel maize production, hydro-electricity or windfarm developments on peatlands. Nevertheless, 80% of the CO_2 emissions from agricultural land use in Europe are derived from peatlands (Joosten, Tapio-Biström and Tol 2012).

In other parts of the world, peatland destruction has only started in recent decades. Especially in the tropics, loss of peatlands is now taking place at an unprecedented scale. In South East Asia, peat swamps are rapidly deforested to make room for short-lived oil palm and pulp wood plantations. Estimates of loss exceed 60% of the original resource and the extent of pristine peat swamp forest in western Indonesia (Kalimantan and Sumatra) has already become negligible (Dommain, Couwenberg and Joosten 2011; see also Chapter 14). The degradation is leading to increased incidences of severe fires, flooding and threats affecting health and livelihoods of communities. In the boreal region in North America, Canada is experiencing rapid peatland destruction for tar sand extraction with extensive loss of habitat.

In the majority of cases, exploitation of peatlands for agricultural and forestry produce as well as for fuel (provisioning services, see below) is a major driver of change (Bonn *et al.* 2009) leading to dramatic impacts on the potential of peatlands for ecosystem-based climate mitigation and adaptation, water regulation, biodiversity conservation and ultimately human well-being.

1.3 Policy context

Peatland restoration and sustainable management therefore should be at the heart of high-level national and international strategic decision making to deal with climate change and the way land and water is managed. There is encouraging progress, including the renegotiation of the Kyoto Protocol and other instruments under the United Nations Framework Convention on Climate Change (UNFCCC), the Wetland (Ramsar) Convention and the Convention on Biological Diversity (CBD), the European Union (EU) Common Agricultural Policy (CAP) reform, and the implementation of the EU Water Framework Directive (WFD), which all recognise the need to conserve peatlands for their essential ecosystem services and for underpinning biodiversity.

Specifically with regard to climate change mitigation and adaptation, peatlands are of major current interest because of their importance as carbon stocks and the potential for climate change-induced changes to the carbon stored in peat. Interest in restoration of degraded peatlands is likely to increase in order to help meet stringent targets to offset greenhouse gas (GHG) emissions established by recent intergovernmental negotiations. Global climate change discussions under the Kyoto Protocol have agreed that carbon savings from rewetting drained peatlands may be used to meet emissions reduction targets, alongside those from other land use and land-use change and forestry (LULUCF) activities such as new forest planting (see Chapter 15). This is an important decision in giving global legitimacy to peatland restoration. Likewise, the 2010 Nagoya protocol (COP 10 Decision X/33) specifically recommends the restoration of degraded ecosystems and ecosystem functions in particular with regard to peatlands as major carbon stores.

Restoration of peatlands is a low hanging fruit, and among the most cost-effective options for mitigating climate change.
Achim Steiner, UN Under-Secretary General and Executive Director UN Environment Programme (UNEP, 2007)

Internationally, land management for carbon has been recognised by the Food and Agricultural Organization of the United Nations (FAO), who launched a Global Organic Soils and Peatlands Climate Change Mitigation Initiative in May 2012 to share knowledge and promote sustainable land use and restoration of organic soils, including peatlands, to increase the mitigation potential through agriculture (Joosten, Tapio-Biström and Tol 2012).

Nationally, there are a number of high-profile government initiatives for new peatland policy and practice, as well as recent country-wide peatland assessments such as the IUCN UK Commission of Inquiry on Peatlands (Bain *et al.* 2011), the BOGLAND Sustainable Management of Peatlands in Ireland report (Renou-Wilson *et al.* 2011), the peatland habitat assessment in Finland (Kaakinen *et al.* 2008) and others.

Peatland restoration can therefore play a pivotal role in fulfilling international and national obligations and safeguarding important ecosystems services for society.

1.4 Practice context

In practice, there are encouraging signs that these policy signals from the international community are translating into practical action to conserve and restore peatlands with increasing expertise to restore damaged peatlands across the world. The relevance of peatlands and peatland restoration is reflected progressively in the quantity of public and private expenditure on restoration. In Europe, major peatland restoration efforts are on the way in many countries supported by agri-environment schemes and the EU LIFE programme. Over 210 major EU LIFE projects funded by the European Commission have included peatland restoration, and, for example, over 120 peatland restoration projects have been conducted in the UK alone (www.peatlands.org.uk). After the 2010 fires, extensive peatland restoration was launched in the Moscow area of the Russian Federation. In North America, a lot of wetland restoration takes place, e.g. the multi-million-dollar restoration project of the US Everglades. Wetland restoration initiatives are generally less specifically focused on peatland restoration, except for some re-vegetation after peat extraction (see Chapter 10). In the tropics, the Association of South East Asian Nations (ASEAN) has endorsed an ASEAN Peatland Management Strategy providing the framework to guide interventions for managing the peatlands in the region (Chapter 19). Progressively, private carbon markets for peatland restoration are also being explored (Bonn *et al.* 2014; Von Unger *et al.* 2015).

Across the globe, there is increasing experience in peatland restoration for biodiversity and ecosystem services. Embracing an ecosystem service framework, new avenues are being trialled as exemplified by case studies throughout this volume through:

- planning and decision making;
- participatory conservation approaches involving stakeholders across sectors through innovative public–private partnerships;
- dealing with novel techniques and technical difficulties in peatland restoration and monitoring success;
- wise use and sustainable management of peatlands (Joosten and Clarke 2002; Quinty and Rochefort 2003).

1.5 Scientific context

The scientific study of peatlands has expanded rapidly (Charman 2002; Wieder and Vitt 2006; Rydin and Jeglum 2013), in particular in response to the increasing recognition of the role of peatland systems in global carbon cycling (e.g. Baird *et al.* 2009; Page, Rieley and Banks 2011a). Scientific research on restoration of peatlands (Box 1.1) has typically been less extensive. Despite some excellent work on approaches to restoration (Wheeler *et al.* 1995; Brooks and Stoneman 1997a; Quinty and Rochefort 2003; Schumann and Joosten 2008a) and on restoration impacts (e.g. Kivimäki, Yli-petäys and Tuittila 2008; Carroll *et al.* 2011), this field has had a lower profile than global peatland science.

Recently, however, the balance between peatland science engaged with the Earth System Science agenda and applied work on degraded and restored systems has become more even. In part, this is a function of the emerging appreciation of peatland carbon storage and the growing apprehension that peatland degradation may constitute a significant feedback to global climate change. Together with the increasing focus of environmental policies on land use and land-use change, this concern has stimulated the study of peatland restoration and the impacts of restoration on ecosystem function and services.

Peatlands have to be addressed in a fundamentally interdisciplinary way drawing on, among others, the disciplines of ecology, geomorphology, hydrology, soil chemistry and socio-economics. One of the hindrances to restoring peatlands is that the various disciplines have not fully joined up to provide a cohesive evidence base for peatland action. For example, where and how will restoration bring the greatest GHG benefit? How do vegetation, peat type and spatial distribution of drainage blocking influence runoff attenuation and how do these affect downstream floods? How can we learn from the environmental archive preserved in peat about recovery and timing of land-use and climate change, and apply this knowledge for future management? Which political tools and economic incentives are needed to align restoration and sustainable livelihoods in these economically marginal areas? This volume, written by scientists from across the disciplines, practitioners and policy makers will attempt to address some of these key questions.

Box 1.1
What are peatlands?

Peatlands are areas with a naturally accumulated layer of peat at the surface. As permanently waterlogged ecosystems, peatlands have no closed nutrient cycle. Semi-decomposed plant material, mainly of mosses, reed and sedges but – especially in the tropics – also wood, is laid down as peat, thereby removing carbon from the atmosphere. These conditions explain the unique capacity of peatlands for long-term carbon sequestration and storage, including the preservation of palaeo-environmental and archaeological organic remains.

Peatland ecosystems are highly diverse and vary from extensive boreal paludified forests and tropical peat swamps to upland blanket bogs and small spring mires (see Chapters 2 and 3). Overall, peatlands constitute around 20 wetland categories in the Ramsar Convention Classification System, over 40 habitat types of the EU Habitats Directive and over 60 types of Endangered Natural Habitats of the Bern Convention (Joosten 2008). Peatland distribution is mainly determined by climate and topography, with a high prevalence of peatlands in the subarctic, boreal and temperate-oceanic regions and in the tropics, particularly in South East Asia (Lappalainen 1996).

The emphasis of this book is on temperate and boreal peatlands across the Northern Hemisphere, as the science on peatland functioning and ecosystem service provision is best developed for these. However, tropical peatlands are covered in a special chapter on restoration of South East Asian peat swamps and in the policy chapters, and where chapters refer to a range of case studies across the world.

1.6 Peatland restoration

Ecological restoration can be defined as 'the process of assisting the recovery of an ecosystem that has been degraded, damaged, or destroyed' (SER 2004). Restoration activities range from removal of pressures through land-use change to active habitat management, such as rewetting through channel blocking, altering livestock numbers, removing non-native trees or re-vegetating bare peat. The overall goal is to re-wet the degraded peatland to the extent that peat accumulation and associated biodiversity and ecosystem services (see Box 1.2) can redevelop.

Recently there have been calls to define the goals of restoration more clearly, as different people value environmental features in different ways, to take into account both ecological and socio-economic considerations (Choi 2007; Temperton 2007), and to consider synergies and trade-offs between various goals. Typically, provisioning services, such as food and timber supply are more easily valued than regulating or cultural services, such as water purification and aesthetic values of landscapes, or biodiversity. While the focus on provisioning services has often led to the degradation of peatland ecosystems, the recognition of the full range of services that peatlands provide to people can serve as strong motivation for restoration. Often actions focused on restoring biodiversity also support increased provision of ecosystem services (Rey Benayas et al. 2009).

In practice, restoration action rarely focuses on restoring a single ecosystem service, but aims for the restoration of a range of functions with different perspectives of success over different timescales. It is equally important to appraise the possible trajectories and potential limits of restoration realistically. In some cases a return to the 'original' ecosystem (i.e. similar in structure and function to the former one) may not be possible and novel ecosystems (Hobbs, Higgs and Harris 2009) with a different set of species, but a similar set of services, may emerge.

Importantly, the terms 'ecosystems' and 'restoration' have sometimes been seen to exclude humans. The ecosystem approach, in contrast, aims to align biodiversity conservation with integrated land management and sustainable use (Shepherd 2004). In this volume, we follow the latter approach and look at socio-ecological systems. Human pressures are drivers for degradation, while people are also integral to solutions for restoring biodiversity and ecosystem services to promote human well-being through responsible use of peatland resources and services.

Box 1.2

Peatland biodiversity and ecosystem services

Ecosystem services are functions of ecosystems that provide benefits to human well-being (Mace, Norris and Fitter 2012), such as the carbon sequestration of functioning peatlands leading to climate regulation as a benefit to society. The ecosystem service framework provides a useful tool for increasing the awareness of the relevance of nature to a wide range of sectors (Daily 1997; Potschin and Haines-Young 2011). By appraising ecosystem services we can outline the costs and benefits of different management and policy options, highlighting the best strategies for enhancing sustainable development and human well-being (TEEB 2010). In this way, biodiversity and ecosystem services can be mainstreamed into other sector policies and provide additional arguments for further efforts of conservation and restoration. A failure to account for the full economic values of ecosystems and biodiversity has been a significant factor in their continuing loss and degradation (MA 2005; SCBD 2014). The ecosystem service concept can therefore serve as a tool to enhance our understanding of our dependence on peatland services, to identify (hidden) costs and consequences of peatland management to people. It thereby promotes more informed decision making on trade-offs between immediate human needs and maintaining the capacity of the biosphere to provide goods and services in the long term (Foley et al. 2005).

While the term ecosystem services began to be used in the late 1970s as a communication tool to enhance understanding of the interdependence of society and nature (Gómez-Baggethun et al. 2010), it received global attention with the publication of the Millennium Ecosystem Assessment (MA 2005). This global assessment has been followed by high-profile international and national assessments, such as the study on The Economics of Ecosystems and Biodiversity (TEEB 2010) or the UK National Ecosystem Assessment (UKNEA 2011) that highlighted – including for peatlands (van der Wal *et al.* 2011) – the dangerous loss of ecosystems and the costs of doing nothing to conserve this natural capital. These studies exposed a clear need for evidence-based knowledge of ecosystem services and of the impact of land use and land-use-change drivers, which has led to the establishment of the Intergovernmental Platform on Biodiversity and Ecosystem Services (IPBES, www.ipbes.net).

A variety of classifications may be needed to suit specific needs of stakeholders and ecosystem assessments (Fisher, Turner and Morling 2009), while for comparison of assessments and for environmental accounting across borders it is useful to employ a unified classification system. Therefore, a Common International Standard for Ecosystem Services (CICES; Potschin and Haines-Young 2011; European Commission 2014) has been developed on behalf of the European Environment Agency, the United Nations Statistical Division and the World Bank, as part of the revision of the System of Environmental-Economic Accounting (SEEA). We use the broad framework suggested to identify peatland ecosystem services (see Table 1.1). The CICES framework builds broadly on the approach of the Millennium Assessment (MA 2005), by using three main categories and dividing these into further subcategories. Supporting ecosystem services, such as nutrient cycling, are classed as intermediate to these final services.

Provisioning services relate to the provision of material and energy by ecosystems, such as wild foods, crops or timber as well as drinking water or biomass-based energy sources.

Regulating services relate to the maintenance of environmental conditions, such as climate regulation through carbon storage and sequestration, regulation of water quality through filtration of pollutants or hazard regulation to protect from disasters.

Cultural services relate to the provision of non-material benefits, such as opportunities for recreation, spiritual and aesthetic experiences as well as the gaining of information and knowledge, e.g. through learning from the peat palaeo-environmental archive about past cultures and climate.

Biodiversity, i.e. the variety of life from genes to species and ecosystems, is linked in various aspects to ecosystem services (Mace, Norris and Fitter 2012). It supports the ecosystem processes that provide ecosystem services, e.g. through nutrient cycling or photosynthesis, often summarised as supporting services. Some specific aspects of biodiversity may directly link to provisioning services, such as crop or livestock species for nutrition, or some species may be linked to cultural services through enjoyment of e.g. wildlife watching. However, not all elements of biodiversity, such as the wide variety of genetic diversity or the breadth of species and ecosystem types, can be directly linked to a current ecosystem service, and to many people biodiversity also has an existence value irrespective of services. For these elements a precautionary approach of biodiversity protection will keep options open for providing future ecosystem services, especially in the light of changing environmental conditions, societal demands or individual preferences.

Table 1.1 Peatland ecosystem goods and services, following the proposed Common International Standard for Ecosystem Services (CICES, Haines-Young and Potschin 2012; European Commission 2014).

Section	Final Services		Examples of benefits provided by peatlands	
	Division	Group	Possibly compatible with peat accumulation	Peat* consuming
Provisioning services	Nutrition	Cultivated crops	*Shorea* species for oil, sago	Carrots, potatoes, oil palm, etc. on drained peatland
		Wild plants and their outputs	Berries, mushrooms, sago, honey	
			Flavours: mire plants for flavouring drinks (e.g. *Menyanthes*, *Acorus*, *Hierochloe*)	Peat flavouring of whisky
		Reared animals and their outputs	Reindeer, red deer	High-density populations damage peat though trampling and grazing
			Low-intensity grazing livestock products (mainly meat)	High-intensity grazing livestock products, most dairy farming
		Wild animals and their outputs	Game, wildfowl, fish	Associated game management may cause drainage and peat damage
		Water for drinking purposes	Drinking water	High abstraction may lead to drainage
	Materials	Construction materials	Plant materials from undrained peatland for roofing, insulation, building, thatching, wattling and veneer	Peat as foundation, building and insulation material, wood from drained peatland
		Paper pulp, cellulose	From undrained peatland: *Phragmites*, *Phalaris*, *Papyrus*	From drained peatland: *Pinus*, *Acacia*
		Absorption, filter and bedding materials	Straw litter	Peat moss litter in stables, peat filters, peat as oil spill absorbent
		Growing media/ potting soils*	Peatmoss biomass, composts	Peat
		Fertiliser/soil improvement	Composts from fen plant material	Peat ashes as K fertiliser, fen peat as N fertiliser, peat as soil improver

Section	Final Services		Examples of benefits provided by peatlands	
	Division	Group	Possibly compatible with peat accumulation	Peat* consuming
		Pharmaceuticals	Medicinal plants (and animals), e.g. *Drosera*, *Menyanthes*, *Ledum*	Humic preparations, peat baths and poultices, peat-based fungi- and bactericides, activated carbon from peat
		Water for non-drinking purposes		Irrigation/cooling water
	Energy	Biomass-based energy fuel*	Reeds, sedges, wood	Peat, palm oil, maize, wood, sugar cane
Regulating services	Mediation of wastes	Bioremediation	Denitrification, nutrient retention and sequestration	Waste treatment
		Dilution and sequestration	Clean water supply to dilute downstream pollution, filtration of atmospheric pollutants	Waste treatment
	Mediation of flows	Mass flows	Erosion control	
		Water flows	Attenuation of runoff and discharge rates, mitigation of downstream floods	
	Maintenance of physical, chemical and biological conditions	Atmospheric composition and climate regulation	Global climate regulation by carbon sequestration, GHG flux mediation	
			Micro- and regional climate regulation	
		Water quality regulation (chemical condition of freshwaters)	Nutrient retention	Waste treatment
		Soil formation and composition	Carbon storage	
		Life-cycle maintenance, habitat and gene pool protection	Pollination and seed dispersal Wildfire control Maintaining nursery populations and habitats; rare and specialised species	
		Pest and disease control	Control of pathogens and parasites, e.g. ticks, malaria	

Table 1.1 (*cont.*)

Section	Final Services		Examples of benefits provided by peatlands	
	Division	Group	Possibly compatible with peat accumulation	Peat* consuming
Cultural Services	Physical and intellectual interaction with biota, ecosystems and landscapes	Physical and experiential interactions: recreation and community activities;	Experiential use: charismatic or iconic wildlife or habitats, e.g. for wildlife watching, conservation activities, volunteering	
			Physical use of landscapes: outdoor recreation (walking/cross-country skiing); leisure hunting, fishing or collecting	Damaging if management for activities affects peat formation, e.g. through track building
		intellectual and representative interactions	Scientific: stratigraphical archive function and pollen record, extreme conditions and special adaptations, self-organisation and -regulation, reference for naturalness	
			Scientific/cultural heritage: historic records, archaeological artefact preservation in peat	
			Educational: subject matter for wildlife programmes, books, guided tours	
			Aesthetic: cultural landscape – notions of cultural continuity, sense of place, appreciation and inspiration in arts and literature	Traditional peat extraction
			Entertainment: *ex situ* viewing/experience of natural world through different media	
	Spiritual, symbolic and other interactions with biota, ecosystems and landscapes	Spiritual and/or emblematic	Symbols and mascots: hunting trophies, Canadian Beaver as symbol of Canada, Japanese Crane as symbol of Japan	
			Wilderness, naturalness, tranquillity, isolation	
			Notions of ecological and evolutionary connectedness temporal continuity, age, naturalness	

Section	Final Services		Examples of benefits provided by peatlands	
	Division	Group	Possibly compatible with peat accumulation	Peat* consuming
		Other cultural outputs	Sacred places and species, e.g. cemeteries or woodland temples Existence: enjoyment provided by wild species and ecosystems Bequest: willingness to preserve plants, animals, ecosystems, landscapes for the experience and use of future generations; volunteering	

* CICES classifies peat as a subsurface asset, similar to coal, that is not renewable over short timescales and therefore not an ecosystem service. The exploitation of benefits from peatlands may in many instances lead to damage to the main characteristics of peatland ecosystems: peat formation and long-term peat storage. We therefore distinguish between benefits that may be delivered sustainably and those that impact on peat formation capacity and the peat stock.

Recognising the value of ecosystem services to society and integrating values into decision making does not preclude or replace the intrinsic value of nature, nor the moral imperative to conserve it (Ehrenfeld 1988; Nash 1989; Daily et al. 2011). Ethical concerns are equally relevant and important in reaching decisions towards management of sustainability and biodiversity conservation (Jax et al. 2013), and the ecosystem service concept complements this by broadening our understanding of how society depends on nature, and in this way reach out to audiences that are otherwise not amenable to ecological or moral arguments to conservation.

1.7 Scope of this volume

The aim of this book is to identify and discuss key directions in peatland conservation and restoration, and to provide an outlook towards managing vibrant peatland ecosystems into a changing future. The scope is global and geared towards identifying solutions and lessons to be applied across science, practice and policy. The book embraces the ecosystem service framework, through its structure and within each chapter.

As ecosystem services delivered from peatlands are multifaceted, this volume has a strong interdisciplinary scope bringing together experts from science, policy and practice, highlighting and debating the importance of peatlands from an ecological, social and economic perspective and demonstrating perspectives of restoration. The various chapters provide up-to-date scientific background information, address policy-related issues and lay out pressing land-management questions.

This volume is structured in three parts. The first section discusses principles of peatland science by reviewing the state and trends of peatland ecosystem services and biodiversity and evaluating the impacts of peatland degradation on these services. The section starts with a global assessment of the peatland resource and condition, and drivers for their deterioration (see Chapter 2). Chapter 3 outlines the importance of peatlands for biodiversity and the scope of restoration to enhance the resilience of peatlands to land use and climate pressures. The next chapters focus on four key regulating and cultural peatland ecosystem services (see Box 1.1), namely climate regulation through moderating GHG flux and maintaining carbon storage (Chapter 4) and water service regulation for both water quality and water flow attenuation and discharge (Chapter 5). As waterlogged systems, peatlands offer a wide range of cultural services. They conserve vast archives of information about past cultural, land use and climate change (Chapter 6), offer opportunities for enjoyment and spiritual enrichment, and provide a sense of place to many communities (Chapter 7). Climate, next to topography, is a main determinant for peatland distribution. While damaged peatlands are predicted to become more vulnerable to degradation with a changing climate and suitable climate space for new peat-forming conditions may contract, peatland restoration may contribute to ecosystem-based mitigation and adaptation (Chapter 8).

The second part of the book applies the principles of the first section to case studies across the globe and provides perspectives of peatland restoration and sustainable management for multiple benefits. The case studies exemplify peat restoration practice in different geographical and socio-economic contexts, including, for example, Canada, Finland, Belarus, Poland, Germany, the UK, China and Indonesia. Overall these case studies set the context to explain the drivers and policies that led and lead to degradation, evaluate the benefits of restoration and review the evidence for enhancements to ecosystem services. Authors assess solutions and lessons learned, as well as research gaps and monitoring needs. The section starts with an evaluation of restoration of blanket bogs in the UK (Chapter 9). Drawing from the Canadian experience of restoring bog vegetation after peat extraction, Chapter 10 develops a framework for restoration of cutaway peatlands. Next to peat extraction, most temperate fen peatland systems in continental Europe and North America have been heavily impacted for centuries through drainage and conversion to agricultural usage. Chapter 11 provides insight into restoration potential along a gradient of degradation across different semi-terrestrial and aquatic fen types, and shows how understanding of biogeochemical and biological processes can aid restoration of ecosystem function and services. Another main driver for peatland degradation in the twentieth century has been afforestation for commercial timber production, especially in Northern temperate and boreal peatlands in Scandinavia, Russia, the Baltics, the UK and Ireland, often supported by tax incentives. With a shift in public preferences and change in public subsidies, efforts now focus on restoring the climate regulation potential and biodiversity values of these peatlands (Chapter 12). On the high-altitude peatlands of China, centuries of livestock grazing complemented by drainage in recent decades have led to widespread erosion, resulting in desertification and increase of downstream flood risk, threatening local livelihoods. Integrated and interdisciplinary approaches to restoration, in close collaboration with affected communities, restore ecological health to the land and help to alleviate poverty (Chapter 13). As highlighted by the headline opening of this introductory chapter, South East Asian peat swamps are not only global hotspots of biodiversity, but also key targets for very recent degradation through exploitation for palm oil and paper pulp. The unprecedented rate and scale of drainage and degradation have turned these peatlands into a huge liability for global climate and regional air and water quality, especially by increasing the risk of fire, thereby affecting local and global populations alike. Restoration efforts in the tropics are only beginning, and the potential to return ecosystem service provision is crucially linked to global economies and political will (Chapter 14).

The third section of this volume assesses socio-economic and political tools for managing natural capital and peatland ecosystem services to embed peatland restoration in practice and policy. The authors identify and critically evaluate political and socio-economic tools to foster peatland restoration in current and future regulatory frameworks. Given the prime importance of peatlands for global climate regulation, international carbon politics may act as new drivers for peatland restoration and for finding new ways to integrate and embed conservation in business and policy

(Chapter 15). As the benefits of healthy peatlands, as well as the welfare costs caused by degraded peatlands, have in the past been undervalued in economic accounting, a comprehensive valuation of peatland ecosystem services is needed. Chapter 16 discusses how to incentivise restoration through innovative finance mechanisms, such as payments for ecosystem services, and outlines opportunities and challenges to this approach. Where return to original conditions is not feasible or not aspired to, other socio-economic avenues may align peatland restoration and sustainable rural development through paludicultures (Chapter 17). Three-way learning at the science–practice–policy interface and embracing an ecosystem approach have allowed innovative public–private partnerships to be instrumental in enhancing peatland conservation (Chapter 18). Chapter 19 reviews major global and regional policy drivers that provide obstacles and solutions towards safeguarding peatland ecosystem service provision and biodiversity.

The concluding Chapter 20 draws a synthesis of lessons learnt on how to address the major challenges of peatland restoration and how to take forward a research and action agenda.

1.8 Outlook

Writing this book has been a very rewarding and fruitful collaboration with all authors. Many of the contributions have been based on in-depth collaboration with peatland practitioners across the world. Much of peatland restoration has been driven by immediate and practical needs to conserve valued habitat. Scientific understanding of the impacts of restoration is now beginning to catch up with practice so that restoration of ecosystem services can build on a stronger understanding of the drivers of ecosystem change and the succession of restored ecosystems.

We hope this book will provide baselines for informed discussions between organisations, scientists and practitioners relating to conservation, restoration and sustainable management of peatlands.

1.9 Acknowledgements

We thank Mark Reed, Marion Potschin, Sabine Wichmann and Roy Haines-Young for valuable comments and discussions on this chapter.

PART I

Peatland ecosystems services

CHAPTER TWO

Peatlands across the globe

HANS JOOSTEN
*Institute of Botany and Landscape Ecology Ernst Moritz
Arndt University of Greifswald, Germany
Partner in the Greifswald Mire Centre*

2.1 Introduction

More than 80% of the globe's 4 million km² peatland area is still in a largely natural state. In contrast, hardly any mire has survived in regions with a large population pressure. Degraded peatlands, i.e. 0.3% of the global land area, are responsible for a disproportionate 5% of global anthropogenic CO_2 emissions (Joosten 2009c). For such a small area of the globe to generate such substantial emissions suggests that peatlands have some remarkable qualities.

This chapter describes the main characteristics of peatlands, provides an overview of peatland distribution across the globe, presents trends in peatland use, describes peatland degradation and its root causes in various parts of the world, and discusses consequent restoration potentials and necessities.

2.2 Peatland characteristics and ecosystem services

2.2.1 Introduction

In most natural ecosystems the production of plant material is counterbalanced by its decomposition through the actions of bacteria and fungi. However, in wetlands where the water table is stable near the surface, the dead plant remains do not fully decay but partly accumulate as peat. Such wetland is called a *mire*, whereas an area with peat is called a *peatland* (see Box 2.1; Figure 2.1; Joosten and Clarke 2002). The rate of peat accumulation ('peat growth') in mires is generally in the order of magnitude of 1 mm per year. Where accumulation has continued for thousands of years, the land may thus be covered with peat layers that are many metres thick (Charman 2002).

Peatland Restoration and Ecosystem Services: Science, Policy and Practice, eds. A. Bonn, T. Allott, M. Evans, H. Joosten and R. Stoneman. Published by Cambridge University Press. © British Ecological Society 2016.

Box 2.1
Central terms and concepts

A **wetland** is an area that is inundated or saturated by water for all or part of the year to the extent that it supports soil microbes and rooted plants adapted for life in saturated soil conditions. The Ramsar Convention also includes all open fresh waters (of unlimited depth) and marine waters ('up to a depth of six metres at low tide') in its wetland concept.

Peat is dead organic material that has accumulated in the place where it has been formed.

A **peatland** is an area with a naturally accumulated peat layer at the surface.

A **mire** is a peatland where peat is actively being formed.

Wetlands can occur both with and without peat and, therefore, may or may not be peatlands. A mire is always a peatland. Peatlands where peat accumulation has stopped, e.g. as a result of drainage, are no longer mires. When drainage has been particularly severe, they are no longer wetlands (see Figure 2.1; Joosten and Clarke 2002; Joosten 2008).

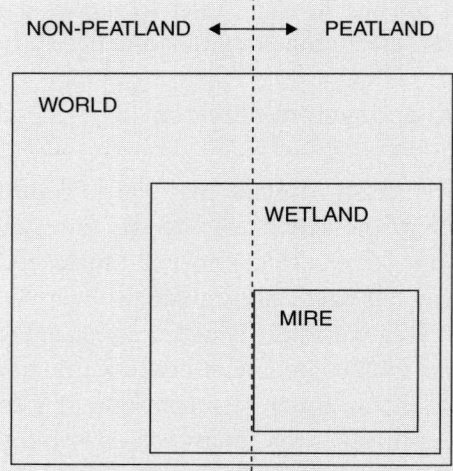

Figure 2.1 The relation between 'peatland', 'wetland' and 'mire' (adapted from Joosten and Clarke 2002).

2.2.2 Peat formation

The accumulation of peat requires an imbalance in the production and decay of dead organic (plant) material. The most important reason for peat accumulation is retarded decay due to water saturation (Clymo 1983). The limited diffusion rate of gases in water leads to a low availability of oxygen, whereas the large heat capacity of water and the large energy demand for vaporisation induce lower than ambient temperatures (Denny 1993; Ball 2000). The resulting anaerobic and relatively cold conditions inhibit the activities of decomposing organisms (Moore 1993; Freeman *et al.* 2001). An important role is played by the recalcitrance of the produced plant material, with some species, organs or substances decaying more easily than others. The production of acids, humic substances and phenolic inhibitors during initial decay also contributes to limiting decomposition.

Peat accumulation only takes place when the water table is – over the long term – just under, at or just above, the ground surface. When the water table is too low, plant remains decay too rapidly because of abundant oxygen, whereas when it is too high, plant production is hampered by insufficient provision of oxygen and carbon dioxide to the submerged parts (Ivanov 1981; Ingram and Bragg 1984; Alexandrov 1988; Sjörs 1990; Lamers *et al.* 1999). With deeper and more fluctuating water tables, a larger part of the organic material decays, leading to less peat accumulation and more strongly humified peat.

Mosses (bryophytes) predominantly determine peat growth in cold (e.g. subarctic and boreal) and wet, cool (e.g. oceanic) regions (see Table 2.1). As mosses lack roots and water-conducting organs they can only produce substantial biomass when the water level during the growing seasons remains close to their growing points and evapotranspiration is restricted. Furthermore, the cold and wet conditions in these climate zones restrict mineralisation and nutrient availability, which suppresses the competitive growth of taller and deeper-rooted vascular plants. Peatland science came into being in such regions (Scandinavia, West and Central Europe), and consequently moss mire growth has become the principal conceptual model of peatland development (see Vitt 2000). This has hampered the appreciation of those peatlands that are *not* dominated by mosses. In temperate-continental and subtropical parts of the world, above-ground plant remains decompose too quickly at the warm and well-aerated mire surface and the drier climate thus forces peat formation to 'go underground'. In these areas, peat accumulates in the first few decimetres below the surface through rhizomes and rootlets of grasses (Poaceae), sedges (Cyperaceae) and other plants being inserted into the older matrix ('displacement peat', Weber 1930). In tropical

Table 2.1 *Characteristic peat-forming plants in different parts of the world (after Prager, Barthelmes and Joosten 2006).*

Climatic zones and sections	Dominant peat formers (physiognomy)	Dominant peat formers (taxonomy)	Dominant peat-forming plant parts
Arctic/boreal/ oceanic-temperate	Mosses	Sphagnaceae, Hypnales	Stems, branches, leaves
Continental-temperate/ subtropic	Reeds, sedges	Poaceae, Cyperaceae, Equisetaceae, Restionaceae	Rhizomes, rootlets
Tropic	Trees	Dipterocarpaceae/ Palmae	Roots

lowlands, peat is formed even deeper under the surface by the deep-rooting lignin-rich roots of tall forest trees (see Table 2.1).

2.2.3 Peatland ecology

Waterlogging and peat formation determine the special site conditions to which peatland organisms are exposed. These conditions typically include (Gore 1983; Joosten 2008; Rydin and Jeglum 2013):

- low redox potential and consequent presence of nitrogen in reduced form (NH_4^+) and toxic reduced ions (Fe^{2+}, Mn^{2+}, S^{2-}) in the root layer
- scarcity of nutrients (and ions in general) as a result of limited supply, slow mineralisation, chemical precipitation and incorporation in the accumulating peat
- acidity caused by cation exchange and organic acids produced by decomposition
- presence of toxic organic substances produced during decomposition and humification
- continuous up-growing soil surface and rising water levels suffocating perennial plants
- spongy soil that means trees are prone to falling over or drowning under their own weight
- generally cooler/harsher climate and stronger temperature fluctuations than the mineral surroundings
- humus-rich 'black' water, complicating orientation and recognition in aquatic animals.

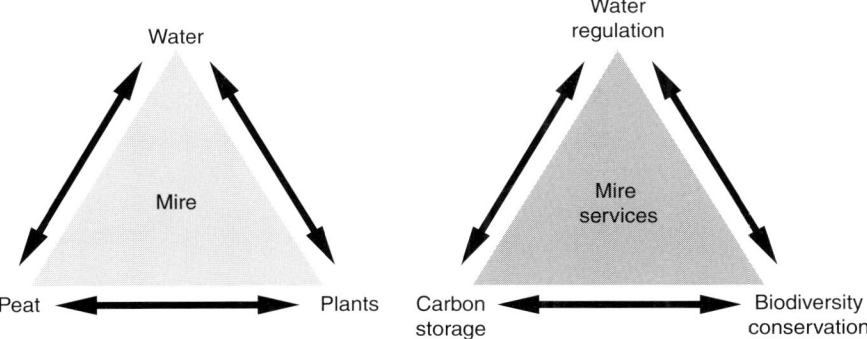

Figure 2.2 Important ecosystem relations and ecosystem services of mires and peatlands.

As a result of these extreme site conditions, natural peatlands are, in general, species poor compared with mineral soil ecosystems in the same biographic region. However, many peatland species are strongly specialised and not found in other habitats, highlighting the biodiversity value of peatlands (Chapter 3).

2.2.4 Ecosystem services

In peatlands, the components *plants*, *water* and *peat* are very closely connected and mutually interdependent (Figure 2.2). The water (hydrology) determines which plants will grow and how much biomass they will produce, whether peat will accumulate and how decomposed and compact the peat will be. Plants determine the type of peat that is being formed as well as its hydraulic properties. The peat structure (pore volume and structure) determines how water will flow and how strongly water tables will fluctuate. These tight interdependencies imply that when any one component changes, the others will change too (Ivanov 1981). As changes take place in the different components, the associated mire ecosystem services, such as carbon storage, water quality and water flow regulation, and habitat provision for wildlife may also change (see Figure 2.2).

2.3 Peatland distribution

Peat formation is primarily a function of climate: net precipitation determines water availability in the landscape, while temperature controls both production and decay of organic matter. Peatlands are therefore especially abundant in cold regions, i.e. in boreal and (sub)arctic zones where evapotranspiration is low, and in wet regions, i.e. in oceanic and humid tropical areas, where precipitation is high (see Figure 2.3; Charman 2002). When

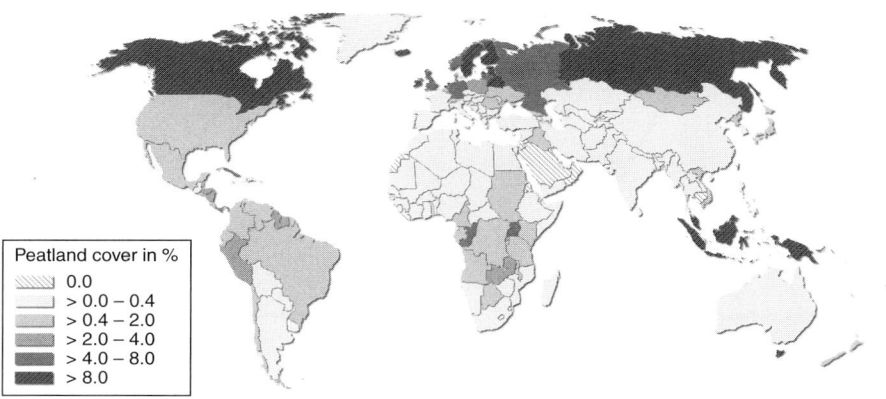

Figure 2.3 Peatland cover per country (in % of national land area) (based on data from the IMCG Global Peatland Database, Joosten 2009c) (map: Stephan Busse).

the balance between precipitation and evaporation is less favourable, peatlands are only found in places where landscape features (relief, bedrock, catchment extent) enable water to collect. The scarcity of peatlands in the southern hemisphere is due to the absence of land in the relevant cool and cold latitudes. As waterlogging is easiest on a level surface, large peatland complexes prevail in extensive flatland areas, such as West Siberia, the Hudson Bay Lowlands (Canada), the South East Asian coastal plains and the Congo and Amazon Basins (Fraser and Keddy 2005). In parts of the world with abundant water supply and limited atmospheric water losses, peatlands may also occur on slopes, forming blanket bogs and hillslope peatlands.

Globally, approximately 4 million km² of peatlands (see Table 2.2) have currently been recorded and peatlands occur in 90% of the countries of the world (Joosten 2009c; Figure 2.3). The general inventory status is, however, inadequate and largely outdated. For some regions very little is known, for example, for large parts of Africa and South America and for the mountain areas of central Asia.

2.4 Peatland types

Globally peatlands are highly diverse, especially with respect to species and community composition (Chapter 3, Steiner 2005; Lindholm and Heikkilä 2012). They have, however, much in common with respect to their eco-hydrological functioning. A globally accepted *mire typology* (and an overview where different types are occurring), however, still does not exist. This deficiency is largely due to the dual origin of mire research in both botany

Table 2.2 Distribution of known peatlands (>30 cm of peat) as of 2008 (data: IMCG Global Peatland Database).

Continent	Total area		Peatlands			Degraded (no longer peat accumulating)	
	km²	% of global area	km²	% of land area	% of global peatland	km²	% of peatland
Africa	30 330 508	19.9	128 173	0.4	3.4	14 215	11.1
North and Central America	26 774 418	17.5	1 396 151	5.2	36.6	16 535	1.2
South America	17 841 262	11.7	157 322	0.9	4.1	5 452	3.5
(Sub)Antarctica	14 038 119	9.2	15 871	0.1	0.4	1 032	6.5
Asia	45 653 482	30.0	1 543 701	3.4	40.4	197 450	12.8
Australasia (Oceania)	8 528 088	5.6	72 845	0.9	1.9	8 261	11.3
Europe	9 482 067	6.2	502 600	5.3	13.2	219 495	43.7
Total	152 647 944	100.0	3 816 663	2.5	100.0	462 440	12.1

and geology and to the many land-use options for which various dedicated – but often incompatible – typologies were developed. The lack of a unified typology severely hampers the identification and effective conservation of mire ecosystem diversity and functionality.

An early, still widely applied approach distinguishes three main types of mire on the basis of overall shape, landscape position and land-use potential:

- *bogs*: convex ('high mires' – *Hochmoore*), elevated over their surroundings, acid and nutrient poor
- *fens*: flat or concave ('low mires' – *Niedermoore*), in depressions, with higher pH and richer in nutrients
- *transitional mires*: with intermediate features.

Dau (1823) was the first to acknowledge that bogs were fed 'by merely rain and dew of heaven'. Since then, mires are classified into *ombrogenous* mires that are only fed by precipitation ('ombrotrophic') and *geogenous* mires that are also fed by water that has been in contact with mineral soil or bedrock ('geo-' or 'minerotrophic') (Sjörs 1948; Du Rietz 1949, 1954). Based on the origin of the feeding water, Von Post and Granlund (1926) subdivided geogenous mires into *topogenous* (= originated as a function of place) and *soligenous* mires (not only fed by direct precipitation water, but 'also by meteoric water running off from the surrounding terrain'; Von Post 1926). Confusingly, the meaning of the terms 'topogenous' and 'soligenous' has changed substantially over time, leading, for example, to a shift of spring mires from topogenous to soligenous (Joosten and Clarke 2002). Since the end of the nineteenth century a distinction has also been made between *terrestrialisation*, i.e. peat accumulation in open water, and *paludification*, where peat accumulation starts directly over a formerly dry mineral soil (Weber 1900; Gams and Ruoff 1929; Moore and Bellamy 1974).

Whereas these approaches focused on classifying mire landscapes, the second half of the twentieth century brought the development and dissemination of more site-oriented typologies. These typologies link vegetation types with abiotic site parameters, especially pH ('soil reaction') and cation concentration (mainly Ca^{2+}) of the mire water. Sjörs (1948, 1950) developed the widely used distinction between *bog* (pH range 3.7–4.2), *extremely poor fen* (3.8–5.0), *transitional poor fen* (4.8–5.7), *intermediate fen* (5.2–6.4), *transitional rich fen* (5.8–7.0) and *extremely rich fen* (7.0–8.4) (see Vitt and Chee 1990; Sjörs and Gunnarsson 2002).

The 'richness' referred to in this typology, which was developed in Scandinavia, relates to specific species richness and level of solutes in the

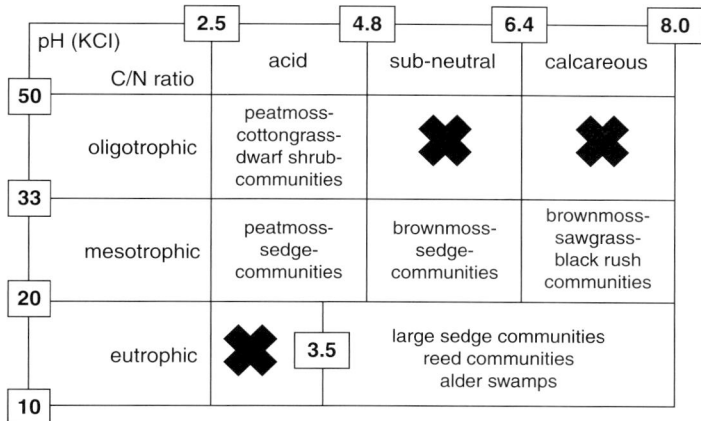

Figure 2.4 Ecological mire types (for freshwater peatlands) for Central Europe with typical plant communities as a function of nutrient availability (expressed as C/N$_{Kjeldahl}$-ratio of the soil) and soil reaction (expressed as pH$_{KCl}$). X = not present in Central Europe (modified from Succow 1988).

water supply – more specifically Ca^{2+} – and not directly to nutrient availability and plant productivity (although important links exist between calcium concentration and phosphorus availability; see Boyer and Wheeler 1989). The more calcareous conditions and wider differentiation in nitrogen mineralisation rates in the warmer Central and Eastern Europe necessitated an explicit separation of the axes 'nutrient availability' and 'soil reaction', which led to the distinction of *ecological mire types* (Figure 2.4). These site-oriented typologies are especially relevant for land-use planning and biodiversity conservation.

In parallel, again on the landscape scale, Kulczyński (1949) pointed out the importance of water movement, laying the foundations for a hydrological mire typology (see Bellamy 1972; Moore and Bellamy 1974; Ivanov 1981). This principle was developed further by Succow (1988; Succow and Lange 1984) and Joosten and Clarke (2002) to a system of *hydro-genetic mire types* (Table 2.3). This typology recognises that the functioning and ecosystem services of peatlands are strongly determined by their hydrological position in the landscape and their consequent peat formation characteristics.

In peatlands in which the surface is sloping, water flow interferes with the hydraulic properties of vegetation and peat in the sense that less pervious vegetation/peat obstructs and more porous vegetation/peat facilitates water flow. This leads to changes in water tables, which again influence the spatial distribution of vegetation types. Through

Table 2.3 Hydro-genetic mire types: an approach to classifying mires according to their hydrology-related peat formation characteristics and their hydrologic position in the landscape.[a]

Hydro-genetic mire types	Succow 1988	Water supply	Internal slope	Internal water storage	Typical example	Main provisioning and regulating services
Schwingmoor mire	Ancient lake mire (*Verlandungsmoor*)	Continuous	None	Large	Floating mat	Water retention and flood control
Immersion mire		Mostly continuous	None	Mostly large	Terrestrialisation mire	
Water-rise mire	Swamp mire (*Versumpfungsmoor*)	Small	None	None	Back swamp mire	Flood control
	Kettle hole mire (*Kesselmoor*)			Rather large	Kettle hole mire	C sequestration and storage
Flood mire	Transgression mire	Periodic	None–small	Small to large	Floodplain mire, mangrove	Flood control, coastal defence
Surface-flow mire	Spring mire (*Quellmoor*) sloping mire (*Hangmoor*)	(Almost) continuous	Small–large	Very small	Spring mire, sloping mire, blanket bog	Food and fodder provision
Acrotelm mire	Raised bog (*Hoch- /Regenmoor*)	Frequent	Small	Rather large	Raised bog	C sequestration and storage
Percolation mire	Percolating mire (*Durchströmungsmoor*)	Continuous	Small	Large	Percolation mire	Flood and base flow control

[a] For linkages between mire types and ecosystem services, see Joosten and Clarke (2002).

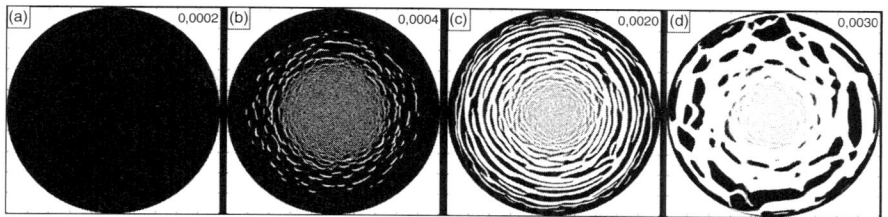

Figure 2.5 Different bog surface patterns (black: dry elements, white: wet elements) may develop as a function of different climates. (a–d) Modelling results with precipitation increasing proportionally to the indicated numbers (from Couwenberg and Joosten 2005).

'self-organisation' based on these feedbacks, mires over time develop high levels of internal coherence, self-regulation and autonomy (Ivanov 1981; Joosten 1993; Couwenberg and Joosten 2005). This is expressed in the development of sophisticated patterns, such as those in string mires/ aapa fens and plateau, concentric (Figure 2.5) and eccentric bogs (Glaser 1999; Couwenberg and Joosten 2005; Dommain et al. 2010). The presence of such patterns has large consequences for biodiversity, water regulation and GHG emissions.

Whereas the hydro-genetic mire typology seems to be universally applicable from the tropics to the (anti)boreal zone, permafrost modifies these types and leads to the formation of special mire types in the (sub)arctic. 'Palsa' (frost mound) and 'peat plateau mires' are found in areas of discontinuous permafrost, where peatlands – with moss vegetation that conducts heat in winter but insulates in summer – are often the *cause* of the formation and persistence of permafrost. Ice wedge formation initiates the formation of 'polygon mires' in (sub)arctic areas with continuous permafrost and little snowfall.

The International Mire Conservation Group has proposed a pragmatic (global) division into 11 main mire types (on a landscape scale), largely based on morphologic features (Table 2.4).

2.5 Peatland use and degradation: root causes and consequences
2.5.1 Introduction

The available data suggest that some 85% of the global peatland area is still in largely natural condition, especially immense areas in remote parts of Canada, Alaska and Siberia. However, worldwide some 500 000 km^2 are disturbed to the extent that peat is no longer formed and the accumulated peat

Table 2.4 *Main global zonal mire types (modified after IMCG Newsletter 2001/3).*

Types	Definition	Principles of subdivision	Main zonal distribution
Bird top mire	Mire originated by guano fertilisation	Location, inclination	(Ant)arctic
Polygon mire	Permafrost ice wedge mire	Shape, size, arrangement	Arctic, subarctic
Palsa mire	Permafrost (ice) core mire	Shape, size, arrangement, shape of complex	Subarctic, subantarctic
Aapa mire	Minerotrophic sloping patterned mire	Shape, size, arrangement of surface elements, developmental stage	Sub(ant)arctic to temperate
Blanket bog	Rain-fed mire, covering entire landscapes including steep slopes	Highland, lowland	Oceanic boreal and temperate
Condensation bog	Mire mainly fed by condensation water	Inclination (vertical, sloping, horizontal)	No zonal distribution
Bog *sensu stricto*	Mire, only fed by rain, elevated above the surroundings	Shape, surface pattern, location	Widespread: boreal to tropics
Open fen	Minerotrophic mire, without forest cover	Alkalinity, nutrient availability, water source and dynamics, shape, vegetation physiognomy	Widespread: arctic to tropics
Forested fen	Minerotrophic mire, with forest cover that contributes to peat formation		Widespread: subarctic to tropics
Coastal mire	Seawater influenced non-forested mire	Vegetation physiognomy	Widespread: subarctic to subtropics
Mangrove mire	Seawater influenced forested mire		Tropics

has partly or totally disappeared (Table 2.2). Pristine peatlands are concentrated in the (sub)arctic and boreal zones (Wieder and Vitt 2006), whereas modified peatlands predominate in the temperate and (sub)tropic zones (Joosten and Clarke 2002). Annually an additional 5000 km² (~ 0.1%) of mires is destroyed by human activities, which means a loss of area ten times faster than the average rate of peatland expansion during the Holocene (Joosten and Clarke 2002). Global peat volumes are decreasing by approximately 0.2% per year (Joosten 2009c). The most important causes of mire losses are linked to drainage for agriculture and forestry, to peat extraction, and to infrastructure development and urbanisation (Chapter 19). Locally mires are also degraded as a result of atmospheric deposition, especially of sulfur (Chapter 9).

2.5.2 Provision of agricultural products

From ancient times, agriculture for food and fodder production has been the most important cause of global mire losses. Peatland agriculture conventionally requires a lowering of the water table. As peat largely consists of water, drainage leads to subsidence and compaction of the peat. Consequently, the hydraulic properties of the peat change, which may decrease the peatland's capacity for water storage and regulation. Drainage also leads to oxidation of the peat layers that are no longer water saturated. As a result drained peatlands lose – depending on the climate – between a few millimetres to several centimetres of peat per year (Couwenberg, Dommain and Joosten 2010). These losses are accelerated by addition of lime, fertilisers, sand or clay, which enhance microbial oxidation (Clymo 1983), by water and wind erosion (Evans, Warburton and Yang 2006) and by (sub-surface) peat fires. The resultant lowering of the peatland surface necessitates a continuous deepening of drainage infrastructure to maintain the same water table, which again enhances peat oxidation, surface lowering and ditch deepening (Figure 2.6). Ultimately subsidence may result in the loss of productive land when the peatland can no longer be drained, is frequently inundated or becomes subject to salt intrusion (Joosten, Tapio-Biström and Tol 2012; Chapter 17).

Peat oxidation leads to increased emissions of GHGs (CO_2 and N_2O) to the atmosphere and nitrate to adjacent surface waters. Degraded peatlands are currently responsible for 2 Gt per year of CO_2 emissions, representing almost 5% of the global anthropogenic CO_2 emissions (Joosten 2009c; Chapter 4).

Particularly in drier climates, water-level fluctuations in drained peatlands cause the formation of fissures in the peat, which impede upward (capillary) water flow and lead to frequent and deeper drying out of the soil. Through the activity of soil organisms, drained peat soils become loosened and fine

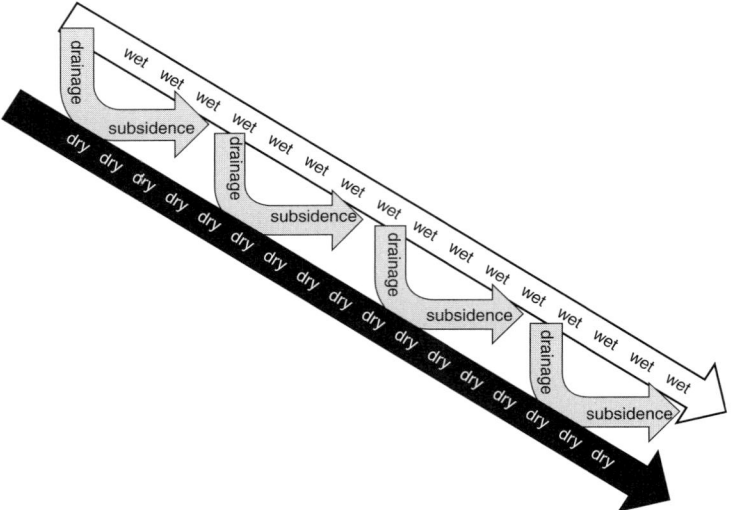

Figure 2.6 The 'bogging-the-bog-down' cascade of drained peatland utilisation, showing continuous losses of elevation, carbon and GHGs.

grained, and may eventually become totally water repellent (Chapter 17). These changes negatively affect:

- characteristic biodiversity (Chapter 3)
- climate regulation and carbon storage capacity (Chapter 4)
- dynamic water storage ability, which reduces the capacity for water retention and flood control (leading to flooding downstream) and for maintaining base flow (leading to less regular supply of water to downstream areas) (Chapter 5)
- agricultural production capacity (Chapter 17)
- to some degree the cultural services (including the palaeo-archive function) peatlands provide (Chapters 6 and 7).

The peatlands that have traditionally suffered most from agricultural reclamation are the often somewhat base- and (after drainage) nutrient-rich fen peatlands in the temperate and subtropical zones of North America, Europe and East Asia (e.g. Bragg and Lindsay 2003). The typical mire type of the temperate zone, the percolation mire, is consequently globally threatened. Where fen peatlands have been utilised long term for low-intensity grazing and hay making, such as in Scandinavia, Poland and Belarus, the mire communities have adapted to these practices and have often become very species rich (Moen 1995; Chapter 10). Abandonment may then lead to a loss of biodiversity (Chapter 17).

In many areas of the world that are unsuited for arable agriculture, peatlands form important grazing lands, e.g. for cattle on the Argentinian pampa mires, alpacas in the Andes, sheep and deer on the British blanket bogs, yaks and horses on the peatlands of the Tibetan Plateau, as well as water buffalo in the humid (sub)tropics. Overgrazing of mountain mires may lead to heavy erosion as in Ireland, Lesotho, Kyrgyzstan, Mongolia and on the Tibetan Plateau (Chapter 13).

Pristine mires in the tropics are increasingly being converted. Large-scale industrial conversion of peat swamp forests is ongoing in Malaysia and Indonesia and increasingly in other parts of South East Asia for palm oil and pulp production, as well as other commercial purposes (Dommain *et al.* 2012; Chapter 14). Drainage for subsistence agriculture also affects large areas in South East Asia (Chapter 14) and impacts substantially on biodiversity and ecosystem services where peatlands are more rare (e.g. in Southern and East Africa).

Until a few years ago the era of agricultural use of peatlands in the boreal and temperate zones of the world seemed to be over and a trend of retreat to the more suitable mineral soils was observable. In Central Europe, this led to the re-wetting of many agricultural peatlands, because the maintenance of drainage infrastructure became economically unacceptable. However, the current quest for land for food, raw materials and energy is driving agriculture back into the peatlands. The demand for biofuels has, for example in Germany, led to a rapidly expanding area of maize for biogas generation into the peatlands where this has instigated deeper drainage (Joosten 2012; Chapters 15 and 17).

2.5.3 Provision of timber and wood fuel

Timber, fuel wood and pulp are the main products for which peatlands have been drained in the boreal zone (Päivänen and Hånell 2012; Box 2.2), whereas in the tropics these products are currently major drivers of peat swamp exploitation (Chapter 14). The largest boom in peatland drainage for forestry took place in the 1970s, when huge areas in Finland, Russia and Sweden were drained to stimulate tree growth (Paavilainen and Päivänen1995). Currently, no further peatland areas are being drained in these countries, recognising that drained peat soils are marginal compared to mineral soils available for forestry. Timber exploitation of peatland forests is, however, largely continued in already drained forests, requiring additional drainage efforts after the first cut. In Russia, where drainage infrastructure is often no longer maintained, a large part of the formerly drained peatland forests is re-paludifying. In the UK, peatland areas that were afforested in the 1970s and 1980s are currently being deforested and rewetted for nature conservation, for example in the Flow Country (Scotland) (Chapter 12). In North America, harvesting of black spruce (*Picea mariana*) and lodgepole pine (*Pinus contorta*) from undrained mires is of economic importance. In South East Asia, tropical swamp forests yield some of the most valuable tropical timbers, for example, ramin (*Gonystylus bancanus*), agathis (*Agathis dammara*) and meranti (*Shorea* spp.) (Joosten and Clarke 2002; Chapter 14).

> Box 2.2
>
> ## Loss of peatlands: the European picture
>
> Its long cultural history, high population density and climatic suitability for agriculture have made Europe the continent with the largest proportional loss of mires. A total of 44% of Europe's present-day peatland expanse is no longer peat accumulating (Table 2.2). If Russia is excluded, then 52% of Europe's peatlands can be considered 'dead', and in many individual European countries the figure is even more than 90% (Joosten 2009c). Around 20% of the original European mire area no longer exists as peatland (and thus does not appear in Table 2.2.), i.e. all peat in these areas has disappeared and the formerly organic soils have turned into mineral soils.
>
> The European experience shows strikingly that an abundance of mires is no guarantee for their survival. Denmark and the Netherlands, which once consisted of 23% and 36% of mires, respectively, have managed to destroy their characteristic landscape type almost completely. Finland (= 'fen'-land; Suo-ma = mire-land) formerly had 96 000 km^2 of mires (28% of the country) but has lost 83% of these, largely since the 1950s by drainage for forestry. In Ireland, 99% of the raised bogs are no longer actively growing. One-third of the remaining living raised bog vegetation was lost between 2000 and 2010 (NPWS 2010), because 'traditional' (but presently mechanised) turf cutting for domestic use could not be controlled. The peatlands of Polesia in Belarus (Bala-Rus = mire-Rus), Poland and Ukraine, one of the most extensive mire complexes of the former Soviet Union, were largely drained between 1960 and 1990 (Tanovitskaya 2011). Only in Latvia, Lichtenstein, Norway, Russia and Sweden have more than half of the mires survived (Joosten 2009c).

2.5.4 Provision of palm oil and pulp

Large-scale peatland clearance is taking place in South East Asia, particularly in Indonesia and Malaysia. Of the original 155 020 km^2 of peatswamp forests in Malaysia, Sumatra and Kalimantan about 75 810 km^2 (49%) were still largely undisturbed by 1990. Twenty years later, only 15 600 km^2 (10%) remained. The expansion of industrial oil palm and acacia plantations has largely been responsible for this change, but small-scale agriculture has also contributed significantly to the destruction of the peatswamp forests. The demand for palm oil and pulp is unrelenting, especially in the rapidly growing economies of China and India. The pressure on peatlands in South East Asia is so great that even protected areas are not safe. Illegal deforestation, drainage, burning and reclamation have been taking place in the Berbak and Sebangau National Parks in Sumatra and Kalimantan, respectively. The only conifer-dominated bog of Borneo in the Kayangeran Forest Reserve (Lawas, Sarawak; Andersson 1961) was recently (2010) destroyed for oil palm cultivation (Figure 2.7). The last largely undisturbed bog dome of Borneo, Mendaram on the border of Brunei and Sarawak, has now on the Malaysian side been released for oil palm production. This will destroy the hydrological balance of the entire peatland, including of the protected Bruneian part with its unique concentric surface structures (see Dommain, Couwenberg and Joosten 2010). The drained peatlands in South East Asia are meanwhile responsible for half (1 Gt) of global peatland CO_2 emissions (Joosten 2009c; Couwenberg, Dommain and Joosten 2010), and the tendency is towards ever-increasing exploitation and consequent emissions.

2.5.5 Provision of peat as an energy source and horticultural substrate

The use of peat for energy provision or as a horticultural growing medium is another strong driver for peatland degradation. Currently, peat extraction is not a nostalgic handicraft but a modern, highly technological industry. Peat as a fuel is important in Finland, Ireland, Russia, Belarus and Sweden. Peat is expensive in extraction and transport and emits more CO_2 per energy unit than other fossil fuel, i.e. 8% more than anthracite coal, 45% more than fuel oil and 103% more than natural gas (IPCC 2006; Couwenberg 2007a, b). Therefore, peat as an energy resource is mainly used where there is an absence of other easily attainable fuels, for securing employment in rural areas and for improving energy-political autarchy.

As in 1973, when the oil crisis roused fresh interest in peat in Finland, Sweden and the United States, and created new interest in fuel peat in Rwanda, Burundi, Senegal, Jamaica and several other states, global

Figure 2.7 The only conifer (*Dacrydium*)-dominated peatland in Borneo (remnants in background) destroyed for oil palm cultivation (foreground) (photo: Hans Joosten).

energy politics and prices are again affecting the use of peat as an energy source. Sweden has in recent years more than doubled its domestic peat extraction volume and imports cheap briquettes from Belarus. Finland plans to expand peat extraction on an additional 1000 km² of peatland, largely in areas of high nature conservation value. The Russian Federation has decided in its National Energy Strategy (2010) to increase peat consumption for energy by more than 500%, which will enable the country to export more oil and gas. In 2011, the government of Belarus released 34 km² of protected peatland sites for peat extraction. In Ontario and Newfoundland (Canada), increasing volumes of peat are used as a 'climate-friendly biofuel'.

Without preferential treatment by subsidies or fiscal advantages, peat could generally not compete with other fossil fuels (Vapo Oy 2006), which have a (sometimes substantially) lower combustion emission factor. Since 1995 (with the EU accession of Finland and Sweden) and increasingly since 2005 (when the Kyoto Protocol entered into force), the peat industry has lobbied – using questionable arguments (Joosten 2007) – for peat to be acknowledged as a 'renewable biofuel'. The lobby, however, fails to acknowledge that burning peat – similar to burning other fossil fuels of botanical origin like coal or natural gas – mobilises carbon from a long-term stock, which would have otherwise remained stored forever (Joosten 2007).

Other than energy generation, the largest consumer of peat is the horticultural industry. Our increasingly urbanising world has a growing demand for permanently available, predictable vegetables, fruits and flowers. As the natural soil is insufficiently homogeneous and reliable for growing uniform, high-quality plants at very high productivity levels, cultivation takes place in specially created 'growing media' that allow the sophisticated, integrated management of water and fertilisers. *Sphagnum* peat has emerged as the foremost constituent of such substrates (Chapter 17). Currently 30 million m^3 of slightly humified *Sphagnum* peat ('white peat') are annually used worldwide in producing growing media. In the hobby market, these media ('potting compost') are used indoors and outdoors to grow pot plants.

Slightly humified *Sphagnum* peat is largely restricted to *Sphagnum* raised bogs, which primarily occur in the (sub)oceanic-temperate and southern boreal zones. Consequently peat extraction for growing media concentrates on a small belt across the globe. In many countries of the European Union, *Sphagnum* raised bog habitat has been reduced to near-extinction and is consequently a priority habitat in the EU Habitats Directive (92/43/EEG). In most countries of Western and Central Europe the stocks of white peat are nearly depleted. To meet demand, peat is instead imported in increasing volumes from Northern and East-Central Europe and Canada. As demand is rising, stocks are decreasing and good alternatives to professional horticulture are not (yet) available, the threat of pristine bogs being opened for extraction is growing. There have been repeated attempts by environmental non-governmental organisations (NGOs) and governments in Europe to reduce the use of peat in horticulture (e.g. Alexander *et al.* 2008; Secretary of State for Environment, Food and Rural Affairs 2011; Schweizerische Eidgenossenschaft 2012). So far, these attempts have had little effect on the overall volume of peat consumed (Denny 2013). The most important reasons for the failure of these policy interventions are the extremely diffuse use of peat ('everybody everyday eats peat': virtually all vegetables consume some peat somewhere in their life cycle) and the limited supply of environmentally friendly, qualitatively and economically competitive alternatives (Schmilewski 2008). For lower demand consumption, such as in gardening and landscaping, the alternatives to peat (compost, wood, bark) are dwindling because of the strong demand for biomass for 'green' energy generation (Bräunlich 2014). In various countries, science and industry are now pioneering the development of high-quality alternatives to peat on the basis of *Sphagnum* biomass (Chapter 17).

2.5.6 Infrastructure development for housing and industry

Traditionally, peatlands have been considered wastelands – areas without value and consequently with low prices and taxes, providing large areas of unoccupied space and thereby opportunities for development. Major cities such as Amsterdam or Saint Petersburg were built on/in peatlands, as are the airports of Kuala Lumpur, Zurich, Ushuaia and many other cities. Peatlands also often serve as urban and industrial waste deposits. Substantial peatlands are located in coastal areas and along rivers, where over 50% of the world's human population lives. Their location near to coastlines makes it tempting to convert peatlands to provide infrastructure for towns, resorts and harbours.

The rising demand for 'green' energy has also had a negative impact on the provision of other ecosystem services of living peatlands or may lead to their direct destruction. Flooding for hydro-electricity is responsible for large losses of peatlands in Canada (7500 km^2) and Scandinavia. Hydro-energy projects that may affect peatlands are planned or in execution in Iceland, Malaysia, Cameroon and Brazil, mainly for aluminium production. Similar developments in other countries, for example, South Africa, Lesotho and Uganda, do not affect large areas but may adversely affect special and rare mire biodiversity.

For several years the generation of wind energy has been rapidly expanding in oceanic and mountain regions, such as in Scotland, Ireland and in Northern Spain, exactly where extensive peatlands (blanket bogs) can be found. On areas of deep peat, the associated infrastructure with roads and drainage can lead to substantial peat losses and careful spatial planning is required (Lindsay 2010).

Last but not least, mires are destroyed worldwide for the exploitation of fossil resources. Infrastructure for oil and gas exploitation is expanding in the peatlands of West Siberia, Sakhalin and Alaska, but also in the Niger Delta (Nigeria). In Georgia (Transcaucasia), a railway, oil terminal and harbour have been built in the Ramsar-protected Kolkheti National Park peatlands in order to carry Caspian oil to the Black Sea while circumventing Russia and Iran. In the oil sands regions of Alberta (Canada) currently the largest open cast mines of the world are developing, and have already destroyed 150 km^2 of peatlands.

2.6 Stages of peatland degradation and their implications for restoration

The strong interrelationship between plants, water and peat in peatlands (Figure 2.2) implies that when one component is disturbed, all components and associated ecosystem services will be affected. The closely interconnected components, however, do not react with the same speed. Generally organisms are more easily affected than the water regime and the latter again more easily than the peat body. Because of these different speeds and the inherent interconnectedness, it is useful to distinguish peatland degradation stages according to the components affected (Table 2.5; see Wheeler *et al.* 1995). To restore a self-regulating fully functional peatland, restoration should start with restoring the components that have the most functional impact (the ones further to the right in Table 2.5).

When only flora or fauna has been impacted, or vegetation has been damaged but hydrological conditions have remained unchanged (degradation stages 1 and 2, Table 2.5), restoration of the original mire type is simple. As soon as the disturbing factor/land use has been removed, the mire will regenerate spontaneously, provided that sufficient diaspores of the key plant species (the relevant ecosystem engineers) are available.

The same accounts for stage 3 after recovery of a recently changed water regime that has not persisted long enough to change the hydraulic properties of the uppermost peat layers. Examples are the spontaneous regeneration of raised bogs used for buckwheat fire cultivation (Joosten 1995) or afforestation (Edom 2001) after collapse or overgrowing of the drainage ditches.

Stage 4 represents peatlands (especially mires that were originally percolation and acrotelm mires, Table 2.3) where peat accumulation has continued but long-lasting utilisation has changed the hydraulic properties of the newly grown peat. In the Biebrza valley (Poland) and on the Ruoergai Plateau (China; Chapter 13), for example, many centuries of low-intensity mowing and grazing have led to the accumulation of more compact peats over the originally loose percolation peats. In the originally treeless mires of Biebrza, the resulting larger water-level fluctuations induce the establishment of scrub and woodland after cessation of mowing, whereas the formation of rainwater lenses in the less permeable surficial peat leads to acidification and the loss of rare species of calcareous habitats (Wassen and

Joosten 1996; Schipper *et al.* 2007). In Tibet, the change in peat type has led to a change from percolation mires to surface-flow mires, which are much more sensitive to overgrazing and erosion (Chapter 13). Similar changes are observed in raised bogs used for grazing where the newly formed, more compact peat no longer possesses the vertically differentiated structure of the original acrotelm and the bog hydrologically starts to resemble a blanket bog. To repair the water regime of the original mire type then requires long-lasting sophisticated management or even the removal of the uppermost compact peat layers over large areas.

Many peatlands in highly populated areas find themselves in degradation stages 5 or 6. Stage 5 represents peatland of which the peat is irreversibly degraded by long-term drainage (Ilnicki and Zeitz 2003) or where a strongly decomposed peat is surfacing as a result of peat mining. Percolation and acrotelm mires require the hydraulic properties of non- or poorly humified peats to regulate their hydrology. Because of the slowness of peat growth, it may take tens to (many) hundreds of years to reinstall new peat deposits with the right properties.

Degradation stage 6 includes peatlands that have lost so much peat by mining, erosion or oxidation that the peatland body is now completely out of hydrological balance. Locally and temporally valuable species, communities and ecosystem services can still be conserved or restored, but restoration of a complete, self-regulating mire ecosystem has become impossible.

When restoration aims at restoring specific ecosystem services, but not necessarily the original mire type, it is important to realise that different ecosystem services are associated with different degradation stages (Schumann and Joosten 2008a). Carbon sequestration, as a major peatland regulating service, is, for example, bound to degradation stages 1 and 2, whereas all provisioning services that directly or indirectly invoke peat degradation (by extraction or drainage; Table 1.1; Chapter 1) lead to stages 3 to 6.

2.7 Global priorities for restoration

Does a global approach to peatland restoration make sense in a world where 80% of the mire area is still undisturbed? Where should restoration be aimed? And where should the priorities be set?

From a global ecosystem service perspective, peatland restoration must focus on those services that are essential to human life and that are prudently expected not to be substitutable within a reasonable human timeframe. These 'vital' services relate to the physical needs of human survival (food, water, shelter, clothing, health care), the liberty to pursue permissible wants, and the autonomy to live according one's own moral position

Table 2.5 Peatland degradation stages (modified after Schumann and Joosten 2008a).

Degradation stage	Peatland components						Site characteristics
	Plants		Water		Peat		
	Single species	Vegetation	Water level	Hydro-physics	Form/relief	Peat deposit	
← Decreasing 1. Minimal restorability							No or minor change in species composition, natural vegetation; undrained, only hunting/gathering; peat accumulating
2. Minor							Vegetation changed by low-intensity grazing/mowing or forestry; not/slightly drained; peat accumulating
3. Modest				not affected			Vegetation changed through recent deep drainage or regular harvesting; no pedogenesis; no/minor peat losses
4. Moderate				slightly affected			Vegetation changed by long-term use or very shallow drainage; some pedogenesis; no/minor peat losses
5. Major				severely affected			Long-term deeply drained or inundated, strong pedogenesis; peatland form altered by subsidence and oxidation
6. Maximal							Intensively drained; strong pedogenesis or compact peats surfacing; peat body damaged by erosion/oxidation/extraction

(Joosten and Clarke 2002). With respect to peatland restoration these vital issues involve:

- the availability of habitable land by avoiding land loss (Chapter 2) and climate change-induced sea-level rise (Chapter 4);
- the maintenance of problem-solving capacities by conserving and restoring biodiversity (Chapter 3) and the peatland archive (Chapter 6);
- the mitigation of global climate change, by conserving and restoring peatland carbon storage and sequestration capacity (Chapter 4);
- the maintenance and enlargement of drinking water provision (Chapter 9) and biomass production capacity (Chapter 17);
- the improvement of health conditions by preventing diseases and uncontrolled flooding resulting from climate change;
- respect for peoples' value systems by restitutive justice (Gorke 2010) and preventing loss of biodiversity (Gorke 2003).

Whereas the provision of many vital ecosystem services has rather local or regional importance (e.g. water supply, food production, flood control, evaporative cooling), two peatland components stand out for their global significance: carbon and biodiversity.

The amount of carbon stored in peatlands is so large that degradation of even a small proportion has global consequences for GHG emissions (Chapter 4). For mitigating climate change, with all its local consequences on vital ecosystem services, it is irrelevant where the emission reduction takes place as the GHGs mix rapidly over the entire atmosphere. For mitigation, restoration must thus be prioritised to those peatlands where most reduction can be achieved, i.e. where the largest extent of degraded peatland combines with the largest emissions per unit area. These criteria concur in the agriculturally drained peatlands of the boreal and temperate zones (especially in Europe) and in all drained peatlands of the (sub)tropics of Asia (Tables 2.2 and 4.3).

Permafrost-underlain peatlands are also relevant from a global climate change point of view, as permafrost melting may induce large emissions of CO_2 and the powerful GHG, methane (Johnston *et al.* 2014; Schaefer *et al.* 2014). The peatlands in the zone of discontinuous permafrost are especially important as they are the cause of the existence of the permafrost, which may vanish when the peatlands are or remain damaged.

Biodiversity is not only relevant because it provides many of the cultural ecosystem services we enjoy. The conservation and restoration of global biodiversity must also be seen as a long-term assurance of provisioning and regulative services under changing conditions, and of cultural benefits that still

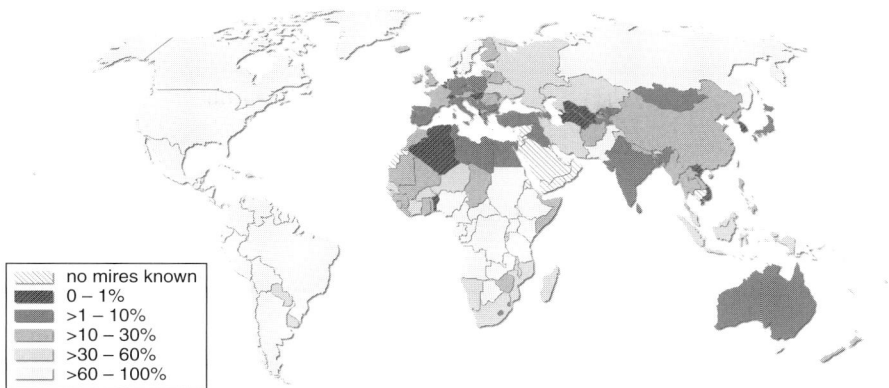

Figure 2.8 Remaining mires (degradation stages 1–4) as a proportion of their maximum distribution during the Holocene (based on data from the IMCG Global Peatland Database, Joosten 2009c) (map: Stephan Busse).

have to be discovered or developed (Joosten and Clarke 2002). Furthermore the conservation of species and ecosystems constitute for many people an important moral obligation.

Similar to carbon, the restoration of peatland biodiversity is most urgent where the largest losses of area combine with the highest biodiversity per unit area (see Chapter 3). Again, these criteria concur in the temperate zone (especially Europe), where the largest proportions of peatlands have been drained (Figure 2.8) and especially the mesotrophic sub-neutral and mesotrophic calcareous peatlands (Figure 2.4) with many associated species have become very rare. The other globally important hotspot is the peatlands of South East Asia (Chapter 14).

The history of peatland use shows a shift from a mere focus on the exploitation of their provisioning services, often in an unsustainable way, to greater recognition of their regulating and cultural values. Conservation and restoration efforts have displayed a similar development, from focusing purely on localised biodiversity to understanding the necessity to restore complete ecosystems. Peatland degradation has now proceeded to the level that restoration maintains its local dimensions with respect to implementation, but must also be pursued for its global effects. Adopting an ecosystem service approach can help to acknowledge the wider relevance of restoration for various beneficiaries, and in this way place local action into global contexts.

CHAPTER THREE

Peatland biodiversity and its restoration

TATIANA MINAYEVA
*Wetlands International, The Netherlands and
Care for Ecosystems, Bonn, Germany*
OLIVIA BRAGG
University of Dundee, Scotland, United Kingdom
ANDREY SIRIN
Institute of Forest Science, Russian Academy of Sciences, Russia

3.1 Introduction

Biodiversity is 'the variability among living organisms from all sources including, *inter alia*, terrestrial, marine, and other aquatic ecosystems, and the ecological complexes of which they are part: this includes diversity within species, between species and of ecosystems' (CBD 1992). Most of the ecosystem services provided by natural peatlands depend ultimately on living organisms, and individual species may directly deliver provisioning and cultural services. In recent years, peatlands have repeatedly been identified by the Ramsar Convention as the most important wetland type for the support of biodiversity and the regulation of natural processes. They also have been singled out for increased attention by both the Convention on Biological Diversity (CBD) and the United Nations Framework Convention on Climate Change (UNFCCC). Nonetheless, the importance of peatlands for biodiversity is still poorly understood among many audiences.

In this chapter, we outline the biodiversity characteristics of natural peatlands and the suitability of different methods for their assessment (Section 3.2), consider how biodiversity is lost and how losses may be quantified (Section 3.3) and explore some implications for the development of effective approaches to the restoration of peatland biodiversity based on the principles of structural-functional ecosystem analysis (Section 3.4).

Peatland Restoration and Ecosystem Services: Science, Policy and Practice, eds. A. Bonn, T. Allott, M. Evans, H. Joosten and R. Stoneman. Published by Cambridge University Press. © British Ecological Society 2016.

3.2 Biodiversity in natural peatlands
3.2.1 Characteristics of peatland habitats and species

The process of peat formation means that part of the peatland biota is directly responsible for creating the habitat (Minayeva *et al.* 2008). Mire massifs form distinct habitat patches that may be spatially separated by large distances, and are characterised by:

- high water level and moisture content
- considerable fluctuations of surface temperature
- low oxygen content
- accumulation of toxic substances and absorbed gases
- limited availability of nutrients
- higher acidity than surrounding ecosystems (in most cases).

These conditions create severe restrictions for living organisms, resulting in intense competition for space and nutrients between individuals even if they have different life forms. Peatlands also influence driving factors (water level, microclimate, matter and water balance, gas exchange, etc.) that affect habitat conditions, and thus biodiversity, for non-peatland ecosystems in the surrounding landscape and downstream.

Most species that are permanently associated with peatlands have developed adaptive strategies during the course of evolution (Rydin and Jeglum 2006), and peatland plants have some distinctive features that are independent of their positions in taxonomic classifications. Typical structural and functional features of the vascular plants include high morphological variability, aeration tissues, extraction mechanisms for toxins and special strategies and mechanisms for nitrogen and mineral uptake, such as insectivory and associations with mycorrhizal fungi. They are predominantly long lived, develop slowly and produce few offspring relatively late in their lifetimes. Thus, they generate populations with stable structure and size. Higher animals (vertebrates) usually use peatlands only at certain stages of their life cycles or during particular seasons, but have also developed adaptations such as the resistance of amphibian and bird egg shells to the acidic environment, specific colourings of fur and plumage, parental care strategies, and synchronisation of life cycles with phenological and weather phenomena. Typically, peatlands host relatively few species (on average no more than 15% of local floras and faunas) but highly specialised species predominate.

3.2.2 Characteristics of peatland ecosystems

Natural peatlands are structurally and functionally organised in a unique way that depends on relationships between plants, peat and water at a range of scales, from the immediate locality to the whole mire massif. Locally, the excess water promotes the dominance of mire plants and impedes decomposition of their dead remains, which consequently accumulate as peat. The physical properties of peat enable it to retain and store a mass of water dozens of times that of its structural matrix. Thus, it can support subsequent generations of living organisms through even the longest periods of normal drought for the prevailing climate. The local conditions depend, in turn, on horizontal connections across the mire massif. A major directional influence is exerted by the lateral movement of water, which both affects and is affected by the presence of plants and peat. This makes peatland a unique ecosystem type in terms of the role that biodiversity plays in its maintenance. Living organisms create and maintain specific abiotic conditions which, in turn, support specialist organisms that are both an integral part of, and highly dependent upon, the ecosystem that is formed. Thus, the peatland ecosystem achieves self-perpetuation on a timescale that is at least one order of magnitude greater than the lifespan of any of the individual organisms involved.

Spatial heterogeneity at various levels is a peculiar feature of most peatlands (Figure 3.1). Different elements of the variously scaled mosaics offer different habitat features, exert different environmental influences and host different ecological processes and phenomena. As a result, ecosystem diversity in peatlands may be described at all spatial levels from the peatland system as a whole down to individual vegetation layers, and biodiversity assessment at the ecosystem level can be carried out within each tier of this hierarchy. For example, the Geographic Information Systems (GIS) archive 'Peatlands of Russia' (Institute of Forest Science, Russian Academy of Sciences) can tell us that the country's peatlands comprise more than 20% permafrost (polygonal and palsa) mire, about 30% transition mire, 18% raised bog, 18% fen and less than 14% ridge-hollow and ridge-pool complexes (Vompersky *et al.* 2005), or that 62% of the total peatland area is treeless, 21% has open woodland and 17% is covered by forest (Vompersky *et al.* 2011). Both are general descriptions of the diversity of peatlands occurring within northern Eurasia but, because they reflect different approaches and refer to different ecosystem levels, they cannot readily be compared. Essentially, there is no single answer to the question of how the biodiversity values and functions of peatlands might best be represented, and the expedient solution is to select either the method that that is most appropriate to the purpose or several methods so that the results can be compared.

The landscape		Description	Scale (m²)
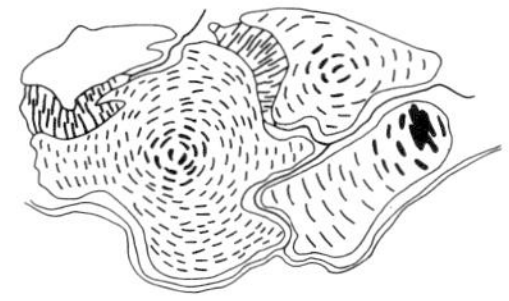	Macrotope	The mire complex (or system; several merged mire massifs)	10^5–10^9
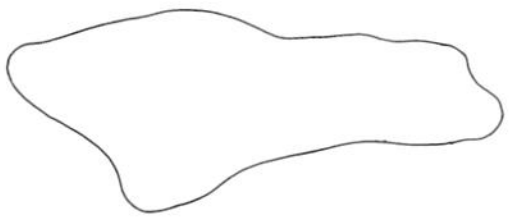	Mesotope	The mire massif (separate raised bog, fen, etc.)	10^2–10^7
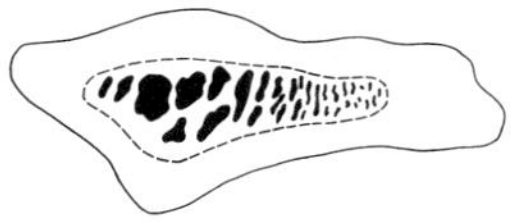	Microtope	Homogeneous element of landscape heterogeneity within the mire massif (hummock-hollow complex, ryam, margin, sedge mat, *Sphagnum* mat)	10^2–10^6
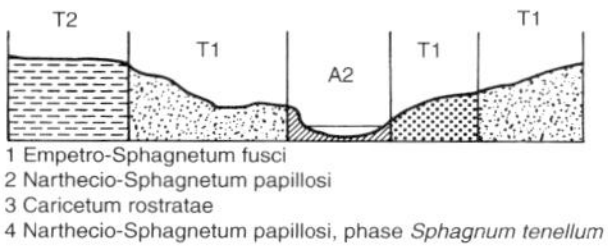	Microform (nanotope)	Hummock, hollow, pool, hillock	10^{-1}–10^1
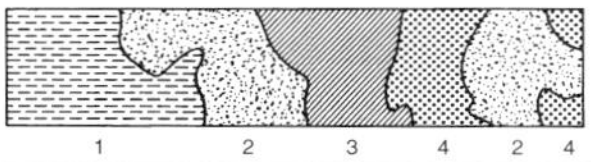	Vegetation mosaic	Microcoenosis, tussock, *etc.*	10^{-2}–10^{-1}

Figure 3.1 The elements of hierarchical mire classification (after Lindsay *et al.*, 1988 and Masing, 1974).

3.2.3 Supporting biodiversity in other ecosystems

The importance of peatlands for the conservation of biodiversity in other ecosystems arises largely from their environment-forming functions, which operate to support wider biodiversity in various ways, some of which are outlined below.

Support of species from other habitats. Peatlands tend to be the best conserved ecosystems in modern landscapes. These assured quiet zones with comparatively natural habitats provide permanent or temporary refuges for relict plant species and for species at the edges of their ranges, which have been displaced from their original habitats as a result of environmental (including climate) change and/or increasing human impact. They also provide temporary habitats for animal species that use them only intermittently and for particular reasons, or have been forced to move into peatlands from other landscapes. Although most of these animals spend much of their lives in other habitats, they have obligatory relationships with peatlands (Minayeva *et al.* 2008; Minayeva and Sirin 2012).

Support of breeding birds. The peatland avifauna of European Russia comprises some 180 species, of which 146 species belonging to 16 orders breed on peatlands. Relatively few of these are specifically associated with peatlands throughout their seasonal and life cycles. The remainder are less consistently confined to peatlands but, rather, choose them so frequently that peatlands are often their principal regional breeding grounds (V. Nikolaev, pers. comm.).

Stopover sites, feeding stations and short-term refuges for birds. Peatlands play a special role in the support of global flyways. The availability of intact peatlands for staging and feeding on migration routes determines bird population numbers in parts of their ranges that may be distant from their breeding grounds, for example, in Scotland, central Asia or Africa for some of the species that breed in the Arctic (E. Strelnikov pers. comm.).

Ecological networks. Due to their relative naturalness, preservation and stability, peatlands play a key role in the support of landscape connectivity. Watershed and floodplain peatlands, with functional connections via peatlands in intermediate positions within river basins, form a network of 'biodiversity-friendly' habitat that makes them especially valuable for nature conservation. Indeed, the establishment and management of ecological networks in which peatlands function as nodes and corridors is regarded as the most effective approach to nature conservation for densely populated regions. This is especially important under conditions of limited humidity such as those encountered in the steppe and forest steppe regions of Eurasia, as well as in the American prairie. In Europe, the ability of peatlands to support well-preserved habitats and contribute to ecological networks has not been sufficiently exploited in environmental conservation, even though peatlands can be included in regional Natura 2000 Special Protection Area (SPA) systems (Minayeva *et al.* 2008).

3.2.4 Criteria and methods for assessment of the biodiversity status of peatlands

The nature of peatland biodiversity is such that not all assessment methods are applicable. In any other ecosystem type, the energy assigned to storage each year would give rise to a high diversity of ecological niches occupied by different species or forms, all of which would interact to create functionality. In mires the energy is stored as peat, which hardly any species can metabolise, and this in turn limits its expression through habitat diversity. Instead, the energetic potential is realised mainly via intimate biological connections and functionally optimal solutions. Therefore, traditional methods for the assessment of biodiversity status, which are based on structural attributes, are unsuitable for mire/peatland

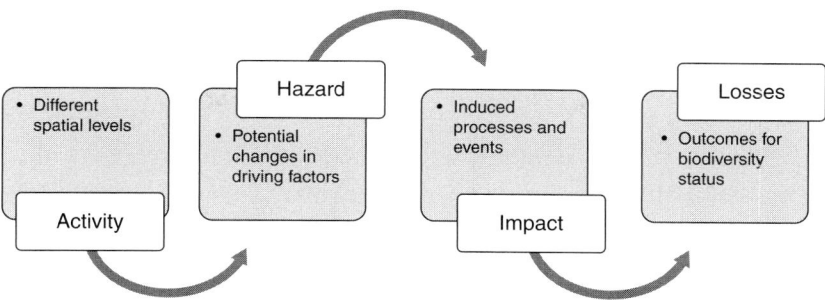

Figure 3.2 The sequence of causality from human activity to biodiversity loss.

ecosystems. Under these circumstances, a functional approach should be applied. Functional effectiveness is often best expressed by the involvement of groups of very small biologically tuned species, such as insects or aquatic invertebrates, which can be used as indicators. Therefore, for peatlands, it is of paramount importance to have an overview of all their components and species and to understand their natural ecosystem processes and functions. Only then might we accurately evaluate their biodiversity status, estimate losses and address these through restoration measures.

3.3 Biodiversity losses

The measures required to restore peatland biodiversity can be identified adequately only on the basis of full information about the causality chain that begins with human activities. These create hazards that may in turn result in impacts leading to biodiversity losses (Figure 3.2). The evaluation of biodiversity losses should follow this chain. It should also be undertaken at different spatial scales, and take account of cumulative effects and biogeographical variability.

The most extensive biodiversity losses are initiated by (macroscale) activities that are applied at landscape level. These activities create hazards such as loss of landscape connectivity and significant changes in climate, hydrology, bedrock, relief, soil (peat), vegetation and species complement which, in turn, impact on natural processes with repercussions that include melting of permafrost, water shortage or flooding, shifts in seasonality, and the disappearance of vegetation cover or even of the peat layer. Some examples of macroscale activities on peatlands are:

- the creation of extensive linear constructions (e.g. roads)
- the construction of large dams and reservoirs
- large-scale opencast mining (e.g. exploitation of oil sands)

- large-scale peat extraction or ploughing for agriculture
- catchment-level overgrazing
- large-scale construction (e.g. airports).

The hazards associated with mesoscale activities, which affect whole mire massifs (Figure 3.1), include shrinkage and compaction of peat. Impacts may be expected across the whole spatial spectrum (microscale to macroscale) and may include changes in hydrology, water level or water quality, the three-dimensional shape of the massif, microtopography, peat thickness and quality, vegetation, species composition and connectivity. Examples of mesoscale activities are:

- drainage or flooding of mire massifs
- small-scale peat extraction
- linear constructions passing through peatlands
- surface pollution and contamination
- small-scale constructions, such as houses
- the conversion of adjacent peatlands into arable land.

Microscale activities alter hydrological factors including water quality, vegetation cover and microtopography. While the primary impacts may occur at microscale, there may be secondary repercussions at mesoscale and above. Microscale activities might include:

- small-scale peat extraction without drainage
- dumping of waste
- pumping in of polluted water
- local water discharge
- construction of recreation facilities including permanent walkways
- industrial berry picking
- lagg or local surface drainage.

As already mentioned, the biodiversity losses arising from impacts at a particular scale may not be restricted to that level in the spatial hierarchy. The relationships between different types of biodiversity loss and the scale of human activities and impacts that may cause them are shown schematically in Table 3.1, and some examples are reviewed in Box 3.1.

Once their nature, origin and potential scale is understood, a quantitative evaluation of biodiversity losses should be within reach. This is important not only for justification and planning of a restoration and/or sustainable management programme, but also to define a baseline condition against

Table 3.1 *The strength of correlation between the spatial scale of impact and type of biodiversity loss.*

Biodiversity losses	Spatial scale of human activity and impact		
	Macro	Meso	Micro
Biodiversity of adjacent land and catchments	strong	weak	weak
Mire massif types	strong	medium	weak
Area/variability of mire complex (pattern) types	strong	medium	weak
Diversity of microform patterns	medium	strong	medium
Peat composition types	medium	medium	medium
Present vegetation communities	medium	medium	medium
Productivity	medium	medium	medium
Diversity of habitats	medium	strong	medium
Native species composition	medium	medium	medium
Alien and invasive species composition	medium	medium	medium
Structure of populations	weak	medium	strong
Morphobiology and forms	weak	medium	strong
Genotypes	weak	medium	strong

Strength of relationship between impact and loss: strong / medium / weak

which the success of restoration measures can be gauged. Like the assessment of peatland biodiversity itself, it is unlikely to follow an existing standard recipe (see Section 3.2.4).

As a general principle, the measurements upon which the evaluation of biodiversity losses is based should reflect real biodiversity characteristics of the peatland in question. Existing practice adopts three distinct approaches to selection of the attributes examined. The first measures structural characteristics and evaluates traditional biodiversity indices (e.g. Fraga *et al.* 2008). The second records functional characteristics and asks how well the ecosystem is working (e.g. Dommain, Couwenberg and Joosten 2010). The third evaluates the socio-economic consequences of biodiversity losses (e.g. Grobler *et al.* 2004). Thus, it is possible to arrive at very different interpretations of a general aim to assess biodiversity-related losses of ecosystem services, depending on the extent of the peatland considered and the focus of the investigator(s). Other treatments (e.g. Page *et al.* 2009) combine all three of the approaches identified.

Box 3.1

From human activities on peatlands to losses of peatland biodiversity: scale changes within the spatial hierarchy

The vegetation or water regime of a peatland may be changed directly by human activities including burning, afforestation, drainage and peat extraction. Because of the close functional linkages between plants, water and peat, any change in one of these components usually affects the others, and impacts need not be restricted to the same level in the structural hierarchy (Figure 3.1). Various authors have observed the consequences of different types of disturbance at individual sites. Some examples chosen to illustrate scale changes are given below.

- Kolomytsev (1993) reports examples from Karelia where small alterations to single components of the plant cover or to the water balance caused dramatic changes in the structure and functioning of the peatland ecosystem, which could lead to complete loss of the mire massif and its associated habitats.
- At Kirkconnell Flow in Scotland, the excavation of a duck pond and a single drainage ditch in the central mire expanse, combined with removal of the uppermost 1–2 m of vegetation and peat from its edges, created conditions that favoured the establishment of self-sown exotic conifer trees across the whole site (Bragg 2004).
- During the first 30–40 years of the twentieth century, the margins of many raised bogs in Scandinavia were partially reclaimed and the upper reaches of streams rising there were canalised. Although only a small and peripheral part of each peatland was disturbed, the ecological consequences were far reaching. The modified peatland edges developed uncharacteristically diverse habitats and species complements, the runoff regime was affected and the chemical composition of the streamwater supplied to habitats downstream was altered. Also, habitats on the mire expanse changed as the peat dome began to degrade (Lindholm and Heikkilä 2006).
- At Puergschachenmoos, a Ramsar peatland in Austria, there was no evidence of direct disturbance on the mire surface but the vegetation changed gradually over a period of decades. Further investigation showed that the functional peatland unit was much more extensive than the designated area, and the remainder had been converted to agricultural use with concealed drainage (Bragg and Steiner 1995).
- At Clara Bog in Ireland, the excavation of peat from the mire margin (Figure 3.3) caused dramatic subsidence of the peat dome that fundamentally altered its drainage pattern, leading ultimately to changes in vegetation (van der Schaaf 1999).

Figure 3.3 Localised peat extraction at the margin of Clara Bog (Ireland) has caused shrinkage and slumping of the peat body and vegetation change on the mire expanse. This site is now protected as a 'natural mire remnant' (photo: A. Sirin).

3.4 Concepts and methods for peatland biodiversity restoration
3.4.1 Concepts for restoration

When losses of peatland biodiversity have been specified, the possibilities for restoration can be explored. The concept upon which we base our consideration of different approaches is close to that developed by the Society for Ecological Restoration (SER), who define (ecological) restoration as 'the process of assisting the recovery of an ecosystem that has been degraded, damaged, or destroyed' (SER 2004). Defined in this way, restoration encompasses the repair of ecosystems and the improvement of ecological conditions in damaged wildlands through the reinstatement of ecological processes. Such integrative approaches to restoration have been widely adopted over the last decade, and most authors suggest that success should be judged on the basis of an indicator of biodiversity status. The strategy is process oriented, and involves directing autogenic processes while taking landscape interactions into consideration (Whisenant 1999; Van Andel and Aronson 2012). This means that, if the techniques for repairing abiotic factors and processes that are described in other chapters of this book are implemented effectively, they will also contribute to biodiversity restoration.

In terms of ecosystem dynamics, the likelihood that biodiversity will be maintained or recover after an external disturbance will depend upon whether the disturbance is transient or a long-term chronic pressure and the ability of the peatland to resist, adapt or recover (its robustness, adaptive capacity and resilience) (Dawson *et al.* 2010). Peatlands are equipped with strong feedback mechanisms that, within limits, tend to move the system back towards a stable state after disturbance (Chapter 2). The stratigraphical record suggests that these mechanisms have enabled mire massifs to spontaneously adapt to, and thus to survive through, past changes in climate. In some cases, the same mechanisms may work to move the system back towards an equilibrium state after disturbance caused by human activities. However, because the changes that humans can impose are more abrupt and usually more severe than climatic changes, active restoration work is often needed to assist the recovery, at least if positive results are to be seen within timescales that are relevant in human terms. The need to reverse the effects of human disturbance becomes more pressing when considered against the current backdrop of climate change because the effects are potentially additive, so that reducing pressure from human causes is the best available means to increase the system's capacity to maintain stability as climatic conditions alter (see also the second example in Box 3.2).

The key drivers in selecting an approach for a particular site are statutory (legal) requirements, policy objectives and the availability of funding. Possible practical approaches can be roughly grouped under the five headings below.

3.4.2 Do nothing

Under favourable conditions, the peatland may recover spontaneously after a source of disturbance is withdrawn, but the degree of self-restoration achieved will depend on the situation. This approach has, in effect, been repeatedly adopted through abandonment of peatlands that have been disturbed in various ways, and must always be worthy of consideration for economic reasons. From this point of view, it is obviously expedient to delay active restoration until there is clear evidence of need, and this can only be obtained by collecting sufficient information to identify trends in the unmanaged situation. A robust monitoring programme will be needed. Although often neglected, an initial phase of monitoring is always a worthwhile investment. If the results eventually show that active intervention is required, the initial monitoring phase will provide a baseline against which the success of restoration measures may be gauged. If, on the other hand, satisfactory progress in spontaneous recovery of ecosystem functions is demonstrated, the considerable expense of active restoration works might be avoided.

3.4.3 Restoration of habitat for populations and species

In some cases, the goal of peatland management is to restore the abundance or population structure of a single target species that has attracted the attention of stakeholders (and funding) because it is rare or endangered. The outcome is usually evaluated on the basis of reproductive success, population size and density, number and variety of individuals, genetic variability or connectivity with other populations. For plants, there are two principal restoration methods. The first reinstates suitable habitats and often relies on natural recolonisation to regenerate the population, but may also involve transplantation. The second involves transplanting specimens of the desired species into existing suitable habitats (Given 1994). For animals, habitat restoration approaches are usually appropriate although reintroduction might be considered in some cases.

This approach to restoration may overlap with restoration of the mire vegetation, the ecosystem, the mire massif or even the landscape. Box 3.2 outlines two cases where conservation requirements for critically vulnerable bird species have indicated needs for peatland ecosystem restoration over large areas. The second example reinforces a recommendation that is common to all available reviews of ecological restoration, namely that species interactions should be taken into account whenever species restoration techniques are applied (Van Andel and Aronson 2012).

On the other hand, there are examples of conservation management for single peatland attributes that negatively affect the natural diversity of the mire ecosystem and/or the biodiversity characteristics of adjacent areas. One is the simulation of historical flax- and hemp-processing activities (Martin and Robinson 2003) by repeatedly excavating pits on bogs for colonisation by *Sphagnum* moss, which promotes the local cover of an important group of mire plants but perpetuates the distortion of natural microtopography and promotes drying out of the surrounding mire surface. Similarly, the reintroduction of grazing or mowing on fen meadows with long histories of traditional extensive management that are no longer required for agriculture (see Chapter 10) may reinstate species-rich 'cultural climax' vegetation, but place a non-natural limit on recovery of the system's peat formation and/or runoff generation functions. Finally, an overriding priority to preserve habitat for the only flock of Taiga bean goose *Anser fabalis fabalis* that winters in Scotland rules out most options for ecological restoration of a flooded peat mine. In cases such as these, where the management of peatland to support single

Box 3.2
Peatland restoration to support vulnerable birds

(a) Aquatic Warbler

The Aquatic Warbler Memorandum of Understanding (MoU) was finalised in Minsk (Belarus) under the auspices of the Convention on Migratory Species (CMS), and became effective on 30 April 2003. It aims to safeguard the globally vulnerable (IUCN Red List) aquatic warbler *Acrocephalus paludicola*. This small migratory songbird was widespread and numerous on European sedge fens at the beginning of the twentieth century but had declined dramatically (by 40% over 10 years) due to drainage of the habitat. Belarus hosts around 40% of the world breeding population (3000–5500 singing males in 2010). To meet the obligations imposed by the MoU, numerous projects to restore aquatic warbler habitat, mainly on sedge fens in the transboundary Pripyat River Basin (Belarus/Poland/Ukraine), followed. Around 15 000 ha of peatland in Belarus, and similar habitats in Western Pomerania and Poland, were restored within EU 'LIFE' projects (Tanneberger et al. 2008) and another 20 000 ha under the auspices of a subsequent German government initiative driven by carbon trading opportunities (Tanneberger and Wichtmann 2011).

(b) Golden Plover

The golden plover *Pluvialis apricaria* is a wader that reaches the southern limit of its global range in the UK, where it breeds on upland heaths and bogs. Given the expected poleward shift in species distributions, the UK population is especially vulnerable to climate change (Pearce-Higgins and Green 2014). One potential problem is climate-related decline of its main food species, the cranefly *Tipula paludosa*. Pearce-Higgins et al. (2010) have demonstrated a negative correlation between golden plover numbers and August temperature, with a 2-year lag, which is explained as follows. Adult craneflies emerging from the surface layers of peat in May and June can provide a super-abundance of food for breeding birds, and more golden plover chicks fledge in years when craneflies are plentiful. Cranefly larvae suffer high mortality when the surface layers of peat dry out in hot weather. Consequently, in the following year, few adult craneflies emerge and few chicks survive to fledge, resulting in a reduced golden plover population the year after that. This understanding can be used as a basis for developing appropriate management strategies. Because the density of cranefly larvae increases with the moisture content of the peat, the negative effect of hotter summers on golden plover might be reduced by managing water levels on peatlands. Peat wetness could be increased by blocking the drainage ditches (grips) that were dug across most UK uplands during the last century in a largely unsuccessful attempt to improve the quality of grazing for sheep. Several conservation organisations are already blocking grips for various purposes including amenity improvement and reduction of fire risk, and recent data show that cranefly increase significantly as a result (Carroll *et al.* 2011). This is one of the first studies to show how the resilience of an ecosystem to climate change might be improved through specific habitat management practices. Importantly, while ditch blocking is already beneficial for peatland conservation, the benefits for birds are likely to increase in the future. This applies not only to golden plover, but also to the wide range of other bird species that feed on craneflies.

facets of biodiversity may limit the potential for recovery of other ecosystem services, a need for especially clear objective setting is indicated.

For the most severely degraded peat bodies, the rehabilitation approach that is most often applied nowadays involves repair of their structure followed by planting to deliver alternative ecosystem services. Especially if a crop such as cranberries, biomass or timber is produced, these activities may be viewed as another type of species-focused restoration practice. Although they aim to establish non-natural plant communities, and thus to create new ecosystem types rather than to restore natural peatland, some peatland habitat conditions may be retained, e.g. peat soil, shallow water table and low nutrient levels. Paludiculture (wet agriculture) is a refinement which involves cultivating crops of wetland species such as reeds and *Sphagnum* on degraded peatland (e.g. Gaudig *et al.* 2014; Chapter 17). In addition to maintaining peatland ecosystem services such as carbon storage and the delivery of pure water to river systems, some peatland biodiversity value may be regained in conjunction with such commercial uses.

3.4.4 Restoration of peatland vegetation

Much of the biodiversity value of an undisturbed mire massif is concentrated in the surface layer that is occupied by living vegetation (including roots), which is termed the 'acrotelm' in at least some mire types (Ingram 1978). The vegetation itself provides a significant fraction of the system's species biodiversity, and furnishes the three-dimensional habitat mosaic that hosts other life forms ranging from birds and mammals to insects and microbes.

The acrotelm also has a pivotal functional role in maintaining the stability of the mire massif. It receives and partitions rainfall so that, whether or not this is the system's only water source, the peat layer is kept sufficiently wet to prevent aerobic decomposition and ensure that new peat continues to form, the water table remains sufficiently high to support specialised biota and maintain any aquatic elements of the microtopographical mosaic, and water of appropriate quality is discharged to aquatic ecosystems downstream in sufficient quantities and with suitable timing to maintain their biodiversity in turn. Thus, if a degraded vegetation layer is restored, we can expect some recovery in all of these functions. Conversely, if the water regime is restored, there will be benefits for vegetation and thus, again, for other ecosystem functions.

Apart from a few examples of species-focused conservation that intentionally prevent the system from returning to its natural condition (Section 3.4.3), peatland restoration usually aims to promote the re-establishment of self-sustaining natural peatland communities (with associated biodiversity value), even if the policy driver (e.g. water quality, fire prevention, coastal protection) is not biodiversity. The requirements for peatland restoration set by environmental regulators in most countries are rather similar. As a rule, active intervention is expected, aiming at least to achieve the presence of a standard list of species, and at best to restore an appropriate assemblage of habitats. A typical restoration project is conceived as a short phase of intervention that will halt degradation and set the system onto a course of recovery towards a self-sustaining equilibrium condition. This often requires manipulation of one or more abiotic factors such as hydrology, relief, nutrient availability or water quality. Occasionally, full ecosystem restoration has been attempted on very limited areas. Grootjans and Diggelen (2002) identify a whole set of example projects where the management goal 'restoration of vegetation' was achieved by manipulating other ecosystem elements including topsoil, seed and other propagule sources, biomass turnover (via grazing or mowing), water regime and even microclimate (by felling adjacent forest).

Degraded peatlands have usually been drained. Therefore, almost universally, measures to reinstate species and habitat diversity are supported by hydrological manipulations that aim to increase surface wetness. Frequently, drainage ditches are closed in order to raise the water table by retarding the discharge of surface water. The other main approaches are to obstruct (and thus slow down) runoff across bare peat surfaces and in erosion gullies by installing bunds, and sometimes to apply materials such as coir matting, straw mulch or brash, which tend to reduce water loss by evaporation even if their main purpose is to provide physical protection or support for re-growing vegetation.

Usually, the vegetation is manipulated to directly reinstate mire plant communities. This may involve the removal of undesirable species, such as invading trees on bogs or planted trees on afforested sites (Brooks and Stoneman 1997b; Vitt and Bhatti 2012; Chapter 12). Alternatively, on bare peat where the primary surface has eroded or been removed, desirable species may be introduced by spreading propagules or planting cuttings and seedlings (e.g. Quinty and Rochefort 2003; Carroll *et al.* 2009; Théroux Rancourt, Rochefort and Lapointe 2009; Chapters 9, 11). Thereafter, imbalanced competitive relationships may be controlled by ongoing vegetation management operations such as sapling removal, mowing or grazing.

In some cases, local microtopography may be adjusted. Ditches on primary mire are usually closed by installing dams which create upstream areas of open water that function as pools. On milled peatland in Canada, pools have been excavated to introduce microtopographical diversity, but their biodiversity was still rather low after 6 years and there may be a need for propagule manipulation (Fontaine, Poulin and Rochefort 2007). Other recent work in Canada has shown that a new *Sphagnum* carpet established on a milled peat surface takes 20 years to develop microstructures comparable to those in natural bogs, and thus to recover ecosystem diversity at this level (Pouliot, Rochefort and Karofeld 2011).

An alternative indirect approach to the restoration of mire vegetation has been adopted for sand-filled oil well platforms in northern Russia and severely eroded peatland in England (Chapter 9). Here, the bare surface is first stabilised by establishing a sward of grasses, with a view to either introducing or allowing natural recolonisation by mire species later. Especially where fertiliser is applied to promote establishment of the grasses, and the grasses are (at least locally) exotic species, the biodiversity benefits may be negative in the initial stages. It is too early to judge longer-term outcomes in general, although the expected replacement of sown timothy grass *Phleum pratense* by a peatland species (arctic cottongrass *Eriophorum scheuchzeri*) occurred in just 4 years at one oil well site in Nenets Autonomous Okrug, Russia (A. Popov, unpublished data).

The intensity of propagule supply is important not only for spontaneous re-vegetation, but also for managed restoration. The scientific literature reports many instances of seed rain/propagule shortage constraining the success of restoration projects, and many techniques to overcome this problem have been developed for various habitat types (e.g. Harper 1977;

Rochefort *et al.* 2003; Klimkowska 2008). Good practice for any biodiversity restoration project should include a full evaluation of seed and propagule sources at an early stage. One of the baseline studies for restoration of the stream-valley fen Drentse Aa (The Netherlands) investigated the soil seed bank, the wind-blown seed rain and the seed influx from the coats of animals as well as in their droppings. The results indicated that grazing animals can be used to carry plant propagules into areas undergoing restoration (Grootjans and Diggelen 2002; see also Vander Kloet *et al.* 2012). Another clever strategy that has been applied on tropical peatlands encourages birds to deposit seed in areas under restoration by installing artificial perches (Graham and Page 2012). For non-peatland ecosystems, the success of restoration work has been enhanced by creating streams to transport propagules (Engström, Nilsson and Jansson 2009), and this technique might be considered for peatlands under some circumstances, although hydrological aspects would need very careful attention. There have also been numerous studies of the role of floods in seed dispersal for riparian habitats which may be relevant to peatland restoration, especially for floodplain mires (Jansson *et al.* 2005; Groves *et al.* 2007).

3.4.5 Mire massif restoration

Where attempts to restore peatland vegetation using the methods outlined in Section 3.4.4 have failed, the cause often lies at a higher level of the structural hierarchy. Vegetation can re-establish successfully only if sufficient water of appropriate quality is available at the ground surface. There is no prospect of achieving this if the total annual loss of water from the peat body as a whole, by seepage, exceeds the net supply. Such imbalances can arise if the base area of the peatland has been reduced (e.g. by peat cutting at the margins as illustrated in Figure 3.3), if its hydrological boundary has been altered by peripheral drainage, or if a groundwater supply has been diverted. In such cases, appropriate restoration measures will aim to establish hydrological stability at the level of the mire massif (Bragg 1995).

If the peat body has been severely disrupted, restoration of the original vegetation may no longer be a viable proposition and the best that can be done is to establish an ecosystem type belonging to an earlier developmental stage. For example, if a bog has been cut down to the fen peat layer, fen vegetation may establish more successfully than bog vegetation. At some Canadian sites where peat extraction had exposed minerotrophic (fen) peat, re-vegetation was relatively rapid but important genera (e.g. *Carex* and *Sphagnum* spp.) failed to colonise spontaneously (Graf, Rochefort and Poulin 2008) so that measures to artificially introduce these key species were still required. If the residual peat layer is very thin and flooding is a problem, lake or swamp may be the only viable target for restoration to a self-sustaining wetland ecosystem. This will at least set a course that could eventually result in establishment of a peat-forming ecosystem.

3.4.6 Landscape approach

In order to realise the full biodiversity potential of a restored peatland, it will be necessary to consider not only the mire massif itself, but also its connections to other similar habitat patches, for example through reproductive and dispersal mechanisms whose ranges vary widely between different peatland species and life forms. If peatlands are too widely spaced within the landscape, recruitment may become impossible for some populations of mire species. Otherwise, population processes occurring under isolated conditions may render them genetically unsustainable. This is the ecological networks concept of interconnectivity, which addresses the need to ensure free movement of wildlife between fragmented habitat patches and may also involve island biogeography theory. Its potential application in the present context is to determine which degraded mire massifs should be afforded the highest priority for restoration in order to achieve a spatial distribution of mire habitat patches within the landscape that is optimal in terms of the interconnectivity requirements of at least the critical characteristic species.

A related consideration is the spatially varying capacity of the physical environment to support peatland systems, insofar as this will influence the degree of correspondence that can be achieved between a practically achievable distribution of mire massifs and the theoretical optimum. This links to the principles of hydro-genetic mire classifications and the extent of peatland losses described in Chapter 2. A legacy of human activities in densely populated areas is that peatlands have disappeared from many physically suitable locations. Their potential extent remains accessible through modelling (e.g. McInnes *et al.* 2007; Franzén *et al.* 2012), which may be required to inform any plans to (re)place missing nodes within the habitat-patch network.

3.5 Conclusion

It is clear that the distinctive biological diversity of natural peatland is much more than a species list. Rather, it is the 'top-level' expression of a combination of ecosystem structure and function that has taken millennia to develop and is responsible for delivery of the majority of peatland ecosystem services. It follows that the restoration of peatland biodiversity at any scale will usually require more than just the reintroduction of missing species. The appropriate management prescription will be site-specific and determined not only by natural site features, but also by the legacy of hazards and impacts created by previous human use. Manipulation of abiotic factors such as hydrology and geomorphology will usually be required, as well as some consideration of climate change effects, and it will almost always take time for the outcome to be fully manifest. Site restoration alone may not be sufficient to achieve the maximum functionality of peatlands as refugia and in providing habitat connectivity to enable the adaptive migration of species in a changing climate. For this, the spatial distribution of mire massifs within the wider landscape will become increasingly important. Given this role of peatlands in supporting species and in the provision of a wide range of other ecosystem services, a broader spatio-temporal approach will be needed to safeguard their full value for biodiversity in the future.

3.6 Acknowledgements

Minayeva and Sirin especially acknowledge the Russian Academy of Sciences Presidium Programme of Fundamental Research 'Living nature: modern condition and problems of development' for partially supporting this study and the project 'Restoring Peatlands in Russia – for fire prevention and climate change mitigation' funded by the German Ministry of Environment (BMUB) within the International Climate Initiative.

CHAPTER FOUR

The role of peatlands in climate regulation

HANS JOOSTEN
Institute of Botany and Landscape Ecology, Ernst Moritz Arndt University of Greifswald, Germany
ANDREY SIRIN
Institute of Forest Science, Russian Academy of Sciences, Russia
JOHN COUWENBERG
Institute of Botany and Landscape Ecology, Ernst Moritz Arndt University of Greifswald, Germany
JUKKA LAINE
The Finnish Forest Research Institute (METLA), Finland
PETE SMITH
University of Aberdeen, UK

4.1 Introduction

Peatlands are the world's most important terrestrial ecosystems with respect to carbon (C) storage, and act as a source and sink for GHGs. In this chapter we outline the importance of peatlands in climate regulation and we describe the effects of drainage and restoration.

4.2 Peatlands and climate regulation
4.2.1 Description, status and trends
Peatlands are the largest terrestrial store of organic carbon
Peatland ecosystems (including peat and vegetation) contain much more organic carbon than other terrestrial ecosystems. In the (sub)polar zone, peatlands contain on average 3.5 times more carbon per hectare than ecosystems on mineral soil; in the boreal zone seven times more carbon;

Peatland Restoration and Ecosystem Services: Science, Policy and Practice, eds. A. Bonn, T. Allott, M. Evans, H. Joosten and R. Stoneman. Published by Cambridge University Press. © British Ecological Society 2016.

and in the humid tropics as much as 10 times more carbon (Joosten and Couwenberg 2008). While covering only 3% of the world's land area, peatlands contain 450 Gt of carbon in their peat (Joosten 2009c; Page, Rieley and Banks 2011a). Peatlands are the largest long-term carbon store in the terrestrial biosphere and among the Earth's most important stores.

The huge carbon stock of peatland ecosystems is attributable to the often thick layers of peat. Peat is a highly concentrated stockpile of carbon because it consists by definition of more than 30% (dry mass) of dead organic material that contains 48–63% of carbon. On average, the peatlands of the world hold a carbon pool in their peat of 1125 t C ha^{-1} (450 Gt/400 × 10^6 ha), which is the largest carbon density of any terrestrial ecosystem. The ecosystem with the second most carbon per hectare is the giant conifer forest in the Pacific West of North America, which, before human disturbance, reached only half the carbon density of the average peatland (Joosten and Couwenberg 2008).

Estimates of soil C stock to 1 m depth range between 1400 and 1600 Gt C (Smith 2004). Further C is stored deeper: 491 Gt C between 1–2 m depth, and 351 Gt C at 2–3 m depth (Jobbágy and Jackson 2000). The atmosphere (in 1990) contained 750 Gt C, mainly as CO_2 and CH_4 (Houghton, Jenkins and Ephraums 1990). The global terrestrial plant biomass carbon stock is estimated to be 654 Gt (IPCC 2001) with total global forest biomass holding 335–365 Gt of carbon (Shvidenko et al. 2005). The carbon stock of global peat is, therefore, equivalent to 20% of all global soil carbon, 60% of all atmospheric carbon, and substantially more than the carbon stock in the entire forest biomass of the world.

Peatlands under natural conditions are a long-term net carbon sink
The peatlands existing today largely originated at the end of the Late-Glacial and in the first part of the Holocene and have continued to accumulate since then (MacDonald et al. 2006; Charman et al. 2008; Yu et al. 2010; Dommain et al. 2014). Over the past 15 000 years peatlands have withdrawn enormous amounts of carbon dioxide from the atmosphere and stored it in their peat deposits. Some scientists consider carbon sequestration in peatlands during interglacials as a major cause of decreasing atmospheric CO_2 concentrations and as an important trigger for the onset of glaciations (Franzén, Deliang and Klinger 1996).

In all terrestrial ecosystems, plants convert atmospheric CO_2 into plant biomass that after death rapidly decays under the influence of oxygen. In peatlands the dead plant material is subject to aerobic decay only for a limited time, because it soon arrives in a permanently waterlogged, oxygen-poor environment where the rate of decay is orders of magnitude lower (Clymo

1984). When the aerobic layer is thin, a large proportion of dead plant material is conserved. When the layer is thick, more material is decomposed with less remaining as peat. When the aerobic layer is too thick, no peat accumulates at all. The permanently anaerobic layer, which is called the 'catotelm', is the true site of peat accumulation. About 5–15% of the net biomass produced is sequestered in the catotelm (Francez and Vasander 1995). Decomposition is slow in the catotelm. As the catotelm becomes thicker, total carbon losses increase because there is more peat to decay. On the other hand, as the easily degradable substances are decomposed first, the rate of decay slows down with increasing age of the peat (Clymo 1992). Because of continuous decay, the peat store would, without continuous addition of new organic material from above, diminish, slowly but inevitably. Active peat formation in living peatlands is, therefore, a prerequisite for the long-term maintenance of the peat carbon store. Peat accumulation rates are dependent on climatic, hydrologic and hydrochemical conditions, and show strong local and regional variation. In general, peat accumulation rates increase from nutrient rich to nutrient poor, from polar to equatorial, and from continental to oceanic conditions (Turunen *et al.* 2002; Prager, Barthelmes and Joosten 2006).

Peat sequestration depends on the delicate balance between production and decay and other losses of organic material. The long-term natural balance is always positive as evidenced by the very present of peat, but many peatlands may be close to the tipping point between carbon source and sink. Peatland carbon sequestration rates may be highly sensitive even to minor climatic fluctuations (Klimanov and Sirin 1997; Charman *et al.* 2008) and show considerable year-to-year variability including negative rates (Alm *et al.* 1999; Roulet *et al.* 2007; Frolking, Talbot and Subin 2014). Lateral expansion of peatlands creates new areas of accumulation and has had a profound effect on Holocene peat carbon dynamics (Korhola *et al.* 2010; Dommain *et al.* 2014), with large areas of relatively young, shallow peatlands contributing considerably to the net rate of accumulation. Worldwide, the remaining area of pristine peatland (>3 million km^2) will presently sequester about 100 Mt C yr^{-1} (Joosten and Couwenberg 2008; Frolking *et al.* 2011).

Fluxes of GHGs from peatlands are complex
Natural peatlands play a complex role with respect to climate by affecting atmospheric burdens of CO_2, CH_4 and N_2O in different ways. They are a considerable global source of CH_4, but make a negligibly small contribution of N_2O to the atmosphere (Frolking *et al.* 2011). In assessing the role of peatlands in global warming, the different time frame and radiative

forcing of continuous and simultaneous CH_4 emission and CO_2 sequestration must be accounted for (Whiting and Chanton 2001; Frolking and Roulet 2007). The climate impact of methane (global warming potential, GWP, integrated over a 100-year time period) is 28 times higher than of CO_2 (Myhre et al. 2013). Frolking et al. (2011) estimated the pre-industrial net climate impact of the world's peatlands to amount to a warming effect of 600 Mt CO_2-equivalents (CO_2-e) per year. However, the atmospheric lifetime of CH_4 is short (12.4 years; Myhre et al. 2013) and the contribution of peatlands to the atmospheric CH_4 concentration soon reaches equilibrium in spite of sustained emissions. In contrast, sequestration of CO_2 (with its much longer atmospheric lifetime) is ongoing and in the long-term peatlands have a considerable cooling effect on the climate (Frolking and Roulet 2007; Frolking et al. 2011).

GHG emissions from peatlands are influenced by a wide range of biological, physical and chemical processes that are interrelated in a hierarchical fashion (Sirin and Laine 2008). Given that these processes are tightly coupled, relationships between GHG emissions and controlling factors can be found (Klinger et al. 1994; Couwenberg et al. 2011). GHG emissions may be strongly influenced by net primary productivity, species composition, community structure, peat characteristics and landscape hydrology. Site-to-site variations in mean GHG fluxes are often closely related to the mean water-table level and for a specific site, for a period without water-table changes, GHG fluxes will tend to follow soil temperature fluctuations (Sirin and Laine 2008).

Water table is the single most important factor influencing peatland ecology and biogeochemistry. The quantity and quality (chemistry) of water coming to the peatland via precipitation, groundwater discharge, upland inflow, flooding or other sources determines its development, functions and processes. Water chemistry has a large influence on the plants that occur in a peatland and therefore on the character of peat that accumulates. The source of water and the hydraulic characteristics of the peat define the key ecological factors – depth to the water table and its fluctuations in time, and the direction and rate of water movement in surface and deep peat layers. Water table and its fluctuations in turn determine chemistry and the hydraulic characteristics of the peat by controlling the availability of oxygen and associated redox potential, which influences hydraulic characteristics through decomposition and loss of pore space. Besides redox potential, temperature plays an important role in mass and energy exchange (and GHG fluxes); there is a strong link between temperature and water regime in peat deposits. Moreover, water delivers various dissolved substances (including GHGs) and suspended particles both upward and downward. GHGs may be released from a peatland horizontally with the lateral outflow (Sirin, Köhler and Bishop 1998, Dinsmore *et al.* 2010), while a significant amount of organic matter may leave the peatland dissolved in water (Evans *et al.* 2014, Koehler, Sottocornola and Kiely 2011, Nilsson *et al.* 2008, Roulet *et al.* 2007), leading to GHG emissions from adjacent aquatic systems like streams, ponds and drainage ditches (Sirin and Laine 2008). Factors affecting peatland ecology and hydrology, therefore greatly influence GHG fluxes from peatlands (see Section 4.2.2).

Vegetation plays an important role in driving GHG fluxes, particularly in providing easily degradable substrate for methanogenesis. Besides providing substrate, plants may furthermore facilitate gas transport between the soil and atmosphere. If methane diffuses upward from the anoxic water-saturated soil layers where it is produced, it has to pass upper, oxic layers, where it is largely oxidised before reaching the atmosphere. Plants with coarse aerenchyma can transport CH_4 from the saturated soil to the atmosphere, bypassing the upper oxic soil layers. When aerenchymous plants are present, CH_4 emissions are usually higher than when such plants are absent (Couwenberg and Fritz 2012). On the other hand, aerenchymous tissue is a plant adaptation to anoxic root zones as it serves as a conduit for oxygen from the atmosphere to the roots, creating an oxic root zone essential for nutrient uptake (Armstrong, Jones and Armstrong 2006). In this oxic root zone methanatrophs thrive that suppress the amount of CH_4 released to the atmosphere (Fritz *et al.* 2011).

4.2.2 Impacts of human intervention on the provision of climate regulation by peatlands

The delicate balance between production and decay causes peatlands to easily become carbon sources following human interventions. Currently, 65 million ha of the global peatland area are degraded, largely as a result of drainage. Peat oxidation from this area (i.e. from 0.4% of the Earth's land surface) is responsible for CO_2 emissions of 1.15 Gt CO_2 yr^{-1} (Joosten 2009c, unpublished update 2014; excluding fires), which is equivalent to 3% of the total 2014 global anthropogenic CO_2-emissions (37 Gt CO_2; Le Quéré *et al.* 2014). When peat fires (mainly in South East Asia, Russia and Canada) are included in the estimates, the global land-use related emissions from peatlands are likely around 2 Gt CO_2 yr^{-1}.

Carbon may be lost from disturbed peatlands through emission of gases (CO_2 and CH_4), efflux of dissolved organic and inorganic carbon, and wind and water erosion of particulate carbon (Figure 4.1). In addition, peat extraction and use and particularly peat fires are most effective in transferring carbon from the peat soil to the atmosphere.

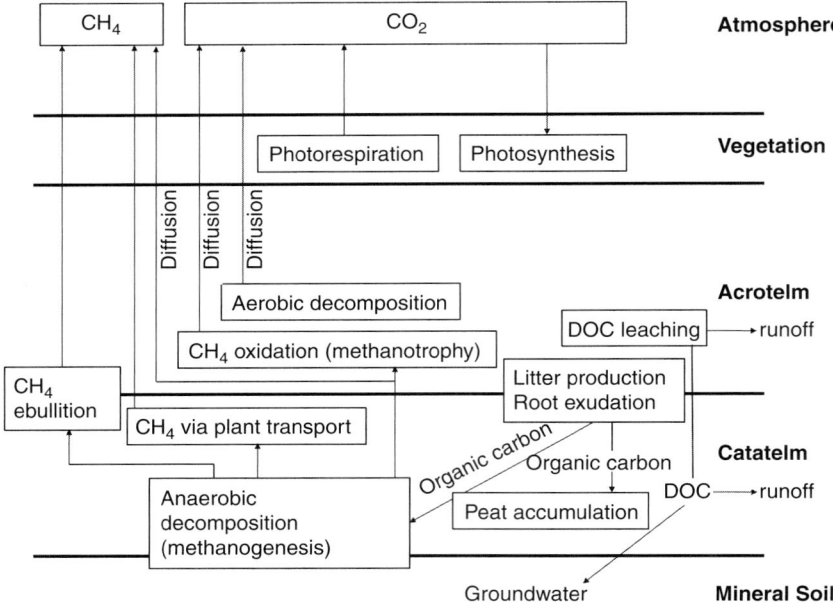

Figure 4.1 Components of the peat carbon cycle (redrawn from Faubert 2004).

The water-saturated conditions of pristine peat soils prevent peatland utilisation for excavation, forestry, agriculture and other purposes in most cases. Conventional land use on peat soils therefore usually involves drainage. The water-level drawdown immediately affects GHG formation and release. Drainage leads to aeration, which stops anaerobic decomposition and the associated emission of CH_4. Aeration also leads to aerobic decomposition of the peat, resulting in the emission of CO_2 and N_2O (GWP 265, Myhre et al. 2013) to the atmosphere. These emissions continue as long as the peatland remains drained or all the peat is oxidised. In addition to the release of CO_2 and N_2O, large amounts of CH_4 are emitted from drainage ditches that also carry increased amounts of dissolved organic carbon (DOC) out of the peatland. This DOC is then largely decomposed off-site and emitted to the atmosphere as CO_2. GHG emissions from drained peatlands generally increase with deeper drainage and warmer climates (Hiraishi et al. 2014b; Table 4.1).

In the sections below, we outline the impact of various human interventions on carbon and GHG fluxes from peatlands.

Peatlands under arable farming
Agriculture on peatlands is commonly associated with drainage, leading to substantial losses of peat through mineralisation and erosion. Under arable farming associated with tillage, peat mineralisation is accelerated

Table 4.1 *IPCC default emission factors for drained peat soils used for arable agriculture, grazing, forestry or peat extraction (after Drösler et al. 2014). Values for CH_4 include emissions from drainage ditches. Calculation of GWP uses a factor of 28 for CH_4 and 265 for N_2O (Myhre et al. 2013).*

	t CO_2 ha^{-1}yr^{-1}	DOC t CO_2 ha^{-1}yr^{-1}	kg CH_4 ha^{-1}yr^{-1}	Kg N_2O ha^{-1} yr^{-1}	total GWP t CO_2e ha^{-1}yr^{-1}
Cropland, boreal	29.0	0.44	58.3	20.4	36.5
Cropland, temperate	29.0	1.14	58.3	20.4	37.2
Cropland, tropical	51.3	3.01	52.0	7.9	57.9
Grassland, boreal	20.9	0.44	59.6	14.9	27.0
Grassland, temperate, nutrient poor	19.4	1.14	60.0	6.8	24.0
Grassland, temperate, nutrient rich, deep drained	22.4	1.14	73.5	12.9	29.0
Grassland, temperate, nutrient rich, shallow drained	13.2	1.14	63.4	2.5	16.8
Forestry, boreal, nutrient poor	0.92	0.44	12.3	0.35	1.8
Forestry, boreal, nutrient rich	3.41	0.44	7.4	5.0	5.4
Forestry, temperate	9.53	1.14	7.9	4.4	12.1
Plantation, tropical	55.0	3.01	46.6	1.9	59.9

compared to grassland due to more intensive aeration (Joosten and Clarke 2002). When the soils are left bare, arable farming may lead to additional losses of particular carbon through water and wind erosion (Holden *et al.* 2006). Also irrigation encourages erosion (Evans 2005b). Arable agriculture always transforms peatlands into sources of GHGs to the atmosphere (first of all CO_2 and very often N_2O; Hiraishi *et al.* 2014b; Table 4.1). CH_4 emissions from drained arable peat soils are virtually prevented, but emissions from drainage ditches constitute a considerable contribution to the total GHG budget (Hiraishi *et al.* 2014b; Table 4.1).

Compared with pristine peatlands, agricultural practices on organic soils lead to a net increase in radiative forcing due to large fluxes of CO_2 and N_2O, despite decreases in emissions of CH_4 (see Table 4.3).

Peatlands used for grazing
Peatlands are often used for grazing. Under grassland, drained bogs and fens in the boreal and temperate zones lose approximately 5 t C ha^{-1} yr^{-1} (Hiraishi *et al.* 2014b; Table 4.1). Livestock production and overgrazing in undrained peatlands can also lead to erosion and consequent carbon losses (Evans, Norris and Rowe 2005), especially in upland peat areas. Overgrazing leaves bare organic surfaces that are susceptible to erosion by water and wind. Poorly drained peats on flat or gentle slopes are particularly vulnerable (Evans 1997), as animal hooves cut through the vegetation into the underlying peat (Evans 2005a). In Ireland, large increases in organic–rich sediments in lakes have been attributed to increasing numbers of sheep (Holden *et al.* 2006). Fertilisation with manure stimulates peat oxidation, resulting in increased release of CO_2 to the atmosphere as well as increased in situ and off-site CH_4 and N_2O emissions.

Peatlands drained and used for forestry
When peatland is drained for forestry, various processes occur simultaneously, with contrasting effects. The integrated effects differ considerably in different areas and over different timescales (Joosten 2000; Sirin and Laine 2008). After drainage, increased aeration of the peat results in faster peat mineralisation and a decrease in the peat carbon store. In the boreal zone this aeration may be accompanied by a lowering of the peat pH and temperature (Laine, Vasander and Laiho 1995; Minkkinen *et al.* 1999), which may again reduce the rate of peat mineralisation. After drainage, forest vegetation (trees and shrubs, etc.) takes the place of the original, lower and more open, mire vegetation. The increased interception and transpiration add substantially to the lowering of the water table, often even more than drainage (Pyatt *et al.* 1992; Vompersky and Sirin 1997; Shotbolt, Anderson and Townend 1998). The peatland biomass carbon store (both above and below ground) increases quickly (Laiho and Finér 1996; Laiho and Laine 1997; Sharitz and Gresham 1998). This store eventually reaches a new equilibrium that is much higher than that of the pristine peatland. Before this stage is reached however, the wood is normally harvested and the biomass store is once again substantially reduced.

Particularly in the boreal zone, where peatland drainage for forestry is common, changes in the litter carbon store are observed. The 'moist litter' in the upper layer of a pristine peatland is generally considered part of the peat, as it gradually passes into the catotelm. The litter in a drained boreal forest (consisting of remains of conifer needles, branches, rootlets, forest mosses, etc.) is of different quality (Laiho *et al.* 2004) and can be considered a separate component. The boreal forest litter, enriched with lignin, is quite resistant to decay (Meentemeyer 1984), but as it accumulates largely under aerobic conditions, the litter carbon store eventually reaches equilibrium and net accumulation stops. Depending on the peatland type and the cutting regime of the forest, it might take centuries before this equilibrium is reached. Peatland drainage for forestry therefore leads to a steady decrease in the peat carbon store, a rapid initial increase in the biomass store that is periodically lost when harvested, and a slow increase in the litter store, which eventually reaches equilibrium.

CH_4 emissions from drainage ditches may have a great impact on the overall GHG budget from drained forested peatlands (Minkkinen and Laine 2006; Hiraishi *et al.* 2014b; Table 4.1). Drainage has been shown to increase N_2O fluxes at nutrient-rich forest sites (Martikainen *et al.* 1995; von Arnold *et al.* 2004; Ojanen *et al.* 2010). The growing tree stand after drainage may have a considerable reducing impact on the albedo of the drained area (Lohila *et al.* 2010), which may change the radiative balance and consequently the radiative forcing from the area. This is an additional climate warming effect, especially from sites with sparse tree stands prior to drainage.

It has been suggested that reduced CH_4 emissions after drawdown of the water table, together with increased C sequestration in trees and litter, may decrease the greenhouse effect of these ecosystems during the first tree stand rotation (Laine *et al.* 1996; Minkkinen *et al.* 2002; Ojanen *et al.* 2010), even though soil CO_2 and N_2O emissions may simultaneously increase. In the long term, however, continued carbon losses from the peat will inevitably outweigh the carbon gains in other pools of the peatland, the faster that more wood is harvested.

Fertilisation of peatlands
Fertilisation of drained peatlands (for cropland, grazing land or forestry) may cause increased N_2O emissions and affect the decay rate, with subsequent changes to carbon GHG flux (Maljanen *et al.* 2010). Anthropogenic nitrogen deposition via air pollution and water contamination could also have an influence on GHG flux from both pristine and drained peatlands. Nitrogen fertilisation on boreal nutrient-poor pristine peatlands did not produce increased N_2O emissions (Nykänen *et al.* 2002), but emissions increased significantly from soils drained for forestry after N addition (Regina *et al.* 1998). Increases were also observed from cropland peat soils (Maljanen *et al.* 2010).

Peatlands managed for hunting and shooting
Many upland peatlands in Britain are managed as grouse moors that require rotational burning to ensure heather regeneration. Garnett, Ineson

and Stevenson (2000) found that this burning reduces peat accumulation. Mismanaged burning can remove all surface vegetation, making the underlying peat susceptible to erosion (e.g Holden *et al.* 2006) and – in the case of deep water levels – vulnerable to unintentional peat fires (Watson and Miller 1976; Maltby, Legg and Proctor 1990).

Peatlands used intensively for recreation
Intensive recreational use of peatlands may lead to peatland erosion. Peatland erosion due to human traffic on footpaths is, for example, a widespread problem in England and Wales (Grieve, Davidson and Gordon 1995). Similar effects are observed as a result of alpine and cross-country skiing in several countries.

Peat extraction
Extraction of peat for fuel, horticulture, landscaping and other purposes rapidly removes carbon from the peatland, leading to a loss of 20–35 t C ha^{-1} yr^{-1} in modern peat fields (Cleary, Roulet and Moore 2005). Peat extraction also leads to substantial carbon losses through vegetation removal during site preparation, drainage of the extraction site and its surroundings, the peat collection process (e.g. milling which increases aeration and oxidation of the upper peat layer) and storage (in stockpiles) (Sundh *et al.* 2000; Cleary, Roulet and Moore 2005; Chistotin, Sirin and Dulov 2006; Alm *et al.* 2007). In addition, the bare dark and lightweight soils are easily warmed, and susceptible to wind and water erosion (Holden *et al.* 2006). After extraction, the extracted peat is immediately (fuel peat) or within some years (horticultural peat) completely mineralised through oxidation. Life-cycle analysis showed that the final decomposition of peat products makes up 71% of the total atmospheric carbon release of nonfuel peat extraction in Canada (Cleary, Roulet and Moore 2005). Land-use change (removal of vegetation, etc.), the transport of peat to the market, and extraction and processing activities comprise 15%, 10% and 4%, respectively. Also peat extracted for bedding, filter and absorbent material, chemistry, balneology, medicine and body care (Joosten and Clarke 2002) is lost completely within a few years. An exception is peat used for long-lasting products like building and insulation material and peat textiles, but their volumes are very small (Joosten and Clarke 2002). Abandoned peat extraction sites that are not rewetted remain important sources of carbon emissions (Mäkiranta *et al.* 2007; Couwenberg *et al.* 2011). Many peatlands previously used for peat extraction and agriculture, especially in Eastern Europe, are now abandoned and have an unclear status. Often the peat surface remains without vegetation for many years after extraction has stopped. The dry conditions resulting from intensive drainage cause rapid peat decomposition, frequent fires, and large carbon emissions.

Peat fires after drainage
Peat fires following peatland drainage are globally important, with current estimated long-term average emissions of more than 0.5 Gt CO_2 yr^{-1}. Whereas peatland fires in many regions of the world have played an important role in natural peatland dynamics (e.g. Zoltai *et al.* 1998), human activities have greatly increased their frequency, intensity and extent (Sirin *et al.* 2011). Peat fires can be smouldering (deep) or flaming (surface) fires and release a mixture of climate relevant gases and particles. Carbon is lost mostly in the form of CO_2, but also as CO, CH_4 and other hydrocarbons as well as soot, volatile organic compounds and polycyclic hydrocarbons. In addition nitrogen oxides (NO_x) are produced with a complex, indirect climate forcing effect. The relative contribution of all these compounds depends on the type of fire and site conditions (Hiraishi *et al.* 2014b).

In recent times, severe peat fires have occurred in European Russia (Sirin *et al.* 2011; Minayeva, Sirin and Stracher 2013) and particularly in South East Asia. The 1997/98 peatland fires on Borneo and Sumatra (Indonesia) released *c.* 700 Mt C to the atmosphere (Heil *et al.* 2007; van der Werf *et al.* 2008). For the period 2000–2006, van der Werf *et al.* (2008) estimated emissions from Indonesian peat fires at 75 Mt C yr^{-1}. Peat fires and the associated haze are a serious health threat to the regional population and can impair air traffic, causing considerable economic losses.

Other human interventions affecting peatland GHG fluxes, but which are less amenable to restoration, include infrastructure development (e.g. urban development, roads, pipelines, etc.), dam building and inundation for creating water reservoirs (Sirin and Laine 2008).

4.3 Perspectives on peatland restoration for climate regulation

The rewetting of drained peatlands to optimise their role in climate regulation entails (a) halting CO_2 emissions, (b) reinstalling peat carbon sequestration, (c) reducing emissions of N_2O and (d) reducing emissions of other climate relevant gases from fires. Rewetting will, however, also increase CH_4 emissions (Table 4.2).

Besides rewetting to restore waterlogged conditions, restoration may involve techniques to stabilise eroding surfaces and re-establish a vegetation cover. Rewetting and restoration of degraded peatlands can restore their sequestration function for atmospheric CO_2 after a number of years (Hiraishi *et al.* 2014b; Günther *et al.* 2015. Even if net sequestration is not achieved, CO_2 emissions are – as a rule – reduced following v. Also, waterborne carbon losses are reduced considerably and studies have shown that after rewetting DOC losses approach those from undrained peatlands. N_2O emissions generally decrease to neglible levels (Hiraishi *et al.* 2014b; Table 4.2).

Table 4.2 *IPCC default emission factors for rewetted peat soils (after Blain et al. 2014). Calculation of GWP uses a factor of 28 for CH_4 and 265 for N_2O (Myhre et al. 2013).*

	t CO_2 ha^{-1}yr^{-1}	DOC t CO_2 ha^{-1}yr^{-1}	kg CH_4 ha^{-1}yr^{-1}	kg N_2O ha^{-1} yr^{-1}	total GWP t CO_2e ha^{-1}yr^{-1}
Rewetted, boreal, nutrient poor	−1.3	0.3	54.7	0	0.6
Rewetted, boreal, nutrient rich	−2.0	0.3	182.7	0	3.4
Rewetted, temperate, nutrient poor	−0.8	0.9	122.7	0	3.5
Rewetted, temperate, nutrient rich	1.8	0.9	288.0	0	10.8
Rewetted, tropical	0	2.1	54.7	0	3.6

CH_4 emissions will increase upon rewettivng (cf. Table 4.2). A recent meta-analysis of available flux data showed that CH_4 emissions from rewetted peatlands do not differ significantly from pristine, undrained peatlands (Hiraishi *et al.* 2014b). However, shortly after rewetting, CH_4 emissions tend to deviate. Particularly on nutrient-poor peat soils left bare after peat extraction, rewetting results in low CH_4 emissions until vegetation re-establishes (Tuitila *et al.* 2000; Waddington and Day 2007). On the other hand, on nutrient-rich peat soils rewetting temporarily often results in (much) higher CH_4 emissions than from pristine sites when vegetation not adapted to wet conditions dies and decays and afterwards high nutrient availability further stimulates methanogenesis (Augustin and Chojnicki 2008; Glatzel *et al.* 2011).

As in undrained peatlands, rewetted peatlands vegetation can play an important role in the production and transport of methane (see Section 4.2.1). The presence of aerenchymous plants will in general result in high CH_4 emissions (Couwenberg and Fritz 2012). As a result, vegetation composition is a good proxy for CH_4 emissions from wet peatlands (e.g. Riutta *et al.* 2007; Dias *et al.* 2010; Couwenberg *et al.* 2011). Recent studies show that mowing of above-ground biomass hardly affects the total GHG balance (Günther *et al.* 2015; Noyce *et al.* 2014).

When accounting for the higher global warming potential of CH_4, increases in CH_4 emissions may reduce or even counteract C savings associated with peatland restoration. The recent IPCC review of published emission values (Hiraishi *et al.* 2014b) indicates that in general emissions are reduced when drained peatlands are rewetted, in some cases with remarkably high savings (Table 4.3).

Table 4.3 Emission reductions expressed in CO_2e ha^{-1} yr^{-1} resulting from rewetting of peatlands with various initial land-use types based on IPCC default values (Blain et al. 2014; Drösler et al. 2014). Emissions from drained and rewetted peatlands and emission reductions include CO_2, DOC, CH_4 from ditches and N_2O. For calculation of the combined effect, a GWP of 28 is used for CH_4 and 265 for N_2O (Myhre et al. 2013).

Initial land use	Emissions drained			Emissions rewetted			Emission reduction		
	boreal	temperate	tropical	boreal	temperate	tropical	boreal	temperate	tropical
Forest land, nutrient poor	1.8	12.1a	59.8a	0.6	3.5	3.6a	1.2	8.6	56.2a
Forest land, nutrient rich	5.4	12.1a	59.8a	3.4	10.8	3.6a	2.0	1.3	56.2a
Cropland	36.5	37.1	57.9	3.4b	10.8b	3.6	33.1	26.4	54.3
Grassland, nutrient poor	27.0a	24.0		0.6	3.5		26.4	20.6	
Grassland, nutrient rich, deep drained	27.0a	29.0		3.4	10.8		23.6	18.2	
Grassland, nutrient rich, shallow drained	27.0a	16.8		3.4	10.8		23.6	6.0	
Peat extraction	11.8	12.4		0.6c	3.5c		11.2	9.0	

a Note that IPCC makes no distinction between nutrient poor or rich and deep or shallow drainage.
b Rewetted croplands are assumed to be nutrient rich.
c Rewetted peat extraction areas are assumed to be nutrient poor.

For peatlands managed for agriculture or forestry, an innovative, carbon-saving alternative to drainage-based peatland agri- and silviculture is 'paludiculture': the sustainable production of biomass on wet and rewetted peatlands (Chapter 17).

4.4 Conclusions and outlook

The enormous stock of carbon in peatlands means that loss of only a small portion of this carbon would have dramatic impacts on GHG emissions. Safeguarding and conserving pristine peatlands is thus an urgent priority in tackling climate change. Numerous human interventions have, however, contributed and still contribute to peatland degradation, limiting the ability of peatlands to provide climate regulation as an v service. The reversal of these interventions offers an opportunity for reducing GHG emissions, with rewetting being the most prominent restoration meassure. Though some residual uncertainty remains in the exact balance of CO_2 and CH_4 emissions after restoration, the best available evidence suggests that, in most cases, there will be a net and often substantial climate benefit. Further evidence from restoration projects needs to be collected to examine the overall short-, medium- and long-term impact on radiative forcing. There are a number of international mechanisms under the UNFCCC and in the voluntary carbon market for incentivising peatland restoration for climate regulation, two of the most important currently being the inclusion of peatland rewetting in the second commitment period of the Kyoto Protocol, and the inclusion of soil carbon in reducing emissions from deforestation and forest degradation (REDD) mechanisms (Chapter 15).

Peatlands should not be managed for the sole provision of one ecosystem service. Instead, multiple services need to be considered. Restoration of peatlands, similarly, should always account for and consider the full range of ecosystem services provided by peatlands. While we have focused on the role of peatlands in climate regulation in this chapter, we recognise the need to balance the services provided by peatlands. However, since a healthy peatland delivers across these multiple ecosystem services, there are few conflicts between managing peatlands to maintain or enhance climate regulation, while safeguarding and strengthening all other ecosystem services that peatlands provide.

4.5 Acknowledgements

This work contributes to the EU FP7-funded projects CarboExtreme (http://www.carbo-extreme.eu/) and GHG-Europe (www.ghg-europe.eu).

CHAPTER FIVE

Peatland restoration and hydrology

JONATHAN PRICE
University of Waterloo, Canada
CHRIS EVANS
Centre for Ecology and Hydrology, Bangor, UK
MARTIN EVANS
The University of Manchester, UK
TIM ALLOTT
The University of Manchester, UK
EMMA SHUTTLEWORTH
The University of Manchester, UK

5.1 Peatlands and water

Hydrological processes strongly control the form and function of peatlands, since the flow of water, dissolved minerals and nutrients dictates the biodiversity and nature of the plant community (Bridgham and Richardson 1993; Zoltai and Vitt 1995) and production and decomposition dynamics (Moore *et al.* 2002) that result in the accumulation of peat. Vegetation and peat, in turn influence the hydrology through their effect on surface flow (Quinton and Hayashi 2005), groundwater (Siegel and Glaser 1987) and evapotranspiration (Lafleur *et al.* 2005). The functional links between plants, peat and water constitute a strongly coupled eco-hydrological feedback system.

There are many approaches to peatland classification (Moore 1984), reflecting in part the closely coupled plant–soil–water system. Because of the fundamental link between peat formation and hydrological conditions, it may be argued that hydrological status is a primary criterion in the classification of peatlands. The most basic distinction between two main mire types, bogs and fens, is based on water source. Fens receive minerogenous (rich in dissolved minerals) surface- and groundwater inputs in addition to

Peatland Restoration and Ecosystem Services: Science, Policy and Practice, eds. A. Bonn, T. Allott, M. Evans, H. Joosten and R. Stoneman. Published by Cambridge University Press. © British Ecological Society 2016.

precipitation. Bogs are peatlands that are entirely ombrogenous (fed only by precipitation) and often develop over fens (Kuhry et al. 1993), as the accumulating peat raises the elevation of the surface and the water table, isolating them from minerogenous water inputs. Further subdivisions of fen and bog are commonly identified through their hydrogeomorphic setting (Brinson 1993; Charman 2002), which is arguably a proxy for water source and water-table regime. In North America, minerogeneous systems are commonly further divided into swamps and fens (NWWG 1997). This distinction is drawn based on vegetation cover (swamps are forested while fens support graminoid and brown moss species), but, in fact, because of the strong plant–water coupling this reflects varying hydrological status with swamps characterised by a strongly variable water table (that allows tree growth), while fen systems have stable high water tables. In maritime climates, such as that of the British Isles and in Newfoundland, very high rainfall supports the development of 'blanket' bogs particularly in upland areas. Blanket bogs are laterally extensive, blanketing the pre-existing topography. Consequently, they typically include both true bog and areas where upslope drainage is a significant component of the water budget (although that drainage in intact mires may be nutrient-poor waters sourced from upslope bogs). Blanket bogs are therefore perhaps more accurately described as blanket mire complexes (Lindsay 1995). For a fuller discussion of peatland classification, refer to Charman (2002).

While the hydrogeomorphic setting controls the water sources, the internal water redistribution in, and water efflux from, peatlands are strongly influenced by the character of the peat. Near-surface peats include the living vegetation and dead, but undecomposed, plant remains while deeper layers comprise more decomposed materials. The upper layer of peatland systems is often referred to as the acrotelm, This zone comprises living and less well-decomposed plant material with high hydraulic conductivity (low water-retention capacity) (Price and Whittington 2010) and high specific yield (Boelter 1976). Consequently the acrotelm is a zone through which water table fluctuates (Ingram 1978), driven by changing meteorological conditions. Hydraulic conductivity can decrease by 4 or 5 orders of magnitude with depth (Baden and Egglesman 1963; Hoag and Price 1995), and the acrotelm is the peat layer where biological activity and nutrient exchanges are highest (Ingram 1983). The lower peat layer (catotelm) is permanently saturated, the hydraulic character is less variable with depth (Chason and Siegel 1986) and the level of biological activity is reduced, facilitating conservation of organic matter (Moore et al. 2002). The acrotelm is more distinct in bogs, ranging from 35–50 cm in thickness (Belyea and Clymo 2001), but often thinner (~10–20 cm) and indistinct in fens (e.g. Price and Maloney 1994) where the water table is typically higher and fluctuates less. We note that Morris *et al.* (2011) believe the diplotelmic model (acrotelm/catotelm) is inflexible and has limited applicability to peatlands disturbed by fire, harvesting, etc.

The two-layered structure (Ingram 1978) which characterises peatlands strongly influences the water table response to wetting and drying, runoff characteristics and carbon exchanges. During periods of high water table, the relatively high hydraulic conductivity of the surface peat layers facilitates rapid near-surface runoff (Evans *et al.* 1999). When the water table drops, saturated flow is confined to the lower, less permeable layers of the acrotelm, and runoff is curtailed or may cease entirely in bogs (Bay 1968). In contrast, some swamp and especially fen peatlands receive more surface or groundwater and are better able to sustain higher water tables and runoff production (Ingram 1983). Horizontal water flow also occurs in the catotelm, but as the hydraulic conductivity is very low this is typically insignificant compared to that in the acrotelm. Because of the variable runoff response, strong when wet and poor when dry, peatlands with strong vertical gradients of hydraulic conductivity are not good regulators of flow (Bullock and Acreman 2003).

Evapotranspiration is commonly the main water loss from peatlands (Ferone and Devito 2004; Lafleur *et al.* 2005), although this is less the case in steeper blanket mires where runoff dominates (e.g. Evans *et al.* 1999, Price 1993). Rates of evapotranspiration are influenced by the nature of the evaporating surface. Price (1994) found greatest losses from open water (average 4.9 mm d^{-1}) but nearly as much can be lost from emergent plants in a *Typha*-dominated fen peatland. Lafleur *et al.* (2005) measured growing season evapotranspiration from a *Sphagnum*-dominated bog at 2.2 to 3.3 mm d^{-1}. During the growing season where vascular plants dominate and the water table is within the rooting zone, evapotranspiration from peatlands is close to the maximum (potential) rate (Kim and Verma 1996). Consequently, evapotranspiration losses are typically higher from fens than bogs (Price and Maloney 1994).

5.2 Hydrological services of peatland systems

5.2.1 Water quality regulation

The influence of peatlands on water quality is closely linked to their capacity to accumulate organic matter. Bogs receive all their chemical inputs from the atmosphere, and can be highly effective at retaining nutrients and other elements. This includes retention and removal of nitrogen from fossil fuel burning and agriculture via biomass uptake and accumulation (Moore et al. 2005), of sulfate via reduction to sulfides and organic sulfur compounds (Brown 1985), and of toxic substances such as metals and persistent organic pollutants (Shotyk et al. 1997, Sanders et al. 1995). The long-term accumulation of these pollutants in peat organic matter prevents their loss to surface waters, which decreases freshwater eutrophication and acidification and improves the quality of drinking water supplies. The significance of peatlands for drinking water supply depends on their landscape position and proximity to population centres; in the UK, where most water supply is obtained from surface sources, and blanket bogs dominate the uplands close to many major cities, peatlands are vital sources of drinking water (Van der Wal et al. 2011)

The role of fens in water quality regulation differs significantly from that of bogs. Nutrient and other solute inputs are much higher because they also receive water through lateral input from surrounding land, groundwater or adjacent river systems. Fens receiving nutrient-enriched agricultural runoff can regulate downstream water quality through denitrification, nutrient assimilation or sediment trapping (e.g. Fisher and Acreman 2004). However, these processes can also lead to the ecological degradation of the fen itself (e.g. McBride et al. 2010), so there is a clear trade-off in the utilisation of fens for this purpose.

In addition to their pollutant retention function, peatlands influence water quality through the release of DOC, which is generated through the incomplete decomposition of organic matter under anaerobic conditions. High DOC concentrations provide the characteristic brown colouration of peatland drainage waters and contribute to their acidity, but also absorb ultraviolet radiation and reduce its detrimental impact on aquatic biota (Zafariou et al. 1984) and provide a major source of carbon for bacterial metabolism, effectively fuelling the food web in many aquatic ecosystems (Wetzel 1992). However, this conversion of peat-derived DOC to reactive forms, and ultimately CO_2, provides an indirect pathway of GHG emission from peatlands (Billett et al. 2004; Evans et al. 2013). In addition, DOC in raw drinking water supplies adds significantly to treatment costs, and can lead to the formation of carcinogenic trihalomethane compounds during treatment processes (e.g. Matilainen et al. 2011), so it is widely viewed as a negative characteristic of peatland water quality in areas used for supply (e.g. McGrath and Smith 2006). Over recent decades, DOC concentrations have risen in surface waters across a large area of Northern and Central Europe and northeast North America (Monteith et al. 2007), raising concerns about peatland degradation associated with land management or climate change. However, DOC increases have occurred across both peats and other upland soils, and appear to be primarily driven by recovery from historic acidification in these industrialised regions (e.g. Evans et al. 2006; Monteith

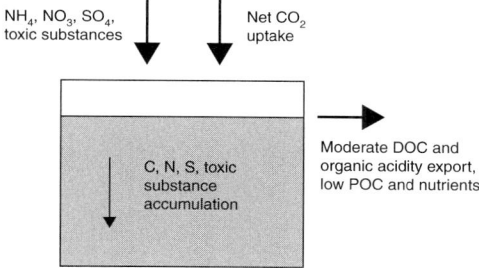
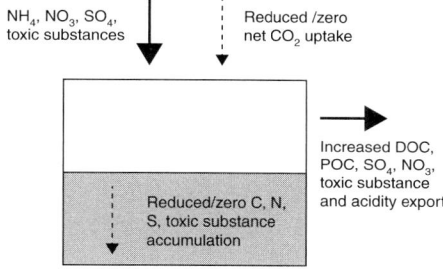
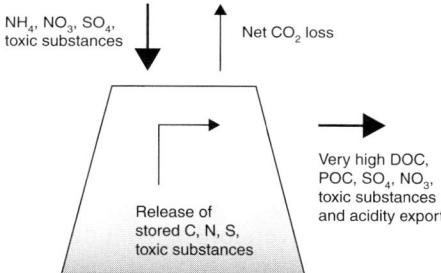

Figure 5.1 Impacts of peatland degradation on peatland nutrient cycling.

et al. 2007). As such, increases in baseline DOC concentrations may reflect a return to natural conditions rather than ecosystem degradation.

Despite evidence that peatlands are responsive to external environmental drivers, it is clear that over-intensive land use, in particular overgrazing, drainage and burning, can have detrimental impacts on many peatland water quality regulation functions (Figure 5.1). These functions are, in general, strongly linked to the capacity of the peat to accumulate organic matter, and therefore key properties such as water table and the presence of peat-forming species such as *Sphagnum*. The loss of bryophyte cover in the English Peak District (due to a combination of air pollution and intensive management) has led to reduced nitrogen retention and high nitrate leaching to surface waters (Curtis *et al.* 2005), while water table drawdown via drainage or gully erosion has reduced sulfur retention via sulfate reduction, exacerbating runoff acidification (Daniels *et al.* 2008a). Various studies suggest that management disturbance can increase DOC loss, due to drainage (Wallage *et al.* 2006; Armstrong *et al.* 2012, 2010; Evans *et al.* 2014b), prescribed burning (Clutterbuck and Yallop 2010) or vegetation change (Armstrong *et al.* 2012). Under the extreme conditions leading to peat erosion, particulate organic carbon (POC) export can increase by several orders of magnitude (Shuttleworth *et al.* 2014), impacting on drinking water quality both directly, and indirectly (via sedimentation of reservoirs, Evans *et al.* 2006; Yeloff *et al.* 2005), and on aquatic filter-feeding organisms (Ramchunder *et al.* 2009).

Overall, it is clear that both local management and external drivers such as climate, and sulfur and nitrogen deposition can impact on water regulation by peatlands. For some issues, such as POC loss, peat restoration will lead to clear and significant water quality improvements. For other issues, notably DOC and water colour, there is greater uncertainty, and in some cases confusion, regarding the relative importance of management versus external factors. Despite this, anticipated reductions in water colour are often a key motivation for peatland restoration, for example in the UK, where the private water company United Utilities initiated its Sustainable Catchment Management Project (SCaMP) project on this basis. On the other hand, other potential water quality benefits of good peatland management and restoration, such as reduced leaching of nitrogen, sulfur, toxic substances and acidity, are rarely considered. This is somewhat surprising given the very large valuation assigned to nutrient regulation by UK inland wetlands by the recent UK National Ecosystem Assessment (£436 ha^{-1} yr^{-1}; Morris and Camino 2011). To set realistic targets for the benefits of restoration activities, it is important that the relative influence of management and external drivers is taken into account; that the full range of potential water quality (and other ecosystem service) impacts are considered; and that monitoring programmes are adequate to identify and attribute the water quality changes that occur.

5.2.2 Water quantity regulation

One of the regulatory functions commonly ascribed to peatlands systems is their capacity to regulate discharge. A commonly used analogy is that of the 'sponge', which can be traced back to the writings of Pearsall (1950) on UK peatlands. Under this model, peatlands are assumed to take up water during wet periods and release it gradually under drier conditions. Evidence for peatlands behaving in this manner comes primarily from fen and swamp systems. For example, Taylor and Pierson (1985) demonstrated that at the scale of the individual storm-hydrograph, valley swamp systems in Ontario, Canada had a significant impact on reducing peak flows, lag times and yields. However, the impact was strongly controlled by antecedent conditions with minimal impact when water tables were high and a limited impact on seasonal patterns of runoff. Similarly Devito *et al.* (1996) demonstrated that forested headwater swamps did not regulate seasonal runoff, but when groundwater recharge was limited in the summer local storage was created through depression of water tables. For peatlands in these contexts to exhibit sponge-like behaviour they must exhibit significant water table drawdown in order to generate sufficient storage capacity to regulate subsequent runoff. They must also have sufficiently high hydraulic conductivity that lateral drainage occurs at a rate sufficient to affect streamwater recharge. Charman (2002) suggests that the woody peats characteristic of forested North American peatlands tend to have higher variation in hydraulic conductivity with depth and greater macropore flow than the relatively dense and homogeneous sedge peats of the oceanic peatlands of Western Europe. Similarly, Evans *et al.* (2014) report data showing that tropical peats tend to have highest hydraulic conductivity followed by fen peats, raised bog, and with blanket peatlands having the lowest values.

Although there are some examples of wetland systems regulating flow, peatlands form under conditions of perennially high water table, so the volume of storage available above the water table is typically low. In raised mires, percolation mires and some fen systems, some additional water storage may be created through 'mire breathing' (Ingram 1983; Charman 2002; Chapter 13). Fundamentally, however, wetlands are highly productive of surface runoff. True ombrotrophic (rain-fed) peatlands maintain near-surface water tables for much of the time. For example, Evans *et al.* (1999) showed water table at or above the surface 83% of the time in blanket bog systems in the North Pennines of the UK. In these systems high water tables are maintained because lateral drainage is very low due to very low hydraulic conductivity in deeper catotelm peats. Water table fluctuations are therefore confined to a relatively narrow range near the surface reaching, in the North Pennine example, depths below the surface of only 400 mm even in severe droughts (Evans *et al.* 1999). Available storage is therefore rapidly filled during storms, minimising the effect of soil storage on regulation of flow. Furthermore, where hydraulic conductivity of the saturated layer is very low, rates of lateral drainage are minimal and there is only a minor contribution from the peat soils to the maintenance of baseflow. Consequently, despite its persistence in the popular understanding of peatlands, the sponge analogy is far from universally applicable and is generally held to be a fallacy at least in relation to blanket peatlands (Baird et al. 1998; Holden and Burt 2003, Bay 1968).

An alternative to the notion that peatlands regulate runoff through soil-water storage and release is to consider the role of peatland surface conditions in controlling runoff. In systems where saturated overland flow or rapid near-surface flow through the acrotelm dominates lateral exchanges of water, the nature of the surface can be an important influence on the velocity of runoff from the peatland. At its simplest this can be expressed through surface water storage. Where raised bog systems have associated lagg fens, surface water storage in the fen can lead to delayed downstream flood peaks. Bragg (2002) reports delays of up to 24 hours in Scottish systems. More generally the roughness of peatland surfaces can impact the rates of surface runoff and therefore significantly influences the time to peak of storm discharge events. Holden et al. (2008) report field experiments which demonstrate a strong influence of roughness on overland flow velocities with the greatest flow velocities occurring on bare peat, followed by peat with a heather/sedge vegetation cover and *Sphagnum*-dominated peatland having the slowest overland flow velocities. Further evidence of the importance of this effect comes from the Trout Beck catchment, a blanket peat system in the English North Pennines where Grayson, Holden and Rose (2010) show an association between changing catchment erosion status and runoff. Higher exposure of bare peat on the catchment slopes led to flashier storm hydrographs and significantly higher mean storm peak discharges.

Despite a widespread acceptance that peatlands play a role in regulation of discharge, there is little firm evidence to generalise the impact of peatlands on discharge regulation beyond a few case studies. One important possible distinction is between rain-fed mires and topographically controlled mires. In topographically controlled mire systems, where water tables are controlled partially by inputs of water from upstream/upslope, higher hydraulic conductivity gives the potential for more rapid lateral drainage and water-table drawdown creating more potential storage and subsequent stream water recharge. Rain-fed raised mire systems, by definition, maintain a water table above the surrounding landscape, and their ability to maintain a raised mire form and elevated water table is controlled by low hydraulic conductivity in basal peats (Ingram 1982). Consequently, water tables are maintained at or near the surface for most of the year, the potential for soil-water storage is low and runoff is generated rapidly through saturation excess overland flow during storm conditions. In such systems, surface character is likely to be a stronger control on the timing of runoff than soil-water storage.

5.3 Degradation of peatlands

Hydrological disturbance of peatland systems can be intentional or unintentional. Unintentional changes arise, for example, from grazing, burning, atmospheric deposition, global warming, large-scale flooding associated with hydroelectric development and mining activities. Intentional changes result from drainage and harvesting and mining activities, mostly those associated with forestry, peat extraction, agriculture, urban development and, more recently, with the development of wind farms on peatlands.

Unintentional disturbance can take place on broad regional or even global scales. Climate change is of great concern since many peatland areas will experience an increased summer water deficit, which could lower peatland water tables by ~14–22 cm (Roulet *et al.* 1992). However, this will be highly spatially variable because of the different properties of peat (Whittington and Price 2006) both within and between peatlands, and also because of high uncertainties in the amount and timing of rainfall predicted by climate models. Lower water tables will induce vegetation change (Strack *et al.* 2006), promote carbon loss (Strack and Waddington 2007) and (other than in the wettest mires) reduce the rates of peat formation (Belyea and Malmer 2004). Broad-scale impacts to peatland hydrology can result from atmospheric deposition of nitrates and sulfates, for example, which can change the vegetation composition and structure (Vitt *et al.* 2003) and accelerate carbon loss, thus altering the composition of peat (Evans *et al.* 2006).

Regional effects on peatlands flooded by hydroelectric developments or water transfers are more difficult to define, since their complete inundation results in the loss of all hydrological function. Peatland adjacent to inundation may be affected (Price *et al.* 1992) as well as regional climate (Rouse *et al.* 1992). Mining can completely remove peatlands (see Price *et al.* 2010) and mine de-watering can desiccate them (Whittington and Price 2012).

Where multiple unintentional changes impact on a peatland system, the resultant degradation can be severe. The most extreme examples of this are the blanket peatlands of the UK and Ireland. Here a combination of industrial acid pollution (associated with the Industrial Revolution) together with overgrazing, wildfire and the climate changes of the last millennium have led to widespread and severe gully erosion and extensive areas of exposed bare peat (Tallis 1997; Evans and Warburton 2007). Extensive gully erosion of peatland systems has two important effects. Firstly the local drawdown of water table by direct drainage can lower water tables significantly. Gully depths in blanket peat are often 2 m or more (Evans and Lindsay 2010) and water table in the adjacent peats can be drawn down by up to 800 mm (Allott *et al.* 2009). This effect is, however, local to the gullies; low hydraulic conductivities in the peat mean that the drainage effect is only significant within about 2–4 m lateral distance of the gullies. Second, the dense dissection of the peatland surface by gullying disrupts downslope flowpaths so that the source area for runoff to downslope locations is reduced, further depressing water tables in gullied systems. This effect occurs across the whole of the dissected peatland. Lowered water tables associated with peat drainage lead to development of macropores in the peat, which are important hydrological links between hillslope and channel, particularly on the initial rising limb of the storm hydrograph (Daniels *et al.* 2008b).

Intentional disturbances to peatlands typically involve some form of drainage to de-water the peat to facilitate agriculture, forest growth and peat extraction. Inevitably the hydrological regime will be affected, including lowering of water table and water content of peat and increasing runoff (Holden *et al.* 2006). Drainage for the purposes of forestry is intended to provide aeration for tree roots, which accelerates forest productivity (Roy *et al.* 1999). Acrotelm function is largely maintained, at least initially, because the direct surface disturbance to the peat is minimal beyond the ditched zone, although soil subsidence affects the hydrology indirectly (see below). In contrast, for peat extraction operations drainage is required to increase the bearing capacity for heavy machinery (see Schothorst 1982), and to lower the moisture content of the peat as part of the production process, whereafter the entire surface layer (former acrotelm) is removed. Therefore, while forestry and peat extraction operations on peatlands require drainage as an initial step, the hydrological consequences differ considerably. Nevertheless, the intentional outcome of drainage is a lowering of the water table, the efficacy of which is inversely related to the distance between ditches, and directly proportional to depth of ditching and the hydraulic conductivity of the peat (Boelter 1972). As with gullied systems, water table drawdown is greatest close to the ditch and diminishes relatively quickly with distance. Price (2003) identifies an effective distance of 15 m in Canadian cutover peatlands. Water tables may also be lowered more widely due to changes in catchment areas.

Peatland drainage causes peat subsidence and changes to the water balance. Peat subsidence is a consequence of decreased peat volume caused by shrinkage and oxidation of peat above the water table, and compression below (Schothorst 1977). As a consequence, the hydraulic properties, including hydraulic conductivity and water retention, are affected. The decrease in hydraulic conductivity (Price 2003) reduces the vertical and lateral movement of water in the peat deposit (Kennedy and Price 2005). However, greater (vertical) capillary flows may occur as a consequence of the new hydraulic geometry, whereby smaller pores in the unsaturated zone exert a stronger pull on the residual water, compared to uncompressed peat at a similar water content (Schlotzhauer and Price 1999). Rothwell *et al.* (1996) concluded that potentially negative effects of drainage can, over a period of several years, be buffered by subsidence, because of this enhanced soil-water retention. Whittington and Price (2006) noted that the surface elevation of fen lawns and mats oscillated with the water table, thus remaining wet under both wet and dry conditions, but lost this ability when artificial drainage was installed.

Changes to the hydrology and water balance are affected by the above noted changes in the hydraulic properties and the lower water table associated with drainage. Holden *et al.* (2006) provide a comprehensive review of the impact of drainage on streamflow from blanket peatlands. They indicate that runoff can become more flashy with drainage, even though lower water tables restrict overland flow. Instead, water conveyance by ditches and macropores that develop in drained peat (especially blanket bog peat) make runoff more efficient (larger proportion of the water budget) (Holden *et al.* 2006). Comprehensive studies of changes in runoff regime in paired catchments are lacking for other peatland types. However, it is noteworthy that some studies have noted a decrease in storm-hydrograph peaks and an increase in baseflow (see Baden and Egglesmann 1970), attributable to greater water storage capacity in a drained system (i.e. lower water table) and continued drainage between storms (Burke 1972). See Holden *et al.* (2006) for a comprehensive discussion.

Changes to evapotranspiration from drained peatlands are related to changes in the position of the water table, changes in vegetation communities and to changes in the hydraulic properties of drained peat. Potential decreases in evapotranspiration caused by a lower water table may be offset by the subsidence of the surface (Lafleur and Roulet 1992), and increased water retention (Rothwell *et al.*1996). Changes in water table can produce significant change in surface vegetation (Lindsay 2010). Modification of the surface vegetation is likely to result in changes to the regime of evapotranspiration, although the degree of change will be closely dependent on the particular nature of vegetation change at a site. Lafleur and Rouse (1988) suggested that the presence of trees in a wet James Bay coastal peatland did not increase the evapotranspiration over a sedge-dominated system. Furthermore, Price (1996) showed that drained cutover peatland near Lac St. Jean, Québec, had similar evapotranspiration losses to a nearby undisturbed site. In the latter example, increased capillary flows of the (more decomposed) cutover peat compensated for the loss of transpiring vegetation. Capillary flow is a key control on surface evaporation in drained peatlands (Schwärzel et al. 2006). Where deep drainage for agriculture, particularly in more continental conditions, dries peats to the extent that they lose capillarity and become hydrophobic (Zeitz and Velty 2002), the effects on vegetation and evaporation are likely to be more significant. The closely coupled nature of the soil–water–vegetation system in peatland systems means that the association of evaporative changes with drainage is complex and subject to numerous feedbacks. The impacts are likely to vary in space and between peatland types, so generalising across peatland types in the absence of empirical data is to be avoided.

5.4 Restoration

Approaches to peatland restoration vary between peatland types and are explored in detail in other chapters in this volume. In the context of hydrological restoration there are two key considerations: first, approaches to restoring water tables and second, the hydrological implications of modifying or re-establishing vegetation cover on degraded systems.

The impact of drainage ditches on water table can persist for decades (Holden et al. 2006; Van Seters and Price 2001); hence, blocking ditches to retain water onsite is an essential feature of all restoration programs. However, changes to the hydraulic properties of the peat are not significantly reversible with rewetting; only some of the consolidation can be recovered (Ketcheson and Price 2011), but oxidative processes cannot (Kennedy and Price 2005). The changes in water storage properties, such as a decrease in the specific yield associated with peat compression and oxidation, result in more variable and deeper water tables, even when the basic water balance has been restored by ditch blocking (Price 1996). To compensate for this, additional surface water retention features such as peat bunds (Shantz and Price 2006a) can be effective in curtailing surface runoff and creating additional storage. However, this may also result in increased evaporation losses (Ketcheson and Price 2011). One approach to restoring the physical properties of drained peats is to remove upper layers of the peat alongside water management. This approach has been applied in fen systems (Klimkowska *et al.* 2015; Chapter 10), where a primary aim is removal of nutrient-rich surface layers, but this approach also removes oxidised and consolidated layers of surface peat, restoring a more typical soil hydrology to the surface.

In gully eroded systems, restoration of water tables is a major challenge. Eroded gullies may be over 2 m in depth and complete blocking of these drainage lines to restore a near-surface water table is not possible. Gully blocking using low dams of wood, plastic or stone has become a common technique on eroded blanket bog systems (Anderson *et al.* 2009), but because the dams are low the impact on water table is limited. The blocks do, however, effectively retain sediment and promote re-vegetation and so impact on hydrology through increases in channel roughness rather than major changes in the water table.

One of the greatest challenges in peatland restoration is establishing a vegetation cover representative of the original system, especially in cutover peatlands where the surface vegetation layer has been completely removed. Drainage of peatland alters the water relations on which the original plant community relied. Removing surface vegetation for peat extraction further alters the soil and water relations, including the seed bank that could contribute to spontaneous regeneration. Lavoie and Rochefort (1996) found *Sphagnum* mosses, the dominant peat-forming plant in bogs, spontaneously recovered on less than 10% of a drained and cutover peatland after 30 years of abandonment, even though other typical (vascular) species had returned. Price and Whitehead (2001) attributed this to low soil-water pressures (below −100 cm of water) in the cutover peat substrate, which desiccates *Sphagnum*, even when the capillary fringe is extensive (Price and Whitehead 2004). The large pores and loose structure of undecomposed mosses cannot generate a strong capillary rise (Price and Whittington 2010). The inability of *Sphagnum* to establish is also in part due to the barrier formed by *Ericaceae* litter that develops on the surface and, in part, to significant transpiration and interception losses from ericaceous shrubs (Farrick and Price 2009), which proliferate on relatively dry drained bog peat (Girard *et al.* 2002). Frost heaving and needle ice also cause damage to the roots of vascular plants (Groeneveld and Rochefort 2005). Once established on cutover peat, *Sphagnum* cushions modify the local environment and somewhat stabilise soil moisture variations, more so in larger cushions (Price and Ketcheson 2009). See Price and Ketcheson (2009) for a comprehensive review of the hydrological changes and challenges associated with restoring cutover peatlands, especially block-cut systems (i.e. older systems dug by hand), and Price *et al.* (2003) for a comparative analysis of restoring block-cut and milled peat (i.e. the most common mechanical extraction) extracted peatlands. Box 5.1 describes the key hydrological changes associated with restoration of cut-over peatlands at Bois de Bel, Québec.

Box 5.1

Bois-des-Bel peatland, Québec, before (1999), during (2000–2002) and after (2010) restoration.

Peatland condition	Characteristics	Key processes	Hydrological consequences
(a) **Figure 5.2a** Abandoned cutover peatland	Vacuum-harvested peatland abandoned in 1980, viewed here in 1999. After 20 years there was very little vegetation, and no *Sphagnum*. Drainage ditches were partially clogged with sediment and *Typha*	Oxidation has lowered the surface by about 10 cm since abandonment. Frost heave, along with harsh hydrological conditions, precluded spontaneous re-vegetation. Oxidation and mechanical subsidence result in high water retention and low specific yield of peat	Water-table depth for unrestored peatland down to 80 cm below the surface. Low specific yield resulted in large water table fluctuations. High water retention of cutover peat resulted in high, sustained evaporation loss. Drainage ditches were still effective, so no ponding or overland flow occurred (Shantz and Price 2006a, b).
(b) **Figure 5.2b** Year 2000, after restoration	Bunds (25–35 cm high) were constructed and ditches were blocked. Straw mulch covered moss and plant fragments taken from a donor site (Poulin *et al.* 2013)	Bunds retained snowmelt water, but were ineffective when water table receded below surface. Mulch altered microclimate, but largely decomposed within 3 years.	Average water table May–Aug 2000–2002 increased by 10.9 cm compared to unrestored site. Evaporation during this period was reduced by mulch to 82% of unrestored site. Average runoff was reduced by 16 mm. Runoff became more dominated by near-surface water, as groundwater loss into ditches was impeded.

Peatland condition	Characteristics	Key processes	Hydrological consequences
Figure 5.2c Ten years after restoration	A 15–20 cm layer comprising mostly *Sphagnum rubellum* cover >90% of the site	Moss layer adjacent to cutover peat formed a capillary barrier, limiting upward water exchange between layers (McCarter and Price 2013).	Water table resided mostly in cutover peat, and was deeper than in an adjacent undisturbed bog
	Bulk density of moss layer much lower than that in a nearby undisturbed bog		Evaporation similar to early post-restoration values, as was runoff More time is required for moss to develop a bulk density profile more similar to natural bogs, whereupon water can be retained in the new moss layer

In fen systems, the primary challenge associated with restoration is hydrological. The challenges are significant because of their dependence on inflowing water to maintain water tables, which may be sourced from other land-use types. Restoration of the water table may be achieved through local blocking of ditches or in heavily modified landscapes may require landscape-scale modification of water flows (Lamers *et al.* 2014). Key considerations are management of water sources and water flow in fens so as to mitigate risks of acidification or eutrophication. Water-table management requires not only raising of the water table, but also the management of the seasonal water table regime. Lamers *et al.* (2014) review the key issues. For a conservation-focused perspective from the UK, see McBride *et al.* (2010).

In the upland blanket peatlands of the UK, where large areas of bare peat have been exposed by erosion, the effects of frost heave described above are a major limitation on re-vegetation. The approach that has been developed to restore these large areas includes aerial seeding of the peat surface with utility grasses, which is applied at the same time as lime, fertiliser and a mulch of cut heather. The aim of this restoration approach is to establish a

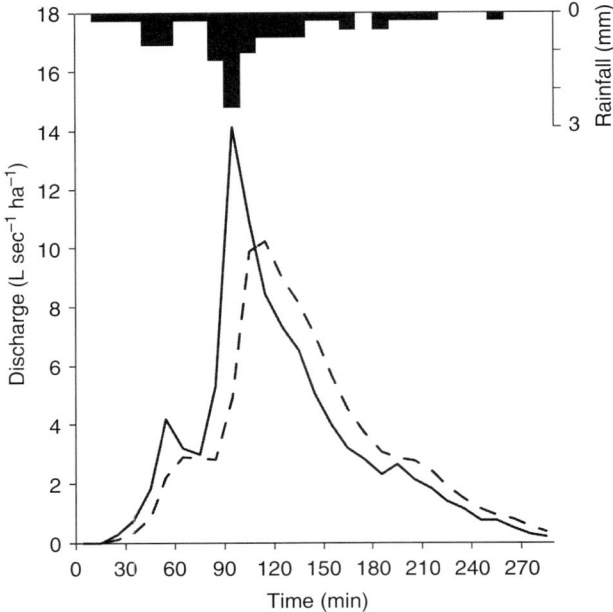

Figure 5.3 Comparison of storm runoff on 19 July 2012 between control (eroded, solid line) and restored (re-vegetated, dashed line) paired blanket peat catchments on the Kinderscout Plateau, South Pennines, UK (Allott and Evans, unpublished data).

nurse crop, which temporarily stabilises the peat surface to allow the colonisation of native species. The approach achieves rapid re-vegetation with grasses and succession to heather and other species (Cole et al. 2014).

Initial data suggest that re-vegetation may lead to slight increases in water table, most likely due to changes in the evaporative regime at the surface (Allott et al. 2009). The other significant hydrological effect associated with the change in surface cover relates to runoff generation. The work of Grayson et al. (2010) on natural re-vegetation suggests that roughness effects may lead to a slowing of surface runoff and reduced flood peaks at catchment scale. Comparison of paired catchments in the South Pennines of heavily eroded control sites to restored sites shows both reduced flood peaks and longer lag times consistent with this pattern (Figure 5.3). Box 5.2 describes the key hydrological impacts of restoration on eroded blanket peatlands.

5.5 Conclusions

Peatlands are a diverse group of ecosystems exhibiting considerable variation in form and function. Given that perennially high water tables are essential to their function, hydrological understanding is integral to achieving restoration of degraded systems.

Box 5.2

Hydrological change in blanket bogs through a cycle of erosion and restoration

Peatland condition	Characteristics	Key processes	Hydrological consequences
(a) Figure 5.4a Intact peatland (Bleaklow Plateau)	Intact peatlands with high water tables, relatively low channelised drainage densities and complete vegetation cover	Dominance of overland flow and near-surface flow Runoff generation associated with saturation overland flow	Rapid runoff, flashy hydrographs
(b) Figure 5.4b Eroded peatland (Kinderscout Plateau)	Highly eroded peatland with gullying creating high drainage density and extensive bare peat	Rapid overland flow over low-roughness surfaces and increased importance of channel flow/ increased slope channel linkage due to gullying Locally reduced water tables due to gullying, which reduces contributing areas and causes local drainage	Lowered water tables Very rapid storm runoff from bare surfaces and in channels
(c) Figure 5.4c Restored peatlands (Bleaklow Plateau)	Restoration of vegetation cover, raised water tables but no restoration of morphology so that the gully systems still create local drawdown and high drainage density	Reductions in overland flow and channel flow velocities due to increased roughness and microscale surface storage	Significant reductions in peak discharge and increased hydrograph lag times emphasise the importance of surface conditions over drawdown storage in controlling peatland runoff

Peatland condition	Characteristics	Key processes	Hydrological consequences
			Stormflow runoff still rapid as this is a characteristic of peatland systems where high water tables predominate

Restoration can involve blocking of drainage lines or manipulating off-site sources of water to achieve appropriate water tables, and requires consideration of mean water levels and water table variability. Restoration of water table is also commonly constrained by physical changes to the peat system, either to the physical properties of the peat (e.g. due to subsidence) or to the morphology of peatland (e.g. due to erosion). These changes are often not fully reversible in the timescales of typical restoration projects or in the case of severe erosion potentially in human timescales. Consideration therefore has to be given to achievable restoration aims, which may not always represent total restoration to a pristine state but, instead, the selective restoration of key ecosystem services/functions. Hydrological ecosystem services are provided by intact peatlands through regulation of both water quality and water quantity.

Hydrological monitoring of restored peatlands is therefore required, not only to assess change in water table, but also to assess fluxes of water, sediment and solute from peatland systems. In intact systems, the eco-hydrological feedbacks that control peatland form and function lead to characteristic equilibrium conditions in the plant–soil–water system. Restoration of peatlands requires consideration of achievable equilibrium points which take into account significant changes to the boundary conditions of the system, whether these are legacy pollution, changes in morphology or shifts in climatic conditions. Evaluation of a desirable balance of ecosystem services is one way to assess the necessary trade-offs that may be required to set restoration targets and hence to assess restoration success at timescales relevant to the project.

CHAPTER SIX

Peatlands as knowledge archives

BENJAMIN GEAREY
University College Cork, Ireland
RALPH FYFE
University of Plymouth, UK

6.1 Introduction

The waterlogged and anoxic conditions within peatlands can result in the exceptional preservation of a diverse range of material, which provides a unique record of past societies and the environment. Organic remains which are entirely lost from the record on dryland sites may be preserved for millennia within peat. Certain of these finds are among the most vivid and also the most vulnerable evidence of past people and cultures that archaeology is able to provide the world over. Peat also preserves a wide range of 'fossil' material that has long been central to understanding patterns of vegetation change and human impact on the environment. Recent work is now beginning to realise the full potential of peatlands as records of climatic change that may be regarded as the terrestrial equivalent of ice core records. Both the archaeological and palaeo-environmental records are fragile, finite and unique resources, the future survival of which is inseparable from the fate of peatlands.

Three interrelated aspects of peatlands as knowledge archives (archaeology, palaeoecology and conservation ecology; Figure 6.1) can be broadly defined which have synergies but has generally different research agendas, although knowledge transfer between the areas of archaeology/palaeoecology and conservation ecology has increased in recent years (see below). One aim of this chapter is to illustrate the distinctive value of the peatland archive for each of these agendas, but also to highlight the specific value of such work within the context of ecosystem services.

Peatland Restoration and Ecosystem Services: Science, Policy and Practice, eds. A. Bonn, T. Allott, M. Evans, H. Joosten and R. Stoneman. Published by Cambridge University Press. © British Ecological Society 2016.

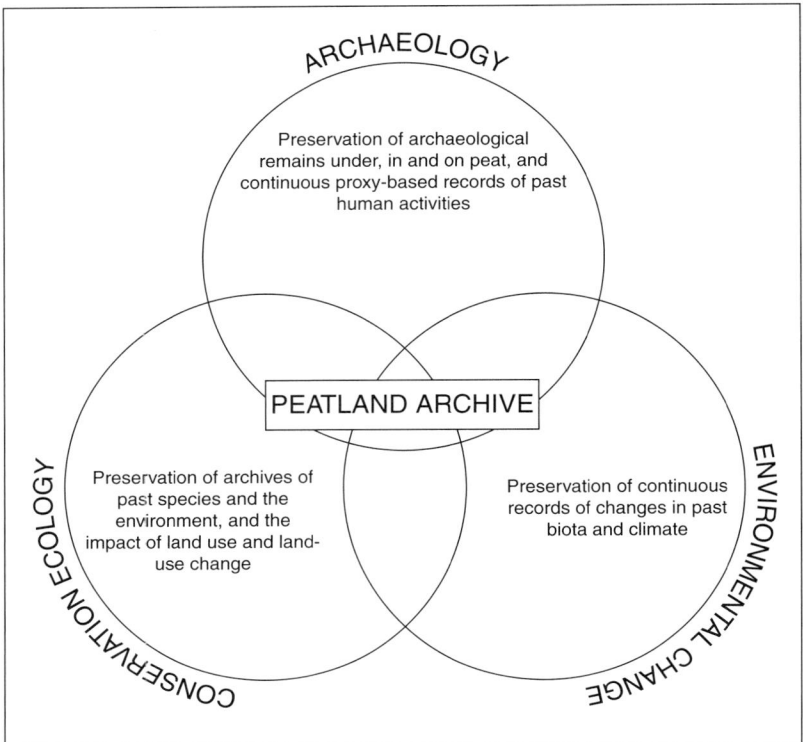

Figure 6.1 Venn diagram illustrating the relationship among the scientific service value of the peatland archive and conservation ecology, the study of environmental change (palaeoecology, palaeo-environmental study) and archaeology.

In particular, by providing long-term records of ecological processes that cannot be attained through 'real-time' monitoring projects, palaeo-environmental data have the potential to inform the future restoration and management of peatlands. Finally, the archaeological and palaeo-environmental archive is also vulnerable to a range of threats, and this chapter discusses the importance of integrated restoration and management to best protect this fragile resource.

6.2 The archaeo-environmental record of peatlands

The archaeological and palaeo-environmental (archaeo-environmental for short) record of peatlands is included in the 'Cultural services' section of the peatland ecosystem services framework within the 'Physical and intellectual interaction with biota, ecosystems, and landscapes' division and the 'Intellectual and representative interactions' group (see Chapter 1; Table 1.1).

6.2.1 The archaeological record of peatlands

A diverse range of sites and artefacts has been found in peatlands, generally from those areas which have been most heavily disturbed, i.e. drained, cutover or reclaimed peatlands in northwest Europe, such as parts of lowland England (e.g. The Somerset Levels, see Box 6.1), the midlands of Ireland, Germany and the Netherlands. Sites can also be discovered during

---

Box 6.1

The Somerset Levels: past cultures from peatlands

The remarkable potential of peatland environments can be well illustrated by considering the Somerset Levels in southwest England. This area saw a period of extensive survey and excavation in the 1970s and 1980s, and is unparalleled in chronological range and richness of the peatland archaeological record. One-quarter of the known surviving wet-preserved sites in England are found here and there are more scheduled examples of such sites than in the whole of the rest of the country combined (Jones et al. 2007). Recognition of the archaeological potential of the Levels dates to the nineteenth century when prehistoric bows and paddles, dug-out canoes and a hoard of bronzes from a wooden box were recovered within peat cuttings (Brunning 2001). Perhaps the best-known sites from this area include the extensive timber-built trackways which indicate human activity in the peatlands over a period of over three-and-a-half millennia from the Neolithic through to the Iron Age, including the well-known Neolithic Sweet Track (Coles and Coles 1986). The range of material culture recovered from the lake village sites of Meare and Glastonbury includes stone (quern stones, grinders and hammer stones), bone, horn and antler (combs, awls and needles), lead and tin (fishing weights and spindle whorls), bronze (rings, broaches, tweezers and needles), glass and amber beads, pottery and wooden containers providing insights into the full span of everyday life in the Iron Age. The peatland archaeological record also incorporates the more mundane items, such as the wooden bowls and implements from Meare (Coles and Coles 1986); objects which would probably have been relatively common during prehistory but are absent from the dryland record.

major infrastructure developments such as the construction of road and rail links which impact upon peatlands (e.g. Larsson 2007). Very little is currently known of peatlands in those parts of the world that remain largely intact, and the difficulty of remotely identifying sites (see below) prevents any informed assessment of their archaeological potential.

Coles (1984) has estimated that as little as 10–25% of the total range of material evidence originally associated with human activity might be inorganic, compared to 75–90% organic, such as wood, leather, plant material and fabrics. The particular value of peatland archaeology is therefore centred upon the preservation of such organic remains, which are rarely, if ever, recovered from other terrestrial archaeological contexts. The conditions that make peatlands suitable for the preservation of organic remains, i.e. waterlogging in anaerobic conditions limiting decomposition of remains, often also favour the survival of inorganic material (Fell and Williams 2004). Some classes of material, however, may preserve less well in peat, as acidic conditions tend to destroy ferrous metals and bone.

There are no comprehensive international synthetic archaeological overviews of the numbers or character of peatland archaeological sites and artefacts, although some general national estimates are available: Brzeziński (1992) concluded that of around 6000 archaeological sites excavated in Poland between 1967 and 1987, some 300 were regarded as 'wetland in character', although this makes no distinction between peatlands and other wetlands. It is clear that some areas possess a significant resource. The most intensively investigated peatlands in Europe are those of the Republic of Ireland, where archaeological survey of c. 64 000 ha of peatland between 1990–2009, associated with intensive and extensive drainage and peat cutting of these lowland raised mires, has recorded over 4300 archaeological sites, very few of which will be preserved *in situ* or recorded by detailed archaeological excavation (Gearey et al. 2013). Plunkett and Foley (2006) identified 41 trackways in both lowland and upland contexts in Northern Ireland, only five of which sites were known to survive. A recent survey of the archaeological resource identified over 12% of archaeological sites in wetland contexts, although again no distinction was made between peatlands and other types of wetland (Gormley et al. 2009).

Coles and Coles (1989) concluded that there were around 1000 known trackways from peatlands in Ireland, the United Kingdom, the Netherlands, Denmark and Germany dating from the Neolithic period to the first millennium AD. The broad stylistic similarities between these structures led Raftery (1996) to view this as demonstrating the emergence of a: 'commonly executed, but independently conceived, method of traversing wet bogs'. While 'functional' sites, such as trackways and platforms, designed

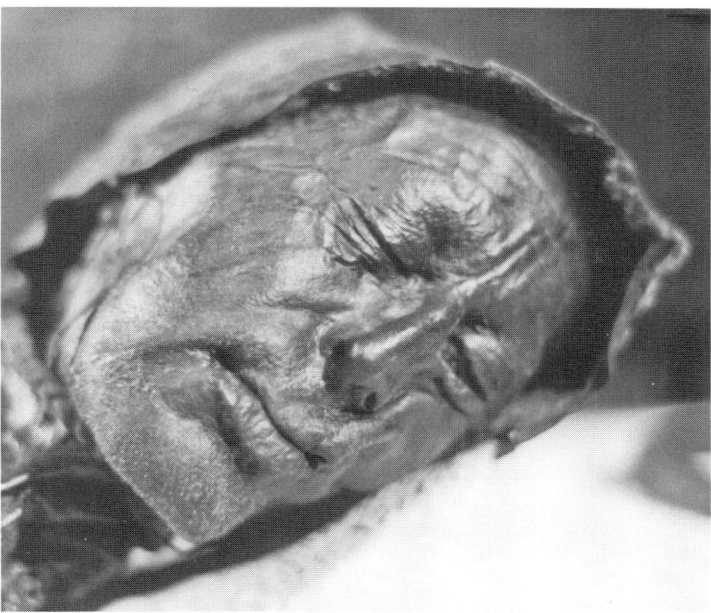

Figure 6.2 The face of Tollund Man, a bog body dating to the pre-Roman Iron Age discovered in a peat bog on the Jutland Peninsula in Denmark (photo: Sven Rosborn).

to cross or access peatlands probably form the greater part of the cultural remains recorded to date, the range of material is diverse and includes fragments of prehistoric boats from Norway (e.g. Henriksen and Sylvester 2007), the remains of wheeled vehicles from Lower Saxony (Hayen 1987), Britain's oldest known bow from the Moffat Hills, southwest Scotland (Sheridan 1993), Iron Age wooden vessels from Ireland (Moore 2000), exceptionally well-preserved human remains or 'bog bodies' (Van der Sanden 1996; Sanders 2009; see Figure 6.2) and prehistoric carved wooden figurines from peatlands across northwest Europe (Van der Sanden and Capelle 2001). Some artefacts such as the Gundestrup Cauldron (Kaul 1995), the largest known example of Iron Age silver work, which was discovered in a Danish bog, were deliberately deposited as part of prehistoric rites centred on these places (Bradley 1990). Other sites also appear to reflect the use of peatlands for ritual practices, such as the Neolithic stone row found within blanket peat on Cut Hill, Dartmoor (Fyfe and Greeves 2010).

Entire palaeolandscapes, with associated archaeological sites and monuments, may be wholly or partially sealed *beneath* peatlands. Since archaeological sites beneath peat are by definition associated with the landscape prior to the extensive spread of wetland environments, they are often similar to sites found in dryland contexts. The Céide Fields in western Ireland

(Caulfield 1983) are one of the best examples of this where entire field systems dating to the Neolithic are preserved beneath blanket peat (see Box 6.2). Likewise, the Copney Stone Circle complex in Northern Ireland, part of the Mid-Ulster Stone Circle Complex, was constructed during the Bronze Age (*c.* 2500 BC) on dryland that was only later subsumed by peat growth (Foley and MacDonagh 1998). Other remains include discrete artefacts, such as Mesolithic cultural material in the form of fragments of stone tools found eroding from beneath blanket peat in areas such as the Pennines and the North Yorkshire Moors (e.g. Manby 2003) of northern England. Such pre-peat sites can be regarded as especially important since the overlying peat means that artefact distributions have been preserved *in situ* in a manner rarely found in other contexts (Spikins *et al.* 2002).

> Box 6.2
> ## The Céide Fields: Neolithic field systems
>
> The Céide fields are the name given to a complex of rectangular field systems and associated oval settlement enclosures and megalithic tombs in County Mayo, Ireland, which were subsequently sealed beneath blanket peat that has effectively 'fossilised' an entire Neolithic landscape (Figure 6.3). Survey and excavation (Caulfield 1978, 1983; Caulfield, O'Donnell and Mitchell 1998) has demonstrated that the field systems cover some 1000 ha and extend over an area of *c.* 5 km northwest to southeast and 4 km southwest to northeast. Palaeo-environmental data (e.g. O' Connell and Molloy 2001), including pollen analyses and radiocarbon dating of the peat and pre-peat landsurfaces, are key to the understanding of the timing and nature of human activity and also the processes by which peat subsequently spread across the landscape. Radiocarbon dating suggests that the construction of the fields began during a phase of largely pastoral farming, with some evidence for cereal cultivation in the early Neolithic around 5700 BP. This was associated with large-scale clearance of woodland, probably on both the local and regional scales, prior to a marked reduction in farming around 5200 years before the present. Peat accumulation appears to have been strongly diachronous, but by 4200 BP had probably spread across much of the landscape although the relationship between the abandonment of the field systems, the formation of peat and possible climatic change remains unclear. There is evidence for other such pre-peat archaeological sequences in a wide area around Céide Fields (Caulfield 1978), which continue to provide detailed archaeological and palaeo-environmental data regarding early settlement and agriculture (e.g. Verrill and Tipping 2010).

Methods for realising and demonstrating the archaeological resource of peatlands can be extremely challenging. While in theory archaeological monuments in peatlands can be identified in much the same way as for drylands, through field walking of drains and other exposures (see Coles 1984; McDermott 2007), this is limited to areas which have already to some extent been disturbed and in practice may be significantly restricted by conditions on the ground, such as high water tables. Remote-sensing techniques such as Earth Resistance have been used to delimit known areas of archaeological remains within wetlands, and other methodologies, including aerial photography, ground penetrating radar, Light Detection and Ranging (LiDAR) and microtopographic surveys may, under certain circumstances, provide useful information regarding aspects of the buried resource (e.g. Chapman and Van de Noort 2001; Cox *et al.* 2001; Chapman and Gearey 2013).

However, it is currently beyond the scope of geophysical methods to explore spatially extensive peatlands to locate or map archaeological sites within or beneath peat (but see Armstrong 2010), due to both the scale of the task and in certain instances the specific physical properties of waterlogged sediments (Coles and Coles 1996). As discussed above, it has long been recognised that our knowledge of the archaeological record of peatlands is thus significantly biased towards those areas that have been most heavily impacted by human activity and are hence by definition already at threat.

6.2.2 Palaeoecology

The value of peatlands as archives of long-term environmental processes has been known for over a century and a half, following the recognition that sub-fossil remains of tree stumps within bogs and variations in peat stratigraphy reflected changes in the prevailing climate (e.g. Dau 1829; Sernander 1908). The manner in which peat accumulates means that deposits have stratigraphic integrity: a core or section through a peatland represents a chronological transect back through time, from the present-day surface through to the oldest deposits at the base. The waterlogged conditions can preserve pollen from plants that grew both on and around the peatland, fragments of insects, fungal spores and organisms, such as testate amoebae. Palaeo-environmental studies are now beginning to realise the potential of peatlands for such study across the world (e.g. Estonia, Newberry *et al.* 2007; Poland, Lamentowicz *et al.* 2010; South East Asia, Page *et al.* 2010; the Amazon Basin, Lähteenoja *et al.* 2011). Recently, significant progress has also been in the application of organic and inorganic geochemistry and stable isotope analyses to peat deposits (e.g. McClymont, Pendall and Nichols 2010).

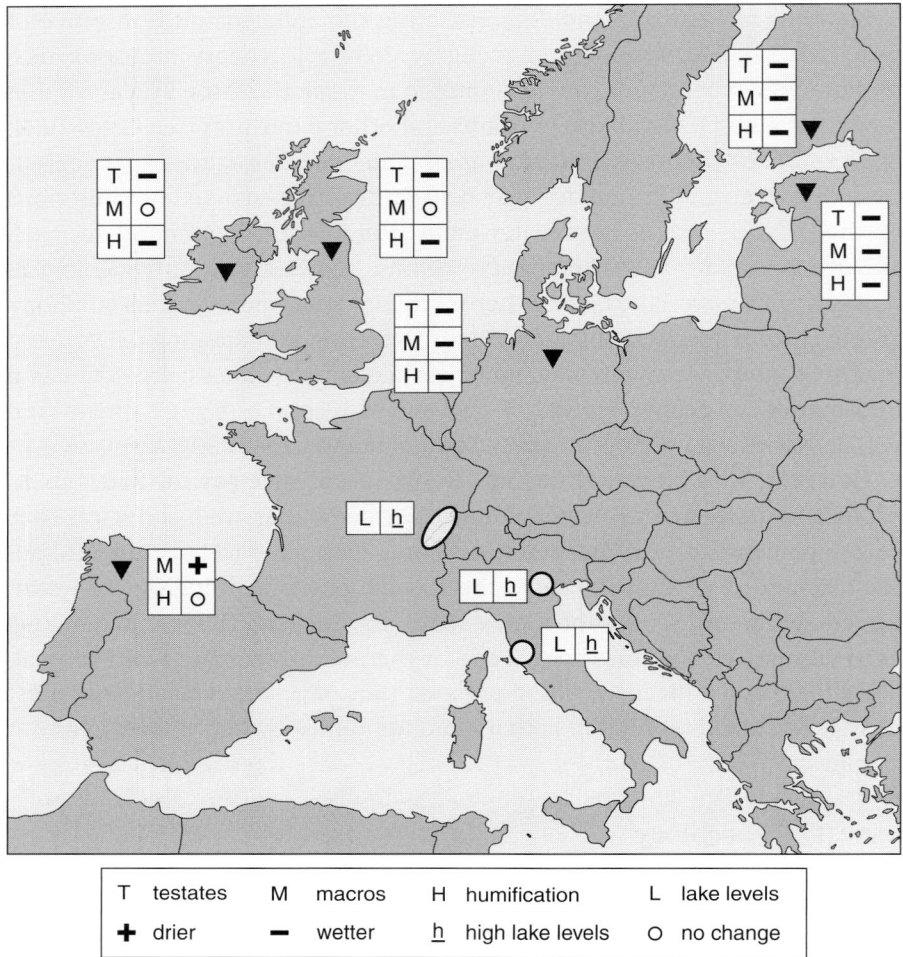

Figure 6.3 Schematic ACCROTELM project map (adapted from Chambers *et al.* 2010) summarising data from six bog sites (closed triangles) and three lake sites showing the direction of change in the century following climatic deterioration around 2700–2800 BP, as indicated by up to three proxy-climate records at each of the bog sites and coincident high water level records of lake sites.

As well as providing unique opportunities to understand the growth and long-term evolution of peatland ecosystems themselves (Charman 2002), the scientific study of this material preserved within peat can be used to elucidate past changes in vegetation and human impact upon the environment, variations in temperature, hydrology and other processes such as the cycling of carbon (Charman *et al.* 2013).

The high organic content of peat means that absolute chronologies can be constructed using radiocarbon and other radioisotope dating of discrete macrofossils or bulk samples of sediment, permitting the relative dating of environmental changes inferred from proxies such as those outlined above. The precision and accuracy of radiocarbon chronologies have in recent years been significantly improved via advances in accelerator mass spectrometry (AMS) dating, calibration and mathematical modelling (Bronk Ramsey 2008). Layers of volcanic ash (tephra), preserved within peat can be geochemically 'finger-printed' to their source eruption (e.g. Plunkett 2006), the exact calendar date of which may be known, while other techniques including ^{210}Pb and spheroidal carbonaceous particles (e.g. Yang et al. 2001) can provide further dating control. The chronological precision of palaeo-environmental records can in some cases now approach the decadal over periods of several millennia (Blauw et al. 2010).

Such methodological advances have in part permitted significant expansion and progress in the study of peatlands as archives of palaeoclimate (Chambers and Charman 2004). This has also followed from the hypothesis that ombrotrophic peatlands, such as blanket bogs and raised bogs, preserve records of past hydrological changes, as the growing surface of the system is directly coupled to rainfall, temperature and humidity (Barber 1981). Past changes in bog surface wetness (BSW) throughout the depth of a peatland can be reconstructed using a range of techniques, including the estimation of relative hydrological shifts derived from changes in the composition of the peat-forming vegetation and the degree of peat 'humification' (decay). The analysis of testate amoebae has probably been the most important development in this area, with quantitative estimates of the depth of past water tables now possible (e.g. Woodland, Charman and Sims 1998; Charman, Hendon and Woodland 2000).

It has been hypothesised that BSW records are strongly related to the summer moisture deficit, reflecting changes in summer precipitation (Charman 2010). Integrated study of an east–west transect of bogs across Europe under the auspices of the ACCROTELM project (Abrupt Climate Changes Recorded Over The European Land Mass; Chambers et al. 2007a) demonstrated the spatial variability in climate over the last 4500 years. However, there is also evidence for episodes of coherent climatic change across their study area; for example, increased BSW is apparent in many European bogs around 2800 years before the present (Figure 6.3; Chambers et al. 2010). This may coincide with a marked reduction in solar variability recorded in the rise in concentrations of cosmogenic isotopes in other records (Van Geel and Mauquoy 2010). It has been hypothesised that evidence for a wet shift in a sequence from an Argentinean peatland around 2800 years before present may suggest coherent climatic changes and teleconnections between the Northern and Southern Hemispheres (Chambers et al. 2007b).

Similar palaeohydrological studies have been carried out in North America; work in the Great Lakes region of eastern North America indicates that: 'many high-magnitude fluctuations in water balance during the past 3,000 years were spatially extensive, extending from the western United States into eastern North America' (Booth, Jackson and Notaro 2010). Records from mires in eastern North America and Europe may also record evidence for coincident Holocene climatic changes (Hughes et al. 2006). In the current context of a changing global climate system, peatland-derived records, therefore, provide not only critical service value in terms of understanding the character and timing of past climate changes but are also significant in terms of understanding the possible response of peatlands to future fluctuations (see below).

Another important and related area of research is the use of peat records to study vegetation change and the impact of human activity on the environment, i.e. land use and land-use change. The peat archive preserves pollen and spores reflecting wider regional vegetation changes over millennial timescales, which can in turn be closely linked to archaeological evidence for human activity and cultural change (e.g. Simmons and Innes 1987; Fyfe et al. 2008), alongside microscopic and macroscopic charcoal relating to both on- and off-site fire histories (e.g. Bal et al. 2011). Where palaeo-environmental analyses are carried out in association with archaeological sites such as those discussed in the previous section, the combined records can provide exceptional, closely integrated evidence of the timing, patterns and processes of cultural and environmental change both within a particular peatland and for the wider landscape (e.g. Coles and Coles 1986; Tipping et al. 2008).

The identification of trace amounts of metals in peat deposits can provide records of atmospheric loading of pollutants associated with industrial activities, demonstrating pollution sources and how human activity has impacted upon the atmospheric geochemical cycle of lead and other metals (e.g. Mighall et al. 2002). For example, analyses of peat sequences from European bogs have produced reconstructions of atmospheric Pb (lead) deposition linked to mining activity and evidence for deforestation in associated pollen records (De Vleeschouwer, Le Roux and Shotyk 2010).

6.3 Conservation and restoration ecology

The added value of palaeo-environmental data as a means of providing a record of 'long-term ecology' has been recognised for some time (e.g. Barber 1993), and recent years have seen more concerted attempts to integrate these data into modern practice (e.g. Willis et al. 2005; Hodder et al. 2009; Davies 2011; Dietl and Flessa 2011). The input palaeo-environmental study might have into contemporary peatland conservation and management in particular was recognised from at least the early 1990s (e.g. Simmons 1989; Schoomaker and Foster 1991), as the analysis of sequences from networks of peatland sites allows detailed reconstruction of the past environment in both time and space (e.g. Mitchell 2011). Recent case studies highlight the value of palaeoecological datasets derived from peat deposits for conservation and management.

For example, the so-called 'Vera-hypothesis', which postulated that large herbivores maintained an open rather than closed woodland environment during the early Holocene, has been extensively tested and largely falsified using palaeoecological data from peatland records spanning the last 10 000 years (e.g. Bradshaw, Hannon and Lister 2003; Mitchell 2005). The study of sub-fossil Coleoptera from the lowland peatlands of Thorne and Hatfield Moors in eastern England has also illustrated the importance of palaeo-environmental data in conservation biology (Whitehouse *et al.* 2008) as the list of sub-fossil beetles recovered from Thorne: 'contains 45% of the species known to have been extirpated from Britain during the last 3000 years' (Buckland and Dinnin 1997). Chambers *et al.* (2007c) studied blanket peat accumulation during the last *c*. 500 years at the sites of Hirwaun Common and Mynydd Llangatwg (mid- and south Wales) using multiple proxies including plant macrofossils, pollen and charcoal, with dating provided by radiocarbon and the record of 'fly ash' particles. The results indicated that blanket mire degradation, including the replacement of *Sphagnum austinii* by *Molinia caerulea*, was related to changes in atmospheric inputs and grazing pressures in the post-industrial revolution period, with burning also playing a role at Mynydd Llangatwg. The conclusions suggest positive management and restoration strategies for maintenance of bog-forming species by modifying grazing regimes and reducing burning and pollution and associated measures aimed at promoting hydrological stability, information directly relevant to the management of upland moorland and blanket bog.

The plant macrofossil record can also reveal further processes driving changes in bog vegetation. Hughes *et al.* (2007) showed with palynological evidence that the decline of *Sphagnum austinii* in peatlands in Wales and Ireland was closely associated with landscape-scale woodland clearance by humans over the last 200 years. The decline of *Sphagnum austinii* may be related to a complex of factors including hydrological change, land-use intensification and the deposition of dust particles, with nitrogen loading possibly a critical factor. Likewise, plant macrofossil analyses of peat sequences from ombrotrophic mires in Cumbria and the Scottish Borders explored a regional decline in *Sphagnum austinii* at around AD 1030–1460, concluding that this may have been related to climatic change, inter-specific competition among *Sphagnum* species (particularly *Sphagnum magellanicum*) and the deposition of atmospheric dust as a result of increased agricultural activity in the wider landscape (Mauquoy and Barber 1999).

Other palaeocological studies have provided information regarding the long-term context of blanket peat erosion in the uplands of the United Kingdom, the causes of which remain poorly understood and are a major source of concern for the conservation of these habitats (e.g. Tallis *et al.* 1997). For example, Ellis and Tallis (2001) investigated the palaeoecology of a hummock-and-hollow complex in partially eroded blanket peat at the Migneint, North Wales, and attributed evidence of peat erosion since 2000 years before present to the impact of woodland clearance by prehistoric human communities on catchment hydrology. These data support similar evidence from the southern Pennines (e.g. Tallis 1997) implying that mire erosion is not necessarily a direct result of recent anthropogenic disturbance.

Palaeo-environmental data can also provide information on processes of peatland regeneration following past disturbance, which may offer unique perspectives on the future restoration of damaged peatlands. Joosten (1995) drew attention to the value of palaeoecological research in terms of providing reliable long-term data on patterns and processes of peat accumulation and bog vegetation following anthropogenic disturbance, reviewing the evidence for regeneration of peatlands following burning, grazing and peat cutting. Palaeo-environmental data may also provide critical information regarding the relationship between carbon cycling in peatlands and climatic factors (e.g. Novak *et al.* 2008) and in the prediction of possible future responses of peatlands to climate change.

In terms of future peatland management and restoration, information such as this represents a key approach to coping with the 'surprise factor' (see, for example, Gorham *et al.* 2001), or the apparent anomalies within the behaviour of environmental systems that appear to have no short-term precedent but may have analogues within the palaeorecord. For example, analysis of BSW records from Northern Ireland and northern England have been interpreted as showing periods of widespread 'drought' during the mid-late Holocene, apparently associated with episodes of increased solar activity (Swindles *et al.* 2010). Widespread patterns of drought such as those during the Medieval Climate Anomaly are also recorded in peatland records from the western United States, the Great Plains and the Great Lake regions, and it has been suggested that these patterns are similar to a mode of climate variability experienced during the early twentieth century (Booth *et al.* 2010).

In these cases, despite phases of extended summer water deficit, undisturbed systems continued to grow suggesting resilience to allogenic forcing such as that associated with climatic change. However, it has been argued that certain future climate change scenarios may have no direct analogues within the Holocene record (see Table 6.1). Mauquoy and Yeloff (2008) concluded that: 'the response of raised bog peat to future changes in climate may occur in decades, with losses in characteristic *Sphagnum* species and increases in vascular plants' (see Table 6.1). Further work is required in terms of using palaeodata to assess the future development of peatlands under different scenarios of climate change, but it is clear that disturbed peatlands will be significantly less resilient to climate change than healthy systems.

6.4 Threats to the intellectual services of peatlands and the benefits of restoration

Once an organic archaeological site or artefact is exposed or removed from its burial environment, degradation begins very rapidly: 'to excavate into a waterlogged archaeological site is to initiate its destruction' (Coles 1984). The survival of the archaeo-environmental (i.e. the integrated archaeological and palaeo-environmental archive) record is therefore inextricably linked with the fate of peatlands themselves (e.g. Coles and Coles 1986; Coles 1995). Sub-fossil remains of pollen, insects and plants are highly susceptible and there is some evidence that these components may be the first to degrade following de-watering of peat and other organic sediments (e.g. Brunning *et al.* 2000). This contention is supported by recent study of upland peats on Exmoor, southwest England which suggests that long-term drawdown of water tables may impact on the preservation of the palaeoecological archive (Davies, Fyfe and Charman 2015).

The recognition of the value of, and threats to, peatlands and wetlands more generally is reflected in the adoption of legislation which can be utilised in the protection of the archaeological heritage of these environments (Harte 1997; Olivier 2004, 2013; Chapter 19). The most significant of these internationally is the Convention on Wetlands of International Importance (Ramsar 1971), although a range of other instruments are relevant such as the Convention Concerning the Protection of the World Cultural and Natural Heritage (UNESCO 1972), the Convention on the Conservation of European Wildlife and Natural Habitats (The Bern Convention, Council of Europe 1979) and the related European Union Habitats Directive (European Commission 1992).

Various studies of the preservation of the archaeological resource of peatlands and wetlands have been carried out (e.g. Croes 1995; Pedersen *et al.* 1997; Zhilin 2007; Brunning 2013). While it is well established that preservation of organic material under waterlogged conditions is related to a complex of factors including temperature, pH and oxidation–reduction (redox)

Table 6.1 Possible future responses of oceanic northwestern European raised bog to climate change. UKCIP02 low-emission scenario (northwestern England and Scotland), potential summer temperature rise of 1–2.5°C by the 2080s and decrease of summer precipitation by up to 30%. Medium-high, summer mean temperatures to rise 1.5–3.5°C and summer precipitation to decrease by up to 50% (adapted from Mauquoy and Yeloff 2008: 2143).

	Natural climate change: cooler–wetter	**Natural climate change: drier–warmer**	**Greenhouse warming UKCIP02 scenarios: low emission**
Raised bog vegetation response	Expansion of hollow microforms: increases in *Sphagnum* section Cuspidata spp., *Eriophorum angustifolium*, *Rynchospora alba*	Expansion of hummock microforms; increases in *Sphagnum fuscum*, *S. capillifolium*, *Calluna vulgaris*, *Empetrum nigrum*	Expansion of hummock microforms: increased abundances of *Sphagnum fuscum*, *S. capillifolium*, *Calluna vulgaris*, *Empetrum nigrum* and reductions in hollow microform elements
	Increases in low-slope elements: *Sphagnum papillosum*, *S. tenellum*	Reductions in hollow microform element	Possible tree colonisation? *Pinus sylvestris* and *Betula* spp.
Holocene analogue	Little ice age	Medieval warm period	**Holocene climatic optimum** **Medium-high emission** No analogue Extreme reductions in lawn and pool *Sphagnum* spp., expansion of *Calluna vulgaris*, *Empetrum nigrum* Tree colonisation Possible loss of raised mire ecosystem?

potential, recent research demonstrates that the exact parameters which control processes of microbial decay under different conditions are highly complex and beyond the scope of this chapter to consider in detail (e.g. Caple 1994, 2004; Douterelo, Goulder and Lillie 2011).

Physical destruction of peat will of course lead to the loss of any archaeological or palaeo-environmental information preserved within or on the peat matrix, and the exposure of archaeological remains sealed beneath the peat. Other threats may, initially at least, have a less direct but ultimately no less damaging impact on the resource: any process that leads to a reduction in the levels of water saturation or to the quality of the water itself can impact negatively on the long-term survival of the archaeo-environmental record. It is clear that organic material such as wood is especially vulnerable, but inorganic archaeological remains including stone may also be at risk (e.g. Warke *et al.* 2010).

Land use is clearly the most significant threat and activities that physically disturb or remove peat are highly detrimental to the long-term survival of the archive. While preservation may be better under a pastoral rather than arable land use, data from the Somerset Levels indicate rates of peat wastage in pasture fields of 0.44 to 0.79 m over the past century (Brunning 2001). In the Fenland of East Anglia, England, assessments of wastage rates under an arable regime suggest losses of 3.83 m per 100 years (Hutchinson 1980) and 2–3 m per 100 years (French and Pryor 1993). This area has lost much over the last millennia and a half of peat accumulation (Hall 1987), and thus the entire scientific service value of the peatlands from at least the Romano-British period.

High water tables are a key to the preservation of the archaeological and palaeo-environmental resource. Water table instability is often a feature of damaged mires (e.g. Money and Wheeler 1999), but seasonal lowering of water tables may also be desirable for certain aspects of nature conservation and biodiversity. This can be damaging to the scientific service value of deposits, especially within the zone of hydrological fluctuation (e.g. Chapman and Cheetham 2002). Low water tables may have an indirect but potentially damaging effects on the *in situ* preservation of the archaeological and palaeo-environmental resource: study at the late Bronze Age site of Flag Fen, Peterborough, England, has demonstrated the difficulty in preserving archaeological sites where water abstraction and drainage have lowered the water table and compromised the preservation of the archaeology *in situ* (Lillie and Cheetham 2002). This has also been illustrated by ongoing studies of the burial environment of the internationally important Mesolithic site of Star Carr (Mellars and Dark 1998) in the Vale of Pickering, Yorkshire, England, where peat containing the archaeo-environmental deposits appears to have become highly acidic following isolation from the influence of circum-neutral groundwater (Boreham *et al.* 2011).

The processes controlling the successful preservation *in situ* of archaeological sites and deposits within wetland sites are complex and dynamic (e.g. Van de Noort, Chapman and Cheetham 2001a), and conserving the surviving record remains a conspicuous problem in peatlands across Europe. For example, the Bourtanger Moor in the northeastern Netherlands and northwestern Germany was the largest contiguous peatland area in Europe, within which numerous archaeological sites were found, such as the Neolithic Nieuw Dordrecht timber trackway (see above). The area has been almost entirely depleted by peat cutting (Van Heeringen and Theunissen 2007), while the surviving section of the trackway site is threatened by desiccation. However, this provides one of the few examples in the Netherlands where efforts are underway to stabilise the burial environment and help preserve the archaeological record (Theunissen *et al.* 2006). While the work of the National Service for Archaeological Heritage (National Service for Archaeology, Cultural Landscape and Build Heritage after 2006) in the Netherlands is an example of a national concerted and integrated approach to understanding the physical environment of wet-preserved archaeological sites, this initiative is very much the exception rather than the rule.

Current heritage policy for the UK at least stresses that, wherever possible, archaeological sites should be preserved *in situ* (Gregory, Helms and Henning 2008); a principle which is also asserted by the Council of Europe in the Valletta Treaty (e.g. Willems 1998). However, it has recently been stated that despite this supposed protection and recognition: 'The well proven, extensive and rapid destruction of waterlogged archaeological deposits in European peatlands should be regarded as a significant crisis' (Brunning 2007). While few robust figures of the scale of this loss are available, it has been estimated that in England alone, some 2020 sites have destroyed in upland and lowland peatlands over the last 50 years (Van De Noort *et al.* 2001b).

Hence there is a pressing need for restoration and conservation measures that will protect the surviving scientific service value of peatlands. Generally, this protection should be favoured by measures that:

- stabilise peat and reduce erosion
- halt the physical removal of peat
- maintain high water tables
- promote active peat formation.

These actions provide significant positive gains for the protection and preservation of the historic environment record of peatlands. Where conflicts arise with restoration measures, they tend to surround the methods by which different goals are achieved; for example, peatland restoration undertaken in collaboration with historic environment specialists provides a mechanism for assessing and safeguarding archaeological and palaeo-environmental remains (see Table 6.2). As outlined above, it must be ensured that restoration does not impact directly or indirectly on the *in situ* integrity of the record. There are both synergies and trade-offs in restoration strategies directed at different ecosystem service and biodiversity goals, a consequence of which may be unintentional damage to the archaeological and palaeo-environmental resource (e.g. Gill-Robinson 2008).

6.5 Summary and conclusions

This chapter has attempted to demonstrate the remarkable value, range and scope of the intellectual and experiential services of peatlands, but not to provide an exhaustive review of palaeo-environmental and archaeological research and knowledge. The known distribution of the often unique archaeological remains within peatlands across the world is the result of both chance finds and specific survey and research projects. Archaeological fieldwork tends to concentrate upon areas of present destruction and threat, such as the peatlands of Somerset in southwestern England, those of the Bourtanger Moor in the Netherlands, and the midlands of Ireland where drainage and peat cutting have exposed sites which would otherwise remain concealed and protected. Hence, the significant bias in archaeological knowledge is towards the heavily disturbed peatlands in many parts of northwestern Europe. The study of peatland archaeology is therefore frequently reactive and more often than not, effectively on 'the back foot' with all the resource restrictions and limitations associated with this situation.

Future restoration strategies must take account of these specific difficulties and challenges and ensure that any measures regarded as essential to the successful restoration of peatlands do not have inadvertently deleterious effects on the archaeo-environmental resource. It is difficult to overstate the exceptional cultural value and rarity of the archaeological record of peatlands in particular, and while restoration cannot restore those sites and artefacts which have already been lost or damaged, it can seek to enhance protection for those that do survive. The palaeoecological record is also vulnerable and it is important to note in this context that all peatlands will have some intellectual service value through their palaeo-environmental record, although this value will depend on other factors such as the state of preservation of the material.

Palaeoecological data represent the only available information regarding the growth and long-term evolution of peatlands, but the scientific service

Table 6.2 *Potential areas of synergy and 'trade-offs' between archaeo-environmental services of peatlands and other properties or drivers.*

Drivers	Synergies	Trade-offs
1. State of peatlands	Knowledge of the extent and condition of peat Understanding peat depth and properties in 3D	Terminologies and mapping of peat Methodologies for defining condition of peatlands
2. Climate change	Provision of an evidence basis for past change	Disturbance of *in situ* peat during restoration
3. Biodiversity	Promotion of functioning peat-building systems Maintenance of high water tables Provision of an evidence basis for past change in species composition Removal of scrub and higher vegetation (plantations)	Focus on vegetation and peat surface, not on peat matrix Disturbance of peat matrix for habitat creation Disturbance of *in situ* peat during peat restoration
4. Restoration	Promotion of functioning, peat-building systems Maintenance of high water tables Opportunities for generating understanding of historic environment	Loss of visible, surface, evidence of peatland exploitation Disturbance of *in situ* peat during restoration works Disturbance of *in situ* peat during rehabilitation
5. Burning	Provision of an evidence base for past change through palaeo-records Increased visibility of heritage assets on surface	Degradation of peat surface
6. Hydrology	Provision of an evidence base for past change from palaeo-records Maintenance of high water tables	Seasonal lowering of the water table for management Disturbance of *in situ* peat during restoration works

value extends far beyond this: the palaeorecords derived from proxies such as pollen, plant macrofossils, fungal spores, beetles and geochemical and isotope analyses provide evidence of environmental changes across timescales from the decadal to the millennial and on scales ranging from the local to the global. Such a 'nested' perspective is essential for understanding the character of past ecosystems; for assessing their response to factors such as human impact and climate change; and for elucidating the complex and recursive relationship between different drivers and processes.

Peatlands have been described as: 'witness[es] of the impact of human activity during centuries and indicators of the health of our planet' (Zaccone *et al.* 2007). In terms of understanding and planning for future environmental change, recent years have seen enormous advances in understanding of the relationship between peatlands and past climates. This work illustrates that dynamism and flux have been an integral part of the Holocene climate system and that undisturbed peatland ecosystems have often been able to adapt to perturbations. However, future climate change may exceed the critical threshold beyond which certain systems are unable to adjust (Mauquoy and Yeloff 2008) and further work is required to investigate this issue (see also Chapter 8).

Current advances in the geographical range of studies, as well as developments in analytical techniques and approaches, mean that the scientific service value of peatlands has considerable scope to provide further critical perspectives on both past and future patterns and processes of environmental change. Such development will ultimately only be possible through informed and integrated restoration and management that takes account of the exceptional value and vulnerability of the archaeological and palaeo-environmental records that peatlands provide.

6.6 Acknowledgements

Thanks are due to the IUCN UK Peatland Programme. This chapter is based in part on the IUCN 'Peatlands and the Historic Environment' review (team members: Dr N. Bermingham, Dr H. Chapman, Prof. D. Charman, Dr W. Fletcher, Dr J. Heathcote, Prof. R. Van de Noort and J. Quartermaine). Thanks to Nick Hogan for assistance with the figures. This chapter has been improved by the comments of anonymous referees and the editors of this volume.

CHAPTER SEVEN

Peatlands and cultural ecosystem services

KERRY A. WAYLEN
Social, Economic and Geographical Sciences Group, The James Hutton Institute, UK
ROBERT VAN DE NOORT
University of Reading, UK
KIRSTY L. BLACKSTOCK
Social, Economic and Geographical Sciences Group, The James Hutton Institute, UK

7.1 The importance of cultural ecosystem services

This chapter argues that peatlands across the world provide many types of cultural ecosystem services, and so these should be reflected in peatland management. Chapters 2–5 and 17 convincingly demonstrate how peatlands provide essential provisioning and regulating services, but as human well-being is a multi-dimensional concept (UNDP 2010), it is important that we recognise and support the role that nature can play in meeting other needs as leisure, religiosity, identity and freedom (Church, Burgess and Ravenscroft 2011).

Although this idea is (arguably) easy to relate to intuitively, it has proved challenging to articulate a precise and comprehensive definition of cultural ecosystem services (Daniel *et al.* 2012). The European CICES classification for ecosystem services (Chapter 1) describes them as: 'the provision of non-material benefits, such as opportunities for recreation, spiritual and aesthetic experiences as well as the gaining of information and knowledge'. This definition is useful as it embraces everything from symbolic (aesthetic and spiritual meanings) to experiential (derived from more physical experiences, such as recreation, community activities) and intellectual benefits (such as scientific research and knowledge-building). The idea of non-material benefits offers a useful way to start thinking about cultural

---

Peatland Restoration and Ecosystem Services: Science, Policy and Practice, eds. A. Bonn, T. Allott, M. Evans, H. Joosten and R. Stoneman. Published by Cambridge University Press. © British Ecological Society 2016.

services, but it should not be interpreted strictly binding: as examples in this chapter show, culture can drive consumptive use while virtually all services that provide material services have cultural dimensions.

We begin by discussing some of the current challenges in understanding of peatland cultural services, before going on to explain and provide detail of the varied and interconnected ways in which peatlands provide cultural ecosystem services, and the implications for management.

7.2 Challenges for describing the value of cultural ecosystem services

The properties of cultural services mean that it is often difficult to measure their importance in monetary terms (Abson and Termansen 2011). First, many are 'non-material' uses that do not entail consumption (harvesting) of the resources – as for aesthetic appreciation of a peatland landscape – and these are typically not valued in conventional markets. Second, many goods in this category are 'common goods' or 'public goods', where it is hard to exclude users or charge for use. Third, many cultural services and benefits are interconnected with each other, and with other ecosystem services (Chan, Satterfield and Goldstein 2012). Chapter 16 in this volume provides a detailed discussion of valuation challenges. In short, although there are metrics and proxies that can allow us insight into some cultural values, expressing the value of cultural ecosystem services in monetary terms is at best challenging, requiring new datasets unique to each place, almost certainly only partially capturing 'value' and at worst judged inappropriate (e.g. for religious values). Therefore, it will often be more appropriate to seek to describe cultural services in non-economic terms, perhaps favouring qualitative approaches to describing and contextualising cultural ecosystem services associated with a site (Chan, Satterfield and Goldstein 2012; Bieling 2014).

A connected challenge comes from how people relate to peatlands. Generally, people respond to their perceptions of landscapes (consisting of a mosaic of habitats) rather than specific habitats (Setten, Stenseke and Moen 2012). Therefore, the cultural benefits provided by peatlands are often inseparable from those provided by neighbouring habitats (e.g. native woodlands and freshwater systems) and the topography of the wider landscape (e.g. hills and mountains). And, since peat soils form under many climatic and environmental conditions (Chapters 2 and 8), so the nature of peatland landscapes can be highly variable.

At smaller scales, people may relate to specific localities, but even here there will be a relationship with a particular place, which means the value of a peatland cannot be meaningfully disentangled from the environmental and social settings. 'Sense of place' is the symbolic meanings that people come to assign to spaces as they live and learn about them, and work on this concept has emphasised social construction of meanings, with less attention to how attributes of the physical environment contribute to people's feelings (Neugarten et al. 2011). However, it is clear that these relationships can occur at different scales, from the scale of 'socially valued landscapes', such as a remote national park, which are recognised by many sectors of society near and far from it, or in 'local places', such as a peatland in the neighbourhood used for recreation and dog walking.

Therefore, the meanings ascribed to place cannot be generalised or predicted from a knowledge of habitat type or landscape topography. Because some relationships and meanings are specific to local places, some aspects of peatlands' cultural values will necessarily vary from place to place, and often cannot be generalised. Furthermore, the services themselves usually depend actively on human practices such as land management (Bieling 2014), and perceptions of services are mediated by societal values and preferences (Curry 2009). Therefore, different individuals and sectors of society may vary how they relate to any one place (Greider and Garkovich 1994) and hence in their perception and value for different services provided by peatlands (Suckall et al. 2009).

Values held will also vary over time. A well-documented shift in ideas comes from the UK, where the idea of remote moorlands as sublime, exhilarating landscapes for visitors did not exist before the eighteenth century – prior to that, these places were seen as inhospitable and dangerous (Hanley et al. 2009). Variations in place, space and time pose a major challenge for researchers who are beginning to try to understand how biodiversity and ecosystem function provide ecosystem services (Tengberg et al. 2012), but this challenge may be particularly acute for cultural services since time- and place-specific associations can limit the ability to transfer or generalise findings. Many of the examples of cultural ecosystem services of peatlands in this chapter are from the UK and Europe even though care has been taken to seek examples from all parts of the world. This is because there is little literature specifically devoted to cultural ecosystem services of peatlands (Kimmel and Mander 2010), except for Joosten and Clarke (2002) and van der Wal et al. (2011) who provide an explicit discussion of cultural ecosystem services derived from peatlands globally and in the UK, respectively. We acknowledge that our examples are only a small sample of the wide range of services provided by peatlands to humankind: as we will explore, cultural services delivered by these complex systems differ between places and among individuals, communities and over time.

7.3 Religious and spiritual values and experiences

Religious and spiritual values are usually quite distinct and unrelated to provisioning or regulating ecosystem services, and their importance is not quantifiable. Therefore, they are an excellent starting point for exploring the range of peatland benefits that are characterised as cultural services, and the challenges of doing so.

Spirituality is a quality sometimes associated with wild and beautiful terrain and experiencing uninterrupted views (Natural England 2009). Although peatlands can be found in a variety of settings – from lowland bogs, to upland blanket mires, fens, or peat swamp forests – those settings with qualities of remoteness and wilderness can provide a setting for spiritual and religious reflection. Undrained wetlands are generally inhospitable to intensive agriculture or urban development, and so it is particularly likely that peatlands in wetland ecosystems have (or had) spiritual and religious values attached to them. Remoteness seems associated with deities: the Dieng Plateau in Central Java, Indonesia, is a mysterious remote area of high-altitude peatland which at one time homed 400 temples and whose name originally meant 'Abode of the Gods' (Michell 1977). Here, as in many other places, past religious associations no longer exist. For example, in northern Europe peat bogs are not now regarded as religious sites, but are thought to have had considerable ritual significance to Bronze Age and Iron Age peoples, who considered them associated with gods, spirits and/or ancestors (Schafer and Bell 2002). Human remains have been found across this region, almost perfectly preserved by the anoxic and acidic conditions, and some are thought to be prehistoric ritual sacrifices (Müller-Wille 1999 in Joosten and Clarke 2002). Many of the religious or spiritual beliefs that led to these actions are no longer appreciated by contemporary societies, and indeed we should be glad that activities such as ritual sacrifice no longer exist! However, it is an interesting question as to how understanding of these past attachments should affect current management practices. Preserving these sites undisturbed is often considered appropriate, and this may seem especially suitable when it accords with other management goals (e.g. to maximise carbon storage services). Although there is a possibility for conflict when considered against other services (e.g. peatland extraction), there are options to reconcile and enhance the delivery of some services: for example, appropriate use of information and visitor facilities can reconcile current recreation needs with the desire to preserve and respect the past.

Peatlands in certain places may contain specific features that prompt spiritual or religious associations. This can include remote pathways used for pilgrimages: for example, in Northumbria in the UK, much of a 100 km trail called St. Cuthbert's Way passes through or near peat moorlands and marshes. Peatlands are particularly likely to be associated with burial sites, perhaps because wet peatlands are unsuitable for agriculture or building construction. For example, Bunhill Fields in London was used as a burial site, to the extent that the ground level eventually rose and became suitable for building on (Black and Backman 1990). Now, any exhumed bodies are treated with respect, but in the past, this and other such places were used for burial simply because they were not regarded as suitable for other uses. As such, it is interesting to note that cultural services valued by us now, may sometimes arise from the lack of other values ascribed to peatlands by previous generations.

7.4 Aesthetic values

Similar to those features which inspire spiritual feeling, aesthetic features commonly associated with peatland landscapes include: remoteness, bleakness, tranquillity, open space and distinctive plant and animal communities (SAC 2005). Across the world (particularly in developed countries), most live in urban areas: for these people the chance to experience remoteness and tranquillity can be distinctive and valued. In the UK, a survey by the Department for Environment, Food and Rural Affairs (DEFRA 2002) reported 58% of people as saying that tranquillity was the most positive feature of the countryside, but it is not known whether this would be a widespread view in other countries.

The qualities of remoteness and tranquillity – even bleakness – can be associated with feelings of freedom and wilderness. In the past, such places may have inspired fear, but today wilderness is valued, at least by contemporary Western societies (Arts, Fischer and Van der Wal 2011). For example, a survey of visitors and residents in Scotland's Cairngorms National Park found that 70% of the respondents and 82% of the residents stated that it was important for Scotland to have 'wild' places (SNH 2008). The same effect is found with lowland-altitude peatlands, with the UK's distinctive Norfolk Broads in East Anglia also receiving many visitors. Accordingly, these 'socially valued landscapes' have received many landscape and biodiversity designations (van der Wal *et al.* 2011).

Of course, preferences towards and ways of engaging with these places and landscapes will vary across demographic, socio-economic and cultural groups (Suckall *et al.* 2009). Therefore, although openness and remoteness in landscapes can be linked to feeling calm and relaxed (Natural England 2009), other potential reactions can include exhilaration, anxiety and fear. Some will see peatlands as dangerous or hostile places, even as 'wet deserts' (Johnston and Soulsby 2000), with little positive value perceived.

Perceptions of peatland aesthetics will also be mediated by relationship to specific places for local communities, whether this be small rural communities with a long history of relationship with one location, or nomadic herders (from northern tribes in Lapland, to Central Asian herders) who relate to wider-scale landscapes. In these situations, specific features of a place may come to be aesthetically prized, layering with a general aesthetic reaction to landscape. Aesthetic values held by communities can be strong enough to limit or affect the use of these landscapes for other services. For example, in northern Scotland, when there are local objections to proposals for windfarm developments, aesthetic impacts are among the main objections cited (Chapter 9).

Aesthetic values of peatlands will vary from judging them to be forbidding hostile places, through to places which are beautiful and allow a fulfilling connection to nature. Management of peatland places should also recognise that negative aesthetic qualities can be perceived for peatlands – such as bleakness and hostile wilderness – which, if respected, could provide a rationale for management prioritising other ecosystem services, or a barrier to societal engagement and resourcing for peatland conservation and restoration. However, it is sometimes claimed that there is growing public appreciation and perception of peatlands as having positive aesthetic qualities (Čivić and Jones-Walters 2010). If true, this appreciation could provide a basis for the goals of peatland management, leading to these landscapes being used as sites for physical recreation and mental refreshment and subsequently providing livelihoods based on leisure and tourism.

7.5 Identity and sense of place

Peatlands provide many people with a 'sense of place' (Bain *et al.* 2011). Often these connections are historically rooted in whole ways of life and livelihoods dependent on the distinctive peatland landscapes, such as fenland communities in East Anglia evocatively described by Sly (2007) or the peatland-dependent Ojibwe and Dakota peoples in North America (Vileisis 1999). However, peatlands often do not carry positive connotations and this was particularly true in the past: many societies have regarded peatland swamps as wild places best avoided or drained. Residents of the 'Black Sluice' district of Lincolnshire, England, spent over six centuries petitioning for surrounding fenlands to be drained and 'reclaimed' (Wheeler 1896). In the nineteen century, the ills of 'ague, poverty and rheumatism' associated with the lifestyles of the remaining fen 'slodgers' caused a remarkable level of opium use and addiction (Berridge and Edwards 1981). Drainage or 'reclamation' was thus often seen as a mark of progress (e.g. Blackbourn

2011), though at present there is an increasing trend for conserving and even reversing these past reclamation actions (see the example of Wicken Fen, Box 7.1).

Where lifestyles have changed so that peatlands are no longer essential to livelihoods, peatlands and their associated traditional uses may still be strongly prized as part of cultural heritage. For example, in the Southeast Pahang peat swamp forest in Peninsular Malaysia the indigenous Jakun people traditionally had a strong interdependence with wetlands. Despite changing lifestyles, their wetland forests are still held as culturally and religiously important, with substantial areas designated as having spiritual or ancestral significance. Several museums in Europe focus on remembering peatlands and the people whose lives they supported (http://www.peatand-culture.org). These offer interesting examples of how cultural heritage can be retained and valued even if livelihoods no longer directly depend on peatlands.

Landscapes associated with peatlands can be linked to group identities at various scales. This can be at the national level: in Scotland, two recently designated National Parks, which contain significant areas of upland peatlands, were important symbolic projects for its newly devolved Scottish Parliament (Rennie 2006). Equally, they can be linked with assertions of group identity: for example, a mass trespass on the peat moorlands of Kinder Scout in 1932 was organised to protest for access rights, a political act linked to frustrations over class and power inequalities (Stephenson, Holt and Harding 1989). Of course, many associations are more subtle, though equally telling of links to identity. Scotland's iconic and most famous drink – whisky – is sometimes described as having a peaty flavour, which occurs when peat-fuelled smoky fires ('peat reek') are used to dry the ingredient malt (Harrison and Priest 2009). Such use can contribute to supporting both economies and identity. Traditional practices such as 'heft' (accustoming sheep to places in northern England) or even small-scale arrangements for foraging also connect culture with livelihoods and economies. This highlights that the concepts of cultural services are not always neatly distinct from provisioning services.

Whisky production entails a relatively small amount of peat cutting. However, the cutting for fuel is a provisioning service that is non-renewable and thus now discouraged. However, where there are long histories of peat cutting it may be seen as part of some communities' identity. Preserving traces of past cutting can help to protect and recall industrial heritage (Rotherham 1999), and where cutting continues its use is likely be linked with particular social arrangements and institutions, such as 'turbary' in Ireland (the right to cut an area of peat). Such processes can be argued to contribute to social capital and cultural heritage, providing a link to historic ways of living in areas where social ties may otherwise be under threat (e.g. Burton *et al.* 2009). However, they can also lead to uncompromising and intransigent views as to how peatland should be used and managed, and to persistent unsustainable uses (Bullock and Collier 2011). It is challenging to engage with such complex 'intermixed' views on rights, traditions and uses (Garrity *et al.* 2001), but peoples' underlying attachment may offer a basis for building awareness that peat extraction is not sustainable.

7.6 Heritage crafts and artistic outputs

In order to retain links with the past, many choose to practice heritage crafts and produce traditional handicrafts, which may relate to peats or resources collected from peatlands. For example, in Wicken Fen in England, visitors can purchase traditional handicrafts and attend training courses in traditional skills (see Box 7.1).

There is growing interest in the use of mosses and fibres from peatlands to make paper, garments or even decorative felting: while some crafts enjoy a revival, others are entirely new. Of course, not all traditional uses for peatlands are completely unproblematic from the perspective of sustaining peat availability and maintaining the various services they provide: drainage quickly damages key wetland features, while vegetation harvesting can be problematic if carried out to excess. Conversely, actively promoting traditional skills and practices can also be part of active interventions to encourage appreciation and sustainable management of peatlands, as in Malaysia, where encouraging traditional weaving of reed handicrafts was part of a larger project to conserve Pahang peat swamp forests (GEF 2001). The key to achieving sustainable management may be to carefully balance the activities promoted, and to capitalise on interest for awareness-raising on sustainability.

The aesthetic appreciation and associations of peatlands across the world are expressed in numerous forms of artistic output, such as sculptures, paintings or folk music. A sculpture park Lough Boora in Ireland, for example, contains some sculptures made from natural peat products, and states that it is 'inspired by the rich natural and industrial legacy of the bog lands' (www.sculptureintheparklands.com).

Peatlands also inspire literature and poetry. The Nobel Prize-winning poet and author Seamus Heaney (2009) has been influenced by Irish peatlands: directly, as in the poems 'Digging' (1966) and 'Bogland' (1969), and more indirectly, as he has claimed his writings have been influenced by attachment to the soil and the process of Irish peat formation (Meredith 1999). The ancient archaeological finds within peat have also inspired his eloquent work, as expressed vividly in his poems 'The Grauballe Man' (1975) and 'Tollund Man' (1980). It is also a feature and setting for stories in many other countries, though often as a sinister wilderness. In traditional stories from Scandinavia, elves are associated with mires, while sirens called Huldra were thought to pose as beautiful young women to lure men into danger, either into dark woods or mires (Littleton 2005). In both traditional myths and modern literature, it is interesting to note that the peatlands are often depicted as dark, dangerous or mysterious places. As such, this can be seen as a case where positive cultural value is derived from negative cultural associations: this highlights that historic uses and perceptions must be appreciated for a balanced understanding of present-day cultural services from peatlands.

Box 7.1

Cultural services and Wicken Fen

The history of human relationships with Wicken Fen in Cambridgeshire, England, exemplifies many of the interlinked aspects of cultural ecosystem services discussed in this chapter.

Wicken Fen is a remnant of the topogenous mires of East Anglia. In the past, East Anglian fens were subject to frequent but irregular incursions from the North Sea and freshwater floods from nearby rivers. However, in 1630, 'Adventurers' from the Netherlands were employed to drain the fens to create land suitable for grazing, hay making, and arable farming. During this time, undrained fens were seen as unproductive and backward, dangerous places – perhaps a classic case of humankind focusing on enhancing provisioning over other types of ecosystem services. Sedge reeds were harvested for roofing, eels and birds were hunted and the peat was cut for fuel, but by the early twentieth century there was less demand for these products.

Wicken Fen was not drained, and first came to the attention of naturalists in the late nineteenth century because of the variety of butterflies that could be found there. In the twentieth century it became clear that other groups of organisms (e.g. birds, beetles and vascular plants) were also found there – many endemic to the fen. These biodiversity benefits (about 7000 species in around 525 ha) motivate many visits from naturalists and scientists. Some species (such as the *Molinea* purple moorgrass community) are of international importance.

Understanding the cultural services of successional change and active management required to maintain these species communities has contributed to the scientific understanding of ecological successions and the role of human interventions in influencing biodiversity in some landscapes. It is now well accepted that in the fen, activities such as sedge cutting and grazing are needed to conserve the unique fenland species communities. Ongoing research and monitoring, particularly regular bird-ringing surveys, continue to inform our understanding of ecological communities and the effects of conservation efforts.

Wicken Fen also attracts many other types of visitors, with adults and families coming for physical recreation, and children in school parties coming to learn about the natural world and heritage crafts. Traditional uses of fen products are now also valued and sustained by Wicken Fen. Activities such as sedge and willow weaving are of strong interest, particularly to those interested in cultural heritage and identity, and many visitors go on to attend courses to learn these skills. Sales of these handicraft products, made from the fen's resources (such as bowls made from bog oak), by local makers, are available for visitors to buy. The aesthetic benefits of the fen are reflected in a wide range of paintings and drawings.

Wicken Fen demonstrates how peatland habitats can sustain many types of cultural ecosystem services – from heritage valuers through to aesthetic inspiration, recreation and intellectual benefits. Its story also shows how values can change over time, for many of the benefits and services prized today would not have been two centuries ago. Lastly, it shows that although many of these services are not directly monetised, they can influence management and decisions for land management, sometimes taking priority over other ecosystem services: by the end of the twentieth century conservation and heritage groups were reclaiming agriculture land for restoration to fen.

The website www.nationaltrust.org.uk/wicken-fen-nature-reserve contains more information about current activities at the fen, while a detailed exploration of its story is contained in Friday (1997).

7.7 Knowledge and education provided by peatlands

Peatlands have made significant contributions to building scientific knowledge. They have been enormously important in archaeology, and are increasingly recognised as an archive of past processes of environmental change, since the unique anoxic and acidic properties of healthy peatlands can provide conditions which preserve records of past environments over the last 10 000 years (Simmons 2003). These records provide fascinating insights into our past environment and culture as well as current understanding of climate change (Chapter 8), sea-level rise, the nature of past human impact and fire regimes on the natural environment (Brunning 2001; Blackford et al. 2006; Yeloff et al. 2007). Chapter 6 in this volume discusses these contributions in more detail.

Research based in peatlands has also contributed to increased knowledge of a range of ecological processes (e.g. Moore 1989), and our knowledge of biodiversity is advanced by the continual discovery of new species in peat ecosystems, particularly in the tropics (e.g. Kottelat et al. 2006). Our improving understanding of natural processes helps us to better understand how peatland-supporting services underpin regulating services such as carbon sequestration and provisioning services such as agriculture.

In addition to supporting ecological, environmental and historical research, peatlands also support learning by both children and adults. Simply spending time in nature can help to communicate a sense of permanence (Natural England 2009), but more active promotion of learning (through guided walks, interpretation panels, audio-trails, linked websites, visitor centres, excursion programmes and school visits) can promote widespread understanding and interest in natural processes. For example, in England, the Peak District National Park Authority is providing outdoor classrooms for life-long learning in and about upland landscapes which include peatlands. These learning experiences often connect with or lead into more active involvement with peatland landscapes for recreation, conservation and restoration. Where this occurs, peatland restoration is likely to create new landscapes that supply new combinations of ecosystem services to future generations (Collier 2014).

7.8 Recreation

Peatlands currently support a range of recreational activities which vary in their compatibility and links to other services.

Field sports and hunting – Hunting is a common activity in peatlands, for peat swamps are often rich in fish and wading birds, while other peat forests and moorlands can be host to many terrestrial birds and game mammals. In subsistence societies, hunting is an activity essential for supporting livelihoods (and therefore would be classed as a provisioning service). However, where hunting is driven by motivations for recreation and sport, it is a cultural service.

Fishing – Many people enjoy fishing for the tranquillity and experience of spending time in nature, not just for the necessity of catching fish. There are no reliable estimates of the numbers of anglers, particularly not for peatlands on their own, but in the UK alone angler numbers have been estimated at over 1 million (Environment Agency 2010), with many more across the world. Likewise, there are many who enjoy the experience of hunting, and they and others enjoy consuming the resultant game meat. Because many people are willing to pay to hunt, markets exist to provide an insight into the value of this service, and accordingly, in some countries, there have been high private investments in establishing and maintaining heather moorlands on blanket bogs for field sports (PACEC 2006). For example, in the UK there are approximately 450 grouse-shooting moors covering about 7% of the UK's area (Richards 2004), on which approximately 47 000 people have taken part in shooting (PACEC 2006). This also supports some livelihoods, including gamekeepers, hunt helpers and the hospitality industry. This often connects to associations with cultural identity and heritage. For example, a certain style of shooting using a punt gun is evocative of past hunting for ducks in East Anglian fens (Sly 2007). In other countries, equivalent activities would be moose and reindeer hunting, or bear trapping. Although popular, where these sports are pursued intensively there can be disturbance and adverse habitat impacts (i.e. trampling by high prey populations) that impacts on the delivery of other ecosystem services such as carbon storage and water regulation (Chapter 9).

Sports and exercise – Most simply, walking or running and cycling in moorlands brings great enjoyment and a sense of freedom (linked to aesthetic values). These are often widely encouraged as an easy and accessible way for people from all backgrounds to improve their health and fitness, although popular trails can suffer from erosion and habitat degradation. Bog snorkelling is a rather more recently invented pastime, and although currently regarded as 'weird' by the majority (Connolly 2011), it illustrates that services and values change over time, and can be hard to predict!

Relaxation – Cut peat can also be used to support recreation via gardening, and via balneotherapy (bathing spa therapies), where it is used in poultices, muds and suspensions (Crebbin-Bailey, Harcup and Harrington 2005). This promotes health and relaxation. However, similar to cutting for fuel (see earlier section on identity), these consumptive uses of peat are controversial because the use of non-renewable resources conflicts also with the sustainable delivery of other services from peatland. It is hard to justify these activities if there are reasonable substitutes (such as peat-free compost) and more significant health benefits to be derived from alternative recreational uses of peatlands, such as walking and running.

Volunteering – Peatlands associated with particular places can also support local social networks that foster and sustain relationships. Opportunities for environmental or archaeological volunteering can engender a sense of ownership and reduce problems of anti-social behaviour, while also providing environmental benefits by supporting monitoring or restoration: a good example comes from the Unites States, where volunteers for 'Rocky Mountain Wild' help to protect peatland habitats and species as part of their wider work to conserve that unique ecoregion.

Wildlife appreciation – Peatland habitats are often associated with rare or charismatic species of fauna and flora, biodiversity which is valued by naturalists near and far, and are linked to intellectual, aesthetic and spiritual values (such as a perception of intrinsic values). For example, Indonesian peat swamp forests are thought important for supporting hundreds of species of rare tree and fish species (Dudgeon 2000). Appreciation of biodiversity may be expressed through tourism focused on aspects of wildlife and nature (ecotourism).

Recreation and tourism are often dependent on infrastructure such as footpaths and car parks, and management of these – perhaps linked to volunteering – offers opportunities to avoid or control degrading activities (such as off-road mountain-biking) while providing access and opportunities for enjoyment.

7.9 Tourism as an indicator of multiple cultural values

The numbers of visitors to peatlands, as well as the conservation and landscape designations received by many of the peatlands visited, provide perhaps the strongest evidence of the importance of cultural ecosystem services provided by peatlands.

People seek to visit peatlands for all of the cultural services discussed, from heritage through spiritual values. The resulting tourism industry can bring significant economic value. Although many tourism and leisure activities – such as walking and enjoying scenery – are informal and non-commercial, tourism activity does allow a partial monetisation or quantification of these cultural values. These are often focused on peatlands in protected areas. For example, day and overnight visitors to Peak District moorlands spend on average £14.97 and £96.40, respectively, per trip for food, accommodation, travel, equipment and souvenirs (Davies 2006). No visitor figures exist solely for peatlands, but a study over the last decade (Joosten and Clarke 2002) listed several million visitors to peatland reserves in just 13 countries; since then the numbers of visitors have doubtlessly grown. Where peatlands form a significant part of protected areas (as in the swamp forests of Indonesia or the upland national parks of the UK), it is reasonable to suggest that the tourism industry partly depends upon them. Ecotourism is widely thought to be a growth industry (Wearing and Neil 2009), so these benefits may grow in future.

For example, the *Rough Guide* series of travel guidebooks recommends the Caroni Swamp (partly underlaid by peat soils and host to Trinidad's national bird, the scarlet ibis) as one of the top four 'things not to miss' in the island (De-Light and Thomas 2005).

Many of these areas used by tourists are legally designated in some way for protection and conservation. Such legal protections and designations may, in themselves, also indicate the extent to which cultural services from peatland landscapes are valued, even if they are not explicitly formulated in terms of ecosystem services (Pleasant *et al.* 2014). Of course, areas receive designation for many reasons, with ideas evolving across countries and in time, but those designated in the early twentieth century were often spurred by the desire to protect the perceived intrinsic and aesthetic values of nature, at least as perceived by powerful elites (Adams 2009). Today, cultural values are perhaps most explicitly recognised and prioritised for those peatlands designated as World Heritage Sites (www.worldheritagesite.org/).

7.10 Conclusions

Peatlands provide significant and varied cultural ecosystem services across the world. Their importance is demonstrated by a myriad of traditional practices, spiritual associations, recreational uses, artistic and literary outputs, protected area designations, tourist visits and volunteer activities. Cultural services are often interlinked with landscapes rather than habitats, vary with place and time and are often co-produced with other services: this poses significant challenges to their characterisation and valuation, particularly in terms and scales commensurate with how other services may be described.

Nevertheless, peatland management decisions must be made regardless of ongoing methodological and conceptual challenges. At present, cultural values may be underrepresented in decision making (e.g. Collier and Scott 2008), so efforts should be made to redress this. An appreciation of cultural services can inform objective setting – for example, to prioritise views that are aesthetically prized – and also inform appropriate means for management: for example, a rewetting intervention that blocks a traditional pilgrimage route would probably receive little popular support. Assessing the diverse experiential, symbolic and intellectual benefits and values encompassed by cultural services will require the use of diverse methods to explore stakeholder views (Chan, Satterfield and Goldstein 2012), informed by insights from fields such as landscape management (Setten, Stenseke and Moen 2012).

Since cultural ecosystem services are often associated with non-consumptive uses, careful management (e.g. to minimise degradation from recreational use) may typically allow their delivery with minimal risk of peatland degradation, and even reinforce management for regulating and supporting services (such as carbon sequestration). However, in other cases, cultural services may themselves act as a barrier to sustainable management, particularly where there are strong traditions of extractive use. This is a significant management challenge, posing complex and even ethical dilemmas, since it may be deemed that some traditions cannot be maintained if peatlands are to be safeguarded and the delivery of other services is to be sustained. Existing literature on resource and conflict management (e.g. Buckles 1999) offers useful insights for handling these trade-offs between ecosystem services and differing views. Stakeholder engagement, based around people's values for and relationships to place (Williams and Stewart 1998), may offer the best starting point for identifying cultural services, discussing trade-offs and seeking management strategies that are socially acceptable and practically sustainable. However, understanding how best to assess and incorporate cultural ecosystem services within peatland management is an ongoing challenge.

CHAPTER EIGHT

Peatlands and climate change

ANGELA V. GALLEGO-SALA
University of Exeter, UK
ROBERT K. BOOTH
Lehigh University, USA
DAN J. CHARMAN
University of Exeter, UK
I. COLIN PRENTICE
Imperial College London, UK
ZICHENG YU
Lehigh University, USA

8.1 Introduction

The fundamental reason for the presence of peatlands is a positive balance between plant production and decomposition of organic matter. Organic matter accumulates in these systems because prolonged waterlogged conditions result in soil anoxia (i.e. exclusion of oxygen), and under these conditions decomposition rates can be lower than those of primary production, as seen in Figure 8.1. Climate therefore plays an important role in peat accumulation, both directly by affecting plant productivity and decomposition of organic matter, and indirectly through its effects on hydrology, water balance and vegetation composition (for a summary, refer to Yu, Beilman and Jones (2009)). Climate provides broad-scale controls on peatland extent, types and vegetation, and ultimately, ecosystem services such as carbon sequestration and storage, as well as water and hazard regulation (Chapters 4 and 5). Peatlands can therefore play a vital role in ecosystem-based adaptation in helping society mitigate and adapt to climate change.

Future climate change is likely to alter the hydrology and soil temperature of peatlands, with far-reaching consequences for their biodiversity, ecology and biogeochemistry, and interactions with the Earth system.

Peatland Restoration and Ecosystem Services: Science, Policy and Practice, eds. A. Bonn, T. Allott, M.Evans, H. Joosten and R. Stoneman. Published by Cambridge University Press. © British Ecological Society 2016.

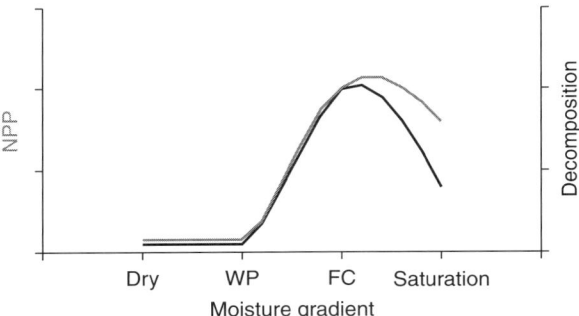

Figure 8.1 Conceptual diagram indicating how net primary production (NPP) and decomposition (heterotrophic respiration) vary along a stylised gradient of soil moisture content. Below the wilting point (WP), water is bound to clay minerals and is inaccessible to plants. NPP increases with soil moisture from the wilting point to field capacity (FC). Above field capacity, NPP is limited by anoxia as oxygen is unable to diffuse rapidly through the soil to the plant roots. In all but the wettest environments soil carbon content tends to an equilibrium, so that the total rate of decomposition matches NPP. In cold climates where the rate of decomposition (per unit soil carbon and time) is slow, this process results in the accumulation of large soil carbon stores. In permanently wet soils, decomposition is strongly inhibited by anoxia, resulting in a disequilibrium (excess of NPP over decomposition), manifested as the accumulation of peat, which can be sustained over thousands of years.

For example, the possibility of drier conditions allowing peat erosion and increases in CO_2 emissions that would result in a positive feedback to climate change (Turetsky 2010). Peatlands that have been damaged by human activity are more vulnerable to climate-induced changes in hydrology and temperature, but suitable management strategies may make them more resilient to changes and help to stabilise the delivery of ecosystem services (Chapter 1).

This chapter describes the interactions between climate and peatlands in three sections. The first section explains how present climate influences peatlands, by documenting how climate limits peatland geographical extent globally, and how bioclimatic envelope models can predict peatland extent. We indicate how each type of peatland is linked to a specific climate range, and introduce the concept of how climate controls peatland ecosystem function and services. The second section looks into the past. It describes how peat preserves a record of past climates and environmental conditions that can be deciphered to reveal the history of peatland vegetation, hydrology and carbon accumulation changes in relation to past changes in climate. We highlight lessons that can be learned from the palaeo-record preserved in

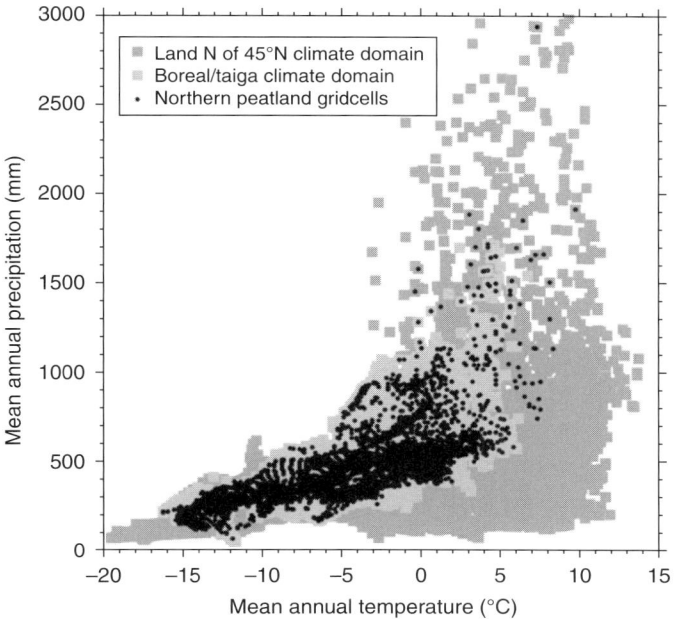

Figure 8.2 The climate space of mean annual temperature and precipitation of total land area north of 45°N latitude (dark grey), the boreal/taiga biome (light grey) and northern peatland regions based on 0.5° × 0.5°-gridded instrumental climate data for the period 1960–90. Adapted from Yu, Beilman and Jones (2009).

peat. The final section discusses the potential effects of present and future climate change on peatlands, their extent and their provision of ecosystem services, in particular climate regulation through carbon storage and GHG exchanges as well as fire hazard and coastal flood control. We also consider how increases in sea level and CO_2 concentration, and decreases in the extent of permafrost, are likely to affect peatlands.

8.2 Modern climate controls of peatland distribution and type
8.2.1 Climate and peatland extent: the basis for bioclimatic envelope models

The geographical distribution and extent of peatlands is largely determined by climate, although at local and regional scales, topography is an important factor that controls peatland boundaries through its effects on both hydrology and mesoclimate. Peatland ecosystems exist therefore within well-defined climatic thresholds (Vitt 2006; Yu, Beilman and Jones 2009). Because peatland extent is dependent on climate, it is possible to describe peatland distribution using a bioclimatic envelope model. This type of model characterises the climatic tolerance limits or thresholds of a species or ecosystem in terms of one or more climatic variables, and has successfully been used to map the regional distributions of peatlands in Canada (Gignac, Halsey and Vitt 2000) and Fennoscandia (Parviainen and Luoto 2007), and to project potential changes of peatland extent under future climate scenarios (Tuck *et al.* 2006; Clark *et al.* 2011). Figure 8.2 shows that peatlands in the northern boreal region occur across a wide range of mean annual temperature ranges from −16°C to around 5°C, with peatlands in warmer regions limited to areas of high rainfall.

The limitations of bioclimatic envelope models for species distribution have been extensively described and mainly stem from neglected factors such as biotic interactions, evolutionary change or dispersal ability, and it has been suggested that dynamic vegetation models are better equipped to predict changes in species distribution (Pearson and Dawson 2003). For applications to understanding peatland distribution, bioclimatic envelope models may not be able to capture all peatland types, for example, those peatlands such as percolation mires or valley mires that are strongly dependent on topography.

8.2.2 Climate limits and controls of peatland types

Climate influences not just the extent but also the type of peatland that is found in each region, because peatland type is primarily a function of vegetation and water source (Vitt 2006; Chapter 2). Precipitation is the only source of water in many peatlands (i.e. ombrotrophic peatlands or bogs). This means that a combination of high precipitation frequency (high number of wet days) and low evapotranspiration (cool wet climates with low air moisture deficit) maintains high water tables and peat anoxia. However, ombrotrophic peatlands can also form in much warmer climates if there is adequate precipitation (e.g. in tropical areas such as Borneo). Other types of peatlands (minerotrophic peatlands or fens) are fed by both groundwater and precipitation. Although fens are less reliant to climate, they still only occur in areas with a positive climatic water balance.

If we define a climate space by mean annual precipitation and temperature, it is possible to place major peatland types within a certain region of this space, i.e. each peatland type has a minimum and maximum threshold of temperature and precipitation (Vitt 2006; Yu, Beilman and Jones 2009; Yu *et al.* 2010). Within the boreal peatland region (Figure 8.3), at the coldest extreme of temperatures (annual mean temperature below 0°C) and lowest precipitation, we find the peat plateaus in permafrost environments of Arctic tundra areas and palsa mires in subarctic areas. Palsa mires are characteristic of the zone of discontinuous permafrost, where ice lenses

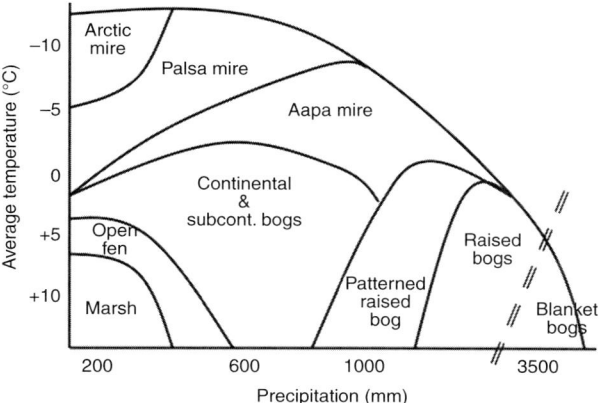

Figure 8.3 Relationship between climate (temperature and precipitation) and major peatland types in the boreal region (adapted from Vitt 2006).

develop inside the palsa mounds and permafrost conditions are maintained by the thinner snow cover on the mounds (Seppälä 1986; Luoto, Fronzek and Zuidhoff 2004). At the opposite extreme, in climates with warmer annual mean temperatures (~5 to 10°C) but with extremely high precipitation all year round (>1000 mm), blanket bogs are found (Gallego-Sala and Prentice 2012). Blanket bogs are so called because of their tendency to cover almost the entire landscape, developing even on sloping surfaces. Outside the boreal region, the temperature–precipitation space also can represent the climate constraints of peatland types. For example, tropical peatlands in wet and warm climates, including in South East Asia and the Amazon, tend to dominate in areas with relatively high temperature and moderate precipitation. In southern high latitudes, such as in Patagonia and New Zealand, peatlands occur where precipitation is high (up to 4 m yr^{-1}) and mean annual temperatures are mild (~5°C).

8.2.3 Climate control on ecosystem functioning and ecosystem services

Warmer temperatures result in the lengthening of the growing season, especially in high-latitude peatlands that experience cold winters. A prolonged growing season increases plant production, but at the same time warmer temperatures increase decomposition rates in peat soils (Dorrepaal *et al.* 2009). In certain nutrient-rich peatlands, the effect of a warmer, drier climate seems to increase both productivity and decomposition similarly (Flanagan and Syed 2011). However, carbon accumulation rates in peatlands have been shown to be most positively correlated to the amount of

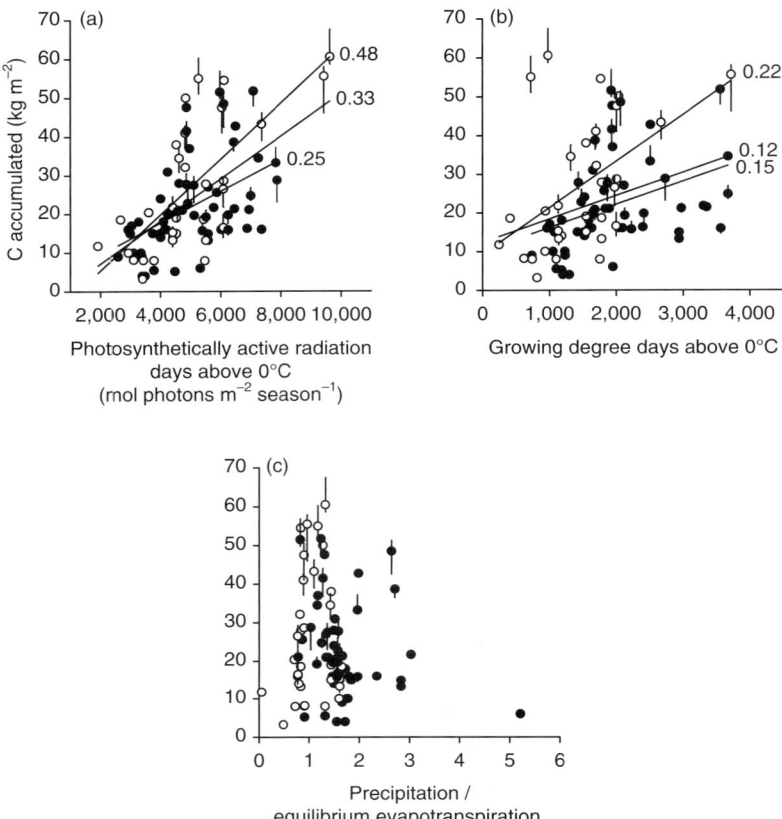

Figure 8.4 Controls on peat C accumulation. The total C accumulated over the last 1000 years at 90 sites compared to: (a) photosynthetic active radiation integrated over those days above 0°C (PAR0), (b) growing degree days above 0°C (GDD0), and (c) the ratio of precipitation to equilibrium evapotranspiration. Open circles represent fen data, closed circles represent bog data. Lines of best fit for fens (top), bogs (bottom) and both (middle) are shown for GDD0 and PAR0. Adapted from Charman et al. (2012).

photosynthetic active radiation (PAR) during the growing season (Figure 8.4; Charman et al, 2012). Thus, the length of the growing season is an important climatic control on carbon accumulation rate but so is cloudiness, with very high cloudiness promoting peatland occurrence (because of low potential evaporation), while keeping carbon accumulation rates low (because of low incident PAR). Overall, intact peatlands therefore perform important climate-regulating services through carbon accumulation and, more importantly, long-term carbon storage (Chapter 4).

While taking up atmospheric CO_2, peatlands are generally net sources of the two other important biogenic GHGs, methane and nitrous oxide. At high water tables that maintain anoxia, the amount of methane produced under warmer temperatures and increased productivity will also be higher (Chapter 4). When water tables fall, methane emissions decrease because oxygen can diffuse down into the aerated peat, and decomposition to carbon dioxide becomes the most energetically favourable path of organic matter decay. Nitrous oxide fluxes are also elevated when the water table drops, especially in nutrient-rich fen peatlands (Martikainen *et al.* 1993).

8.3 What we know from peat-core records: past climates and peatlands

A unique feature of peatlands is that they record their own history and development via the accumulation of well-preserved organic remains of past plant communities and other organisms that can collectively be used to reconstruct the vegetation, hydrology and geochemistry of the peatland (Chapter 6). Many peat characteristics can also be used to infer changes in the past climate and broader areas of the landscape than the peatlands themselves. Several key points emerge out of a consideration of this evidence:

1. The initiation of peat growth has mostly been climatically determined, reflecting either prevailing climate conditions that have persisted over an extended period of time, or a change to a climatic regime more favourable to peat formation (MacDonald *et al.* 2006).
2. Peatland growth has resulted in continuous sequestration of CO_2 in the world's peatlands, amounting to almost 600 Gt C (Yu *et al.* 2010). This valuable ecosystem service continues in pristine peatlands but is reversed in many damaged peatlands (Page *et al.* 2002).
3. Peatland carbon sequestration has varied significantly over time as a function of both internal processes, such as successional change, and external factors, such as climate and human disturbance.
4. The development of northern peatlands over the postglacial period has influenced the atmospheric concentration of methane (Yu *et al.* 2013).
5. While peatlands are responsive to past climate change, they have shown remarkable resilience to the natural changes that have occurred in the postglacial period. The extent of this resilience is now challenged by more rapid future climate change and human disturbance.

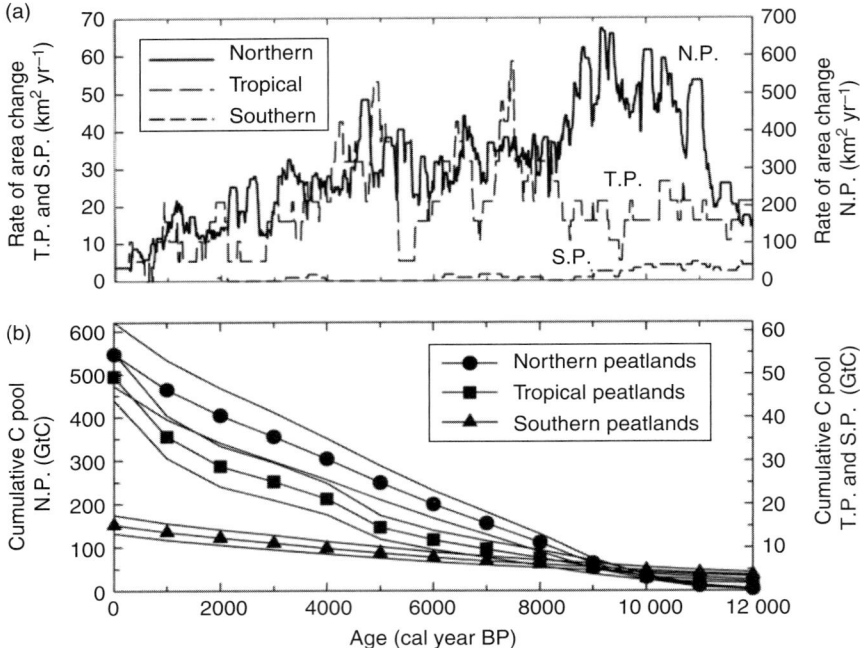

Figure 8.5 Changes in the rate of global peatland expansion and size of the cumulative peatland carbon pool divided into northern, southern and tropical regions (Yu et al. 2010). The changes in extent are estimated from basal peat ages and an assumed linear expansion since inception. The change in the size of the cumulative pool is based on accumulation rates from multiple ages in peat cores.

8.3.1 The history of carbon sequestration in peatlands

The initiation of peat growth marks the transition of the ecosystem to a net accumulator of carbon. Thus, we can learn something about the contribution of peatlands to the global carbon cycle simply by reconstructing the extent and initiation patterns of peatlands in the past (Figure 8.5). In western Canada, patterns of peatland expansion followed known trends in millennial-scale climate change, with initial peatland establishment in suitable areas following deglaciation, and expansion further into other regions as cooler conditions were established from about 6000 years ago (Halsey, Vitt and Bauer 1998). Across the whole of the circumarctic region, peat shows a similarly rapid development early in the Holocene with new peatlands continuing to develop later as climatic and soil conditions became more suitable (MacDonald et al. 2006). Peatlands also have implications for methane emissions. The early Holocene rise in methane may have been partly driven by the development of northern peatlands (Smith et al. 2004; MacDonald *et al.* 2006); and the later spread of peatlands from about 5000 years ago could also have contributed an additional pulse of methane to the atmosphere (Korhola *et al.* 2010).

8.3.2 Lessons for future peatland carbon accumulation from past records

Variations in the rate of peat accumulation over time are important in understanding the contribution of peatlands to global atmospheric CO_2 variations. If peat grows faster, it will sequester more carbon from the atmosphere. Conversely, if peat growth slows down or stops, peat will become a smaller CO_2 sink or even a CO_2 source. Reconstructing changes in accumulation rates through time is not as straightforward as establishing the time of initiation, because the detection of rate changes is dependent on highly precise dating throughout the profile and this information is not always available.

Studies at individual sites and over small regions show that changes in the rates of peat growth vary widely, but large-scale data compilations again reveal some basic patterns (Yu, Beilman and Jones 2009). In boreal peatlands, peat growth rates were fastest in the early Holocene, associated both with the early phases of peat growth and warmer conditions. The pattern was different for tropical peatlands (Yu *et al.* 2010), and the links with climate variability there are less clear. Further evidence for a broad-scale link between temperature and accumulation exists for northern peatlands. Very well-dated individual sites suggest that peat growth was faster during short, warm phases such as the 'Medieval Warm Period' when compared to the later Little Ice Age (Mauquoy *et al.* 2002). Spatial patterns in carbon accumulation for the last 2000 years across a north–south temperature gradient in Siberia also show faster rates of peat accumulation in warmer areas (Beilman *et al.* 2009).

There is thus a strong suggestion from palaeo-environmental reconstructions that peat accumulation (and hence carbon sequestration) are higher under warmer climates, as long as there is sufficient moisture to maintain a high water table (Yu *et al.* 2011; Charman *et al.* 2012). This has important implications for future peatland response to climate change. Small increases in temperature may actually increase peat growth rates in the future in areas where productivity is limited by short growing seasons and low temperatures. There also seems to be scope for peatlands in more temperate regions to increase peat growth rates to some extent. However, projected climate changes for the next century are much greater than the small-amplitude, slow changes that peatlands have experienced in the past, and the response of peatlands is likely to be non-linear. At some point, peat accumulation will probably reach a threshold and will decline as temperature rises, but we do not yet know what that threshold will be. Furthermore, natural fire risk is likely to increase while human activities and land-use change could exacerbate climatically induced pressures on accumulation rates.

8.4 Future climate change and peatlands
8.4.1 Predicted climatic changes

There is overwhelming scientific agreement that continued GHG emissions will cause further atmospheric warming and changes in the climate of the Earth during the twenty-first century (IPCC 2007). The Intergovernmental Panel on Climate Change's Fourth Assessment Report (IPCC AR4) predicts a warming of 0.2°C per decade for the next two decades, then further warming depending on the emission scenario, with the warming being greater (a) at high latitudes and (b) over land (Trenberth et al. 2007). As a result, the snow cover will decrease and the thaw depth of permafrost regions, including the vast expanses covered in boreal peat, will increase. Precipitation patterns are expected to change, with increases at high latitudes and decreases in subtropical regions. Climatic extremes, such as heatwaves and heavy precipitation events, are also likely to increase. All these changes are anticipated to affect peatland regions, since boreal, tropical and mountainous regions have been highlighted as being especially vulnerable to the predicted climatic changes (IPCC 2007). These changes are likely to lead to degradation of peat climate regulation services, including loss of carbon storage due to decreased water tables and increased decomposition of peat, increased erosion and sediment flux, and reduction in water regulation services due to potential degradation of water quality (Turetsky 2010).

8.4.2 Changes in the global extent of peatlands

Since climate largely determines the extent of most peatlands, we can assume that changes in the climate will result in changes in the overall extent of these ecosystems. Bioclimatic models at the regional scale also predict that the suitable bioclimatic envelope for peatlands will retreat towards higher latitudes in the future due to climatic changes (Gignac, Nicholson and Bayley 1998; Clark et al. 2011; Gallego-Sala et al. 2011). This retreat is mainly driven by increases in temperature. Equally, peatland ecosystems at lower latitudes may not be well adapted to survive the more frequent extreme heat waves predicted in Europe and North America (Meehl and Tebaldi 2004; Bragazza 2008).

Future precipitation predictions are particularly uncertain and present more regional variation, so the effect on peatlands will be more localised.

For certain peatlands, precipitation increases may counterbalance the effect of higher temperatures on evapotranspiration, but the effects will be dependent on local factors, including mire type (Parish *et al.* 2008). For most peatlands, changes in the distribution of rainfall towards more frequent extreme events, i.e. drought and/or flooding, are likely to exacerbate the effect of increased temperatures and become a further stress on peatlands, making them more vulnerable to, for example, peat erosion.

The treeline is likely to also advance towards higher latitudes and altitude where there might have been peatlands before, leading to a decrease in albedo (Parish *et al.* 2008). The effects may depend on peatland type and, for example in the case of northern oceanic peatlands, it has been proposed that they may be increasing in area, due to a retreat of the treeline and an ecological succession towards bogs where there were previously forests (Crawford, Jeffree and Rees 2003). Although oceanic mires may in the future expand towards mountainous and northern areas, their present location may still be under threat from increasing summer and annual temperatures (see Box 8.1).

It is important to highlight that peatlands are resilient and adaptive ecosystems, able to respond to and survive variations in their environment, and their exact response to changes in the climate remains ambiguous (Lindsay 2010). If a bioclimatic model predicts that a peatland falls outside

---

Box 8.1

Are blanket bogs under threat?

Blanket bog is a distinctive type of mire that is very rare at the global scale, and almost restricted to the fringes of continental land masses in mid- to high latitudes (Chapter 9). Blanket bog requires the highest year-round rainfall of all peatlands, combined with low summer temperatures, restricting this mire type to the hyperoceanic regions of the world. Blanket bogs are ombrotrophic (rain-fed) mires that cover the landscape with a blanket of peat broken only by the steepest slopes. A simple process-based bioclimatic model, PeatStash, was used with climate change projections from seven global climate models to study the fate of blanket bogs globally (Gallego-Sala and Prentice 2012). The results (Figure 8.6) show dramatic shrinkage of its bioclimatic space with only a few, restricted areas of persistence. However, shrinkage of the bioclimatic space for blanket bog does not necessarily entail complete or swift disappearance of these peatlands and the associated loss of the accumulated carbon to the atmosphere. The resilience of peat to environmental changes has been highlighted previously (Hogg, Lieffers and Wein 1992; Lindsay 2010), and rapid carbon losses may be avoidable, especially if vegetation cover is maintained. Nevertheless, regions falling outside the envelope will be under stress from climate change and unlikely to continue growing and acting as carbon sinks. It is worth noting that even assuming no further carbon sequestration, the loss of carbon to the atmosphere is likely to be slow and it would take in the order of millennia to deplete all the stored carbon in blanket bogs (Billett et al. 2010). Protection of these mires, including good water management and fire and grazing control, is critical to preserve these rare peatlands and mitigate the effects of a changing climate on blanket bogs (Parish et al. 2008).

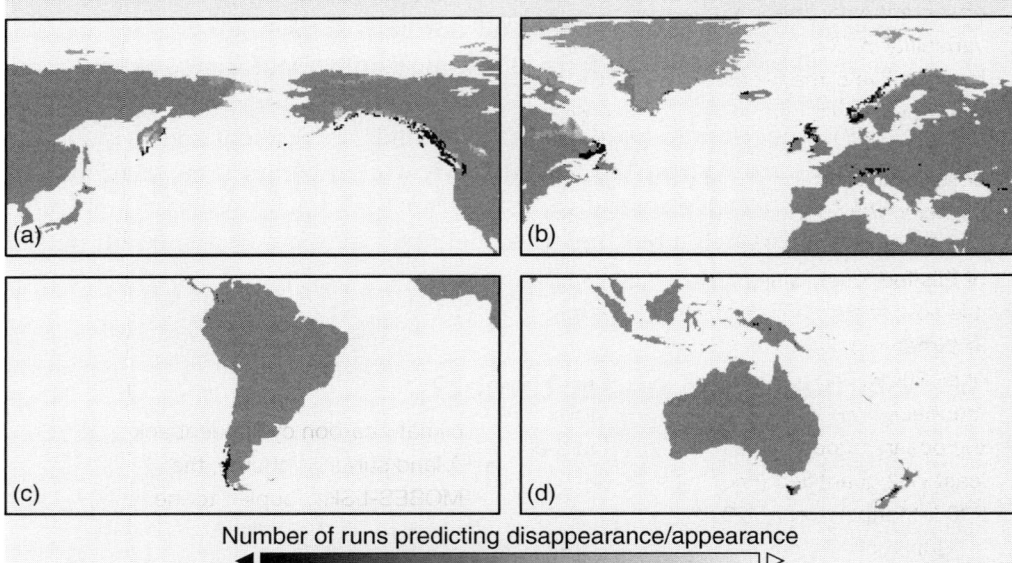

Figure 8.6 Projected changes to blanket bog bioclimatic space for seven climate change scenarios compared to the standard period for (a) Kamchatka and Western North America, (b) Eastern North America and Europe, (c) South America and (d) Australasia. The scenarios were derived by pattern scaling, assuming a 2°C warming by 2050, resulting in a warming of 3.9 to 4.5°C over land during 2070–99. The grey scale represents number of climate models predicting new appearance (white) or disappearance (black) of blanket bog bioclimatic envelope area (adapted from Gallego-Sala and Prentice, 2012).

Box 8.2
Peatlands as part of carbon cycle models

Changes in the atmospheric concentration of CO_2 are the primary driver of contemporary climate change, but climate change also influences the amount of CO_2 in the atmosphere by affecting plant productivity and decomposition processes in soils. The carbon cycle, climate and atmospheric carbon dioxide concentration form a feedback loop (Friedlingstein et al. 2006). Earth system model results and observations of interannual and historical variability in CO_2 concentration point to a positive climate-carbon feedback, whereby climate change results in a larger fraction of anthropogenic carbon dioxide emissions remaining in the atmosphere, further warming the climate (Friedlingstein and Prentice 2010). However, the strength of this feedback is highly uncertain, indeed it is now one of the largest uncertainties in climate change science (Gregory et al. 2009). The terrestrial carbon cycle feedback is both the dominant term (over the ocean carbon cycle feedback) and the least well quantified (Friedlingstein et al. 2006, Matthews et al. 2007).

Until recently, models have completely ignored the potential contribution of peatlands, even though they contain 530–694 Gt C (Yu et al. 2010). Most model-derived estimates of global carbon storage treat all soils as mineral soils of fixed depth, and thus disregard the dynamic nature of peat growth. Yet, with the widespread acknowledgement that peatland ecosystems play an important role in the carbon cycle and the climate comes an increasing interest in representing peatlands in terrestrial carbon cycle models. Some initial efforts have already been made to include peatlands in global models:

- A methane emissions model for northern peatlands within the Lund–Potsdam–Jena Dynamic Global Vegetation Model (LPJ-WHyMe and LPX) has been developed which includes permafrost dynamics and peatland vegetation and hydrology (Wania et al. 2009; Spahni et al. 2012).
- A model that uses a topographic index to calculate inundation as a proxy for peatland/wetland extent has been developed as part of ORCHIDEE, the Institut Pierre-Simon Laplace land surface scheme (Ringeval et al. 2011). This model also calculates methane emissions and their role in the climate-carbon cycle feedback.
- A land surface scheme, the MOSES-LSH, coupled to the Met Office climate model, uses a topographic index to assess the extent of peatlands and can also calculate methane emissions (Gedney et al. 2004). This model's results suggest that global wetlands' response to climate change will amplify the total anthropogenic radiative forcing at 2100 by about 3.5–5% via increases in methane emissions.

- The McGill Wetland Model is currently being developed from previous peat accumulation models (e.g. the Peat Decomposition model, Frolking et al. 2001) in order to be coupled with the Canadian Centre for Climate and Model Analysis (CCCma) coupled general circulation model (St-Hilaire et al. 2008). This latter model has already been applied at the regional scale to a raised bog in Canada, and it predicts low sensitivity of the net carbon balance to variations in water table because of opposing responses in plant productivity and decomposition. On the other hand, the net carbon balance of this particular bog in Canada was extremely sensitive to temperature increases that could switch the balance from a sink to a source of carbon (St-Hilaire et al. 2008).
- The climate model of the Institute of Atmospheric Physics of the Russian Academy of Sciences (IAP RAS CM) has also been coupled with a model of soil thermal physics and the methane cycle, and initial results predict a global increase in methane emissions from wetland ecosystems under all future IPCC scenarios, together with a decrease in the area covered by permafrost (Eliseev et al. 2008).
- Finally, a simple wetland distribution and methane emissions model has been incorporated into the Goddard Institute for Space Studies (GISS) GCM (Shindell et al. 2004). Simulations using this model under carbon dioxide levels double that of the pre-industrial time show an increase in annual average wetland methane emissions from 156 to 277 Tg yr^{-1}, a rise of 78%.

Most of these peatland models are able to make predictions of how methane emissions from wetlands or peatlands may change in the future, but are not advanced enough yet to give us a clear picture of the overall role of peatlands in the carbon cycle. Only one of these models (LPX) has recently been run to allow predictions of how carbon accumulation rates may change under a warmer climate (Spahni et al 2012). Mostly, global peatland models cannot predict whether the radiative forcing of peatlands will vary, or whether peatlands extent may change. There are many challenges ahead for the peat-modelling community, some of which will involve developing modules able to calculate the extent of peatlands dynamically, better representation of the hydrology of peatlands as distinct from mineral soils and improved representation of the biogeochemical processes that occur in peat. Models will have to tackle the challenge of small-scale heterogeneity and self-regulation of northern peatlands (Baird et al. 2009). Future models should aim to simulate the long-term responses of peatlands to climate change observed in the past record.

its bioclimatic envelope in the future, it would not imply a sudden and complete loss of the peatland habitat, its carbon storage capabilities or any other ecosystem service it presently provides, because of the resilience of the established peatland system. Although bioclimatic models are unable to make predictions about the rate of carbon loss or possible resilience of peatlands to a changing climate, they can help identify which peatland regions may be particularly vulnerable to future climate changes.

8.4.3 Climate effect on peatland hazard regulation service: wildfire risk

Fires in peatlands have considerable consequences in terms of ecosystem services. They release large amounts of carbon into the atmosphere in the form of carbon dioxide, carbon monoxide, methane and other volatile organic compounds, together with nitrous oxide (Hamada *et al.* 2010). In this way, they are a large point-source of GHGs and contribute to climate change. The smoke and haze from fires can have major health implications for people (Johnston *et al.* 2012) and may affect air traffic. Vegetation loss after fire may be long-lasting depending on the type of vegetation, its regeneration capabilities and the depth and intensity of the fire. The loss of vegetation may lead to erosion, peat subsidence and a potential increase in surface waters and subsequent flooding, as well as degradation of water quality due to DOC losses and sediment flux (Charman 2002). The surface layer of peat may be lost, slowing the rate of peat accumulation. All these changes are likely to modify the characteristics of the peatland, and depending on the severity of the fire, some of the changes may be irreversible.

Both people and climate play a role in determining fire patterns, especially where mires have been artificially drained and are therefore most at risk. Considering the economic and natural losses involved in large-scale peat fires, peatland restoration is a cost-effective fire mitigation strategy. For example, the Russian authorities, in conjunction with Wetlands International Russia, have been working on the Meschera National Park in the Vladimir province, to rewet 2000 ha of degraded peatland as a fire prevention measure (http://russia.wetlands.org/). Other restoration projects are in place in tropical peatlands, for example in the Central Kalimantan province in Indonesia, which has involved the blocking of drains (Chapter 14). Restoration of peatlands through rewetting and re-vegetation is a complex and lengthy process, but a reduction of fire risk may lead to subsequent reduction in carbon dioxide emissions, a reduction in peat subsidence and a decrease in dissolved organic matter in runoff waters and an increase of biodiversity, which ultimately benefits the local communities (Parish *et al.* 2008; Chapter 14).

Analysis of sedimentary charcoal records has revealed that there is a close correlation between large-scale temperature trends and biomass burning (Marlon *et al.* 2008). One implication is that global warming is very likely to increase fire frequency, and several modelling studies have made this prediction, globally or for specific regions (e.g. Scholze *et al.* 2006; Balshi *et al.* 2009). On the other hand, the effect of climate change on fire is unlikely to be spatially uniform and some regions could see reduced fire risks due to increasing rainfall (Pechony and Shindell 2010).

In tropical peatlands, especially in Indonesia, the compound effects of drought, deforestation and fire have been responsible for tremendous losses of carbon to the atmosphere in recent years. It has been calculated that ~1.45 Mha of peatlands were burnt in Indonesia in 1997 alone, an El Niño year, releasing 0.81–2.57 Gt C to the atmosphere: equivalent to 13–40% of the global annual CO_2 emissions from fossil fuel burning (Page *et al.* 2002). Drainage and deforestation are continuing to give way to oil palm and other biofuel crops in the region, which in addition to the predicted increase in the frequency of extreme weather events, drought and heat waves, is likely to increase the fire frequency (Page *et al.* 2002; Miettinen, Shi and Liew 2011). Unless there is a clear management change in these peatlands, involving major fire risk management and mitigation, and restoration and rehabilitation programmes, the impact of fires on ecosystem services is likely to escalate in the future (see also Chapter 14).

Model predictions suggest the areal extent of extreme fire danger risk is also likely to increase in boreal regions (Stocks *et al.* 1998). The intensification of extreme weather events, in particular drought and heat waves, has already resulted in the number of wildfires escalating in boreal regions (Riordan, Verbyla and McGuire 2006). For example, unprecedented drought conditions, combined with an extended heatwave, resulted in widespread forest and peatland fires in western Russia during 2010 that burnt hundreds of thousands of hectares (Stocks *et al.* 2011). Some areas of Russia are extremely fire prone, due to drainage for peat mining in the past and abandonment since the beginning of the 1990s.

It has been suggested that at a global scale, temperate peatland fires may emit up to 0.32 Gt C during drought years (Poulter, Christensen and Halpin 2006). As drought frequency is predicted to increase in the future, fires from mid-latitude peatlands could also become more frequent. For example, in the UK, moorland fires are likely to increase due to changes in the climate and increased visitor access to peatland areas (McMorrow *et al.* 2009).

8.4.4 Changes in water table, dissolved organic carbon and greenhouse gas exchange

To a degree, the limited hydraulic conductivity and large storage coefficient of peat allow it to maintain the water table at a certain level, although inevitably the water table in peatlands is greatly affected by rainfall and groundwater inflow. Future changes in precipitation will impact the water table level and therefore have far-reaching effects on all microbial processes occurring in peatlands. Predicted precipitation changes are different depending on the region. Annual precipitation is predicted to increase in higher northern latitudes, while summer precipitation will decrease in mid-northern latitudes, and tropical regions may experience an increase of precipitation (Amazon) or a decrease (Indonesia) depending on the area. In South East Asia, drained peatlands experience subsidence and have become large sources of CO_2 due to peat oxidation, this source being larger than that from peatland fires in the region, while methane fluxes become negligible when water tables are lowered (Couwenberg, Dommain and Joosten 2010). Similarly, drained peatlands in Europe are also negligible sources of methane, and large sources of carbon dioxide (Couwenberg *et al.* 2011). However, the effect of the water table is not always straightforward. In a water-table drawdown experiment, lowering of the water table resulted in peat subsidence, an increase in vascular plant cover and decreased methane fluxes, but did not have a significant effect on carbon dioxide fluxes (Strack and Waddington 2007). However, generally peatlands that experience increased precipitation and higher water table level in the future are likely to produce and emit more methane. On the other hand, those peatlands with lower water table levels in the future will release more nitrous oxide, which is also a GHG (Martikainen *et al.* 1993). DOC will also be affected by changes in precipitation patterns; for example, DOC has increased in surface waters in the UK over past decades, and the results obtained by Tang *et al.* (2013) suggest that an increase of drought events will decrease the amount of DOC but change DOC quality, making water treatment more costly. Finally, peatlands that experience a lowering of the water table level are likely to become more forested, while peatlands with increasing water table level may become deforested (Parish *et al.* 2008).

8.4.5 Changes in permafrost

Peatlands at high latitudes have experienced warming over past decades that have led to a lengthening of the growing season, an increase of the potential evapotranspiration and warming and/or melting of permafrost (Riordan, Verbyla and McGuire 2006). An increase in the thickness of the snow pack and an early establishment of the snow cover also enhances permafrost melting because of the insulating properties of snow (Zhang, Barry and Haeberli 2001). Permafrost degradation can have a number of different ecological consequences, depending on the terrain, soil characteristics and hydrology. It can result in conversion of forests to peat-forming ecosystems, or to improvement of drainage in upland areas (Jorgenson and Osterkamp 2005). Different studies show markedly different effects of permafrost melting on peatlands. For example, Alaskan remote-sensing observations since the 1950s have shown drying of lakes and wetlands of the discontinuous permafrost region, which was thought to be mainly due to an increase in evapotranspiration and improved drainage (Riordan, Verbyla and McGuire 2006). A more recent study offers an alternative explanation to the observed drying of lakes in Alaska: terrestrialisation, i.e. the formation of peatlands on previously existing lakes (Roach et al. 2011). A study of subarctic peatlands in Canada during the same period based on long-term ecosystem monitoring found that rapid melt of permafrost due to increasing snow thickness favoured the rise of water tables, with subsequent formation of thermokast lakes and expansion of fens and bogs (Payette et al. 2004). The overall effect on peatlands may vary with peatland type and topographic characteristics, but certain mires, for example palsa mires, which contain peat mounds that are permanently frozen, are likely to be threatened by the increasing temperatures, and the area occupied by these mires is likely to decrease (Fronzek, Luoto and Carter 2006).

The consequences of permafrost degradation seem to be different depending on local characteristics, but even then, they are likely to affect the provisioning and climate regulation services provided by peatlands that currently lie on permafrost areas (Riordan, Verbyla and McGuire 2006). The disappearance of permafrost and subsequent variations of the water table could have profound consequences for provisioning services. For example, in Alaska, where water tables may lower, the breeding grounds of many wild animals would be affected, especially waterfowl and shorebirds, and the subsistence lifestyles of indigenous people would also be impacted (Riordan, Verbyla and McGuire 2006). In Fennoscandia, the shrinking of the area covered in palsa mires would have devastating consequences on the avian biodiversity of subarctic mires (Fronzek, Luoto and Carter 2006).

In terms of climate regulation services, future climatic changes may favour carbon sink conditions in subarctic peatlands because of the rising of water table levels leading to both an expansion of peatlands and rapid peat accumulation (Vitt, Halsey and Zoltai 2000; Payette et al. 2004). However, the capture of carbon dioxide may be offset by large increases in methane emissions once discontinued permafrost peatlands have melted (Turetsky, Wieder and Vitt 2002). The net effect of permafrost melting in terms of 'global warming potential' is a still a matter of debate.

8.4.6 Changes in sea level: inundation of coastal peatlands and loss of flood protection

Due to thermal expansion and glacial and ice sheet melting, sea levels are projected to rise by between 0.20 and 0.35 m by the end of this century, depending on the emission scenario (Bindoff *et al.* 2007), with significant risk of a much larger rise due to the rapid melting of the Greenland icesheet (Gregory, Huybrechts and Raper 2004; Overpeck *et al.* 2006). Sea-level rise will have unavoidable consequences for coastal peatlands. Worldwide, as much as 150 000 km^2 of low-lying coastal peatlands may be vulnerable to sea-level rise (Henman and Poulter 2008). These peatlands may suffer from shoreline erosion, salt intrusion and/or inundation. When coastal peatlands are inundated by seawater, they experience vegetation die-off, peat subsidence and a shift from methane production to sulfate reduction in the decomposition process. Inundation of coastal peatlands is likely to be a positive feedback to climate change, because the combination of factors is likely to release the carbon store to the atmosphere (Henman and Poulter 2008). In certain areas, sea intrusion will cause forest retreat and replacement by salt marshes (Williams *et al.* 1999); in others, freshwater peatlands may become saltmarshes. An added issue is that in many cases, human populations are concentrated on these coastal peatlands, which have been drained to give way to agriculture and grazing. Drainage of peatlands in coastal areas leads to subsidence with a lowering of the surface that is much faster than the expected rise in sea-water level. In this way, former and current drainage of coastal peatlands accelerates the local rate of sea-level rise (Borger 1992). This is a serious problem in many populous countries, for example, the Netherlands and also in the United States (Gulf Coast), but especially in tropical peatlands with extreme rainfall, such as Indonesia (Kalimantan, Sumatra), where expensive pumping facilities could not be sustained.

8.4.7 Changes due to CO_2 fertilisation

Plant life is not only being exposed to climatic changes but also to the direct physiological effects of an increase in the atmospheric concentration of CO_2, which has risen from 280 ppm in pre-industrial times to the current 390 ppm (Forster *et al.* 2007). The continuing CO_2 concentration increase is likely to affect vegetation photosynthetic rates and water-usage efficiency, with one study measuring markedly increased plant productivity under CO_2 enrichment, especially in more nutrient-rich sites, and a slight shift towards vascular flora and loss of mosses (Freeman *et al.* 2004). The combined effect on plants, also called the CO_2 fertilisation effect, seems to be variable dependent on a series of factors that may limit its extent, such as temperature, nitrogen availability and plant type. A number of FACE (free-air CO_2 enrichment) experiments have been carried out on peatland vegetation to study the CO_2 fertilisation effect on these ecosystems. The prevalence of mosses, especially *Sphagnum* sp., and other bryophytes coexisting with vascular plant species such as sedges, grasses and rushes, means that the composition of peatland vegetation is unique and there is no clear reason *a priori* to expect that the response to CO_2 would be the same as in, for example, forests or grasslands; although it might be anticipated that strong nutrient limitations in ombrotrophic peatlands would constrain the magnitude of the CO_2 effect. Some experiments have found no effect on *Sphagnum* moss biomass growth (Berendse *et al.* 2001), but an increase of *Sphagnum* moss height, which may give it an advantage over lower-lying plants (Heijmans *et al.* 2001). A study of bogs in Finland found no CO_2 fertilisation effect on either above- or below-ground productivity and attributed this to nutrient limitations (Hoosbeek *et al.* 2002), although the statistical power of this study to detect a change was limited. In any case, higher CO_2 atmospheric concentrations may well enhance the growth of vascular flora of nutrient-rich peatlands. The limited available evidence suggests that CO_2 fertilisation is likely to be less significant for *Sphagnum* than for vascular plants.

8.5 Conclusions and implications for peatland restoration and research

Climate change is expected to have far-reaching consequences for peatlands and the ecosystem services they provide. Peatland geographical distribution is likely to change. Bioclimatic models predict shrinking of the geographical distribution of climatically suitable areas for peatlands, with some peatlands falling outside their bioclimatic envelope in the future. These peatlands will be at risk in the future and will require more carefully considered management to mitigate the effects of climatic changes. In addition, coastal peatlands will be exposed to the consequences of sea-level rise due to climate change, including inundation and erosion. At the same time, the melting of the permafrost is likely to increase the area covered in peatlands at the northern boundary.

It is important to highlight that intact and well-functioning peatlands can be resilient ecosystems, as palaeoecological evidence shows they have survived past changes of climate (Charman 2002). Intact peatlands have greater potential to retain provision of vital ecosystem services than damaged peatlands. There is also some evidence to suggest that intact peatlands may accumulate carbon more rapidly in the future (Charman *et al.* 2012), but overall, the role of peatlands in the carbon cycle in a warmer climate remains uncertain.

Once the water balance of peatlands is disturbed and peatlands are in a degraded state, they become more vulnerable to climatic changes. Drainage leads to peat subsidence and oxidation and an enhanced risk of peatland fires. Climate change in the form of rising temperatures and drought, as well as more frequent severe weather events, will exacerbate the degradation process in these peatlands. This further degradation forms a feedback loop, worsening climate change through increases in GHG emissions. Globally, a recent report by Wetlands International gives an estimate of carbon loss from peatland degradation of 1.3 Gt C yr^{-1} in 2008, an increase of 20% since 1990 (Joosten 2009c), compared to the estimated carbon sink from northern peatlands (not including tropical peatlands) of 0.076 Gt C yr^{-1} (Gorham 1991).

Peatland conservation management and restoration can be cost-effective climate mitigation activities to reduce CO_2 emissions from peat oxidation and peatland fires (Joosten, Tapio-Biström and Tol 2012; Chapter 15). A first priority should be the preservation of those peatlands that are still intact. The next priority should be to restore or improve the conditions of degraded peatlands, as management can reduce but not always reverse emissions to those of intact peatlands (Chapter 4).

Additional external stressors from land management, such as inappropriate grazing and managed burning regimes and mining, exacerbate the problems due to climate change alone. Targeted fire prevention and control management will need to address predicted increases in fire risks in order to prevent catastrophic carbon losses and risk to human health, such as those seen in recent years in South East Asian and Russian peatlands. For agriculture and forestry on peatlands, new management strategies, such as wet agriculture or paludiculture (Chapter 17), should be promoted as an alternative to drainage to generate sustainable productivity from peatlands without compromising the ecosystem services they provide.

Challenges for the peatland research community will be to inform peatland managers of the best way to deal with the impacts of climate change. There are large peatland areas that have received little interest and have not been the focus of many studies to date (e.g. tropical and remote regions of the Hudson Bay lowlands and East Siberia). These areas should be targeted by new projects based on their relevance to providing evidence on the effect of climate on peatland ecosystem services (Yu *et al.* 2011). Also of importance to peatland ecosystem management is long-term monitoring to obtain high-quality baseline data that clarify the main drivers of change (Bonn, Rebane and Reid 2009). To profit fully from the richness of information contained in the peat record, a more concerted effort should be made to integrate palaeo- and contemporarary observations (Yu 2012). Finally, efforts to include the complexity of peatland dynamics into Earth System models should continue so that more reliable predictions of the future contribution of peatlands to the carbon cycle can be taken into account. There is a need to generally increase and improve knowledge exchange and promote increased awareness of the value of peatlands in the public (Bonn, Rebane and Reid 2009).

PART II

Perspectives on peatland restoration

CHAPTER NINE

Blanket mire restoration and its impact on ecosystem services

TIM THOM
Yorkshire Wildlife Trust, UK
MARTIN EVANS
The University of Manchester, UK
CHRIS EVANS
Center for Ecology and Hydrology, Bangor, UK
TIM ALLOTT
The University of Manchester, UK

9.1 Introduction

Blanket mire is a rare resource representing less than 3% (120 000 km^2) of global peatlands (Tallis 1997). The largest concentration of blanket mire occurs in the uplands of the UK and Ireland (approximately 20% of global blanket mire (Tallis 1998)). The global rarity of blanket mire and concerns over its current condition in the UK (see Box 9.1) have led to it being included in protective legislation (European Commission 1992) and in national conservation strategies (JNCC and DEFRA 2012).

Blanket mire condition in the UK has been impacted by multiple pressures, including drainage, afforestation, atmospheric pollution and burning. The most intensely impacted areas are severely eroded, with large areas of bare peat and erosion gully networks (Evans and Warburton 2007), with artificial drainage additionally affecting over 1.5 million hectares of blanket mire (Parry *et al.* 2014). Although the extent of erosion of blanket mire in the UK and Ireland is not widely replicated elsewhere in the world, analogous peat erosion has been reported from North and South America, Asia and Australia (Evans and Warburton 2007). For example, increasing levels of erosion of sloping mires in Tibet (Joosten and Schumann 2007; Chapter 13) demonstrate that the requirement to manage upland peat is not just a UK

Peatland Restoration and Ecosystem Services: Science, Policy and Practice, eds. A. Bonn, T. Allott, M. Evans, H. Joosten and R. Stoneman. Published by Cambridge University Press. © British Ecological Society 2016.

concern. The focus of this chapter is therefore on the ecosystem service benefits of blanket mire restoration in the uplands of the UK and Ireland, as an exemplar for peatland restoration which may become more widely applicable.

The chapter is in three sections. The first summarises the main ecosystem services of blanket mire; the second describes the main drivers for the condition of blanket mire in the UK; and the third outlines the impact that blanket mire restoration has on ecosystem services. Readers are also directed to the review by Parry *et al.* (2014), which provides further details on blanket mire degradation, the restoration techniques employed in the UK and the response of ecosystem service features to restoration practices.

Box 9.1

The current condition of blanket bog in the UK

- Only 20% of blanket bog is in a natural or near-natural condition (Littlewood *et al.* 2010).
- Only 58% of the blanket bog in protected sites is in favourable condition (JNCC 2011). Of the remainder only 15% is recovering.
- Reported peatland erosion across the UK varies from 10–30% (Evans and Warburton 2007).

9.2 Ecosystem services from blanket mire systems

Blanket mires contribute a range of ecosystem services, briefly summarised below following the proposed Common International Standard for Ecosystem Services (Haines-Young and Potschin 2013; see Table 1.1 in Chapter 1).

9.2.1 Provisioning services

Reared animals (sheep and deer farming)

The low fertility of blanket mire systems has generally limited agricultural activities to grazing, predominantly with sheep across the UK, and sheep and deer in Scotland. Grazing rates have been on an upward trajectory since the land enclosures and agricultural improvements of the early 1700s culminating in the post-war drive for agricultural self-sufficiency where numbers peaked at the end of the 1980s (Condliffe 2009). Deer numbers in Scotland have been increasing since the 1920s (van der Wal *et al.* 2011). In the 1990s it was recognised that this increasing grazing pressure was damaging the uplands and livestock numbers were reduced through agri-environment schemes (Condliffe 2009).

Drinking water supply
Blanket peat catchments are important for water supply, particularly in the upland regions of the UK. Peatlands leach DOC and so downstream rivers, lakes and reservoirs are often characterised by coloured water which has to be treated by water supply utilities at high cost. DOC leaching, however, is higher in damaged blanket peat catchments than in intact catchments (e.g. Wallage, Holden and McDonald 2006; Armstrong *et al.* 2010), and treatment costs are significantly enhanced. Undisturbed blanket peatlands therefore provide an important ecosystem services benefit for drinking water supply (Bain *et al.* 2011).

9.2.2 Regulating services
Climate regulation
Intact peatlands perform two globally important climate regulation functions: (1) they store carbon and (2) they sequester carbon from the atmosphere in the form of CO_2 through photosynthesis (Chapter 8). UK peatlands store over 3200 million tonnes of carbon (Worrall *et al.* 2010), the majority of which is in blanket mire, approximately 20 times that stored in UK forests. In the UK, blanket mires may also sequester 30–70 t C km^{-2} yr^{-1} from the atmosphere (Billett *et al.* 2010; Worrall *et al.* 2010). Due to their high water tables, peatlands will also act as natural sources of the GHG methane. However, their long-term climate influence is generally accepted to be net cooling (Frolking, Roulet and Fuglestvedt 2006).

Water quality regulation
Blanket mires buffer against acidification and eutrophication by locking up nutrients and other elements (e.g. sulfur, nitrogen and heavy metals from atmospheric deposition) in accumulating organic matter and therefore buffer downstream surface waters against the impacts of atmospheric pollutants (Chapter 5). The loss of peat-forming species may cause leaching of acidity, metals and nitrates into watercourses (Helliwell *et al.* 2007), with subsequent impacts on water quality and aquatic ecosystem condition. Blanket mires also act as sources of DOC, which is considered detrimental to drinking water supplies but may also provide some ecological benefits (e.g. Evans, Monteith and Cooper 2005).

Flood risk regulation
Blanket mires are saturated systems with little fluctuation in the water table, which is generally close to the surface, and have little capacity to store significant additional water (van der Wal *et al.* 2011). However, surface flows in *Sphagnum* species-dominated mires are lower than in mires dominated by other vegetation types or degraded mires (Holden *et al.* 2008), and

the loss of *Sphagnum* cover and increases in bare peat can increase peak flow and reduce runoff lag times (Grayson, Holden and Rose 2010). Holden *et al.* (2006) also indicate that runoff from blanket mires can become more flashy after peat drainage. There is therefore growing evidence that blanket mire condition influences storm runoff characteristics and therefore downstream flood risk (Chapter 5).

9.2.3 Cultural services

Recreational and community activities
Many peatlands are in remote areas and offer experiences of wilderness and solitude, physical challenge and inspiration not easily experienced elsewhere (Bonn, Rebane and Reid 2009). The peatland-dominated upland English National Parks, for example, receive close to 60 million day visitors a year (Bain *et al.* 2011). Blanket mires also form parts of privately owned upland estates managed for recreational shooting of red grouse (*Lagopus lagopus* subsp. *scotica*) or for red deer (*Cervus elaphus*) stalking in Scotland. An estimated 4428 km^2 (56%) of the English uplands is managed for shooting, providing 120 full-time jobs and 5700 shoot days per year (Sotherton *et al.* 2009).

Scientific and cultural heritage
The anaerobic conditions in peat make it an excellent preservative of archaeological artefacts, and blanket mires provide a detailed archaeo-environmental record of environmental change through the preservation of pollen, plant remains, insect fragments, fungal spores and testate amoebae (Chapter 6).

9.2.4 Biodiversity

Blanket bogs are priorities for conservation under the EC Habitats Directive and are designated as Special Areas for Conservation (SAC) in much of the UK (Bain *et al.* 2011). A large proportion of peatlands in the UK are designated as Sites or Areas of Special of Scientific Interest (SSSI/ASSI) and for their landscape value as National Parks and Areas of Outstanding Natural Beauty. Peatlands support a range of rare, threatened or declining species which are adapted to waterlogged, acidic and nutrient-poor conditions, such as *Sphagnum* species (e.g. *Sphagnum austinii*) and the bog hoverfly (*Eristalis cryptarum*) (Littlewood *et al.* 2010). In terms of avian fauna, blanket mires in the UK are especially important for waders such as golden plover (*Pluvialis apricaria*), greenshank (*Tringa nebularia*) and dunlin (*Calidris alpina*), as well as other species such as the red-throated diver (*Gavia stellata*) and common scoter (*Melanitta nigra*).

9.3 Drivers for the current condition of blanket mire and their impacts on ecosystem services

The drivers for the current condition of blanket mire in the UK can be either indirect or direct (Parry, Holden and Chapman 2014). The source of direct drivers is within the blanket mire management unit itself, and the main direct drivers are grazing, peat extraction, forestry, fire, drainage and development. Indirect drivers are unrelated to local blanket mire management, but can still have a direct physical impact on the blanket mire. The most significant indirect drivers are policy, climate change and atmospheric pollution.

9.3.1 Indirect drivers

Policy

Upland land-use policy relating to agriculture, forestry and conservation dating from the Enclosures Acts (Bevan 2009) through the two World Wars (Condliffe 2009) and in the early stages of post-war European cooperation provided incentives for increased drainage, grazing and burning to improve agricultural productivity and increase timber production. More recently, growing recognition of the damage being caused to natural habitats led to a fundamental shift towards environmentally focused rural policies. Designation afforded protection from damaging operations and provided incentives for conservation and restoration. Agricultural policies also changed from the 1980s to provide agri-environment funding for positive environmental management (Condliffe 2009).

The European Union Water Framework Directive (WFD) increased recognition of the role upland peatlands play in regulating downstream water quality (Martin-Ortega *et al.* 2014; Chapter 19), and the Environment Agency in England is funding a number of restoration programmes across England including the Yorkshire Peat Partnership and Moors for the Future. A substantial amount of restoration work has also been driven by drinking water quality objectives, with OFWAT (the statutory regulator in the UK) supporting £26 million worth of peatland restoration work through water company-led programmes (Chapter 19).

Atmospheric deposition

The deposition of atmospheric pollutants has been a major driver of change in UK blanket mires since the Industrial Revolution. As sulfur emissions rose through the twentieth century, acid deposition in the southern

Pennines was a major cause of ecological damage, in particular the loss of peat-forming *Sphagnum* species, and has been a contributory factor in the onset of peat erosion across this region (Tallis 1987). Although sulfur emissions have declined by around 90% since the 1970s (RoTAP 2012), peatlands are slow to recover (e.g. Daniels *et al.* 2008a). Blanket mires in some parts of the UK also store large amounts of heavy metals such as lead and arsenic deposited from industrial processes (Rothwell *et al.* 2010). The deposition of nitrogen compounds, which has increased since the mid-twentieth century and remains above the 'critical load' (the threshold above which damage is expected) for 40% of all bog habitat in the UK (van der Wal *et al.* 2011), has the potential to trigger species change through their role as a nutrient.

Changes in blanket mire vegetation associated with atmospheric deposition have a range of impacts on ecosystem service. Excess nitrogen and the displacement of *Sphagnum* spp. by more competitive species (Berendse *et al.* 2001; Sheppard *et al.* 2011) can lead to the cessation of peat formation and potential release of CO_2. Historical sulfur deposition and the associated loss of *Sphagnum* may have resulted in increased DOC (Armstrong *et al.* 2012), and recent large regional DOC increases have been linked to reduced sulfur emissions since the 1970s (Evans, Monteith and Cooper 2005). Increased nitrogen supply can enhance heather (*Calluna vulgaris*) growth, but increase susceptibility to late winter injury (Carroll *et al.* 1999).

Climate change
Bioclimatic models suggest that by 2080 almost all of the blanket mires in England and Wales will exist outside their current climate envelope (Clark *et al.* 2010) and may, therefore, be vulnerable to pressures associated with higher temperatures, lower precipitation rates, higher decomposition due to increased soil temperature and climatic extremes (Chapter 8). For example, carbon accumulation rates may decrease due to higher rates of decomposition or changes from *Sphagnum* species to competitive vascular plants. Increased drought frequencies may also affect chemical controls on decomposition, increasing the loss of DOC (Freeman *et al.* 2001). The return period of high-magnitude wildfires is also expected to increase (McMorrow *et al.* 2009), leading to GHG emissions and the loss of stored carbon. However, it is important to note that the bioclimatic envelope models do not necessarily mean that blanket mire will be lost as they do not take full account of the influence of topography (Chapter 8), or the resilience and adaptability of blanket mires to climatic variations (Lindsay 2010). Additional considerations are that a wet peatland is likely to be more resilient to climate change than a drained one, rainfall rather than temperature is the overriding control on peat formation (Lindsay 2010), and there is significant uncertainty

in predication of future UK precipitation under climate change. Our current understanding of the likely responses of blanket mires to future climate change is therefore restricted.

9.3.2 Direct drivers

Grazing
Sheep are the dominant herbivore in the UK uplands. By 1986, 71% of peatland was stocked at rates greater than that considered to be sustainable (two sheep per hectare) (Holden *et al.* 2007), and this can have a significant impact on the ecosystem services provided by blanket mire through vegetation change towards more vascular species (Ward *et al.* 2007), and by trampling and grazing initiating and enhancing peat erosion (Evans and Warburton 2007). For example, heavy grazing on blanket mire can lead to dominance by *Molinia caerulea* and *Eriophorum vaginatum* (Shaw *et al.* 1996) and *Sphagnum* species decline under heavy grazing pressure (Rawes and Hobbs 1979). Trampling by sheep and associated sheep tracks can increase overland flow generation (Holden, Gascoigne and Bosanko 2007), with subsequent peat erosion increasing sediment loads into watercourses and reducing water quality (Evans 1998). Alternatively, the impacts of grazing on blanket mire carbon sequestration are not clearly established, although Garnett, Ineson and Stevenson (2000) found no differences in peat accumulation rates between grazed and un-grazed plots.

Peat cutting
Upland blanket mire was a source of peat for fuel, as litter for animals in stalls and as an agricultural soil improver after being burnt (Ardron 1999). Evidence of peat cuttings can still be seen across much of the uplands of the UK and small-scale peat cutting is still practised in parts of Scotland.

Forestry
Government incentives led to the planting of conifers on at least 190 000 ha of deep peat in the UK, with significant impacts on ecosystem services through associated land preparation (ditching) and the direct impact of tree growth (Chapter 12). In addition to the direct physical loss of the blanket mire habitat, afforestation leads to additional soil organic carbon losses through CO_2 efflux, particulate erosion or as DOC in runoff. This may be offset by accumulation of soil organic carbon through litter formation and incorporation into soils, carbon accumulating in growing trees and, on drained sites, reductions in methane emissions. The available data suggest that CO_2 efflux from the soil outweighs the increased rates of sequestration in the growing trees

(Morison et al. 2010). In terms of water quality, initial ground preparation for forestry on blanket mire releases suspended sediments (particulate organic carbon) into watercourses, and forest canopies increase atmospheric pollutant deposition and enhance nitrate and aluminium leaching from organic soils to surface waters (Evans et al. 2013). Drainage for afforestation also alters water quantity regulation from blanket peatlands, the main impact being increased water flow during prolonged dry periods (Chapter 12).

Fire
Fire is a significant driver of change in eocosystem services on UK blanket mires. Wildfire is common on blanket mires and may occur naturally due to lightning strikes, failure to control managed burning, ignition due to human carelessness or by arson. Where wildfire burns into the roots of the vegetation, rapid erosion over considerable areas may ensue (Maltby, Legg and Proctor 1990; Evans and Warburton 2007) and where the vegetation cover fails, exposure of the bare peat surface follows leading to erosion and the dissection of the peatland surface by deep gullies. Sediment yields from eroding blanket mires impacted by wildfire can exceed 200 t km^{-2} (Evans, Warburton and Yang 2006).

Prescribed management burning of small patches on rotations has been used in northern England and southern Scotland for the last 150 years or so to promote the growth of *Calluna vulgaris* and support red grouse for shooting. The expansion of *Calluna* cover can be beneficial to biodiversity, for example, to avians such as stonechat (*Saxicola torquata*) and golden plover (*Pluvialis apricaria*) (Pearce-Higgins and Grant 2006). However, managed burning on blanket mire has expanded in recent decades as the popularity of red grouse shooting has increased (Yallop et al. 2006), and the impacts on blanket mires have been the subject of considerable debate (Holden et al. 2012). Evidence for negative impacts on peat ecology and hydrology, peat chemistry and physical properties, river water chemistry, river ecology and flood risk is becoming more established (e.g. Brown, Holden and Palmer 2014). Burning on cycles of 3–6 years favours the replacement of *Calluna* and other ericoid shrubs with grasses, while cycles of about 10 years favour *Eriophorum vaginatum* on wetter ground (Ramchunder, Brown and Holden 2013). Yallop, Clutterbuck and Thacker (2010) report that areas of new burn are associated with increased water colour (DOC), and Palmer et al. (2013) report higher and more variable concentrations of DOC and particulate organic carbon (POC) in streams draining burnt catchments than in unburnt catchments. Prescribed burning also causes near-surface macropore blocking, decreasing infiltration into the surface peat layers and leading to increased surface runoff (Holden et al. 2014). Stormflow in streams draining burnt catchments is flashier in response to rainfall, with greater rainfall to runoff efficiencies than unburnt catchments (Holden *et al.* 2013). Burnt catchments also produce higher drainage water suspended sediment concentrations (Ramchunder, Brown and Holden 2013), causing detrimental changes to downstream invertebrate populations (Brown *et al.* 2013).

Drainage

The peatlands of upland Britain have been extensively drained since the 1950s with the aim of improving livestock and red grouse production. By 1970, 100 000 ha of land were being drained annually (Robinson and Armstrong 1988) but there is little evidence that drainage achieved any increase in productivity (Stewart and Lance 1983). Drainage was also carried out as part of afforestation programmes (Cannell, Dewar and Pyatt 1993). In some regions of intense peat erosion such as the English Peak District, large networks of gullies also act as drainage routes and in some of the most degraded mire systems these gullies are the primary drainage system (Evans and Lindsay 2010a).

Drainage leads to declines in *Sphagnum* spp. cover to be replaced by grasses and dwarf shrubs (Lindsay 2010). Peat drainage leads to rapid loss of water and as the water table drops, oxygen penetrates more deeply causing oxidative wastage, which converts the stored carbon into CO_2 and other products such as DOC (Lindsay 2010). This is counterbalanced by reductions in methane production. Where drainage leads to the loss of the peat-forming layer, carbon sequestration may cease, so 45–50 g C m^{-2} yr^{-1} is no longer transferred to carbon storage (Lindsay 2010). Similarly, Evans and Lindsay (2010b) report oxidative losses of carbon from erosion gullies >50 g C m^{-2} yr^{-1}. Drainage can increase DOC production (Wallage, Holden and McDonald 2006; Armstrong *et al.* 2010), and there is evidence of higher POC flux in drained or gullied catchments (Evans *et al.* 2009; Wilson *et al.* 2011). Bare peat in the drains also becomes susceptible to wind, rain, frost and summer dessiccation leading to erosion, overdeepening (Holden, Gascoigne and Bosanko 2007) and mass failure of peat slopes (Warburton, Holden and Mills 2004). Drainage modifies the peat structure and hydrological flow pathways, and depending on topography runoff can become more flashy, even though lower water tables restrict overland flow (Holden *et al.* 2006; Chapter 5).

Development

The main development pressure on UK blanket mire is the development of windfarms, as open upland landscapes are associated with high wind speeds. In Scotland, a third of the land area is covered by peat soil and windfarms are a key part of the Scottish government's renewable energy strategy. Construction of windfarms with associated access tracks, peat removal and drainage can be damaging to peatlands (Stunell 2010), resulting in changes to landscape aesthetics, habitat loss, disturbance to species (Fraga *et al.* 2008; Pearce-Higgins *et al.* 2009), reduction of carbon sequestration and storage in the peat (Nayak *et al.* 2010) and increased DOC and sediment (POC) loads to streams (Grieve and Gilvear 2008).

9.4 Ecosystem service benefits of blanket peatland restoration

Over the last decade there has been a significant increase in the number of blanket peat restoration projects in the UK (Cris *et al.* 2011; Parry, Holden and Chapman 2014), and knowledge of the impacts of restoration and associated ecosystem services benefits has increased. Two approaches to the restoration of blanket mire can be identified: (1) removal of external pressures and (2) active intervention through local land management. The former is achieved through policy interventions (e.g. to control grazing or to reduce air pollution), and removal of these indirect drivers of degradation may in some cases be sufficient to promote natural re-vegetation of bare peat surfaces (Evans and Warburton 2007). Nevertheless, in most cases active, location-specific intervention has been required (see Box 9.2) and three main types of local management intervention have been adopted:

1. Restoration by pressure removal, including managing grazing, deforestation and reducing burning
2. Restoration by rewetting, including ditch and gully blocking
3. Restoration by re-vegetation, particularly of bare peat.

Assessing the evidence for the impacts of restoration on ecosystem services is complex due to the large spatial and long temporal scales of ecosystem response to treatment. Most studies do not extend for more than a few years after restoration and the majority fail to include pre-restoration monitoring. Many have also failed to clearly identify the habitats on which their research is based, making it difficult to determine whether their findings apply to drier heathland or blanket mire communities. In a number of studies, control sites which were described as 'pristine' were in fact altered by drainage or land management and there is a pressing need to improve the experimental design of many studies (Lindsay 2010). Nevertheless, the evidence base for the benefits of blanket peat restoration is increasingly substantial.

Box 9.2

Examples of techniques for blanket bog restoration in the UK

Drainage channel blocking aims to rewet the peat mass by raising water tables using peat turves, heather bales or plastic piles to create dams.

Gully blocking is, analogous to drainage channel blocking, aiming to rewet the adjacent peat mass through raising water tables and stabilising erosion and carbon loss from the gully system. A range of gully-blocking methods have been adopted including wooden dams, low stone walls, wool bales and plastic piling. Sediment deposition behind the blocks creates locations for re-vegetation by common cottongrass.

Gully reprofiling is carried out where the sides of gullies are actively eroding and too steep for stablisation by re-vegetation, with the aim of controlling the erosion. The Yorkshire Peat Partnership working in the Yorkshire Pennines re-profiles the vertical sides of eroding gullies to a 33-degree slope and utilises turves from the surrounding area to cover any bare peat surfaces. Where insufficient turves are available, bare peat is treated using re-vegetation techniques. The Moors for the Future Partnership working in the South Pennines used geotextiles to stabilise slopes and then applied bare peat restoration techniques to establish a vegetation cover.

Bare peat re-vegetation is used to preserve the existing peat mass. Typically re-vegetation occurs through seeding with a nurse crop and with heather seed from a mulch of cut heather (Anderson, Buckler and Walker 2009), which stabilises the peat and allows colonisation by natural bog species. This includes application of lime to raise the soil pH, fertiliser to support root establishment and amenity grass seed to provide a nurse.

***Sphagnum* reintroduction** to blanket peatlands is being trialled in several projects. The Yorkshire Peat Partnership has been trialling spreading a bryophyte-rich mulch, which creates a thin moss layer on the bare peat. Moors for the Future has been working with a horticultural company (Microprop Limited) to develop Beadamoss which delivers *Sphagnum* propagules over large areas, and the Yorkshire Peat Partnership has been trialling mechanical spreading of fragments of *Sphagnum* species.

9.4.1 Restoration by pressure removal

Grazing reduction

Explicit evidence for the impacts of grazing reduction on blanket peat restoration is still relatively sparse, and there are few studies which clearly demonstrate benefits to (for example) flood risk management, water quality and biodiversity from reductions in heavy grazing and in the absence of other restoration treatments. Vegetation recovery following stock exclusion depends on the initial grazing intensity, and where grazing rates are already low the impacts on ecosystem services are probably also low. However, grazing exclusion from high-altitude, species-poor blanket bog produces the biggest changes (Adamson and Kahl 2003). Reduced trampling and the presence of sheep can reduce both overland flow routes and flood risk (Holden, Gascoigne and Bosanko 2007), and the prevention of livestock-induced erosion scars reduces sediment delivery and so mitigates against water deterioration (Evans 1998). The removal of grazing animals from areas which have been overgrazed has proved an effective first step in the recovery of blanket mire vegetation (Bain *et al.* 2011), and stock exclusion is often considered a prerequisite for the success of large-scale blanket mire restoration, in particular where re-vegetation of bare peat is required (e.g. Anderson, Buckler and Walker 2009).

Removing forestry

Although it is too early to be definitive about the full ecosystem service impacts associated with the removal of trees from commercial forests on UK blanket bogs, the number of projects monitoring such impacts is increasing and evidence for selected ecosystem service benefits emerging (Chapter 12). For example, the Border Mires project in the north of England has restored blanket peat by a combination of the removal of trees (pressure reduction) and the blocking of drainage ditches (rewetting), leading to higher water tables and increases in *Sphagnum* species cover (Chapter 12). Similarly, Stephen *et al.* (2011) found that average *Sphagnum* cover increased from 15% to 25% within 6 years after the deforestation of a Caithness (Scotland) blanket mire. Anderson (2010) has reported significant hydrological and mire vegetation benefits from a restoration experiment of afforested blanket bog in Caithness, supporting evidence that a combination of tree removal and ditch blocking is more effective than either one of these restoration techniques in isolation.

Reducing blanket mire burning

Blanket mire burning, particularly where it alters vegetation structure, has the potential to increase DOC concentrations and sediment yields, reduce the carbon store, reduce water quality, increase surface runoff and degrade biodiversity through replacement by competitive species (e.g. Bain *et al.* 2011; Holden *et al.* 2012). There is also increasing evidence that recovery can take place over time if burning is not repeated for at least 15–25 years. In particular, space-for-time experiments have shown that surface infiltration rates, and hence surface runoff characteristics, may recover if the mire surface is not burnt for 15+ years (Holden *et al.* 2014). Similarly, Palmer *et al.* (2013) report that streamwater DOC and POC concentrations are lower in catchments draining areas of burn 15–25 years old than in catchments dominated by recent burns.

9.4.2 Restoration by rewetting

Many blanket peatland restoration projects in the UK have focused on rewetting the peat mass, either by the blocking of peat drains or (in severely eroded peatland) the blocking of erosion gullies. Until recently there has been uncertainty over the ecosystem service benefits of drain and gully blocking, largely due to the short-term nature and limited spatial extent of most studies. A small number of studies are starting to provide evidence that, in the longer term, drain blocking can improve water quality, biodiversity and (potentially) downstream flood impacts. For example, studies comparing drained and drain-blocked catchments have reported reduced DOC concentrations (water colour) following restoration (e.g. Wallage, Holden and McDonald 2006; Armstrong *et al.* 2010; Wilson *et al.* 2011). Drain blocking has also been found to significantly reduce suspended sediment and fine particulate organic matter (Holden, Gascoigne and Bosanko 2007; Wilson *et al.* 2011), leading to improvements in invertebrate populations in downstream aquatic ecosystems (Ramchunder, Brown and Holden 2012). Rewetting may reduce *Calluna* cover, and therefore food for red grouse (Pearce-Higgins and Grant 2006), but Carroll *et al.* (2011) report significant increases in cranefly abundances after drain blocking with benefits for both grouse and breeding wader populations. Wilson *et al.* (2010) report reduced peak flows following drain blocking in a Welsh catchment, but the degree to which drain blocking alters peak flows will vary depending on the topographic configuration of the drainage and drain networks (Holden *et al.* 2004), and changes in vegetation cover type are potentially a more important control on peak flow and storm lag times and therefore on downstream flood risk (see Parry *et al.* 2014).

9.4.3 Restoration by re-vegetation

A limited number of studies have focused on the impacts of restoration by re-vegetation of bare blanket peat, which has been a particularly prevalent type of restoration in the South Pennines. These demonstrate clearly that sediment delivery and POC loss can be dramatically reduced by restoration

Box 9.3
Restoration of eroding blanket peat on the Bleaklow plateau, South Pennines, UK

The blanket mires of the South Pennines are the most severely eroded peat systems on the globe, with 34% of the area of the Bleaklow plateau being eroded (Evans and Lindsay 2010a). The predominant erosion type is a pattern of tightly dissected gullies, with smaller areas of extensive bare peat 'flats'. In 2003, a landscape-scale programme was initiated to re-vegetate bare peat (see Figure 9.1a, b) and block eroding gullies (see Anderson, Buckler and Walker 2009).

In gully-blocked catchments, water tables were raised and water storage increased with reduced stream discharge from the system (O'Brien et al. 2008). On re-vegetated sites there was some initial evidence of a rise in water tables (Allott et al. 2009) and reductions in particulate carbon flux from 155 g C m^{-2} yr^{-1} on bare peat sites to 6.4–7.9 g C m^{-2} yr^{-1} at restored sites (Worrall et al. 2011).

Estimates suggest carbon benefits from restoration of between 122 and 833 g C m^{-2} yr^{-1} (Worrall et al. 2011).

(a)

(b)

Figure 9.1 Progress of restoration by re-vegetation of an eroding South Pennine blanket mire over three years (photos: T. Allott). (a) Bare peat is first stabilised with a mulch of heather brash, before the addition of lime (to raise the soil pH above 4.0) and fertiliser. A nurse crop of agricultural and amenity grasses is then applied. (b) The nurse crop is progressively replaced by the natural establishment of cotton grasses *Eriophorum vaginatum* and *E. angustifolium* and the growth of heather (*Calluna vulgaris*) from the seed bank within the heather brash.

of bare peat to a vegetated surface (Evans *et al.* 2009; Shuttleworth *et al.* 2014; see Box 9.3). Importantly, these trends take place over short (<2 years) time periods after initial restoration treatment, and have immediate benefits for carbon sequestration (through avoidance of carbon loss) and water quality (through reduced suspended sediment and pollutant export to surface waters) (Worrall *et al.* 2011). Clear evidence is also emerging that re-vegetation and the recovery of *Sphagnum* species surface cover on blanket mire surfaces can reduce peak flows and increase stormflow lag times, thereby potentially contributing to downstream flood risk reduction (Chapter 5). Grayson, Holden and Rose (2010) showed that flood peaks in a northern England catchment were strongly related to the changing proportion of bare peat within the catchment, and Holden *et al.* (2008) demonstrated that surface runoff is significantly slower over *Sphagnum*-covered blanket peat than over bare peat or degraded vegetation cover.

9.5 Integrated assessments of restoration impacts on ecosystem service provision

While ongoing empirical work on the impacts of restoration on ecosystem services continues, there has also been a need to develop approaches to integrated assessment of the impacts of multiple restoration approaches on a range of service provision. One approach to this problem has been the development of predictive models which link ecosystem modifications to impact on particular ecosystem services. For example, Worrall *et al.* (2009) modelled the impact of drain blocking, and removing burning and grazing, on the carbon balance of 1 km grid square in the English Peak District. Modelling multiple scenarios identified optimum treatments and allowed analysis of costs of restoration in the context of carbon savings. The results showed that management interventions could increase the size of the peatland carbon sink and that at over half the sites the value of carbon stored in a 30-year time window would, if monetised through carbon markets, exceed the cost of restoration. This conclusion was reinforced by economic analyses presented by Moxey and Moran (2014) who, assessing UK degraded peatlands as a whole, concluded that in many cases the carbon sequestration benefits alone were sufficient to justify the cost of restoration, but that additional benefits further strengthen the economic case for action. Assessing the full range of ecosystem services changes affected by restoration requires a quantitative understanding of drivers and responses, and Glenk *et al.* (2014) argue that further research on the complex and sometimes non-linear responses to restoration interventions is required to deliver fully integrated ecosystem service assessments. Recent work by Evans *et al.* (2014) develops the concept of quantitative pressure–response functions linking modes of peatland degradation (drainage, burning, etc.) to specific ecosystem functions and associated services. The response curves presented by Evans *et al.* are partly conceptual but offer a potential way forward for further work to develop quantitative integrated assessments of the impact of restoration on the full range of peatland ecosystem services.

9.6 Conclusions

The evidence reviewed here demonstrates the value of blanket peats and blanket peat restoration to ecosystem services, and the increasing body of evidence that blanket mire restoration has overall positive benefits for the ecosystem services of climate regulation, water quality regulation, flood risk regulation and biodiversity conservation. The growing number of successful landscape-scale restoration projects in the UK suggests that a healthy blanket mire is more resilient in the face of environmental change, and knowledge of the ecosystem services effects of peat restoration can significantly inform future blanket peat restoration practice. Perhaps unsurprisingly, the clearest evidence of ecosystem service benefits associated with restoration comes from carefully controlled studies based on local land management interventions, such as through deforestation or the blocking of drainage ditches. It is also notable that some ecosystem service benefits associated with blanket peat restoration are realised very rapidly, such as with the re-vegetation of bare peat, whereas much longer-term studies will be required to fully evaluate the impacts of changing drivers over longer timescales, such as the ongoing trends in atmospheric deposition.

An important consideration is that, although blanket mires in the UK have been extensively studied, scientific analysis of the benefits to ecosystem services of blanket mire habitats is still based on a relatively small number of short-term studies over limited spatial scales, and with methodologies that have not always fitted the hypotheses being tested. At present there remain considerable unknowns about the net benefits of the restoration work carried out, and many decisions on restoration approaches still have to be made by practitioners based on observation and local knowledge of conditions on individual sites. The modelling approaches described in section 9.5 may offer a potential way forward for more scientific spatial planning of restoration approaches. Key challenges remain for blanket peatland restoration at the UK scale. The likely effects of future climate change on these peat systems remain uncertain, and further assessment of the extent to which restoration can mitigate the impacts of climate on peatlands is required. The emerging evidence that prescribed burning has a detrimental impact on blanket mire condition and associated ecosystem services also provides an example of a key policy challenge. Management of blanket peat for red grouse, largely through rotational burning, is a major economic priority for landowners in southern Scotland and northern England. Natural England has recently concluded that 'burning on blanket bog [...] should be phased out' (Natural England 2014), but realising such a policy intervention for blanket peat restoration will be a major challenge, and to be successful will require significant continued dialogue between scientists, restoration practitioners, policy makers and landowners.

The UK Peatland Strategy outlined by the IUCN Commission of Inquiry on Peatland (Bain *et al.* 2011) identifies four key aims: (1) conserve peatland in good condition, through management that maintains a favourable state; (2) restore partially damaged peatlands through land-use changes and active habitat management and return them to a peat-forming state with typical peatland vegetation; (3) intervene to repair severely damaged peatlands through major operations such as woodland removal, gully blocking and re-vegetating bare peat; and (4) communicate the contributions peatlands make to environmental, economic and social goals – critically to help combat climate change and to halt the loss of biodiversity. The evidence base to date provides some confidence that achieving these aims will go a long way to restoring the ecosystems services provided by peatlands. The focus of ongoing work will be to integrate current understanding to fully quantify this assertion and use the available evidence to plan and prioritise ongoing restoration work.

CHAPTER TEN

Restoration of temperate fens: matching strategies with site potential

WIKTOR KOTOWSKI
University of Warsaw, Poland
MICHAEL ACKERMAN
Centre for Ecology and Hydrology, Oxfordshire, UK
AB GROOTJANS
University of Groningen and Radboud University of Nijmegen, The Netherlands
AGATA KLIMKOWSKA
Eco-Recover, Ecosystem Restoration Advice, The Netherlands
HOLGER RÖßLING
Naturschutzfonds Brandenburg, LIFE Project 'Alkaline fens of Brandenburg', Germany
BRYAN WHEELER
University of Sheffield, UK

10.1 Introduction

Fens are mire ecosystems that, in addition to precipitation, receive ground or surface water (minerotrophic peatlands), whereas bogs are exclusively fed by precipitation water (ombrotrophic peatlands; Gore 1983; Bridgham *et al.* 1996). For a more extensive discussion of different peatland types we refer to Moore and Bellamy (1974), Wheeler and Proctor (2000), Joosten and Clarke (2002) and Chapter 2.

The framework of fen restoration includes a variety of different concepts and techniques, which have been developed with different objectives and for diverse target states. Assessment of success can vary considerably, depending on the identified criteria, be it bird diversity, rare plants, peat formation or nutrient status. Some authors distinguish restoration of fens (i.e. returning damaged fens near to the pre-disturbance state) from mire

Peatland Restoration and Ecosystem Services: Science, Policy and Practice, eds. A. Bonn, T. Allott, M. Evans, H. Joosten and R. Stoneman. Published by Cambridge University Press. © British Ecological Society 2016.

rehabilitation (i.e. re-establishment of their selected functions, which may result in systems that have not existed at the restoration site in the past) (Wheeler *et al.* 1995; Grootjans *et al.* 2012), whereas others focus on restoring key ecosystem functions of fens, such as peat formation and role in carbon cycling, formulating long-term targets (Joosten and Clarke 2002). In this chapter we attempt to structure the discussion around fen restoration by identifying challenges and trade-offs in this field and to clarify how close these different concepts come to the objective of reinstalling or improving the provision of key ecosystem services. We focus on lowland fens in West and Central Europe (UK, The Netherlands, Germany, Poland). We will first discuss the concept of fen ecosystems, their 'naturalness', resilience and stability, and the ecosystem services they provide. Next, we introduce the main ecological gradients in fens, the drivers of fen degradation and the consequences for ecosystem services, followed by an overview of constraints, synergies and conflicting targets in fen restoration. We conclude with an overview of gains and trade-offs of various restoration strategies.

10.2 The concept of fen

The diversity of fen restoration concepts can partly be explained by different understandings of the compass of fen ecosystems. Some fen concepts only include peat-forming ecosystems, whereas others also cover derivative ecosystems, such as wet meadows and pastures on drained fens. In this chapter, we will use the term *fen* only for peat-forming systems. Ground- and surface water-fed peatlands that have lost their peat-forming character due to drainage we call 'drained fens', 'former fens' or 'fen meadows'. In many situations, however, such altered fen systems are the only feasible goal of restoration (which may lead to conflicts and trade-offs in fen restoration). Whereas the presence of a peat layer determines fens as peatlands, one should note that comparable telluric water-fed vegetation types (often of high biodiversity) occur on mineral soil, exposed calcareous lake sediments or sites with tufa deposition (Grootjans and Jansen 2012). These, sometimes very species-rich, systems may develop into peat-forming fens. 'Living' fens include a wide array of hydrological types and reflect in the diversity of vegetation types a considerable variation in productivity and pH. While some authors restrict the term *fen* to low-productive (oligo- to mesotrophic) systems with a vegetation dominated by small sedges and brown mosses (e.g. Moen 1995), we also include eutrophic systems dominated by tall sedges or reeds, as well as fen forests (carrs), as peripheral elements of the fen continuum (Wheeler and

Proctor 2000; Kotowski and Van Diggelen 2004). In a broader sense, it might be more appropriate to use the term *fen (landscape) system*, proposed by Grootjans and Van Diggelen (1995), to address the whole range of fen and fen-related ecosystems, together with mechanisms determining their occurrence in the landscape, such as groundwater flows or mowing management.

10.3 Ecological gradients in fens

Three main, functionally interrelated, ecological gradients control the distribution of plant species and explain the spatial diversity and temporal variation of fens, including their response to human impact (Wheeler and Proctor 2000): variation in base-richness, productivity and moisture. The base saturation gradient refers to pH and the abundance of ions in groundwater, permitting the differentiation of poor, moderately rich and extremely rich fens. The productivity gradient, which is related to differences in nutrient availabilities, segregates species by their ability to compete for light (Kotowski and Van Diggelen 2004) and their efficiency in nutrient acquisition and use (Aerts and de Caluwe 1994). In general, low-productivity systems support higher biodiversity and are therefore the focus of restoration and conservation efforts (Wheeler and Shaw 1991; Wassen *et al.* 2005). The third gradient that structures vegetation in fen systems is defined by hydrological variables, in particular flooding frequency and hydrological factors, that determine whether the upper layers of the soil are anoxic. This hydrological gradient can also be related to the gradient of productivity, because lowering of the groundwater level can cause peat mineralisation and, in many cases, release of nutrients. In hydrologically undisturbed riverine fen systems, productivity and moisture gradients form apparent zonation patterns, with hydrologically dynamic and eutrophic systems occurring nearer to the river and hydrologically more stable conditions with low-productive fens developing along the valley flanks (Wassen *et al.* 1996; Bartoszuk and Kotowski 2009).

10.4 Naturalness, semi-naturalness and resilience

A feature of fens is that similar plant communities can in some circumstances exist as entirely natural systems, while in other situations their persistence depends on regular vegetation management, which prevents succession to scrub or forest communities. Under natural hydrological conditions, fens can remain nearly unchanged for thousands of years (Pałczyński 1975; Michaelis 2002), which illustrates their high resilience and resistance to environmental disturbance and change (Peltoniemi *et al.* 2012; Turetsky *et al.* 2012). Intrinsic feedbacks between water flows, plant and microbial life, and peat formation have enabled the original large groundwater-fed fens to remain treeless and with low productivity. Several authors have argued, however, that such fen systems are resilient until an environmental change reaches a certain threshold, beyond which they switch into another stable state (Eppinga *et al.* 2009; Granath *et al.* 2010). Such changes have occurred gradually over a period of several centuries, with transformation of pristine unmanaged fens into mown and grazed fens with ongoing peat accumulation (but of another type), and later into fen meadows which no longer formed peat. As a result of changed landscape hydrological and peat hydraulic conditions, cessation of traditional management in the second half of the twentieth century caused sudden shifts in fens and fen meadows (see Schipper *et al.* 2007), usually marked by shrub encroachment and a decrease of biodiversity (e.g. Pałczyński 1985; Moen 1995). Regular mowing or cutting of shrubs and trees is now necessary to maintain species-rich plant communities and birds of open wetlands that formerly persisted spontaneously. So, in a sense practically all fens in West and Central Europe have become 'semi-natural'. In addition, there are also 'semi-natural' open fen systems that never have existed as a natural treeless fen but that have originated by tree removal.

10.5 Ecosystem services of fens

Healthy wetland ecosystems may provide considerable benefits to people (Maltby and Acreman 2011). These 'ecosystem services' (Fischer *et al.* 2009) include (1) *regulating functions*, such as flood reduction, control of GHG emissions (CO_2, NH_4, N_2O) or regulation of the mesoclimate; (2) *provisioning services*, such as providing food, fuel, composting material and water; (3) *cultural services,* such as preserving archaeological artefacts, *providing services for* recreation; and (4) *supporting services* for biodiversity conservation.

One of the most important ecosystem services of natural and restored fens is the prevention or reduction of GHG emissions, by conserving peat deposits under anaerobic conditions. This service is to a large extent the legacy of the accumulation of peat over thousands of years. Natural fens have a neutral or slightly positive impact on climate warming in the short term (because of simultaneous CO_2 removal and CH_4 emission) and a cooling effect in the long term (because of the long-term prevalence of the C-sink function) (Couwenberg *et al.* 2011; Chapter 4). Fens may also be important for reducing water flow within their catchments. This service is particularly provided by undrained percolation fens (and to some extent floating fens), which can store water in their peat body that shrinks and swells with changing water supply. The consequent reduced peak outflow of water from the catchment (Joosten and Clarke 2002) contributes to flood prevention.

A similar function is provided by water storage on the surface of floodplain systems, making flood mitigation an important service of floodplain fens and other floodplain wetlands (Platteeuw and Kotowski 2006).

Fens are typically located in the landscape between terrestrial and aquatic ecosystems. They may therefore influence the quality of surface waters significantly by 'filtering' inflowing ground- and surface water (including run-off) and by releasing nutrients, dissolved carbon and other substances. The filtering effect includes both nutrients in the inflowing water being accumulated by plants and partly stored in peat, and denitrification of nitrate under anaerobic conditions. Outflow of nutrients from natural fens is rather small, because of denitrification and limited decomposition of organic matter.

Agriculture and forestry are the best known provisioning services of fens. Natural and near-natural fen systems have regularly been used for wildlife and waterfowl hunting or to obtain low-quality hay for fodder or litter. Similarly, forested fens have provided wood, especially alder (*Alnus glutinosa*). In some areas, reed (*Phragmites australis*) and 'sedge' (*Cladium mariscus*) have been harvested for roof thatching, e.g. in the Netherlands. In many parts of the world, collection of cranberries (*Vaccinium oxycoccos*) or medicinal plants, e.g. *Menyanthes trifoliata*, provides a locally important value of fens. While under natural or near-natural conditions exploitation of (herbaceous or woody) biomass probably does little direct harm to the provision of other services, conflicts can arise when utilisation is intensified by drainage and agricultural reclamation.

In some rural landscapes, the traditional utilisation of fens and the resulting semi-natural vegetation, flora and fauna are an important component of cultural heritage. Traditional management of undrained fens has allowed a close cohabitation of humans and nature (Bartoszuk and Kotowski 2009), with moderate exploitation of ecosystem services. Today, the remaining undrained fens serve as unique objects of scientific exploration, and as reference sites for the restoration of functions and processes lost in degraded fens.

10.6 Main drivers of fen degradation and consequences for biodiversity and ecosystem functions

According to the *Primer of the Society for Ecological Restoration* (SER 2004), degradation of an ecosystem pertains to subtle or gradual changes that reduce ecological integrity and health. The basic process that drives the persistence of a mire ecosystem is the formation of peat. Factors that prevent peat formation are drainage, which turns mires from peat-forming to decomposing systems, eutrophication, acidification, land-use changes and also direct habitat destruction, e.g. by peat extraction or infrastructure development. Whether certain changes are considered to constitute 'degradation' depends, however, on the context and values associated with an ecosystem. In the context of societal goods and services, degradation denotes the reduction of those ecosystem functions that condition delivery of these services, i.e. peat formation and groundwater flows. In terms of biodiversity, subtle changes in productivity and pH may induce degradation by the loss of certain species, while they might not directly affect peat formation and carbon sequestration. Moreover, there may be recursive interactions among some of these processes, for example, when rewetting following peat removal re-initiates new peat formation on surfaces where it had long since ceased because of earlier drainage.

Drainage for agriculture and forestry has been by far the principal cause of fen degradation across the world (Joosten and Clarke 2002), although drainage may also have resulted from other causes, e.g. groundwater abstraction (Van Diggelen, Grootjans and Burkunk 1994). Direct consequences of drainage are enhanced peat mineralisation and, often, release of nutrients, changes in physical properties of peat and a reduction of anoxia stress that prevents the establishment of non-adapted species in mires.

Another important driver of fen degradation is peat extraction. Fen peat has traditionally been used for fuel, but this use has diminished. On the other hand, the use of fen peat in horticulture has gained importance because of depletion and increasing prices of bog peat. Fen peat is less suitable for industrial horticulture than bog peat due to its larger and more variable mineral content and its usually higher degree of humification. Fen peat is, however, used to produce potting composts or applied as fertiliser in agriculture and forestry (Joosten and Clarke 2002).

Whether caused by agricultural drainage, industrial extraction of peat or groundwater, or other hydrological alterations in the landscape, a severe lowering of the groundwater tables can lead to a competitive displacement of specialised mire plants by grasses, tall forbs, trees or shrubs (depending on the management). As well as for pastoral farming and haymaking, drained fens in many parts of the world have also been used for arable agriculture, which enhances peat oxidation and subsidence of the peatland surface by regular tillage (Chapter 4). Also the physiochemical properties of the peat change after drainage.

While the availability of N or P limits productivity in natural fens, drained fens may develop P or K limitation or co-limitations, which triggers a shift to a new, usually higher, level of plant productivity, which is defined by the most limiting nutrient (Olde Venterink *et al.* 2009). Phosphorus limitation may occur in fens rich in calcium and iron, which under aerobic conditions following drainage form insoluble complexes with phosphate, decreasing its availability to plants (Lamers, Smolders and Roelofs 2002; Smolders et al. 2006; Zak et al. 2010). Increased P-limitation may actually enhance biodiversity after modest drainage (Wassen et al. 2005). Potassium limitation can be induced by intensive drainage, because K^+ ions are easily leached from the soil profile (Van Duren, Boeye and Grootjans 1997), especially in combination with no fertilisation and long-lasting mowing, which removes this nutrient from the system (Olde Venterink et al. 2009).

To counteract decreasing productivity of fen soils by nutrient depletion and limitation, farmers usually apply mineral fertilisers. This practice leads not only to an almost complete loss of fen biodiversity but also to increased nutrient loads in the peat soils, thereby constraining the restoration potentials (Lamers, Smolders and Roelofs 2002).

External atmospheric deposition of nitrogen is also an important source of eutrophication in Europe, due to the high density of road transport and agricultural fertilisation. In some areas, like the Netherlands or Belgium, atmospheric deposition of nitrogen can exceed 50 kg N ha^{-1} yr^{-1} (Wassen et al. 2005), thereby largely preventing restoration of oligo- to mesotrophic fens, except perhaps where these are strongly P limited.

Increased acidification is an important driver of degradation, especially in rich fens. The resilience of rich fens depends on their inherent buffering capacity, with fen soils rich in $CaCO_3$ generally showing little short-term response to acid inputs. Acidification can be caused by external factors, such as atmospheric deposition of nitric and sulfuric acids, but can also be triggered by lowering of groundwater levels, which enables infiltration of acidic rainwater in the uppermost layer of peat, favouring establishment of *Sphagna*, which further acidify the environment through a positive feedback loop (Van Wirdum 1993; Van Diggelen, Molenaar and Kooijman 1996). Such a switch from rich fen to bog, triggered by water-table lowering, is generally regarded as an irreversible ecosystem shift (Granath et al. 2010), in which fen species are displaced due to the toxicity of H^+ and reduced forms of aluminium, iron and other elements. However, palaeoecological studies have shown that shifts from bog to calcareous fen have also occurred in the past as a consequence of increased discharge of groundwater (Michaelis 2002; Hájková et al. 2012). Acidification may, through hummock development, also facilitate establishment of woody species on top of tussocks and eventually a shift towards forests (Giller and Wheeler 1988).

As implied by the overview above, management is a necessary tool to maintain fen ecosystems under sub-optimal hydrologic and trophic conditions, and to counteract the spread of rank herbaceous vegetation and trees. Cessation of traditional land use is, next to drainage, the second most important driver of fen degradation, although its importance is to a large extent secondary to drainage. Sudden expansion of woody species has been observed in many semi-natural systems, including sites with only little-disturbed hydrological regimes, such as the Biebrza Valley in north east Poland (Pałczyński 1985; Bartoszuk and Kotowski 2009). Whether it is possible to reinstall the natural resilience of such systems and what would be the costs of doing so, is one of most important unanswered questions in fen restoration.

10.7 Consequences of fen degradation to ecosystem services

When fens are converted to farmland their regulatory services are replaced by provisioning services, which in many cases also become defective over time (Maltby and Acreman 2011). As mentioned before, the most important regulatory services of fens, such as climate and catchment regulation, or provision of clean water, depend on well-functioning peat-forming processes. Drainage turns peat-forming fens into sources of environmental degradation, for instance due to increased emission of GHGs to the atmosphere, increased loss of nutrients to surface waters, and accumulation of toxic substances in the peat itself (Smolders *et al.* 2006). Drained fens have on average a greater climate-warming potential than drained bogs, especially under arable use, when GHG emissions can exceed 40 t CO_2 e ha^{-1} yr^{-1}. Half of this emission value is reached under grassland use (see: Oleszczuk *et al.* 2008; Chapter 4). Given the large area of fens drained for agriculture and forestry, their contribution to climate warming is remarkable, most important sources being Eastern Europe, the European Union, China and the United States (Florida Everglades) (Joosten 2009c).

The ability of certain types of fens to store water on the surface is not directly affected by drainage (in fact, drained fens may store even more floodwater because of their subsidence and aerated soil), but agricultural reclamation of floodplain fens has frequently been combined with embanking, designed to separate them from river floods. Natural fens can also have a damming effect on groundwater flow (Kulczyński 1949), causing over the long term a rise of groundwater levels in the upstream part of the catchment. Consequently, drainage of fens may lead to a considerable drop in regional groundwater levels.

10.8 Fen restoration measures and their limitations

In terms of mechanistic ecology, ecosystem restoration is the removal of environmental and ecological constraints that prevent the establishment and maintenance of key properties and functions of this ecosystem. These constraints relate in particular to hydrological processes, such as water flow to and through the peatland, as well as ecological processes, such as species establishment and their competitive interactions. Below, we list the main measures applied in fen restoration and point to constraints and trade-offs that may limit their applicability or effects.

10.8.1 Rewetting degraded peat: hydrological constraints and trade-offs with nutrient status

Re-establishment of high groundwater levels is necessary to stop soil peat decomposition, and soil anoxia is the condition *sine qua non* for new peat formation. Rewetting is usually achieved by damming or blocking drainage ditches in agriculturally transformed systems (cf. Boxes 10.1 and 10.3). However, such measures may not be effective if groundwater flows have markedly deteriorated (Klimkowska *et al.* 2010b), e.g. due to straightening of rivers, abstraction of groundwater (Van Diggelen, Grootjans and Burkunk 1994) or open-cast coalmining activities. Changes in surface water levels in rivers or lakes can trigger similar effects in floodplains and spring-fed fens, due to lowering of the regional groundwater level (Schot *et al.* 2004).

The degree to which rewetted fens come to resemble original ecosystems largely depends on the degree of peat decomposition. After drainage, the hydraulic conductivity of the peat may have decreased up to 1000 times by increased compaction, an increased proportion of macro- and micropores and a decreased volume of mesopores (Brandyk and Szatyłowicz 2002). In extreme situations degraded peat may even become hydrophobic! Re-establishment of groundwater flow through the peat, the basic mechanism to ensure hydrological stability and low productivity in percolation fens, is usually impossible in such cases and a new porous peat layer must develop to reinstate accumulation. Assuming a peat accumulation rate of 1 mm yr^{-1}, it takes 1000 years to build a 1 m-thick layer of undecomposed peat to buffer hydrological fluctuations and enhance the resilience of the fen ecosystem (however, much more rapid accumulation of loose peats can occur in wet hydroseral circumstances). Reinstalling groundwater discharge in degraded peatlands may result in groundwater surfacing at the flanks of system, forming new erosive springs and rivulets that enhance peat erosion (Wołejko *et al.* 1994).

Another important constraint of rewetting is its interaction with nutrient availability. Drained fen peats often contain high amounts of nutrients originating from peat decomposition and fertilisation, which usually become increasingly available to plants after rewetting. Ground or surface water can deliver potassium (K), which commonly limits productivity in severely drained fens (Olde Venterink *et al.* 2009), whereas reinstatement of soil anoxia and low redox potential may release phosphate from insoluble complexes. These two processes usually switch rewetted fens from K or P limited to N limited at higher levels of productivity than in drained situations (Smolders *et al.* 2006). Eutrophication can also be enhanced by the replacement of groundwater by surface water, due to nutrient input and sulfate-induced mobilisation of phosphate (Lamers, Smolders and Roelofs 2002).

High nutrient availability in rewetted fens hampers the re-establishment of typical fen species and keeps biodiversity at low levels due to intensive competition for light (Kotowski and Van Diggelen 2004). Such highly productive systems may, however, be desirable, when restoration of the C-sink function of fens is the main objective, provided that peat-forming species with high lignin content are established (Timmermann *et al.* 2006). Although high methane production from rewetted fens leads to a net increase of their global warming potential in the first years after rewetting, emission of methane decreases as initially flooded biomass becomes decomposed. A period of at least 50 years is needed to achieve climate-neutral status. It is important to recognise that when this approach is applied in severely degraded fens, it will usually not deliver high botanical diversity in the short term, but may attract wetland birds, especially if mowing is applied to complement the effects of restoration. In Belarus, large areas of productive fen have been restored by rewetting former bogs and poor fens (Tanneberger and Wichtmann 2011). The high productivity of rewetted peatlands can also make them appropriate for harvesting biomass, which can be used to produce energy or other products (Chapter 17).

Lowering of GHG emissions from drained peatlands does not necessarily require re-establishment of peat-forming processes. In fact, any rise of groundwater levels reduces peat mineralisation. Moderate rewetting, with water tables 20–60 cm below the surface, can limit GHG emissions and nitrogen losses to groundwater, while maintaining meadow management (Box 10.1). Under low-intensity agricultural use such systems can contribute to the conservation of wading birds (Kloskowski and Krogulec 1999) or wet meadow butterflies (see Box 10.2). However, options for re-establishing weakly competitive fen plants into highly productive vegetation are not very promising. Protracted mowing and hay removal can help to reduce productivity by inducing K limitation (Olde Venterink *et al.* 2009).

Box 10.1
The Somerset Levels and Moors wetlands: compromising trade-offs in ecosystem services by water management schemes

Mike Acreman

The Somerset Levels and Moors (SLM) wetland system in southwest England comprises a mosaic of wet grasslands, fens, bogs and wet woodland. It provides important ecosystem services locally, regionally and globally, including agricultural production (grazing for cattle), carbon sequestration, floodwater storage, recreation, biodiversity, cultural heritage and archaeology. However, these wetlands are under pressure from peat extraction and conversion, by drainage, to intensive agricultural production. Future climate change is likely to increase water stress during late summer and autumn (Acreman et al. 2009). To demonstrate the values of these wetlands, Acreman et al. (2011) used ecosystem services as a means of comparing the implications of raised water levels and low (pumped) water levels.

- **Health:** key human-biting mosquitoes recently found on the SLM include *Anopheles claviger*, a species capable of transmitting *Plasmodium vivax* (the probable causal agent of historical malaria in the UK).
- **Water storage:** the SLM has a high volume of available flood storage that reduces flood risk downstream. Raising water levels can reduce flood storage by a small percentage.
- **GHGs:** local measurements show a trade-off between reduction of carbon dioxide (CO_2) emission and an increase of methane (CH_4) emission after rewetting (Figure 10.1a, b).
- **Archaeology:** the Sweet Track, dating from 3806 BC, is the best preserved ancient trackway in the UK.
- **Recreation:** the Ham Wall wetland bird reserve receives around 35 000 visits per year, primarily to watch the 6–10 million starlings roost at night during the winter.
- Biological uniqueness and diversity; the SLM represents the largest remaining area of lowland wet meadows in England (more than 20% of the resource). In the short term, overall botanical diversity may decline with raised water levels. In the longer term, diversity may exceed that of the drained system.

Some services were found to be synergistic and reinforcing, e.g. maintaining wet conditions supports wetland bird life, protects archaeological artefacts and reduces CO_2 emissions. However, a trade-off in ecosystem services was also identified, because raising water levels may reduce potential floodwater storage, augment methane

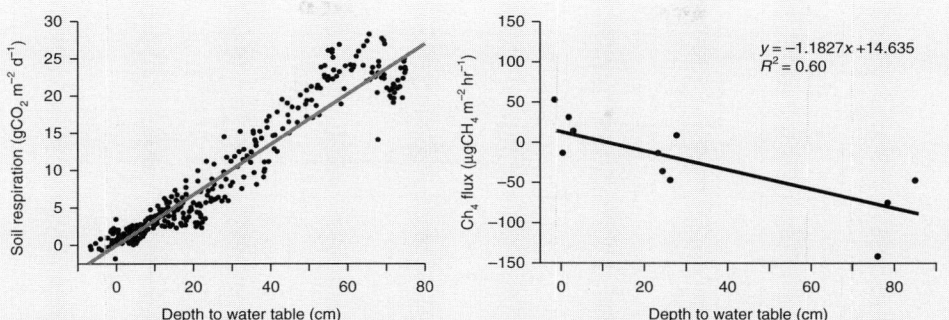

Figure 10.1 (a) Water table control on CO_2 flux at Tadham Moor, Somerset (Acreman et al. 2011); (b) water table control on methane flux at Tadham Moor, Somerset (Acreman et al. 2011).

emissions (especially during the first few years after rewetting) and increase health risks. Management decisions affecting wetlands may necessitate a trade-off of ecosystem services.

During the 1980s, the Environmentally Sensitive Areas (ESA) scheme was introduced to nearly 30 000 ha to provide incentives to encourage agricultural practices that would restore, safeguard and enhance areas of particularly high landscape, wildlife or historic value. Under ESA, land owners were encouraged to operate a more natural water level regime, for which they could receive annual subsidies of up to £430 per hectare. There were several options for raised water levels: for example, Tier 3 had a target of maintaining ditch water at mean field level during the winter and 30 cm below this level during the summer. The Tier 3 seasonal water regime provides a cycle of multiple ecosystem services, including peat conservation, wildlife habitat for over-wintering birds, diverse wet grassland plant communities, traditional summer grazing and hay making. These tiers and supplements are the main mechanism for achieving the Biodiversity Action Plan targets in the area, and almost 17 000 ha have been placed in the ESA scheme. Slight variations on the prescription can be implemented to make the optimum trade-off, such as on the Parrett floodplain grazing meadows (Figures 10.2 and 10.3; Morris et al. 2008).

This strategy largely led to an increase of bird populations: e.g. the West Sedgemoor, managed by the RSPB, now has the largest lowland population of breeding wading birds in southern England, such as lapwings, snipe, curlew and redshanks.

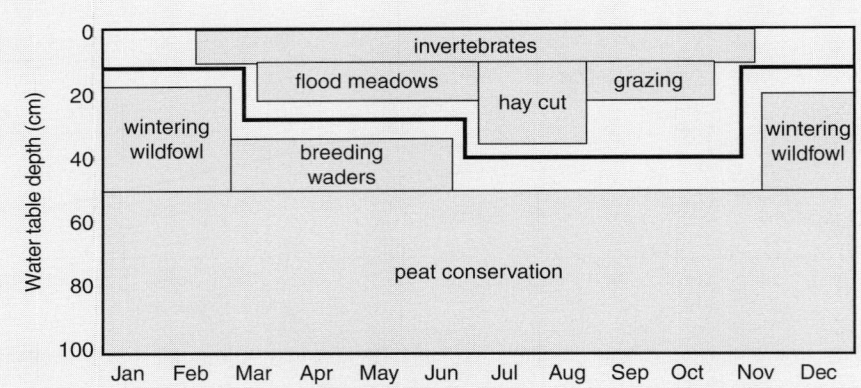

Figure 10.2 Water level regime (solid line) set to optimise multiple delivery of ecosystem services (boxes) on the Parrett floodplain, Somerset Levels and Moors (after Morris *et al.* 2008).

Figure 10.3 Tadham Moor, Somerset Levels and Moors (photo: M. Acreman).

10.8.2 Topsoil removal and hay transfer

Removal of the decomposed peat layer is an effective but costly procedure that can simultaneously lower nutrient availability, increase water tables and remove an unwanted soil seed bank of opportunistic, competitive species (Klimkowska *et al.* 2010b; Box 10.2). Based on a meta-analysis of 36 restoration sites, Klimkowska *et al.* (2007) concluded that topsoil removal was more effective than rewetting in restoring target species of fen meadows (provided that target species were introduced, see below). Observations at Redgrave Fen (England) suggest that the short-term success of topsoil removal depends on the underlying substratum. In this case the process was particularly effective where an underlying layer of marl ($CaCO_3$) had been exposed (see also Grootjans and Jansen 2012).

Topsoil removal can reduce nutrient leaching to groundwater and decrease GHG emissions faster than with rewetting, because no readily decomposable organic matter remains in the system. On the other hand, removal of large amounts of decomposed peat from the system must be accounted for when assessing the net carbon balance. Klimkowska *et al.* (2010d) identified several commercial uses for removed topsoil, such as tree nurseries, agricultural fertiliser or production of potting material after composting. In some cases, degraded topsoil could replace peat that is normally used to produce potting composts and reduce demands for raw peat.

Box 10.2
Experimental restoration of a severely degraded fen by topsoil removal

Agata Klimkowska and Wiktor Kotowski

Całowanie Fen (Central Poland, 52°00'40"N, 21°21'00"E) was originally a groundwater-fed fen, *c.* 1.500 ha in size, which was drained for agriculture. Due to intensive drainage, fens and derivative species-rich fen meadows have changed into severely degraded meadows. A heavily decomposed soil with granular or pulverised peat structure, with little water-holding capacity, was found to *c.* 30 cm depth. Mineralisation has led to nutrient release and eutrophication of the site, as in many other degraded fens of Central Europe.

Small-scale peat cutting, which was practised here until the 1960s, resulted in the establishment of shallow water bodies which, after drainage of the fen, re-vegetated with fen flora which persists today. However, deeper lakes created by mechanised peat cutting remained as open water. Since the 1990s, commercial peat extraction has been facilitated by deep drainage, causing a drastic drop in groundwater levels (Klimkowska *et al.* 2010b).

The good, spontaneous regeneration of fen plants in old, shallow turf-pits was the main reason for testing topsoil removal as a restoration method. Topsoil was removed on a pilot scale, first from 0.25 ha (2004) and later from 2 ha plots (2009) (Figure 10.4a, b). To help establishment of target species, seed-containing hay was

Figure 10.4 Całowaie restoration site (a) during topsoil removal and (b) 4 years later.

transferred from neighbouring species-rich meadows in old peat-cuts. Between 2004 and 2009, vegetation development was monitored in relation to removal of 20 or 40 cm topsoil, application of hay transfer and the presence or absence of large animals, mainly wild boar (*Sus scropha*) (using fences). From 2006 onwards, annual mowing with biomass removal was applied. The vegetation was monitored in a 2 × 2 m grid at each restoration treatment. Vegetation data were also collected in degraded meadows and local reference sites. Soil seed bank data after topsoil removal were also acquired and the seed content of the transferred hay was assessed. A redundancy analysis (Figure 10.5) shows the development of vegetation in different treatments over time, in comparison to degraded meadows, reference meadows and composition of the soil seed bank and hay seed content. Re-vegetation in the 40 cm topsoil removal treatment with hay addition was most similar to that of the reference vegetation, whereas shallow removal plots with hay were most similar to the degraded meadows. The plot without hay transfer developed in a very different way, resembling neither reference nor degraded vegetation, remaining dominated by pioneer species associated with flooded, organic soils or ruderal communities. Re-vegetation with deep peat removal and hay addition was more similar to the reference vegetation when animals were excluded, probably indicating sensitivity of early assembly processes to disturbance (see Klimkowska et al. 2010a for more details).

In the second phase of the project (starting in 2009), topsoil was removed over a larger area (2 ha) and was deeper (50–70 cm). The deeper removal was applied because of large fluctuations in groundwater tables in the previously restored plots. Our unpublished results indicate that CH_4 emissions from topsoil removal sites are c. 100 times lower than in experimentally rewetted plots, and still c. 20 times lower than those noted in reference fens (Kozub and Kotowski,

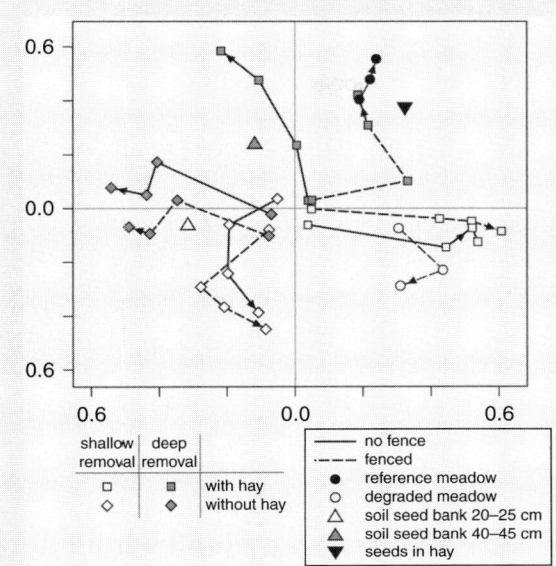

Figure 10.5 RDA analysis of vegetation development under different restoration treatments in Całowanie Fen (Klimkowska et al. 2010a) © Restoration Ecology, John Wiley and Sons. reproduced with permission.

unpublished data). Similar discrepancies have been observed with regard to N and P contents of the pore water, which are highest in rewetted sites and lowest in topsoil removal sites, indicating that topsoil removal can significantly lower the negative environmental impacts of drained fens.

10.8.3 Terrestrialisation of open water

Restoration of rich fens through terrestrialisation of open calcareous water bodies (fen lakes) has been proposed in the Netherlands as an alternative to the reinstatement of sedentary peat accumulation in (semi-)terrestrial fens (Lamers, Smolders and Roelofs 2002). The assumption is that floating mats of macrophytes, e.g. *Stratiotes aloides* or *Calla palustris*, initiate the terrestrialisation processes, later to be overtaken by mosses and specialised fen sedges. This approach effectively mimics the processes by which some fens have naturally developed, and some turbaries have spontaneously re-colonised (Giller and Wheeler 1986, 1988). However, the dynamics of rafting are not well understood (e.g. appropriate water depth) and rafting often does not take place readily (Geurts et al. 2008).

10.8.4 Overcoming dispersal constraints by species introductions

Most wetland plants have very limited seed dispersal (Middleton, Van Diggelen and Jensen 2006), which impedes their natural recolonisation of restoration sites. These constraints can be overcome by reintroductions (Graf and Rochefort 2008; Hedberg and Kotowski 2010), e.g. direct seeding, planting or transfer of fresh biomass. Relying on spontaneous colonisation by target species can significantly hamper restoration and favour light-seeded, potentially invasive, wetland species, such as *Typha* sp. or *Salix* sp. (Thompson, Bakker and Bekker 1996). However, acquisition of sufficient seeds or plants may be difficult for large-scale restoration projects, and a more feasible option may be to allow spontaneous re-vegetation by ubiquitous plants in most of the area while making targeted species reintroductions to selected core areas.

Multi-species reintroductions seem especially important in sites restored by topsoil removal, where bare soil becomes exposed to new colonisers. In such a situation, hay transfer is often recommended as an approach that combines seed dispersal with mulching, which protects seedlings against drought or frost and prevents establishment of light-seeded colonisers. While such projects are usually small scale and reintroduction is carried out by hand (e.g. Boxes 10.2 and 10.3), large-scale mechanical transfer of plant material from donor fens has been proposed by Graf and Rochefort (2008) for some Canadian mined bogs, from which peat had been removed down to the minerotrophic layer, exposing undecomposed fen peat, following a similar approach to that developed for bog restoration (Chapter 11).

Box 10.3

Alkaline fens of Brandenburg (Germany): restoring hydrological processes

Maxsee, 52°27′54″N, 13°58′30″E

Holger Rößling, Michael Zauft, Janine Ruffer, Pamela Hafner

One hundred and fifty years ago, alkaline fens were still abundant in Brandenburg. Today only small areas remain (Thormann and Landgraf 2010). Alkaline fens are now among the rarest and most endangered habitats in Brandenburg. From 2010 to 2015, an EU 'LIFE-Nature' Project conducted by Stiftung Naturschutzfonds

Brandenburg has aimed to preserve and restore alkaline fens in 14 NATURA 2000 areas (Figure 10.6).

The largest and least-disturbed alkaline fens were selected for restoration because they have the greatest potential for regeneration. In the past, sloping spring and percolation fens have been transformed to agricultural land by digging a large number of small drainage ditches. When agricultural use of these areas was no longer profitable, the fens were abandoned with the drainage systems still in place, thus continuing peat degradation and eutrophication. Reed, willow shrubs and trees developed, suppressing characteristic fen plants.

Restoration measures within the project were aimed at restoring natural hydrologic conditions. Carrying out such actions requires close collaboration with all stakeholders. That is why our restoration activities were preceded by the following steps:

- **Land acquisition:** the land had to be acquired either by purchase or by long-term agreements with land owners.
- **Removal of tall vegetation:** reed mowing (*Phragmites australis*) or shrub removal was sometimes necessary to allow re-establishment of mosses and typical fen species.
- **Filling-in of drainage ditches:** all drainage ditches in sloping fens were completely filled with degraded peat. About 15 to 20 cm of the top layer of the adjoining peatland was used to fill the ditches. This had the additional advantage that less degraded peat became exposed. Weirs were built in the larger water courses and dead wood was inserted to slow down flow velocities.
- **Reintroduction of species:** seeds and vegetative material of typical fen species were collected from 'undisturbed' fen sites and dispersed in the restoration areas.
- **Monitoring:** effects of restoration measures were monitored (water levels, vegetation composition in permanent plots).

To date, restoration measures are promising but whether all damage done in the past is reversible will hopefully become evident in the near future.

10.8.5 Removing shrubs and trees to reverse succession

Removal of woody species that spread after the cessation of management can enhance the establishment of fen plant species by increasing light availability (Sundberg 2012, Kotowski *et al.* 2013a). Similarly, removal of planted trees can

Figure 10.6 In the 'Maxsee', a NATURA 2000 area, 40 km southeast of Berlin, more than 5 km of ditches have been filled with peat or blocked by dams in about 20 ha of drained peatland. Water levels rose considerably within a month after eliminating the drainage system.

help to restore fen vegetation in peatlands drained for forestry (Hedberg *et al.* 2012). The response to tree and scrub removal depends partly on the extent and richness of the residual herbaceous flora (Madaras *et al.* 2012). In many cases shrub and tree removal has been carried out to enhance the habitat conditions of fen-related bird species. In the Biebrza Valley (northeast Poland), for instance, open fens were restored after 20–30 years of successional forest and scrub development over several thousands of hectares to protect the endangered aquatic warbler (*Acrocephalus paludicola*). The prospects for such activities are favourable (Kloskowski and Krogulec 1999) as long as the effect is maintained by mowing, otherwise cleared areas may quickly become overgrown again (Klimkowska *et al.* 2010c). Note, however, that mechanised mowing may also affect plant diversity by compaction, possibly modifying the functioning of a fen ecosystem (Kotowski *et al.* 2013b). Removal of shrubs and trees can also lead to increased groundwater levels, by lowering evapotranspiration (Huxman *et al.* 2005), and can complement other rewetting measures. On the other hand, maintenance of shrub or tree cover can in time permit the development of fen woodlands with rich and unique biodiversity.

10.9 Summing-up and conclusions

Two major thresholds have marked human impact on fen mires. The first took place centuries ago and gradually changed many fens from natural to semi-natural systems in cultural landscapes. At this stage, exploitation of fen provisioning services did not directly hamper their key regulatory services, though the natural resilience of fens may largely have been lost. The second step was made during the last 200 years, when the majority of fens were effectively destroyed by intensive agriculture, forestry and peat excavation. The few residual examples of little-disturbed sites provide an appreciation of their role in the conservation of biodiversity and our environment. Moreover, drained fens, instead of delivering services, can pose threats to the environment by emitting CO_2 and forming important sources of water pollution. While fen restoration has already developed into a scientific discipline, the framework of ecosystem services calls for a fresh view on what should be regarded as realistic and sustainable in restoration.

One way to deal with the trade-offs inherent in peatland restoration is to compromise various needs in a multifunctional approach, such as the water management programme for the Somerset Levels and Moors in England (Box 10.1). In that case, maximisation of multiple gains has been achieved by adjusting water levels several times over the season. Though the long-term sustainability of such an approach can be questioned due to limited long-term predictability of the socio-economical mechanisms that drive this system, this may be the only way to deliver regulating or supporting ecosystem services while maintaining basic provisioning functions in highly populated and transformed landscapes. Also the policy context, with a subsidy system favouring low-intensity agricultural landscapes, is an important driver of multifunctional restoration strategies. In the case of Całowanie Fen in Poland (Box 10.2), restoration of semi-natural meadows through topsoil removal and rewetting was considered the most realistic option. Here, deterioration of the local hydrological system made the site unsuitable for the redevelopment of low-productive peat-forming communities (Klimkowska *et al.* 2010b), while maintenance of floristically similar fen meadows can currently be supported by EU agri-environmental payments.

An alternative approach is to set long-term goals and prioritise processes that may allow for the development of more resilient and more natural mire ecosystems in the future. In a fen restoration project in Brandenburg (Box 10.3), the main aim is to restore natural hydrological processes responsible for the long-term maintenance of brownmoss alkaline fens. Rewetting by groundwater may in time help to establish new peat layers, facilitating species-rich low-productive fen communities. Finally, we also should recognise that in highly transformed sites, novel ecosystems

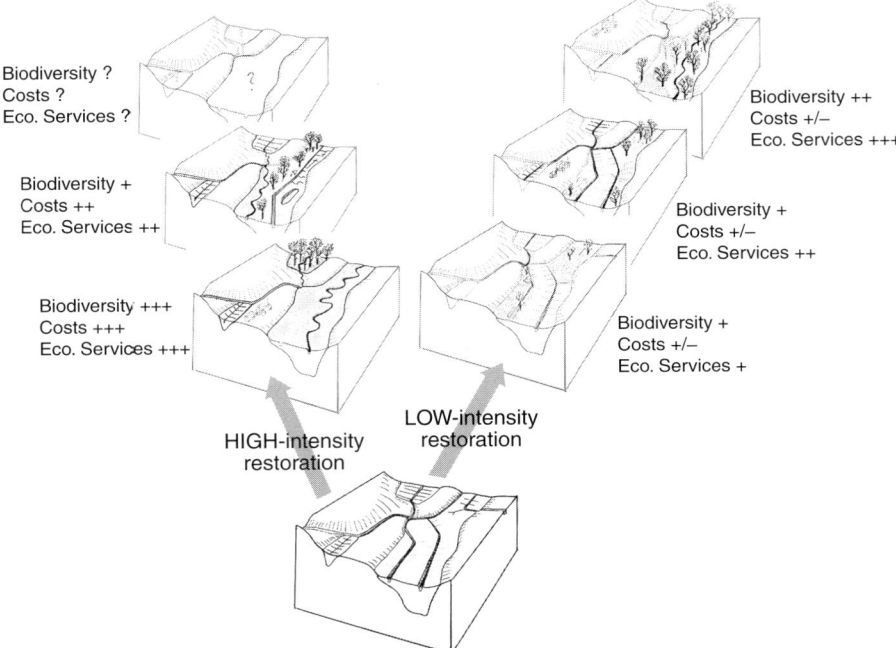

Figure 10.7 Starting from a highly impacted landscape subject to intensive agricultural use, restoration efforts may proceed along two different pathways. High-intensity restoration may be carried out during periods in which society is willing to invest heavily to redevelop a high-biodiversity landscape which also provides many ecosystem services. But when money for maintenance of such landscapes is lacking due to loss of political support, or failure to establish sound economic drivers for nature conservation, such restoration efforts may be frustrated by the introduction of competing land uses, which destroy the original restoration efforts. Lack of financing can also lead to low-intensity restoration, when intensive land-use practices are abandoned and natural succession can take its course. This can be accompanied by appropriate hydrological interventions to restore hydrological systems in the landscape and facilitate other processes to support, as much as possible, the functioning of fen systems. In time, novel wet ecosystems could develop that might harbour moderately high biodiversity and regain most of the ecosystems services that wetlands can provide. The outcome of this low-intensity restoration trajectory is greatly influenced by the establishment of economic drivers for the use of such wetlands.

(Hobbs and Harris 2001) that are different from those that ever existed in the restored site might function as well, or better, than the original ones, but at lower cost.

While clear formulation of the ultimate goal of restoration certainly helps to develop long-term strategies, the reverse approach is also important: the choice of restoration targets has to be realistic, matching local constraints. Fen restoration has to be economically sound, especially in the context of ecosystem services, i.e. it must deliver maximum services for the lowest possible price and at low risk of failure. To illustrate this, we can recognise two different restoration pathways that may result from contrasting initial strategies (Figure 10.7): (1) high-intensity restoration, in which the initial costs are very high, and (2) low-intensity restoration, where restoration costs are low and follow the trend in land-use changes, rather than directing such trends. Both options may be appropriate in certain landscape and economy settings, but it is low-intensity restoration that carries the lower risk of failure.

The timescale of restoration appears to be a key issue that needs to be reassessed when applying an ecosystem approach to fen restoration. Biodiversity targets have usually been formulated on a short-term basis and evaluated within a few years or decades after restoration. The re-establishment of key ecosystem functions of fens that are crucial for the provision of services, such as peat formation, may not be possible in the short term, depending on the context and restoration options. Much of the success of ecosystem services and accompanying biodiversity will depend on developing economic drivers for these services, and they may not always be directly related in a positive way. To upscale fen restoration and benefit from re-established ecosystem services, we need a vision that employs time and succession processes in restoration and which extends beyond our current limits and perspectives, so that the restored systems occupy an appropriate trajectory for long-term resilience while simultaneously giving rare species the best chance of sustainable long-term survival.

CHAPTER ELEVEN

A conceptual framework for ecosystem restoration applied to industrial peatlands

MARTHA D. GRAF
Leibniz Universität Hannover, Germany
LINE ROCHEFORT
Université Laval, Canada

11.1 Introduction

The extraction of peat for fuel on an industrial basis started in the seventeenth century in eastern and northern Europe as the supply of wood for energy declined. The use of peat for energy in North America has always been small in scale. The demand for horticultural peat rose steadily after World War II on both continents (http://peatmoss.com/what-is-peat-moss/the-history-of-peat/). Currently, Europe and North America use peatmoss-peat extensively for landscaping, professional greenhouse production, hydrocarbon spills and waste water treatment. To date, in Canada, the main horticultural peat producers have impacted close to 20 000 ha. To place this into context, Canada's peatland extent is estimated to be around 125 000 000 ha with industrial activities mostly located on the southern margins of the peatland distribution. Most of the industrial peatlands are still in operation (16 000 ha), whereas close to 2000 ha have been restored according to the approach described below.

With the rising awareness of goods and services provided by wetlands in the 1980–90s (Costanza *et al.* 1997), the international industrial peat sector recognised the impacts their activities had on peatland functions and developed a strategy for responsible peatland management. Several countries have since developed their own strategy and encourage the restoration of industrial peatlands (Clarke and Rieley 2010). For the case of Canada,

Peatland Restoration and Ecosystem Services: Science, Policy and Practice, eds. A. Bonn, T. Allott, M. Evans, H. Joosten and R. Stoneman. Published by Cambridge University Press. © British Ecological Society 2016.

peatland restoration is particularly driven by their main US horticultural clients, who demand responsible management of wetlands, driven by their interior policy on wetlands (NAWCA 1989).

Based on two decades of trial-and-error experiments on restoring industrial peatlands, we have created a restoration framework. This framework draws on the ideas of assembly rules and restoration ecology. In this chapter, the framework is applied to restoring peatlands, but it should be applicable to the restoration of any ecosystem.

11.2 Assembly rules and restoration ecology

The union of assembly rules and restoration ecology should be beneficial for both areas of ecology (Keddy 1999; Temperton *et al.* 2004). Assembly rules are a helpful tool for restoration because, if the constraints of community membership are defined, restoration efforts can focus on manipulating these constraints to steer succession towards the desired community (Temperton *et al.* 2004). Restoration ecology has been criticised for being a haphazard collection of individual cases (Keddy 1999). A recent study found that 63% of articles on wetland restoration between 2001 and 2006 were trial-and-error accounts of habitat restoration (Wagner *et al.* 2008). An assembly rules approach would aid restoration ecology in becoming a more rigorous discipline with repeatable methods (Keddy 1999). Restoration, on the other hand, provides the ultimate test for community ecologists. If community ecologists truly understand the mechanisms of the ecosystem, they should be able to recreate it (Jordan, Gilpin and Aber 1987; Keddy 1999).

Most literature on assembly rules views a community as a series of species pools where species are filtered out through various constraints (Figure 11.1; Belyea 2004). In such filter models, all species found in the region are represented by the total species pool. Due to environmental and dispersal constraints, only a subset of the total species pool, the ecological species pool, actually establishes in a given community. Eventually, some of the species from the ecological species pool will be filtered out due to internal dynamics within the community, such as competition among species. The actual species pool consists of species from the ecological species pool that persist in a community (Figure 11.1; Belyea 2004).

While the assembly rules approach is an important tool for community and restoration ecology, differences between these areas of ecology make filter models insufficient for repeated success in restoration projects. Filter models provide insight into what limits each pool's species membership and help identify restoration strategies. However, filter models provide little information about community structure or ecosystem function (Belyea 2004), which are the crux of restoration ecology (Ehrenfeld and Toth 1997).

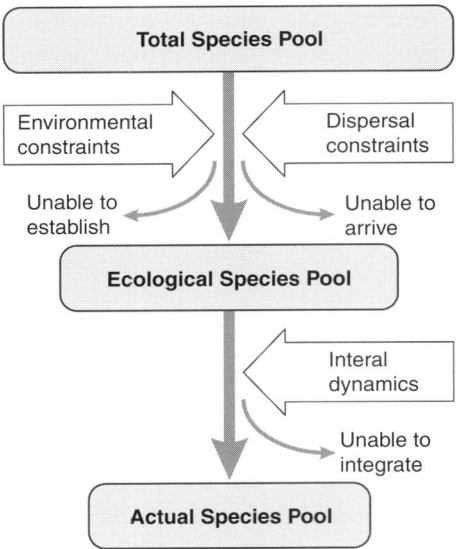

Figure 11.1 A filter model of plant colonisation based on the assembly rules approach of changes to a system during stages of colonisation. The rectangles represent species pools. The total species pool is the largest as it represents all species in a given region. The ecological species pool consists of species that successfully establish in a community despite environmental and dispersal constraints. The actual species pool consists of the species which persist in the community despite internal dynamics, such as competition. The open arrows represent constraints which limit membership to the species pools located below each arrow. Simplified from Belyea 2004, reproduced by permission of Island Press, Washington, DC.

For restoration, it is important to understand structural and functional differences between degraded and undisturbed sites. Once these differences are understood, a target species pool, including species necessary to the return of the system's structure and/or function, can be identified. Another limitation of filter models is that the total species pool is less important in restoration ecology because some target species are no longer found in the region and are therefore not included in the total species pool but could be important for the restoration of some ecosystem functions (Figure 11.1; White and Walker 1997). For example, *Sphagnum austinii* (formerly *S. imbricatum*) used to be an important peat-accumulating species in the peatlands of Northwestern Europe but has largely disappeared due to episodes of heavy pollution in the past or land-use changes (Chapman and Rose 1991); one could now envisage reintroducing it in restoration projects. Finally, filter models are static and are ideal for a passive understanding of a system. In contrast, active manipulation of the constraints is needed to achieve restoration. A framework for restoration ecology should include manipulation of the system's constraints.

11.3 A new framework

We propose a new framework inspired by the assembly rules theory, but tailored to restoration ecology. The new model begins with comparing the structure and function of degraded species pools (species present on sites targeted for restoration) with those of an undisturbed species pools of the same region (Figure 11.2A and B). For the case of industrial peatlands, the undisturbed species pool could be the site before extraction occurred, an undisturbed peatland with similar physiochemical properties, or species identified through paleoecological studies of the restoration site's residual peat. This comparison will allow target species to be identified. Once target species have been identified, restoration strategies can be tested to improve environmental and dispersal constraints for these species (Figure 11.2C and D) such as with Sphagna for boreal bogs. Restoration manipulations might be designed in a way to reduce exotic or locally invasive species, if the aim is to remove or reduce the abundance of a degraded species. The combination of species from the target and degraded species pools represents the novel species pool.

In order to ensure that the target species can persist on the restoration site, the internal dynamics between species should be monitored (Figure 11.2E). If aggressive competitors are part of the degraded species pool, they might out-compete the target species. In the northern hemisphere, some of the most infamous aggressive species of post-industrial sites are birches (*Betula* spp.), cottongrasses (*Eriophorum* spp.), rushes (*Juncus effusus*), grasses (*Molinia caerulea*) and ferns (*Pteridium aquilinum*) (Smart, Wheeler and Willis 1989; Cooper and McCann 1995; Tomassen *et al.* 2004; Lavoie, Saint-Louis and Lachance 2005; Fay and Lavoie 2009). On the other hand, target species establishment may be improved by facilitation. Eventually, the restored species pool, which should be similar in structure and/or function to the undisturbed species pool, should be reached. This regional undisturbed species pool is also referred to as reference system in restoration ecology (White and Walker 1997; Ehrenfeld 2001). Long-term monitoring can verify whether the community structure and environmental functions of the restored site are indeed similar to those found on undisturbed sites. This framework is applicable to any restoration project where reference sites are available, but in this chapter it will be applied to peatland restoration.

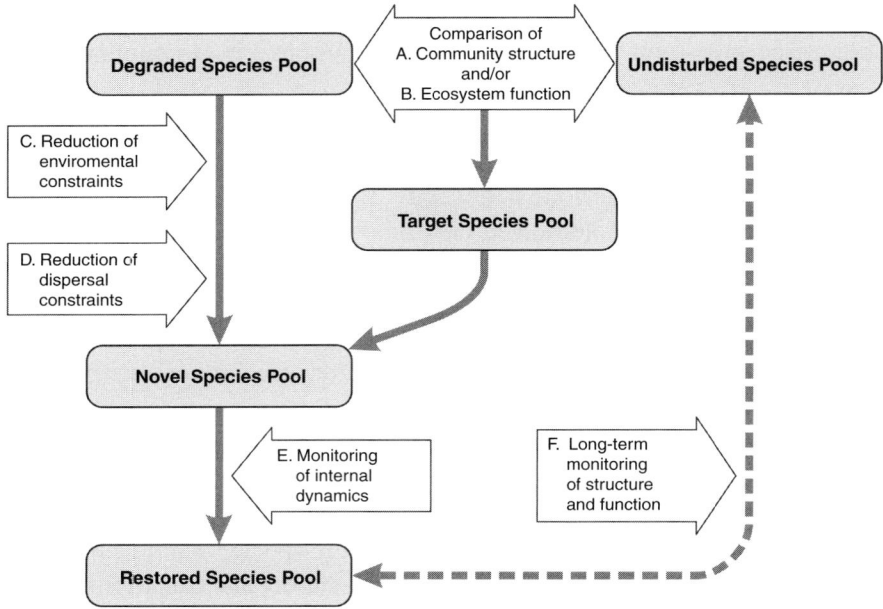

Figure 11.2 A new framework for restoration projects inspired by assembly rules approach. The rectangles represent species pools which are pertinent to restoration. Open arrows represent active measures which should be explored to develop strategies for restoring a degraded system. Solid arrows represent the direction of the species pool development during restoration and the dashed arrow represents similarity between species pools.

11.4 Peatland restoration

Peatlands are disturbed by the following land uses: conversion to agricultural lands, peat extraction for horticultural peat and peat fuel, drainage for forestry production, infrastructure building and energy sector development (i.e. hydro-dams or oil sands in Canada; Rooney, Bayley and Schindler 2012). In some cases (i.e. conversion to agricultural lands), the disturbance to the peatland is so extensive that a return to the original ecosystem is not possible because the peat properties have changed radically (Pfadenhauer and Grootjans 1999; Lamers, Smolders and Roelofs 2002). In other instances, no natural remnants remain and deciding on a target ecosystem is difficult, as is often the case in Western Europe. For such cases, restoration with a novel species mix may be acceptable if these species aid the return of desired ecosystem functions.

Our peatland restoration research has focused on the restoration of Canadian peatlands harvested for horticultural peat. Modern peat-extracting techniques use tractor-pulled vacuum machines. This intensive method requires a complete drainage and removal of the top living vegetation layer of large (up to 100 ha) peatlands (Poulin *et al.* 2005). Consequentially, many of the peatland's ecosystem services are lost (Table 11.1). For the most part, the restoration of such sites is feasible and local undisturbed remnants or paleoecological data can be used to target vegetation communities to reintroduce (Rochefort and Lode 2006).

This restoration framework was developed from research projects carried out by the Peatland Ecology Research Group (www.gret-perg.ulaval.ca). Through our experiences with hundreds of research projects that varied from Petri dish experiments to landscape-scale restoration (see Box 11.1), we gleaned the most important aspects to create this restoration framework. The majority of research has been carried out on restoring bog vegetation. However, work on restoring fen plant communities has recently begun (Cobbaert, Rochefort and Price 2004; Graf and Rochefort 2008, 2009, 2010). We hope that this framework will enable researchers faced with the restoration of peatlands or other ecosystems to organise and concentrate their efforts in an effective manner.

Table 11.1 Ecosystem services lost due to industrial use of peatlands. The corresponding variable measured is shown. The references listed compare the corresponding measured variable among peat-extracted and undisturbed sites.

Ecosystem services lost	Variable measured	Reference(s)
Carbon sequestration	Net ecosystem (CO_2) exchange	Waddington, Strack and Greenwood (2010)
Water regulation	Water table and water flow	Price, Heathwaite and Baird (2003)
Water purification	Water chemistry	Andersen, Rochefort and Landry (2011)
Soil erosion protection	Dissolved organic carbon	Strack *et al.* (2011)
Flora and fauna habitat	Species inventories	Calmé, Desrochers and Savard (2002) (birds); Fontaine, Poulin and Rochefort (2007) (pool vegetation); Mazerolle, Desrochers and Rochefort (2005) (flora and fauna in pools)

Box 11.1
Bois-des-Bel peatland research station

The Bois-des-Bel peatland (Figure 11.3) is over 7000 years old and covers 100 ha. It was partially exploited from 1972 to 1980 over an 11.5 ha surface. The peat was extracted using large, tractor-drawn vacuum machines leaving a peat deposit circa 2 m deep. Twenty years post-extraction, little vegetation had recolonised the site; typical peatland plants were practically absent (see points A, B and C below). A moss layer transfer technique that had been tested on small-scale plots was tested for the first time on an ecosystem scale at this site. Research carried out at this experimental station over the last 15 years has allowed us to better understand how a restored ecosystem evolves in terms of vegetation patterns, hydrology, biodiversity, carbon cycles and principle chemical components over a long period of time.

A. An economic activity
Peat is made up of peatmoss (*Sphagnum*; Figure 11.4) and other partially decomposed plants. Its performance as a growing medium lies in its particular anatomical structure that allows the substrate to **retain water and nutrients** while providing **good aeration**. This is

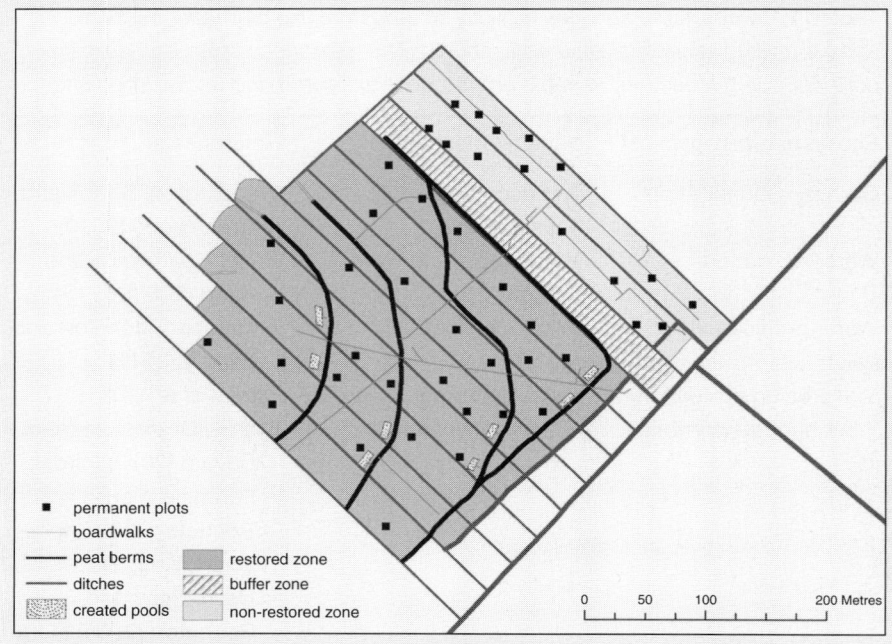

Figure 11.3 The restoration site of Bois-des-Bel (Peatland Ecology Research Group).

due to the cylindrical and porous structure of the *Sphagnum* cell. Furthermore, peat is a natural organic product which is void of contaminants, making it an excellent **growing medium for interior plants and gardens.**

B. Spontaneous recolonisation

A disturbed environment is often a hostile environment for the establishment and growth of pre-existing vegetation. After peat extraction the substrate is unstable and prone to extreme dryness, thereby preventing the re-establishment of peat-moss, as was the case at Bois-des-Bel. And, in Canada, without *Sphagnum*, most peatlands cannot develop.

Polytrichum moss (*Polytrichum strictum*), a moss that looks like a miniature coniferous tree, is important in peatland restoration because it readily colonises organic soils. As a pioneer plant, it is one of the first to establish after disturbance. Its ability to tolerate dryness, an instable substrate and burial by wind-blown peat make it a perfect nurse plant for the establishment of *Sphagnum* and other peatland plants. *Polytrichum* (Figure 11.5) forms colonies that **stabilise the soil** and improve the microclimate for *Sphagnum* growth. Once *Sphagnum* has established, it will slowly replace *Polytrichum*.

C. Disturbances

Peat harvesting has two major effects on peat soils: notably **frost heave** and **peat**

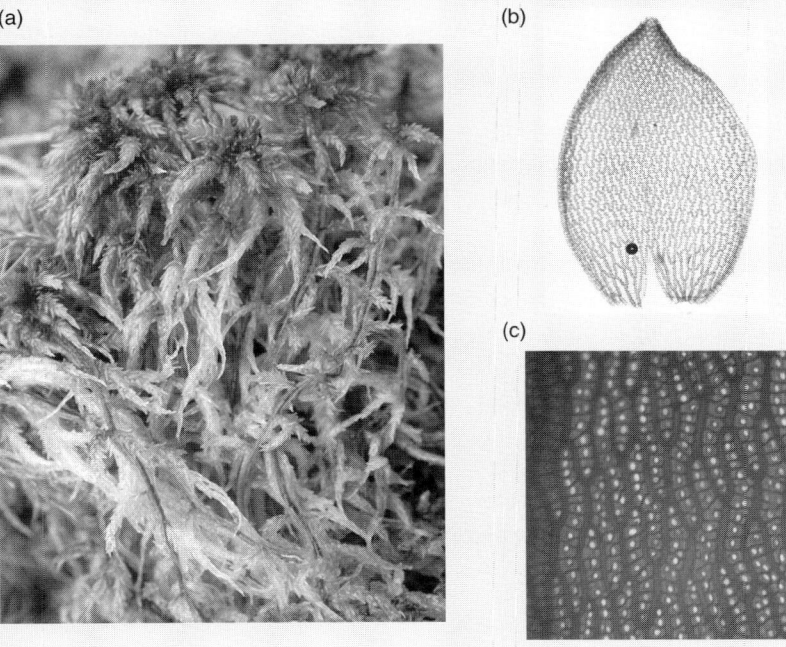

Figure 11.4 *Sphagnum* moss (a) with photo-micrographs illustrating cell structure (b and c) (photo: Gilles Ayotte).

Figure 11.5 *Polytrichum* moss (photo: Maude Létourneau-Baril).

oxidation. Frost heave occurs when the water contained in peat freezes and creates needles of ice (Figure 11.6), raising the ground by a few centimetres (up to 12 cm in some areas), thereby making the substrate unstable. This phenomenon impedes plant recolonisation because the ice needles damage the seeds and root systems of newly established plants. There are even instances where the ice has unearthed small tufts of cottongrass and young birch trees.

When a peatland is drained and void of vegetation, ground surface temperature increases resulting in a better oxygenation of the soil and an increase in microbial activity. The increased oxidation and decomposition of peat allows carbon to be released in the form of gas into the atmosphere. We can observe the drop in peat level by the appearance of old stumps which were originally buried in the peat deposit. Once a carbon sink, the peatland becomes a source of carbon. Therefore, it is important to restore peatlands promptly once peat extraction has ceased.

D. Ecological restoration

Sphagnum moss is considered the keystone species for bogs, not only because it is the most prevalent plant but also because this small moss has the ability to transform its environment. *Sphagnum* mosses have the ability to acidify their environment, thereby reducing the availability of nutrients to vascular plants. Furthermore, by maintaining the water level near ground surface, they limit

Figure 11.6 Needle ice in surficial peat causing frost heave (photo: Vicky Bérubé).

the amount of oxygen close to the roots, consequently decreasing the growth of other plants and reducing the decomposition of organic matter. Finally, *Sphagnum* moss is a poor conductor of heat. Its presence decreases the temperature of its environment and thus the growing season of other plants. Hence, *Sphagnum* moss does not adapt to the conditions of peatlands, but rather **transforms its environment into a perfect habitat for itself**.

The **success of peatland restoration** is determined by **reintroduction of *Sphagnum*,** engineer of its own environment. In order to do this, it is necessary to reintroduce moss fragments. At Bois-des-Bel, the *Sphagnum* moss carpet is now well established. We can observe that the *Sphagnum* moss has already grown by 15 to 35 cm since restoration work began (2000) (Figure 11.7).

E. Habitat diversity

A peat bog is made up of several **microhabitats**: pools, lawns, hummocks, hollows, tree thickets and lagg (peatland border). Variations in water levels favour different vegetation and allow for greater biodiversity. However, peat harvesting flattens the ground and homogenises the landscape structure. To overcome this problem and restore the peatland's natural look, pools can be constructed.

The construction of **pools** at Bois-des-Bel was effective in increasing

Figure 11.7 Thick *Sphagnum* cover in the restored site (photo: Line Rochefort).

biodiversity because pool plants differed from plants found on the rest of the site (Figure 11.8). Numerous frogs and insects inhabit the pools. This newly created habitat increases the **richness of this ecosystem**, thus bringing it closer to a natural peatland. However, animals and plants typically found in natural pools are not always found in these artificially constructed pools. It is therefore important to continue research to improve the construction design of pools in restored peat bogs.

Figure 11.8 Constructed pools at Bois-des-Bel (photo: Peatland Ecology Research Group).

11.5 Fen restoration of cutaway peatlands

In several northern countries, peat for energy production is extracted from fens or from the fen layers of a peatland, thus leaving exposed peat which is rich in base cations once the industrial activities have finished. Additionally, new techniques for peat extraction have enabled horticultural peat companies to remove deep layers of peat. In such cases, the residual peat is minerotrophic (fen) peat, even though these sites were previously ombrotrophic peatlands (bogs). For such sites, a restoration towards a fen plant community is desirable (Wind-Mulder, Rochefort and Vitt 1996).

The assembly rules framework proved valuable in pinpointing important research areas for fen restoration of cutaway peatlands. A comparison of community structure (A in Figure 11.2) among 28 degraded species pools and 11 undisturbed species pools revealed that *Carex* and fen bryophytes are largely absent from degraded species pools (Graf, Rochefort and Poulin 2008). The degraded species pools can be characterised by wetland species, such as those from the genera *Scirpus, Juncus, Solidago* and *Spirea*. Although these are wetland species, are they functionally similar to preferential fen species?

In the next step, the peat-accumulating potential, an important peatland function, was compared between species abundant in degraded species pools and those common to undisturbed species pools (B in Figure 11.2). *Scirpus*, an abundant species of the degraded species pool, showed the highest peat-accumulating potential due to its high production rates (Graf and Rochefort 2009). This study indicated that restoration measures might not be necessary if peat accumulation is the ultimate goal; however, a long-term study of peat accumulation potentials in restored sites would give a better indication. Other ecosystem functions have yet to be tested.

A chronosequential successional study provided further information about the abiotic filters present on cutaway peatlands. Degraded species pools are more diverse on cutaway peatlands where drainage canals have been blocked, showing that hydrology is one of the major environmental constraints to re-vegetation (Graf, Rochefort and Poulin 2008). Keddy (1999) found that hydrology is the most important filter in controlling wetland composition (C in Figure 11.2). Field experiments provided further information about dispersal and environmental constraints present on cutaway peatlands (Cobbaert, Rochefort and Price 2004; Graf and Rochefort 2010). The highest plant cover and richness were observed on plots when a diaspore reintroduction technique was used. Many studies have shown that *Carex* species have difficulty in dispersing over great distances, and active introduction of rhizomes is the most effective means for re-establishment (van der Valk, Bremholm and Gordon 1999; Cooper and MacDonald 2000; Patzelt, Wild and Pfadenhauer 2001). On the other hand, moss spores can disperse over long distances (Campbell, Rochefort and Lavoie 2003), and therefore if fen mosses are in the regional species pool they could spontaneously establish on the site without active reintroduction.

Additionally, environmental constraints were improved by applying fertiliser and straw mulch (C in Figure 11.2). When a light dose of phosphate fertiliser was applied, *Carex* species showed a higher establishment rate (Graf and Rochefort 2008). Covering introducing plant material with straw mulch increased fen plant richness (Cobbaert, Rochefort and Price 2004).

Spontaneous re-vegetation of wetland plants does occur without active reintroduction of species. Whether vegetation should be reintroduced depends on restoration goals and largely the time frame allowed for restoration (Figure 11.2). If emphasis is put on restoring community structure, *Carex* species and fen bryophytes should be reintroduced to cutaway peatlands. Two vegetation reintroduction methods have been tested: (1) the hay transfer and (2) *Sphagnum* transfer (Graf and Rochefort 2008). The *Sphagnum* transfer method, commonly used for bog restoration of dry, abandoned peatlands (Rochefort *et al.* 2003), proved to be the more effective way to reduce the dispersal constraints for fen bryophytes (moderate-rich *Sphagnum* species) and *Carex* species.

When the internal dynamics of the novel species pool (species from the degraded and target species pool; E in Figure 11.2) were examined, shade from herbaceous plants was shown to improve the regeneration of bryophytes (Graf and Rochefort 2009). The effect of shade was studied in a field experiment, using an herbaceous layer (50% cover), and in a greenhouse experiment, using shade nets. Both experiments showed that shade allowed for a higher regeneration rate for eight of nine tested fen bryophytes (Graf and Rochefort 2010). This indicates that spontaneous vegetation, creating a certain herbaceous cover, facilitates the regeneration of introduced bryophytes. Other authors (Callaway *et al.* 1996; Nuñez, Macelo and Ezcurra 1999; Bruno, Stachowicz and Bertness 2003) have made similar observations in other harsh environments. Therefore, reintroduction of fen species will be more successful on spontaneously vegetated fens than on bare peat surfaces. However, the vascular plant cover should not be too dense: Kotowski (2002) found that herbaceous fen species were unable to compete with large, dominant plants. Pouliot, Rochefort and Karofeld (2011) also found that if the herbaceous layer is too dense, it will create too much shade for moss establishment and/or persistence on the restored bog site.

The field plots where the *Sphagnum* layer transfer method was tested were similar to a restored species pool (Figure 11.2). After 3 years, these plots had *Sphagnum* and Cyperaceae (family mainly comprising *Carex*) covers which were similar to surveyed undisturbed sites (Graf, Rochefort and Poulin 2008). Long-term monitoring of ecosystem function should be carried out to determine to what extent the functions (peat accumulation, nutrient cycling and water absorption) of the degraded species are similar to those of the undisturbed species pool.

11.6 Bog restoration of cutover peatlands

Sphagnum-dominated peatlands often contain a type of fibric peat highly valued as horticultural growing media. From the beginning to the middle of the twentieth century, peat blocks were cut manually and then ground to produce the growing media. The residual landscape of this extraction method resulted in a combination of baulks and trenches, which spontaneously re-vegetated relatively well. Vegetation reintroduction was included in this harvesting technique as workers discarded the living surface vegetation over their shoulders, back into the trenches (Poulin *et al.* 2005; Poschlod *et al.* 2007). With the mechanisation of peat extraction activities, the peat was milled over large areas and collected by large vacuums drawn by tractors or harvested by the Haku method (by means of conveyor belts). These industrial peatlands are more problematic to restore. The restoration framework was developed to restore this type of extensive disturbance. A general restoration goal promoted in North America for these large, milled peatlands is the re-establishment of bog plant communities, which will allow for the return of the peat-accumulating function defining peatland ecosystem (Rochefort 2000).

A comparison of community structure (A in Figure 11.2) between natural peatlands and vacuum-milled sites in eastern Canada revealed a strong discrepancy between the degraded species pool and the undisturbed species pool. A typical abandoned peat field was characterised by large surfaces of bare peat (70%) with only *c.* 1% cover of *Sphagnum* mosses, whereas denuded peat is virtually absent in natural peatlands and *Sphagnum* moss cover averaged close to 70% (Table 11.2). Also notable is the greater abundance of ericaceous shrubs in natural peatlands, averaging 58% compared to 17% in milled peatlands (Table 11.2). Another vegetation survey based on plant frequency shows a similar ecological distance between the natural and disturbed sites (Desrochers, Rochefort and Savard 1998; Table 11.2).

Once the spontaneous plant communities are established, they tend to be mono-dominant and can remain stable over decades (Poschlod *et al.* 2007).

The second component of comparison in our model is the peatland functions (B in Figure 11.2). *Sphagnum* bogs are known to be great peat-accumulating systems (Rydin and Jeglum 2006; Wieder and Vitt 2006) but on post-industrial peatlands the main plant groups responsible for carbon accumulation in bogs are missing if post-milled peatlands are left unrestored (Table 11.2). Clearly, the degraded species pool is not as productive as the undisturbed species pool in terms of carbon accumulation potential. Drained peatlands result in a 100–400% increase in CO_2 emissions to the atmosphere, owing to an increase in soil respiration and the destruction of the carbon-fixing vegetation when the acrotelm is removed (Waddington and Price 2000). The ecological distance between the two species pools can even increase over time, as older cutover sites (7–8 years old and drier) have been found to lose more carbon (290%) than recently abandoned (2–3 years old and wetter, 260%) cutover sites when compared to a natural site (Waddington, Warner and Kennedy 2002). The ecological difference detected by carbon flux measurements is also seen in the few above and below-ground primary production values available comparing abandoned milled and natural peatlands (Table 11.3). The 100% greater above-ground net primary production (ANPP) of the herb strata in the degraded site

Table 11.2 *Summary of three studies presenting the ecological distance between natural and post-vacuum-harvested peatlands in terms of community structure.*

Stratum	Site perturbation		Origin of data
	Natural	Post-vacuum	
Sampling effort	576 quadrats[a]	395 peat fields	Poulin et al. (2005) Desrochers, Rochefort and Savard (1998):
	12 bogs	7 cutover bogs	- Plant cover
	300 quadrats	11 grids (100 points/grid)	- Frequency
	13 bogs[b] (130 quadrats)	1 bog (20 quadrats)	Triisberg, Karofeld and Paal (2011)
Bare peat	0%	67%	Triisberg, Karofeld and Paal (2005)
	12%	73%	Desrochers, Rochefort and Savard (1998)
	0%	89%	Triisberg, Karofeld and Paal (2011)
Sphagnum **moss**	66%	1.7%	Poulin et al. (2005) Desrochers, Rochefort and Savard (1998)
	71%	0.8%	- Plant cover
	40%	0%	- Frequency
	92%	0.3%	Triisberg, Karofeld and Paal (2011)
Ericaceous plants	48%	19%	Poulin et al. (2005) Desrochers, Rochefort and Savard (1998)
	69%	14%	- Plant cover
	50%	14%	- Frequency
	15%	19%	Triisberg, Karofeld and Paal (2011)

[a] See Poulin, Rochefort and Desrochers (1999) for more details on the sampling effort.
[b] Pouliot, R. (Université Laval, unpublished data).

compared to the natural site is due to the typical good establishment of *Eriophorum spissum* and ericaceous shrubs (Tuittila, Vasander and Laine 2000; Lavoie, Saint-Louis and Lachance 2005).

Early in the process of developing a restoration method to rehabilitate industrial bogs, *Sphagnum* mosses were identified as a key ecosystem-engineering plant group essential to the success of restoring commercial peat fields (Rochefort 2000). Indeed when a young *Sphagnum* carpet was re-established successfully in a restored milled peat field, *Sphagnum* net production rate was equivalent or greater (average 276 g m^{-2} yr^{-1} across species and years) to moss production in natural peatlands (average 200 g m^{-2} yr^{-1} across species and years; Waddington, Rochefort and Campeau 2003). A similar result was found with net ecosystem CO_2 exchange of a restored site (170 g C m^{-2}) when compared with the natural adjacent site (138 g C m^{-2}; Waddington and Price 2000). Even though a whole array of plant diversity is added in a landscape comprising bogs, particularly with specialists such as orchids and carnivorous plants, it was judged that the main target species pool should concentrate on *Sphagnum* peat mosses to ensure the construction of the ecosystem basement: a wet, acid and carbon-accumulating ecosystem. We believe that if one can succeed in re-establishing a thriving *Sphagnum* moss carpet with the aim of restoring the acrotelm and catotelm hydrological layers and the organic matter accumulation function, the habitat will then be suitable to receive the associated specialised fauna and flora diversity.

A study on the immigration potential of plants colonising industrial peatlands after the cessation of milled peat extracting activities revealed that dispersal constraints (D in Figure 11.2) are not important in explaining

Table 11.3 *Differences in above-ground net (ANPP) and below-ground net primary production (BNPP) between a milled sector abandoned 30 years ago and the adjacent natural bog of the Bois-des-Bel peatland (Peatland Ecology Research Group, unpublished data).*

	Milled bog (abandoned 30 yrs)	Natural bog
ANPP (g m^{-2} yr^{-1})		
Sphagnum mosses	0	135
Shrubs	5	94
Herbs	23	11
BNPP (g m^{-2} yr^{-1})	2.7	23

the poor spontaneous regeneration of *Sphagnum*-dominated peatlands (Campbell, Rochefort and Lavoie 2003). Early on in the research process of restoring industrial peatlands, it was noted that the environmental constraints are hydrology, carbon and hydrochemistry (Wind-Mulder, Rochefort and Vitt 1996; Price 1997; Waddington and Price 2000). To reintroduce *Sphagnum* mosses successfully, a whole array of restoration actions has been designed to alleviate the severe environmental constraints found on bare peat (Figure 11.2C): blocking the drainage ditches (Price 1997), the addition of mulches (Price, Rochefort and Quinty 1998), surface reprofiling (Bugnon, Rochefort and Price 1997), passive seepage reservoirs (LaRose, Price and Rochefort 1997; Schlotzhauer and Price 1999), pumped seepage reservoirs (Price 1998), terracing with bunds (Price, Healthwaite and Baird 2003) and addition of P fertiliser (Ferland and Rochefort 1997). Several of these actions are site-dependent (Rochefort and Lode 2006; Graf, Bérubé and Rochefort 2012).

To date, 47 sites greater than 1 ha in size (one site up to 100 ha) have been restored in North America. Through long-term monitoring (F in Figure 11.2), it has become apparent that large-scale rewetting brings about another serious environmental constraint to plant establishment: frost heave. In view of this important environmental constraint, the target species pool had to be adjusted to include *Polytrichum strictum* in the reintroduction material, to stabilise the peat substrate during frost events (Groeneveld and Rochefort 2005). When the internal dynamics of the novel species pool are examined, the microclimates and safe sites provided by a *Polytrichum* moss carpet make it a good nurse crop for *Sphagnum* moss establishment (Groeneveld, Massé and Rochefort 2007). The intensive monitoring of one restored site over 8 years revealed how some species of the novel species pool were abnormally high in the restored species pool in the first 3–4 years post-restoration (Isselin-Nondedeu, Rochefort and Poulin 2007). These species are *Eriophorum vaginatum*, an important element in the degraded species pool, *Polytrichum strictum*, specifically targeted in the plant material transfer method, and *Chamaedaphne calyculata*, favoured by wetter conditions. Long-term monitoring shows a reduction in their abundance through internal dynamics and changes through time of species composition (Poulin, Andersen and Rochefort 2012) and structure (Isselin-Nondedeu, Rochefort and Poulin 2007). Comparisons with regional reference systems have demonstrated a move towards an ecosystem similar to the undisturbed species pool. Along with the return of species which are also found in the undisturbed species pool, several peatland structures and functions show signs of recovery (moving at least on a trajectory towards the regional reference system), i.e. regulation of the water table (Price and Ketcheson 2009), carbon sequestration

(Lucchese *et al.* 2010), plant nutrient retention (Andersen, Rochefort and Poulin 2010), microbial community structure (Andersen *et al.* 2010) and plant composition (Poulin, Andersen and Rochefort 2012).

11.7 Transferring theory into practice

The ultimate goal of peatland restoration is to promote the return of ecosystem functions, especially peat accumulation, within a reasonable timeframe of a human generation. A methodology for the restoration of *Sphagnum*-dominated bogs is well developed (Rochefort and Lode 2006; Graf, Bérubé and Rochefort 2012). The best practical example of our conceptual framework is our *Sphagnum* moss layer transfer restoration protocol (Figure 11.9). Restoration work at Bois-des-Bel (see Box 11.1) took place in several stages during the fall seasons of 1999 and 2000. First, a donor site was identified where *Sphagnum* mosses from sections Acutifolia or Sphagnum have to be present in companionship with *P. strictum* mosses (Figure 11.9a). Second, the ground was flattened and bunds were created along contour lines to uniformly rewet the site (Figure 11.9b). Then, live *Sphagnum* was collected from the donor site (Figure 11.9c), transported to the restoration site (Figure 11.9d) and spread over the site in a 1 to 10 ratio (Figure 11.9e). This means that 1 m^2 of material was required to restore 10 m^2 of peatland. Because the peatland is found in a continental climate, it was necessary to spread straw (Figure 11.9f) over the moss to protect it from drying out, which improves its survival rate until it can form a self-regulating carpet. Usually it is advisable to fertilise with phosphate rock (Figure 11.9g) to favour the germination of *Polytrichum* spores, a good nursing plant to facilitate the establishment of a *Sphagnum* carpet. The next step was to block the drainage ditches to assure that the water level was high enough for *Sphagnum* growth (Figure 11.9h). The last step was to design a monitoring programme to assess restoration success (Figure 11.9i).

11.8 Conclusions

The strengths of this new model are that it includes particular measures to be carried out within the framework of an assembly rules model. Additionally, this new model allows restoration practitioners to target species or vegetation groups which are important to the return of community structure and function. As returning key ecosystem functions and services to restored sites is often the goal of restoration (Hobbs and Harris 2001), knowledge of what species are most strongly linked to these functions is critical. In the context of restoration of industrial peatlands in Canada, the main long-term goal is to restore the defining characteristic of that ecosystem: carbon sequestration. Identifying the right 'novel species pool' conducive to carbon accumulation as a first step of the restoration has been the primary driver. For bogs, the early establishment of a mix of *Polytrichum* and *Sphagnum* species from the Acutifolia or Sphagnum taxonomic sections has been found to be a successful combination. For fens, this is still an area of active research. Finally, this model integrates adaptive management into an assembly rules model, which to date has been absent in the literature (Temperton *et al.* 2004). The success or failure of a restoration project can be quantitatively assessed by measuring variables which correspond to ecosystem functions (Table 11.1) deemed important at the start of the restoration project.

Figure 11.9 Common steps used to restore cutover bogs in North America using the *Sphagnum* moss layer transfer method. (a) Donor sites; (b) recontouring; (c) *Sphagnum* harvesting; (d) *Sphagnum* transported to recipient site; (e) spreading *Sphagnum*; (f) application of straw mulch; (g) fertiliser application; (h) blocking of ditches; (i) monitoring restoration success (photos: Peatland Ecology Research Group; (g) reproduced under CC3.0 license from Tractor and Construction Plant Wiki). (Figure continued overleaf.)

Figure 11.9 (*cont.*)

One shortcoming of this model is that the costs of such an in-depth study may not be feasible for small or poorly funded restoration projects. Moreover, this model does not include a socio-economic filter, which is often a very important factor in restoration projects (Higgs 2003). Additionally, such a framework is not suited for ecosystems that exhibit a high degree of variability in species and environmental conditions due to difficulties in defining target groups that would be appropriate for several restoration projects. Although this new model also has its limitations, such as the presence of a reference ecosystem, it should provide a useful framework for practitioners to systematically approach restoration projects.

11.9 Practical implications:
- Assembly rules are a useful tool for organising restoration projects. These aim to identify the major filters acting on a given ecosystem, which can be manipulated to achieve optimal succession.
- The new framework for restoration aims to: (1) identify target species; (2) reduce dispersal and environmental constraints that inhibit the target species from establishing or include restoration measures to reduce invasive species forming the novel species pool; and (3) monitor the competition or facilitation occurring between species on restoration sites.

CHAPTER TWELVE

Afforested and forestry-drained peatland restoration

RUSSELL ANDERSON
Forest Research, Northern Research Station, Roslin, UK
HARRI VASANDER
University of Helsinki, Finland
NEVILLE GEDDES
Forestry Commission, North East England Forest District, Hexham, UK
ANNA LAINE
University of Helsinki, Finland
ANNE TOLVANEN
Natural Resources Institute Finland and the University of Oulu
AILEEN O'SULLIVAN
Coillte Teoranta, Newtownmountkennedy, Ireland
KAISU AAPALA
Finnish Environment Institute, Finland

12.1 Introduction

Restoration of afforested peatlands was initially driven by recognition of the high biodiversity value and increasing scarcity of peatlands in their natural state. Now we recognise that peatlands also play an important role in climate regulation, raising the question: should we be restoring afforested peatlands on a large scale as a climate change mitigation measure? This needs careful consideration because it involves sacrificing the initial investment in afforestation and taking land out of economic production. And what if we realise when it's too late that the peatland forests were benefiting us in previously unrecognised ways? We need to consider all the goods and services that afforested peatlands provide and weigh these up against those they will supply if we restore them. This chapter provides the background to the restoration of afforested peatlands, looks at the scientific evidence on how afforestation and restoration affect ecosystem services, summarises lessons

Peatland Restoration and Ecosystem Services: Science, Policy and Practice, eds. A. Bonn, T. Allott, M. Evans, H. Joosten and R. Stoneman. Published by Cambridge University Press. © British Ecological Society 2016.

learned from practical projects and attempts to answer the question: should we be doing more of this in future?

The chapter focuses on temperate and boreal peatlands. Tropical peatlands are dealt with in Chapter 14 of this book. This chapter deals with the restoration of naturally forested peatlands that have had the growth of their natural tree cover boosted by forest drainage (forestry-drained peatlands) and naturally treeless peatlands that have been afforested by planting (afforested peatlands). Much of it also applies to peatlands that have become forested naturally as a result of drainage or peat cutting (sometimes also termed 'afforested').

There are two main contexts reflecting differing degrees of natural tree cover on mires and different peatland forestry practices. In the northern coniferous forest or boreal zone, some mire types have a natural cover of slow-growing trees. During the twentieth century, in Finland, Sweden, Norway, the Baltic countries, Russia, and to a lesser extent in Canada and the United States, forest drainage was undertaken on these wooded peatlands to stimulate growth of the existing tree cover and thus form productive forest stands. Drainage for forestry has been the most extensive use of boreal peatlands, affecting more than 15 million hectares, 90% of which is in Scandinavia or Russia (Paavilainen and Päivänen 1995). The total area of peatland drained for forestry in Canada was estimated in 1995 to be less than 25 000 ha, much of this in Québec (Paavilainen and Päivänen 1995). In contrast, in the temperate vegetation zone, particularly in Ireland and the UK, where most peatlands are naturally treeless, many bogs have been afforested by ploughing, drainage, planting with non-native conifers and application of fertiliser. Small areas of peatland have been afforested in France, Belgium and Germany. In the United States, peatland forestry is practised on riverine and depressional peatlands in the southeast of the country (Minkkinen, Byrne and Trettin 2008).

Decisions to afforest and to restore mires are based on values to society at the time. The value of timber was recognised in afforestation decisions but that of their other ecosystem services, including peatland habitats was generally not. The value of bogs and fens as wildlife habitats has since been recognised, particularly in countries where there are few peatlands left in a natural state, as in the British Isles and in areas where few of a particular peatland type are left, such as nutrient-rich mires and pristine forested mires in Finland.

Other values affected by afforestation have come into consideration. The role of peatlands in climate regulation, via protection of carbon stored as peat and greenhouse-positive sequestration of further carbon, is now acknowledged, as are the climate change mitigation benefits of carbon sequestration in wood and soil by forest trees. Production of wood fuel from forests has been promoted because this can replace the burning of fossil fuels and thus reduce GHG emissions. We also recognise that quantity and quality of water in streams and rivers flowing from peatlands can be affected by afforestation. In Finland, undrained mires are also recognised as versatile natural water filters with a capacity to buffer nutrient-loaded water from adjacent forestry operations (Hyvönen *et al.* 2000; Silvan *et al.* 2002, 2003; Silvan, Vasander and Laine 2004; Väänänen *et al.* 2008; Vikman *et al.* 2010; Hynninen *et al.* 2011).

Restoration of afforested peatland to open or naturally wooded peatland appears to be a relatively new activity, pioneered during the last 25 years as a land-use change option for peatland forests (Figure 12.1). In Finland, Ireland and the UK, restoration has been attempted during a number of EU LIFE projects (Raeymaekers 2000) and independently by state forestry and conservation bodies, NGOs, community woodland groups, private landowners and increasingly by windfarm developers. There may be longer experience of restoring peatland in the United States, where a shift from drainage to protection and restoration is said to have occurred in the mid-1970s prompted by the recognition of the many values of peatlands (Mitsch and Gosselink 2007). A search for peatland restoration examples from countries other than Ireland, UK and the Fennoscandian countries failed to find any, although there is thought to be some activity in Germany (Hasch *et al.* 2009), Belgium (Raeymaekers 2000) and France (Dupieux 1998).

The Finnish Forest Research Institute (METLA) identified 830 000 ha of drained peatlands no longer economically viable for forestry, forming a massive potential area for restoration. Reasons given for undertaking restoration as stated by different large restoration projects, e.g. LIFE projects, in Finland, Ireland, UK and the United States in project briefs included biodiversity and landscape measures, such as:

- management to repair damage in protected areas
- landscape mosaic re-naturalisation
- scarce habitat area expansion
- endangered species conservation.

In addition, several ecosystem service enhancement goals have been mentioned, such as:

- soil carbon protection/carbon sink reinstatement
- water quality buffering between forestry land and streams/stream water quality improvement
- flood and drought reduction/flood and storm protection

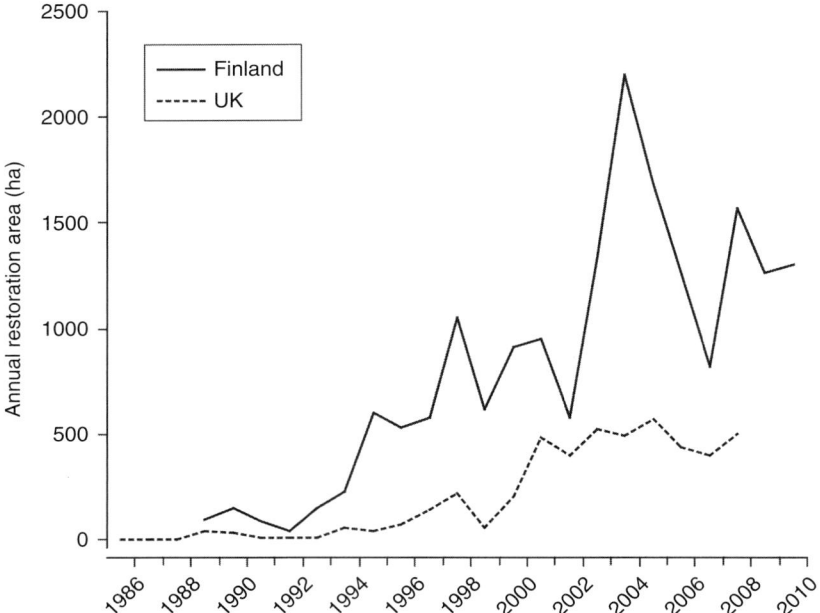

Figure 12.1 Rate of restoration of afforested and forestry-drained peatlands in Finland and the UK. Finnish rates are for protected areas only (source: Metsähallitus: Finnish Forest and Park Service). UK rates are for projects known to the authors and are probably underestimates.

- recreational and educational opportunities
- game bird population enhancement
- nutrient and sediment filtering.

However, these goals have rarely been monitored (Chapter 18). In this chapter we aim to provide evidence for the above goals.

12.2 Effects of peatland afforestation on ecosystem services

As the focus in this chapter is on restoration, it will serve as useful background to first briefly consider how ecosystem services are affected by afforestation. The most obvious effects are the loss of the former peatland habitats and their biodiversity. This is only partly balanced by the gain of generally less valuable woodland habitats, and the gain in the provision of timber and wood products. There are knock-on effects in the form of important gains in climate regulation when wood fuel replaces fossil fuels or wood replaces cement-based products in the construction industry. The

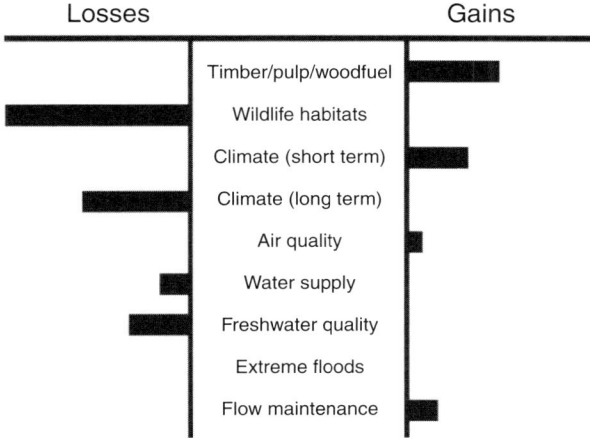

Figure 12.2 Effect of peatland afforestation on ecosystem services. Sizes of the gains and losses are subjective estimates based on the evidence presented in the text. Other ecosystem services affected are not shown because the effect on them is strongly site dependent or unknown.

full effects on climate regulation and water supply are less obvious. The main effects are shown in Figure 12.2.

12.2.1 Peatland habitats and biodiversity

The environmental impacts of peatland drainage for forestry have been discussed in detail (Laine, Vasander and Laiho 1995; Laine, Vasander and Sallantaus 1995; Laine *et al.* 2006). Some major ecological effects are given here. Water-level drawdown affects the soil environment by increasing the aerobic limit, lowering the pH, causing subsidence and resultant changes in bulk density and changing the decomposability of the peat matrix due to altered above- and below-ground litter inputs (Straková *et al.* 2010). By changing crucial soil properties, drainage induces a secondary vegetation succession that continues until the plant community has adjusted to the new conditions. Initially the existing community undergoes changes in root-to-shoot ratios and species abundances (Weltzin *et al.* 2000, 2003). This is followed by slower, more drastic changes in composition when species better adapted to the new conditions gain dominance; trees and shrubs proliferate and graminoids decline (Laiho *et al.* 2003). Mire species adapted to waterlogged conditions, i.e. those found in hollows and lawns, are replaced by (upland) forest species (Vasander, Laiho and Laine 1997). Hummock species, however, may remain in the species assemblage especially in nutrient-poor sites (Laine, Vasander and Laiho 1995). Ecological effects of afforesting treeless peatland were described by Anderson, Pyatt and White (1995) and Anderson (2001) (Figure 12.3).

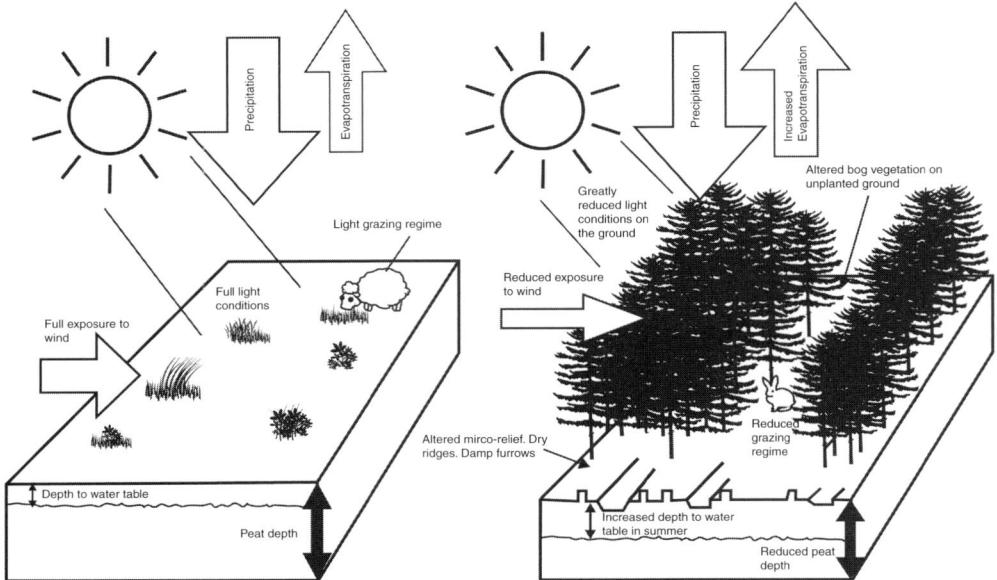

Figure 12.3 Diagram illustrating the effects of afforestation on previously open peatland.

Laine, Vasander and Sallantaus (1995), reviewing literature on how forestry drainage of peatland affects the plant and animal species present, concluded that specialised peatland species tend to be lost and generalist species previously common in the landscape tend to increase. In biodiversity terms, it led to a short-term increase in the biodiversity of individual sites but a long-term decrease in biodiversity of the whole landscape. Afforestation of open peatland likewise leads to losses of specialised species (e.g. Gustafsson 1988; Oxbrough et al. 2006).

12.2.2 Climate regulation: soil carbon stocks

As a whole, drained peat soils are thought to release carbon (Byrne et al. 2004; Couwenberg 2009; Chapter 4). However, due to large spatial variation individual, drained peatland ecosystems may be either sinks or sources. Studies suggest that forests on fertile Finnish peatlands decrease their soil carbon stocks as a result of drainage (on average by 130 g CO_2 m^{-2} yr^{-1} for those studied), while those on nutrient-poor sites increase their stocks (by 510 g CO_2 m^{-2} yr^{-1} on average) (Minkkinen and Laine 1998; Minkkinen et al. 1999). Finnish GHG reporting assumes a loss of soil carbon (average 140 g CO_2 m^{-2} yr^{-1}) for forestry-drained peat soils (Statistics Finland 2012).

Accumulation of carbon in the growing tree stands exceeds any decrease in soil carbon, so that these ecosystems are strong carbon sinks until they are harvested (Laurila *et al.* 2007; Chapter 4). Von Arnold *et al.* (2005) estimated that peat soils in Sweden release carbon (autotrophic + heterotrophic activity) at a rate of 900–1900 g CO_2 m^{-2} yr^{-1}. However, when the annual net primary production of forests was added, all drained sites were net sinks of carbon (von Arnold *et al.* 2005). This agrees with the conclusions of Minkkinen, Byrne and Trettin (2008) that in boreal conditions in the short term the C gains of growing tree stands often exceed the losses of C from the soil. Whether trees are a short- or long-term storage depends on cuttings and future use of raw wood.

12.2.3 Climate regulation: carbon sequestration and emissions

Afforestation of treeless peatland replaces a weak carbon and GHG sink with a stronger but shorter-term sink (Worrall *et al.* 2011; Chapter 4), but at the same time it may cause leakage of carbon from the enormous and previously secure store of the peat deposit (Hargreaves, Milne and Cannell 2003). The carbon loss rate is slow and only after many years does the accumulated loss overtake the gain accumulated due to faster carbon sequestration. The reversibility of this breaching of the peat carbon store is crucial to whether afforestation of peatland is sustainable.

12.2.4 Water regulation: flood risk, drinking water provision, water quality

Water from a peatland area may be affected in several ways by afforestation (Chapter 5). The Coalburn catchment study (e.g. Birkinshaw *et al.* 2014) has measured these effects over 45 years. Rapid channelling of rainwater by plough furrows and drains increases the size of minor peak flows but makes no difference to the size of major peak flows (i.e. once-in-a-year floods and greater) (Robinson, unpublished data), because these occur when soils are saturated and the runoff rate equals the rainfall rate (David and Ledger 1988). Enhancement of the minor floods normally decreases over time as the drainage system deteriorates and the trees grow.

In some peatlands, drainage for afforestation increases water flow from a peatland during prolonged dry periods when streams fall to their lowest levels (Robinson *et al.* 2003). This maintains drinking water supply and may allow water abstraction for industrial use to continue when it would otherwise have had to stop to protect the flora and fauna of peatland-fed streams. At Coalburn, afforestation doubled low flows, with the effect reducing over time but still present after 40 years. This water regulation benefit comes at a cost in that continued water supply to streams results in deeper and more prolonged water table drawdown and, presumably, increased peat decomposition, a loss in terms of climate regulation.

Water yield increases after afforestation but then gradually declines as the evapotranspiration of the growing trees increases, levelling out at a somewhat reduced value (perhaps 5% lower) compared to pre-afforestation. This reduces the supply of water from the forest until it is felled, when the cycle starts again. The effect is often unimportant but becomes more significant the larger the proportion of the catchment the forest occupies.

Disturbance of peat by forestry ploughing, draining and harvesting can cause the release of peat particles into drainage water. Besides GHG flux effects dependent on the ultimate fate of this peat, it may affect drinking water provision by increasing the cost of filtration. The effect is temporary and short lived but recurrent. A more prolonged release of carbon into drainage water occurs in the form of DOC related to drying of the upper peat. DOC affects water colour, and its removal from drinking water requires expensive processing. The amount of DOC released depends on how the forest is managed and particularly on the degree and depth of peat drying.

Water quality is affected in other ways. Phosphorus–potassium fertiliser is applied once or twice to nourish the trees and a proportion, perhaps 10%, gets released into streams over a period of 3–5 years. Later, when the trees are harvested, further release can occur. The potassium has little effect downstream but the phosphate can have adverse impacts on the more sensitive inhabitants of oligotrophic waters, such as freshwater pearl mussel (*Margaritifera margaritifera*). In general, fish are likely to benefit from the enhanced productivity.

The even topography, dense moss cover and favourable physical, chemical and biological properties of surface peat in pristine condition (e.g. anoxia, porosity, cation exchange capacity and microbial retention) give it the ability to filter and buffer water carrying sediment and nutrients. By lowering the water table, drying the peat and allowing water to bypass the natural filter, forest drainage disables this useful function (Sallantaus, Vasander and Laine 1998).

Forests scavenge acidic pollutants from the air, helping to regulate air quality (NEGTAP 2001) but affecting water quality in streams. In the past, when atmospheric deposition was much worse than it is now, this effect more often resulted in acidification of acid-sensitive streams and damage to their ecosystems. Today, pollutant levels are only 20–30% of those during the 1970s, mainly due to greatly reduced sulfur deposition (RoTAP 2012), and the problem is reduced.

12.2.5 Cultural services: opportunities for recreation

Blanket mires are often major components of largely treeless landscapes. In Europe, such landscapes tend to be sparsely populated and confined to northwestern fringes, where they are a valuable draw for tourists. Afforestation can alter otherwise barren landscapes and may adversely affect their tourism potential. Conversely, well-designed forests catering for recreation and outdoor pursuits may improve the tourism potential of a remote area.

12.3 Effects of restoring afforested peatlands on ecosystem services

When an afforested or forestry-drained peatland is restored, we hope to regain the ecosystem services lost due to the original land-use change and presumably we will lose those that were gained. We will certainly lose the provision of timber and wood products, the scale of the loss reflecting the economic viability of forestry on these sites before restoration. Other things being equal, the balance of ecosystem service gains and losses will be more positive for uneconomic forestry sites than for more profitable ones. Thus ES-based targeting of sites may allow restoration programmes to proceed without too serious a loss of forestry production.

Some of the change processes involved will be fast, like felling the trees, but others, for example recolonisation by lost plant species and re-establishment of an equilibrium among competing plant species, will be much slower. And we can expect to see transitionary effects, some of which may be in opposite directions to the long-term effects. This section sets out the scientific evidence of changes resulting from restoration. The main effects on ecosystem services are summarised in Table 12.1 and Figure 12.4.

12.3.1 Provision of habitat for peatland species

Vegetation and water table monitoring are commonly undertaken in restoration projects to demonstrate that valuable habitats are being created. Often, results are reported only up to the end of the project funding period, by which time only the earliest vegetation changes have occurred. Signs of successful habitat restoration are usually very tentative.

During the restoration of the forest-drained mire Kirkkaanlamminneva, cutting trees and damming ditches raised the water table and increased the cover of some mire species, particularly hare's-tail cottongrass *Eriophorum*

Table 12.1 *Conceptual effects of restoration of afforested peatlands on ecosystem services.*

Restoration measures	Effects on ecosystem services
Re-establish light conditions at ground level by removing the tree canopy	- **climate regulation (– –)**: stops carbon sequestration by trees, - **climate regulation (+)**: increases albedo when canopy is removed - **climate regulation (+)**: encourages *Sphagnum* recovery, renewed peat formation - **habitat provision (+)**: increases suitability for peatland species colonisation - **recreational and cultural values (+)**: increases open space and scenery
Minimise plant nutrients in soil, litter and vegetation (except on rich fens)	- **water purification** (– in the short run after restoration, + in the long run when the restored site is stabilised again): reduces nutrient export
Raise the water table to as close to the surface as possible	- **provisioning services (– –)**: limits wood production - **climate regulation (++)**: reduces oxygen levels in peat, safeguarding stored carbon - **climate regulation (+)**: restarts peat accumulation, long-term carbon sequestration - **climate regulation (–/?)**: increase in methane emissions - **water regulation (?)** - **habitat provision (++)**: limits nutrient availability, favouring bog specialists - **cultural services (+)**: regional level increase in biodiversity - **supporting services (+)**: increase in area of peat-forming vegetation

vaginatum, and in wetter areas the sedges *Carex magellanica* and *Carex limosa* (Heikkilä and Lindholm 1995).

The water table rose markedly in response to rewetting treatments at the fen and bog restoration sites Konilamminsuo and Viheriäisenneva in southern Finland (Komulainen *et al.* 1999; Jauhiainen, Laiho and Vasander 2002). Hare's-tail cottongrass increased to dominance within one year of restoration on the restored fen, the ground layer of which saw a moderate increase in *Sphagnum angustifolium*. Vegetation changed more slowly at the bog site, where terrestrial lichens disappeared and crowberry *Empetrum nigrum*, ling heather *Calluna vulgaris*, hare's-tail cottongrass and Baltic bog-moss *Sphagnum*

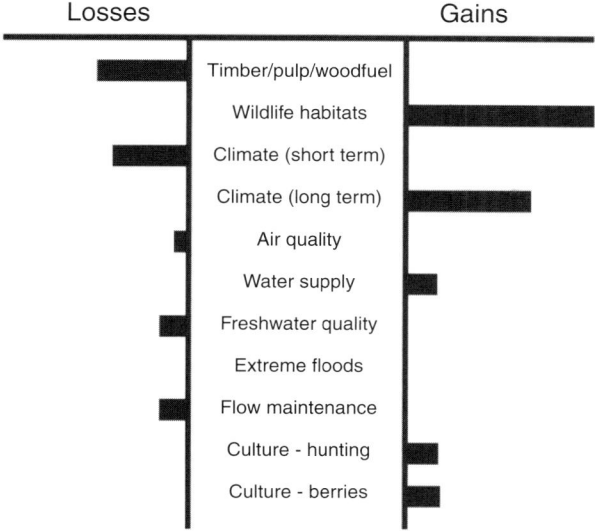

Figure 12.4 Subjective assessment of ecosystem service gains and losses resulting from restoration of afforested peatlands.

balticum increased. These sites appeared to be changing towards functional mires again (Jauhiainen, Laiho and Vasander 2002).

Restoration has resulted in succession of plant communities towards the targeted peatland vegetation of wetter conditions, with decreased abundance of species benefiting from drainage and an increase in peatland species (Komulainen *et al.* 1999; Jauhiainen, Laiho and Vasander 2002; Haapalehto *et al.* 2011). However, many species typical of pristine mires were still missing after 10 years, including wet bog hollow vascular plants like Rannoch rush *Scheuchzeria palustris* and mud sedge *Carex limosa*, and fen Sphagna like *S. fallax* and *S. flexuosum* (Haapalehto *et al.* 2011). Their failure to reappear may be due to the poor dispersal ability of the specialist vascular plants and to generalist *Sphagna* hindering immigration of the specialist *Sphagna* (Rydin 1993).

During blanket bog restoration at 14 sites in Ireland, it became clear that re-vegetation was more rapid where the former forest had not closed canopy (Box 12.1) and there was still some bog vegetation under the trees (Conaghan 2009). Purple moor grass *Molinia caerulea* returned rapidly, commonly covering 75% of the ground within 3 years of restoration. This overwhelming *Molinia* dominance may be transient but if not, the restored bog will have little representation of specialised bog species and limited biodiversity value. Vegetation recovery was much slower where the former forest had closed canopy and shaded out the remaining bog vegetation. *Molinia* was prominent here too, along with mosses such as *Hypnum cupressiforme* and *Sphagnum capillifolium*.

Box 12.1

Restoring afforested and partly cutover raised bogs in Ireland

Ireland's raised bogs represent a significant conservation resource. At one time, they formed extensive wetlands over the midlands and mid-west but commercial peat harvesting has used up over 80% of the area, with a further 2% planted with conifers under the national reforestation programme. However, Ireland retains an important part of the active raised bog habitat in Europe, and Irish raised bogs constitute a unique oceanic variant. Today, the margins of most remaining raised bogs have been cut for fuel so the dome of 'high bog' is surrounded by a strip of cutover bog, where the peat has been drained and cut but not totally removed.

During the 2004–08 EU LIFE project Restoring Raised Bog in Ireland (LIFE04 NAT/IE/000121), Coillte undertook the restoration of active raised bog on afforested portions of 14 bogs within candidate Special Areas of Conservation. Forests had been established on both high bog and adjacent cutover. The project involved the removal of 450 ha of plantation forest. Project actions also included blocking drains to raise the water table, removing spontaneously established trees from open, unplanted bogs and protecting raised bog perimeters against fire.

Water levels were monitored before and after the restoration work (Derwin 2008). Intact areas of high bog had a higher water table and a lower range of fluctuation than cutover or planted bog. The water table fell during the summer months, but less so on intact high

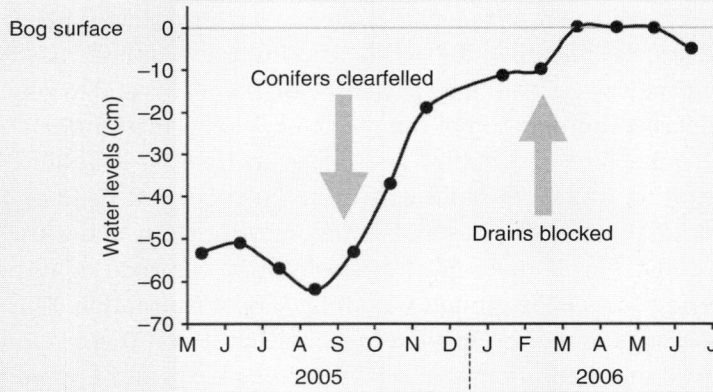

Figure 12.5 An example of the water table level during restoration operations at Killyconny Bog, Ireland. The average rise was less than in this dramatic example.

bog. Removal of forests led to a rise in water table level – in one case dramatic (Figure 12.5). Blocking drains facilitated the rewetting of damaged areas. Over time, the water table is expected to rise to levels comparable to those on intact bog.

Following clearfelling, there was a reduction in bare peat and an increase in the number of pioneer species, with limited appearance of the higher plants, mosses and lichens characteristic of raised bogs. Ling heather, purple moor grass and bramble *Rubus fruticosus* agg. were prominent re-colonisers. Species preferring wet conditions, e.g. *Sphagnum* spp., white beak-sedge *Rhynchospora alba* and sundews *Drosera* spp., are regenerating but will take some time. However, at some sites, abundant and widespread *Sphagnum* regeneration, particularly in and around blocked drains, was very encouraging.

The rate of recolonisation of bog vegetation was strongly influenced by the stage of the conifer crop that had been removed. Prospects for restoration appeared better on sites where the conifer crop had not yet closed canopy. This was because the ground vegetation was still present so it could recover quickly and the forest had not yet lowered the water table sufficiently to change the hydrology and peat properties. Post-project monitoring has shown significant regeneration of lodgepole pine *Pinus contorta* and downy birch *Betula pubescens* at some sites. Lessons learned from the project should give consideration to questions about the balance between practical matters, such as management inputs and costs, and the ecological benefits obtained.

Restoration of afforested blanket bogs in Caithness, Scotland, resulted in a rise in the water table to a level close to but slightly lower than that of pristine bog (Figure 12.6) (Anderson 2010). Forest floor mosses declined while hare's-tail cottongrass, a key bog plant, expanded rapidly. Hare's-tail cottongrass, along with ling heather, showed a similar rapid response to restoration after closed-canopy lodgepole pine forest was removed from a lowland raised bog, Flanders Moss, in east-central Scotland (Anderson 2010). Wavy hair grass *Deschampsia flexuosa* also increased after restoration, suggesting increased nutrient availability compared with pristine bog.

During the restoration of forest-drained peatlands that originally had a dense tree cover, particularly spruce mires (Box 12.2), the whole tree cover is usually left intact when the drains are dammed (Metsähallitus 1999). In

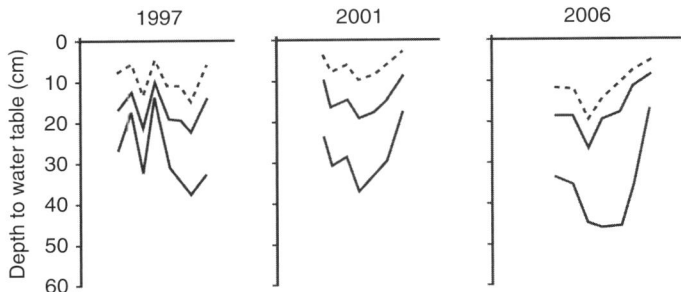

Figure 12.6 Water levels 1, 5 and 10 years after restoration of afforested blanket bog in Caithness, Scotland, in the afforested (bottom line), restored (middle line) and pristine (top line) state.

time, this increases the amount of fallen and decaying wood, benefiting fungal and insect biodiversity and thus providing valuable supporting services.

12.3.2 Climate regulation

While restoration may be important in reviving the carbon exchange function of mires, the full climatic effects of restoration are not known and need further study (Strack 2008).

Box 12.2

Restoring boreal spruce mires: vegetation response

Boreal spruce mires are naturally forested peatlands with tree stands dominated by Norway spruce *Picea abies* with a low density of deciduous species. These are important habitats for both forest and mire species and thus natural centres of biodiversity in boreal landscapes. In southern Finland, most have been drained for forestry and they are one of the most important forested habitats in need of protection. After drainage, mire species decrease or disappear and forest species increase or colonise. The natural uneven tree stand structure remains for some time, but further management levels it up later.

Soukonkorpi, a 13 ha spruce mire in the Liesjärvi National Park, Finland, and a Natura 2000 site, was drained in the 1930s, long before it became part of the national park. It was restored in 1995, using an excavator to dam the drains with peat.

Before restoration the lowest water-table level was approximately 50–60 cm below the surface. Three years after restoration the water table level in these areas had risen approximately 40 cm. In other parts of the restored mire, changes in the water table level were more moderate.

Relict populations of *Sphagnum girgensohnii*, *S. russowii*, *S. angustifolium*, *S. magellanicum* and *S. wulfianum* started to recover immediately after restoration and, after 15 years, had similar cover to those in pristine spruce mires (Figure 12.7a). The forest moss species, mainly *Pleurozium schreberi*, *Hylocomium splendens*, *Dicranum polysetum* and *D. scoparium*, had clearly declined. The small moss species growing on litter or dead wood, such as *Lophocolea heterophylla*, *Plagiothecium* sp. and *Tetraphis pellucida*, had more or less disappeared.

In the field layer, the cover of blueberry *Vaccinium myrtillus* decreased but cowberry *V. vitis-idaea* showed no strong response to restoration. *Carex globularis* increased strongly in the favourable light and nutrient conditions after restoration, but after 10 years it declined rapidly (Figure 12.7b). Species typical of disturbed sites, like rosebay willowherb *Epilobium angustifolium* and raspberry *Rubus idaeus*, rapidly colonised the restored site but have now almost disappeared.

The high water table level and the recovery of *Sphagnum* to the level of pristine spruce mires gives reason to assume that supporting services such as peat formation have been restored. The restored mire provides several cultural services as it is used actively as a demonstration and study site with a boardwalk built through it. The vitality of the remaining shoots of blueberry has greatly improved and its berry yield has increased after restoration.

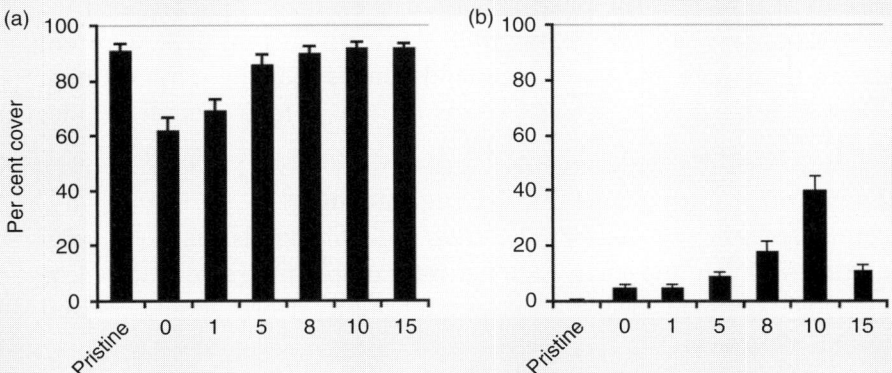

Figure 12.7 Cover of (a) bog mosses *Sphagnum* spp. and (b) the sedge *Carex globularis* over 15 years after restoration by using an excavator to dam the drains with peat but leaving the tree stand intact, compared to mean cover on pristine spruce mires (error bars represent ± one standard error of the mean; Aapala and Tukia, unpublished data)

Restoration is not always able immediately to improve the balance of GHG emissions, due to land use. Worrall, Bell and Bhogal (2010) compiled data on peatland drain blocking. They argued that most published studies find decreased soil respiration, increased primary productivity and increased CH_4 release. In their analysis, Worrall, Bell and Bhogal (2010) concluded that the measure results in only a 35% probability that the GHG budget will be improved as a consequence of blocking drains.

The succession of vegetation and peat methanogenic microbial activity both take time (Box 12.3). Similarly, the fluxes of the most relevant GHGs in peatland ecosystems under restoration, CO_2 and CH_4, and the balance of these GHGs evolve until a self-sustaining peatland ecosystem has eventually formed (Chapter 4). Published studies of GHG exchange on peatlands under restoration concern mostly boreal and temperate climatic zones. Literature on GHG fluxes is available for peatlands restored from abandoned grasslands, or other agricultural use, and barren residual peat after peat extraction. Corresponding gas exchange studies for previously forestry-drained peatlands are scarce. In one of the earliest studies, the initial impact of rewetting after clear-cutting and ditch blocking in a boreal peatland forest was studied by Komulainen *et al.* (1999), who found a rapid change in vegetation towards mire species, followed by net CO_2 sequestration in ground vegetation and peat. Methane emissions were not measured. Thus, there is a great need for GHG measurements and life cycle analysis calculations for restored afforested peatlands. Meanwhile, it may be wise to assume that the pre-drainage GHG balance might be returned some decades, perhaps 50 years, after successful restoration. A recent review on temperate and boreal peatlands shows that the establishment of a peat-accumulating ecosystem seems to take at least several decades (Höper *et al.* 2008).

12.3.3 Water quantity and quality regulation

Phosphorus may be released by felled trees or felling debris left on site after restoration and can appear in high concentrations in stream waters (e.g. O'Dea 2008). Removing whole trees and all felling debris should prevent this problem occurring.

There are examples of restored buffer zones or small peatlands restored in the vicinity of drainage areas decreasing the nutrient content of waters from forestry operation areas (Hyvönen *et al.* 2000; Silvan *et al.* 2002, 2003; Silvan, Vasander and Laine 2004; Väänänen *et al.* 2008; Vikman *et al.* 2010; Hynninen *et al.* 2011). Silvan *et al.* (2002, 2003, 2004) reported that a restored peatland was very effective in retaining nitrogen and phosphorus. Approximately 15% and 25%, respectively, of experimentally added high

Box 12.3
The Green Belt Life project: research closely linked to practice

The Green Belt of Fennoscandia extends over 1000 km along the Finnish–Russian–Norwegian border and includes areas impacted by forestry. In the Green Belt LIFE project (LIFE04 NAT/FI/000078), all the drained peatlands in three Natura 2000 sites in Kainuu region, eastern Finland, were restored.

The Finnish Forest Research Institute (METLA) established a research program to follow the impacts of restoration on 11 pine fens drained for forestry in the 1970–80s and restored in 2007 (Laine et al. 2011). In these nutrient-poor fens, post-drainage succession had not proceeded noticeably during the three decades following drainage. While the tree cover had increased, the field and ground layer vegetation was similar in managed and pristine fens, with mire dwarf shrubs and *Sphagnum* mosses dominating. Restoration was carried out by removing three-quarters of the tree stand volume to equal that of pristine pine fens and using excavators to fill the ditches.

The study concentrated on monitoring water levels and vegetation. Before restoration, the water table was significantly lower in the forestry-drained fens but immediately after blocking the ditches it returned to the same level as in the pristine fens. The water table in the restored fens behaved similarly to that of the pristine fens. The return of the high water table is crucial, since it regulates several peatland functions, such as slow decomposition, which are important for carbon accumulation (Laiho 2006). Blocking the ditches is likely to slow down runoff from the fens, restoring their capacity for flood control. Restoration had little impact on the vegetation in the first 2 years after restoration, indicating that species were tolerant of the rising water levels.

Restoration aims to return the natural functioning of peatlands, including nutrient and carbon cycles. Return of the high water table reduces soil respiration rates and increases methane emissions, depending on water table height and vegetation composition (Komulainen et al. 1997, 1999; Couwenberg et al. 2011). While the tree stand of the managed fens was relatively small and its carbon binding expected to be low, restoration is likely to have improved the CO_2 balance by reducing respiration. Since the vegetation is composed of shrubs and *Sphagnum* mosses, and the water table is generally below the peat surface, methane emissions are likely to be low, as in pristine pine fens. Therefore, restoration improves the capacity of these fens to bind carbon.

Directly after restoration, peatlands may not appeal to recreational users because the felling debris gives them an unnatural look and makes them difficult to walk over. However, removal of the tree stand as part of the restoration quickly creates a typical mire–forest mosaic landscape. Restoration is expected to increase the occurrence of mire berries, such as cranberry *Vaccinium oxycoccos* and cloudberry *Rubus chamaemorus*, and improve the conditions for game birds, therein increasing cultural services from these peatlands.

loads of N and P were retained by microbes while the vegetation retained 70% and 25%, respectively. Large restored buffers (>1% of the catchment area) may bind 70–100% of the added N, 100% of the added P and >70% of the suspended solids. Less than 3% of the added N escaped to the atmosphere as N_2O (Hynninen *et al.* 2011). Also, during the 2002–07 LIFE project *Restoring active blanket bog in Ireland*, it was shown that sites which had a vegetated riparian buffer zone had lower concentrations of P in water after felling than a site without a buffer zone (O'Dea, 2008). This water-purifying capacity is a valuable regulating service that also contributes to provisioning services by making it possible to practise peatland forestry in areas near water courses.

12.3.4 Cultural services: recreation, volunteer involvement, education, field sport

Local community involvement in restoration projects can have benefits in fostering understanding of the ecological rationale and even a sense of ownership. Similarly, people can gain education into the value of peatlands under different land uses through working as volunteers on these projects (Box 12.4), and this may also contribute to their health and well-being. Project sites can, and often do, provide educational opportunities at various levels, from primary schools to postgraduate students. Projects can also give value by educating people on peatland use and its changes during different economic–political situations. Local economic benefits can result from peatland restoration, such as by the Royal Society for the Protection of Birds (RSPB) at its UK Forsinard Flows Reserve, where a programme of restoring afforested blanket bog has played a part in attracting 4000 visitors per year, who contribute £190 000 to the local economy (Cris *et al.* 2011).

Gearey and Fyfe (Chapter 6) detail the scientific service value of peatland (i.e. its value as a record of human activity and past environmental conditions). They highlight the importance of keeping sites as wet as possible for the preservation of the palaeo record. Provided restoration aims to rewet sites it should prevent further loss of its scientific service value, which might continue to diminish otherwise. Forestry activity should then become another episode stored away in the peat's stratigraphic record.

In Finland, restoration of forestry-drained peatlands is needed to strengthen forest grouse populations, which have declined because of land-use/predator interactions exacerbated by climate change (Ludwig 2007). Grouse-breeding success can be improved by restoring peatlands that are not economically viable for continued forestry use. Increased populations

Box 12.4
The Border Mires: a partnership approach

The border mires is a group of bogs located within Kielder Forest in northern England and managed by the Forestry Commission (FC). They consist of 55 discrete mires, 29 of which are SSSIs, covering an area of 2850 ha. Most were partially afforested or drained with surrounding land after World War II, resulting in loss of hydrological condition and vegetation cover. Work on Berry Hill Moss in the early 1990s demonstrated the feasibility of recovery to active mire with restoration of the native vegetation and protection of the carbon store. Since 1986, management has been aimed at maintaining the intact mires and restoring the hydrology and vegetation of the modified sites, both to maintain or re-establish mire vegetation communities and prevent carbon release through oxidation of the peat.

Management of the mires has been directed through the Border Mires Committee, consisting of representatives of the stakeholder organisations Northumberland Wildlife Trust, Natural England (NE), RAF Spadeadam, Northumberland National Park and Newcastle University, and chaired by the Forestry Commission. The joint nature of this management approach has brought together a variety of delivery and funding mechanisms ranging from the FC's own budget, through National Park and NE grants to the Wildlife Trust providing a massive in-kind contribution in the form of enthusiastic volunteers. Notable delivery periods included a European Union LIFE project in 1998–2003 and an FC-funded project in 2006–2009, which has seen all the SSSI mires finally brought into favourable or recovering condition.

Most of the restored mires now have a more or less continuous carpet of *Sphagnum* mosses. This has been achieved through a programme of drain blocking, using peat dams and plastic piling, and the removal of tree crops. Where economically practical, tree removal was self-funded through harvesting, and where not, it was done by mulching or chipping. Finally, naturally established trees seeded in from the surrounding forest were pulled or cut. Mire condition is monitored by fixed-point photography and more formally through NE's condition monitoring programme for SSSIs. In future, the remaining forest cover on the non-SSSI mires is programmed for removal. Ongoing maintenance of the dams will be required, plus removal of naturally regenerated trees.

Opportunities have been taken to provide recreational and educational benefits through the construction of interpretive boardwalks on two of the mires, plus the production of the booklet 'The Border Mires: a conservation history' (Lunn and Burlton 2010) and a visitor leaflet. The project has also provided volunteering opportunities through Northumberland Wildlife Trust.

of forest grouse draw more people to the restored sites as hiking and/or hunting areas.

Waylen, Van der Noort and Blackstock (Chapter 7) show that there are many forms of cultural value attached to peatlands. Some of these will be affected where peatland has been afforested or forestry-drained, and most could be regained in the long term by restoration. There will also be cultural values attached to forests created on peatland (e.g. Tittensor 2009), some of which may be lost if the forest were to be cleared for peatland restoration.

12.3.5 Supporting services: nutrient cycling

When a peatland is receiving water of the correct chemical composition, the nutrient status of the peat layer may return to its original level. Haapalehto *et al.* (2011) reported that 10 years after restoration, peat mineral elements (Ca, K, Mg, Mn and P) in the studied bog and fen ecosystems had concentrations corresponding to those of comparable pristine peatlands. The authors concluded that ecosystem functionality in terms of nutrient cycling between peat and plants had recovered.

12.4 Conclusions

The first experiences of restoration are promising. This land-use change seems to be feasible in most situations. Exceptions include raised bogs or aapa mires so severely dry as a result of peripheral peat cutting or drainage that they cannot be rewetted. Afforested bogs with advanced peat cracking (Pyatt 1987) may be another exception, but these are only known in the UK, where they seem to be restricted to the drier peatland areas. Climate change may work against restoration of afforested blanket bogs in places that become more prone to summer droughts. Where restoration is successful, it will bring the expected gains and losses in ecosystem services over a timescale of a few decades. The picture will initially be confusing, due to transitionary effects such as a temporary decrease in drainage water quality.

Most peatlands restored so far are in the early stages of post-restoration succession. Existing research sites should continue to be studied long enough to cover both transient transitionary fluxes and the new equilibrium state. Future restoration projects should be closely linked to monitoring and research to determine the extent to which peatland functions are restored and to show other long-term effects of restoration (Kuuluvainen *et al.* 2002). For example, long-term monitoring of vegetation at a sample of sites (Aapala, Sallantaus and Haapalehto 2008) is needed to confirm whether they support a plant community likely to accumulate peat in future, or revert to woodland. Also, research on target species is needed to ensure that restoration actions lead to successful results (Rassi *et al.* 2003). For example, better understanding of metapopulation dynamics of butterflies and rich fen vascular plants and of the autecology of rich fen bryophytes (Mälson and Rydin 2007, 2009) can inform restoration theory and practice so that restoration can be targeted to maximise its biodiversity benefits.

The full climatic effects of restoration are not known (Strack 2008), and the change in GHG fluxes resulting from restoration is a crucial topic for further research. Studies should be conducted to determine how the overall net GHG balance changes when an afforested peatland is restored. The studies must measure or reliably estimate all the component fluxes, including the aqueous ones, must include an adequate baseline and must continue for long enough to cover both transient transitionary fluxes and the new equilibrium state. If the peat carbon store can be re-secured by restoration, then the balance of all ecosystem services may be for or against peatland afforestation but if the peat carbon store continues to leak despite best efforts at restoration, then there is a strong argument against further peatland afforestation.

In future, when peatland restoration increases in scale, it will be important to study and develop the ecological and economical efficiencies.

CHAPTER THIRTEEN

Restoration of high-altitude peatlands on the Ruoergai Plateau (Northeastern Tibetan Plateau, China)

XIAOHONG ZHANG
Wetlands International China Office, Beijing, China
MARTIN SCHUMANN
Ernst Moritz Arndt University of Greifswald, Germany
YONGHENG GAO
Chinese Academy of Sciences, Chengdu, China
J. MARC FOGGIN
Mountain Societies Research Institute, University of Central Asia, Kyrgyzstan
Institute of Asian Research, University of British Columbia, Canada
SHENGZHONG WANG
Northeast Normal University Changchun, China
HANS JOOSTEN
Institute of Botany and Landscape Ecology, Ernst Moritz Arndt University of Greifswald, Germany

13.1 Introduction

All over the world, high-altitude peatlands are the product of co-evolution between nature and pastoral communities. Over thousands of years, people, looking for subsistence and resources, have changed the character of fragile mountain landscapes and their peatlands through deforestation and livestock grazing (Trimble and Mendel 1995). Increasing population pressure, the quest for mineral resources and perverse policies have in recent times intensified these changes.

The character of high-altitude peatlands can be paraphrased as 'cold and steep and wet and sheep'. The high altitude induces colder and more humid conditions and – upwind of the mountain – more precipitation. Excessive exposure to ultraviolet radiation at high altitudes requires special adaptation

Peatland Restoration and Ecosystem Services: Science, Policy and Practice, eds. A. Bonn, T. Allott, M. Evans, H. Joosten and R. Stoneman. Published by Cambridge University Press. © British Ecological Society 2016.

of the biota, whereas the climatic island character explains the disjunct distribution of species and the high degree of endemism (Körner 2003, 2008; Spehn *et al.* 2010). The colder climate also discourages arable agriculture so that pastoralism – with a wide variety of livestock – is the principal form of subsistence. High rainfall and relatively steep slopes generate surface run-off, exposing the landscape and the sensitive peatlands to strong erosive forces (Evans and Warburton 2007).

The world's largest concentration of high-altitude peatlands is found in the northeastern part of the Qinghai–Tibetan Plateau (China). There, in the provinces of Sichuan and Gansu right in the heart of China (Figure 13.1), the Ruoergai (or Zoige[1]) Plateau is located at an altitude of about 3500 m a.s.l. In contrast to the drier western and central parts of Tibet, the Ruoergai Plateau, a plain glacial landscape with low mountain ranges of some hundred metres in height, has a humid climate with long winters and short summers (Lehmkuhl and Liu 1994) which have facilitated the development of 474 000 ha of peatlands (Schumann, Thevs and Joosten 2008).

In this chapter, we explore the history and drivers of peatland degradation on the Ruoergai Plateau, the loss of important ecosystem services and the impact of such loss on livelihoods. We discuss how integrated projects may facilitate the restoration of ecosystem services and biodiversity while contributing to poverty alleviation. Case studies present the various approaches and illustrate how participatory community involvement is integral to the successful implementation of peatland conservation and restoration programmes.

13.2 Peatland development and degradation: root causes and consequences

Peatland development on the Ruoergai Plateau started with the improving climate at the beginning of the Holocene, around 11 000 years ago (Thelaus 1992). Palynological records (Liu and Qiu 1994; Yan *et al.* 1999; Zhou *et al.* 2010), soil studies (Yang *et al.* 2004; Klinge and Lehmkuhl 2005, Kaiser *et al.* 2006; Kaiser, Schoch and Miehe 2007) and studies of recent vegetation (Schmidt-Vogt 1990; Winkler 2000; cf. Miehe *et al.* 2006) indicate that in the first half of the Holocene most mountain ranges were covered by trees (Ren 2000). Schumann and Joosten (2008b) suggest that at that time, slightly sloping percolation mires (see Joosten and Clarke 2002) were the prevalent

---

[1] Zoige and Ruoergai are names for the same plateau (and a county in the centre of the plateau). While Zoige was earlier translated directly from Tibetan into English and used in most English maps and documents, Ruoergai is the Chinese *pinyin* spelling of the area and has more recently also been used in English (Yan and Wu 2005).

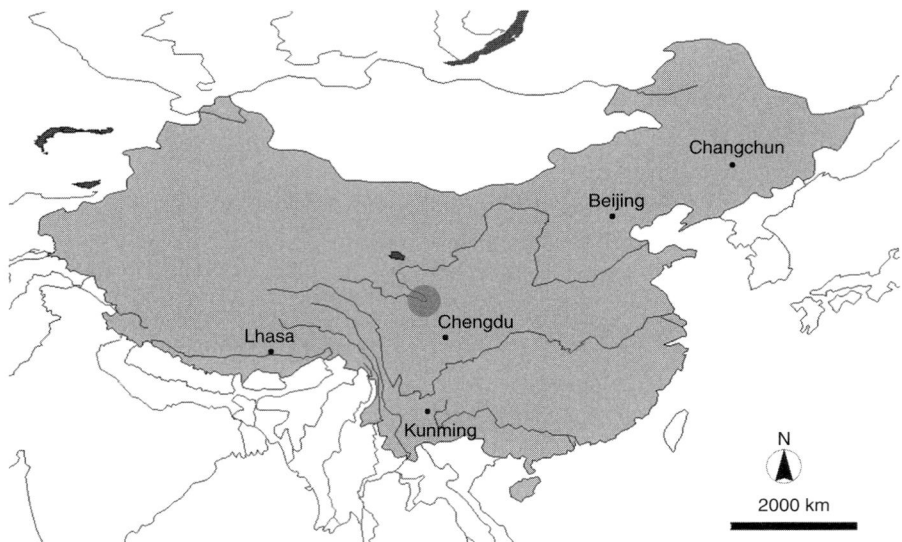

Figure 13.1 Location of the Ruoergai Plateau, a major headwater of the Yellow River in the northeastern part of the Qinghai–Tibetan Plateau (33°03'N, 102°36'E).

mire type of the Ruoergai Plateau. The steady water supply from the tree-covered catchments kept the mires permanently wet. Their open sedge vegetation produced a slightly decomposed and loose herbaceous peat with high hydraulic conductivity and large storage capacity (Large et al. 2009).

Whereas hunter/gatherers had arrived on the Qinghai–Tibetan Plateau 20–50 000 years ago (Aldenfelder and Zhang 2004), permanent settlement with domesticated animals can only be traced back 5000 years BCA. The first settlers lived at the margins of the wide valleys (Brantingham and Gao 2006), using only the edges of the mires for grazing. As the low demand for fuel was supplied by wood and yak dung, peat and sods were cut only for constructing walls and fences to shelter animals from the winter winds (Foggin 2000; Wiener, Jianlin and Ruijun 2003). The tree stands on the hills stayed largely intact until 3000 years BCA when – simultaneously with a change in climate – the growing population resulted in higher demand for fuel and rangeland (Chai and Li 1988; Holzner and Kriechbaum 1998; Ren 2000; Winkler 2000; Joosten, Haberl and Schumann 2008; Zhou et al. 2010; cf. Herzschuh et al. 2010a, b). Recurrent traces of charcoal in the peat reveal that the herders may have used fire to open up the landscape (Miehe et al. 2006; Kaiser, Schoch and Miehe 2007).

Logging, grazing and burning and the resulting deforestation and vegetation damage in the uplands induced a cascade of developments. Aeolian transport and runoff water carried clay, silt and sand, which was no longer retained by vegetation, into the valley peatlands (Thelaus 1992; Schumann and Joosten 2007; Joosten, Haberl and Schumann 2008; cf. Wang, Wang and Yang 2010). There the increased load of these sediments caused compaction of the hitherto accumulated loose peat and changed peatland hydrology pervasively: the water was increasingly hindered in percolating through the peat body and was forced to overflow the peatlands. In this way the prevalent percolation mires changed to a large extent into surface-flow mires (cf. Joosten and Clarke 2002; Joosten and Schumann 2007), which are currently the dominant peatland type on the Ruoergai Plateau.

The compacted and hence more accessible peat soils now allowed steady grazing of the mires, which caused further compaction of the newly formed peat (Joosten, Haberl and Schumann 2008). Over time a sustainable pastoral system developed, which included the sharing of common grazing lands and their seasonal, rotational use (Ekvall 1968; Clarke 1987; Goldstein and Beall 1990). The number of animals was optimised between the need for stable subsistence and the threat of mass starvation during times of severe cold or drought (Wu 1997).

As the peat body had largely lost its capacity to oscillate and store water dynamically, retardation of water flow had from then on largely to be achieved by the peatland vegetation cover (Schumann and Joosten 2008b). The replacement of the high retention capacity of the percolation peat deposits with the much lower capacity of the above-ground biomass decreased the volume of water that could effectively be regulated, while at the same time the water supply from the deforested uplands increased and became more irregular. Furthermore the water-regulating system became more vulnerable to external impact because a subsurface regulator, the peat body, was exchanged for a superficial one, the vegetation. Especially on intensively grazed sites, where the protective vegetation cover was cropped down and vegetation density reduced, concentrated water flow could incise into the weak peat and create drainage channels (see Evans and Warburton 2007; Figure 13.2).

Long before the recent intensification of peatland use, traditional grazing had thus already rendered the peatlands prone to degradation, and large extents of peatlands were indeed already degraded (Schumann, Thevs and Joosten 2008).

The speed of degradation increased dramatically, however, when new roads opened the Ruoergai Plateau to settlers from other parts of China and the demand for food and fuel rose. Expanding livestock numbers, overgrazing and the resulting decrease in pasture quality fuelled the demand for new rangeland and led to increased pressure on the hitherto undrained peatlands (Wiener, Jianlin and Ruijun 2003; Wang *et al.* 2006; Gao *et al.*

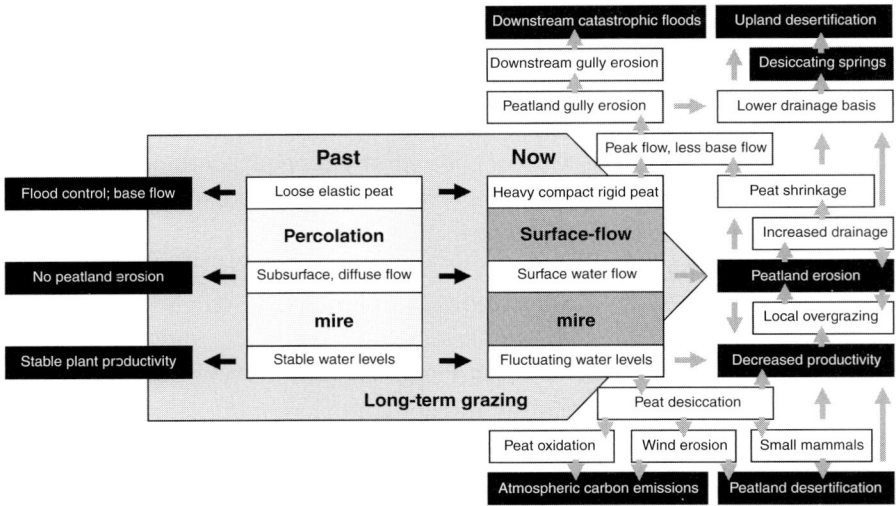

Figure 13.2 Long-term grazing on the Qinghai–Tibetan Plateau changed percolation mires into surface-flow mires, which altered ecosystem functioning and made it prone to degradation, with consequent loss of ecosystem services (modified after Joosten and Schumann, 2007).

2009). Since the 1970s, almost 50% of the peatlands on the Ruoergai Plateau have been drained (Yang 2000) to make the wet peatlands more suitable for pasture (Qiu *et al.* 2009). In order to increase milk and meat production for the growing population of China, traditional husbandry generally was replaced by a more market-oriented economy. Following privatisation and distribution of collective livestock and pastures to individual families, livestock numbers increased tenfold from about 3 (Li 1989) to over 30 yaks per km^2 grazing land (Cai *et al.* 1986; Long and Ma 1997).

However, rather than a sustainable increase in vegetation productivity and livestock-carrying capacity of the peatlands, the opposite was achieved. Many families with pastures in the peatlands sought ways to drain the wetlands and clear the water retaining tussocks (Yan and Wu 2005). Ditches, erosion gullies, subsidence and peat oxidation lowered the drainage base in the peatlands, resulting in a falling groundwater head in the adjacent uplands (Figure 13.3). As a consequence, hillslope springs dried up, upland vegetation suffered from drought stress, desertification increased and more mineral sediments were deposited on the peatlands (Dong *et al.* 2010). Small burrowing mammals, such as pikas (*Ochotona* spp.) and plateau zokors (*Myospalax fontanierii*), colonised the already overgrazed dry peatlands, increasing erosion by digging holes and burrows and decreasing the forage available for domestic animals (Figure 13.4; Liu, Zhang and Xin 1980; Shen and Chen

Figure 13.3 Gully erosion (photo: Hans Joosten).

1984; Zhong, Zhou and Sun 1985; Retzer 2007; Xiang *et al.* 2009; cf. Smith and Foggin 1999; Wilson and Smith 2015). This increased the grazing pressure on the remaining land, leading to further decline in peatland quality, whereas the area of cold alpine steppes and even deserts in the uplands steadily increased (Foggin and Smith 1996; Holzner and Kriechbaum 2000; Qian *et al.* 2006).

13.3 Peatland degradation: effect on ecosystem services

The change of percolation mires to surface-flow mires and the associated change in ecosystem functioning had major effects on the ecosystem services of the Ruoergai peatlands (Figure 13.2). At landscape scale, percolation mires can provide important water-regulating services by acting as sponges. During periods of plentiful water supply they absorb and retain water in their swollen peat body, whereas in times of water deficit they slowly and diffusely release water. Percolation mires thus reduce peak flow, prevent erosion, reduce downstream flooding and guarantee a steady base flow supply to downstream areas (Joosten and Clarke 2002). This functioning is particularly relevant in the case of the Ruoergai peatlands. On a national scale, the Ruoergai peatlands are situated strategically in the 'first bend' of the Yellow (Huanghe) River (Figure 13.1), where they act as a major interface between the humid source area of that river and

Figure 13.4 Yak grazing on degraded peatland (photo: Hans Joosten).

the largely (semi-)arid North China Plain downstream. At a local scale, the peatlands mediate between the local uplands and rivers that provide the Yellow River with water. On this scale the peatlands maintain high groundwater in the uplands, which stabilises the productivity of rangelands. The reduced speed of water flow enables peat and vegetation to filter the water effectively and to provide output water of good quality. The oscillation capacity of their peat body keeps the water table constant at the mire surface in spite of changes in water supply and discharge, which results in well-developed percolation mires being among the most stable in existence (Couwenberg *et al.* 2001).

The stable productivity of percolation mires was barely used, because of their limited accessibility and the absence of human 'consumers' on the plateau. The human-induced change to surface-flow mires with their compact peat soils provided for a substantial expansion of rangeland. This increase of provisioning services was of great relevance to the development of livelihoods on the Ruoergai Plateau, with cattle husbandry (mainly yaks, but also sheep, horses and goats) as the main source of subsistence (Wu 2000; Wiener, Jianlin and Ruijun 2003). Cattle husbandry also allowed the development of a unique cultural heritage, in which livestock have multiple important functions including social status and sense of identity (Wu 1997; Foggin and Torrance-Foggin 2011).

Simultaneous with the increase in provisioning services, the change from percolation to surface-flow mires weakened the water-regulating function of the peatlands (see section 13.2). Regional climate altered because peatland degradation led to a decrease in evaporation, an increase in summer temperatures and a significant decrease in local precipitation (Bai *et al.* 2013).

The global climate-regulating function also decreased: the surface-flow mires continued to accumulate peat and to sequester carbon, but probably at a substantially slower rate than the former percolation mires (Joosten, Haberl and Schumann 2008). At present the Ruoergai peatlands hold an estimated 500–750 Mt (Björk 1993; Chen *et al.* 2014), some 25% of the total Chinese peat carbon stock (Joosten 2009c).

Yet because of insufficient local hydropower and coal and oil resources, local people used this peat as their major energy source, with 138 large and 82 medium-scale peat mines scattered over the plateau. Furthermore, peat is mined for local use in factories, schools and apartments and to produce compound fertiliser (Xiang *et al.* 2009). In many cases, peat extraction causes heavy peat erosion.

A peculiar provisioning service of the Plateau is that, since the 1990s, the bones of zokors have been used in traditional Chinese medicine. As a result of this commercial value, millions of plateau zokors have been killed annually (Zhang, Zhang and Liu 2003).

Until the second half of the twentieth century, the decrease in regulating services may have been balanced by an increase in provisioning services. The subsequent efforts to boost productivity, however, involved the impairment of various regulating and supportive functions. The initially strongly increased productivity of the peatlands soon spiralled down into severe degradation, not only of the provisioning but also the regulating services (Li *et al.* 2010; see section 13.2; Figure 13.2). The progressive degradation of the peatlands has decreased base flow and increased peak flow towards the North China Plain, where 140 million people need drinking and irrigation water and protection against floods (Kaczmarek 1998).

Between 1977 and 2007 the area of degraded peatlands on the Ruoergai Plateau almost doubled, whereas less than 20% of the total peatland area remained as percolation mires of good quality (Schumann, Thevs and Joosten 2008; see Bai *et al.* 2008; Pang *et al.* 2010). Many thousands of hectares of previously tree-covered upland have changed to severe desert over recent decades (Qiu *et al.* 2009; Zhang, Liu and Xing 2011).

In spite of large-scale degradation and the associated loss of biodiversity (Yan and Wu 2005), the area still is home to numerous endangered and endemic species (Tsuyuzaki *et al.* 1990; Ekstam 1993; Schaller 1998) and plays an important role in biodiversity conservation. On World Wetlands Day 2008, the Ruoergai peatlands were designated as Wetlands of International Importance under the Ramsar Convention.

Recently, tourism has been developing rapidly in parallel with the development of road and air transport infrastructure. Tourists from the hot, crowded and polluted Chinese lowlands are attracted by the pleasant summer climate of the high plateau, its openness and wilderness, its clean air and lakes, as well as Tibetan culture. The number of tourists visiting the plateau increased from 50 000 in 2000 to 1.3 million in 2013, indicating the extent to which tourism may contribute substantially to local economies (Zhang, Liu and Xing 2011). It is expected that more local people will shift from livestock-based economies to the tourism service sector, at least as a subsidiary economic activity.

13.4 Peatland restoration: lessons learned

The first peatland restoration initiatives were undertaken by Wetlands International China and local administrative counterparts. Various awareness-raising, capacity-building, pilot and implementation projects were carried out with financial support from UNDP-GEF (1999–2007), the Global Peat Initiative (2002–2003), UNEP-GEF (2003–2006) and the EU-China Biodiversity Conservation Programme (2007–2010) (Zhang *et al.* 2012). Peatland restoration on the ground started in 2004 in Ruoergai and Hongyuan counties in Sichuan Province and was later also extended to Maqu and Luqu counties in Gansu Province (see Boxes 13.1, 13.2 and 13.3). Field studies were carried out to assess the status of peatlands (Schumann and Joosten 2007), whereas concrete restoration activities focused on the two main drivers of peatland degradation: drainage and overgrazing. In a 'learning by doing' approach, drainage channels and erosion gullies were blocked with a variety of techniques and results. Complete refilling of ditches hardly occurred because of lack of resources. There are strong parallels here with the development of restoration techniques in eroded blanket peatlands in the UK, which are the nearest parallel in terms of widespread erosion of upland peats (Chapter 9).

In Hongyuan, rewetting of a peat extraction site with a concrete dam was at first successful but cracks in the concrete gradually decreased its effectiveness, whereas its heavy weight caused the dam to sink into the deep peat. Erosion gullies were initially blocked with plastic bags filled with sand and gravel. Especially at the exposed downstream side of the dams, ultra-violet radiation, frost and mechanical damage rapidly destroyed the bags and the dams

Box 13.1
Rewetting of degraded peatlands on the Ruoergai Plateau, China

Project duration:	2004–2009
Location:	32°–34° N/102°–103° E, average altitude 3400 m a.s.l.
Peatland type:	Predominantly surface-flow peatlands
Aim of the project:	Peatland rewetting
Background:	Peatlands in Ruoergai County have been drained by 380 km of drainage canals, which doubled the area for cultivation and brought about rapid expansion of the livestock population. Simultaneously drainage made the peatland environment prone to degradation.
Aim of measures:	Reinstallation of former hydrological site conditions, by: - stopping further drainage - raising water levels by blocking canals.
Realisation:	Damming of ditches with PVC pipes in the dams to release water flow when water levels in the canals are sufficiently high. Erection of fences to protect the dams from damage by cattle.
Results:	Water levels in the canals raised significantly, but this only led to rewetting of limited parts of the adjacent peatlands. Some aquatic vegetation re-established in situ. Herders greatly appreciated the dammed-up canals as a new source for providing drinking water to yaks.

failed. Since 2008, large erosion gullies have instead become blocked by jute bags filled with peat mixed with grass seeds, so that the roots would stabilise the bag filling; the establishing vegetation slowed down water flow over the dam and no artificial material had to be used (Figure 13.5).

In several cases, the dams were too narrow or insufficiently anchored into the stable sides of the drains such that they tipped over due to increased water pressure. Other dams were eroded away by overflowing water, especially when made of pure peat. Later peat dams were equipped with PVC pipes to discharge the surplus water, but this only worked well at sites with minor discharge. It was soon apparent that to prevent erosion the speed of water had to be reduced; this could be achieved by creating gentle slopes

> **Box 13.2**
> # Rewetting of degraded peatlands in Hongyuan
>
> | | |
> |---|---|
> | **Project duration:** | 2005–2009 |
> | **Location:** | 33°21'–33°34' N, 102°37'–103°10' E, average altitude 3400–3650 m |
> | **Peatland type:** | Surface flow-dominated peatlands |
> | **Aim of the project:** | To prevent further erosion |
> | **Background:** | Drainage and peat mining caused degradation of peatland used as rangelands for food production. Peat primarily covered the energy demands of a local milk-powder factory and of local people as no coal or hydropower was available. Mining ceased in 2003 with the supply of electric power. |
> | **Aim of measures:** | Reinstallation of former hydrological site conditions, by:
- cessation of peat mining
- refilling of peat extraction site. |
> | **Realisation:** | At the upper part of the mined area, a concrete dam of 120 cm height was built to raise the water level in the deep (>2 m) peat-cutting site. The steep sides of the mined site were flattened. A 1600 m-long metal-net fence was constructed to keep yaks out. Some 50 kg of seeds were sown to stimulate re-vegetation on the bare surfaces. |
> | **Results:** | The water table in the former peat-mining area increased by 30–50 cm and effectively reduced the decomposition of peat. A lake formed, which attracts waterbirds and amphibians. The mined site is now covered with dense vegetation. |

on the downward side of the dam. The best way to prevent erosion from overflowing water is to make the dams higher than the adjacent peat surface and to force the surplus water to flow away across the peatland surface, where the flow is retarded by vegetation (Figure 13.6).

In a less degraded remnant percolation mire near Waqie, simple weirs made of wooden planks raised the water table effectively in the narrow ditches, which facilitated the expansion of typical wetland species (mainly

Eriophorum angustifolium) that quickly filled the ditches (Figure 13.7). Regretfully, the planks were readily removed by local people, as the raising water level made the grazing land inaccessible for yaks. In the end, peat as a locally available and cheap material was found to be the optimal material for building dams in the remote peatlands of the Ruoergai Plateau, where acquisition of other construction material often poses unsolvable problems.

The spacing of dams also is crucial in sloping peatlands to prevent water level differences on both sides of the dam being too great (Brooks and Stoneman 1997a; Evans *et al.* 2005; Edom *et al.* 2007). The best way to rewet sloping sites is to infill the drainage ditches completely and to allow the water to spread diffusely over a wide area.

Box 13.3

Controlling gully erosion in Luqu

Project duration:	2007–2009
Location:	Gongba, Luqu County, 34°09′17.0″ N, 102°33′48.5′ E, along the national Lanzhou–Langmusi road
Peatland type:	Sloping surface-flow peatlands
Aim of the project:	To prevent water and soil erosion
Background:	Peatlands degradation caused by gully erosion. Gullies incise with very steep (25–30°) slopes in the flat terrain. The prevailing meadow communities are dominated by *Polygonum marophyllum* and grazed by sheep only in winter. The land still belongs to the state and is not fenced.
Aim of measures:	To reinstall former hydrological site conditions by controlling gully erosion.
Realisation:	Six peat dams were constructed with a membrane at the base. This approach has not been employed at other restoration sites.
Results:	The water table between dams was raised significantly, to the top of the terrain. Also the groundwater in the terrain was raised, as shown by the ex-filtration of iron-holding water at the surface.

Figure 13.5 Jute bags filled with peat and seeds to back up water (photo: Xiaohong Zhang).

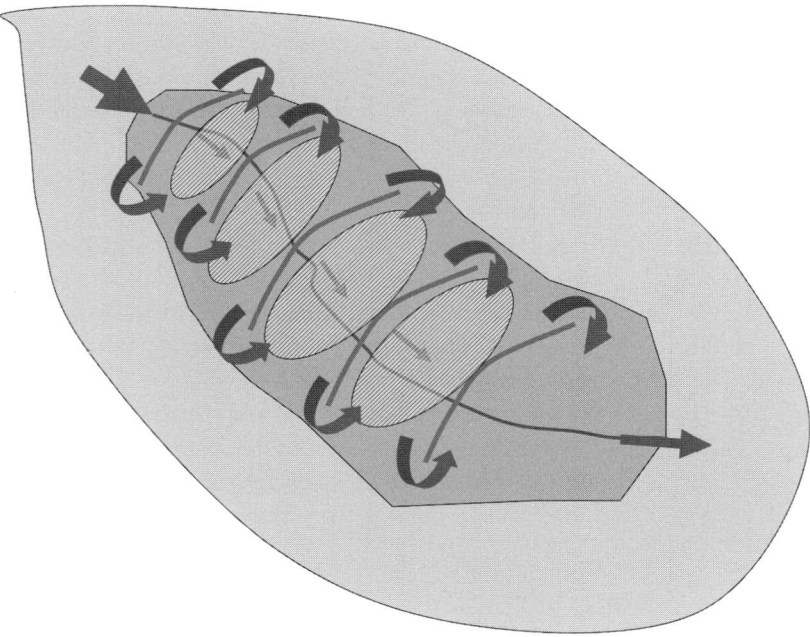

Figure 13.6 Deviating water flow into the peatland expanse.

Figure 13.7 Rewetting a drained percolation mire with simple weirs of planks (photo: Hans Joosten).

To reduce the erosive power of water and to prevent the development of preferential flow paths, a dense vegetation cover has to be restored or maintained by restricting grazing. Gao *et al.* (2011) showed that a reduced grazing intensity increases the water and nutrient content of the soil. On a small scale, degraded areas were fenced and sown in pilot projects. Fencing of the peat dams, until a stabilising vegetation cover had established, appeared to be the most successful strategy. In some cases, additional peat dams were built to enable cattle to cross the impounded drainage ditches.

Importantly, groups of households were encouraged to reduce their number of livestock and to share (i.e. commonly manage) rangelands so that cattle could graze less intensively than before. The group thus keeps the number of livestock of each household in check and takes care that a surplus is sold on the market.

Conversely, fragmentation of the landscape by fences also brought negative effects. As surface water is unevenly distributed, the fences led to water scarcity on many private estates. Formerly, all livestock were taken to a nearby river to drink and various households shared the same water source, e.g. a stream, a spring or a well. With the privatisation and fencing of individual estates, this was no longer possible and several households had to dig wells on their own lands. The fencing of large areas equally has negative impacts on biodiversity as this prevents the movement of wildlife in search for food, especially during periods with deep snow when they depend on access to lower, snow-free areas (Yan and Wu 2005).

In 2007 and 2010 the Provincial People's Congresses of Gansu and Sichuan, respectively, approved Wetland Conservation Regulations, which prohibit drainage, peat mining and reclamation of peatlands without licence and prescribe restoration measures if disturbances cannot be avoided. The Sichuan Regulation explicitly encourages local people and organisations to become involved in peatland restoration and allocates 0.3% of the provincial annual fiscal income to peatland restoration. In response, prefectural governments likewise have developed resource management programmes to control erosion and to reduce livestock numbers in order to ensure a more sustainable use of these resources.

13.5 Peatland restoration: effect on ecosystem services

Although some yaks drowned in the rewetted gullies, the restoration activities, including the reduction of stock numbers, were widely accepted. The local herders increasingly realised that forage yield on the plateau is inherently low and that stock numbers have to be reduced in order to manage the grazing land sustainably. It appeared that with reduced stock numbers they can earn more cash than before, as the wider availability of forage allows the cattle to gain more weight. Raised water levels were found to increase biomass production (Zhang *et al.* 2010), whereas reduced grazing intensity changed the vegetation composition towards herbs with higher forage quality. Peatland restoration is furthermore positively received by the herders because the damming also increased drinking water availability in the previously dry drainage canals; previously, livestock had to walk for several kilometres to access water. Effects on the restoration of regulating functions is plausible but has not yet been quantified.

13.6 Effects on livelihoods

The livelihood of Tibetan herders, similar to that of many pastoral communities in Africa and Asia (Khazanov 1984; Bennett 1988; Galaty and Johnson 1990; Wu 1997; Chatty 2007; Behnke 2008), involves a rational utilisation of natural resources in a harsh, unpredictable environment. An adaptive suite of socio-economic practices has developed over time, including the seasonal mobility of grazing livestock. Typical for the Tibetan Plateau is the yak with its many values as provider of transportation, fresh milk and related dairy products, shelter (yak hair traditionally is woven into strips of cloth, then sewn together to make tents), leather and meat. In fact, it would have been very difficult for Tibetan pastoralism to develop successfully on the high plateau without domestication of the yak (Bailey *et al.* 2002; Wiener, Jianlin and Ruijun 2003).

While Tibetan nomadic pastoralism has been practised for centuries, life is not always easy for herders. As with most pastoral populations around the world, their health status (Foggin *et al.* 2006) as well as levels of (formal) education, literacy, economic achievement and other human development indicators generally lag far behind most other regions or sectors of society in China (Wu 1997; UNDP 2005; Yan and Wu 2005; Foggin, Torrance and Foggin 2009).

China's rural reform of the late 1970s aimed to replace the commune system with greater autonomy in farm management at the level of individual households. As a classic 'tragedy of the commons' (Hardin 1968), this led to dramatic overstocking, as the ownership of large herds and flexible land management arrangements, including stock mobility, are among the few rational production risk avoidance mechanisms available to local herders (Simpson, Cheng and Miyazaki 1994) – but the latter option was removed through privatisation, leaving only livestock numbers as the main variable that could be managed by local resource users.

Several programmes have been introduced in recent decades in China to improve socio-economic conditions in the Tibetan plateau region (Foggin 2008). Programmes that have recently impacted pastoral areas include the 'Four-Part Programme' (*sipeitao*), which supported the construction of winter homes, livestock shelters, fencing and planting of winter forage. This national programme not only sought to improve living conditions, but was also aimed at 'modernising' Tibetan herders' livelihoods through sedentarisation. The greatest effect on China's grass- and peatlands has come from the 'Grain to Green' programme (*tuimu huancao*), which has returned vast tracts of traditionally used rangeland to 'natural grassland' by excluding herders from the land for 10 years. This policy is the largest programme under the 'Great Western Development Strategy' (*xibu dakaifa*), which began in 2000 in order to redress the emerging economic and social development disparities between eastern and western China. Such policies have been initiated to alleviate poverty, improve living conditions and restore the ecological functions of grass- and peatlands. They may, however, inadvertently also involve significant changes in the socio-cultural realm and introduce other disparities or even increase poverty. The Ecological Migration policy (*shengtai yimin*, also known as 'Ecological Resettlement') is a prime example, with its emphasis on relocating Tibetan herders away from grassland environments into new towns, or to the periphery of towns, for environmental conservation purposes (Figure 13.8). Recently, more participatory models of land and resource management are being explored as well (Box 13.4; Foggin 2014).

Large-scale resettlement of pastoralists involves long-lasting challenges with respect to employment, education and health care, which are not easy to manage. Increased centralisation removes the possibility for herder children to receive an education in their rural home areas and results in loss of traditional culture and ecological knowledge (Lu, Wu and Luo 2009). Under the banner 'ecological animal husbandry', many herders are now still required to modify their traditional practices and to consider alternative livelihood options.

Box 13.4

Collaborative management in the headwaters of the Yangtze River

Project duration:	2005–present
Location:	Grassland and mountain areas, 34°09′ N, 93°58′ E, at an elevation around 4700 m in the centre of the Tibetan Plateau near the high-altitude vegetation line (around 4800 m)
Peatland type:	Peatlands on slopes and in valleys
Aim of the project:	To enhance local community participation in conservation agendas through increased opportunity for dialogue between partners, learning opportunities and the development of long-term partnerships between multiple stakeholders
Background:	Loss of endangered wildlife due to poaching (mostly by outsiders), changes in water availability and local desiccation, and the establishment of nature reserve with varied management zones (core zone, buffer zone, experimental zone) required the development of a viable environmental management plan with clear roles for community members resident in the reserve. Various other development policies encouraged – directly and indirectly – the movement of herders away from traditional pastures and peatlands. Key problem addressed: to determine whether pastoralism and pastoralists (herders) were causal in the observed environmental changes and whether local herders could be part of the solution. The project has sought to trial and demonstrate how nature reserve managers and government can work effectively together with herding communities as genuine partners to attain local and national conservation goals.

Aim of measures:	Increase community participation in habitat and species conservation through development of 'community co-management' in partnership with the nature reserve.
Realisation:	Through agreed priority areas for cooperation between the Sanjiangyuan National Nature Reserve and a Tibetan herding community (Muqu, Suojia), facilitated by an international organisation (Plateau Perspectives), collaborative work has been carried out for several years in a priority conservation area with significant peatland. The focal topics included: • the survey, monitoring and protection of the endangered snow leopard (with a concomitant raising of environmental awareness); • the mitigation of conflicts with brown bears (which break into herders' homes) through the introduction of solar-powered electric fences; • improvements in local people's quality of life through the provision of enhanced rural health services by a broader cooperation with government authorities.
Results:	A more inclusive, people-centred approach to environmental management has been introduced to the project area, and accepted by a national nature reserve as valuable for achieving conservation goals. Collaborative management helps to empower communities, transfers certain rights and responsibilities, and increases their overall involvement and commitment to development and conservation agendas held by multiple partners. Several different collaborative approaches are now considered for broader application across the Sanjiangyuan region in southern Qinghai Province. Local snow leopard conservation has been enhanced, and a new means to reduce conflicts with brown bears has been proven to be effective.
Website	http://www.plateauperspectives.org/en/projects/collaborative-management/

13.7 Conclusions

Population growth in many parts of the world has led to the intensification of peatland use, with subsequent failure of ecosystem functions and their services. Of critical importance in mountain peatlands such as those in Central Asia is the use of peatlands as part of local livelihood strategies

Figure 13.8 Resettlement houses arranged alongside straight dirt roads (photo: Marc Foggin).

based on livestock grazing; household-level farming and herding is a core element of global sustainability (Hodges *et al.* 2014).

Human impact on peatlands of the Ruoergai Plateau started long before intensified land use directly affected them through drainage. The human-induced change of percolation to surface-flow mires made the peatlands prone to degradation by overgrazing. Today the majority of peatlands on the Ruoergai Plateau is moderately or severely degraded. As the change of percolation to surface-flow mires involves a change in the hydraulic properties of the peat body, this change is virtually irreversible. Therefore, the highest priority for land management is to prevent any further degradation, which implies the strict protection of the last percolation mires, a low-intensity use of the surface-flow mires, and a restoration of eroding sites. This can only be effectively achieved by simultaneously taking into account the inseparable interrelations among plants, water and peat (Chapter 2).

Additionally, integrated management regimes must consider the needs of the local population. Local communities are often both the immediate source and the direct victim of peatland degradation, and central players in the elaboration and implementation of conservation solutions. The development of more inclusive and participatory approaches to planning and decision making will increase their acceptance and indeed partnership in remediation efforts.

CHAPTER FOURTEEN

Ecosystem services, degradation and restoration of peat swamps in the South East Asian Tropics

RENÉ DOMMAIN
Institute of Botany and Landscape Ecology, Ernst Moritz Arndt University of Greifswald, Germany
INGO DITTRICH
Dr. Dittrich and Partner Hydro-Consult GmbH, Dresden, Germany
WIM GIESEN
Euroconsult/BMB Mott MacDonald, The Netherlands
HANS JOOSTEN
Institute of Botany and Landscape Ecology, Ernst Moritz Arndt University of Greifswald, Germany
DIPA SATRIADI RAIS
Wetlands International – Indonesia Programme, Bogor, Indonesia
MARCEL SILVIUS
Wetlands International Headquarters, The Netherlands
IWAN TRI CAHYO WIBISONO
Wetlands International – Indonesia Programme, Bogor, Indonesia

14.1 Introduction

The coastline of Sarawak appears to the casual observer monotonous and uninteresting. A coastal fringe of littoral forest or mangrove merges quickly into a flat plain behind which the inland mountain ranges appear in the distance. […][F]rom the mouth of the Batang Lupar to Kedurong Point – a distance of 200 miles – there is no high ground in the vicinity of the coast. Apart from the immediate coastal or riparian fringe, subject to regular or occasional inundation, the whole plain has been and still is largely covered in swamp forest growing on peat, recorded depths of which may exceed fifty feet.

(Anderson 1963).

Fifty years later this nearly untouched world in northwest Borneo no longer exists. Of Sarawak's original 1.4 million hectares of peat swamp forest, 80% is already lost. Most of the peat swamp forest has been drained and cleared to

Peatland Restoration and Ecosystem Services: Science, Policy and Practice, eds. A. Bonn, T. Allott, M. Evans, H. Joosten and R. Stoneman. Published by Cambridge University Press. © British Ecological Society 2016.

make way for plantations of African oil palm *Elaeis guineensis* to boost the production of highly valued palm oil (Wetlands International 2010; Miettinen *et al.* 2012a). This situation exemplifies the overall trend of peat swamp destruction and conversion in South East Asia. Of the original 15.5 million hectares of South East Asian peat swamp forests, less than 5 million hectares (32%) remains today, mostly in some state of degradation. Commercial and illegal logging and fire have affected nearly all remaining peat forests in western Indonesia and Malaysia, including conservation areas. There are now no untouched peat swamp forests and not one hydrologically intact peat dome remaining in Malaysia, Kalimantan and Sumatra (e.g. Silvius and Giesen 1996; Miettinen and Liew 2010; Wetlands International 2010). If current rates of deforestation continue, this region will lose its last peat swamp forests by 2030 (Miettinen *et al.* 2012b). The possible exception is the small state of Brunei, where most peat swamps are well protected.

In Europe, the region with proportionally the greatest peatland losses worldwide, most peatland degradation took place over the past four centuries and halted in the 1980s (Joosten 2009b). In contrast, South East Asian peatland destruction is a very recent phenomenon that largely started in the 1970s and has dramatically accelerated over the last 20 years. Compared to other major peatland regions on Earth, the scale of peatland destruction in South East Asia is unprecedented in extent, speed and impact. Logging-, clearing- and drainage-based land-use activities jeopardise the survival of globally endangered species such as orang-utan *Pongo* spp. and Sumatran tiger *Panthera tigris sumatrae* in these high-biodiversity peatlands (Box 14.1). They also impact on crucial ecosystem services, especially those relating to global climate and regional water regulation, whereas peat fires and associated haze harm human health and regional economies (Box 14.2). Peat oxidation from drained areas and peat fires are estimated to release over 200 million tonnes of carbon (Mt C) annually to the atmosphere (Couwenberg, Dommain and Joosten 2010). The anthropogenic peat fires during the 1997/98 El Niño event contributed to the steepest annual increase in atmospheric CO_2 concentrations since global records began in 1958 (Page *et al.* 2002). Consequently, peatland degradation in South East Asia has become one of the most significant sources of GHG emissions from land use, land-use change and forestry (LULUCF), being responsible for c. 20% of the annual global LULUCF carbon release (van der Werf *et al.* 2009).

Whereas peatland cultivation, from the 1970s to 1990s, was largely promoted by national policies to increase or establish rice and crop production in undeveloped swamp areas, the continuous destruction of peat swamps ever since has been driven by global economies and the growing demand for palm oil, biofuel, food, pulp and timber on the world market. Moreover, as the population of South East Asia already stands at over 300 million people and continues to grow, further peat swamp conversion in the near future is highly likely. While it is essential to strictly protect the few remaining pristine peat swamp forest areas, restoration of degraded areas and the implementation of appropriate crops and land-use techniques that do not require drainage are urgently needed to reduce peat fires, trans-boundary haze, CO_2 emissions, soil degradation, subsidence, habitat destruction and biodiversity losses. In this chapter, we summarise the impacts of land use on the peat swamps of Indonesia (excluding Papua), Malaysia, Brunei and southern Thailand (Figure 14.1) and on their ecosystem services. We address restoration activities that were undertaken over the past decade, with special attention to techniques applied, achievements and shortcomings. Finally, we propose an integrated approach to peat swamp restoration and land use that considers the unique hydrological characteristics of domed peat swamps.

14.2 Distribution and ecology of peat swamps

Sundaland, the region consisting of Peninsular Malaysia and the islands of Sumatra, Borneo and Java, harbours the largest concentration of tropical peatland worldwide with a total area of about 15.5 million hectares (Figure 14.1).

These peatlands are largely restricted to the coastal lowlands, where they occur as either rainwater-fed peat domes located on interfluvial divides or freshwater swamps in river floodplains, on the landward side of mangroves or in topographic depressions (Anderson 1983). Domed peatlands, analogous to European lowland raised bogs, are the prevailing peatland type in insular South East Asia but these are restricted to Borneo, Sumatra and the southern part of Peninsular Malaysia, whereas freshwater swamps occur across all of Sundaland. Coastal peatlands extending over more than 13 million hectares constitute the largest portion of peatland in Sundaland, while peatlands in inland Borneo (Kalimantan) cover *c.* 2.7 million hectares in suitable topographic settings (Dommain, Couwenberg and Joosten 2011; Figure 14.1). Importantly, South East Asian peatlands, including peat domes, are naturally forested with up to six forest types (or phasic communities; Anderson 1983).

Crucial for conservation and restoration is the understanding that a living peat swamp dome is an organic landform that is raised above the surrounding landscape and therefore only fed by rain. Although equatorial South East Asia receives high annual precipitation of 2000 to 4000 mm, rainfall is highly variable on daily to interannual timescales. Periods of water deficit are most pronounced during El Niño events (Aldrian and Susanto 2003). Moreover, southern Sumatra and southern Borneo experience a distinct dry

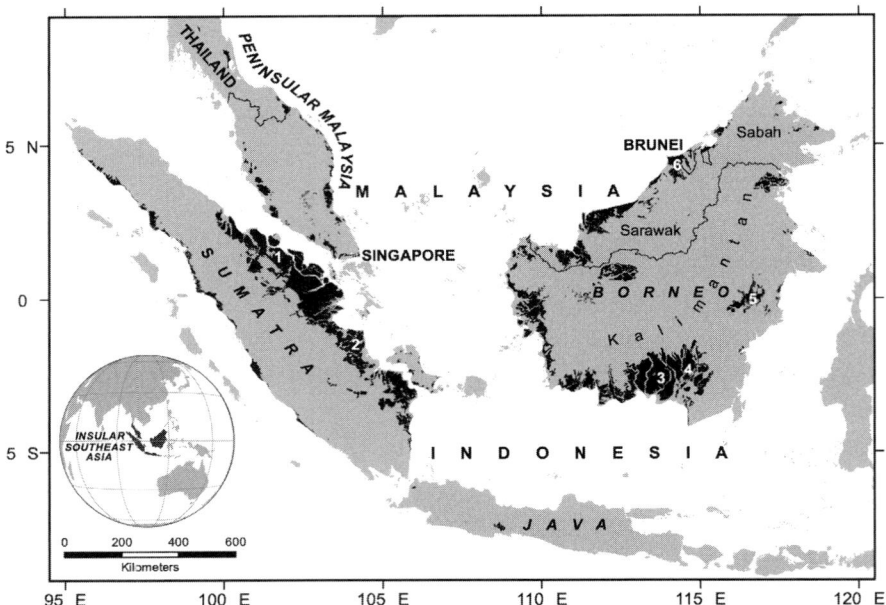

Figure 14.1 Peatland distribution in insular South East Asia. Black areas represent peatlands. White numbers denote locations mentioned in the text: (1) Siak Kecil, (2) Berbak National Park, (3) Sebangau National Park, (4) Block A north – Ex-Mega Rice Project area, (5) Mahakam peatlands and (6) Baram-Belait peatlands.

season from July to September under the influence of the southeast-monsoon (Aldrian and Susanto 2003; Putra *et al.* 2008).

To maintain water-saturated conditions – the basic precondition for accumulation and long-term preservation of peat organic matter – water supplied in periods of surplus needs to be stored. In tropical peat domes, surface roughness resulting from numerous mounds, depressions and various kinds of above-ground roots creates a series of hydrological feedback mechanisms that retain runoff, attenuate water table fluctuations and maintain prolonged flooding of forest floor depressions (Dommain, Couwenberg and Joosten 2010). Continuous addition of fresh litter maintains a zone of high storage capacity above the saturated, less permeable peat deposit (Hooijer 2005). These mechanisms convert an intermittent rainfall-derived water supply into a steady supply to the peat dome, ensuring water availability also during dry spells. The peat swamp forest floor is thus functionally analogous to the hummock–hollow surface pattern of northern *Sphagnum* bogs (Dommain, Couwenberg and Joosten 2010). On the sloping edge of tropical

Box 14.1

South East Asian peat swamps: a unique element of a global biodiversity hotspot

Peninsular Malaysia and the islands of Sumatra, Borneo and Java belong to the biogeographic region of Sundaland, a global biodiversity hotspot with 25 000 vascular plant species including 15 000 endemics (Myers *et al*. 2000). The peatlands of Sundaland are habitat for over 1300 vascular plant species, including 720 tree and shrub species (Anderson 1963; Posa *et al*. 2011; Giesen 2013). Currently about 50 plant species are known to be strictly confined to peat swamp forests (pers. observation). Plant species richness of peat swamp forests is lower than that of the South East Asian dipterocarp rainforests on mineral soil, but much higher than that of the non-tropical peatlands. However, almost monospecific peat swamp forest stands of the Dipterocarp *Shorea albida* were once common in northwest Borneo (Anderson 1983).

Peat swamp forests are inhabited by a diverse fauna. Numerous species are naturally restricted to this ecosystem and many threatened lowland species now find their last refuges in peat swamps because dry lowland forests have largely disappeared. Globally endangered vertebrate species include *Panthera tigris sumatrae* (Sumatran tiger), *Dicerorhinus sumatrensis* (Sumatran rhino), *Elephas maximus sumatranus* (Sumatran elephant), *Pongo pygmaeus* (Bornean orang-utan), *Pongo abelii (*Sumatran orang-utan*)*, *Symphalangus syndactylus* (siamang), *Tapirus indicus* (Malayan tapir), *Lutra sumatrana* (hairy-nosed otter), *Tomistoma schlegelii* (false gharial), *Ciconia stormii* (Storm's stork) and *Asarcornis scutulata* (white-winged wood duck). The acidic blackwater streams and forest pools are home to a unique, diverse and highly endemic fish fauna, which includes the world's smallest known vertebrate species *Paedocypris progenetica* (Kottelat *et al*. 2006). Due to progressive habitat isolation by peat dome formation, upward growth and associated acidification single-peat domes can hold their own stock of endemic fish species. In Peninsular Malaysia, around 30 fish species (10% of total) are confined to peat swamps and perhaps around 180 species throughout South East Asia (Ng 1994).

Deforestation and peat swamp conversion has reduced habitat of all of these and many other species. Significant extinctions, e.g. of fish or dragonflies, were ongoing, even before species could be described (e.g. Ng 1994; Kottelat *et al*. 2006). The peat swamps of the eastern lowlands of Sumatra were a stronghold for the Sumatran tiger, which requires large home ranges of up to 250 km^2. This magnificent species is impacted by poaching, but also the ongoing destruction and fragmentation of peat swamp forests has left few areas large enough to sustain viable populations (Wibisono and Pusparini

> 2010). Currently the largest populations of Bornean orang-utan are dependent on remaining peat swamp forests in Indonesian Borneo (Morrogh-Bernard et al. 2002), which are under constant threat of conversion to oil palm plantations and of forest fires. The well-protected peat swamp forests of Brunei, unfortunately, do not host the orang-utan, presumably as a result of prehistoric hunting (Rijksen and Meijaard, 1999). Habitat destruction by logging, drainage, fire and plantation development also threatens the false gharial, a once common crocodilian specific to peat swamps, throughout its range (Stuebing et al., 2006). Further biodiversity surveys in peat swamps are paramount (1) to generate or update species inventories; (2) to identify centres of endemism; and (3) to regularly monitor populations of endangered species. Such information will be critical in prioritising and designing conservation and restoration activities.

peat domes, higher nutrient levels and higher water table fluctuations lead to the prevalence of bigger trees, which often possess supporting plank buttress roots that delay runoff (Anderson 1983). On the flat dome plain, higher water tables induce the prevalence of trees with lower girth and stilt, and prop roots that facilitate runoff.

14.3 Drivers of peatland degradation in South East Asia

Traditionally, peat swamp forests were only used marginally. These forests provided construction timber and non-timber forest products (NTFPs) and fish (provisioning services) to indigenous people and early settlers (section 14.7).

Government-sponsored swampland reclamation started in Indonesia in the 1930s, but really took off in the 1970s and 1980s when people from densely populated Java, Bali and Madura were resettled in the less populated outer islands. The focus of the early *transmigrasi* programmes was on dryland and mineral soil swamps, but as these better soils became scarce, the emphasis shifted towards shallow and later deep-peat areas. Initially Sumatra was the focus for transmigration, but after the mid-1980s Kalimantan (Indonesian Borneo) became the target region, whereas the transmigration programme itself began to move from smallholding to tree crop agriculture (Gellert 1998; Field et al. 2009).

In 1995, in an attempt to compensate for lost rice cultivation capacity on Java, the Government of Indonesia initiated the Central Kalimantan Peatland Development Project – commonly known as the Mega Rice Project

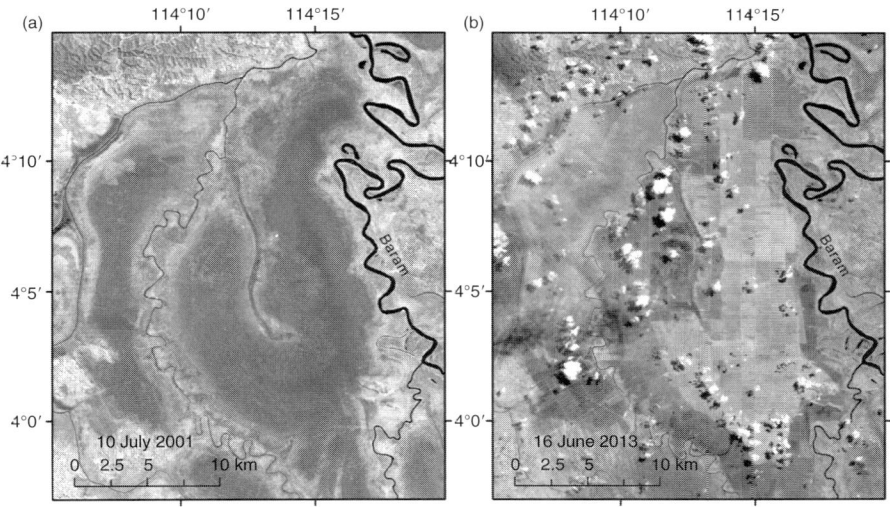

Figure 14.2 Conversion of the originally forested Baram peat dome (2001, a) in Sarawak (Malaysia) to an oil palm plantation (2013, b). The Baram peat dome was globally one of only three peat domes covered with all six phasic forest communities described by Anderson (1983) and represented one of the last undisturbed peat swamp forests of Sarawak. This nearly 5000-year-old and over 11 m-thick peatland was completely deforested and drained between 2006 and 2013, exemplifying rates of current peatland conversion to oil palm plantations in Malaysia and Indonesia. Landsat images (scene IDs: LE71190572001191SGS00; LC81190572013168LGN00). Location in Borneo shown in Figure 14.1.

(MRP). This project aimed to convert 1.4 million hectares (900 000 ha) of peatland and lowland swamp for rice cultivation and moving 300 000 transmigrant families into the region. Over 4400 km of canals were excavated, often through deep peat and across entire peat domes. However, the converted peatlands proved unsuitable for the cultivation of rice. Of over 15 000 transmigrant families that were moved to Block A of the MRP area, more than half had fled within the first 10 years (Euroconsult Mott MacDonald/ Deltares-Delft Hydraulics *et al.* 2008). In 1997/98 during a major El Niño event, massive fires broke out in the drained peatlands of the MRP area affecting 474 000 ha of peatland of which more than half was still peat swamp forest (Page *et al.* 2002; Box 14.2). As a result, government-sponsored programmes for swamp development were shelved for a decade.

After 1990, industrial-scale establishment of plantations for oil palm and *Acacia*-based pulpwood induced the highest annual deforestation rates in South East Asia in peat swamp forests (Figure 14.2). Between 2000 and 2010, Sumatra lost 40% and Sarawak 55% of their remaining peat swamp

Table 14.1 *Peat swamp forest cover (ha) in Malaysia and western Indonesia (Sumatra and Kalimantan). Note: differences in the extent of forest cover relate to differences in resolution of available satellite imagery, in mapping approaches and in the definition of forest.*

Original*	1990	2000	2008	2010	Reference(s)
15 562 415					Mutalib et al. 1992; Wahyunto et al. 2003, 2004
15 502 000	11 624 000**		6 472 000**		Miettinen and Liew 2010
15 528 000				5 249 000	Miettinen et al. 2012a
	10 227 400	6 996 200		4 783 300	Miettinen et al. 2012b
		7 793 818***			Hooijer et al. 2010
		7 600 000		5 218 000	Miettinen et al. 2011

* Original (i.e. pre-disturbance) peat swamp forest cover is estimated based on extent of peat soils and assumed natural forest cover of all peatland.
** Sum of 'pristine peatswamp forest' and 'degraded peatswamp forest', excluding 'tall shrub/secondary forest' and 'mangrove'
*** Excluding 'mangrove forest'

forest, mainly due to plantation conversion (Miettinen *et al.* 2011). By 2008, *c.* 5 Mha of peatland in Malaysia and western Indonesia were already under agricultural use (Miettinen and Liew 2010; Table 14.1). By 2010, over 3 Mha or 20% of the peatland area of this region was in use for industrial tree crop plantations (Miettinen *et al.* 2012a). Over-dimensioned pulp mills in Sumatra create an insatiable demand for wood and over 800 000 ha of *Acacia* plantations have by now been established on cleared peatland (Barr and Cossalter 2005; Miettinen *et al.* 2012a). By 2010, almost 800 000 ha (>30%) of Malaysia's peatlands were cultivated with oil palm (of which, *c.* 500 000 ha in Sarawak), exceeding the extent of the remaining Malaysian peat swamp forest of ~570 000 ha (Miettinen *et al.* 2012a; e.g. Figure 14.2), while Sumatra hosted over 1 Mha (75%) of western Indonesia's oil palm plantations (Miettinen *et al.* 2012a). At present, Malaysia and Indonesia produce over 44 million tonnes or almost 90% of the world's palm oil (FAS/

USDA 2011). Since the global demand for palm oil (for food and biofuel) is growing continuously, Indonesia plans to double its production to 40 million tonnes by 2020. Whereas the oil palm and pulp sectors provide significant employment and income, the related destruction of peat swamp forest resources impacts traditional livelihoods.

Also the international demand for tropical hardwood timber drives both concession-based and illegal logging, accelerating the losses of peat swamp forests in South East Asia. Traditional logging was technically constrained and allowed natural forest regeneration. With the rise of commercial logging, high-impact techniques were widely introduced, involving the excavation of transport canals and the use of heavy machinery such as traxcavators (Bruenig 1996). Also illegal loggers constructed transport canals, often at high density (Suryadiputra *et al.*, 2005), facilitating access to remote areas for further resource exploitation and forest conversion and causing considerable drainage to peat domes. Intensive logging had significant impacts on biodiversity (Box 14.1) and deprived local tree populations of valuable hardwoods, in particular of the now threatened *Shorea albida* (Alan), *Shorea* spp. (Meranti), *Koompassia malaccensis* (Kempas) and *Gonystylus bancanus* (Ramin) (Bruenig 1996).

In 1990, peat swamp forests still covered between 10–11.5 Mha of Peninsular Malaysia, Borneo and Sumatra, while in 2010 the extent of forested peatlands was reduced to only 5 Mha (Tab. 14.1) of which probably less than 1.5 Mha were still pristine (Miettinen and Liew 2010; Wetlands International 2010). In contrast, Indonesian Papua still holds 5.97 Mha of forested peatland (Miettinen *et al.* 2011).

Degradation of peat swamp forests and widespread poverty forces local people to seek jobs in the plantation sector or to (over-)exploit remaining peatland resources mainly by illegal logging, illegal mining or slash-and-burn agriculture. These destructive activities create a poverty trap through the continuous degradation and declining availability of peat swamp resources. Poverty rates in Indonesian peatland regions such as Central Kalimantan are consequently higher than those in other areas (CKPP 2008).

14.4 Human impacts on ecosystem functioning and ecosystem services

Land use always alters or even destroys peat swamp ecosystem structure and functioning and affects valuable ecosystem services, specifically the regulation of climate and water and the mitigation of environmental hazards, in addition to the provision of forest products and cultural services (see examples in Table 14.2). In tropical peatlands, a gradient in degradation

Box 14.2
Peat fires

Large-scale peat and forest fires are the greatest environmental disaster arising from South East Asian peat swamp transformation and fragmentation. These fire events have contributed excessively to the build-up of atmospheric CO_2 levels and caused the formation of enormous haze plumes, with substantial impacts on regional air quality.

Large fire events arising from deforestation and colonisation were already occurring in the 1960s in Sumatra, while in Kalimantan, fire prevalence has increased since the 1980s (Field et al. 2009). Annual clearing of agricultural fields by fire is a common practice and a main cause of uncontrolled fires during dry seasons. Intentional fires are also set to convert forest to plantation, for traditional slash-and-burn agriculture, for swamp rice cultivation (*sonor*), for hunting, for the expansion of fishing grounds or simply as arson (e.g. Bowen et al. 2001; Musa and Parlan 2002; Chokkalingam et al. 2005, 2007).

Human-induced fires substantially contribute to the loss of peat swamp forest, particularly in Indonesia where most peat fires occur (Langner and Siegert 2009). In recently logged forests, fire susceptibility increases significantly (Siegert et al. 2001). Forest fires often arise from illegal logging as happened, for example, in the interiors of the national parks Sebangau and Berbak (Page et al. 2002; Giesen 2004; Figure 14.1). Such fires can destroy entire tree stands (of up to 10 000 ha) and burn deeply into the surface peat (Siegert et al. 2001; Ballhorn et al. 2009).

The frequency and spread of fires are both at a maximum during prolonged drought periods, which are primarily induced by El Niño events, positive Indian Ocean dipole conditions or a combination of both phenomena (Putra et al. 2008; Field et al. 2009). Surface fires develop into peat fires when groundwater tables drop more than 40 cm below the surface (Usup et al. 2004; Putra et al. 2008). On average, peat fires have a combustion depth of over 30 cm, release between 20 and 30 kg C m^{-2} as CO_2, CO and CH_4 and produce high levels of particulate matter, which contributes to haze plumes (Usup et al. 2004; Heil et al. 2007; Ballhorn et al. 2009; Couwenberg, Dommain and Joosten 2010). Repeated burning can convert peatland areas into temporal or permanent lakes, as was the case in Berbak National Park, Sumatra (Wösten et al. 2006; Figure 14.1), along the Siak Kecil River in Riau, Sumatra (van Eijk et al. 2009; Figure 14.1) and in the Mahakam peatlands, Eastern Borneo (Chokkalingam et al. 2005; Figure 14.1).

During the 1982/83 El Niño drought, fire destroyed 3.5 Mha of rainforest in East Kalimantan of which 550 000 ha was peat swamp forest (Goldammer 2007). Over 900 000 ha of peat swamp forest in Borneo and over 600 000 ha in Sumatra were destroyed by fires during the major El Niño event of 1997/98, compared to 'only' ~1800 ha in Peninsular Malaysia (Liew et al. 2001; Langner and Siegert 2009; Musa and Parlan 2002). Ten per cent of Sundaland's peatland was burnt in 1997/98 – an area almost as large as the total peatland area of the UK. During the following El Niños of 2002 and 2006 ~590 000 and ~895 000 ha of Bornean peat swamp forest were affected by fire, respectively (Langner and Siegert 2009). Even in the wetter non-El Niño years, ~200 000 ha of peat swamp burn on average per year in Borneo (Langner and Siegert 2009). The Indonesian provinces of East and Central Kalimantan have suffered worst, presumably because of the pronounced dry season and the high El Niño sensitivity of this region (see Aldrian and Susanto 2003). Annual peat fire emissions from Borneo and Sumatra averaged c. 75 Mt C for the period 2000–2006 (van der Werf et al. 2008). During recent El Niño events, generally more than 100 Mt C were released from peat combustion alone: in 1997/98 around 700 Mt C, equivalent to 10% of the global fossil fuel emissions in 1997 (Heil et al. 2007; van der Werf et al. 2008).

Air pollution during fire episodes can reach hazardous levels and have a direct impact on human health and well-being, with many people suffering respiratory problems and eye irritation (e.g. Aditama 2000; Kunii et al. 2000). The mortality rate during the 1997/98 fire event tripled in fire-affected localities, mainly related to higher incidence of respiratory failure, bronchitis and other lung diseases (Aditama 2000; Kunii et al. 2000). The 2006 fire haze caused acute respiratory tract infections in over 90% of infants in Central Kalimantan in February 2007 (CKPP 2008). Besides serious health impacts, the smog from Indonesian peat fires caused the closure of schools and hospitals and the cancellation of hundreds of local and international flights, both locally and regionally in overseas Malaysia and Singapore (e.g. Gellert 1998). The fire episodes over the last two decades have resulted in economic losses in the order of several billion US dollars for the forestry, tourism and transport sectors. The total fire- and haze-related costs of the 1997/98 event are estimated at USD 2.3–3.2 billion (Tacconi 2003).

exists ranging from selectively logged peat swamp forests through to completely deforested, deeply drained peatlands subject to frequent, recurrent fires (Table 14.2; Page et al. 2009; Dommain, Couwenberg and Joosten 2010; Yule 2010). Depending on the degree of degradation, the provision of peat swamp-specific ecosystem services may decrease, may cease entirely or turn into damage. The induction of positive feedback effects may provoke complete shifts in ecosystem structure and functioning. Fires, for instance, destroy peat swamp forest vegetation, which is hydrologically self-regulating and fire resistant, and favour vegetation types (e.g. fern shrubs) that promote fire recurrence. All land use affects biodiversity and ecosystem-inherent supporting services, which maintain all other ecosystem services (Chapter 1).

14.5 Climate regulation and greenhouse gas emissions

Sundaland's peatlands form an important terrestrial carbon reservoir that largely accumulated over the Holocene period (Dommain, Couwenberg and Joosten 2011). The size of Sundaland's peat carbon reservoir is *c.* 40–45 billion tonnes of carbon (Wahyunto *et al.* 2003, 2004; Page *et al.* 2011). Coastal peat domes sequestered on average 77 g C m^{-2} yr^{-1} during the Holocene, which is the highest long-term carbon accumulation rate known from ombrotrophic peatlands globally. In contrast, some inland peat domes in southern Borneo seem to have largely stopped accumulating peat during the last millennia (Dommain, Couwenberg and Joosten 2011).

With an average Late Holocene carbon accumulation of 0.7 t C ha^{-1} yr^{-1} over an approximate area of 13 million hectares of coastal peatland, the natural carbon sink strength of the lowland peatlands prior to human disturbance can be estimated at 9 Mt C yr^{-1}. Natural methane emissions, which are remarkably low (Couwenberg, Dommain and Joosten 2010) most likely did not offset the CO_2 drawdown in terms of radiative forcing.

Modern land use has severely disturbed the climate regulatory service of tropical peatlands. Most land-use activities require lowered water tables (i.e. drainage), which reduces peat carbon stocks through oxidative peat losses in the form of CO_2 emissions. Carbon emissions from tropical peatlands that have been drained tend to rise linearly with lower water tables (Couwenberg, Dommain and Joosten 2010; Hooijer *et al* 2012). In oil palm and pulp plantations, water tables are on average lowered to −70 cm, resulting in an emission of ~70 t CO_2 ha^{-1} yr^{-1}, while the peat soil subsides by up to 5 cm yr^{-1} (Hooijer *et al.* 2012; Jauhiainen *et al.* 2012). Many plantations, especially smallholder plantations, have no or very limited water management structures, resulting in still deeper drainage levels (Table 14.3). Agriculturally drained and fertilised peatlands may furthermore emit extremely large amounts of the strong GHG nitrous oxide (3–40 g N_2O m^{-2} yr^{-1}, equalling 10–120 t CO_2-equivalents ha^{-1} yr^{-1}; Takakai *et al.* 2006).

Total CO_2 emissions from peatland drainage in Malaysia and western Indonesia can be calculated by combining the extent of different land-use types with respective emission factors and making simple assumptions on proportional drained area (see Table 14.3). Accordingly, carbon emissions from drainage related peat decomposition more than doubled between 1990 and 2008. It is estimated that in 1990, 66 Mt C yr^{-1} were emitted from drained and degraded peatlands. The largest contribution came from smallholder fields and degrading, drained forests. Around 5 Mt C yr^{-1} may still have been sequestered as peat in 7.5 Mha of pristine peat swamp forest. Until 2008, the annual emissions from oxidative peat decomposition likely grew to 144 Mt C yr^{-1}, of which a third came from industrial plantations. Even under optimistic assumptions, only 1 Mt C yr^{-1} was annually being sequestered as peat in the remaining 1.5 Mha of primary peat swamps. Clearly, drainage-related degradation massively reduced the long-term carbon sink function of South East Asian peatlands. We estimate that over 9 Mha of drained peatland (~70% of the total) currently function as a carbon-emitting ecosystem (Table 14.3). These drained peatlands release on average over 20 times more carbon (16 t C ha^{-1} yr^{-1}) than they would have sequestered when undrained (0.7 t C ha^{-1} yr^{-1}).

Combining oxidative carbon losses from drainage with average emissions from Bornean and Sumatran peat fires of 75 Mt C yr^{-1} (Box 14.2) results in annual carbon emissions of ~220 Mt C yr^{-1} for the last decade. In years with high fire activity (i.e. strong El Niño events) the entire region emits over 300 Mt C, resulting in an atmospheric burden of over 1.1 billion tonnes CO_2-equivalents considering the global warming potential of fire-emitted gases. The main goal of restoration must therefore be to avoid emissions, much more than reinstating peat carbon sequestration.

14.6 Restoration of peat swamps

Restoration projects in South East Asian peatlands began a decade ago. These pioneering projects aimed primarily at restoring the climate- and water-regulation services while at the same time reinstalling provisioning services of peat swamps and reducing poverty by actively involving local communities in restoration and rehabilitation. A number of technical restoration guidelines and reports provide detail on the activities and outcomes of these projects (e.g. Giesen 2004; 2009; van Eijk and Leenman 2004; Adinugroho *et al.* 2005; Nuyim 2005; Suryadiputra *et al.* 2005; Wibisono *et al.* 2005; CKPP 2008; Hooijer *et al.* 2008; Euroconsult Mott MacDonald/Deltares-Delft Hydraulics *et al.* 2008, 2009a, b; Giesen and van der Meer 2009).

Table 14.2 Impacts of human activities on peat swamp forest ecosystem services. Note that impacts of low-intensity land use (e.g. selective logging) on ecosystem functioning and services as described in the upper part always occur with higher severity under more intense land use such as clear-cutting or agricultural conversion. (Sources: Silvius et al. 1984; Bruenig 1990, 1996; Klepper 1992; Silvius and Giesen 1996; Kobayashi 2000; Giesen 2004; van Eijk and Leenman 2004; Hooijer 2005; Wibisono et al. 2005; Limin et al. 2007; Cochard et al. 2008; Hooijer et al. 2008, 2012; Page et al. 2009; Couwenberg, Dommain and Joosten 2010; Dommain, Couwenberg and Joosten 2010; Yule 2010; Jauhiainen et al. 2012).

Severity of degradation	Human activity	Affected ecosystem function	Impact on ecosystem function	Affected ecosystem service and specific damage	Restoration approaches
+	Selective logging of valuable timber without artificial drainage	Forest stability, resilience and succession; natural tree regeneration	Reduced tree regeneration, change of forest structure and productivity, lower biodiversity and less habitat for pollinators	Provision of timber and NTFPs – reduced resource availability	Enrichment planting and management
			Disruption of natural ecosystem development and reduction of functional diversity and resilience	Cultural services: spiritual, religious and educational values – loss of pristine forest, sacred places and wilderness	Potentially irreversible impact, ban of any further use and complete protection
		Biomass growth and peat accumulation	Reduced above-ground tree biomass	Climate regulation – reduced long-term carbon storage in timber	Replanting of native (late successional) peat swamp tree species

Intensity	Disturbance	Ecosystem function	Impact	Ecosystem service affected	Restoration measure
++	Intense logging with artificial drainage	Detention of runoff, (sub)surface storage	Reduced below-ground biomass growth and thus reduced peat formation	Climate regulation – reduced peat carbon sequestration	Replanting of mound- and buttress-forming tree species
		Water storage, maintenance of base flow	Reduced water storage and higher runoff losses, larger water-table fluctuations	Water regulation – increase in streamflow extremes (floods and low flows) in adjacent rivers	
			Reduced water storage, higher runoff losses, reduced and partly ceasing base flow	Provision of freshwater – reduced water availability particularly during dry periods	Canal blocking in cascade arrangement and reforestation; control of spreading secondary vegetation (ferns, vines) possibly needed; fire control likely required
		Persistence of wet, evergreen and fire-suppressing forest	Desiccation and proliferation of fire-adapted species, reduced fire suppression	Air quality and fire hazard regulation – increased fire risk, haze production, health hazards	
+++	Clear-cutting	Genetic inheritance, evolution, adaptation and speciation	Extinction of local populations and endemic species, loss of genetic variability	Provision of genetic resources – loss of unique genetic information due to local or global extinctions	Irreversible in case of global extinctions, animal species might be reintroduced from captivity

Table 14.2 (cont.)

Severity of degradation	Human activity	Affected ecosystem function	Impact on ecosystem function	Affected ecosystem service and specific damage	Restoration approaches
		Forest stability, resilience and natural regeneration	Failing regeneration in absence of parental seed sources and dispersal agents	Provision of timber and NTFPs – completely depleted forest resources, local poverty	Requires water-table management (canal blocking/filling), fire control and extensive reforestation programmes, including mound planting; rewetting constrained by subsidence, reforestation hampered by fires and/or flooding. It will take decades to develop natural water storage and retention structures, thus artificial structures (ridges, pools) may be needed; rehabilitation by paludiculture.

Forest floor stability	Peat erosion and loss of dissolved and particulate organic carbon (DOC, POC)	Mass flow (erosion) regulation – higher sediment load and deposition and reduced water quality in rivers, lakes and sea
Nutrient cycling and retention	Leaching of nutrients	Water quality regulation – additional nutrient supply to adjacent rivers, lakes and sea
	Disruption of nutrient cycling and depletion of nutrient stock	Soil quality regulation and provision of fertile land – loss of soil fertility and ecosystem productivity
Forest transpiration	Loss of tree-mediated transpiration, meso- and microclimatic change	Climate regulation – warmer ambient temperatures and decreasing rainfall

Table 14.2 (cont.)

Severity of degradation	Human activity	Affected ecosystem function	Impact on ecosystem function	Affected ecosystem service and specific damage	Restoration approaches
++++	Agricultural conversion including deep drainage, liming and fertilisation	Biomass growth and peat accumulation	Peat consolidation and continuous subsidence, acid sulfate soil exposure and related acidification	Food provision – reduced crop yields, loss of productive land, poverty	After protracted use, adaptation (by diking and pumping) is very expensive; restoration to peat swamp forest impossible under inundated conditions. Rehabilitation by paludiculture
			Rapid peat oxidation	Climate regulation – high CO_2 and N_2O emissions, global warming	
		Near coast: lateral dome expansion, freshwater discharge	Loss of surface height and peat mass, increased deep flooding, permanent inundation, salt water intrusion and salinisation	Hazard regulation (flooding) and provision of freshwater – reduced shoreline protection, increased tsunami vulnerability, reduced freshwater availability, loss of productive/habitable land	

Note: Severity of degradation: + low, ++ moderate, +++ high, ++++ very high

Table 14.3 Annual CO_2 emissions in 1990 and 2008 from drainage-related peat decomposition for Malaysia and western Indonesia (Sumatra and Kalimantan) (fire-related emissions excluded).

Land-cover type*	Year			1990				2008			
	Mean drainage depth (cm)	CO_2 emissions (t ha^{-1} yr^{-1})	Area drained (%)	Land-cover area (ha)	%	Total CO_2 emissions (t yr^{-1})	Emission contribution (%)	Land-cover area (ha)	%	Total CO_2 emissions (t yr^{-1})	Emission contribution (%)
Water	0	0	0	70,000	0.4	0	0	69 000	0.4	0	0
Seasonal water	0	0	0	207 000	1.3	0	0	306 000	2	0	0
Pristine PSF	0	−2.57	0	7 581 000	48.9	−19 457 900	0	1 560 000	10.1	−4 004 000	0
Degraded PSF	35	35	50	4 043 000	26.1	70 752 500	29	4 912 000	31.7	85 960 000	16
Tall shrub/ sec. forest	35	35	50	753 000	4.9	13 177 500	5	1 311 000	8.5	22 942 500	4
Low shrub/ ferns	35	35	50	708 000	4.6	12 390 000	5	1 673 000	10.8	29 277 500	6
Smallholder agriculture	80	80	100	1 515 000	9.8	121 200 000	50	2 759 000	17.8	220 720 000	42
Industrial plantations	70	70	100	304 000	2	21 280 000	9	2 278 000	14.7	159 460 000	30
Built-up area**	–	0	–	19 000	0.1	0	0	32 000	0.2	0	0

Table 14.3 (cont.)

Land-cover type*	Mean drainage depth (cm)	CO_2 emissions (t ha^{-1} yr^{-1})	Area drained (%)	Year 1990				Year 2008			
				Land-cover area (ha)	%	Total CO_2 emissions (t yr^{-1})	Emission contribution (%)	Land-cover area (ha)	%	Total CO_2 emissions (t yr^{-1})	Emission contribution (%)
Cleared/burnt area	35	35	50	235 000	1.5	4 112 500	2	551 000	3.6	9 642 500	2
Mangrove	0	0	0	69 000	0.4	0	0	51 000	0.3	0	0
Total				15 502 000	100			15 502 000	100		
Total annual CO_2 emissions (t)						223 454 600				523 998 500	

PSF = peat swamp forest. *Land-cover distribution based on Miettinen and Liew (2010). ** Built-up area assumed to be completely sealed. CO_2 emissions are based on a linear relationship with drainage depth: 10 t CO_2 ha^{-1} yr^{-1} for each 10 cm of drainage (see Couwenberg, Dommain and Joosten 2010, Hooijer et al. 2012); CO_2 emissions continue to increase up to a drainage depth of 100 cm (Hooijer et al. 2012). Peat carbon sequestration in pristine peat swamp forest is assumed to be 0.7 t C ha^{-1} yr^{-1} (Dommain, Couwenberg and Joosten 2011) and indicated by negative CO_2 emissions.

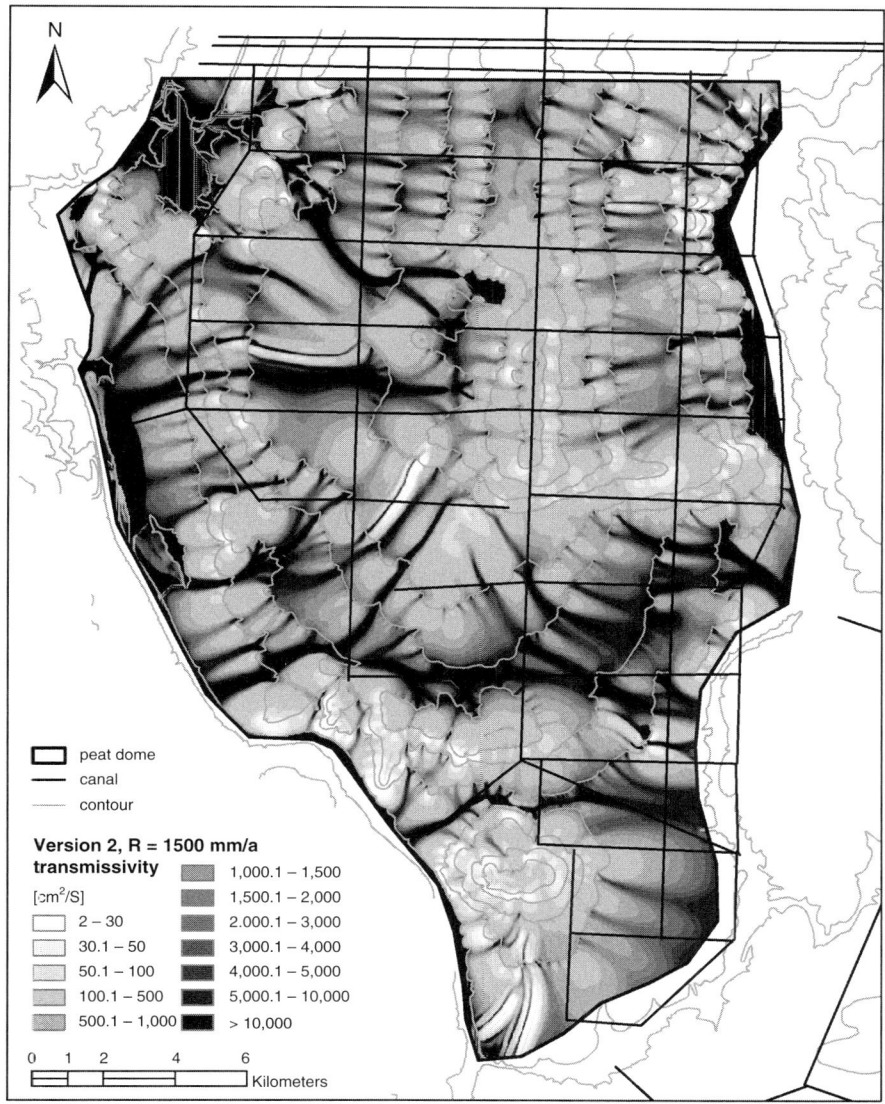

Figure 14.3 Transmissivity of Block A north – Ex-Mega Rice Project area, based on a digital elevation model with 1 m contour intervals (grey lines) and water balance modelling for the period January 2007 to November 2008. Note the dense network of drainage canals (black lines).

14.6.1 Hydrological restoration

Under the humid equatorial climate, most months of the year experience atmospheric water surplus (Hooijer 2005; Dittrich 2009). In pristine peat swamps most of this excess water cannot be stored in the (saturated) peat deposit and will run off over the peat dome surface to adjacent rivers. This

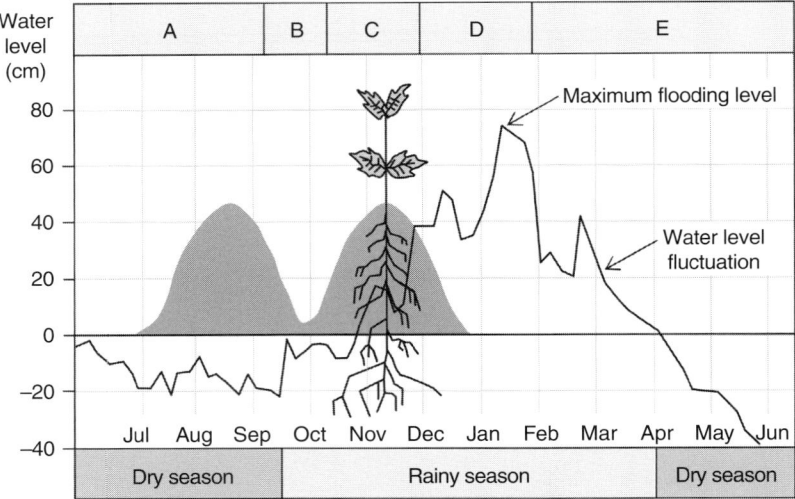

Figure 14.4 Mound-planting reforestation strategy in relation to changing water levels as implemented in the CCFPI project (modified from Wibisono et al. 2005). Planting stages are: A = mound construction, seedling preparation and hardening off; B = seedling transportation; C = planting; D = stop activity; E = seedling maintenance.

runoff follows a coherent pattern (Figure 14.3) that has evolved over thousands of years in an iterative, self-organising process of dome shape development and vegetation structure adjustment (Dommain, Couwenberg and Joosten 2010). Water flow intensity is consequently unevenly distributed over a peat dome (Figure 14.3), with different adapted vegetation types characterising these different areas. Human activities have impacted both water flow intensity and direction (by impacting vegetation and excavating drainage canals), and dome shape (by fires, peatland subsidence and peat decomposition). Restoration must aim at bringing vegetation, hydrology and dome shape into balance again in order to stop or reduce degradation.

When the original flow paths are interrupted and shortened by drainage canals or clear-cutting, long-distance flow lines change to short-path flows and both the volume and duration of surface and subsurface storage decrease. Ditches parallel to the slope increase discharge to the dome edge, whereas ditches cut perpendicular to the slope cut off water supply to downslope areas. In order to increase water storage, reconnect former flow paths and restore recharge to downstream areas it is essential to block drainage canals. With the aid of a flow path model such as shown in Figure 14.3, optimal locations for dams can be identified. Natural flow channels should not be blocked as this would likely result in dam failure, especially during

Table 14.4 Canal-blocking activities in Indonesia.

Project	Location(s)	No. of dams	Size of dam	Year	Agency	Remarks
CCFPI	Merang (South Sumatra)	12	small	2004	WIIP	Dams removed following conversion to plantations in 2006
	Block E (Mawas), Block A north (ex-MRP area), (Central Kalimantan)	7	large (14–27 m wide)	2004–2005	WIIP	Most stable design: steel wire reinforcement, constant maintenance
CKPP	Block A north (ex-MRP area), (Central Kalimantan)	18	large (11–20 m wide)	2005–2008	WIIP	Overall 900 people employed in canal blocking, constant maintenance and hydrological monitoring network
	Sebangau NP (Central Kalimantan)	6	large (9–17 m wide)	2005–2008	WWF	
		263	small	2005–2008	UNPAR, WWF	
RESTOR-PEAT	Block C (ex-MRP area), (Central Kalimantan)	7	large (up to 25 m wide)	since 2004	CIMTROP	
	Sebangau NP, (Central Kalimantan)	50	small	since 2004	CIMTROP	

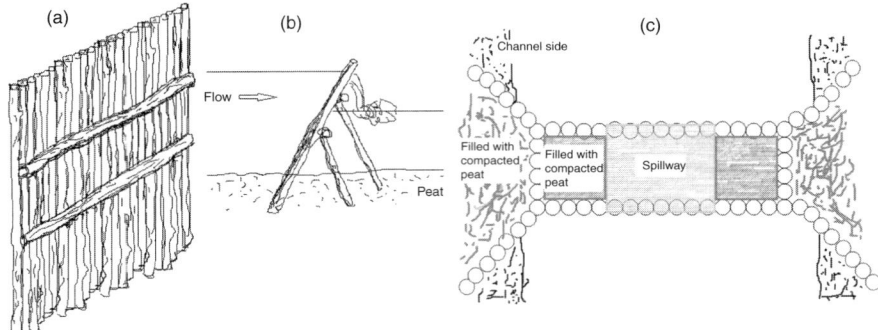

Figure 14.5 Dam designs. (a) Traditional vertical palisade design; (b) leaning palisade design; (c) double-palisade design with modification adopted to CKPP dams (figures not to scale). Drawing by Dipa S. Rais.

Figure 14.6 Dam construction by Wetlands International as part of the CKPP project: construction using (a) traditional techniques by local people; (b) palisade dam; (c) double-palisade dam with spillway.

the wet season, and would also reduce recharge to downslope areas. Closing canals is, however, not sufficient to restore the hydrology, as the vegetation performs an important hydrological function through temporal storage of surplus water at the surface and subsurface through both stagnating and porous plant material (Dommain, Couwenberg and Joosten 2010). Here a flow path model also provides a template for reforestation, because location, density and species to be planted must be compatible with the local flow intensities determining hydrologic stability. In areas with high-profile discharge, flood-tolerant or floating species that form highly conducting vegetation (e.g. *Pandanus* spp., *Hanguana malayana*, *Mallotus sumatranus*,

Combretocarpus rotundatus) are more promising (for more species, see van Eijk and Leenman, 2004; Giesen 2009). Areas with low-profile discharge are preferable sites for planting with buttress- and mound-forming trees to increase surface roughness and depression storage.

Vegetation structure and dynamics can regulate surface hydrology much more finely than static dams, for instance by spreading water flow. While the development of natural forest structures will take decades, artificially constructed mounds and ridges can mitigate the effects of an over-steepened slope in strongly subsided areas by reducing runoff velocities. Mounds also facilitate the establishment of tree seedlings in areas of large water table fluctuations (section 14.6.2; Figure 14.4). To be successful, restoration therefore has to combine closing artificial drainage paths with the re-establishment of tree cover.

Projects that included hydrological restoration activities (i.e. canal blocking) were implemented in Indonesia (mainly in the province of Central Kalimantan; Table 14.4) and on a small scale in Selangor state, Malaysia. In the projects Climate Change, Forest and Peatlands in Indonesia (CCFPI) and the Central Kalimantan Peatland Project (CKPP), and in WWF's hydrological restoration programme for Sebangau National Park, wooden dams were constructed in a vertical palisade design based on traditional technology (Figure 14.5) and placed in cascade arrangement up the peat dome slopes (Suryadiputra *et al.* 2005; CKKP 2008). The sharpened logs are manually inserted, preferably down into the mineral subsoil (Figure 14.6). Spillways on large dams allow discharge of excess water (Figures 14.5 and 14.6). Some of the blocked canals were also used as fish ponds to provide livelihood benefits to local communities (Suryadiputra *et al.* 2005; CKPP 2008). Dam construction costs vary depending on size, design, accessibility of the area and distance to material sources. Small dams (2 m wide) cost between USD 80 and 220 each, whereas the large double-palisade dams (15–30 m wide) built by the Wetlands International – Indonesia Programme (WIIP) cost between USD 2750 and 11 000 each (Suryadiputra *et al.* 2005).

14.6.2 Peat swamp reforestation

Peat swamp forest reforestation has been attempted in South East Asia during the past decade with mixed success. Some examples are summarised in Table 14.5. In Thailand, replanting has been relatively successful using nursery seedlings and improving soil fertility (Nuyim 2000, 2005). In Malaysia, reforestation activities never moved beyond an early stage. In Indonesia, at least 31 indigenous tree species (out of over 700 known peat swamp forest trees; Box 14.1) have been used in various reforestation projects and planting trials in Sumatra and Kalimantan. Some programmes involved replanting of

Table 14.5 *Peatland reforestation activities in South East Asia.*

Country	Activities and experiences	References
Thailand	The Royal Forest Service has over the last 10 years replanted 640 ha with nursery-grown seedlings, the most successful regeneration occurring with *Ganua motleyana*, *Melaleuca cajuputi*, *Syzygium oblatum*, *Syzygium pyrifolium*, *Sterculia bicolor*, *Sandoricum beccarianum*, *Alstonia spathulata*, *Calophyllum teysmannii*, *Ixora grandifolia* and *Alstonia spathulata*.	Nuyim (2000, 2005)
Malaysia	Limited to trials and small-scale activities undertaken by the Forestry Department and Forest Research Institute Malaysia (FRIM). Of various techniques used, the most successful was through open planting of *Anisoptera marginata*, *Ganua* (*Madhuca*) *motleyana*, *Gonystylus bancanus* and *Shorea platycarpa*.	Ismael Parlan (2006, pers. comm.); Giesen and van der Meer (2009)
Indonesia	The most successful regeneration programme was the planting of 2120 ha of mainly *Dyera polyphylla* by PT Dyera Hutan Lestari in Jambi province of Sumatra, who then extracted latex from the plantation. Sadly, the plantation succumbed to fire in 2008 and was abandoned. Elsewhere in Sumatra and Kalimantan, at least 31 indigenous tree species have been used by various reforestation projects and planting trials. Both young seedlings from remaining peat swamp forest and nursery-grown seedlings have been used.	Wibisono *et al.* (2005); Wibisono and Wardoyo (2008); Euroconsult Mott MacDonald and Deltares/Delft Hydraulics (2009a); Giesen and van der Meer (2009a)

seedlings collected in the wild, but most involved seed collection, establishment of nurseries and planting and tending programmes.

Naturally regenerating tree species should preferably be used in replanting activities (van Eijk *et al.* 2009). The major constraints for reforestation are fires (following clearing and drainage) and flooding (following (repeated) fires) (Giesen 2004; van Eijk and Leenman 2004; Wösten *et al.* 2006; van Eijk *et al.* 2009). Hydrological restoration to reduce fire incidence and raise water levels in drained areas is thus essential for successful reforestation. To increase survival rates of seedlings they can be planted on artificial mounds (30–50 cm tall), which reduce the risk of prolonged inundation (Figure 14.4; Wibisono *et al.* 2005). However, deep flooding can cause complete failure of replanting trials and over deeply inundated areas (water levels >100 cm) have no prospect of sustaining tree regeneration and reforestation (Wösten *et al.* 2006; van Eijk *et al.* 2009).

The total cost of a 3-year peat swamp forest rehabilitation programme is about USD 1000 per hectare; this includes sourcing of planting material, site preparation, labour, transportation costs, planting, immediate tending, maintenance and monitoring in years two and three, and replacement planting (Euroconsult Mott MacDonald and Deltares-Delft Hydraulics 2009a).

14.6.3 Fire prevention and mitigation activities

Linking of fire prevention and mitigation measures are crucial to restoration activities, and were carried out in the CCFPI and CKPP projects through awareness-raising campaigns, the establishment of early warning systems and use of fire brigades. For example, in 2006 the Wetlands International – Indonesia Programme conducted training with farmers from Mantangai subdistrict (ex-MRP area) to practice zero burning in land preparation and to use compost in rice cultivation. In the CKPP project, 25 village fire brigades (total of 399 firefighters) with an extinguishing capacity of 1.75 ha per hour were established and trained under the coordination of CARE and the University of Palangka Raya. Over 120 deep-water wells were drilled in the ex-MRP area and in the buffer zone of Sebangau National Park, and regular fire monitoring and reporting was conducted (CKPP 2008). During the 2006 El Niño event, fire-fighting teams extinguished fires over an area of 4650 ha – a little more than 1% of the 400 000 ha fire-affected ex-MRP area in that year. Fire control remains an enormous problem.

14.6.4 Challenges in peat swamp restoration

Peat swamp restoration can only be a long-term success if peat domes are taken as hydrological units and piecemeal approaches are abandoned. Off-site drainage effects emerge as a major challenge in the conservation of peat swamp forest remnants, with future restoration sites requiring costly hydrological isolation measures (e.g. sheet piling). Entire peat domes are normally not available for restoration. Most peat domes are now fragmented into different land-use types and concessions do not follow hydrological catchment boundaries. This situation worsens with the rapid expansion of tree crop plantations into most remaining peat swamp areas outside national parks. When restoration areas border such actively drained areas on the same peat dome, water levels cannot be raised sufficiently because drainage and associated subsidence of the used peat dome areas continuously lower the water table mound that sustains the entire peat dome (Hooijer et al. 2012). Peat dome fragmentation may consequently offset any rewetting efforts in restoration areas.

Regional climate seasonality can also limit rewetting success. Water balance modelling shows that Central Kalimantan experiences periods of pronounced water deficit, which may last for up to 4 months (Dittrich 2009). Even in undrained peat domes these droughts diminish the soil-water storage to an extent that base flow to rivers may cease and fire risk increases. These results differ from the hydro-climatic situation in Sarawak, where such periods are extremely rare (Hooijer 2005), and highlight that water storage prior to and during the dry season is of paramount importance in peat swamp restoration in Indonesia. Large-scale deforestation and drainage in Kalimantan might have already exacerbated drought severity while the long-term climate effects of deforestation in South East Asia certainly include reduced precipitation (e.g. Hoffmann et al., 2003) – an issue that needs further scientific attention.

Restoring the hydrology of tropical peat domes is not a simple process, due to the complexity of the hydrology and effects of peat subsidence. The major difficulties in rewetting densely drained and deforested peat domes are illustrated by the example of Block A north (Ex-MRP area, Figures 14.1 and 14.3), which is the largest rewetting effort in Indonesia to date. Rewetting extensively subsided peatlands through canal blockage may only affect parts of the restoration areas along dammed canals. Dam construction in Block A north resulted in a difference of canal water levels up- and downstream of dams of 1 m in the wet season and up to 2.5 m during the dry season. Despite such substantial water retention in the canals, the dry season groundwater table near canals was still around 1 m below the surface, leaving the peat soil still highly fire prone with subsidence and oxidative peat decomposition continuing at high rates. Hydrological modelling for this area indicates that the actual rise of groundwater tables is restricted to a 600 m-wide zone around canals and that groundwater tables consequently rose over less than 25% of the area (Hooijer *et al.* 2008). Remote-sensing data indicate an even smaller rewetted area, but show that fires during the 2009 El Niño did not spread into this wetter zone (Jaenicke *et al.* 2011). Depending on canal gradients, the influence of canal blocking normally extends only a few kilometres upstream of a dam. In most rewetting schemes dam spacing thus needs to be narrower to allow raising of the groundwater to desired levels. Reaching the target level of 40 cm below surface in the dry season in Block A would require at least 90 dams instead of the existing 25 (e.g. Hooijer *et al.* 2008). Successful rewetting in Block A is furthermore constrained by a decade of severe peat subsidence forming a new surface relief of mini-domes (approximately 2.5 × 5 km in size) across the original interfluvial peat dome. Drainage canals now lie in depressions 1 m or more below the adjacent peatland surface, so that dams have little effect beyond the immediate vicinity of the dam (Hooijer *et al.* 2008; Euroconsult Mott MacDonald and Deltares-Delft Hydraulics 2009b).

In order to increase success, hydrological restoration efforts need to:

- involve indigenous and local communities in all project stages in order to clarify and respect land-tenure and land-use rights
- use hydrological models to predict the ideal locations, arrangement and number of dams (general rule: head differences <0.4 m between two dams)
- ensure stable dam design (filling material preferably sand and clay bags; steel wire enforcement)
- ensure regular maintenance of dams (also beyond project lifetimes)
- apply 'green engineering': plant trees and herbaceous plants with different flooding tolerance in canals and along canal sides to increase hydraulic resistance (Giesen 2009; Giesen and van der Meer 2009)
- infill canals mechanically in accessible areas.

(For further technical details see Euroconsult Mott MacDonald and Deltares-Delft Hydraulics *et al.* 2009a,b)

Next to technical and eco-hydrological challenges, social aspects may limit the success of hydrological interventions. Even though community engagement in previous CCFPI and CKPP restoration projects in the Ex-Mega Rice Project area was unprecedented, not all communities could be involved, either due to funding limitations or occupation preferences. Most local people participating in the projects were farmers and fisherman. Hunters and gatherers were reluctant to participate as they regarded dams as obstacles to their daily occupation. With the disappearance of nearby forests in the ex-MRP area, these people need to travel long distances to reach remaining forests and often use canals as transportation routes (Suyanto *et al.* 2009). In consequence, they may intentionally damage dams or dig new navigation canals around them. Also in other areas local people or illegal loggers breach dams on purpose to access timber or other forest resources. Success of hydrological restoration for climate and water regulation can only be guaranteed when hydrological measures are paralleled by restoring the provisioning services of peat swamps, through enrichment planting, reforestation or paludiculture.

14.7 Sustainable land management: paludiculture

Restoration measures in uncultivated peatlands alone are not sufficient to effectively reduce fire occurrence and carbon emissions from peatlands. Conventional agriculture on peatland in South East Asia involves drainage and, in the case of smallholder farming, the annual use of fire. Therefore, substantial emission reductions require a shift from drainage-based agriculture on peat soils to wet (i.e. waterlogged) cultivation techniques (Chapter 17). Paludiculture in South East Asia should principally be tree based to ensure peat preservation and possibly peat formation. Establishment of paludicultures can provide economic incentives to develop degraded areas into wet buffer zones around remaining 'pristine' peat swamp forest areas, and contribute to poverty alleviation. Paludicultures can build up existing wet production techniques and be adopted in ongoing smallholder farming, but also in industrial plantation settings, and may include wet, mixed agroforestry and intercropping schemes (see Kartawinata and Satjapradja 1983). Of the more than 1300 plant species found in undisturbed peat swamp forests, at least 534 have one or multiple known uses, including 222 timber species, 221 medicinal plants and 165 food species (Giesen 2013). Many of these were in the past used by indigenous people. However, the knowledge on these species is rapidly lost with ongoing destruction of swamp forests and changing livelihoods. Use of peat swamps is not restricted to harvesting profitable timber, but also includes a wide range of NTFPs which played an essential role as livelihood sources prior to the era of commercial logging, and still do so in remaining peat swamp forest patches (Suyanto *et al.* 2009). The variety of NTFPs providing peat swamp plants (> 500 species) includes edible fruit trees (e.g. *Durio carinatus*, *Nephelium* spp., *Mangifera* spp*.*, *Garcinia* spp.), rattan palms (*Korthalsia flagellaris*, *Calamus* spp), fat/oil-producing plants (e.g. *Shorea* spp., *Palaquium* spp.), latex-producing trees (e.g. *Dyera polyphylla*, *Palaquium* spp.), resin-producing trees (*Shorea* spp.), dye/tannin-producing plants (e.g. *Fibraurea tinctoria*), fibre plants (e.g. *Pandanus* sp., *Lepironia articulata*) and medicinal plants (e.g. *Alseodaphne coriacea, Ilex cymosa*) (e.g. Soepadmo 1995; Ramakrishna 2004; Giesen and van der Meer 2009;

Suyanto *et al.* 2009; Giesen 2013). The popularity of several of these species (e.g. *Dyera polyphylla*, *Alseodaphne coriacea*) and of commercially valuable timbers (e.g. *Gonystylus bancanus*) has often caused overexploitation or even local species extinction in the natural habitat (e.g. Bruenig 1996; Suyanto *et al.* 2009). A first step to counteract product scarcity and improve species stocks is the establishment of mixed-tree gardens or plantations of these useful plants. Such wet agroforestry would be a quasi *in situ* conservation measure for the cultivated species. Many peat swamp species have commercial value, which should stimulate market-oriented cultivation not only by local communities, but also by the private and public sectors. For example, mixed rattan plantations with native trees as support were established in Central Kalimantan peatlands in the 1960s in response to growing demand for rattan (Suyanto *et al.* 2009). Furthermore, the large diversity of medicinal plants offers another lucrative area that deserves more attention (Soepadmo 1995).

Paludiculture in South East Asia could be applied in the following approaches:

- food production, intercropping and agroforestry in agriculturally used peatland such as transmigration areas or the Ex-Mega Rice Project area
- community forests and agroforestry in buffer zones of protected and rehabilitated peat swamp forests
- Production of bioenergy plants in deeply flooded areas with no prospect for reforestation
- large-scale mixed plantations of commercial peat swamp species as alternatives to drainage-based plantations.

14.7.1 Wet, mixed agroforestry and intercropping schemes for food production and NTFP products

In order to secure food production (a priority in peatlands inhabited by people), wet agroforestry and wet intercropping with native peat swamp forest trees and less flood-tolerant species growing on mounds and ridges on the shallow-sloping peat dome margins can be established. At least 84 fruit and 47 vegetable species from peat swamps are (locally) consumed and could be cultivated (Giesen 2013). Sago palm (*Metroxylon sagu*) is a suitable food crop because its yield is around ten times larger than that of rice on peat (Rijksen and Persoon 1991). Sago grows in freshwater swamp and on waterlogged, shallow peat soil with some throughflow. Still, it is of utmost importance to identify more food plants that grow on undrained peatland.

14.7.2 Community forests and agroforestry

In Indonesia, *hutan desa* (village forest) concessions allow both limited timber utilisation and agroforestry. These are similar to timber concessions but confined to an area of no more than 10 000 ha and only given to villages, not companies. Spatial zonation is possible through a combination of strictly protected and utilised areas. Ideally, *hutan desa* concessions should be combined with ecosystem restoration concessions. This new concession type is intended to protect and restore the ecosystem of degraded production forests over time spans of 60 or more years. It promotes replanting and the collection of NTFPs, but does not allow harvesting of timber. The synergistic use of both concession types would allow the utilisation of forest edges and adjacent agroforestry schemes by local communities (under *hutan desa*) while at the same time promoting the regeneration of disturbed peat swamp forest interiors (under ecosystem restoration) and thus reduce leakage by activity shifting in the case of carbon conservation projects.

14.7.3 Production of bioenergy plants in deeply flooded areas

Bioenergy paludiculture plants are successfully cultivated on rewetted peatlands in Europe (Chapter 17), and this seems similarly possible in South East Asia. Herbaceous plants for bioenergy production are available in flooded areas previously burnt. The sedges *Lepironia articulata* and *Eleocharis* spp. (both known as purun) often attain dominance in such now widely available environments. The below-ground biomass of *L. articulata* forms peat (Ikusima 1978), whereas the above-ground shoots are harvested as weaving material (Ramakrishna 2004). Its use as a biofuel, together with other available reed and aquatic species, needs to be explored. Herbaceous plants could be planted in blocked canals and other permanently flooded areas after rewetting.

14.7.4 Large-scale mixed plantations of commercial peat swamp species

The commercial plantation approach is intended (1) to transform existing drainage-based plantations into wet plantations and (2) to establish wet plantations of indigenous peat swamp trees on drained and deforested peatland fallows. A number of *Shorea* species from mineral and alluvial soils produce *tengkawang*, or illipe nuts, from which high-quality edible oil similar to butter fat is extracted (Kartawinata and Satjapradja 1983; Blicha-Mathiesen 1994). *Shorea* as typical elements of Bornean peat swamp forests are ideal species for paludiculture plantations, and test trials from West Kalimantan demonstrate that several oil-producing *Shorea* species can grow on peat and are tolerant to flooding (Giesen and van der Meer 2009; Giesen 2013). These *tengkawang* species are an alternative to oil palm on peat – certainly in terms of sustainability and product quality. Another promising species for commercial plantations is the latex-producing tree Jelutong (*Dyera polyphylla*) that has already been widely planted (e.g. Muuß 1996). For timber pulp production, exotic *Acacia* species are preferred for their low cost and extremely fast growth. Possible substitutes for *Acacia* are the species *Alstonia pneumatophora*, *Combretocarpus rotundatus* and *Macaranga pruinosa*. These species are fast-growing, partly fire-resistant pioneer species that often dominate early secondary forest stages after clearance or fires in peatlands and can partly withstand flooding (Nuyim 2000; van Eijk and Leenman 2004; Giesen and van der Meer 2009).

The successful spread of paludiculture requires demonstration sites and economic cost–benefit analyses to encourage local communities and political authorities. Funding can be sought from the industrial sector, avoided emission schemes (e.g. Verified Carbon Standard (VCS); Chapter 15) or the Bio-rights mechanism (Box 14.3). Special market incentives, for instance the certification of paludiculture products that would offer higher prices, could also attract farmers or plantation companies to move from drainage-based cultivation to paludiculture.

Paludiculture is an ideal component of reforestation and restoration projects as it guarantees peatland access and use of valuable species by local communities. This approach reduces conflicts between maintaining and enhancing carbon stocks and biodiversity, and maintaining local livelihoods and traditional land-use rights in specific project cases. It therefore also qualifies for Climate, Community and Biodiversity Standards. Paludiculture would sustain the peat swamp forest resources (peat, plants and water) and therefore counteract the poverty trap inherent in drainage- and fire-based agriculture or illegal land-use activities.

14.8 Conclusions and outlook

Restoration of damaged tropical domed peatlands is of pivotal importance for global climate regulation and biodiversity conservation. We showed that South East Asia's peat carbon stock is now rapidly being depleted, at a rate 24 times faster than it was sequestered. It is obvious that drained and burning peatlands emit disproportionally more carbon than pristine peatlands can sequester. Given the effects of continued drainage and the complexity of restoration, immediate action is required as severe degradation of tropical peatland is essentially irreversible. A major practical problem for restoration is the strongly varying water table, which is either too high or too low

Box 14.3

Payments for ecosystem services: the Bio-rights approach

Peatland degradation and destruction in South East Asia contributes to the spread of poverty in rural areas. With the destruction of peat swamp forests and adjoining ecosystems, local communities lose their traditional livelihoods and, as a consequence, often turn to environmentally non-sustainable activities such as illegal logging. In order to combat poverty and improve environmental conditions simultaneously, payments for ecosystem services to local communities are required. The experience of past and ongoing restoration projects has demonstrated that the involvement of local communities is a crucial factor for the success of conservation and restoration activities. Neglecting local communities may cause substantial resistance towards internationally funded projects. The Bio-rights approach is a financing mechanism that aims to harmonise conservation and restoration activities with poverty reduction (see van Eijk and Kumar 2009 and www.bio-rights.org). In the Bio-rights approach, business contracts are established between a global stakeholder, such as a NGO or a government, and a local community partner. The Bio-rights approach then involves three main steps (van Eijk and Kumar 2009):

- Local communities are provided with micro-credits to offset their opportunity costs from abandoning non-sustainable land-use practices and to allow for sustainable economic development while conserving natural resources and biodiversity.
- Interest is not repaid as money but in the form of biodiversity conservation or the protection of other ecosystem services, such as carbon sequestration.
- With successful delivery of conservation targets, micro-credits may be transformed into definitive payments or community-based revolving funds.

This funding mechanism thus guarantees sustainable livelihoods for local communities and the protection of ecosystem services and natural resources for future generations.

Since 2001, the Bio-rights approach has been implemented in peatland projects in three Indonesian provinces (Jambi, South Sumatra and Central Kalimantan) under the coordination of the Wetlands International – Indonesia Programme and with the support of international funding. Under the Wetlands and Poverty Reduction Program (WPRP) funded by the Dutch Ministry of Foreign Affairs (DGIS), local communities of West Tanjung Jabung district (Jambi) and Musi Banyu Asin district (South Sumatra) received micro-credits to improve their income through various agricultural activities, in exchange for their collective efforts in peatland rehabilitation programmes (i.e. planting indigenous

> trees in degraded peatlands). In Central Kalimantan, local communities of Mentangai village were actively involved in the CCFPI and CKPP projects. They received financial support for livelihood improvement as rewards for their active role in reforestation (Jelutong plantations), fire prevention and canal blocking.

for the regeneration of peat swamp forests. The narrow range of water table fluctuations in natural peat swamps can, if at all, only be restored with substantial technical interventions over large areas and considerable human resources over long time horizons.

A major challenge for peat swamp conservation and restoration is human-induced fires. Fires threaten all peatland forests and create a very large source of GHGs. Another El Niño-induced fire event of the severity of that in 1997/98 might totally destroy the remaining peat swamp fragments. Climate models predict future reduction of dry season rainfall over parts of South East Asia (Li et al. 2007), which implies an increasing risk of fire. This risk calls for urgent and widespread rewetting of all drained, disturbed and unused peatlands and proactive fire control measures to mitigate fire risk. Wherever possible, restoration should address entire peat domes as hydrological units.

Next to fires, marine inundation due to continuous subsidence will become a serious problem for the prevalent coastal peatland areas, particularly in view of ongoing and future sea-level rise (cf. Hooijer et al. 2015). Restoration will therefore contribute to the preservation of coastal areas, productive land and human settlements.

The destruction of South East Asia's tropical peat swamp forests is undoubtedly one of the most severe ecological disasters of recent times. In Malaysia vast areas of peat swamp forest have been destroyed and converted to monotonous oil palm plantations, including the entire, 420 km^2, globally unique Baram peat dome with its six phasic peat swamp forest communities – a classic site of peat swamp forest research (Anderson 1983; Figure 14.2). Brunei has most peat swamp forests included in the transboundary 'Heart of Borneo' conservation initiative, but its best remaining peat domes in the Belait District (Figure 14.1) are threatened by cross-boundary drainage and fire from adjacent Sarawak. Indonesia's ambitious CO_2 emission reduction pledges, strong support for REDD+ and new draft regulations to conserve peat swamps (RPP Gambut, RPP

Rawa) stand in sharp contrast to the continuing allocation of peatland areas to agricultural conversion (see Miettinen *et al.* 2012a). To meet its CO_2 emission target reduction of 26% by 2020 (Presidential Decree No. 61 2011), Indonesia must strictly protect all remaining peat swamp forests (including the nearly 6 million hectares in Papua), stop the conversion of degraded peat forests to plantations, and start rehabilitating degraded sites by enrichment planting, rewetting and paludiculture. The newly created ecosystem restoration concession type seems to be a promising tool to make extensive forest rehabilitation and conservation a reality. This concession type, in which the Indonesian government sets aside land for restoration and implicitly carries the short-term opportunity costs of alternative land use, might be the only possibility to make conservation of natural peat swamp ecosystem services (Table 14.2) – for the lasting benefit of the Indonesian people – competitive with highly profitable, but unsustainable, palm oil production (Silber 2011).

The future of the peat swamp forests of Sundaland hangs in the balance. A window of opportunity remains to halt the disaster, to conserve the last remnants and to begin the restoration of this forest with its extraordinary biodiversity and carbon reservoir. It is, though, a window of opportunity that is rapidly closing.

Acknowledgements

The Central Kalimantan Peatlands Project (CKPP) and the Master Plan for the Rehabilitation and Revitalisation of the Ex-Mega Rice Project area were funded by the Dutch Ministry of Foreign Affairs (DGIS). The authors wish to thank the CKPP consortium partners: World Wide Fund for Nature (WWF), The Borneo Orang-utan Survival Foundation (BOSF), CARE International Indonesia and the University of Palangka Raya. The CCFPI was funded under the Canada Climate Change Development Fund by the Canadian International Development Agency (CIDA). Special thanks go to Alue Duhong, Jill Heyde, Reza Lubis, Yus Rusila Noor, Nyoman Suryadiputra and Aswin Usup. Karin Kessler kindly produced the flow path model. We thank John Couwenberg, Paul Glaser and an anonymous reviewer for constructive comments on the manuscript. R.D. and H.J. acknowledge support from the German Federal Ministry of Education and Research (BMBF) for the project 'VIP – Vorpommern Initiative für Paludikultur' (no. 033L030A).

PART III

Socio-economic and political solutions to managing natural capital and peatland ecosystem services

CHAPTER FIFTEEN

International carbon policies as a new driver for peatland restoration

HANS JOOSTEN
Institute of Botany and Landscape Ecology, Ernst Moritz Arndt University of Greifswald, Germany
JOHN COUWENBERG
Institute of Botany and Landscape Ecology, Ernst Moritz Arndt University of Greifswald, Germany
MORITZ VON UNGER
Atlas Environmental Law Advisory, Belgium

15.1 Introduction

When – in 2006 – experts and advocacy groups for the first time raised the issue of GHG emissions from degraded peatlands at the United Nations Framework Convention on Climate Change (UNFCCC), they met with negotiators, many of whom had never heard of 'peat' in the first place. Six years later, the UNFCCC allowed countries to comply with their reduction commitments by peatland rewetting and included peat soils in the REDD+ mechanism to reduce emissions from tropical deforestation. After years of neglect, peatlands have gained the attention that they deserve in the face of their enormous emissions and mitigation potential (Chapter 4).

This chapter discusses the potentials and complications of using climate change mitigation policies for stimulating and financing peatland restoration using the Climate Convention, in the context of voluntary carbon markets and through policies with indirect climate targets.

Many land use-oriented mitigation mechanisms have been developed with a forest bias, i.e. from the perspective of biomass carbon stocks. In using existing approaches to address peatlands, concepts and criteria thus have to be modified, complemented or newly developed to accommodate the specific peculiarities of peatlands – often after wearying awareness raising.

Peatland Restoration and Ecosystem Services: Science, Policy and Practice, eds. A. Bonn, T. Allott, M. Evans, H. Joosten and R. Stoneman. Published by Cambridge University Press. © British Ecological Society 2016.

Market-based instruments are recognised as important elements of the international climate finance architecture. Since the entry into force of the Kyoto Protocol (2005), about 3 billion Kyoto units, each of these representing 1 t CO_2e, have been traded at least once for prices ranging from less than 1 EUR per unit to 20 EUR and more. The annual market value of national and subnational cap-and-trade systems (outside Kyoto) stands at USD 30 billion (World Bank 2014). These large sums, in combination with the huge carbon stocks in peatlands, have nurtured the idea that peatland restoration is an effective way of tapping into climate finance. However, reality is more complicated – as this chapter will show.

Beyond carbon trading proper, this chapter also addresses some future options for stimulating peatland restoration. Large peatland emissions occur both in industrialised and developing countries (Figure 15.1), and the ongoing negotiations within the post-2020 climate framework offer various opportunities to create peatland restoration incentives.

15.2 The United Nations Framework Convention on Climate Change (UNFCCC)

15.2.1 Introduction

The UNFCCC was adopted at the United Nations Conference on Environment and Development (UNCED) in Rio de Janeiro (1992) and entered into force in 1994. At present (2015), UNFCCC has 196 parties, including all United Nations member states, as well as Niue, Cook Islands and the European Union. The UNFCCC has as its ultimate objective to achieve 'stabilisation of GHG concentrations in the atmosphere at a level that would prevent dangerous anthropogenic interference with the climate system' (UNFCCC art. 2).

Progress with respect to this goal is monitored by means of GHG inventories that all parties regularly have to submit. Reporting covers six sectors: energy; industrial processes; solvents; agriculture; land use, land-use change and forestry (LULUCF); and waste. With regard to LULUCF the reporting is done for six land-use categories, which – while tolerating national approaches – are strictly defined. These categories have a distinct hierarchy with forests at the top and wetlands at the lower end (Table 15.1). Only GHG fluxes from land management are included, those from natural, undisturbed ecosystems are not.

'Peatland' is explicitly mentioned in the definition of the land category Wetlands, but in fact emissions from peatlands (organic soils) may occur in all LULUCF categories (and the sector agriculture). Countries should – but often fail to – apply different rules to mineral and organic soils in their UNFCCC reporting and Kyoto Protocol accounting (see below). Indeed, the

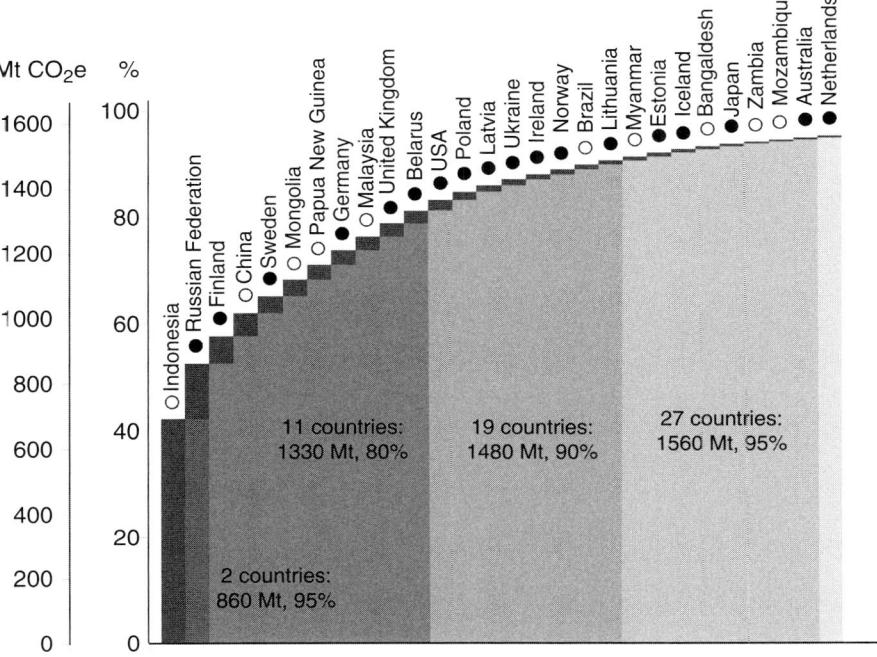

Figure 15.1 Key countries with emissions from organic soils (peat; emisisons from fire excluded). The graph shows the amount of GHG emissions in a cumulative way in Mt CO_2e per year (Mt = million tonnes), with each country's black bar representing the percentage of the total global emissions from degrading organic soils. Emissions are shown for the 28 countries responsible for most of the emissions, in descending order. White circles denote non-Annex 1 (developing) countries, black circles Annex 1 (developed) countries. The five shades of grey indicate where the 50, 80, 90 and 95 per cent marks are crossed. Data collated by Alexandra Barthelmes, John Couwenberg and Cosima Tegetmeyer; analysis and figure by John Couwenberg.

presence or absence of peat has enormous consequences for the GHG emissions from land (Chapter 4).

15.2.2 The Kyoto Protocol (KP)

The Kyoto Protocol is the only legally binding mechanism within the Climate Convention. The Protocol was adopted in 1997 and entered into force in 2005. Currently (2015), the Protocol has been ratified by 192 of the 196 UNFCCC Parties, the most important exception being the United States, in 1990 by far the largest emitter worldwide. Other non-members are Andorra and South Sudan; Canada cancelled its membership in 2011, when facing

Table 15.1 Overview of land categories in the UNFCCC and activities that are mandatory or can be voluntarily elected in Kyoto Protocol accounting for the first (2008–12) and second (2013–20) commitment periods. In principle, Kyoto Protocol activities have no relation to UNFCCC categories, although with respect to forest management and cropland management a compelling link is made.

Land-use categories under the UNFCCC		Activities under the Kyoto Protocol			
Name	Definition (after IPCC 2003 GPG LULUCF)	Name	Definition (after 16/CMP.1)	2008–12	2013–20
Forest land	All land with woody vegetation, including vegetation that currently falls below, but is expected to exceed, the threshold of forest land	Afforestation	The direct human-induced conversion of land that has not been forested for a period of at least 50 years to forested land	Mandatory	Mandatory
		Deforestation	The direct human-induced conversion of non-forested land to forested land	Mandatory	Mandatory
		Reforestation	The direct human-induced conversion of forested land to non-forested land	Mandatory	Mandatory
		Forest management	A system of practices for stewardship and use of forest land aimed at fulfilling relevant ecological … economic and social functions of the forest …	Voluntary	Mandatory

Cropland	Arable and tillage land, and agroforestry systems where vegetation falls below the threshold used for forest land	Cropland management	The system of practices on land on which agricultural crops are grown and on land that is set aside or temporarily not being used for crop production	Voluntary	Voluntary (unless chosen in the first commitment period)
Grassland	Rangelands and pasture land that is not considered as cropland, including vegetation that falls below the threshold used in forest land	Grazing land management	The system of practices on land used for livestock production aimed at manipulating the amount and type of vegetation and livestock produced	Voluntary	Voluntary (unless chosen in the first commitment period)
Other land	Bare soil, rock, ice and all unmanaged land areas that do not fall into any of the other five categories	Re-vegetation	A direct human-induced activity to increase carbon stocks on sites through the establishment of vegetation that … does not meet the definitions of afforestation and reforestation	Voluntary	Voluntary (unless chosen in the first commitment period)

Table 15.1 (cont.)

	Land-use categories under the UNFCCC		Activities under the Kyoto Protocol		
Name	Definition (after IPCC 2003 GPG LULUCF)	Name	Definition (after 16/CMP.1)	2008–12	2013–20
Wetlands	Land that is covered or saturated by water for all or part of the year (e.g. peatland) and that does not fall into the forest land, cropland, grassland or settlements categories	Wetland drainage and rewetting	A system of practices for draining and rewetting on land with organic soil … The activity applies to all lands that have been drained since 1990 and to all lands that have been rewetted since 1990 and that are not accounted for under any other activity	Not applicable	Voluntary
Settlements	All developed land, including transportation infrastructure and human settlements of any size, unless they are already included under other categories				

Table 15.2 *Peatland rewetting and drainage practices and the Land Use, Land-Use Change and Forestry Activities under which these practices have to be accounted in the second commitment period of the Kyoto Protocol (2013–2020).*

Land-use practice	Accounted under activity	Type of accounting
Felling and drainage of a forest on organic soil and conversion to cropland or grassland	Deforestation[a]	Gross-net
Forest harvesting that by reduced evapotranspiration results in much higher water tables so that re-establishment of forest is prevented	Deforestation[a]	Gross-net
Rewetting that raises the water table to such an extent that forest cannot persist or regenerate	Deforestation[a]	Gross-net
Rewetting and felling of forest, e.g. to restore a non-forested peatland	Deforestation[a]	Gross-net
Drainage of a (non-forested) peatland for forestry, e.g. when a treeless or sparsely treed peatland is drained to stimulate tree growth	Afforestation/ reforestation[a]	Gross-net
Rewetting of a (non-forested) peatland for forestry, e.g. when a grassland on organic soil is rewetted and afforested with alder trees	Afforestation/ reforestation[a]	Gross-net
Drainage of forest on organic soil that remains a forest, e.g. when a forested peatland is drained to stimulate tree growth	Forest Management[a]	Reference level
Rewetting of forest on organic soil that remains a forest, e.g. when an ash forest on organic soil is rewetted and replaced by an alder forest	Forest Management[a]	Reference level
Drainage of a non-forested peatland and conversion to cropland	Cropland Management[b]	Net-net
Rewetting of a cropland on organic soil that remains a cropland, e.g. when a potato field is rewetted for paludiculture	Cropland Management[b]	Net-net
Drainage of a non-forested peatland to improve grazing	Grazing Land Management[b]	Net-net
Rewetting of a grassland on organic soil that remains a grassland, e.g. when a drained grassland used for dairy husbandry is rewetted to a grassland for water buffalo husbandry	Grazing Land Management[b]	Net-net

Table 15.2 (cont.)

Land-use practice	Accounted under activity	Type of accounting
Re-vegetation and rewetting of a (non-forested) peatland, e.g. when a bare peat extraction site is converted to a vegetated wetland	Re-vegetation (if elected)[b]	Net-net
Rewetting or drainage (after 1990) of a (non-forested) peatland that is not yet accounted for under any other mandatory or elected activity	Wetland Drainage and Rewetting (if elected)	Net-net

[a] mandatory accounting; + if elected.
[b] accounted if elected; mandatorily accounted if elected in the first commitment period.

penalties after overshooting its emission target (17% above 1990 emissions instead of 6% below them, as agreed under the Protocol). For the first commitment phase of the Protocol (2008–12), 37 industrialised countries and countries in transition to a market economy (both groups are referred to as 'Annex I Countries') had committed themselves to reducing their emissions collectively by 5.2% compared to 1990.

The Kyoto Protocol was developed primarily to curb industrial GHG emissions. Simultaneously, the possibility was opened to use the LULUCF sector for compensating these emissions by improved land management. Whereas the UNFCCC reporting of greenhouse fluxes from land is 'land based', i.e. follows the land-use categories, accounting under the Kyoto Protocol is 'activity based', i.e. follows specifically defined human activities (Table 15.1).

The land-use activities that first came to mind as carbon sinks were afforestation and reforestation, and consequently accounting for these activities (and their reverse – deforestation) was from the outset made mandatory (KP art. 3.3). In contrast, accounting for all other types of land use (i.e. forest management, cropland management, grazing land management and re-vegetation; Table 15.1) was made voluntary (KP art. 3.4), and countries were allowed to choose whether to account for these activities or to neglect the associated GHG fluxes.

For the first commitment period only 4 of the 37 Annex I countries chose cropland management, only two grazing land management and only three re-vegetation. Reasons for the reluctance to choose these activities were the complexity in monitoring and the assumed negative consequences for the national GHG budget. In contrast, 23 countries chose forest management, because the monitoring of carbon stock changes in forests (as a proxy of GHG fluxes) was easier and a positive outcome for the national carbon budget was expected.

As GHG emissions from drained peatlands are substantial (Chapter 4), rewetting would be beneficial for the climate irrespective of the land-use activity. The Kyoto Protocol, however, did not allow countries to account solely for rewetting of drained peatlands. A country may only choose an activity in its entirety and then has to account for all practices on all lands subject to that activity.

If, for example, Germany had chosen the activity grazing land management in order to claim emission reductions from the 600 km^2 of peatland meadows it has rewetted since 1990, it would also have had to account for the remaining 6000 km^2 of grassland on drained peatland and for the 60 000 km^2 of grassland on mineral soil. Then, it would not only have had to monitor the effects of rewetting, but also of fertilising, ploughing and all other practices that might affect the GHG fluxes from all this land. The imbalance between workload and expected reduction gains has further discouraged countries from electing the voluntary activities. In other words, until recently, the accounting rules of the Kyoto Protocol were such as to frustrate efforts to rewet peatlands.

Peatlands under the Kyoto Protocol: the second commitment period

Since 2008, the UNFCCC has been striving to find a way out of this impasse (Joosten 2011a) and in 2011 a new (voluntary) Kyoto Protocol activity was adopted – under the confusing name 'Wetland Drainage and Rewetting' – to make peatland rewetting directly accountable. For the second commitment period of the Kyoto Protocol (2013–20), UNFCCC also expanded the number of mandatory activities with forest management and with all activities that countries had already chosen for the first commitment period (Table 15.1).

Wetland drainage and rewetting enables the accounting of rewetting of peatlands that fall outside other mandatory and voluntarily elected activities. The activity has deliberately been created to support a hotspot approach for peatland rewetting, as long as no complete wall-to-wall accounting for land has been achieved or not all art. 3.4 activities have become mandatory.

Table 15.2 illustrates the complicated and inconsistent set of rules and regulations that has evolved for LULUCF accounting of peatlands under the Kyoto Protocol. The Intergovernmental Panel on Climate Change (IPCC) has meanwhile produced extensive guidance on how to report and account for peatland emissions and emission reductions (Hiraishi *et al.* 2014a, b).

Trading emissions under the Kyoto Protocol

Parties (countries) with the obligation to reduce their GHG emissions under the Kyoto Protocol do not have to do that 'on their own'. The 'flexible mechanisms' of the Protocol allow for emissions trading ('carbon trading'), i.e. using reductions achieved elsewhere to comply with domestic reduction obligations. These mechanisms consist of:

- International Emissions Trading in which an Annex 1 country sells (part of) its national surplus in 'carbon credits'[1] to another Annex 1 country with a deficit in carbon credits.
- Joint Implementation (JI) in which an Annex 1 country finances a GHG emission reduction project in another Annex 1 country and in return receives the carbon credits achieved by that project.
- Clean Development Mechanism (CDM) in which an Annex 1 country finances a GHG emission reduction project in a Non-Annex I, i.e. a developing country and in return receives the carbon credits achieved by that project.

Only JI and CDM are project based, i.e. there is a direct connection between an emission-reduction intervention and cash transfer (through carbon credit generation). The CDM, however, in its current state, only allows for afforestation and reforestation projects in its land-use portfolio. JI has fewer restrictions and, in theory, could integrate peatland rewetting interventions, but as the European Union has excluded JI from its emission trading system (EU ETS), which has been responsible for virtually all demand from both CDM and JI, there has been a negligible demand for JI credits.

Topical developments
In 2012, the UNFCCC has decided to add a new commitment period under the Kyoto Protocol, and negotiations are ongoing to put more focus on LULUCF interventions, including peatland interventions, through enhanced accounting rules and more refined mechanisms. Some important peatland countries, however, have withdrawn from the Protocol entirely (Canada) or have abstained from taking commitments for the second commitment period (New Zealand, Japan and Russia). The other Annex 1 countries have yet to decide which activities they will choose to account for.

---

[1] In climate policy various concepts related to 'carbon credits' are distinguished, including Assigned Amount Units (AAUs), Emission Reduction Units (ERUs), Removal Units (RMUs) and Certified Emission Reductions (CERs), which may or may not be interchanged in Kyoto Protocol accounting, plus various types on the voluntary market. For simplicity we all call them 'carbon credits' here.

As part of the negotiations on LULUCF accounting, Parties agreed to explore more comprehensive accounting of GHG fluxes to reduce the selective opportunism that has thus far characterced LULUCF accounting. To date, discussions have not produced any significant progress, except that any outcome will only be valid after 2020 (SBSTA 2013).

15.2.3 Peatlands in developing countries

Thus far, developing countries have not been required to set legally binding emission reduction targets and only participate in UNFCCC-regulated emission reductions via the CDM. In recent years, however, Parties have been vigorously negotiating the development of a new mechanism targeting specific interventions in developing countries: Reducing Emissions from Deforestation and forest Degradation (REDD+). Much progress has been achieved with respect to reference levels, safeguards, implementation phases and jurisdictional approaches. REDD+ development has furthermore been supported by strong bilateral and multilateral activities, e.g. the United Nations Collaborative Initiative on REDD (UN REDD) and the Forest Carbon Partnership Facility. Some 50, mostly tropical, countries have started building a REDD/REDD+ implementation framework, supported by a large number of developed countries.

In developing countries, emissions from peatlands are even more important than in developed countries both in absolute and relative terms (Figures 15.1 and 15.2). Initially, REDD+ merely focused on forest biomass and neglected the important role of peat soils. In the tropics, however, most peatlands are indeed forests ('peat swamp forests') and they follow a similar fate of deforestation, drainage and degradation. Their enormous peat carbon pool – on average per hectare ten times larger than the biomass carbon stock of tropical forests (Joosten and Couwenberg 2008) – makes peat swamp forests fundamentally different from other forests in their emission behaviour. Emissions from deforestation on mineral soils are largely restricted to the removal and oxidation of forest biomass. The associated emissions may be large, but stop shortly after the forest has been cut and may be reversed when it grows back. In contrast, emissions from deforestation and drainage on peat soils stop only when the area is effectively rewetted or when the entire peat is depleted, which may take decades to centuries (Figure 15.3).

In 2011, the UNFCCC implicitly decided to include peat soils in the REDD+ mechanism by ruling that 'significant pools and/or activities should not be excluded' (decision 12/CP.17). Nonetheless, the REDD+-*cum*-peatlands discourse still has a limited audience, and few countries have yet committed to a dedicated peatland agenda, Indonesia being a notable exception.

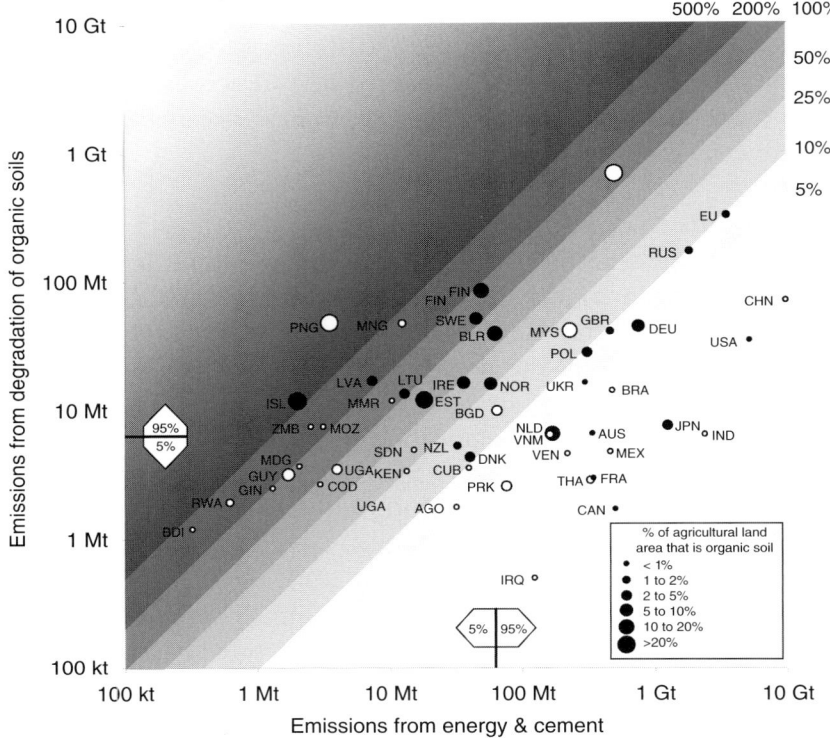

Figure 15.2 Emissions from degrading organic soils (vertical axis) in relation to emissions from energy and cement (horizontal axis) for 50 countries and the EU. Emissions are shown on a logarithmic scale (kt = 10^3 tonnes, Mt = 10^6 tonnes, Gt = 10^9 tonnes CO_2e). Countries are denoted by their ISO 3166-1 alpha-3 three-letter code. White circles denote non-Annex 1 countries, black circles Annex 1 countries. Shades indicate where emissions from organic soils are equivalent to more than 5, 10, 25, 50, 100, 200 and 500% of emissions from energy and cement. Flags on the horizontal axis separate the countries responsible for 95% of total emissions from energy and cement from the remaining 5% of countries (not all countries plotted); flags on the vertical axis do the same for emissions from the degradation of organic soils. Data on emissions from organic soils are calculated from the most recent national reportings to the UNFCCC and the IMCG Global Peatland Database, corrected with the latest IPCC emission factors. Data on emissions from energy and cement are taken from the Global Carbon Project. Data collated by Alexandra Barthelmes, John Couwenberg and Cosima Tegetmeyer; analysis and figure by John Couwenberg.

The most contentious issues in the UNFCCC REDD+ discussions to date concern the establishment of a rigorous measuring, reporting and verification (MRV) framework and the integration of REDD+ in the international carbon markets. Common ground is emerging around the concepts of

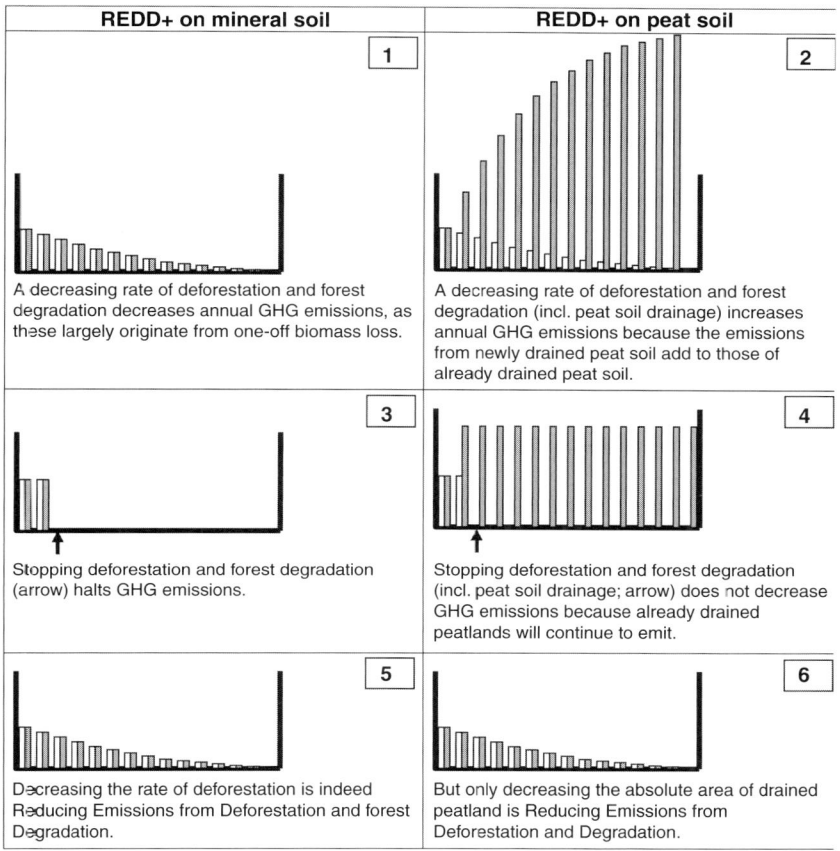

Figure 15.3 The relation between annual land-use change (1–5)/land use (6) (ha yr^{-1}, white) and total annual emissions (t yr^{-1}, grey) when considering REDD+ on mineral soil (left) and on peat soil (right). Modified from Wibisono *et al.* (2011).

result-based action and result-based funding, with the biggest finance initiative involving peatlands being the REDD+ Partnership that Norway and Indonesia have entered in 2010. In this partnership, Norway will support – with up to USD 1 billion – the efforts of Indonesia in reducing emissions from deforestation and degradation of forests and peatlands.

15.2.4 The UNFCCC after 2020

In the coming years the international community will be struggling to substantiate the Paris Agreement, to enter into force by 2020. Intensive discussions have been taking place in and outside UNFCCC on the role of the land sector in the post-2020 scheme (e.g. La Vina *et al.* 2012; Canaveira 2013; Iversen *et al.* 2014; Parker *et al.* 2014; Von Unger *et al.* 2015). Despite the uncertainty over the direction the concrete international rules on climate will take, the policy prospects and opportunities for integrating peatlands in the climate change architecture have never been better.

The Paris Agreement presents an opportunity to improve the current system of land-sector accounting that over the years has indeed become increasingly complex (Table 15.2). The disproportionally large emissions from drained peatland offer an excellent opportunity to focus as a priority on peatlands as a first step towards the full coverage of land. Such a 'hotspot' approach has the advantage that the mitigation efforts (i.e. peatland rewetting) and the MRV efforts can be concentrated on areas where a disproportionally large reduction of emissions and a fair return on investment can be achieved. Furthermore, peatland rewetting is an excellent way of integrating climate change mitigation and adaptation, certainly when combined with paludiculture (Chapter 17).

15.3 Regional climate policies

The global aims of the UNFCCC have led to the implementation of regional legal policies to reducing GHG emissions, some of which pay explicit attention to peatlands.

Following the prolongation of the Kyoto Protocol, the European Union has sharpened its own LULUCF accounting rules with Decision No. 529/2013/EU of 21 May 2013. Under the new EU rules, accounting for GHG fluxes from cropland management and grazing land management shall become mandatory for EU member states from 2021 onwards, while accounting for Wetland Drainage and Rewetting remains voluntary. With respect to peatlands, the decision's recitals state that 'the Union should endeavour to advance the issue at the international level with a view to reaching an agreement within the bodies of the UNFCCC or of the Kyoto Protocol on the obligation to prepare and maintain annual accounts' for wetland drainage and rewetting, 'with a view to including this obligation in the global climate agreement'.

Despite the voluntary nature of Wetland Drainage and Rewetting accounting, the new EU decision effectively imposes mandatory accounting for most peatland rewetting activities, as agricultural peatlands (constituting half of the drained peatland area) will fall under cropland management or grazing land management and forested peatlands (which constitute one-third of the drained peatland area) under forest management, which is anyhow mandatory. Accounting for wetland drainage and rewetting proper would thus cover little more than rewetting of current and former peat extraction sites.

On the other hand, European Union Directive 2009/28/EC, which aims at the promotion of the use of energy from renewable source, requires that 'Biofuels and other bioliquids [...] shall not be made from raw material obtained from land that was peatland in January 2008, unless it is proven that the cultivation and harvesting of this raw material does not involve drainage of previously undrained soil' (Art 17 (5)). This article factually forbids the cultivation of biofuels on all drained peatland, because all peatland is 'previously undrained' (otherwise there would not be any peat, Joosten 2009a), but is interpreted to mean that biofuels may continue to be cultivated on peatlands that have been drained before 2008.

However, cultivation on peatland drained before 2008 also leads to continuous and enormous GHG emissions from oxiding peat (see Figure 15.3) that cannot be compensated by the GHG saving of the produced biofuels or bioliquids (Couwenberg 2007b). The Executive Board of the CDM, for its part, has recognised (albeit rather late, in September 2010, CDM-EB-56) this inherent characteristic of peatlands and decided that plantations on peat soils will no longer be supported. In contrast, the EU policy (and derived national policies) that allows continued use of these lands for the (perverse) production of biofuels frustrates the necessary rewetting of these emission hotspots.

On the side of EU-internal nature conservation, the Habitats Directive – together with the Birds Directive – forms the cornerstone of the European Union's nature conservation policy. The Directive protects over 1000 species and over 200 habitat types, including a wide variety of mire and peatland types. The Directive has as a target that these habitats and species should be maintained or restored at favourable conservation status. A timetable when this target should be reached is not given. The EU Biodiversity Strategy to 2020 aims 'to halt the deterioration in the status of all species and habitats covered by EU nature legislation and achieve a significant and measurable improvement in their status'. The Strategy includes a 'restoration subtarget' to restore at least 15% of degraded ecosystems until 2020.

An important financial instrument to realise the Habitat Directive has been the LIFE programme. Since 1992, LIFE has co-financed over 4000 projects, including hundreds of peatland restoration projects, contributing over 3 billion EUR to the protection of environment and climate.

The new LIFE Programme 2014–20, with a budget of 3.4 billion EUR, has a general objective 'to contribute to the shift towards a resource-efficient, low-carbon and climate- resilient economy, to the protection and improvement of the quality of the environment and to halting and reversing biodiversity loss, including the support of the Natura 2000 network and tackling the degradation of ecosystems', which opens ample synergetic perspectives for peatland restoration.

This general goal notwithstanding, peatland agriculture is responsible for the vast majority of emissions from peatlands in the countries of the European Union. The reformed Common Agricultural Policy (CAP), the cornerstone of EU policy making in agriculture, is the EU's largest subsidy scheme with over 400 billion EUR for the period 2014–20. Over 75% of this sum is directed towards direct payments under the so-called first Pillar, in which the 'cross-compliance mechanism' ties direct payment support for farmers to compliance with standards of environmental care. Farmers are, among others, required to avoid deterioration of the habitat, maintain soil organic matter and protect and manage water. Non-compliance should lead to reductions in subsidy and development payments. Perversely, the soil organic matter criterion of the cross-compliance regime only matches mineral soils, so that climate-hostile agriculture on deeply drained peat still receives unrestricted EU direct payments.

The focus of the second Pillar on sustainability includes measures beneficial for environment and climate that farmers undertake voluntarily. For agri-environmental climate measures, organic farming, Areas of Natural Constraints, Natura 2000 areas, forestry measures and investments which are beneficial for environment or climate, at least 30% of the budget of each rural development programme must be reserved, which may become a strong incentive for peatland conservation and restoration, including paludiculture (Chapter 17).

In California, with similarly heavily emitting agricultural peatlands in the Sacramento–San Joaquin River Delta, the Global Warming Solutions Act (Assembly Bill 32) aims to stabilise state-wide emissions by 2020 at the level of 1990. Having started in 2013, the programme had phased in participation of economic sectors to cover 85% of the state's emissions by 2015. Peatland restoration is not yet acknowledged in its own right, but a 2013 scoping paper on a 'Reserve Peatland Protocol' found that the emission reduction potential of peatland restoration is 'significant', that 'existing tools, methods, and primary data would make the development of a suitable protocol feasible and relatively simple', and that it 'could generate sufficient revenues to make some activities economically feasible' (Climate Action Reserve 2013).

In South East Asia, the Association of South East Asian Nations (ASEAN) Member States has developed the ASEAN Peatland Management Strategy (2006–20) to address fires on drained peatlands (Chapter 14) and the associated trans-boundary smoke haze pollution.

Next to these domestic and regional programs, countries bilaterally support peatland rewetting for climate benefits in other countries: Canadian, Dutch and Australian funding supports rewetting in Kalimantan (Chapter 14), the International Climate Initiative of the German government supports large peatland rewetting projects in Belarus and Russia. Also, the UNEP-GEF and UNDP-GEF support to, for example, China (see Chapter 13), South East Asia and Belarus must be mentioned in this context.

15.4 Other peatland and climate-relevant international policies

Peatland restoration with a climate change mitigation co-target is also supported by international policies that do not aim directly at climate benefits. Here we present a selection of such policies.

The Convention on Wetlands of International Importance (Ramsar Convention, www.ramsar.org), an intergovernmental treaty for the conservation and wise use of wetlands, has paid explicit attention to peatlands since 1996. At its 6th Conference of the Parties (COP 6), the Convention noticed that peatlands represent 50% of the world's terrestrial and freshwater wetlands but that only 75 of the designated 778 Ramsar sites – with 3 million out of 52 million hectares – had peatland as their dominant habitat (Rubec 1996). Immediately the Convention took steps to correct this underrepresentation. COP 8 (Valencia 2002) adopted several peatland and climate-relevant resolutions with Resolution VIII.3, calling upon all relevant countries 'to minime the degradation, as well as promote restoration, and improve management practices of those peatlands and other wetland types that are significant carbon stores, or have the ability to sequester carbon'. COP 10 (Changwon 2008) urged relevant Contracting Parties 'to take urgent action ... to reduce the degradation, promote restoration, improve management practices of peatlands and other wetland types that are significant GHG sinks, and to encourage expansion of demonstration sites on peatland restoration and wise use management in relation to climate change mitigation and adaptation activities', and called for 'joint policies and measures that are aimed to reduce anthropogenic GHG emissions from wetlands such as peatlands' together with the UNFCCC. COP 11 (Bucharest 2012) encouraged Contracting Parties and relevant organisations 'to undertake studies of the role of the conservation and/or restoration of both forested and non-forested wetlands in relation to [...] climate change mitigation. Finally, COP 12 (Punta del Este 2015) stressed the importance of peatland restoration in its resolution on 'Peatlands, climate change and wise use'.

Peatlands were firstly brought onto the agenda of the CBD (www.cbd.int) in 2004, when resolution VII/15 was adopted. This resolution mentions peatlands as valuable ecosystems, providing habitats and carbon storage and sequestration. In 2007, the global 'Assessment on Peatlands Biodiversity and Climate Change' (Parish *et al.* 2008) was endorsed by the CBD's Subsidiary Body on Scientific, Technical and Technological Advice. In 2008, CBD COP 9 recognised 'the importance of the conservation and sustainable use of the biodiversity of wetlands and, in particular, peatlands in addressing climate change'.

The Strategic Goals and Aichi Targets adopted by CBD's COP10 (Nagoya 2010, Decision X/2) are of special relevance for peatland conservation and restoration, especially:

- Target 14: 'By 2020, ecosystems that provide essential services, including services related to water, and contribute to health, livelihoods and well-being, are restored and safeguarded.'
- Target 15: 'By 2020, ecosystem resilience and the contribution of biodiversity to carbon stocks have been enhanced, through conservation and restoration, including restoration of at least 15 per cent of degraded ecosystems, thereby contributing to climate change mitigation and adaptation and to combating desertification.'

15.5 Voluntary markets

15.5.1 Introduction

The reluctance of countries to implement and account for peatland rewetting and other land-based mitigation practices under the Kyoto Protocol has stimulated the voluntary carbon market to fill the gap. In spite of its very small volume (<0.3% of the global carbon markets; Ernst and Young 2012), the voluntary market is a very distinct market. It serves the realm of corporate and consumer social responsibility and offers companies, organisations and individuals the opportunity to compensate for their unavoidable emissions and to become 'carbon neutral'.

A number of high-quality standards have emerged, among them the Verified Carbon Standard (VCS), the Gold Standard (which incorporates the previous Carbonfix standard), Plan vivo, the American Carbon Registry and the Climate, Community and Biodiversity Standard. Some of these lean heavily on the criteria of the CDM.

Even stronger than compliance policies and markets, voluntary markets require clear criteria and procedural methods to prove that claimed reductions indeed have taken place. Important criteria include 'additionality', i.e. that the emission reduction would not have happened without the revenue from the sale of credits; the 'reference level' against which reductions are expressed (see Table 15.2); 'permanence', i.e. the guarantee that emission reductions cannot be reversed; 'leakage', i.e. consideration of GHG emissions outside the project boundary as a result of the project; 'measurability' and 'verifiability', i.e. that the claimed emission reductions are reliably quantified and can be verified by independent parties; 'conservativeness', i.e. providing certainty that at least the agreed amount is provided; 'reliability', i.e. that the ownership of credits is transparent and documented; and 'sustainability', i.e. that the project contributes to the improvement of local socio-economic conditions and does not impair other ecosystem functions. An extensive discussion on these criteria with respect to peatlands is presented by Joosten et al. (2015a).

According to estimates, in 2013, about 80 million voluntary carbon credits were traded with a financial volume of USD 380 million. Land-use projects (especially forestry) comprised some 45% of the voluntary market size (Peters-Stanley and Gonzalez 2014).

15.5.2 Global standards

A standard defines all the specific requirements for developing projects and methodologies including their validation, monitoring and verification.

The VCS (www.v-c-s.org) is the most important standard for land-use projects, and the only one that has developed an explicit programme for peatland projects (VCS 2013; Tanneberger and Wichtmann 2011). Whereas Afforestation, Reforestation and Re-vegetation (ARR), Agricultural Land Management (ALM), Improved Forest Management (IFM) and Reducing Emissions from Deforestation and Degradation (REDD) have been included in the VCS AFOLU programme since its inception in 2007, Peatland Rewetting and Conservation (PRC) was added in March 2011 and later expanded to Wetlands Restoration and Conservation (WRC). With respect to peatlands, VCS distinguished three basic types of activity: 'restoration of degraded peatlands', 'avoided drainage of wet peatlands' and 'avoided conversion to open water', which all can be combined with other land-use activities and practices. Thus far, VCS has validated only one peatland project. Additional methodologies and projects are being prepared.

15.5.3 Regional and local standards

As global standards want to maintain a high level of credit quality, generating carbon credits under these standards may involve substantial costs. For new project types (like peatland rewetting) a methodology must be developed that details how emissions and emission reductions are assessed. Such a methodology must then be verified by independent consultants. The next step is to create a project design document (or 'PDD' in the terminology of the CDM, or

Box 15.1
Regional carbon standards MoorFutures® and the UK Peatland Code

MoorFutures® (www.moorfutures.de) is a regional standard developed by the Ministry of Agriculture of the German federal state of Mecklenburg-Western Pomerania and Greifswald University. The standard is based on the criteria of the VCS and the Kyoto Protocol, but avoids high administrative costs by keeping validation and certification in its own hands.

In 2009, the annual GHG emissions from drained peatland were about 6.2 million tonnes CO_2e, making peatlands the largest source of GHGs in the federal state (MLUV M-V 2009). To procure funds for rewetting, MoorFutures® were introduced in 2010 as the first carbon credits issued for peatland rewetting in the world. Other German federal states soon adopted the standard and its philosophy (www.moorfutures.de).

MoorFutures® strives for regionality in order to (1) facilitate proximity between buyers, sellers, project developers and coordinating bodies; (2) exploit regional expertise (e.g. local universities) with respect to quality control; and (3) facilitate regional identification, specialisation and diversification.

Since 2010, MoorFutures® has been further developed to quantify and integrate additional ecosystem services (including biodiversity) into its carbon credits (MoorFutures® 2.0; Joosten et al. 2015a).

Compared to global standards, good regional standards deliver carbon credits of the same quality but at considerably lower organisational costs (Joosten et al. 2015a). They usually operate within a fixed and stable set of national juridical rules and regulations that need not be assessed independently. Moreover, they address a different market that is far more personal and transparent compared with the anonymous global carbon market. The MoorFutures® scheme has meanwhile allowed for the rewetting of several peatland areas, which were and will be entirely financed by credit revenues (www.moorfutures.de).

The United Kingdom is now piloting a UK Peatland Carbon Code (Reed et al. 2013; Bonn et al. 2014) to incentivise the restoration of UK peatlands, of which over 80% have been degraded (Bain et al. 2011). After the Government's 2011 Natural Environment White Paper had emphasised the creation of new markets for ecosystem services, and DEFRA's Ecosystem Markets Taskforce had ranked a UK Peatland Code as a top opportunity, the Code was launched in September 2013. It started for an initial 18-month period with a number of pilot peatland restoration projects. The Code, owned by the International Union for the Conservation of Nature (IUCN) UK National Committee, sets out principles, requirements and guidance for the eligibility of projects, how projects are governed and documented, and how the climate and other benefits of restoration should be monitored.

project description or 'PD' in the terminology of the VCS, respectively) that details the project objectives, estimates of emissions, and practical measures. Besides the practical costs of acquisition, technical implementation, management and monitoring, additional costs arise from independent validation of the project and verification of its results. The strict requirements imply administrative costs of several tens of thousands of euros, making it prohibitively expensive to apply a global standard like VCS to small-scale projects. For this reason, also regional standards have been developed, of which we present some examples (Box 15.1; see also Bonn *et al.* 2014).

15.6 Outlook and recommendations

People and governments around the globe have started to realise the emission reduction potential of peatland conservation and restoration and the comparably moderate costs it involves. Science and practice have developed methodologies that have made peatland reporting more comprehensive and robust (see Hiraishi *et al.* 2014a, b). Voluntary trade mechanisms for carbon credits generated by peatland rewetting and conservation are in place and the necessary methodologies are available or under development. Now policy makers are challenged, at the international, supranational (EU), domestic and local level, to further develop and implement appropriate instruments and incentives to deliver on the potential in the most effective and efficient way.

Much has already been achieved. Accounting for peatland emissions within the UNFCCC – an exotic item, when the Kyoto framework was first drawn up – has been consistently strengthened in recent years. A new activity, 'Wetland Drainage and Rewetting', has been adopted, enabling a dedicated hotspot approach for peatland rewetting under the Kyoto Protocol. Accounting for Forest Management, including that of forests on organic soil, as well as for all other activities already chosen by Parties for the first commitment period, has become mandatory, which will benefit peatland rewetting in several important peatland countries of Annex I. A new reporting process, consisting of Biennial Reports and International Assessment and Review, promises to strengthen the reporting capacity across sectors including peatland emissions. New mechanisms like REDD+, Nationally Appropriate Mitigation Actions (NAMAs), the New Market Mechanism (NMM) and the Framework of Various Approaches (FVA) are under development under the UNFCCC, which will allow accounting for peatland conservation and restoration in the developing countries, where peatland emissions often constitute a substantial portion of their total emissions (see Figure 15.2) and which together are responsible for over 60% of the world's anthropogenic peatland emissions (see Figure 15.1).

The EU LULUCF Accounting Decision manifests the emergence of a more thorough and comprehensive accounting capacity by going further than the respective UNFCCC rules, and phases in mandatory accounting for activities that are responsible for the large majority of peatland emissions.

But many challenges still have to be met. Many decision makers, also within UNFCCC, are still insufficiently familiar with the relationship between peatland restoration and climate change mitigation. Extensive information campaigns on the peculiarities of peatlands are still necessary.

In the field of reporting and accounting, improvements would include the mandatory accounting of peatland-related emissions both in the developed and in the developing world. This would, without major risks for compliance and excessive monitoring costs, stimulate peatland rewetting substantially. It would, however, also require the strengthening of the technical and institutional capacity including – first and foremost – the accurate assessment of peatland distribution and drainage status in the major peatland countries (Chapter 20), and the development of cost-effective monitoring and verification procedures. There is no reason to assume that – with a dedicated 'readiness for peat' programme – these challenges cannot be met before 2020.

Also many potential investors on the voluntary market are not yet acquainted with peatlands. Regional embedding, such as with MoorFutures®, offers an instrument to communicate content and increase awareness with high public visibility. The association with wider ecosystem services and other benefits that have the potential to justify higher prices per tonne of carbon may make peatland projects extra attractive for corporate social responsibility schemes.

A wide series of options exists to improve the perspectives of peatland restoration via market-based mechanisms. These include, for example, earmarking part of the proceeds from auctioning allowances from emission trading schemes for peatland mitigation actions, broadening the scope of CDM to include peatland related measures, adding a dedicated peatlands window to the REDD+ mechanism, and establishing a sectoral peatlands approach under NMM and FVA (Von Unger *et al.* 2015). Another option would be to link peat-rich developed countries with peat-rich developing countries across the globe. Public funds, mobilised from participating developed countries, would be used to establish a common accounting framework and to prepare all participating countries for implementing robust conservation and restoration measures. Implementation itself would be financed through a peatland emissions trading scheme connecting all participating counties, with allowance and compliance quotas established per country, balancing economic and political considerations (Von Unger *et al.* 2015).

Given their enormous emissions when drained (Chapters 4 and 14), countries should prioritise protection of tropical peat swamp forests by implementing an immediate halt to conversion, introducing no-go zones for undisturbed peatlands, revoking peat swamp concessions and shifting to mineral soils, rewetting and restoring drained and degraded peatlands, and adopting paludiculture for severely degraded peat soils.

Much will have to be reflected on, discussed, developed and decided upon with respect to carbon policies and their role in peatland restoration, and much is still unsure. What is, however, beyond dispute is the recognition of the important role which peatlands can play in climate change mitigation. Peatlands have arrived in mainstream politics and they are there to stay (Joosten 2011b).

CHAPTER SIXTEEN

Valuing peatland ecosystem services

SABINE WICHMANN
Institute of Botany and Landscape Ecology, Ernst Moritz Arndt University of Greifswald, Germany
LUKE BRANDER
Institute for Environmental Studies, VU Amsterdam, The Netherlands; Division of Environment at Hong Kong University of Science and Technology, Hong Kong
ACHIM SCHÄFER
Greifswald Mire Centre, Germany
MARIJE SCHAAFSMA
Geography and Environment, Centre for Biological Sciences University of Southampton, Southampton, UK
PIETER VAN BEUKERING
Institute for Environmental Studies, VU Amsterdam, The Netherlands.
DUGALD TINCH
University of Sterling, UK
ALETTA BONN
Helmholtz Centre for Environmental Research (UFZ) | Friedrich-Schiller-University Jena | German Centre for Integrative Biodiversity Research (iDiv) Halle-Jena-Leipzig | IUCN UK Peatland Programme, UK

16.1 Introduction

Throughout history, peatlands have been inhospitable places for humans; feared as wilderness, despised as wasteland and often remained as unsettled borderlands (Silvius, Joosten and Opdam 2008). They became seen as *valuable* only since being drained for agriculture, forestry or peat extraction. This biased focus on direct provisioning services has long ignored the destructive effects of peatland exploitation on regulating and cultural services (e.g. loss of biodiversity, emissions of CO_2 and nutrients, declining water quality and quantity).

The degradation of ecosystem functions inspired the recognition of human dependence on nature (e.g. Leopold 1949; Ehrlich and Ehrlich 1981;

Peatland Restoration and Ecosystem Services: Science, Policy and Practice, eds. A. Bonn, T. Allott, M. Evans, H. Joosten and R. Stoneman. Published by Cambridge University Press. © British Ecological Society 2016.

De Groot 1992; Daily 1997) and stimulated attempts to include ecosystem values in planning and political decision making (e.g. Krutilla 1967; Krutilla and Fisher 1975; Pearce and Nash 1981). Over the last two decades the concept of ecosystem services (Chapter 1) and their valuation have raised increasing interest. Within the scientific community it is represented by an exponential growth in publications (Fisher, Turner and Morling 2009). In addition, the policy world has boosted the concept by initiating major comprehensive studies such as the Millennium Ecosystem Assessment (MA 2005), The Economics of Ecosystems and Biodiversity (TEEB 2008, 2010) and several initiatives on the national scale such as the UK National Ecosystem Assessment (UK NEA). Launching the Intergovernmental Platform on Biodiversity and Ecosystem Services (IPBES) established an interface between the scientific community and policy makers comparable to the IPCC. It reflects as much the hope as the political challenge connected to the ecosystem service approach bridging nature conservation and human well-being.

This chapter aims to introduce the concept of ecosystems service valuation to readers with no economic background, gives an overview of valuation studies on peatlands, including three case studies (Boxes 16.2–16.4), shows that expressing damage to peatlands as welfare costs provides economic reasons for conservation and restoration, and identifies instruments for the remuneration of benefits provided by functioning peatlands.

16.2 Valuing nature

The great variety of benefits derived from ecosystems is reflected by the distinction between economic value (welfare), socio-cultural value (well-being) and ecological value (ecosystem integrity and life-support functions) (e.g. MA 2005; De Groot *et al.* 2006). The valuation of ecosystem services integrates ecology (understanding and quantification), ethics (e.g. intergenerational justice), politics (setting objectives) as well as economics, psychology and sociology (disclosing the underlying values and motivations of people). Concepts of values as well as techniques for valuation differ across disciplines. There is not one 'correct' concept of values or ecosystem service valuation but rather a need for conceptual pluralism (Farber *et al.* 2002).

The concept of Total Economic Value (TEV) (Pearce 1993) recognises that the economic value of a natural resource depends not only on whether it can be used as an input in production but also on other benefits that it can provide to people. TEV distinguishes between (direct or indirect) use values and non-use values (Figure 16.1). This distinction is also relevant for choosing appropriate valuation methods (Table 16.1). The concept is embedded in an anthropocentric utilitarian framework and widely used in economic valuation.

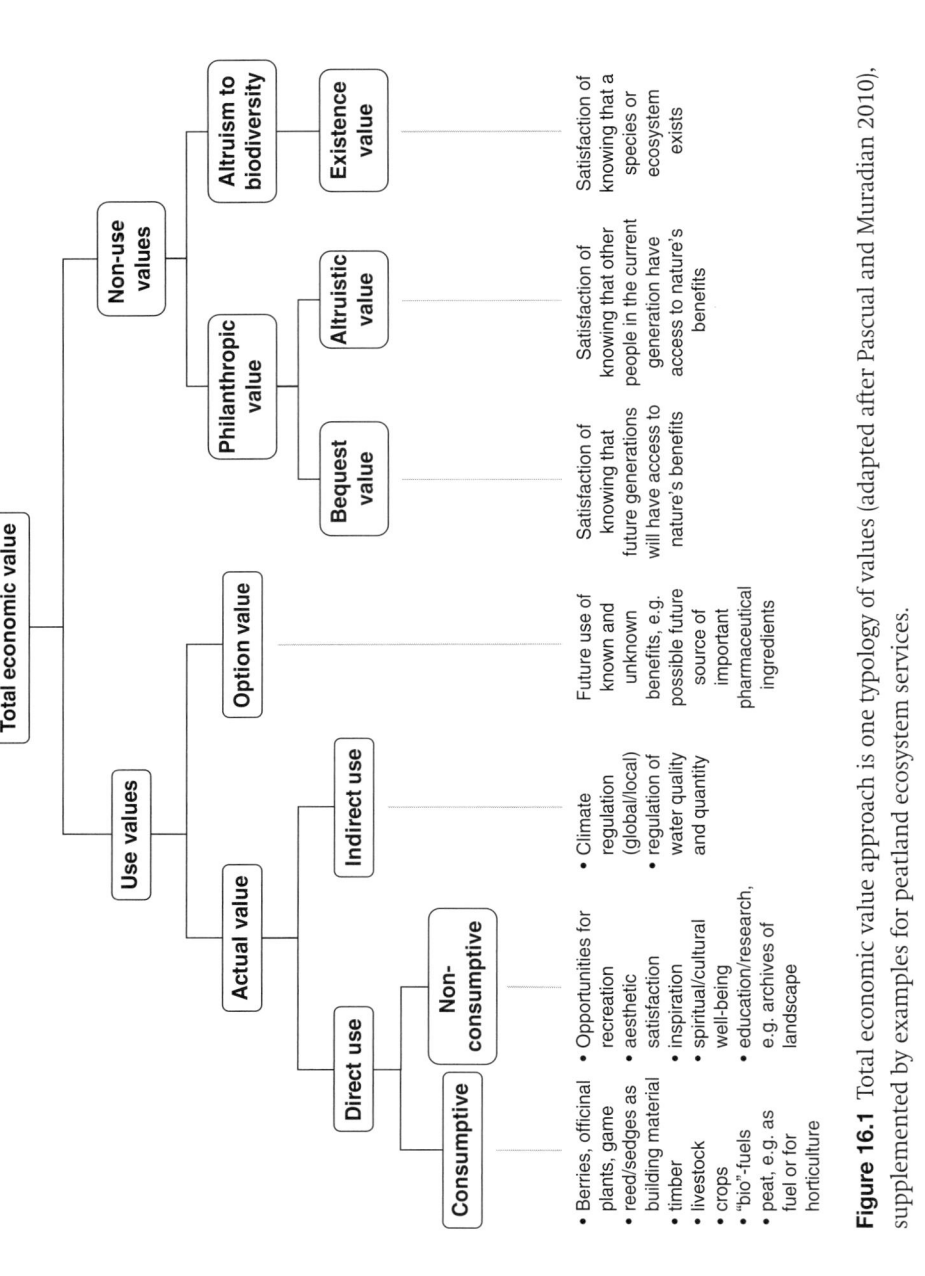

Figure 16.1 Total economic value approach is one typology of values (adapted after Pascual and Muradian 2010), supplemented by examples for peatland ecosystem services.

Table 16.1 Relation between monetary valuation methods and assessable ecosystem values (after De Groot et al. 2006; Turner, Georgiou and Fisher 2008; Pascual and Muradian 2010).

Approach		Valuation method	Description/example	Direct use	Indirect use	Non-use	Box
Market valuation	Price based	Market prices	The value of goods (food, peat) and services (cultural: opportunity for recreation, regulating: carbon storage) equals their market price	✓	✓		
	Cost based	Costs of avoiding damages	The value of the flood control equals the estimated damage if flooding occurs	✓	✓		**16.2, 16.3**
		Costs of replacing services	The value of high-quality water supply equals the costs of obtaining water from an alternative source	✓	✓		**16.3**
		Cost of restoration/ mitigation	Cost of moderating effects of lost functions or of their restoration (e.g. the value of carbon storage equals the cost of peatland rewetting to reduce GHG emissions)	✓	✓		
	Production based	Production function/ Net factor income	Measures effect of peatland services on loss (or gains) in earnings and/ or productivity (e.g. recreational enterprises dependent on a peatland)		✓		

Table 16.1 (cont.)

Approach	Valuation method	Description/example	Direct use	Indirect use	Non-use	Box
Revealed preference	Travel cost method	The recreational value of a peatland equals the costs (in time and money) of reaching the peatland	✓	✓		
	Hedonic pricing method	The value of a peatland equals the price difference between an adjacent residence and similar real estate without the clean air, aesthetic view and identity	✓	✓		
Stated preference/ Simulated valuation	Contingent valuation method	Respondents are asked to express their willingness to pay for the restoration of a peatland site or their willingness to accept the degradation of a peatland site	✓	✓	✓	

Method	Description				Section
Choice modelling	Respondents choose among alternative proposed peatland policies with different effects on biodiversity conservation and restoration of ecosystem services, as well as different increase in annual tax; *methods*: choice experiments, contingent ranking, contingent rating, pair comparison	✓	✓	✓	16.3, 16.4
Deliberative group valuation	Interactive group process allows capturing value types that may escape individually based surveys (e.g. social justice) and addressing shortcomings of traditional methods (e.g. preference construction during the survey, lack of knowledge of respondents about what they are being asked to allocate values to)	✓	✓		

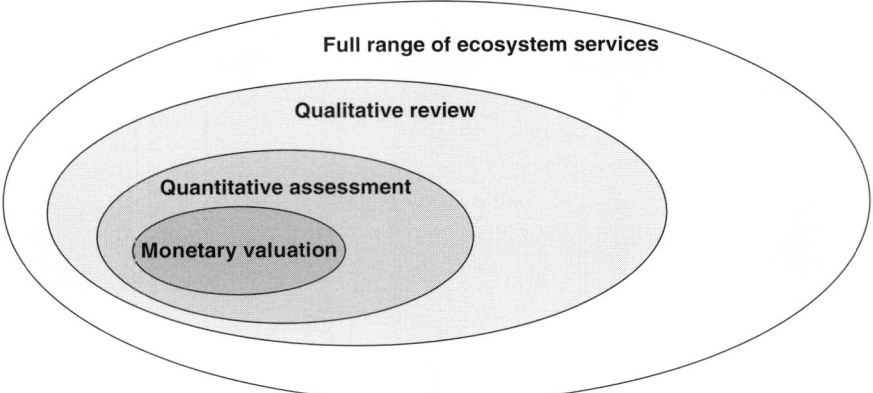

Figure 16.2 Qualitative, quantitative and monetary estimation of ecosystem services (adapted after Ten Brink in TEEB 2008).

The aggregated value of benefits in a given state (output value, akin TEV) should be complemented by the insurance or resilience value, which reflects an ecosystem's capacity to maintain a sustained flow of benefits in the face of variability and disturbance (Pascual and Muradian 2010). Because of insufficient knowledge about ecosystem functioning, the insurance value is difficult to capture.

Valuation starts with identifying those ecosystem functions that are important for humans and are therefore called ecosystem services. The qualitative recognition of benefits may already be sufficient to raise awareness for ensuring conservation and sustainable use (TEEB 2010a). Because of lack of ecological knowledge, only a subset of ecosystem services can be quantified and an even smaller subset monetised (Figure 16.2). Monetary valuation can therefore capture only part of the total value, but providing the most inclusive and accurate estimate of value as possible is crucial for enabling a more rational and informed use of nature.

16.3 Attaching monetary value to nature

16.3.1 Reasons and methods

A characteristic of peatlands is that the use of their provisioning services, such as the provision of food, timber and fuel – which are largely marketable products – has often resulted in the degradation of their other services (but see Chapter 17). These other services provided by living peatlands include a range of regulating and cultural services, which are commonly viewed as public goods. Public goods are charactered by non-rivalry as well as non-excludability. For example, the climate regulation provided by an actively growing peatland will not change with the number of beneficiaries, and nobody can be excluded from these benefits. For this reason, public goods are not traded in existing markets so that market prices are not available to reflect their costs and benefits (market failure). Therefore, nature is often given a zero value in decision making. Missing markets for public goods result in a lack of incentives for individuals to consume these goods at socially optimal levels or to ensure their supply to meet the needs of other people. They consequently are responsible for continued loss of biodiversity and degradation of ecosystems.

In cases where the use of a resource is not at a socially optimal level, expressing values in monetary terms allows economic accounting for the effects of an individual's behaviour on the welfare of others (external effects or externalities). Monetary valuation:

- raises awareness for the costs of losing peatland benefits through degradation
- improves decision making by displaying non-marketable services
- allows optimising efficient allocation of scarce financial resources, and
- may provide information and justification for introducing payments from beneficiaries to providers of services.

For example, restoring a peatland – ranging from conservation, adaptive management to intervention – may be more cost-effective for society than bearing the costs of the damaged peatland now and in the future.

Three methodological approaches to economic valuation can be distinguished: using existing markets for the relevant goods and services (*direct market valuation*); eliciting the value of goods and services indirectly through analysing related markets or observing behaviour (*revealed preference approaches*); and asking people directly about the value they attach to goods and services (*stated preference approach*). (See Table 16.1 for a more detailed description of specific valuation methods.) The methods employed to value peatlands (see Table 16.2 and Boxes 16.2–16.4) largely reflect the nature of the services being valued, with market values and net factor income used to value provisioning services, replacement or damage costs used to value regulating services, and contingent valuation or choice experiments used to value cultural services. All methods have their advantages, disadvantages and limitations (see, for instance, Freeman III 2003).

The perceived importance of a service and therefore estimated values vary depending on:

Time

- *Increasing scientific knowledge*: This may change valuation and politically set objectives. For example, resulting from the formulation of global climate objectives (politics) and the increased knowledge on stocks and emissions (science), carbon storage in peatlands has developed within a few years from an unvalued function to a highly appreciated ecosystem service (see also Chapter 12: change from afforestation to restoration efforts).
- *Service provision may change over time*: For example, peatlands drained for agriculture may lose their value as grassland after several decades of intensive use because of the degradation of the peat soils (see also Chapter 17).
- *Discounting*: Benefits and costs occurring in the future are considered less important for the present time. In economics their future value is discounted to their 'present value'. The value is considered the smaller the further in the future it appears and the higher the applied interest rate.

Place

- *Geographic location of peatlands and number of beneficiaries*: For example, recreation or flood mitigation values are higher if peatlands are closer to urban population centres.
- *Cultural context*: For example, peat cut for fuel is not only a provisioning service, but at low levels of extraction for personal use is also of cultural value, such as domestic turf cutting in Ireland.
- *Socio-economic context*: For example, the existence of structural poverty and power asymmetries in developing countries may lead to the acceptance of low compensation for the provision of ecosystem services – 'the poor sell cheap' (see Kosoy and Corbera 2010).

Scale

- *Individual preferences versus social preferences*: Individual preferences may take community interests into account only to a limited extent into account (see different valuation methods, Box 16.1).
- *Scarcity of goods or services*: For example, continued degradation of peatlands increases the existence value of remaining pristine mires.
- *Service provision and beneficiaries*: Understanding the relationship between the scale of provision of services and the scale at which service-related benefits are distributed (see Figure 16.3) is crucial for informing planning processes for restoration and payments for ecosystem services schemes. There can be differences in terms of place (i.e. the provision of services and their beneficiaries can be far apart), spatial scale (i.e. local, regional,

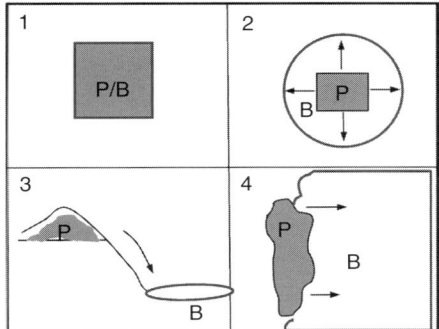

Figure 16.3 Spatial relationships between service production area (P) and service benefit area (B) (from Fisher, Turner and Morling 2009). Shown are the following categories (1) in situ benefits, e.g. a recreational walk through a peatland; (2) benefits without directional bias (omni-directional), e.g. carbon sequestration; (3) + (4) directional benefits due to flow direction, e.g. attenuation of runoff rates (uphill–down slope) or flood protection to a coastline. In addition, scale qualifiers can be used: local (example 1), regional (example 3 + 4) and global (example 2).

global) and time (i.e. services are produced at a different point in time from when they are consumed). For example, local populations in South East Asia bear the costs of mitigating GHG emissions providing a global service, which benefits future generations (see Box 16.4 or Chapter 14).

16.3.2 Valuation: key considerations

Three common misunderstandings about monetary valuation have to be rectified (after Pearce 1993):

1. It is not the economist who places a monetary value on nature. In fact, economists just disclose underlying valuations of people.
2. It is not the value of nature, ecosystems or biodiversity as such that is assessed, but people's preferences for or against marginal changes in the provision of goods and services. Functions which are irreplaceable or indivisible, e.g. the sun or the biosphere, cannot be monetised (Hampicke 1999). Aggregating marginal values and scaling-up to a national or global value is methodically questionable.
3. There are values of nature which cannot and should not be measured in monetary terms. Moral limits to monetary valuation concern intrinsic value, intangible goods (e.g. human life) and fairness towards future generations that cannot communicate their preferences (Hampicke 1999). Therefore, legitimatising nature conservation can be informed by economics but eventually should be based on ethical argumentation.

> **Box 16.1**
>
> ## Combining valuation approaches
>
> Valuation of ecosystem services is one important tool to provide information on how policy or land-use choices will affect human well-being. To overcome the constraints of single methods of monetary valuation, it is recommended to use a wide range of instruments to facilitate better decision making. Important interactive or non-monetary valuation methods include:
>
> - deliberative and participatory approaches considering community-based social preferences instead of individual preferences that usually form the basis in monetary valuation, e.g. focus group discussion (Box 16.4);
> - biophysical valuation estimating physical costs of producing goods and services instead of using preferences for monetisation, e.g. ecological footprint; or
> - multi-criteria analysis integrating multiple values and applying ordinal ranking of assigned relative weights without needing to express how much more one option is worth than another.

16.4 Monetary valuation of benefits from and damage to peatland functions

16.4.1 Review of literature on monetary valuation of peatland ecosystem services

Whereas the economic valuation literature on wetlands is very broad (a recent review found 272 studies for inland wetlands; TEEB 2010b), peatland ecosystem services have, to date, been rarely assessed. Furthermore, the results of several existing peatland valuation studies cannot be standardised to a common set of units (e.g. to USD ha^{-1} yr^{-1}) and therefore do not allow a comparison. We present an overview of seven primary studies providing 18 monetary value estimates for peatland ecosystem services (Table 16.2). Peatlands have generally been valued in combination with other ecosystems, including non-peatland grassland and other wetland types such as lakes. The range of ecosystem services considered includes provisioning services (peat extraction, hunting and fishing), regulating services (flood protection, nutrient filtration) and cultural services (recreational opportunities, existence values).

Table 16.2 Summary of the literature on monetary valuation of peatlands.

Source	Country	Location	Ecosystem type	Ecosystem service	Valuation method	Value (USD ha^{-1} yr^{-1})
Marangon et al. 2002	Italy	Veneto	Wet woodland, peatland and grassland	• Recreational (picnic, walking, wildlife viewing)	Contingent valuation	479
		Friuli-Venezia Giulia	Peatland	• Recreational (picnic, walking, wildlife viewing)	Contingent valuation	2096
Gerrard 2004	Lao	Vientiane	Freshwater marsh, seasonally flooded grassland and shrublands, peat shrubland	• Flood protection	Replacement cost	6002
				• Aquaculture, capture fisheries, mammals, birds, etc.	Market prices	3443
				• Wastewater purification	Replacement cost	148
				• Rice cultivation, vegetable gardens	Market prices	855
Azmi et al. 2009	Malaysia	Pahang State	Peat swamp forest	• Existence value	Contingent valuation	10
Hein et al. 2006	Netherlands	Overijssel	Lowland peatland	• Provision of fish (non-recreational)	Net factor income	31
				• Membership/donations to conservation (biodiversity)	Market prices	490
				• Reed for cutting (used mainly for thatched roofs)	Net factor income	107

Table 16.2 (cont.)

Source	Country	Location	Ecosystem type	Ecosystem service	Valuation method	Value (USD ha^{-1}yr^{-1})
				• Recreational activities (including recreational fishing)	Net factor income	374
Folke 1991	Sweden	Gotland Island	Fresh water, peatland, fen	• Water supply	Replacement cost	41
				• Water quality/nutrient filtration	Replacement cost	61
				• Habitat and nursery	Replacement cost	12
				• Biodiversity	Replacement cost	10
Gren 1995	Sweden	Gotland Island	Fresh water, peatland, fen	• Nitrogen abatement	Contingent valuation	27
				• Water buffering, supply of peat, provision of habitat	Replacement cost	20
Hanley and Craig 1991	UK	Northwest Scotland	Blanket peat bog	• Habitat for unique flora and fauna (reasons for visiting: touring, walking, work, birdwatching)	Contingent valuation	24

All values have been standardised to a common set of units: They represent the annual flow of the ecosystem services from a hectare of peatland, in USD at 2007 price levels.

In this review, we have excluded carbon sequestration and storage as this is covered extensively in Chapter 4. The provision, and therefore value, of this service is variable across peatlands but in some cases is high and marketable (Chapter 15). Furthermore, there has been a scientific debate about the cost of carbon (Nordhaus 2007; Stern 2007) which resulted in recommendations of different standard values in different countries (see Boxes 16.2 and 16.3).

The value of provisioning services from peatlands in the evaluated studies ranges from 12 to 3443 USD ha^{-1} yr^{-1}, of regulating services from 27 to 6002 USD ha^{-1} yr^{-1}, and of cultural services from 24 to 2096 USD ha^{-1} yr^{-1} (Table 16.2). These very wide ranges of values reflect differences in services valued and the context of the study site. This prohibits making general inferences about the value of peatland services without considering the socio-economic and ecological context such as the number of beneficiaries, their income and preferences, and the availability of alternatives. Services and values will differ widely between pristine, degraded and restored peatlands with degraded peatlands generating high 'negative values' related to nutrient and CO_2 emissions. As peatland degradation is poorly assessed in most studies, it is difficult to draw conclusions on how ecosystem quality influences service provision and subsequent values. Only few studies have assessed external costs of peatland degradation or have compared benefits and costs of restoration (see Boxes 16.2–16.4; Kimmel and Mander 2010).

16.4.2 Benefit transfer using value information from other types of ecosystem

There is a growing policy interest in the potential to 'transfer' value information from other types of ecosystem that provide similar services for the following reasons:

- limited availability of value information for peatlands
- relative abundance of value information for other ecosystems, and
- high costs of conducting primary valuation studies.

For example, can the value of recreational activities at a freshwater wetland, e.g. birdwatching or hiking, be used to predict the value of the same activities in a peatland? The accuracy of value transfer has been shown to be questionable and context sensitive (Rosenberger and Stanley 2006; Johnston and Rosenberger 2010). It is therefore necessary to carefully account for differences between the 'study sites' for which value information is available and the 'policy sites' to which values are transferred. A number of studies have specifically examined the transferability of values between wetlands, and found high average differences between primary and predicted values (Brander, Florax and Vermaat 2006; Brander *et al.* 2010).

Box 16.2
Benefits and damage derived from German peatlands in respect of carbon cycling

Country: Mecklenburg-Western Pomerania, Germany
Peatland type: drained and rewetted fens
Ecosystem service: carbon storage
Stakeholders: political decision makers
Valuation method: damage costs, avoided damage costs
More information: www.eea.europa.eu/teeb/teeb/peatland-restoration-for-carbon-sequestration-germany-1

Case
In Germany, 930 000 ha of peatlands under agricultural production release 20 million tonnes of CO_2-equivalents (CO_2 e) per year (Schäfer 2009). These largely avoidable emissions nearly equate to the 22 million tonnes that need to be reduced annually by German households and traffic to fulfil national climate change goals (National Allocation Plan period 2007–2012). The unsound use of peatlands neither meets the demands of sustainable land use nor the principles of good agricultural practice. Without environmentally harmful subsidies, such as direct payments within the EU Common Agricultural Policy or incentives of the German Renewable Energy Sources Act for biofuels, most peatlands would be abandoned and left to natural succession.

Ecosystem services under valuation
Rewetting drained peatlands is a reliable tool of climate change mitigation since GHG emissions are substantially reduced, and in some cases, carbon sequestration through peat formation is enhanced (Chapter 4). Additionally, rewetting peatlands may provide multiple benefits by enhancing water retention and purification and contribute to achieving the EU 2020 biodiversity target by producing species-rich meadow habitats, reed-marshes, alder forests and other valuable habitats for rare and threatened species. Furthermore, paludicultures on wet peatlands (Chapter 17) allow for the production of agricultural commodities while maintaining ecosystem services (Wichtmann et al. 2010).

Methodology
Each GHG unit not released into the atmosphere provides a small benefit in the mitigation of climate change. Estimating the marginal costs of avoiding an incremental GHG unit (mitigation cost) and the marginal costs of avoided damage are two important economic approaches for valuing the damages of drained, and the benefits of rewetted, peatlands.

The economic valuation has been carried out for drained peatlands used for agriculture and for a programme of peatland restoration in the Federal State of Mecklenburg-Western Pomerania in Germany. The global warming potential of land-use alternatives has been estimated by applying the GHG Emission Site Types (GEST) approach that allows the assessment of reductions in GHG emissions from peat soils with simple proxy parameters, such as mean water-table fluctuation and vegetation (Couwenberg et al. 2011).

Results
Damage costs of agricultural use on drained peatlands versus its added value

Marginal damage costs have to be considered with 70 EUR per tonne CO_2 in cost–benefit calculations of public projects in Germany (Federal Environment Agency 2008). The damage costs of the 20 million tonnes CO_2e emitted by agriculturally used peatland are in this case in the magnitude of 1.4 billion EUR, or approximately 1500 EUR ha^{-1} yr^{-1}. The net farm income of a well-placed milk farm in Mecklenburg-Western Pomerania is on average 585 EUR ha^{-1} yr^{-1} (Schäfer 2009). The collateral damage costs of the farm through enhancing GHG emissions are therefore much higher than its value-adding contribution of livestock production. While unsustainable agriculture on degraded peatlands is encouraged by environmentally harmful subsidies, other sectors in Germany, such as households, energy and traffic, have substantial costs for reducing emissions.

Avoided damage costs as proxy for GHG mitigation benefits from rewetted peatlands

The ambitious peatland conservation program of the Federal State of Mecklenburg-Western Pomerania rewetted approximately 30 000 ha of drained peatland in 2000–2008. This resulted in a GHG emissions reduction of about 300 000 tonnes CO_2 e per year (MLUV MV 2009). Using the carbon value above, the benefit of the programme amounts to more than 21 million EUR yr^{-1} or 728 EUR yr^{-1} for every hectare of rewetted peatland (Schäfer 2009).

Comparing mitigation costs of land use-based mitigation measures

Most paludiculture, such as the cultivation of reed or alder, can compete with normal drainage-based agriculture. Furthermore, mitigation costs of paludiculture on rewetted peatlands are considerably lower than for other agricultural mitigation measures, such as biofuel production on mineral soils requiring high subsidies (cf. Table 16.3). In contrast, biofuel production on drained peatlands leads to peat oxidation causing CO_2 emissions that are up to ten times higher than those released by the combustion of fossil fuels such as peat or oil (Couwenberg 2007b).

Table 16.3 *Mitigation costs of reed and alder paludiculture on organic soils compared to those of biomass production for biogas and biofuels on mineral soils.*

	EUR per t CO_2	Reference
Cultivation of reed (*Phragmites australis*)	0	Wichtmann and Schäfer 2007
Cultivation of alder (*Alnus glutinosa*)	0–2	Schäfer and Joosten 2005
Biogas*	52–387	Isermeyer *et al.* 2008
Biofuels*	193–578	Isermeyer *et al.* 2008

* on mineral soils

Box 16.3

Valuation of restoring degraded peatland on the Bleaklow plateau

Country:	Bleaklow, Peak District National Park, UK
Peatland type:	degraded upland bog
Ecosystem service:	regulation of water quality, carbon storage, non-use values
Stakeholders:	local, regional, national bodies
Valuation method:	replacement costs, avoided damage costs, choice experiment
More information:	eftec (2009); van der Wal *et al.* (2011), www.moorsforthefuture.org.uk

Case

The Bleaklow restoration site is a highly degraded blanket bog which has seen significant damage through industrial pollution, wildfires and overgrazing, resulting in loss of vegetation, erosion gullies and acidification of soils. Restoration efforts by the Moors for the Future Partnership have been directed towards re-establishing the natural vegetation by erosion control, nurse crops, liming and fertilising. The Bleaklow restoration site covers 6 km^2 of the Bleaklow plateau, which feeds the reservoir system of the Derwent Valley providing water to surrounding cities such as Sheffield and Derby.

Ecosystem services under valuation

Restoration changes the provision of

services of the site, such as climate regulation, potentially water quality regulation and cultural services. Recreational values were omitted in the analysis due to the risks of double-counting with non-use values and a lack of accurate visitation data for this site.

Methodology

Carbon values are based upon calculated reductions in losses of carbon following restoration management and UK Government-stipulated values for CO_2e (DECC 2008). These values take into account the potential costs of future climate change by increasing over time to factor in the changing impact (currently 27 GBP rising to 196 GBP in 2109). Water quality values are based upon the treatment costs of water, mainly for chemical coagulants required to remove water colour (DOC) to comply with Drinking Water Standards. Further costs may occur for dredging the reservoir network. Non-use values are based upon a choice experiment applied across the East Midlands Severely Disadvantaged Areas (Hanley et al. 2007), of which the Bleaklow restoration site covers 0.6%, equivalent to c. 1.8 million households.

Results

The value of the Bleaklow peatland restoration (Table 16.4) is predominantly related to cultural/non-use value. Its net present value (over 50 years) relates to a value of c. 3 million GBP compared with that of carbon storage of c. 0.4 million GBP. Water quality changes, although important, could not yet be established and therefore valued. This lack of evidence limits the valuation and is currently being addressed through further studies. Given uncertainties in the valuation approach, this conservative analysis allows a suitable value to be derived for policy analysis and is indicative that the restoration costs of 1.75 million GBP (c. 2900 GBP yr^{-1}) are met by even the lower bounds of this limited set of service values which can be expected from restoration.

Table 16.4 Selected values of ecosystem services amended by restoration activities on the Bleaklow plateau (adapted and abbreviated from eftec 2009, van der Wal et al. 2011).

Service	Baseline	Impact of Restoration	Values and Notes
Climate regulation through carbon storage	Data for a range of carbon pathways provided in Worrall et al. (2011b)	Reduced carbon loss: 93–319 t CO_2e km^{-2} yr^{-1} Carbon benefit dominated by avoided losses (Worrall et al. 2009, 2011b)	Conservative reduction of c. 600 t CO_2e over 6 km gives a net present value of c. 370 000 GBP over 50 years.

Service	Baseline	Impact of Restoration	Values and Notes
Water quality regulation	High rates of DOC loss 34–72 t CO_2e km^{-2} yr^{-1} (Worrall et al. 2011b) High sediment losses of up to 267 t sediment km^{-2} (Evans, Warburton and Yang 2006)	Reduced levels of DOC expected, but currently no measurable benefit of re-vegetation on DOC to date Significant reduction in erosion rates up to an order of magnitude (Worrall et al. 2011b)	Conservative estimate: value of zero. Likely future value, but high uncertainty as dependent on management of surrounding areas. A full estimation needs a catchment approach
Non-use values from cultural landscapes	Highly degraded landscape	Change to good conservation	Willingness to pay (WTP) of 0.12 GBP per household (Hanley et al. 2007) results in c. 200 000 GBP for the Bleaklow restoration site Amount may well be higher because large populations live in adjacent regions (Northwest, West Midlands)

A promising approach to controlling for differences between study and policy sites in value transfer is the use of value functions estimated using meta-analysis (EEA 2010). Meta-analytic function transfer uses results from a collection of studies together with information on parameter values for the policy site to estimate values. This results in the inclusion of greater variety in site characteristics, e.g. socio-economic and physical attributes, and study characteristics, e.g. valuation method, than a single primary valuation study, which allows for the specific characteristics of a policy site to be better represented in the transferred value.

16.5 Payments for ecosystem services

Valuation – i.e. identifying, quantifying and, where applicable, monetising ecosystem services – can inform and justify many forms of economic and policy instruments to allow accounting for externalities. In this regard, the instrument of payments for ecosystem (or environmental) services (PES) has become very popular in recent years. Creating markets for public goods may prevent mismanagement of ecosystems and ensure protection of biodiversity. PES are voluntary transactions in which those who protect and manage the provision of a well-defined ecosystem service are paid (in money or in-kind) for providing that service (see Wunder 2005). In reality, the term PES is often used for describing any kind of market-based mechanism for conservation (Engel, Pagiola and Wunder 2008). This broader understanding includes regulatory (non-voluntary) policies, indirect incentives and payments for vaguely defined services, with examples from conservation concessions and watershed protection, via forest-carbon plantations and agri-environmental schemes, to eco-certification of products and entrance fees for tourists. Box 16.4 provides proposals for a PES scheme for local communities in Central Kalimantan to cooperate in peatland restoration.

Only a few PES mechanisms have been carefully documented (Engel, Pagiola and Wunder 2008). Nevertheless, many financing instruments can be used or adapted to provide payments for peatland ecosystem services:

- **Carbon storage and sequestration:** REDD+ as global PES system, as well as standards, for global (VCS-PRC) and regional voluntary markets (e.g. MoorFutures® in Germany, www.moorfutures.de) have been established (Chapter 15). The German International Initiative for Climate Change Mitigation (ICI) finances peatland restoration projects in Belarus, Ukraine and Russia (see Tanneberger and Wichtmann 2011) with money generated by trading emission certificates on the European market.
- **Water quality:** Water companies paying land users for adapted watershed management is probably the most common example of a PES scheme, known particularly in Latin America (e.g. Kosoy *et al.* 2007). Drawing on the EU Water Framework Directive, peatlands are rewetted with water and sewage fees (e.g. Schleswig-Holstein, Germany) or with taxpayers' money (e.g. Brandenburg, Germany) to improve water quality of lakes, rivers and the Baltic Sea.
- **Biodiversity:** EU-Life+, the European Commission's financial instrument supporting environmental and nature conservation projects throughout

the EU, has been financing many peatland restoration projects in, for example, the UK, Ireland, Finland, Germany, Poland and Lithuania, both for protecting biodiversity and restoring ecosystem functions.

- **Agri-environmental schemes:** The EU and United States provide a wide range of payments to farmers for sensitive environmental management, including reducing erosion and protecting habitats for endangered species. Similarly, payments for paludiculture (wet peatland agriculture and forestry) could stimulate peatland rewetting and reinstalling peatland ecosystem functions (Chapter 17). Even more urgent is redesigning environmentally harmful subsidies and perverse incentives that sustain and encourage drainage of peatlands, such as direct payments for agriculture and incentives for biofuels (see Box 16.2).
- **Health and safety:** Wildfires in peatlands have high negative impacts on human life and lead to serious economic losses. Hazards can be avoided by payments for adapted peatland management (e.g. in Indonesia, Box 16.4, Chapter 14). After extensive peat and forest fires in 2010, affecting especially Moscow, Russia has rewetted 65 000 ha of drained peatlands in the Moscow region (involving 100 million EUR) to prevent further fires.

The monetisation of ecosystem services and their commodification through payment schemes is critically discussed (e.g. Kosoy and Corbera 2010; Gómez-Baggethun *et al.* 2010). Focusing payments on single services can lead to unbalanced decision making ignoring trade-offs with other objectives, e.g. the rapidly developing carbon market can aggravate the loss of

---

Box 16.4

Valuation of restoring degraded peatland in Central Kalimantan

Country:	Central Kalimantan, Indonesia
Peatland type:	degraded tropical peatland, former peat swamp forest
Ecosystem service:	provision of timber and NTFPs from local species, co-benefits for climate change mitigation, biodiversity conservation and health
Stakeholders:	local and international communities

Valuation method:	quantitative (choice experiment) and qualitative (focus group discussions)
More information:	van Beukering *et al.* (2008)

Case

The peatswamp forests of Central Kalimantan, Indonesia, have been heavily degraded by logging and drainage for conversion to agricultural land and oil palm and pulp plantations (Jaenicke, Englhart and Siegert 2011, Chapter 14). The resulting degradation of natural resources has led to large carbon emissions and annual peat fires with supra-regional negative effects on health due to smoke and haze (Page *et al.* 2009). In combination with unfavourable agricultural conditions of peatland soil, these hazards contribute to levels of poverty that are two to four times higher than in the rest of Indonesia (Silvius, Joosten and Opdam 2008), while enormous areas of land are left fallow. The objective of the study was to assess the compensation needed by local communities in Central Kalimantan to cooperate in peatland restoration programmes, where local farmers would reforest these fallow lands with local tree species suitable for peatland soils.

Ecosystem services under valuation

Changes in peatland management require significant short-term investments in alternative land-use practices, providing longer-term local benefits in terms of income from timber and non-timber forest products, and reduced health and safety risks related to peatland fire prevention. The international community could benefit in terms of climate change mitigation, biodiversity conservation and reduced health risks.

Methodology

The development of successful compensation schemes involves the design of the payment mechanisms catering to the needs of local communities (Engel and Palmer 2008). The measurement of the required payments should reflect the costs and benefits that communities may face when environmental programmes are implemented. In this study, a combination of quantitative and qualitative approaches was used (cf. Powe, Garrod and McMahon 2005). A quantitative valuation method (choice experiments) was used for the assessment of the necessary payments through estimation of costs and benefits.

In a developing-country context, results of stated preference approaches may be less reliable due to cross-cultural differences. For instance, Whittington (1998) argues that 'yes'-answers to a willingness to pay question are a polite way of saying 'no' in Indonesia and may result in inflated value estimates. Nevertheless, group discussions are not suitable for estimating monetary values, and therefore quantitative methods are necessary.

> Qualitative focus group discussions were used to develop the design of the payment mechanism and to cross-check the results of the choice experiment and the underlying motives, which is more difficult within survey methods such as choice experiments.
>
> **Results**
> The results indicate that farmers are willing to change from current agricultural practices to reforestation and sustainable agroforestry. One of the reasons is that many local farmers found it difficult to make a living from the infertile peatlands. However, farmers' cooperation is conditional on secure and stable income and food supply and, therefore, farmers prefer to continue using part of their land for household consumptive production. Compensation in the form of agricultural and technical assistance, training and advice to help farmers grow local tree species is not valued highly by local communities. Farmers preferred to receive financial compensation in the form of loan and grant schemes, paid directly in order to avoid corruption. Environmental awareness about the benefits of conservation and engagement of local communities in peatland management are vital for acceptance of new land-use policies, such as a change in crop type. Willingness to change to the cultivation of local species also depends on the availablity of nurseries and the development of and access to markets. Further recommendations for peatland conservation measures are to create a system of secure tenure rights and policies, reducing the risk of food and income shortages (Engel and Palmer 2008).
>
> Combining the quantitative method with qualitative focus group discussions helped to better understand the underlying attitudes and motives that drive the valuation outcomes of the choice experiment, and to confirm that the choice experiment results provide reasonably reliable information for ecosystem valuation. The focus group discussions were necessary to
>
> - understand preferences regarding the distribution of costs and benefits over time;
> - understand differences in the preferences of respondents arising from environmental awareness and ecosystem characteristics; and
> - provide further detail about the specific terms and conditions on which respondents will accept land-use change scenarios.

biodiversity, which is not globally commodified. Furthermore, incentives need to be carefully designed and adapted to local circumstances, since appealing to economic self-interest may change the behaviour of people and undermine possibly existing intrinsic motivations for conservation based on moral or communal obligations (crowding-out, see Bowles 2008).

16.6 Conclusions and outlook

Peatlands deliver a wide range of services contributing to human well-being, which can be classified as ecological, socio-cultural and economic values. Only part of the overall value can be captured in monetary units due to the methodological constraints of valuation, lack of knowledge and ethical considerations. Nevertheless, valuation is regarded as vital for raising awareness about the importance of ecosystem services may facilitate better-informed decision making (e.g. on peatland restoration), the correction and creation of markets through the introduction of effective and efficient schemes to capture benefits (e.g. PES, supporting paludicultures) and raising 'new' money for nature conservation by considering expenses for conservation and restoration of peatlands as investments rather than costs.

Any robust valuation of ecosystem services depends on good underpinning science. In contrast to many other ecosystems, the literature on the value of peatlands is limited and almost completely restricted to monetary valuation. To enable a better accounting for peatland ecosystem services in decision making, further research and monitoring is needed

- to quantify services to provide reliable and replicable evidence for valuation
- to explore possibilities for benefit transfer across ecosystem boundaries
- to broaden valuation with more comprehensive methods capturing socio-cultural and ecological values (see Daily *et al.* 2009).

Despite the challenges and limitations of valuation and PES in the scientific arena, the political world considers monetisation of ecosystem services and remuneration of their provision as promising tools for tackling globally important problems such as climate change, loss of biodiversity, ecosystem degradation and poverty. However, monetary valuation as a tool to inform the design of policy instruments and PES as a possible policy instrument should not be seen as a panacea. They are merely instruments to pursue objectives set by deliberative processes based not only on economic values but also on ethical considerations, and should be applied in very specific contexts in addition to other methods and policies. Nonetheless, providing reliable information on the benefits provided by functioning and especially on the damages resulting from degraded peatlands, identifying winners and losers of changes in ecosystem health today and in the future, as well as comparing cost–benefit ratios of ensuring ecosystem service provision and of alternative options, will considerably support decision making in policy and management and may strengthen arguments for conservation, restoration and sustainable use of peatlands.

CHAPTER SEVENTEEN

Paludiculture: sustainable productive use of wet and rewetted peatlands

HANS JOOSTEN
Institute of Botany and Landscape Ecology, Ernst Moritz Arndt University of Greifswald, Germany
GRETA GAUDIG
Institute of Botany and Landscape Ecology, Ernst Moritz Arndt University of Greifswald, Germany
FRANZISKA TANNEBERGER
Institute of Botany and Landscape Ecology, Ernst Moritz Arndt University of Greifswald, and Michael Succow Foundation, Greifswald, Germany
SABINE WICHMANN
Institute of Botany and Landscape Ecology, Ernst Moritz Arndt University of Greifswald, Germany
WENDELIN WICHTMANN
Michael Succow Foundation Greifswald, Germany

17.1 Introduction

The origin of mainstream Western agriculture lies in the 'fertile crescent' of the Middle East and, in this cradle of arable farming, dryland plants were domesticated that currently constitute some of our major cereal, legume and fibre crops. This 'semi-desert' agriculture installed the idea that productive land must be dry, a paradigm that ever since has been applied also to wet, organic soils. We deeply drain peatland to grow arid maize *Zea mays* in Germany, strongly water-demanding sugar cane *Saccharum* spp. in Florida and the desert species *Aloe vera* in Indonesia. Practices like this have made agriculture the main driver of global peatland loss (Joosten and Clarke 2002, Chapter 2) and drained peatlands are thus primarily found in regions that are climatically favourable for agriculture, i.e. in the temperate zone and the (sub)tropics (Chapter 2).

Peatland drainage causes inherent peatland degradation, a substantial financial and environmental burden and eventually the loss of the productive value of the peat soil (Joosten, Tapio-Biström and Tol 2012). These problems

Peatland Restoration and Ecosystem Services: Science, Policy and Practice, eds. A. Bonn, T. Allott, M. Evans, H. Joosten and R. Stoneman. Published by Cambridge University Press. © British Ecological Society 2016.

are increasingly being recognised: worldwide several thousands of square kilometres of drained agricultural peatlands have been rewetted in recent years for climate change mitigation, for biodiversity, or simply because maintaining drainage infrastructure had become too expensive. Rewetting has indeed re-established major regulating and cultural services of wet peatlands, including carbon storage, flood control, water purification, archive function and biodiversity (Theuerkauf *et al.* 2006; Limpens *et al.* 2008; Trepel 2010; Tanneberger and Wichtmann 2011; Joosten *et al.* 2015a; Chapter 6). The provisioning services of these formerly productive lands, however, were mostly lost as the rewetted areas were generally earmarked for nature conservation with the condition that they would no longer be used agriculturally.

On the other hand, the quest for productive land is rapidly growing worldwide. This demand will continue to increase, because of the inevitable growth of human population and the justified demands for food security and more welfare. The demand will also grow, because biomass from cultivated land will increasingly have to replace the resources that until now were obtained from the wilderness (wood, non-timber forest products, bushmeat) and the bedrock (coal, oil, gas, minerals). Both the persistent use of drained peatlands for agriculture and the conversion of agriculturally used peatlands to unused wetlands imply that we are losing productive land at a time when we need it most. Therefore new production techniques have to be urgently developed that allow the productive use of peatlands while simultaneously restoring or maintaining the ecosystem services of wet peatlands (Joosten, Tapio-Biström and Tol 2012).

Management innovation is also required to stop the widespread loss of biodiversity from traditionally used wet peatlands. Gathering hay and litter from fen mires was a common practice in Europe, to which the ecosystems over centuries have adapted. As labour-intensive scything provides limited income opportunities, many former fen mires and fen meadows have been converted to drained and fertilised highly productive grasslands, which has caused a loss of habitat of many fen-typical plant and animal species (Kotowski 2002; Hodgson *et al.* 2005; Wassen *et al.* 2005; Chapter 10). Many areas have also been abandoned, which similarly leads to a loss of biodiversity because of lack of regular biomass removal and consequent macroforb and shrub encroachment (Chapter 10). Restoration and conservation of typical semi-natural fen diversity thus require new, cost-effective conservation management tools to sustain habitat quality.

This chapter presents an overview of 'paludiculture', wet peatland agriculture and forestry, and illustrates the experiences of this innovative concept to date. Special attention is paid to paludiculture in the temperate zone.

17.2 Drawbacks of drainage-based peatland utilisation

Conventional peatland agriculture and forestry requires a lowering of the water table, which substantially impacts on ecosystem services. Drainage leads to an increase in GHG emissions to the atmosphere (Chapter 4), an increase in nutrient emissions to ground- and surface waters (Sapek *et al.* 2007; Mališauskas and Kutra 2008), a decrease in evaporative cooling (Joosten *et al.* 2015a) and to a loss of typical mire biodiversity (Chapter 3). Drainage also causes compaction of the peat, which changes its hydraulic properties and reduces the capacity of the peatland for water storage and regulation (Edom 2001; Joosten and Clarke 2002; van den Akker 2010).

Drained peatlands furthermore loose – depending on climate and land use – from millimetres up to several centimetres of height per year by peat oxidation (Succow and Joosten 2001; Couwenberg, Dommain and Joosten 2010). This inevitable subsidence necessitates – in the case of continued exploitation – a continuous deepening of the drainage ditches, which again enhances subsidence, ditch deepening, etc., a phenomenon known as 'the vicious circle of peatland utilisation' (Kuntze 1982; Chapter 2). In the Netherlands (the 'Low Countries'), a millennium of peatland drainage has led to almost half of the country existing below sea level (Borger 1992). As a result of progressive subsidence, gravity drainage becomes increasingly more difficult so that the land eventually becomes too wet for conventional use unless a polder system with embankments, permanent pumping and ever-increasing management costs is installed. Drainage-induced subsidence furthermore increases the risk of floods and salt water intrusion in many low-lying and coastal peatlands, be it in the Sacramento–San Joaquin Delta of California (Deverel and Leigthon 2010), the peat polders of Northern Germany or the extensive coastal peatlands of Malaysia and Indonesia (Chapter 14).

In more continental and warmer climates, water-level fluctuations in drained peatlands and the associated shrinkage and swelling cause the formation of fissures in the peat, which impede capillary water flow and lead to more frequent and deeper desiccation. Soil organisms then make the drained peat so loose and fine-grained that the soil eventually becomes irreversibly hydrophobic (Ilnicki and Zeitz 2003; Litaor, Reichmann and Shenker 2011) and unsuitable for agriculture (Figure 17.1). In this way a wet peatland may change to a dry desert within a few decades. Abandoned drained peatlands continue to emit CO_2, and the lack of management and cessation of control may lead to the outbreak of catastrophic fires (Minayeva, Sirin and Stracher 2013).

Figure 17.1 Heavily degraded desiccated agricultural peat soil in Chernigiv region, Ukraine (photo: Hans Joosten).

It is clear that peatland exploitation by peatland drainage is not sustainable and that new, wetland utilisation techniques have to be developed (Verhoeven and Setter 2010; Knox *et al.* 2015).

17.3 The concept of paludiculture

In contrast to conventional agriculture, paludiculture (Latin '*palus*' = swamp) utilises biomass from wet and rewetted peatlands in a way that the peat body is preserved, natural peatland ecosystem services are maintained or restored and (ideally) peat accumulation is re-established or continues (Box 17.1). In the temperate zone (especially its more continental parts), the subtropics and the tropics, peat is often formed by roots and rhizomes (Chapter 2) and the above-ground biomass of such peatlands can (partially) be harvested without substantially harming peat formation and conservation (Wichtmann and Joosten 2007).

Paludiculture comprises any biomass use from wet and rewetted peatlands, from using spontaneous vegetation on natural sites (Boxes 17.2 and 17.3) to harvesting artificially established crops on rewetted sites. Besides traditional yields of food, feed, fibre and fuel, the biomass can be used as a raw material for industrial biochemistry in the production of high-quality liquid or gaseous biofuels and for further purposes like extracting and synthesising pharmaceuticals and cosmetics.

Box 17.1
What is paludiculture?

Paludiculture is a peat-conserving sustainable form of productive land use on peatland, which avoids the GHG emissions and other forms of pollution resulting from drainage-based land use. The objective of paludiculture is to maintain and restore the multiple services provided by wet peatland ecosystems, while at the same time allowing biomass harvest. Paludiculture is thus an agri- (or silvi-)cultural production system: it targets the production of plant- or animal-based commodities.

Paludiculture is the use of peatlands under wet site conditions and implies an agricultural paradigm shift. Instead of draining mires for producing biomass and increasing load-bearing capacity, peatlands are used under peat-conserving hydrological conditions. Deeply drained and highly degraded peatlands have, from an environmental point of view, the greatest need for action, and provide the largest land potential for paludiculture (Wichtmann, Schröder and Joosten 2016).

17.4 Paludiculture in the temperate zone

17.4.1 Introduction

Low-intensity forms of paludiculture include hunting/gathering of plants and animals with little land management intervention. In the boreal zone of Eurasia a wide variety of berries and mushrooms are gathered from peatlands for food and vitamins (Joosten and Clarke 2002; Box 17.2), and the safeguarding of these provisioning services has been a major argument for protecting and restoring mires in the Russian Federation and Belarus. In other parts of the world a variety of plants for human nutrition or medical use are collected from wet peatlands, such as wild rice *Zizania aquatica* (North America), bogbean *Menyanthes trifoliata*, calamus *Acorus calamus* and sweet grass *Hierochloe odorata* (Europe) or sago palm *Metroxylon sagu* (Malaysia) (Joosten and Clarke 2002; Abel *et al.* 2013).

More intensive land-use options include crop cultivation on wet and rewetted peatlands. This may include both the revival of traditional land use through modified utilisation schemes and the cultivation of novel crops for new market demands (Table 17.1). The following sections illustrate the various options.

Box 17.2
Valuation of cranberry harvest in Maročna bog (Belarus)

Sviataslau Valasiuk and Aliona Shushkova

In a study on the local use of cranberry *Vaccinium oxycoccos* resources in the Maročna raised bog (4200 ha), Brest region (Belarus), representatives of 149 households (10% of the total number) of the adjacent villages, Haradniany and Hlinka, were interviewed to assess the socio-economic characteristics of the households, the volumes of cranberries annually collected, marketed or domestically consumed, prices paid, alternative employment opportunities, and the willingness to pay (WTP) for conserving the bog in its current semi-intact state (Figure 17.2).

The annual value of the provisioning service was estimated as the difference between the income from selling cranberries and the costs of labour and alternative income opportunities expressed in monetary terms.

The survey revealed that, in 2009, the average cranberry harvest per household amounted to 125.5 kg, implying an annual harvest of 39.5 kg ha^{-1}, which is equal to the average natural productivity of bogs in Belarus (Baginski 2007). A total of 60% of the households reported using the cranberry

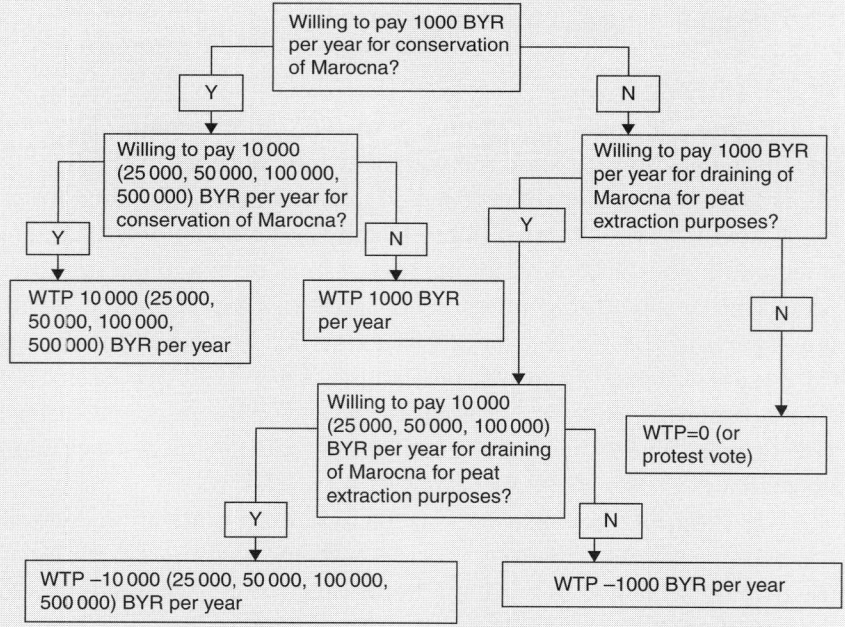

Figure 17.2 Contingent valuation scheme to assess the WTP of households to conserve the adjacent Maročna bog (Belarus).

resources of Maročna regularly. Of the harvest, 85% was sold, providing an average net income per collector household of 392 000 Belarusian rubles (BYR) per year (2009 prices, 1000 BYR is ~0.30 EUR). Extrapolation to all households of Haradniany (752) and Hlinka (675) provided an overall net value of 314 million BYR.

Most respondents (including 82 collector and 40 non-collector households) proved to have a positive average WTP of 26 900 BYR per household per year for conserving the site. The total annual WTP for the conservation of Maročna was BYR 7100 ha^{-1}, which is almost 10 times less than the value of the cranberries per hectare.

The study showed that cranberry harvesting contributes substantially to the welfare of local households. The interviews, however, showed a substantially lower contribution than estimated by experts, which might be explained by respondents' strategic behaviour to conceal part of their income. The relatively low willingness to pay for conserving Maročna shows that most respondents do not associate the need for preserving the bog with its value as a cranberry resource.

Table 17.1 *Provisioning services provided by paludiculture in temperate Europe with an indication of associated regulating and cultural services, using peat accumulation as a proxy (Chapter 2). Modified after Joosten et al. (2015b)*

Division	Product	Source	Quality demand	Origin	Harvesting time	Peat accumulation
Nutrition	berries and other fruits	shrubs, dwarf shrubs	+	S, A	autumn	+
	mushrooms	mushrooms	++	S	summer/ autumn	+
	meat	game, fowl, fish		S	hunting season	+
	in situ fodder (grazing)	wet meadows, reeds	++	S	entire year	±
Material	*ex situ* fodder: hay, silage	wet meadows, reeds	++	S	early summer	±
	roofing materials	reeds	++	S, A	winter	+
	building panels/ boards	reeds	++/0	S, A	winter	+

Table 17.1 (cont.)

Division	Product	Source	Quality demand	Origin	Harvesting time	Peat accumulation
	insulation materials	reed, cat-tail	++	S, A	winter	+
	timber/veneer	alder, birch, pine	++	S, A	winter-frost	+
	wattle- and basketware	willow, bullrush	++	S, A	autumn	±
	moulds	wet meadows, reeds	+	S, A	autumn/ winter	+
	growing media	peat moss	++	S, A	entire year	±
	litter	sedge meadows, reeds	0	S, A	summer/ autumn	±
	compost	wet meadows, reeds	0	S, A	late summer	±
	pharmaceuticals	many herb and forb species	++	S, A	early summer	±
	flavours	various herb, forbs and grasses	++	S, A	summer	±
	cosmetics	various herb species	++	S, A	summer	±
Energy	direct combustion	alder/birch/ willow, reeds	0	S, A	autumn/ winter	+
	pellets, briquettes	wet meadows, reeds	0	S, A	winter/early spring	+
	biogas	wet meadows, reeds	±	S, A	early summer	±
	liquid biofuels	wet meadows, reeds	0	S, A	entire year	+
	biochar	wet meadows, reeds	0	S, A	winter	+

S = spontaneous occurrence; A = artificially established; ++ = high; + = medium; 0 = no; ± = possible; – = negative.

> **Box 17.3**
> # Grazing fen peatlands with water buffalo
>
> **René Krawczynski**
>
> Cattle grazing for meat and dairy production on peatland generally involves drainage, but also on drained sites the fodder often does not meet the increasing quality needs of high-production dairy cows. As a consequence, grasslands on peat soils are often abandoned or only subject to minimalist management in order to secure EU direct payments (Chapter 15). An alternative use of such grasslands after rewetting is grazing water buffalo, *Bubalus bubalis*. Water buffalo are well adapted to permanent wet conditions and forage on biomass with low energy content. They are much less sensitive to parasites and hoof diseases and move better on wet soils than domestic cattle (Krawczynski, Biel and Zeigert 2008). Buffalo can be kept outside even at temperatures below –20°C, provided that they have shelter from the wind and a straw bed to lie on. Under good pastoral management the animals can gain about 800 g of weight per day at a livestock density of 1.5 per hectare, without supplementary feeding (Müller and Sweers 2016). Water buffalo rearing for beef production is economically feasible, at least with direct marketing, with the reproductive performance of the animals being decisive for economic results (Sweers, Möhring and Müller 2014).

17.4.2 Energy crops from fens

The substitution of fossil fuels and resources is a key challenge of our times, and biomass may play an important role in this substitution. Within the European Union, for example, the use of biofuels is promoted by the Renewable Energy Directive (RED–Directive 2009/28/EC), which established a target of 10% of energy for road transport derived from renewable sources by 2020.

Peatlands have also been subject to the recent expansion of energy crops, e.g. the large-scale cultivation of maize for biogas production in Germany and of oil palm *Elaeis guineensis* for palm oil in South East Asia (Chapters 14 and 19).

Similarly to other agriculture, the cultivation of energy crops on drained peatland leads to major environmental and sustainability problems. Biogas produced from maize cultivated on drained peatland, for example, may cause over 800 t CO_2e of GHG emissions per terajoule energy produced, whereas generating the same amount of energy by burning coal produces only 100 t CO_2e (Couwenberg 2007b). From a climate change mitigation point of view, it is thus far better to burn fossil fuels than to cultivate 'biofuel' crops on drained peatland (Couwenberg 2007b). The practice of biofuel production on drained peatland is, however, perversely supported by the Kyoto Protocol, the European Union and national subsidy systems like the German Renewable Energy Act, which consider biofuels as climate neutral in the energy sector, but largely fail to account for the huge peat carbon losses from the land that produces the energy crops (Chapter 15).

On wet peatlands, winter mown common reed *Phragmites australis* can economically compete with energy crops from mineral soils (cereal straw, Miscanthus, *Miscanthus × giganteus*), even when special machinery for harvesting is required (Wichtmann, Wichmann and Tanneberger 2010, see Wichmann 2016). With an average yield of 8 t dry weight (DW) ha^{-1} yr^{-1} and a lower heating value of at least 17.5 MJ kg^{-1} DW (Wichmann and Wichtmann 2009), common reed from 1 ha can replace fossil fuels (fuel oil) in a combined heat and power plant that would otherwise emit 10 t CO_2e. With emissions from handling (mowing, transport, storage, delivery and operation of the co-generation plant) amounting to 2 t CO_2e ha^{-1} (Wichtmann, Couwenberg and Kowatsch 2009), the emission reduction from rewetting (18 t CO_2e ha^{-1} yr^{-1}; Chapter 4) and replacement of the fossil fuel (10 t CO_2e ha^{-1} yr^{-1}) adds up to about 25 t CO_2e ha^{-1} yr^{-1}.

Reed canary grass, *Phalaris arundinacea* harvested under wet site conditions with adapted standard grassland machines in summer results in higher costs per unit than reed, as yields are lower (5 t DW ha^{-1} a^{-1}) and drying on site is necessary (Wichtmann and Wichmann 2011b). The type of utilisation (liquid biofuels, biogas, direct heat supply to single consumers, combined heating power for regional heating and others) eventually determines the economic revenues from paludiculture energy crops.

Implementation of paludiculture on 19% (57,000 ha) of the peatland area of the German federal state of Mecklenburg-Western Pomerania would annually provide 456,000 t DW of biomass, representing a gross energy yield of 8 million GJ (ca. 188,000 t fuel oil equivalents), which could supply 400 local energy plants with 800 kW each (Schröder et al. 2012). This would reduce GHG emissions by 1.5 million t CO_2 e, i.e. 9% of the total emissions of the federal state. Energy plants fed with biomass from wet fens (Schröder, Wichtmann and Körner 2013) decrease the local dependency on global energy policies and prices and – by purchasing biomass – also facilitate regional nature conservation management (Box 17.4) and water quality improvement (Box 17.5).

Box 17.4

Energy from conservation management in Central and Eastern European fens

Jarosław Krogulec, Uladzimir Malashevich, Christian Schröder, Franziska Tanneberger and Wendelin Wichtmann

The vast fen peatlands of the Biebrza River Valley and the Lublin region (Eastern Poland) are a stronghold of biodiversity, with as a flagship species the globally threatened aquatic warbler *Acrocephalus paludicola*, with 25% of the global population. After traditional hand-scything had ceased around 1970, successional overgrowth became the main threat to this habitat, affecting over 15 000 ha by 1999. A project funded by EU LIFE and run by OTOP BirdLife Poland catalysed the implementation of landscape-wide restoration and sustainable management. Since 2007, machinery capable of mowing large areas of delicate peatlands has been tested and, since 2009, adapted mountain piste-bashers, colloquially called 'ratrak', have been used (Lachmann, Marczakiewicz and Grzywaczewski 2010). Recently, some 10 000 ha of public lands were made available for mowing under lease agreements in several peatland areas in Eastern Poland. Targeted aquatic warbler agri-environment packages provide a financial incentive for local farmers and enterprises. In a follow-up EU LIFE project (2011–15), a facility to turn the biomass into fuel briquettes/pellets was set up in Trzcianne. This has operated since 2013, with an annual target of *c*. 4,500 tonnes of dry biomass. Pellets are sold mainly to wholesalers (power plants) and by retail for households heating (Cris *et al.* 2014).

Overgrowing vegetation is a major threat also at Sporava (Belarus), another key aquatic warbler breeding site, with *c*. 5% of the global population. Vegetation management with conventional agricultural equipment started in 2006 but appeared to be too weather and water-level dependent. A feasibility study and business plan (2010) showed that the most cost-effective way of using biomass from Sporava is the production of fuel briquettes. A 'ratrak' funded by the German International Climate Initiative was delivered to Belarus in 2011 and facilitates mowing of *c*. 200 ha annually. An EU/UNDP Clima East project (2015–20) currently aims at using the biomass for producing fuel briquettes/pellets. Building on the experiences from Sporava, similar measures are also planned for one of the most important aquatic warbler fen sites in the world, Zvanets (16 000 ha). Another EU-funded project (EU-AID) cooperates with a peat briquette factory in order to substitute peat by sustainably produced peatland biomass (Wichtmann *et al.* 2014).

In the Peene River Valley (northeast Germany), biomass harvesting from wet fens has been tested by an EU LIFE project (2005–11) and a project funded by the German Ministry for Education and Research (2010–14). New products from wet fens such as insulation materials, plaster bases, fire-resistant panels, pellets and briquettes have been developed. Since 2014, a heating plant covering the demands of 1000 apartments, a school and a kindergarten in the city of Malchin operates on fen biomass. The biomass of $c.$ 300 ha is harvested in bales by machinery adapted for the site (Schröder, Wichtmann and Körner 2013).

These recent developments illustrate new possibilities for managing open fen habitats for specialised flora and fauna. However, long-term monitoring will be important to assess the impact of mechanical mowing on peat formation, decomposition of organic matter, vegetation productivity, stability, resistance and resilience to invasive plants, and on soil organisms, which play an important role in nutrient cycling and form an important part of the food webs in these peatland habitats (cf. Kotowski, Jabłońska and Bartoszuk 2013).

Box 17.5
Cattail for bioenergy and nutrient recovery in Manitoba, Canada

Richard Grosshans

Cattail, *Typha* spp., are very tolerant of water-level fluctuations and extremely competitive. Cattail plants spread clonally or by seed and produce a large leaf area, particularly under drawdown or dry conditions (Grace and Wetzel 1982). In North America, broadleaf cattail *Typha latifolia* and the European introduced narrow-leaved cattail *Typha angustifolia* are common. These species hybride to form the highly invasive *Typha × glauca*, with many intermediate forms between the parent species, which outcompetes native species (Stevens and Hoag 2006; Kirk, Connolly and Freeland 2011). Cattail can be readily transplanted as plants or from bare rootstock from other sites. Seedlings from container stalks can be used, or seeds collected in fall when seed heads are dry or slightly immature (Stevens and Hoag 2006). Rootstock or seedlings are preferred for re-vegetating areas with standing or moving water, while seeds will germinate readily on moist soils providing a cost-effective means for larger areas.

By assimilating nutrients into accumulated biomass, cattail effectively removes nutrients that cause eutrophication in aquatic systems (i.e. nitrogen and phosphorus) and consequently they are commonly used in constructed wetlands for wastewater treatment (Kadlec and Knight 1996). They can produce significant biomass within a single growing season. The bioenergy potential of cattail has been known for well over 30 years (Dubbe, Garver and Pratt 1988), but the feasibility of utilising it as an economically viable bioenergy feedstock with major environmental and economic co-benefits has not been demonstrated until recently (Grosshans et al. 2011b).

In Manitoba, Canada, the International Institute for Sustainable Development (IISD), University of Manitoba and Ducks Unlimited Canada evaluated harvesting cattail for water quality improvement and nutrient capture and recycling, while adding significant economic opportunities through combined heating and power (CHP) generation, GHG reduction credits and recovery of phosphorus – a limited strategic agricultural resource critical for global food security (Grosshans et al. 2011b). When harvested, nutrients locked in plant tissue are prevented from being released into the environment via natural decomposition. Late summer/early fall harvests removed 20–60 kg ha^{-1} yr^{-1} of phosphorus while maintaining a healthy plant community, and removal of overlying plant material opened the area to sunlight, allowing plants to emerge earlier the following spring (Grosshans et al. 2011a). Cattails reach maturity in less than 90 days with average biomass yields of 15–20 t DW ha^{-1} yr^{-1}. Combustion trials show an average calorific heat value of 17–20 MJ kg^{-1}, an average potential energy yield of 300 GJ ha^{-1} yr^{-1} and an ash content of 5–6%. No major concerns were identified regarding combustion emissions and ash (Dubbe, Garver and Pratt 1988; Grosshans et al. 2011a).

Cattails can be compressed into densified fuel products to provide a standardised feedstock and to reduce storage and transport costs. In Switzerland, harvested cattail was converted into compressed pellets for heat and pyrolysis (Wyss 2004), while in Manitoba, Canada, it was compressed into pellets, high-density cubes and logs for coal displacement and heat (Grosshans et al. 2011a). High-efficiency conversion for heat and CHP, as well as ethanol, has also been pursued in North America and Europe (Cicek et al. 2006). The estimated GHG mitigation potential for small-scale distributed coal displacement is significant. One tonne of cattail biomass used to displace coal for heat production would generate 1.05 t of CO_2 offsets. As an additional co-benefit, elements can be recovered in the ash following combustion (Grosshans et al. 2011a). From an agricultural context, this biomass resource is presently undeveloped.

17.4.3 *Sphagnum* farming for producing horticultural growing media

The most important raw material for growing media in professional horticulture is slightly decomposed moss peat ('white' or 'blond' peat, 'peat moss'), which has been deposited by *Sphagnum* mosses in living bogs. About 30 million m³ of white peat are globally used for this purpose annually. This use presents two major problems:

- peat extraction destroys important ecosystem services of bogs, e.g. biodiversity conservation, carbon storage, water regulation and their function as palaeo-archives
- peat is a finite resource. In most countries of Western and Central Europe the deposits of white peat are nearly exhausted.

A non-polluting alternative ensuring a lasting and sustainable supply of high-quality growing media for professional horticulture is urgently needed. Fresh peatmoss biomass, which has similar physical and chemical properties to white peat, is currently emerging as such an alternative. In recent decades the introduction of peatmosses was established as a measure of re-vegetating and restoring cutover peat extraction sites in Canada (Quinty and Rochefort 2003; González and Rochefort 2014; Chapter 11). These experiences have been further developed for the cultivation of peatmosses to provide a renewable substitute for fossil peat (Gaudig *et al.* 2014; Pouliot, Hugron and Rochefort 2014).

Since 2004, the perspectives of cultivating peatmoss as a raw material for horticultural growing media ('*Sphagnum* farming') have been systematically studied in greenhouse and field experiments by research institutes and industrial partners (Gaudig, Kamermann and Joosten 2008). A pilot site of 1200 m² on rewetted cutover bog in Germany demonstrated the feasibility of *Sphagnum* farming and harvesting, attaining long-term yields of over 3 t DW ha^{-1} yr^{-1} (Kamermann and Blankenburg 2008). The establishment of *Sphagnum* farming on formerly drained and degraded bog grassland appears successful, with the maintenance of constant high water tables being crucial for reaching high productivity (Gaudig *et al.* 2014). Plant cultivation experiments show that growing media based on *Sphagnum* biomass – even up to a proportion of 100% – allow professional plant cultivation without loss of quality compared to the established use of white peat (Emmel 2008; Blievernicht *et al.* 2011, 2013; Joosten, Gaudig and Krebs 2013; Jobin, Caron and Rochefort 2014).

17.4.4 Common reed and cattail as industrial raw material

From a climatic perspective, the use of biomass for construction or handicraft is to be favoured over its use as a fuel, as the sequestered carbon remains stored over the long term. With respect to using fibre from peatlands, common reed for thatch has a long tradition in Europe (Rodewald-Rudescu 1974; Moir and Letts 1999; Häkkinen 2007; Figure 17.3) and is well established in the United Kingdom, Germany, the Netherlands and Denmark. In Western Europe the demand for high-quality reed cannot be satisfied by inland supply and most reed is imported from Southern and Eastern Europe, Turkey and China (Wichmann and Köbbing 2015). Weaving of reed is a long-established way of manufacturing construction and insulation materials (Köbbing, Thevs and Zerbe 2013). In Iraq, reed is even used for constructing complete houses (Thesiger 1964). The culms (stems) are weaved in single layers when mats are used for plaster porter, for insulating garden plants against frost or for privacy screens. For insulation mats, thicker layers of reed are put onto the loom and enmeshed with stainless steel netting (Table 17.1) (Tanneberger and Wichtmann 2011).

The economics of reed as a construction material are more favourable compared with its use for energy (Wichmann 2016), but strongly depend on processing and use (Schäfer 1999). Thatch produced from wet peatlands showed negative revenues when high costs for planting and processing met low biomass yields and prices, but calculated proceeds turned positive in more realistic settings (Schäfer 2004). Further mechanisation of planting, improved harvesting, and development of new products may improve the results (see papers in Wichtmann and Couwenberg 2013).

Cattail cultivation (Wild *et al.* 2001), with an average yield of 17 t ha^{-1} yr^{-1} with 86% dry matter content, proved to be profitable in pilot trials in Donaumoos (Germany) when used for the production of high-quality insulation materials and other panels or boards, but not when used for combustion (Schätzl *et al.* 2006).

17.5 Synergies and trade-offs with other ecosystem services

Compared to land use on drained peat soils, paludicultures on rewetted peatlands may support substantial co-benefits (Wichmann and Wichmann 2011a; Wichmann *et al.* 2012), including preservation and sequestration of carbon, adaptation to local climate change (by increased evaporative cooling), regulation of water dynamics (flood control) and quality (purification), and conservation and restoration of peatland typical flora and fauna (see Joosten *et al.* 2015a; Wichtmann, Schröder and Joosten 2016). In the vast

Figure 17.3 Harvesting of reed for thatch in Northern Germany (photo: Philipp Schroeder).

areas of deeply subsided peatlands that are threatened by flooding, paludiculture strongly reduces the costs of pumping.

Combining bioenergy generation and rewetting of drained peatlands makes paludiculture an extraordinary cost-effective climate change mitigation option that can generate income from both carbon credits and biomass production (Tanneberger and Wichtmann 2011).

Paludiculture may also support typical peatland biota, as has been demonstrated for species-rich fen vegetation in Switzerland (Güsewell and Le Nédic 2004) and the UK (Cowie et al. 1992) and for the globally threatened aquatic warbler in Poland (Tanneberger et al. 2009, Kubacka et al. 2014). Especially when mowing does not take place annually and parts of the site are left unmanaged, creating a mosaic of ages, harvesting of fen biomass can benefit invertebrate (Schmidt et al. 2005) and bird (Kubacka et al. 2014) conservation. In *Sphagnum* farming sites in north-west Germany, several red list plant species and various rare spider species became established within a few years (Joosten et al. 2015b; Muster et al. 2015).

Using wet grasslands for buffalo grazing may create a more heterogeneous soil and vegetation structure (Gulickx, Beecroft and Green 2007), benefit plant diversity (Kazoglu and Papanastasis 2001; Walton 2009; Wiegleb and Krawczynski 2010; Sweers et al. 2013), provide reproduction habitats for amphibians (e.g. fire-bellied toad *Bombina bombina*) (Wiegleb and Krawczynski

2010), and improve – in combination with late mowing – habitat conditions for threatened meadow-breeding birds (H. Pegel pers. comm). As water buffalo hardly need medication, their dung is not contaminated by anthelmintics and supports abundant microflora and fauna, which form the basis for a rich food web.

Rewetting intensively used agricultural peatlands often leads to nutrient-overloaded wetlands, with limited rare species occurrence. By harvesting biomass in summer, significant amounts of nutrients may be removed (see Box 17.5), which in time improves habitat quality for characteristic mire species of more open and more nutrient-poor conditions. In contrast, by harvesting dead biomass in winter, most nutrients are left on site and stable yields can be achieved over long periods of time, as exemplified by the long-standing harvest of reed for thatch (Wichmann and Köbbing 2015).

Biomass use may, however, also conflict with nature conservation, e.g. when early mowing for biogas production destroys breeding habitats or when winter harvesting leaves insufficient old-growth reed for breeding habitats. Sound monitoring may then allow for adaptive management, whereas agri-environmental schemes can offer compensation to farmers when exploitation has to be restricted. In sites designated for conservation, paludiculture must be considered as a cost-effective management option, instrumental but ancillary to conservation (Wichtmann *et al.* 2010).

Last but not least, paludiculture can improve rural livelihoods by counteracting rural unemployment and social disintegration and can thus substantially increase the acceptance of peatland rewetting programmes. Paludiculture can provide income from provisioning services from sites that formerly were abandoned or where unsustainable land use took place. Autumn and winter harvest leads to more consistent employment throughout the year, whereas paludiculture biomass processing may create net added value and generate additional jobs. Paludiculture furthermore can contribute to both energy autarchy and economic regionalisation (Wichtmann, Schröder and Joosten 2016).

17.6 Outlook

The total global area of drained peatlands amounts to some 500 000 km^2 (Chapter 2), with degradation-associated problems occurring everywhere (Joosten, Tapio-Biström and Tol 2012). Practical experiences and model calculations indicate that paludiculture can compete with drainage-based peatland agriculture and forestry, certainly when external costs are considered (Wichmann 2016; Chapter 16). Paludiculture enables peatlands to provide provisioning services, while maintaining and restoring the supply of important regulating and cultural services. It softens the tension between the productive use of peatlands, which was hitherto drainage based, and the demands of conservation and environmental protection, which require peatlands to be wet. Paludiculture thus contributes to a multifunctional use of peatlands which is a more space-efficient use of this increasingly scarce land resource. Paludiculture also allows the rewetting of drained peatlands that otherwise would not be available for climate change mitigation and adaptation (Joosten *et al.* 2015a), and has the potential to offer sustainable economic returns to strengthen rural livelihoods.

Various conditions, however, still hamper large-scale implementation. Rewetting of peat soils must often involve a substantial area or an entire hydrological unit (polder, catchment) as it is impractical, or even impossible, to keep stable high water levels in single plots surrounded by fields that continue to be drained. Rewetting will thus often demand hydrological restructuring, land reallotment and consolidation of a similar scale to the (often huge) projects that drained the peatlands in the first place.

Paludiculture furthermore implies a major change in operational management and substantial investment in adapted machinery so that a change to paludiculture is virtually irreversible on the level of the individual enterprise. Because of the important ecosystem services generated for wider beneficiaries, it is reasonable that peatland rewetting and paludiculture projects are supported by central planning and public financing (Joosten *et al.* 2015b).

In order to implement paludiculture, the entire life cycle from field to market must be in place. The recent emergence of this concept, however, means that various steps of this life cycle still need development and optimisation. This especially concerns (Joosten 2014, Joosten *et al.* 2015b):

- the identification, selection and propagation of optimal species, provenances and cultivars
- the development of low-soil pressure machinery and the identification of adequate logistics
- the development of new products and the adaptation of existing production lines to new types of biomass
- the assessment and communication of the co-benefits of paludiculture
- the improvement of agricultural consultation for site-adapted peatland use
- the involvement of participatory stakeholder deliberation to increase acceptance
- the adjustment of laws, rules and regulations that fail to accommodate for paludiculture

- the abolition of subsidies that stimulate drainage-based peatland agriculture
- the implementation of payments for ecosystem services to reward external benefits.

Research, development and realisation are not only necessary for the temperate zone, where paludicultures will mainly be implemented on formerly drained and degraded lands. Especially in the tropics, paludicultures are required as an alternative for rapidly expanding unsustainable drainage-based agriculture and forestry (Chapter 14). If (near-)natural peatlands have to be claimed to achieve growing production targets, they must be managed sustainably: if you really need to use them, use them wet! (Joosten, Tapio-Biström and Tol 2012).

Drained peatland use is not a sustainable land use as it destroys its own subsistence base and that of adjacent conservation areas (Chapter 14). In a world hunting for land, the loss of productive land through peatland degradation must be stopped. There is a need to distract the inherently expanding destructive peatland use away from the declining areas of wilderness. Managing peatlands sustainably requires rewetting already degraded peatlands and restoring their capacity to provide biomass. If we want to protect natural mires, paludiculture is the final frontier.

CHAPTER EIGHTEEN

Peatland conservation at the science–practice interface

JOSEPH HOLDEN
University of Leeds, UK
ALETTA BONN
Helmholtz Centre for Environmental Research (UFZ) | Friedrich-Schiller-University Jena | German Centre for Integrative Biodiversity Research (iDiv) Halle-Jena-Leipzig | IUCN UK Peatland Programme, UK
MARK REED
Newcastle University, UK
SARAH BUCKMASTER
University of Aberdeen, UK
JONATHAN WALKER
Moors for the Future Partnership, Peak District National Park Authority, UK
MARTIN EVANS
The University of Manchester, UK
FRED WORRALL
Durham University, UK

18.1 Introduction

The conservation and management of peatlands by practitioners is often assumed to work best when guided by science (e.g. Maltby 1997). However, there are also many excellent peatland management and restoration projects, which have built upon years of practical experience (sometimes through trial and error), undertaken by organisations involved in hands-on peatland conservation. Parry, Holden and Chapman (2014) provide many examples of techniques developed through common sense and ingenuity on the part of practitioners, often with little input from the science community. Often restoration projects have to make progress well before

Peatland Restoration and Ecosystem Services: Science, Policy and Practice, eds. A. Bonn, T. Allott, M. Evans, H. Joosten and R. Stoneman. Published by Cambridge University Press. © British Ecological Society 2016.

the science is fully understood. Significant investment is being poured into peatland management projects across the world (Parish *et al.* 2008), and it is important for those investing resources in peatland environments that there is some evaluation of the impacts of such investment. Evaluating the success of peatland management projects may involve the scientific community (e.g. taking measurements of carbon fluxes). In many instances, however, practitioners may involve less stringent measures with success measured by recording some simple visible changes to the landscape. The evaluation of success may indeed be an economic one (Kent 2000) based on cost–benefit analyses (Christie *et al.* 2011) of, for example, money spent on restoration that has been or will be saved elsewhere through, for instance, improved water quality entering water company treatment works. The observations for measuring peatland conservation success may depend on spatial and temporal scale, geographic settings and project targets, as well as available expertise and funding. There are therefore questions about how we measure success and how scientists, practitioners and policy makers can work closely together to deliver the best outcomes for peatland ecosystem services. Careful attention should be given to the mechanisms for science knowledge exchange between science and practical application so that practical experience and knowledge by those managing peatlands is transferred into the scientific understanding of peatlands. Scientists value the opinions and ideas of the restoration community and there have been recent attempts to move towards improved co-design of research and co-production of knowledge of science and practitioner communities in peatland restoration environments (Reed 2008; Reed *et al.* 2009).

Taking an ecosystem services approach to peatland conservation means that scientists, practitioners and policy makers have to understand the wider interconnectedness of peatland processes that lead to the provision of goods and services to society. Whereas peatland conservation has traditionally focused on biodiversity targets, adopting a wider ecosystem services approach may create an atmosphere which encourages collaboration between scientists, practitioners and policy makers (Bonn, Rebane and Reid 2009). This chapter seeks to understand whether by incorporating ecosystem services into peatland conservation at the science–practice interface we can bring added value. Interspersed throughout the chapter is a case study based on a questionnaire survey of the UK peatland conservation community to identify: (1) their assessment of the success of their conservation and restoration works and (2) their needs for support by the science community. The findings have international relevance and applicability to other peatlands across the globe.

18.2 Peatland conservation drivers

Peatland conservation projects have traditionally focused on protecting and restoring biodiversity (Chapters 15 and 19). Important policy drivers have involved designating protected areas and thereby placing peatland sites under legislation that enforces conservation efforts (Bain 1997). For example, the main mechanism of conservation in the West Siberian Lowland is through a formal network of refuges, nature reserves, national parks and nature monuments (Solomeshch 2005) that protect the landscape and encourage restoration of degraded areas. This is also exemplified by the UK case study. Here we consulted in 2008 government bodies, agencies, non-governmental organisations, academics and water companies via a questionnaire on UK peatland restoration and conservation projects, which resulted in a compendium website that still remains open (Box 18.1). The 2008 survey data incorporated 56 UK projects providing information from a total of 412 separate peatland sites (most projects operated over more than one site), with project area sizes varying from 5–8000 ha.

Box 18.1

The peatland compendium web tool

The peatland compendium web tool is available online at www.peatlands.org.uk for peatland restoration practitioners and scientists anywhere in the world. The tool consists of an online questionnaire which enables people to upload information about their restoration or peatland management project. Details include: (1) location, administration and funding; (2) initial site conditions, project justification and objectives; (3) restoration and management methods; and (4) methods of evaluation and monitoring, perceived success, revised site condition assessment and future plans. The website has a clickable map showing the location of projects. Much of the questionnaire allows qualitative information to be added on the restoration techniques being used, area covered and any innovation. There are also quantitative sections which aid evaluation of the content. The tool can be used by practitioners to see what methods have been used by other projects and any nuances to those methods that have been developed. It is hoped that projects can learn from each other and build on each other's experience (see also Cris *et al.* 2011).

An important policy driver reported for peat conservation projects was the implementation of the UK government target to achieve favourable or 'unfavourable recovering' condition status for 95% of the Sites of Special Scientific Interest (SSSI) in England by 2010 (English Nature 2003). All but one peatland restoration project site had a conservation designation status (e.g. SSSI or Area of Outstanding Natural Beauty (AONB), EU Natura 2000 site, Special Area of Conservation or Special Protection Area). A total of 13% of the projects were located on Ramsar sites and 89% were on SSSIs. Most sites (87%) had more than one conservation status, while 43% of the sites had four or more different conservation designations. This reflects both the importance of peatlands and the role of such designations in ensuring that restoration and management projects take place by levering political and financial support.

In the UK survey, project representatives were asked to rate justifications (categories of targets) for their project on a scale of 0 to 5 with rising importance (information available for 54 projects). Biodiversity targets were most important and provided a strong justification for all projects (Figure 18.1). Other ecosystem services were considered less important. Water quality regulation, for example, was perceived by only 31% of projects as extremely

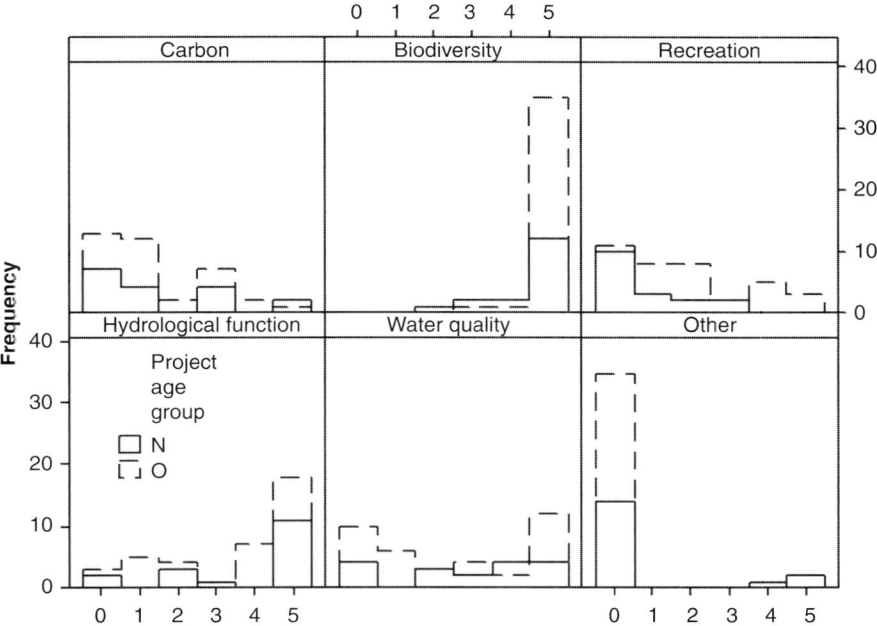

Figure 18.1 Project justification scores for 54 restoration and conservation projects on UK peatlands (0 = not important, 5 = extremely important). The plots show the number of projects giving each score (situation 2008). N = projects which started since 1 January 2005, O (dashed lines) = projects which started prior to 1 January 2005.

important and by 26% of projects as unimportant. Carbon storage and sequestration, i.e. climate regulation, was used as a justification for 63% of the projects, but was considered as extremely important only in three cases, similar to recreation targets. Clearly, the project justifications map onto policy and funding priorities. However, these priorities may shift over time, for example, with the development of carbon markets (Bonn *et al.* 2014; Chapter 15) or legislation on water quality such as the EU Water Framework Directive (Martin-Ortega *et al.* 2014; Chapter 5). Figure 18.1 plots data separately for projects which started after 2005 and those that started prior to 2005 to assess a change in objective setting. While there is little difference in the patterns, climate regulation through carbon storage and sequestration seems to have become of slightly greater importance in later years in regard to justifying peatland restoration or management.

The UK system of designating and assessing conservation status is strongly rooted in notions of biodiversity and habitat preservation. This is also aligned to EU legislation such as the Habitats Directive (Raeymaekers 1997). Therefore, it was not surprising that biodiversity was the major restoration objective and driver for UK peatland restoration projects. The role of legislation and policy targets is therefore pivotal in the drive towards adequate peatland protection and restoration. Therefore, acquiring a designated conservation status may be the most crucial step towards protection and restoration for peatland sites, while in general landscape-scale approaches should be adopted for conservation rather than a focus on protected areas only (Lawton *et al.* 2010).

In addition, communicating the relevance and importance of services from peatlands and adopting an ecosystem services approach in decision making and management can broaden the scope of peatland projects. As a result this can bring added value by facilitating and broadening cross-sectoral partnerships, opening up new sources of funding, developing understanding, focusing research and ultimately informing policy.

18.3 Measures for achieving success

18.3.1 Partnerships

While there are a wide range of peatland conservation and restoration techniques available (Chapters 9–14), it is equally important to consider the broader governance measures for achieving conservation objectives. Partnerships embracing the breadth of ecosystem services delivered by peatlands allow for addressing conservation under different headings for multiple benefits, so that stakeholders can be included across a range of concerns. Under tighter funding regimes, public–private partnerships are one possible way forward. Indeed, this may work well if a broad range of ecosystem services are part of the decision-making process. For example, a private water company may foster peatland restoration since degraded peatlands impact water quality entering its reservoirs and raw water intakes (e.g. Buytaert *et al.* 2006; Wallage, Holden and McDonald 2006), while government conservation bodies may seek peatland restoration to achieve biodiversity targets (statutory or otherwise). Thus, through a partnership between the private water company and the public sector, multiple benefits can be realised through peatland restoration while the cost burden may be shared. In the UK case study just over half of the projects were managed as part of a partnership, with 63% having a government agency involved in their management. Some 13% of projects were managed by a private business, while 34% were managed by charities.

18.3.2 Investment

Partnerships allow for cross-sectoral engagement, major funding or match-funding of grants, and can also provide some organisational inertia to buffer against short-term risks and funding waves. The partnership approach through understanding multiple benefits of ecosystem services has already facilitated additional funding in many peatland locations and developed new finance avenues, including core matched funding to attract successful multi-million dollar grants from national and international sources. Other possible finance tools include payments for ecosystem services schemes (Chapter 16), voluntary carbon reduction markets with verification programmes (Chapter 15; see also Worrall *et al.* 2009; Bonn *et al.* 2014) or corporate social responsibility schemes, such as that developed by the Cooperative Bank supporting *Sphagnum* propagation for peatland restoration in the Peak District National Park through the Moors for the Future partnership.

18.3.3 Community engagement and knowledge exchange

Community involvement in many peatland conservation projects is crucial, and consultation is a common theme for peatland conservation projects. In the UK case study, 48% of projects involved very wide consultation with local tenants, landowners and other stakeholders about the restoration and management projects to either gain agreement or win hearts and minds. This was found to be particularly important in locations where the land ownership is mixed and/or rights to use resources provided by that land are mixed (e.g. the right to access the land for recreational walking or for game hunting). In the UK survey of peatland conservation projects, it was found that mixed land ownership created problems for implementation of projects. Another problem was that many peatland conservation projects covered several different types of peatland (e.g. raised bog, fen, blanket peat) and this complicates the approaches and engagement required because suitable restoration approaches may differ between different peatland habitat types. Engaging stakeholders in peatland restoration processes requires early participatory involvement of all key players. However, in many cases, the more aggressive approach of land purchase was seen as part of the solution and was included in project budgets, although in a number of cases land purchase had not proved possible and budgets were unspent. This clearly demonstrates that in many situations, politics and social relationships are more important than technological advances or money for making conservation and peatland restoration happen (Koontz and Bodine 2008).

To move forward and achieve effective and sustainable management of our peatlands, it is therefore imperative that we share emerging knowledge about peatland conservation as widely and effectively as possible. It is only through effective collaboration between scientists, practitioners and the policy community that we will be able to develop effective solutions for peatland conservation. This means moving away from one-way knowledge transfer and towards two-way knowledge exchange and a way of joint working that values all forms of knowledge equally (Fazey *et al.* 2014).

Knowledge exchange has been defined as 'collaborative problem-solving between researchers and decision makers, and should take place through the processes of prioritising, planning, conducting and disseminating new research' (Graham *et al.* 2006). As such, knowledge exchange needs to be seen as an integral part of the research process and not simply viewed as an 'add-on' at the end of the research project. Knowledge exchange can be seen as part of a broader collection of approaches to managing knowledge, ranging from the storage and one-way transfer of knowledge to two-way knowledge exchange and the co-generation of knowledge between researchers and end-users (Fazey *et al.* 2014). The trend towards these latter forms of knowledge management emphasises the role of learning, as knowledge is passed from person to person through social networks and via other means (Reed *et al.* 2010). In the context of peatlands, the huge diversity of stakeholders with differing goals and circumstances means that knowledge exchange, and where possible the co-production of knowledge, are essential to ensure that new knowledge emerging from the research findings may be put to multiple uses.

Although science is generating a growing knowledge system of underlying processes and effective management of peatlands, the results of scientific research have all too often failed to influence the policies and practices that could help society (Phillipson and Liddon 2010). To ensure that research results in practical applied outcomes for peatlands and, as a result, benefits society as a whole, all forms of knowledge must be valued. Deciding which knowledge is relevant, reliable and valid for peatland ecosystem services requires a continuous process of negotiation between scientists, practitioners and the policy community. Furthermore, iterative stakeholder reviews of knowledge exchange mechanisms must be supported to move forward in working collaborations. Working together with the people that live, work and manage peatland environments in research projects may lead to more resilient conservation strategies, as well as an increasing likelihood of the scientific evidence being accepted and implemented. As exemplified by the case study of the Sustainable Uplands project (Box 18.2), engaging a wide range of stakeholders throughout the research process can result in increased relevance of research questions, design and outcomes.

Box 18.2
The Sustainable Uplands project

The Sustainable Uplands project has practised knowledge exchange and knowledge co-production in a range of peatland contexts (http://sustainableuplands.org/). Sustainable Uplands was a GBP 1 million Research Council-funded project, helping people to anticipate and adapt to future change across UK uplands between 2005 and 2013. By combining local knowledge with social and natural science, the project identified contrasting futures (or 'scenarios') facing UK uplands, based on policies to intensify or extensify land management. The project shows the potential to quantify and map how policy decisions are likely to affect multiple ecosystem services (the benefits society derives from nature) in future. In this way, policies can be designed to avoid the worst trade-offs, and where possible, benefit multiple ecosystem services for generations to come.

A strong focus was placed on the joint production of knowledge with a wide range of stakeholders being involved at all stages of the project – from the identification of research questions to the dissemination of research outcomes. To facilitate stakeholder input from the very beginning of the project, a Sustainable Uplands Advisory Panel was established and joint site visits hosted by stakeholders were organised to discuss land management issues, thereby also actively reducing the number of scientist-led workshops in formal meeting rooms. Local stakeholders commented that they felt themselves to be an integral part of the project and, as a result, the project benefited from a rich knowledge base incorporating both scientific and local knowledge. This led to increased relevance of research questions and outputs of the project.

The communication of research developments and final outputs employed a wide range of strategies to ensure information was accessible to a range of users. Information was shared through websites, newsletters, social networks such as Facebook and Twitter, as well as targeted workshops or policy and practice briefing notes. In particular, following suggestions from stakeholders, four short films were jointly developed and edited to effectively communicate the research objectives and outcomes. These films were distributed widely as DVDs to upland tourist centres and local shops and colleges, and are accessible online via the project website and YouTube. The exchange of knowledge and information happens through multiple channels, including informal networks (Phillipson and Liddon 2010), and effective social interaction can add great value to a research project. The Sustainable Uplands project used various strategies to share knowledge through social interaction, whether through meetings and site visits or interaction via Twitter and one-to-one dialogue between project members and individual key stakeholders. This developed a sense of trust between scientists and practitioners, as well as increasing the relevance of research. This implies that staff and financial resources must be allocated to knowledge exchange activities. The Sustainable Uplands project employed a full-time Knowledge Broker who ensured consistent two-way communication. This resulted in greater buy-in from a large number of local stakeholders and led to increased participation in the project, and ultimately increased relevance and uptake of the research outputs.

18.4 Peatland conservation project evaluation

Peatland environments are not static. Undisturbed peatlands change over time as the landscape evolves. For example, palaeo records show that a fen can naturally become a bog and then back to a fen again before becoming a bog (Hughes and Dumayne-Peaty 2002). Even within one particular type of peatland the landscape naturally evolves over time due to both internal feedbacks and external climatic drivers (Clymo 1991). Therefore, conservation needs to take account of change. Traditional conservation efforts either targeted moving the landscape back to some former state that was deemed to be more 'natural' or tried to lock the landscape into a particular state. Another conservation approach is to aim for restoring or conserving ecosystem function. This approach would reduce vulnerability and increase resilience in the face of climate change. It would also enable acceptance of changes in peatlands and enable success to be evaluated, not on the basis of the current appearance of a peatland but on the operation of ecosystem processes and their potential to provide a wide range of ecosystem goods and services.

In the UK practitioner survey, respondents were asked to score initial and present site conditions from 0 (peatland completely destroyed) to 100 (perfect condition). Staff also scored how they perceived the status of the initial and present hydrological condition, percentage area that the target biodiversity community covers, percentage area of peatland intact, and a score between 0 and 100 for their perceived condition for carbon storage potential and the overall success of their projects (Table 18.1). Clearly, this way of reporting success (differences between initial and present condition with some subjective judgements made by project staff) may not provide uniform comparisons *between* projects, but it is one way of identifying how successful practitioners deemed the restoration projects to be. Importantly, practitioners reported that they typically scored on the basis of overall impression rather than a detailed analysis of data available from a site, although any available monitoring data to which the practitioners had access were often used to inform that impression. Project staff were also asked to report on the nature of monitoring data that were being collected at each site.

Scores for the biodiversity category and the proportion of peatland that was intact did not differ significantly between the initial and the current assessment (Table 18.1). The main success story of restoration strategies appears to be for site hydrology. To some extent this may have influenced the staff perception of whether the peatland is actively functioning as a carbon store and uptake route, since only a few projects monitored carbon fluxes (Table 18.2). Improvements in the perceived climate regulation of the peatland (i.e. positive balance of carbon sequestration and emission) were found to be significant at the 95% confidence level. The mean overall perceived success rate for the 56 projects was 67%, while the median was 75%. In order to examine the role of project age in determining success, the present overall site condition and project success score were both plotted against the age of the project (Figure 18.2). There was no significant relationship between either of these pairings. However, there were no projects older than 9 years that had success scores lower than 75%. In

Table 18.1 Percentage scores evaluating the initial site condition and current site condition for each UK peatland project, with 100% indicating perfect condition. P-values are from the Mann–Whitney U test comparing initial and current site condition for each category. Probability is for improvement in the category to be zero.

Category	Median, %	Mean, %	Standard deviation, %	p-value
Overall initial site condition[a]	50	46	25	0.001
Overall current site condition[a]	63	61	19	
Initial hydrology[b]	50	46	26	<0.001
Current hydrology[b]	70	67	24	
Initial biodiversity[c]	60	60	36	0.374
Current biodiversity[c]	55	63	31	
Initial intact peat[d]	75	70	25	0.422
Current peat intact[d]	70	71	25	
Initial carbon storage potential A[e]	50	50	25	0.047
Current carbon storage potential B[e]	60	60	25	
Overall success[f]	75	67	26	

The questions asked:

[a] What was the overall condition of the site (%)? 0 = completely destroyed, 100 = pristine
[b] What was the hydrological status of the site (%)? 0 = completely drained, 100 = hydrologically intact
[c] What percentage area does your target biodiversity community cover?
[d] What percentage of the original peat deposits remains? 0 = none of original (expected) deposits remain, 100 = all the original (expected) peat deposits remain
[e] What is the condition of your site for carbon storage (%)? 0 = entire site is a carbon source, 100 = entire site is a fully functioning carbon sink
[f] What is the overall success of the project to date (%)?

other words, those projects that have run for longest are most likely to have been deemed successful. There were no differences between upland and lowland peatlands in this regard. Figure 18.2 illustrates interesting patterns in the reporting of project success. Figure 18.2b suggests a trend whereby perceived project success increases rapidly through the first three years of a project before levelling off at 80–100% thereafter. In contrast, the perceived site condition data show relatively little pattern in time and much greater variation (Figure 18.2a).

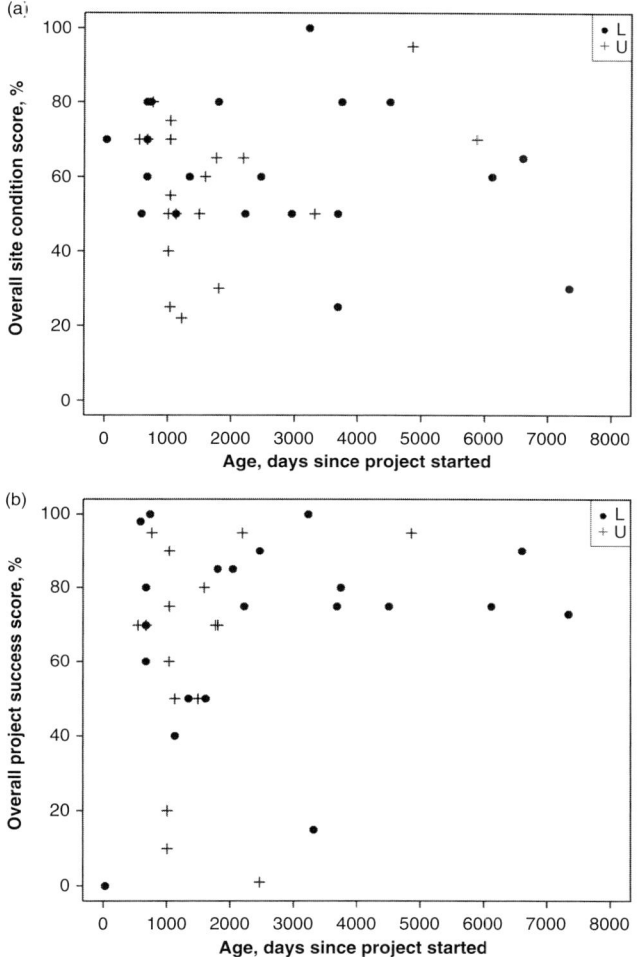

Figure 18.2 Plots showing practitioner perception scores for (a) site condition and (b) project success with age of project for upland and lowland peatland projects (circles = lowland, crosses = upland) for UK peatlands.

As noted above, biodiversity targets were cited as the most important goals for peatland restoration projects in the UK, followed by hydrological targets. Consequently biodiversity indicators were the most commonly monitored components of restoration projects. However, while biodiversity was the main aim and the projects were, on a holistic basis, deemed to be 75% successful by project staff, there were no significant changes in the scores for biodiversity when comparing initial to current site conditions. In other words, peatland biodiversity indicators had not improved in condition and yet the projects were still deemed to be highly successful. An interesting pattern was

Table 18.2 Number of UK projects monitoring peatland restoration indicators and methods by which they are doing so. There was an option to enter 'other' methods on the forms, but no entries were received under this category

	Total	Ground surveys	Remote sensing*	Air photos	Infrared images	LiDAR+
Vegetation	53	53	26	26	9	11
Invertebrates	27	27	0	0	0	0
Birds	31	31	0	0	0	0
Hydrology/ water quality	39	39	6	3	2	4
Carbon/ GHGs	8	8	2	2	1	1
Peat erosion	10	10	2	2	1	0
Climate	8	8	1	1	1	0
Pollution	4	0	0	0	0	0
Other	4	4	1	0	0	1

+ Light Detection and Ranging
* Includes air photos, infrared images, LiDAR and other techniques.

also seen in overall project success scores by age of project, whereby there appeared to be a desire to claim success within a typical 3-year funding window. This is despite the fact that peatland restoration can be a slow process.

Hobbs and Harris (2001) identified the setting of appropriate goals and success criteria as a major challenge for ecological management projects. The potential difficulties are clearly exemplified by the mismatch between measured and reported success in UK peatland restoration projects presented above. It is necessary that clear, sharp, verifiable and thus often quantifiable aims should be set with adequate identification of suitable indicators to monitor and evaluate success. Of course, the goals of projects often change during the course of an ecological management project, but targets with the identification of clear evaluation techniques should still be set carefully. Here, an approach to adaptive management, incorporating feedback loops to allow learning from experience and continuous monitoring, is needed. This is most easily achieved in a 'no blame' management culture that allows for mistakes to be accepted and subsequent management changes to be welcomed, if based on emerging evidence. Overall projects will benefit from an ecosystem services approach to target setting and evaluation, by incorporating a holistic view of success and thereby providing background data to assess synergies and trade-offs from management actions.

18.5 Monitoring, data and research

There is clearly a need for early monitoring to be integrated into projects to help measure success and enable projects to be accountable. Monitoring varied in type and intensity between the projects surveyed in the UK case study. Biodiversity indicators were the most commonly monitored components of restoration projects, with vegetation monitored in 95% of projects, birds in 55% and invertebrates in 48%. Vegetation monitoring occurred mainly through ground survey, but was assisted in about half of the cases by air photos and other remote-sensing techniques (Table 18.2). Hydrology was monitored by ground survey in 70% of projects. This typically involved sampling dipwells to gauge water-table level, usually through manual sampling rather than automated recording. Small-scale stream gauging was also conducted by some projects. Further biodiversity monitoring of invertebrates and birds was also common, occurring in more than 50% of projects, while carbon flux and climate regulation, peat erosion and pollution were only monitored in a few cases. Most vegetation monitoring was delivered in-house, with most monitoring for other variables delivered by external organisations; academic collaborators mainly performed the carbon and climate monitoring. There was widespread use of GIS and remote sensing. Ten project questionnaire responses stated that GIS or remote sensing was 'essential' to the projects. Many respondents noted that technological advances were helping them, and they would have used GIS and remote-sensing imagery such as aerial photographs and Light Detection and Ranging data (LiDAR) (Holden 2005) to a greater extent had these been available at the start of their project. Such levels of monitoring described above do imply that there is a wide resource of monitoring data that should be shared and analysed between projects to inform future project design and enable success to be evaluated. Importantly, this will need to involve also monitoring control sites without restoration treatment, which is rarely conducted. Another key concern is the lack of shared protocols for monitoring between peatland sites. This makes any meta-analysis of data being collected across projects difficult. Scientifically robust monitoring guidelines and training are needed for practitioners. These need to be developed in partnership with practitioners so that the feasibility of undertaking the measurements is incorporated into monitoring design. Standardisation of monitoring may represent a burden if adopted in parallel with existing monitoring, and practitioners are concerned that standardisation becomes an unnecessary requirement.

Two-thirds of UK projects had expenditure dedicated to monitoring, with approximately 15% of the budget allocated to monitoring for projects whose funding was in the range of GBP 100 000 to 300 000. Data need to be shared between projects and analysed in order to maximise their potential.

However, only a tiny proportion of peatland conservation projects that have included monitoring have released their data or published findings (e.g. Wilson *et al.* 2010, 2011), and there is rarely an impetus for data sharing between peatland conservation projects. A staffed resource (potentially internationally funded) needs to be made available to act as a data repository and to facilitate data analysis and more rapid evaluation of functional responses to conservation efforts in peatlands. The importance of remote-sensing data for peatland restoration planning and monitoring is another area where regional, national and international agencies could help peatland restoration projects by providing advice, common remote-sensing datasets and funding. Many small projects can often not afford the expertise or datasets for restoration or management projects, but they could be greatly assisted if a funded agency existed to provide this service for them.

Strong synergies between restoration for biodiversity and ecosystem services, especially regulating and cultural services, such as carbon storage, seem intuitive and have been shown for a range of ecosystems (e.g. Chan *et al.* 2006; Rey Benayas *et al.* 2009). However, evidence is still limited and scattered. Depending on spatio-temporal scales and types of restoration, relationships may be noisy, non-linear or include trade-offs (Evans *et al.* 2014). To strengthen the evidence base and justify restoration for multiple benefits, many projects are actively engaging with universities and aim for not only more rigorous monitoring but also fundamental research to develop evidence and best practice. Developing focused research through active communication and two-way learning early on between practitioners, researchers and funders is needed to facilitate successful moves forward on ecosystem services approaches to peatland conservation. Furthermore, while monitoring restoration success for biodiversity and ecosystem services (Grand-Clement *et al.* 2013) can take years and decades, modelling approaches can help in understanding change (Holden 2005; Ballard *et al.* 2011) and improvements in both monitoring procedures and modelling are needed for peatland environments.

The timescale of monitoring at conservation sites is also a major concern. At the start of peat conservation projects there is rarely a 'set-up' time for practitioners when priority is given to baseline monitoring. At the end of any restoration activity, most projects have no scope to continue monitoring. For example, EU LIFE projects generally lack funding to continue monitoring peatlands beyond the lifetime of the practical restoration work. However, timescales for restoration of diverse peatland communities may be decades. On UK blanket bogs, for example, a typical restoration timescale has been estimated to be at least 25 years (Crowe, Evans and Allott 2008). Therefore, achieving success with targets to restore biodiversity and habitats is difficult over short timescales for most restoration projects. At short timescales, achievable goals such as restoration of water tables or stabilisation of eroding peat surfaces provide a necessary precursor to full restoration. However, not enough is known about the long-term trajectory of restored peatlands (Money and Wheeler 1999; Holden et al. 2011). It may well be that water tables can be restored successfully and relatively quickly in peatlands, but some other hydrological or water quality parameters may still be degraded several years after full water-table recovery (Worrall, Armstrong and Holden 2007).

Choi (2007) has suggested that restoration of ecosystem function should be the primary aim of restoration, and an approach to setting restoration goals based on function provides a possible solution to the problems of not being able to achieve biodiversity or habitat targets in the short term. Partial restoration of function through reclamation as a staging post to more complete restoration may provide a more achievable success criterion for peatland projects within typical 3–5-year funding windows. It is likely that a median overall success score of 75% for the UK peatland restoration projects we surveyed partially represents practitioners' views of successfully restored ecosystem functions despite no significant improvements in biodiversity. However, it still remains the case that relatively few projects in the UK survey explicitly identified ecosystem functions as restoration drivers. Of course, taking an ecosystem service approach may present difficulties as it might take decades for some services to be restored and just a few months for others. Indeed the choice of relevant ecosystem services will depend on preferences by beneficiaries, and therefore may differ between peatland sites (Bonn et al. 2010). A shift towards recognition of ecosystem functions and ecosystem service benefits of restoration will thus necessitate a more comprehensive engagement of restoration with society. Therefore, although biodiversity is a strong policy driver, understanding the importance of ecosystem functions and services within conservation legislation will be required.

18.6 Conclusions and outlook

The ecosystem services concept applied to peatlands has recently encouraged stakeholder partnerships and engagement, with a wider range of funding sources. The concept can inform policy and highlight cases for potential payments for ecosystem services. It also has the effect of broadening the scope of those who might need to be considered as beneficiaries or sufferers from peatland management outcomes. For example, if peatlands impact water quality or flood storage then consumers or residents many hundreds of kilometres downstream may be affected by conservation practice. The ecosystem services approach applied to peatlands is also encouraging stronger links between restoration projects and academic research to develop better understanding of provision and quantification of ecosystem services.

Combining practical knowledge that may sometimes be locally specific with academic knowledge (e.g. on monitoring protocols or peatland processes) is needed to assist better environmental management of peatlands in the future (e.g. through better understanding of biodiversity change trajectories). These both need to be combined with policy knowledge to make societal system changes that will best use public funds for conservation and wider impacts (e.g. through maintaining research institutes that can successfully monitor long-term changes). Combining these different forms of knowledge is not a simple process (Prell *et al.* 2007; Reed 2008). There is a need for national and international exchange of scientific and practical information, data sharing and meta-analysis. Advances in modern communication technology can surely facilitate good networking and information exchange. Monitoring over longer timescales is also needed, and the creation of an international peatland monitoring network would be useful. Indeed, in many environments an inventory of peatland resources is still far from adequate (e.g. in the Hudson Bay Lowland; Abraham and Keddy 2005), and without this understanding the potential for properly evaluating ecosystem service provision will still be some way off. We therefore conclude with a strong call to the science, policy and practice community to support a move towards framing peatland decision making within an ecosystem services approach, with targeted research, rigorous monitoring and two-way knowledge exchange, so that this new alliance is built on strong foundations. The knowledge exchange process is vital to the future of peatlands and, in order to be effective, it needs to be well resourced. Thus we advocate a funded national and international peatland knowledge exchange hub which will be vital to ensure that peatlands are protected and restored for multiple societal benefits.

18.7 Acknowledgements

The data from the UK practitioner survey were collected as part of DEFRA project SP0556. Holden, Reed and Buckmaster were supported by ESRC grant RES-189-25-0017.

CHAPTER NINETEEN

Policy drivers for peatland conservation

ROB STONEMAN
Yorkshire Wildlife Trust, York, UK
CLIFTON BAIN
IUCN UK Peatland Programme, Scottish Wildlife Trust, UK
DAVID LOCKY
Grant MacEwan University, Canada
NICK MAWDSLEY
Euroconsult Mott MacDonald, The Netherlands
MICHAEL MCLAUGHLAN
Saskatchewan Ministry of Environment, Canada
SHASHI KUMARAN-PRENTICE
Charles Darwin University, Australia
MARK REED
Newcastle University, UK
VICKI SWALES
Royal Society for the Protection of Birds (RSPB), UK

19.1 Introduction

Peatlands have long been recognised as a high priority for protection under international and national wildlife laws and agreements. Over the last half century this protection has essentially been reactionary in the face of more widespread land management policy and market forces, which have encouraged damage to peatlands. This damage has been mainly to support the delivery of provisioning services, such as food, timber and pulp, or the widespread extraction of peat and oil. Across the world, peatlands of different types face a variety of pressures from land use and land-use change as well as pollution (e.g. atmospheric pollution on British blanket bogs), making them more susceptible to impacts of climate change. Within the general framework of international agreements on peatland conservation,

Peatland Restoration and Ecosystem Services: Science, Policy and Practice, eds. A. Bonn, T. Allott, M. Evans, H. Joosten and R. Stoneman. Published by Cambridge University Press. © British Ecological Society 2016.

each country has developed its own approach to tackling the threats with varying degrees of success. While established wildlife conservation policy has helped limit the extent of damage to peatlands in some countries, there is a need and opportunity for a stronger and more urgent public policy response to address the significant ongoing losses of peatland biodiversity and ecosystem services. The recognition of the multiple benefits that peatlands provide has presented new avenues to support sustainably managed peatlands, in addition to reducing peatland loss through active restoration (e.g. Bain *et al.* 2011; Joosten, Tapio-Biström and Tol 2012). This chapter presents an overview of the principal international and national policy drivers, with examples from selected countries across the world to highlight how new resources could be directed at wise use and conservation of peatlands.

19.2 Global overview of policy drivers for peatland conservation

While peatlands have been regarded as wastelands, and areas to be 'improved' for agriculture and forestry since the late eighteenth century (Chapter 2), they are now recognised for their wildlife and increasingly for their ecosystem services. Peatlands, therefore, feature in some of the world's highest-level environmental policies.

One of the earliest global agreements to recognise the importance of peatlands for protection was the Ramsar Convention (1971) that promoted the establishment and management of a network of protected wetlands. In 1996, it was reported that though peatlands represented 50% of the world's freshwater and terrestrial wetlands, less than 10% of the designated Ramsar sites had peatland as their dominant habitat (Chapter 15). Given continuing peatland loss and degradation, Contracting Parties set out guidelines to improve peatland protection (Ramsar 2003).

Peatlands are also a priority identified by the 1992 Convention on Biological Diversity (CBD, United Nations 1992), which recognises biodiversity as underpinning ecosystem functioning and the provision of ecosystem services essential for human well-being. Commitments were extended across all the world's governments to achieve a significant reduction in the rate of biodiversity loss by 2010. A global review of progress (CBD 2010a) concluded that the target had not been met leading to a new strategic plan for 2011–20 (CBD 2010b). This reinforces the need to conserve and restore peatlands, highlighting their role in mitigating and adapting to climate change.

Further traction is exhibited within the Convention on International Trade in Endangered Species of Wild Fauna and Flora (CITES) where it relates to species found on peatlands. A good example is the Bornean and Sumatran orang-utan (*Pongo pygmaeus* and *P. abelii*, respectively) which are both strongly associated with tropical peat swamp forest. Likewise, the signatories to the Convention on the Conservation of Migratory Species of Wild Animals (also known as CMS or Bonn Convention) are more likely to conserve peatlands where there is a strong association with migratory species. An example of such action is work to restore Belarusian fens, which is partly designed to protect the CMS-Appendix 1-listed aquatic warbler *Acrocephalus paludicola* breeding grounds (CMS 2011a).

Of particular pertinence today is the United Nations Framework Convention on Climate Change (UNFCCC) – an international process that provides a framework for action to reduce GHG emissions. Under this Convention, developed nations are committed to protecting and enhancing GHG sinks and carbon stores and promoting practices that reduce emissions from agriculture and forestry. The Convention provides for update protocols that set mandatory emission limits. The principal update is the Kyoto Protocol, which includes specific commitments for relevant parties to reduce emissions and account for land use, land-use change and forestry (LULUCF) activities. Land-use change on peatlands is a recognised activity, and a decision at the Durban Conference in 2011 allows the emission benefits of peatland rewetting to be accounted for (Chapter 15). Under the UNFCCC, developed countries can invest in low-carbon technologies in developing countries, including helping to meet the costs of some peatland restoration action and there are also proposals to also allow investment in avoiding peatland damage/degradation under the REDD programme – see Chapter 15 for more details.

The important message from these high-level policies is to ensure that peatlands, along with the biodiversity that underpins the ecosystem and its services, are conserved and restored to a functioning state. Peatland protection and other relevant policies (e.g. food security, energy and trade) need to be designed to ensure that peatlands and their ecosystem services are maintained or enhanced. Land-use policy and subsidy are often designed to convert peatlands into supposedly more economically productive use, yet this can damage or destroy important ecosystem services – the value of which is only monetised once it is lost. It is interesting that peatland conservation in the high Andes of Ecuador and Colombia is driven more by a recognition of the role of the paramo (including its peatlands) for water supply than necessarily biodiversity conservation (R. Stoneman, pers. obs.).

International policy can also work against peatland conservation. For example, EU Directive 2003/30/EC (European Commission 2003a) established a goal of reaching a 5.75% share of renewable energy in the transport sector by 2010, which included the use of biofuel. This has had the paradoxical effect of driving up demand for palm oil, in turn fuelling the conversion of tropical peat swamp forest into palm oil plantation (Page, Rieley and Banks

2011a), leading the EU to revise its policy to ensure the use of biofuels with a clear and net GHG saving without negative impact on biodiversity and land use (European Commission 2009), in which, however, the climate damaging use of already drained peatlands remained allowed (Joosten 2009a).

The policy context at a global level sends a clear message to individual governments to take strong action to protect and restore their peatlands; the case for peatland conservation is clear, strong and explicit. It is, of course, at a national level that this policy framework should be made to work. In this chapter, the approach and effectiveness of peatland conservation policy is examined in three contrasting parts of the world: in the European Union with a case study from the UK, in South East Asia and from selected regions in Canada.

19.3 Policy drivers in the UK
19.3.1 Context

UK peatlands have historically been seen as wasteland, a resource to be developed typically through drainage to 'improve' agriculture, afforestation and deliberate burning to encourage *Calluna vulgaris* (increasing wild populations of red grouse for shooting). Industrial atmospheric pollution has also had a very significant effect in some areas. Much of this land-use change has been supported by Government policy and subsidy, in particular grant-aided drainage which peaked at 100 000 ha per year from the 1970s to 1990s (Robinson 1990) and associated headage payments (e.g. Condliffe 2009), as well as widespread conifer planting that has dramatically altered *ca.* 190 000 ha of deep peatland through ploughing, drainage and tree planting (e.g. Stroud *et al.* 1988). Some of these perverse incentives have now been removed, in particular tax breaks for forestry (Morrison *et al.* 2010), land drainage and headage payments. There are now agricultural subsidy payments from the European Union for peatland restoration through the Common Agricultural Policy (DEFRA 2011) in recognition of broader public benefits (Van der Wal *et al.* 2011), although new threats have emerged, in particular those from renewable energy developments (windfarms and associated access tracks in particular, Chapter 9) while ongoing commercial peat extraction continues to damage many lowland bogs, especially in Scotland. Burning is still prevalent despite stronger guidance (DEFRA 2007; SEERAD 2008).

19.3.2 International and European policies affecting UK policy on peatlands

As well as being a signatory to the global commitments outlined above, the UK must also comply with a number of important EU environmental obligations. These include specific wildlife legislation (EU Habitats

Table 19.1 *International policies and regulations affecting peatlands globally and in Europe.*

Commitment	Detailed plans	Requirements	References
UN Convention on Biological Diversity (CBD)	Strategic Plan for 2011–2020 and Aichi Targets	Promotes conservation and restoration of peatlands and highlights their role in mitigating and adapting to climate change	CBD, 2010a, b
	EU Biodiversity Strategy to 2020	By 2020, ecosystems and their services are maintained and enhanced by establishing green infrastructure and restoring at least 15% of degraded ecosystems	European Commission 2011
UN Framework Convention on Climate Change	Kyoto Protocol and LULUCF	Protect and enhance carbon reservoirs and account for losses/gains from peatlands	Kyoto Protocol Article 2,1 (a) (ii) (United Nations 1998; Ad hoc working group to the Kyoto Protocol)
Ramsar Convention	Strategic Plan 2009–2015	Establish and manage a network of protected sites	Ramsar Convention 2008
	Global Action Plan for Peatlands	Encourage wise use and recognition of ecosystem service benefits	Ramsar Bureau 2003
EU Habitats Directive (92/43 EEC)	Conservation of listed habitats – blanket bog, raised bog and fens	Classify protected sites and ensure favourable status of peatland habitats across their natural range, including typical species	European Commission 1992

Table 19.1 (cont.)

Commitment	Detailed plans	Requirements	References
EU Water Framework Directive (2000/60/EC)	Wetlands identified in the Directive	Prevent deterioration, protect and enhance aquatic ecosystems including wetlands	European Commission 2000
	Horizontal Guidance on Wetlands	Peatlands included as ecosystems which influence water quality or quantity, as well as those dependent on groundwater	European Commission 2003b

Directive and Wild Birds Directive) targeted at species and habitats, as well as wider environmental legislation such as the Gothenburg Protocol to reduce atmospheric sulfate emissions (United Nations 1979). Table 19.1 shows the UK's main international commitments with specific peatland obligations.

19.3.3 National policy drivers
Designation
The main mechanism for implementing international conventions and European Directives is site designation to guide development and inform appropriate management. All sites deemed worthy of protection under European Directives are designated as Special Protection Areas (SPAs under the Birds Directive) and Special Areas of Conservation (SACs under the Habitats Directive) to form part of the pan-European Union's Natura 2000 ecological network. These internationally important sites and the UK's nationally important sites are designated as Sites of Special Scientific Interest (SSSIs) in England, Scotland and Wales and Areas of Special Scientific Interest (ASSIs) in Northern Ireland, under devolved legislation of the constituent UK countries.

Designation provides protection by prohibiting damage through a process of notification and consent for changes in management and new development. Wider biodiversity duties under the legislation mean that funding and regulatory support for designated site objectives can also come from other public bodies; for example, the Habitats Directive influences the design of agri-environment schemes that are used to help deliver environmental objectives, including the maintenance and restoration of peatlands.

Wildlife designations cover only a portion of the peatland resource since much of the area no longer supports peatland species and habitats of conservation importance. Even within qualifying peatlands, the designations are only a selection of the UK's best known sites and at the site level the boundaries do not always cover the whole peatland hydrological unit. Indeed Lawton *et al.* (2010) concluded that 'England's collection of wildlife sites, diverse as it is, does not comprise a coherent and resilient ecological network even today, let alone one that is capable of coping with the challenge of climate change and other pressures'.

Planning policy
Land-use planning policy across the UK tends to presume against development that could adversely affect protected sites. Non-designated peatland is therefore not as well protected against development of various forms given lower statutory protection, and also receives less funding for positive management. This is a serious limitation in the UK's approach to implementing the Habitats Directive, in which designation as SAC is only one tool of many that EU countries can use to conserve these habitats.

At the local level, land-use planning is implemented by Local Planning Authorities and guided by their local development plans. Many Local Planning Authorities liaise with non-statutory partners such as NGOs (in particular the local Wildlife Trusts) and naturalists to identify Local Wildlife Sites within their local development plans. Local policy directs development away from these sites, although there are few mechanisms to ensure positive conservation management.

Other policy instruments
The protected site system on its own is not adequate to halt the decline of the UK's wildlife (Lawton *et al.* 2010). The EU Habitats Directive obligations go beyond designating sites and require the deterioration of habitats to be avoided (Article 6.2). The use of agri-environment payments and agreements, with specific measures aimed at maintaining and restoring peatlands, is one of the most important mechanisms to address this obligation.

The UK's ratification of the Convention on Biological Diversity led to a planned approach to conserving biodiversity with priorities, objectives and targets (Kerr and Bain 1997). UK Habitat Action Plans were produced for peatlands, with targets for the conservation and restoration of blanket bog, raised bog and fens (HM Government 1994a). Monitoring progress on these plans forms the basis of the UK reporting to the Biodiversity Convention. These plans have helped to steer land management policy; for example, UK forestry policies promote woodland expansion but give safeguards for peatlands and promote peatland restoration. Likewise, voluntary guidance aims to phase out the use of horticultural peat by 2020 (DEFRA 2010).

Governments have a suite of policy instruments available to help protect peatlands (see Table 19.2), though biodiversity objectives are not fully integrated into the policy accounting, e.g. agri-environment expenditure does not facilitate identification of specific habitat action.

Monitoring of the habitat itself shows that the UK still has a long way to go to conserve its peatland. A report on the state of peatlands (JNCC 2011) notes that 80% of UK peatlands have been damaged. Within the internationally designated sites for blanket bog, the most widespread peatland type in the UK, only 45% are in good condition with 14% in a recovering condition, i.e. under some kind of restoration management.

New opportunities
Despite the wide array of instruments available for sustainable peatland management, the balance of these has not been sufficient to meet existing biodiversity targets. Rather than searching for a single policy *silver bullet*, the concept of *smart regulation* (Goulder and Parry 2008) recognises that there needs to be a combination of instruments to deliver policy objectives with regulation and incentives supported by information provision and capacity support. The 2010 CBD COP 10 identified that the way to overcome such slow progress in meeting biodiversity objectives is to recognise and value the multiple benefits that biodiversity brings and attract investment from budgets beyond the limited funds normally allocated for wildlife conservation.

Reform of the Common Agricultural Policy away from public subsidy for private farming businesses towards public benefits is one such approach (e.g. Lyon 2010). Further impetus could result from carbon accounting for peatland rewetting under the Kyoto Protocol (Chapter 15), though the flexibility mechanisms that could finance peatland restoration would require significant changes to the Kyoto Protocol and EU Emissions Trading Scheme before they could be applied to the UK. Meanwhile, voluntary schemes

Table 19.2 *Categories of government policy instruments.*

Category	Type	Peatland examples
Direct state control	Public ownership of land Areas managed by public bodies	State-owned forestry on peatland Peatland managed by Scottish Water/ Northern Ireland Water, Ministry of Defence National Nature Reserves
Classic regulation	Prohibited activities, licences/permits, planning zones, delivery of conservation objectives	Minerals controls on peat extraction Renewable energy policy SSSIs, SPAs, SACs Moorland burning code
Financial instruments	Grants, subsidies, tax breaks, user fees, taxes	Agri-environment peatland measures
Capacity building	Skills training, capital grants, infrastructure funding	None at present
Information provision	Leaflets, websites, research and advisory services	JNCC website and others
Creating new markets	Payments for ecosystem services, voluntary schemes	None at present although DEFRA is currently developing new guidance

are being developed (Rabinowitz and d'Este Hoare 2009). The EU Water Framework Directive provides another driver for action in that many 'failing' water bodies derive from catchments that have peatland-dominated headwaters. A significant proportion of England's drinking water is similarly derived from upland peatland-dominated catchments, and there is strong evidence that re-vegetation and gully blocking lead to significant reductions in sediment and associated heavy metal export from degraded peatland catchments in the uplands (e.g. Worrall and Evans 2009), leading to improved stream biodiversity (Ramchunder *et al.* 2012) and reduced concentrations of dissolved organic matter (Chapter 9).

It is likely that under climate change, many UK peatland catchments will become more vulnerable (Clark *et al.* 2010); preventing deterioration and enhancing peatlands is an important part of the future delivery of the Water Framework Directive and maintaining good drinking water supplies. The statutory water services regulation authority, Ofwat, is allowing water companies to fund catchment solutions to water quality problems. Ofwat has supported GBP 52 million-worth of catchment management work to date. Approximately half of this budget has been specifically spent on peatland restoration. A recent cost–benefit analysis of one such project (the SCaMP project) showed a cost of GBP 7414 million compared with benefits of GBP 13 328 million (White, pers. comm.), while another study for the Keighley and Watersheddles catchment estimated a benefit ratio of 1.3–2.9 for every pound spent on improvement against a 'cost of doing nothing' ratio of −2.0 to −5.3 for every pound not spent (Harlow *et al.* 2012).

As 95% of UK peatlands are blanket bogs and cover often large areas in the landscape, effective management depends on a cooperative approach across multiple ownership boundaries and across sectors. The CBD concept of an ecosystem approach to managing the environment has been successfully applied in a number of landscape-scale peatland projects with public–private partnerships across the UK (Chapter 9). Spatial planning is an important tool and could be used to enable new forms of governance and partnerships for multiple land-use objectives (e.g. Harris and Hooper 2004), potentially extending development benefits beyond the immediate development sites through mechanisms such as the community infrastructure level, Section 106 agreements and biodiversity offsetting.

19.4 Policy drivers in South East Asia
19.4.1 Context

About 60% of the world's tropical peatlands are located in South East Asia, where they are the main wetland ecosystem type (Page *et al.* 2011b). They are found in all ten Association of South East Asian Nations (ASEAN) Member States and are particularly extensive in the coastal lowlands of Indonesia and Malaysia, with Indonesia accounting for almost 90% of the region's peatland (see Table 19.3). Peatlands in South East Asia are naturally forested, have a unique biodiversity and a high economic value due to an abundance of resources: a source of high-quality timber (e.g. Parish 2002), fish (e.g. Dennis and Aldhous 2004) and peatland plants such as rattan and sedge for weaving mats and baskets (e.g. Kumaran 2007). Environmentally, peat swamp forests are also important for a range of ecosystem services including water supply, moderating river flows, preventing tidal flooding in near-coastal areas and as a terrestrial carbon store (e.g. Hooijer *et al.* 2010).

Table 19.3 *Area and condition of peatland within ASEAN member states (sources: Bappenas et al. 2009; Hooijer et al. 2010; Miettinen and Liew 2010; Wetlands International 2010; Parish et al. 2012).*

State	Peatland area (km²)	% of national land area	% ASEAN peatland	Intact/slightly degraded peat forest (km²)	% peatland forested
Brunei Darussalam	909	17%	0.4%	c. 700	80%
Cambodia	45	0%	0.0%	-	-
Indonesia	206 950	11%	87.8%	113 500	55%
Lao PDR	191	0%	0.1%	-	-
Malaysia	24 577	7%	10.4%	4 703	19%
Myanmar	1 228	0%	0.5%	-	-
Philippines	645	0%	0.3%	-	-
Singapore	50	7%	0.0%	-	-
Thailand	638	0%	0.3%	-	-
Vietnam	533	0%	0.2%	-	-
Total ASEAN	235 766	5%	100.0%	118 993	51%

Despite their important and valuable environmental benefits, peatlands in South East Asia have been extensively cleared, drained and/or degraded in the name of economic development (Chapter 14, for example). In the last 20–30 years, a third of peat swamp forest has been converted to agricultural land and another third logged or degraded (ASEAN 2011), while 3 million hectares have burnt, causing large-scale transboundary smoke haze and concomitant environmental, economic and health impacts alongside huge GHG emissions (e.g. Page *et al.* 2002; Government of Indonesia 2010; Hoojier *et al.* 2010). The level and pace of peatland degradation and destruction is extraordinary, such that very few forested peatland domes in the Sundaland bioregion now remain intact. Tropical peatland destruction represents one of the greatest failures of biodiversity conservation by the global community in recent decades, while the scale of carbon emissions is likewise extraordinary (Chapter 14).

19.4.2 Importance of international policy drivers for peatland protection in South East Asia

At the global level, a number of conventions are of particular relevance to the management of peatlands and their biodiversity, see Table 19.4.

Table 19.4 *Status of ASEAN state membership in global environmental conventions, as of November 2010 (sources: official websites of the listed conventions).*

State	CBD	CMS	Ramsar	CITES	UNFCCC
Brunei Darussalam	acs	-	-	-	acs
Cambodia	acs	IOSEA	Contracting Party	Party	acs
Indonesia	rtf	IOSEA	Contracting Party	Party	rtf
Lao PDR	acs	-	Contracting Party	Party	acs
Malaysia	rtf	IOSEA	Contracting Party	Party	rtf
Myanmar	rtf	IOSEA, Dugong	Contracting Party	Party	rtf
Philippines	rtf	Party, IOSEA, Dugong, Sharks	Contracting Party	Party	rtf
Singapore	rtf	-	-	Party	rtf
Thailand	rtf	IOSEA	Contracting Party	Party	rtf
Vietnam	rtf	IOSEA	Contracting Party	Party	rtf
Total	10	1	8	9	10

Notes: *CBD and UNFCCC: All terms, 'ratification' (rtf), 'accession' (acs), 'approval' (apv) and 'acceptance' (acp), signify the consent of a state to be bound by a treaty. The legal incidents/implications of ratification, accession, approval and acceptance are the same. The treaty becomes legally binding on the state or the regional economic integration organisation. All countries that have either ratified, acceded to, approved or accepted the Convention are therefore Parties to it. CMS: Signatories to the CMS Memorandum of Understandings on Turtles (The Memorandum of Understanding on the Conservation and Management of Marine Turtles and their Habitats of the Indian Ocean and South East Asia or IOSEA), dugongs and sharks are listed, although only the Philippines is a Party to the Convention.*

Table 19.5 *The APMS framework with 13 focal areas and 25 operational objectives.*

Focal Areas	Operational Objectives
1. Inventory and assessment	1.1: Determine the extent and status of peatlands in the ASEAN region (including issues of definition)
	1.2: Assess problems and constraints faced in peatland management
	1.3: Monitor and evaluate peatland status and management
2. Research	2.1: Undertake priority research activities
3. Awareness and capacity building	3.1: Enhance public awareness on importance of peatlands, its vulnerability to fire and the threat of haze through implementation of a comprehensive plan
	3.2: Build institutional capacity on management of peatlands
4. Information sharing	4.1: Enhance information management and promote sharing
5. Policies and legislation	5.1: Develop or strengthen policies and legislation to protect peatlands and reduce peat fire
6. Fire prevention, control and monitoring	6.1: Reduce and minimise occurrence of fire and associated haze
7. Conservation of peatland biodiversity	7.1: Promote conservation of peatland biodiversity
8. Integrated management of peatlands	8.1: Promote multi-agency involvement in peatland management
	8.2: Promote integrated water resources and peatland management using a basin-wide approach and avoiding fragmentation
	8.3: Promote integrated forest and peatland management
	8.4. Manage agriculture in peatland areas in an integrated manner
	8.5: Promote integrated community livelihood and peatland management
9. Establishment and promotion of demonstration sites for peatland management	9.1: Promote best management practices

Table 19.5 (cont.)

Focal Areas	Operational Objectives
10. Restoration and rehabilitation	10.1: Develop appropriate techniques for the restoration or rehabilitation of degraded peatlands
	10.2: Rehabilitate burnt, drained and degraded peatlands
11. Peatlands and climate change	11.1. Protect and improve function of peatlands for carbon sequestration and storage
	11.2. Support peatland adaptation process to global climate change
12. Regional cooperation	12.1: Promote exchange of expertise in addressing peatland management issues
	12.2: Establish 'centres of excellence' in the region for peatland assessment and management
	12.3: Contribute to the implementation of other related agreements and regional cooperation mechanisms
	12.4: Enhance multi-stakeholder partnerships to support peatland management
13. Financing of the initiative	13.1: Generate financial resources required for the programmes and activities to achieve target of the strategy

19.4.3 The ASEAN Peatland Management Initiative

ASEAN plays an important role in facilitating international cooperation between member nations on priority regional issues. ASEAN does not have any supranational statutory role (unlike the European Union), but can provide pan-state guidance. In particular, it has developed the ASEAN Peatland Management Initiative (APMI) to provide a framework to reduce transboundary smoke haze. The goal of APMI is to promote sustainable management of peatlands by enhancing understanding and building capacity, reducing peatland fires and promoting better peatland management and fire management.

ASEAN Peatland Management Strategy (APMS)
A principle mechanism is the development of the ASEAN Peatland Management Strategy (APMS; ASEAN 2006). This aims to guide actions on the management of peatlands for 2006–2020. In particular, it requests that member states develop National Action Plans for peatlands (Table 19.5).

National peatland management strategies and action plans
The ten ASEAN member states are at different stages in the preparation of their National Action Plans, but good progress has been made in parts of Indonesia, in Malaysia, the Phillipines and Brunei Darussalem.

19.4.4 Policy drivers in Indonesia

Indonesia has the largest area of peatland in South East Asia and is illustrative of the challenges for peatland conservation in the region. A partnership of state, private sector and local communities is required to overcome these challenges. Most peatland areas are state owned and leased out for various uses. An analysis of five Indonesian provinces (WACLIMAD 2012a) showed that about 90% of the peatland area is *kawasan hutan* or state forest land, of which 40% is already leased to timber plantation or for agriculture (principally for palm oil). Ultimately, it is for the state to ensure that private sector companies comply with regulations though with 4–5 million people living close to these peatland areas, many people's livelihoods have a link to the peatland resource (WACLIMAD 2012b, c). With their pre-existing ownership and use rights not being recognised by the state in many areas (see Lynch and Harwell 2002), land tenure uncertainty and conflict is prevalent and detrimental to the livelihoods of local people and the long-term management and conservation of peatland.

Peatland and climate change policy
The single most important policy change that has prompted interest in peatland conservation is the commitment of the President of Indonesia in 2009 to reduce GHG emissions by 26% domestically and by 41% with international support. As peatlands contribute an estimated 50% of national emissions (DNPI 2010), it would be difficult to achieve these targets without significant action to protect, rehabilitate and manage peatland. The Letter of Intent between the Governments of Indonesia and Norway saw Norway offer Indonesia up to USD 1 billion dollars to achieve emissions reductions through a series of phased actions. A key part of this has been a temporary moratorium on the licensing of primary forest and peatland. While this has enabled a pause in licensing, the extent of peatland that is already licensed but not developed has meant that the moratorium has had a more limited impact on the ground. Its value will only be realised if Indonesia can address some of the key issues identified below.

Legal context: conflicting regulations and the need for evidence-based policy – Under Indonesia's spatial planning and land-use framework (*penataan ruang*), the central dome of peat (deep peat over 3 m in depth) is protected, allowing economic use of shallower peats around the main peat dome while some forested peatland is protected in National Parks. Under the forestry regulations, however, which are far more important given that most peatland is under state forest ownership, forests on peat over 3 m in depth or topographically flat are automatically classified for production (WACLIMAD 2010), resulting in very large areas of peatland under logging or conversion to oil palm plantation. This loophole has to be closed and replaced with regulations that conserve the hydrological integrity of peatland systems ideally targeting development away from peatland areas.

Designation and resources for protection – The land-use planning system can designate forest for conservation (*hutan konservasi*) with focus areas for biodiversity (*hutan lindung*) based on various criteria. However, a critical barrier is the lack of an accurate and independently verified national peat depth map. Current maps all consistently underestimate peat depth, so even if this legislative tool was used, data is not available to support effective conservation. Critically, the Presidential Delivery Unit has started to produce a single verified peat map specifically for land-use zonation, protected area designation and licensing. Once designated, a further barrier to conservation is the lack of dedicated local field staff to address fires and illegal logging. This requires finance that could be developed through a 'peatland' use tax or deployment of international climate change funds.

Private sector interests and economic growth – As noted elsewhere, peatland destruction has been largely the result of the expansion of the palm oil industry and to a lesser extent of the timber and paper industry. This is justified in terms of jobs and economic growth. Interestingly, there is little economic difference between growing oil palm on peatland or mineral soils even if the timber harvest is taken into account. Palm oil yields on peatlands tend to be somewhat lower, while water management and fertiler cost are higher (BAPPENAS 2009); swapping peatland concessions for mineral concessions makes much sense economically and such a process is under way through the Forests and Landscapes in Indonesia project (formerly known as POTICO). project. In tandem, the major oil palm companies are moving away from growing oil palm on peatlands following international pressure from consumers (especially in Western Europe). Clearly, part of the solution lies outside the peatland areas although where peatlands have been cleared, developing paludiculture – agriculture that does not require land drainage – provides another mechanism to conserve peat (Chapter 14).

Fiscal and other incentives – Timber licensing includes land taxes to local government while it is well known that a range of informal payments to expedite applications typically apply. This incentivises local government and officials to sanction peatland destruction and should be reversed. An intergovernmental fiscal instrument could be designed to reward district governments to protect peatland that could be related to a peat tax if set sufficiently high (Goetz 1997). Further policy work is required on this issue.

Institutional drivers – There are further institutional drivers that mitigate against peatland conservation. For example, the Ministry of Forestry makes little distinction between wetland and dryland forests; water management is the responsibility of the Ministry of Public Works, with little cross-working on the issue; and there are few institutional mechanisms to assess wider environmental effects of peatland destruction and degradation. Environmental impact assessment is required (Decree of the Minister of Environment No 5/2000) for wetlands but, in practice, never used (WACLIMAD 2010). Market mechanisms, such as the Round Table on the Sustainable Production of Oil Palm, may be more effective in slowing the rate of peatland destruction given that institutional reform is difficult and slow.

19.4.5 Priority actions and outlook

Peat conservation and management requires four priority actions:

1. **Fire prevention and control** incentives and sanctions are required to stop fires being lit, to reduce the incidence and severity of peatland fires and to facilitate rehabilitation of peatlands. This should include a network of fire response teams and prosecution of offenders (in particular those companies that encourage burning on land they lease).
2. **Conservation and peatland management** to restore functional hydrological landscapes. This requires a step change in funding, for example carbon funds, capacity building and clear and transparent accounting of funding and measures to enable partnerships of state institutions, NGOs and businesses to undertake restoration in the main peatland areas. In some areas, there is a critical need to re-zone peatland forests to substantially expand peatland conservation and protection areas, e.g. in Sumatra.
3. **Rehabilitation of degraded tropical peatlands** With more that 3–4 million hectares of unmanaged degraded peatland in South East Asia, there is a clear need to build on the small-scale peatland rehabilitation pilots that have been developed in Sumatra, Kalimantan and Thailand (e.g. Dohong 2005). Initiatives such as the Kalimantan Forest and Climate Partnership initiated between the Governments of Indonesia and Australia in 2009 need to become the norm.
4. **Community-based management and protection of tropical peatlands** The sustainable management of peatlands requires an integrated approach at all levels – local, regional and national – developing common strategies for management of different uses within each peatland

area. Local communities have an important role as stewards of peatland resources, and should be effectively involved in activities to restore and sustain the use of peatland resources. Enhancing the awareness and capacity of the local community, addressing poverty and inequity, and providing positive incentives are important to tackling the root causes of peatland degradation. In particular, specific local investment models for lowland peat areas in South East Asia need to be piloted based on environmental criteria to reduce pressure on peatland and peat swamp forests while providing local jobs and income. This will require safeguarding local land tenure and working with communities and the private sector to ensure that positive social, environmental and economic outcomes can be achieved.

19.5 Policy drivers in Canada

19.5.1 Context

Canada provides an interesting case study of wetland policy because of the sheer extent (1.27 million km^2, representing about 25% of the world's wetlands and covering 14% of Canada), the variety and the distribution of wetlands (Rubec 1994). Much of the peatland area is located in the remote boreal region and remains fairly intact. However, there have been region-specific losses and degradation due to agriculture, forestry, peat mining and large-scale industrial development (Table 19.6). Additionally, there is the impending threat of climate change and new, grand-scale industrial developments.

19.5.2 Policy

Wetland policy in Canada is applied at the international, national, provincial and municipal levels. However, wetland policy varies widely across provincial and territorial jurisdictions in both scope and efficacy (Locky 2011).

International

Canada is signatory to a range of international policy instruments, including the Ramsar Convention and the Convention on Biological Diversity (see section 19.4.2 above for more details). Notably, however, Canada pulled out of the Kyoto Protocol on climate change, believing that the cost of staying in the Protocol was too high. This decision was upheld by the Supreme Court of Canada.

National

The Federal Policy on Wetland Conservation (Government of Canada 1991) is the guiding policy for federal land, of which the objective is to

Table 19.6 *Drivers of change and damage to Canadian peatlands.*

Driver	Damage to Canadian peatlands
Losses to agriculture	Drainage for agriculture in the Little Clay Belt of north-eastern Ontario has reduced peatland area significantly within the region. Similar losses have been evidenced in other settled areas across boreal Canada.
Impairment by forestry	Peatland forestry with drainage is primarily at the experimental level in Canada. Most significant is the Wally Creek Watershed in north-western Ontario (250 km^2) and at a few, much smaller research sites in boreal Alberta. Peatland forestry without drainage is conducted primarily in north-eastern Ontario and Québec on vast wooded bogs and black spruce swamps. In Alberta, forest clearance associated with conventional oil and gas exploration and development account for double the amount taken during commercial forestry operations (Anielski and Wilson 2001).
Impairment by horticultural peat and peat 'biofuel' production	Horticultural peat harvesting is common in Québec, New Brunswick and Alberta, and to a lesser extent in other provinces, extending to about 17 000 ha. The use of peat for 'biofuels' in Canada is currently a minor activity.
Losses and impairment by large-scale industrial development	Peatland loss and impairment due to large-scale industrial activities is an emerging and significant concern in Canada. Some losses have occurred due to flooding the landscape for hydroelectric generation in Manitoba, Québec and Labrador. Future projects are planned. However, the majority of peatland losses, current and future, are related primarily to the development of oil (tar) sands deposits in Alberta (Locky 2011) – see Box 19.1.
Threats from climate change	Approximately 60% of Canada's peatlands are found in areas that are modelled as severely affected by climate change. A significant proportion of the western boreal region will experience severe to extremely severe impacts of drying.

Table 19.7 *Selection of wetland and peatland policy examples for Canadian provinces.*

Canadian province	Wetland and peatland policy
New Brunswick	New Brunswick's 2002 wetland conservation policy is under revision. Overall policy objectives include a *no-net-loss* policy that will remain intact at two levels: • no net loss of provincially significant wetlands and • no net loss of function for other wetlands (Water Canada 2010).
Nova Scotia	Nova Scotia has recently updated its wetland protection policies (Government of Nova Scotia 2011). The policy is designed to manage human activities on or near wetlands to ensure there are no net losses of *Wetlands of Special Significance* (WSS) or, if not defined as a WSS, then to ensure that any damage sustained is evaluated through environmental assessment and adequately mitigated for.
Ontario	The Ontario government promotes development of wetland policies at the municipal level that align with provincial wetland policy. Protection of provincially significant wetlands is the aim, and overarching is the Provincial Policy Statement on Natural Heritage which includes all wetlands regardless of ownership or size (Rubec and Hanson 2009). Specific to this policy is that: • all coastal wetlands are protected, and • the province is divided into two sections for specific management objectives: the south, which is dominated by mineral soil wetlands, and the north, which is dominated by peatlands. Two novel wetland evaluation systems are used in the two sections of the province. The Southern and the Northern Ontario Wetland Evaluation Systems integrate a degree of wetland function and value within the evaluation metrics (OMNR 1994). Wetlands are evaluated based on biological, social, hydrological and special features (250 points each). Those wetlands that score more than 600 or more or with 200 or more points in the Biological or Special Features components are considered provincially significant and protected, provided the municipality designates this wetland in its official plan. The conservation of less significant wetlands is still promoted, but through municipalities rather than through the province.

Canadian province	Wetland and peatland policy
Saskatchewan	Wetland and peatland conservation in Saskatchewan is accomplished through a variety of programme, policy and legislative instruments. An initial level of conservation of Saskatchewan's wetlands comes from the Saskatchewan Representative Areas Network (RAN). This programme is intended to conserve representative and unique landscapes, both terrestrial and wetland, in each of Saskatchewan's 11 ecoregions (Saskatchewan Environment 2005). The goal of the program is to set aside 12% of the province, in turn set by the province's Biodiversity Action Plan (Government of Saskatchewan 2006). A second level of conservation is the Saskatchewan Wetland Policy, which is promoted by the Saskatchewan Watershed Authority (2002). A third level of conservation and regulation of developments in wetlands and terrestrial environments in the province is the Environmental Assessment Act, which requires developers to receive the approval of the Minister of the Environment before proceeding with a development that is likely to have significant 'environmental' implications (Government of Saskatchewan 2002). The above instruments represent important policy drivers of wetland conservation and regulation in the province of Saskatchewan, but are not the only ones; other levels of regulation exist under legislation such as The Forest Resources Management Act, The Crown Resource Land Regulations and The Environmental Management and Protection Act.
Alberta	Alberta's wetland protection policies have oscillated, from virtually no policy in the early 1990s, to national leader in 2007 (Rubec and Hanson 2009), and currently somewhere in between (Locky 2011). In 1993, Alberta developed two progressive draft wetland policies: one for the southern settled region mostly relating to mineral soil wetlands, and the other covering the northern more sparsely populated region with peatlands. The southern policy provided the template for the Interim Wetland Policy and Compensation Plan of 2004, although wetland losses by then amounted to 64% with the remaining wetlands as small and often in private ownership. Additionally, a much lauded Wetland Restoration/Compensation guide was introduced, based on the no-net-loss concept. This policy, principally for use in the southern region, was designed to avoid impacts, mitigate (minimize) unavoidable impacts, and compensate for irreducible impacts.

Table 19.7 (cont.)

Canadian province	Wetland and peatland policy
	In 2013 a revised wetland policy was initiated (Government of Alberta 2013). Implementation occurred in 2015 for the southern mineral soil wetland region and in 2016 for the northern peatland region. Mitigation is still used as a framework but no-net-loss has been removed and wetlands are valued based on rarity and location. Mitigation now includes investment in research and other tools. Wetland practitioners require certification.
British Columbia	British Columbia recently released a Wetland Action Plan to assist in developing policy (British Columbia Wetlands 2010). The three overarching directives include: • clear and comprehensive information (wetland information and education) • effective legal and planning tools (enhance legal protection and enforcement, integrate wetland protection into strategic planning); and • effective actions and incentives for wetland protection (secure protection of priority wetlands and improve coordination among partners). The Water Resources Act states that the property and the right to the use of water are for all purposes vested in the Crown. Wetlands are identified as bodies of water, permitting the provincial government to assert property rights over wetlands (Rubec and Hanson 2009).

promote the conservation of Canada's wetlands to sustain their ecological and socio-economic functions, now and in the future. As such, the Federal Government, in cooperation with the provinces and territories and the Canadian public, will strive to achieve the following goals:

- maintenance of the functions and values derived from wetlands throughout Canada
- no net loss of wetland functions on all federal lands and waters
- enhancement and rehabilitation of wetlands in areas where the continuing loss or degradation of wetlands or their functions has reached critical levels
- recognition of wetland functions in resource planning, management and economic decision making with regard to all federal programmes, policies and activities

- securement of wetlands of significance to Canadians
- recognition of sound, sustainable management practices in sectors such as forestry and agriculture that make a positive contribution to wetland conservation while also achieving wise use of wetland resources
- utilisation of wetlands in a manner that enhances prospects for their sustained and productive use by future generations.

The policy is backed up by a comprehensive strategy, composed of seven strands, from public awareness to the management of federal lands for wetlands. Canada's federal wetland policy has provided a model for some provincial policy development, particularly the no-net-loss of wetland concept (see below for the provinces). This links to Canada' no-net-loss policies for fish-bearing wetlands passed in 1986 (Rubec and Hanson 2009).

Provincial examples
Most of Canada's provinces and territories have developed wetland policy or utilise Federal wetland policy. Table 19.7 sets out a selection of policy examples from various provinces in an east to west progression, exemplifying different states of policy development and approach.

The table shows widely different approaches taken at a provincial level, albeit in the general framework of international and Canadian Federal policy. However, these difference also reflect geography in that large parts of Canada have such low development and population pressure that the necessity for strong policy is simply not apparent – complacent, perhaps, or simply pragmatic.

19.6 Conclusions

At a global level, peatland protection is recognised in important international conventions and treaties. The Ramsar Covention (1971, 2008) and Convention on Biological Diversity (CBD 2010a, b) explicitly mention peatlands for conserving their biodiversity, while the UNFCCC (via the LULUCF part of the Kyoto Protocol) provides another very strong driver for the conservation of peatlands.

However, international convention only operates within the policies of individual states. In the European Union, for example, international convention may be partly delivered via European Directives but these in turn have to be transposed into member state law. In South East Asia, policy coordination is further diluted and each country essentially has its own approach. The goals of policy also differ between countries. In Canada, the main policy

Box 19.1
The impact of oil sand mining on peatlands

Alberta has the third largest petroleum reserves in the world, most of which are in oil sands. The total area of oil reserves is 142 000 km^2, of which the proven reserves cover 22 500 km^2 (Fig. 19.1). The current approved oil sands operations are currently impacting 4 800 km^2 of Alberta's boreal landscape. These are related to surface deposits of oil sands that are less than 75 m deep and accessed through open-pit mines.

Peatland cover in the oil sands region is approximately 65% of the landscape (Rooney et al. 2011), and losses of peatlands to oil sands mines is estimated at 30 000 ha based on current approved mines, and eventually much higher with future developments (Locky 2011). Current approved plans suggest that the loss of peatlands to oil sands mines will release 11.4 to 47.3 million tonnes of stored carbon, with the carbon sequestration

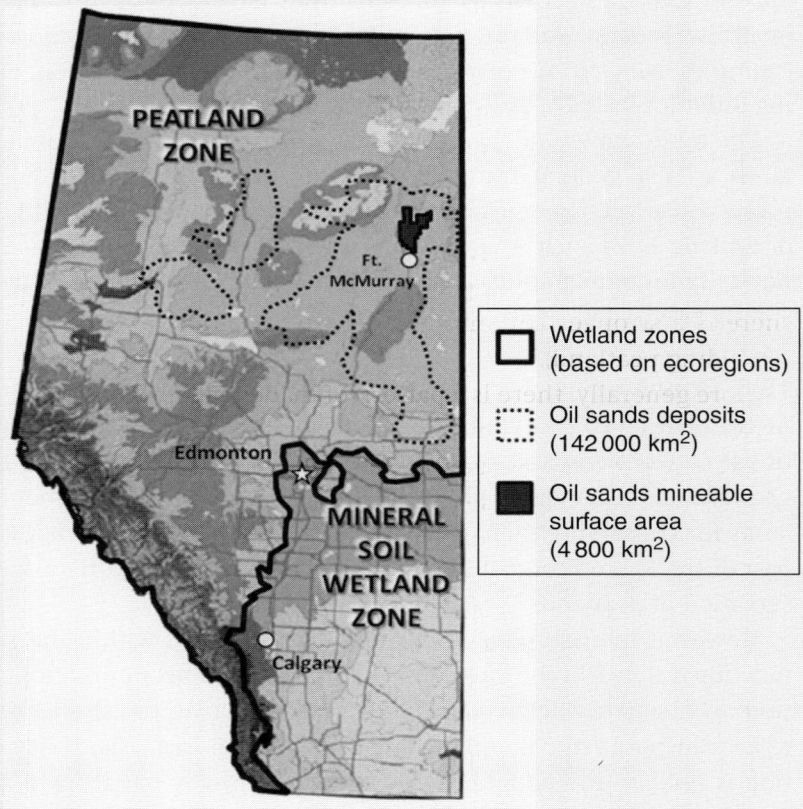

Figure 19.1 Map of Alberta showing oil sands mining area.

> potential reduced by 5734 to 7241 t C yr^{-1} (Rooney *et al.* 2012). Oil sands development is also being initiated in Saskatchewan's oil sands region, another area with high peatland cover (Locky 2011).
>   Restoration of the post-mining landscape is difficult, with only partial success so far for agriculture and forestry. Recreating wetlands is even more challenging although the construction of new mineral soil wetlands has shown some promise on two novel but expensive fen construction research sites at the Syncrude and Suncor sites (Locky 2011).

objective is no net loss, while in Indonesia economic development with limited conservation goal appears to be the *de facto* aim of peatland policy.

Likewise, for many countries, these laws are further refined and/or implemented at a more local level. For the UK and Canada, national policy is further devolved at a country/province (UK) or provincial (Canada) level. In Indonesia, national policy and legislation is implemented by a combination of central agencies within state forest land where the majority of peatland is found and local governments in other lands. Clear differences in implementation are apparent across single countries. In Canada, for example, peatlands in Nova Scotia are rather strongly protected while in Alberta, protection is weaker (although outside the oil sands mines regions, threats to Alberta peatlands are comparatively reduced and related more to cumulative linear disturbances). Within Indonesia, peatland in Sumatra is poorly protected and heavily exploited, while in Papua there is a stronger commitment to protection of remaining forest land (including peatland).

More generally, there is a pattern of inadequate protection of peatlands across the globe. This is particularly so in South East Asia, where international conventions are backed by strong commitments at a pan-country ASEAN level but have little practical impact when applied at a nation state level (with perhaps the exception of Thailand and Brunei Darussalem). The unfolding ecological catastrophe of Indonesian and Malaysian peat swamp forest degradation and conversion to oil palm is a particularly stark failure of state governments to implement international treaty and convention, although the moratorium on forest conversion is perhaps the first indication of a slowing of the pace of peatland forest destruction in Indonesia.

For South East Asia, a huge market failure is apparent where the long-term financial consequences of peatland forest destruction, in terms of the loss of nature tourism potential, flood prevention and a carbon store that may have a high value as the carbon market develops, is not taken into account when compared to the short-term financial gain resulting from logging and conversion to oil palm plantation. Indeed, even the short-term gains are doubtful in some areas where coastal oil palm plantations may fail before a positive economic return on investment is achieved, due to enhanced fire risk and coastal flooding as the peat subsides (Parish, pers. comm.). Moreover, the business case for investing in oil palm on peat as opposed to mineral soils appears to strongly favour mineral soils. Similarly, in the UK, purported economic returns from state-subsided afforestation of open blanket bog and drainage to improve grazing also proved illusory, with substantial onward costs to society in terms of reduced water quality, potentially increased flooding and the current need to restore these peatlands to comply with current regulations such as the European Habitats Directive.

Regulation alone appears to be inadequate to protect peatlands. A range of policy instruments that work in tandem with each other is required to make real progress. In the UK, land-use control regulations, financial incentives (mainly land-use subsidies via the European Union), advice and, in the future, payments for ecosystem services are applied to make progress. Yet even here, such work risks being undone by poor planning for renewable energy, or continued management for agriculture or recreational shooting that impacts on the peat carbon store and wildlife. In Indonesia, regulations are currently characterised by a lack of enforcement and loopholes that enable a business-as-usual approach. Despite discussions about REDD+ in Indonesia, there is limited discussion about the development of fiscal and other policy incentives and disincentives to change the logic of unsustainable peatland use.

With increasing threats to peatlands resulting from land degradation and climate change, active restoration and responsible management of peatlands is more urgently required. The IUCN UK Commission of Inquiry on Peatlands (Bain *et al.* 2011) and the recent report from the Food and Agriculture Organization of the United Nations (Joosten, Tapio-Biström and Tol 2012) identified a number of recommendations:

- a strong national steer from government that peatlands should be conserved and restored
- strategic planning to protect peatlands from damaging development and integrated land-use planning to balance different land-use pressures
- removal of perverse incentives that lead to peatland damage, and introduction of measures to support delivery of conservation and restoration, in recognition of the ecosystem services they provide

- government and private sector investment in peatland conservation/restoration, and attraction of investment aimed at delivering multiple win–wins for carbon, water and biodiversity
- support for local and landscape-scale projects facilitated by project managers, strong stakeholder engagement and coordinated effort across different private and public sectors
- support for ongoing surveying and monitoring of peatland condition and delivery of ecosystem services
- coordination of scientific effort across the different disciplines to provide consensus-based evidence for policy and practical management
- sharing of experiences and expertise on peatland conservation and restoration internationally and within countries, engaging a wide range of land managers and relevant stakeholders.

Well-considered and properly regulated Government policy has a huge role to play in the conservation of peatlands around the world and is essential to address the long-term market failure that bedevils the global conservation of biodiversity, in which short-term financial gains destroy longer-term, but less easily monetised, ecosystem services. Given the enormous significance of the carbon store that the world's peatlands represent and the overwhelming need to address climate change, world governments have a clear and new mandate to develop effective policy to conserve their peatland resource. There are good examples of effective policy, as well as many examples of where policy has not been as effective as wished. The opportunity to protect the world's peatlands is within our grasp.

19.7 Acknowledgements

We thank Line Rochefort, J. Kirkby, Aletta Bonn and Marja-Liisa Tapio-Biström for their valuable efforts to improve the text.

CHAPTER TWENTY

Peatland restoration and ecosystem services: nature-based solutions for societal goals

ALETTA BONN
Helmholtz Centre for Environmental Research (UFZ) | Friedrich-Schiller-University Jena | German Centre for Integrative Biodiversity Research (iDiv) Halle-Jena-Leipzig | IUCN UK Peatland Programme, UK

TIM ALLOTT
The University of Manchester, UK

MARTIN EVANS
The University of Manchester, UK

HANS JOOSTEN
Institute of Botany and Landscape Ecology, Ernst Moritz Arndt University of Greifswald, Germany

ROB STONEMAN
Yorkshire Wildlife Trust, York, UK

'Peatland conservation is a prime example of a nature-based solution to climate change but we urgently need to switch from aspiration to action to secure the benefits that peatlands provide'.

Julia Marton Lefèvre, former Director-General, IUCN

20.1 Introduction

The chapters of this book provide a compelling account of the crucial role of peatlands for human well-being and the role restoration can play in providing nature-based solutions to societal goals. Across the world, natural peatlands provide important ecosystem services, with a special role in climate regulation, water regulation, provision of cultural services, such as historical archives and recreation opportunities, and hosting important habitats for wildlife. In contrast, damaged peatlands on only 0.3% of the earth's land surface contribute disproportionally to global GHG emissions, producing probably up to 50% of the total global land bound and 5% of the total global

Peatland Restoration and Ecosystem Services: Science, Policy and Practice, eds. A. Bonn, T. Allott, M. Evans, H. Joosten and R. Stoneman. Published by Cambridge University Press. © British Ecological Society 2016.

annual anthropogenic CO_2 emissions. Degraded peatlands therefore pose a high risk and, ultimately, a high cost to society.

At the heart of peatland degradation is the unsustainable exploitation of peatland resources, mainly to maximise provisioning services for agricultural and forestry produce (Chapters 2 and 9–14). There are still perverse incentives and economic drivers in place fostering short-term profits (Chapters 2, 15 and 19), while neglecting consequences for global natural capital and sustainable livelihoods. The speed of degradation is alarming, especially in the tropics. Natural peatland habitats in Indonesia have shrunk to just 32% of the original peatland area, with most of those losses occurring in the last two decades as peatlands are drained and logged and converted to oil palm or pulpwood plantations. These plantations often cannot be sustained for more than one or a few production cycles, because subsidence eventually makes drainage of the low-lying peat soils impossible (Chapter 14). In temperate Europe, the majority of the peatlands has already been degraded by land use and land-use change over the past 150 years (Chapters 2, 10, 12). In Canada, recent technological advances and a desire for energy independence have meant that tar sand extraction will destroy peatlands to a significant extent. Also in Europe some of the remaining peatlands remain under current threat from the energy industry. For example, in Ireland, Finland and Belarus valuable peatlands are under threat from peat extraction; in Scotland peatlands are damaged through the siting of wind turbines; in Germany peatlands are being deeply drained for biofuel maize production; while in Iceland, Scandinavia and Canada peatlands are being flooded for hydro-electricity.

The world has failed to reach international targets to significantly reduce the rate of biodiversity and habitat loss by 2010 as set out by the Convention of Biological Diversity and the Ramsar Convention. The cost of inaction to conserve peatlands has not only affected wildlife. Inaction has led to a poverty spiral in tropical peatlands, with threats to livelihood and human welfare due to fires and increased flooding from peat subsidence (Chapter 14), and the likelihood of complete disappearance of coastal land in Sumatra and Kalimantan with sea level rise in the next decades (Silvius 2014). Peatland degradation has left graziers on high-altitude peatlands in Tibet without a basis for sustainable livelihoods (Chapter 13), and across the world peatlands contribute significant GHG emissions affecting populations globally (Chapter 4, 15).

Many peatland areas in the world, however, are still in near-natural state, and awareness of their importance to society may foster measures to safeguard their integrity. For example, the Congo and Amazon basins host many pristine peatland areas which have neither been mapped nor are subject to safeguards and regulations yet (Joosten, Tapio-Biström and Tol 2012).

Importantly, peatlands are extremely sensitive to anthropogenic disturbance and behave differently to other ecosystems. Even when the direct land-use driver for degradation has been removed, damaged peatlands continue to degrade and to emit carbon dioxide until drainage is reversed and a peat-producing, or at least conserving vegetation, has re-established (Chapter 4). It is often very difficult to stop the process of degradation once started (Chapters 2, 9, 10 and 14) and, within a human timeframe, hardly possible to restore a damaged peatland to its former full function and biodiversity.

Conservation of the remaining pristine peatlands is therefore critical. Furthermore, given the extent of degraded peatland and an urgent need to stop continued peat oxidation, especially in the face of a warming climate, peatland rewetting and restoration is a key nature-based solution to mitigating and adapting to climate change. Restoration also decreases peatland vulnerability to environmental change and increases the adaptive capacity of peatland ecosystems and the communities that depend on them. This follows the specific policy framework set by the CBD and the EU Biodiversity Strategy 2020 with the internationally agreed targets of restoring 15% of all degraded habitats by 2020 – a challenging and urgent call to action (Chapter 19; Box 20.1).

Box 20.1

International policy goals regarding peatland ecosystem services and restoration

The **Convention on Biological Diversity (CBD)** Conference of Parties (COP) 9 in 2008, in its decision on Biodiversity and Climate Change, recognised 'the importance of the conservation and sustainable use of the biodiversity of wetlands and, in particular, peatlands in addressing climate change'. The Strategic Goals and Aichi Targets, adopted by COP 10 (Nagoya, Japan, 2010, Decision X/2), is of special relevance for peatland conservation and restoration:

Target 15: By 2020, ecosystem resilience and the contribution of biodiversity to carbon stocks has been enhanced, through conservation and restoration, including restoration of at least 15 per cent of degraded ecosystems, thereby contributing to climate change mitigation and adaptation and to combating desertification.

The **EU 2020 Biodiversity Strategy** Target 2 incorporates the global CBD target agreed by EU Member States and the EU in Nagoya:

By 2020, ecosystems and their services are maintained and enhanced by establishing green infrastructure and restoring at least 15% of degraded ecosystems.

As the chapters in this book show, restoration has considerably progressed the continued provision of both ecosystem services and wildlife habitat. In some European countries, such as the UK, the Netherlands and Germany, a substantial body of experience is building (Chapters 9, 10 and 12); in other areas of the world, especially in the tropics (Chapter 14), restoration efforts are in their infancy.

The range of experience reported in this volume represents the state of the art on the developing understanding of restoration for ecosystem services. Below we draw together some of the recurring themes from the chapters in order to synthesise the core findings and identify the key challenges for future work on peatland ecosystem services in three critical areas: science, policy and practice.

20.2 The science challenge

Climate change represents one of the greatest challenges for restoring peatland, while it is also a major justification for many peatland restoration activities. Climate change increases the vulnerability of peatland ecosystems (Chapter 8) and of the livelihoods of people that depend on them. Restoration increases the resilience of peatlands to additional climate stress (Harris *et al.* 2006; Morecroft *et al.* 2012) and provides a strong, nature-based solution to climate change mitigation and adaptation.

Chapter 4 describes the important role that peatlands play in terrestrial carbon cycling, highlighting the magnitude of carbon stocks in peat soils worldwide. As such, peatland restoration is essential but the challenge gets harder as the climate changes. To some extent, the impact of a changing climate can be lessened through effective management (e.g. Chapter 8). As the links between peatlands and climate are complex, there is a need for a clearer understanding of these relationships to enhance resilience to climate change by more effective restoration and management.

Peatland hydrology links climate change to peatland function and is central in all restoration programmes (Chapter 5). Since peat formation requires high water tables, rewetting is central in all restoration programmes. Where climate change directly impacts on water balance, options for restoring peat-accumulating conditions may be reduced. That said, raising the water table will typically result in a decrease of GHG emissions as peat oxidation is reduced, even if the ecosystem process of peat accumulation may not be restored. The peatland archive holds records of the nature of the mire ecosystem under a variety of past climate regimes (Chapters 6 and 8) and is therefore a critical resource for evaluating likely mire responses to climate change. For example, changes in the dominance between moss species reflect changes in climate-mediated bog surface wetness (Barber 1981).

Under conditions of climatic stress the restoration of anthropogenically impaired systems becomes paramount. While the peatland archive shows that pristine mires exhibit often substantial resilience to climate change (Chapter 8), the combination of climate change alongside further anthropogenic pressures may force the peatland to cross the thresholds into alternative states. These may differ substantially in ecosystem properties so that original ecosystem functions and biodiversity may not be maintained and sustained ecosystem services delivery may severely be impaired or altered. The case of UK blanket peatlands that have suffered catastrophic degradation in response to multiple human and climatic pressures in the last millennium is instructive in this case (Evans and Warburton 2007).

Understanding and managing peatlands under climate change towards resilience is therefore perhaps the defining challenge for wetland science in the twenty-first century. Understanding is better advanced in some peatland types, notably those in temperate and boreal regions. In tropical peatlands the science is advancing rapidly, but a critical research need remains given their fast rate of destruction and potential impacts on global carbon cycling (Chapters 4 and 14).

One area where further understanding is required is the role of time in peatland ecology and restoration. Chapter 4 points to the importance of the timescale for assessing the influence of CH_4 and CO_2 emissions, whereas Chapter 12 assesses the transitional and long-term impacts of peatland forestry. Restoration of the carbon sequestration function may require timescales of decades at least (Lucchese et al. 2010). A fuller understanding of the long-term trajectory of ecosystem development in restored systems is an issue also addressed in Chapter 11, which illustrates the important role of process-understanding of ecosystem structure and function in planning, implementing and predicting the course of peatland restoration.

A further scientific challenge is to establish appropriate success criteria for peatland restoration. Monitoring of restoration projects is typically undertaken in order to assess or to demonstrate the 'successes' of the restoration approach. The most straightforward approach is comparing the restored ecosystem to a representative pre-impact system. This approach has been commonly adopted in North America for restoration projects on mined peatlands (Chapter 11), but presents difficulties in more heavily impacted terrain (e.g. Chapters 9 and 10). Here, the peatlands themselves, as environmental archives (Chapter 6), present an alternative where an analysis of the palaeo-ecological record allows the 'pristine' pre-impact ecosystem structure to be reconstructed as a target for restoration (Chapters 6 and 8). As full restoration of structure may be a very long-term process (e.g. Joosten

1995; Lucchese *et al.* 2010), short-term assessments must enable a judgement of whether restoration activities are successful, i.e. result in developments that go in the right direction, which again requires a detailed knowledge of ecosystem trajectories. For most peatland systems, this knowledge is incomplete because of the scale of peatland degradation (e.g. Chapter 5). A viable alternative approach to determining restoration success, therefore, is to develop peatland restoration targets around ecosystem function and ecosystem services rather than ecosystem species composition and structure (e.g. Hedberg *et al.* 2013; Shackelford *et al.* 2013; Chapters 3 and 18).

As Bradshaw (1996) noted, practical restoration ecology is a key test of ecological theory. The relationship between ecological theory and restoration practice is not a one-way transfer of knowledge, rather it should be an iterative learning process (Chapter 18). It is imperative that appropriate monitoring of peatland restoration is undertaken. Currently, monitoring is often piecemeal and underfunded, due to the vagaries of funding for long-term monitoring programmes and the frequent reluctance of the funders of practical restoration to support monitoring. In this context, one of the more important science challenges becomes the collation of existing data and the development of standardised monitoring approaches to assess the efficacy of peatland restoration. Standard methodologies ensure inter-comparability of data, so that even where the monitoring of particular restoration projects is limited there is potential to assemble meaningful meta-analyses of multiple projects.

Widely implemented standard monitoring methodologies may also offer the possibility of early warning of climatically driven shifts in peatland function. The magnitude of potential carbon release from current peatland carbon stocks (Chapter 4) is such that monitoring to provide early warning signals of threats to the stock (monitoring of intact sites) and to assess the resilience of restored sites (monitoring of restoration) is an ongoing requirement.

The shift from restoration targets around ecosystem structure and biodiversity to targets around ecosystem function defines an interesting intersection of restoration ecology and ecosystem services research. In many ways, restoration targeting ecosystem services is more demanding since it requires an evaluation of a wider range of socio-ecological parameters. It offers, however, the prospect of more nuanced definitions of success and – with a focus on functions and trajectories rather than endpoints – possibly earlier 'success' in restoration projects more in line with funding timeframes. More understanding is required on interactions of anthropogenic drivers and the interplay of linear and non-linear processes (Evans *et al.*

2014), and how management delivers ecosystem services. The evaluation of restoration success with respect to multiple ecosystem services will rapidly require a common currency to assess trade-offs and synergies between particular restoration practices, specific ecosystem service outcomes, wider societal goals and enhanced human well-being.

Ideas around the valuation of ecosystem services developed in Chapter 16 show one way forward to clarify the economic importance of peatlands, to demonstrate the cost-effectiveness of nature-based solutions through restoration, and to develop markets for peatland restoration. But there is a clear need for further development not just of the assessment of socio-economic benefits of restoration (Aronson *et al.* 2010) but also of the science underpinning the quantification of ecosystem service responses to restoration. Care needs to be taken that valuation focuses on holistic assessments of all ecosystem services and various value systems, as not all values may be easily captured by monetary valuation (Chapters 7 and 16). This emphasises again the need for more monitoring of restoration approaches, but also for careful investigation of the process links from restoration activities to ecosystem service responses and the development of modelling approaches towards reasonable prediction.

One of the greatest challenges of an ecosystem service approach to restoration success is the question of 'trade-offs', as an implementation that will optimise one ecosystem service does not necessarily lead to the optimisation of other ecosystem services or biodiversity (Bullock *et al.* 2011). A more formalised approach to valuing each ecosystem service is vital. Emission reduction assessment has already undergone such a formalisation when it was agreed that the varying climate impact of different gases would be expressed as their effect over 100 years compared to CO_2 (Global Warming Potential). This convention made it possible to compare the climatic effect of different GHGs and evaluate them consistently (Chapter 4).

A standardised metric of this type is still pending for other ecosystem services. Standardisation is rather straightforward if the service is independent of location, and can be measured along one single axis. For the global climate, it is irrelevant where the emission reduction takes place because GHGs are well mixed in the atmosphere. However, most ecosystem services depend on both location and time and cannot be evaluated independently of their spatio-temporal context, and metrics need to be developed to incorporate these aspects.

The data demands of adopting an ecosystem service approach to defining restoration success are high, and in some cases this requires more specialist measurements than are typically available to restoration practitioners. There is therefore also an urgent need for more research on linking biodiversity, ecosystem structure and function with ecosystem services and their quantification (Cardinale *et al.* 2012). This will allow for the assessment of ecosystem service performance by proxy, e.g. through the plant communities present in peatlands (Couwenberg *et al.* 2011), and to develop tools to quantify this performance with – depending on the aim – various efforts and varying accuracy (Joosten *et al.* 2015a).

Progress on the key scientific challenges requires an interdisciplinary approach to peatland science. Crucially, as attempted in this volume, this embraces active trans-disciplinary collaborations between scientists, practitioners and policy advisers with active knowledge exchange processes throughout the whole research and implementation process. This will foster the appreciation and enhance the relevance of research into ecosystem service delivery, the inclusion of different knowledge forms, and a quicker uptake of research results into practice (Chapter 18). The resources and capabilities to develop landscape-scale manipulations including restoration of peatland systems lie with the practitioner community, yet the maximisation of scientific return on these investments requires that experimental work and monitoring on these sites are built in at an early stage of planning. There is a need for a continuing dialogue between parties at the local scale, and for structures at national and international scales that facilitate collaboration and exchange.

In summary, we identify five key scientific challenges:

1. Development of restoration approaches towards resilience under a changing climate based on understanding of the peatland hydrology system.
2. Understanding restoration trajectories and appropriate timescales for evaluating peatland restoration projects.
3. Identification of success criteria for key peatland restoration practices and development of proxies or indicators of ecosystem service delivery.
4. Development of standardised monitoring approaches, including the creation of monitoring networks and long-term monitoring, and the use of these to (a) develop restoration theory and practice, (b) monitor risk to the state of peatlands and (c) assess restoration success.
5. Closer engagement of scientists with economists and policy makers to evaluate restoration outcomes in support of policy development.

20.3 The practice challenge

Peatland restoration practitioners need to understand the loss of ecosystem services through peatland degradation, to translate scientific advances into action, to share good practice and to develop adaptive management systems. Where severe degradation of peatlands has occurred, rapid action is required given the lag times between restoration action and the re-establishment of ecosystem functioning and services. In many cases, this means that waiting for near certainty in scientific evaluation of sites and approaches is not practically possible so that restoration actions are decided on the basis of best available evidence. The close collaboration between practitioners, policy makers and the scientific community is vital here to allow for adaptive management.

While knowledge of peatland system functioning and effects of management differs between regions, mire types and services, the key principle of rewetting is soundly established as a cost-effective contribution to mitigating and adapting to climate change. As evident from Chapter 4, halting damaging management to peatlands is not enough to stop peat degradation, but rewetting is required to minimise GHG emissions and move towards functioning peatland ecosystems. In short, the science is good enough to act.

Nonetheless, as shown also for other approaches to climate adaptation, there can be a lack of understanding of how to prioritise and target them, hindering implementation of theory into practice (Oliver *et al.* 2012). There is still a lack of awareness among decision makers of the importance of organic soils for the global carbon cycle. Further, since peatlands can be covered by many different vegetation types, local authorities are not always aware of their position and extent. Therefore, as a first step, it is vital to map the distribution of peatlands, specify drivers of change and identify regions under threat. Chapter 2 provides a global overview, and efforts are underway nationally and internationally to map hotspots and identify priorities (Dommain *et al.* 2012; Biancalani and Avagyan 2014). In addition, bioclimatic envelope models (Chapter 8) can help to assess vulnerability and sensitivity to climate stress in the future.

As a second step, restoration practice knowledge needs to be pooled to collate and synthesise practical experience, techniques and, most importantly, evidence of success as well as failure of restoration practice. Do we know what works to achieve the basic principle of rewetting? Are there common trends for all ecosystem services and for biodiversity across different peatland systems? Overall, synthesis of good practice should identify good technical advice to provide locally based solutions and share innovations, ideally through capacity development involving training and good practice demonstration sites. Importantly, restoration also needs to scale up and move from a site-scale approach to work at a landscape scale to tackle the challenge of restoring peatlands at regional and national scales (Chapter 2).

Accepting ecosystem service delivery as a shared goal across sectors and realising the limits of restoration for biodiversity (Chapter 3), it will be important to realise that restoration may not necessarily return peatlands to their original condition (Chapter 5). Rather, in some cases, we need to accept and work towards 'novel ecosystems' (Hobbs, Higgs and Harris 2009) with a changed set of species and refocus discussions on what functions and services can and should be restored. Conservation needs to consider concepts of sustainable use, too. While conventional 'dry' agriculture on peatlands is unsustainable and often unprofitable, 'wet' agriculture or paludiculture may provide new perspectives (Chapter 17; Joosten *et al.* 2015b).

Embracing an ecosystem service framework, innovative public–private partnerships have been formed to fund peatland restoration for multiple objectives (Chapter 19), and steps taken to align peatland restoration and sustainable rural development (Chapter 17). This can pool funding from different sources such as rural development funds, climate adaptation subsidies or improvement funds for water quality. In addition, innovative financing mechanisms are under development, such as payments for ecosystem services (Chapter 16) or carbon markets (Chapter 15) (Von Unger *et al.* 2014), to find new ways to integrate and embed conservation in business and policy.

We therefore identify five key practice challenges:

1. Identification of global priorities in restoration through mapping peatland distribution, actual emissions and conservation hotspots.
2. Synthesis of good practice and set-up of demonstration projects to raise awareness, to share expertise and innovation and to develop standard guidance for restoration projects.
3. Setting up of ecosystem service-based restoration targets for all projects.
4. Engagement of practitioners with the science community to develop a wider knowledge base for restoration management intervention, effective monitoring that aids project evaluation and adaptive management.
5. Development of novel partnerships across sectors. These can also foster new finance mechanisms for peatland restoration that build on the concept of payments for ecosystem services (including adequate measuring, reporting and verifying methodologies) and that strengthen the identification with these peatland ecosystem services.

20.4 The policy challenge

This volume highlights the range and magnitude of biodiversity and ecosystem services that peatlands provide, services which may at first appear to be provided at no cost to society. While some clear policy goals already exist (Chapter 15, 19; Box 20.1), these have not yet been met, and instead perverse incentives are still fostering further peatland degradation. The absence of economic mechanisms to rectify these losses represents a clear market failure. The damages to ecosystems services through peatland degradation causes substantial costs to society as is evident from the previous chapters.

Effective governmental policies and actions are therefore critical to sustaining the services that peatlands provide. This is particularly critical, since degradation not only results from 'collateral damage' but is often related to deliberate action. For example, in Central Ireland, the extensive Bog of Allan has almost completely disappeared, having been largely cut away by the state organisation Bord-na-Móna to fuel power stations and provide peat for the horticultural industry. In Chapter 14, Dommain quotes Anderson (1963), who noted that over a distance of 200 miles, the coastal plain of Sarawak 'has been and still is largely covered in swamp forest growing on peat, recorded depths of which may exceed fifty feet'. These systems have been entirely lost during the last few decades, and not a single hydrological peat swamp unit remains intact in Malaysia (Chapter 14).

In both cases, this loss of peatland was a direct result of national policy – in Ireland to support a domestic energy industry, in South East Asia to support more 'productive' land use. Similarly, in Canada, the Albertan government licences the destruction of peatland to enable tar sands mining (Chapter 19). In European countries, land subsidies, including those through the Common Agricultural Policy, were deliberately targeted to drain peatlands to increase land productivity, such that most peatlands have been damaged in some way (Chapters 2, 9, 10, 19). In some cases, agricultural policy is less deliberately targeted at peatlands yet still creates negative consequences for the state of peatlands and the services they provide. For example, Chapter 16 highlights the impact of European agricultural subsidies and German legislation (the German Renewable Energy Sources Act) linked to the Kyoto Protocol of the UNFCCC. In these policies, biofuel production is encouraged resulting in maize being grown on drained peatlands, a practice that causes rapid oxidation of peat resulting in GHG emissions that by far outweigh emission savings from replacing fossil fuels (Chapter 17). Likewise, in the UK, renewable energy obligations encourage the development of wind farms on upland peatlands, with negative impacts on the peatland system due to the construction of turbine bases and access roads.

In counterpoint, where suitable policy frameworks support peatland restoration, ecosystem service benefits can be restored effectively and often fairly cheaply and cost-effectively, also compared to other (technical) climate mitigation measures (Moxey and Moran 2014).

Peatlands have been described as *Cinderella* habitats (Lindsay 1993) – overlooked and undervalued, yet immensely important. However, the increased understanding of peatland ecosystem services, which has developed rapidly in the past decade and is exemplified in this volume, has led to a developing recognition by governments and society of the utility and value of peatland systems. Indeed, at an international level there is now a significant body of commitment to conserve the world's peatlands (Chapters 15 and 19). As stated above, commitments in relation to the CBD, the Ramsar Convention and the UNFCCC (via the LULUCF of the Kyoto Protocol and REDD+) all specifically commit national governments to conserve and restore their peatlands.

The path from international treaty to local policy action requires nation states to develop policy to enact those commitments, both nationally and locally. At this level, progress is variable. In some countries, such as the Netherlands, remaining peatlands are strictly protected. In other countries, peatland destruction is rapid, in particular in Indonesia, though even here the Agreement on Transboundary Haze Pollution of ASEAN (Chapters 15 and 19) and the Indonesia–Norway moratorium on peatland drainage (Edwards, Koh and Laurance 2012) give hope for a decline in the rate of destruction. Governments have a range of policy instruments open to them to address the manifest market failure of peatland degradation and destruction:

- **Regulation** – Governments can pass legislation that protects peatlands at a national or regional level. Spatial land-use planning is an important policy instrument in this regard. Site designation to inform authorities to avoid development of designated sites is a common approach (Chapter 18). Other regulatory instruments might include policies of 'no net loss' that are used, for example, in some Canadian provinces and the EU Habitats Directive (Chapter 19), or requirements for environmental impact assessment and subsequent mitigation and management.
- **Incentives** – Direct payments can be made available to address market failure. For example, rather than pay for the cost of drinking water treatment from degraded peatlands (Chapter 5 and 9), UK Government policy is now allowing the UK Water Industry Regulator to enable direct payments from Water Companies to improve the management of blanket bog to reduce water colour. In addition, subsidies through the second pillar of the EU Common Agricultural Policy reform can lever investment through agri-environment schemes for peatland restoration (Reed *et al.* 2014). For developing countries, payments can be made to restore tropical peat swamp forest through the 'Reducing Emissions from Deforestation and Forest Degradation plus' (REDD+) mechanism (Chapter 15).

- **Markets** – Governments can reform markets to provide market incentives for the conservation and restoration of peatlands, for example, through the various mechanisms of the Kyoto Protocol of the UNFCCC (Chapter 15). Likewise, governments could facilitate voluntary carbon markets related to peatland rewetting. Internationally, a high-quality voluntary standard for trading peatland credits has been available since March 2011 (Chapter 15).
- **Guidance** – Crucially, governments can provide guidance to resource managers and decision makers. Government guidance is, for example, set out in the ASEAN Peatland Management Strategy for South East Asia, which aims to guide actions to support the management of peatlands, requiring, in particular, Member States to develop national action plans for peatlands. Similarly, in the UK, Ministers for the Environment in the four constituent nations set out a letter to the statutory conservation agencies that states the Government's intent 'to protect and enhance the natural capital represented by peatlands in the UK and British Overseas Territories', in turn leading to enhanced action by Government departments to protect Britain's peatlands. Switzerland has produced an inquiry on perspectives of peatland restoration for climate change mitigation (Paul and Alewell 2013), whereas Finland recently summarised 25 years of restoration experience in a best practice book (Similä, Aapala and Penttinen 2014). The FAO has produced guidance for climate change mitigation by conservation, rehabilitation and sustainable use of peatlands (Joosten, Tapio-Biström and Tol 2012; Biancalani and Avagyan 2014).

Effective guidance can also come from non-governmental organisations and significantly impact on practice on the ground. In the UK, the IUCN UK peatland programme has re-published the management handbook on conserving bogs as an online resource (Brooks *et al.* 2014), to provide guidance for peatland restoration projects in the UK that want to be sponsored on the basis of their climate and other benefits. While government guidance is non-statutory, it can provide a powerful driver for action by reconfiguring existing public policy towards peatland conservation and restoration.

Given this discussion, we identify five key policy challenges:

1. Further development of public policy commitments from national governments to peatland conservation, recognising their powerful ecosystem service role, in particular in relation to climate regulation and biodiversity conservation.

2. Development of stronger links between the science community and policy makers to ensure public policy is framed from the scientific consensus so that the ecosystem service objectives of policy are clear and quantifiable.
3. Avoidance of perverse subsidies incentivising further peatland damage, and development of stronger regulatory mechanisms and legislation to directly protect and restore peatlands, recognising these as a finite resource and a globally significant store of carbon.
4. Recognition by governments that adequate mechanisms and direct funding are required to undertake critical conservation and restoration work.
5. Market reforms to address market failures that lead to the degradation of peatlands.

20.5 The communication and capacity challenge

Embedding restoration science into practice and policy demands active partnerships and working with stakeholders through awareness raising, engagement and joint learning and action (Chapter 18). The concept of ecosystem services allows engagement across sectors and the framing of environmental and social targets in a different way, without neglecting biodiversity goals. The recognition of the benefits of peatland restoration for ecosystem service delivery and, importantly, the risks of no action will need to be translated into action. Restoration needs to be appreciated and communicated, not as net cost but as a net benefit to society and a high-yielding investment (de Groot *et al.* 2013).

The importance of organic (peatland) soils for climate change mitigation has not yet reached mainstream international policy, let alone public knowledge. Internationally, the FAO has set up, in collaboration with Wetlands International, the Global Organic Soils and Peatlands Climate Change Mitigation Initiative (http://www.fao.org/climatechange/micca/peat/en), to share knowledge and promote sustainable land use and restoration on organic soils, including peatlands, to increase their mitigation potential (Joosten, Tapio-Biström and Tol 2012). Here, specialists communicate their knowledge directly within implementing organisations.

Over the coming years, it will be important to engage with the work programme of the Intergovernmental Platform on Biodiversity and Ecosystem Services (IPBES) and to communicate findings, especially with respect to Deliverable 3(b)(i): 'Thematic assessment on land degradation and restoration'. There are opportunities for scientists and practitioners to engage in the IUCN CEM Peatlands Thematic group alongside the International Mire Conservation Group (IMCG) and others.

In addition, we need to understand and communicate the cultural values of peatlands (Chapters 6 and 7), as peatlands form important historical archives and provide nationally important heritage. In some areas, peatlands form the last wilderness areas and provide an important sense of place (Chapter 7). Through communication of these cultural values, alongside biodiversity conservation goals and solutions to further societal goals, a greater understanding and capacity for safeguarding peatland services can be reached.

We identify five key communication challenges:

1. Communication of the benefits of peatlands to society in terms of ecosystem services and the costs arising from damaged peatland.
2. Identification of the role of peatland restoration in reaching national and international policy targets (especially for climate, water and biodiversity).
3. Communicating cultural values of peatlands to engender stronger ownership by local communities.
4. Building key partnerships to advance institutional mainstreaming of peatland restoration.
5. Celebrating the successes of peatland restoration.

20.6 Outlook

In the face of global change, we need concerted action for peatland environments and their services. The challenge is to urgently address the threats from degraded peatlands, especially in the tropics, and to harness solutions to achieving and maintaining global and local benefits from intact and restored peatland environments. In practice, conservation needs to link active restoration with the responsible use of peatland resources to safeguard peatland environments and the services they provide.

The ecosystem service framework provides a 'common language' that allows the many different constituencies with an interest in the use and management of peatlands to understand the synergies and trade-offs involved in various approaches to peatland management. A key role for the scientific community is to further quantify the association of peatland restoration with ecosystem services. In some cases, this requires generation of new knowledge, but in many instances synthesis and active knowledge exchange can already provide sufficient evidence for peatland restoration and adaptive management (Chapter 19). Proactive collaboration of the science and practitioner community can establish successful monitoring schemes to better understand what practical restoration techniques work and what their impacts are on ecosystem function.

With intensifying competition for land and water under a changing climate, it will become increasingly difficult to allocate peatland areas for a single purpose. Synergies in land use have to be found. This will be the most stimulating challenge for future peatland restoration: to foster integrative approaches that change degraded peatlands into mires which are again productive, supportive and beautiful.

References

Aapala, K., Sallantaus, T. and Haapalehto, T. (2008) Ecological restoration of drained peatlands. In *Finland – Fenland*. ed. R. Korhonen, L. Korpela and S. Sarkkola. Helsinki: Finnish Peatland Society and Maahenki, pp. 243–249.

Abel, S., Couwenberg, J., Dahms, T. and Joosten, H. (2013) The Database of Potential Paludiculture Plants (DPPP) and results for Western Pomerania. *Plant Diversity and Evolution*, 130, 219–229.

Abraham, K.F. and Keddy, C.J. (2005) The Hudson Bay Lowland. In *The World's Largest Wetlands: Ecology and Conservation*, ed. L.H. Fraser and P. Keddy. Cambridge: Cambridge University Press, pp. 118–148.

Abson, D.J. and Termansen, M. (2011) Valuing ecosystem services in terms of ecological risks and returns. *Conservation Biology*, 25, 250–258.

Acreman, M.C., Blake, J.R., Booker, D.J. *et al.* (2009) A simple framework for evaluating regional wetland ecohydrological response to climate change with case studies from Great Britain. *Ecohydrology*, 2, 1–17.

Acreman, M.C., Harding, R.J., Lloyd, C. *et al.* (2011) Trade-off in ecosystem services of the Somerset Levels and Moors wetlands. *Hydrological Sciences Journal*, 56, 1543–1565.

Adams, W.M. (2009) Editorial introduction to volume 1: The idea of Conservation. In *Conservation, Volume I*, ed. W.M. Adams. London: Earthscan, pp. 1–16.

Adamson, J.K., and Kahl, J. (2003) *Changes in Vegetation at Moorhouse within Sheep Exclosure Plots Established between 1953 and 1972*. Merlewood, UK: CEH.

ADB (1999) *Planning for the Fire Prevention and Drought Management*. Asian Development Bank TA 2999-INO. Jakarta: ADB and BAPPENAS (National Development Planning Agency).

Adinugroho, W.C., Suryadiputra, I.N.N., Saharjo, B.S. and Siboro, L. (2005) *Manual for the Control of Fire in Peatlands and Peatland Forest. The Climate Change, Forest and Peatlands in Indonesia Project*. Bogor, Indonesia: Wetlands International – Indonesia Programme and Wildlife Habitat Canada.

Aditama, T.Y. (2000) Impact of haze from forest fire to respiratory health: Indonesian experience. *Respirology*, 5, 169–174.

Aerts, R. and de Caluwe, H. (1994) Nitrogen use efficiency of *Carex* species in relation to nitrogen supply. *Ecology*, 75, 2362–2372.

Aldenfelder, M. and Zhang, Y. (2004) The prehistory of the Tibetan Plateau to the seventh century A.D. perspectives and research from

China and the West since 1950. *Journal of World Prehistory*, 18, 1–55.

Aldrian, E. and Susanto, R.D. (2003) Identification of three dominant rainfall regions within Indonesia and their relationship to sea surface temperature. *International Journal of Climatology*, 23, 1435–1452.

Alexander, P.D., Bragg, N.C., Meade, R., Padelopoulos, G. and Watts, O. (2008) Peat in horticulture and conservation: the UK response to a changing world. *Mires and Peat*, 3, Art. 8, 1–10.

Alexandrov, G.A. (1988) A spatially distributed model of raised bog relief. In *Wetland Modelling*, ed. W.J. Mitsch, M. Straškraba and S.E. Jorgensen. Amsterdam: Elsevier, pp. 41–53.

Allott, T.E.H., Evans, M.G., Lindsay, J.B. *et al.* (2009) *Water tables in Peak District blanket peatlands*. Moors for the Future Report No. 17. Edale, UK: Moors the Future Partnership.

Alm, J., Schulman, L., Silvola, J. *et al.* (1999) Carbon balance of a boreal bog during a year with an exceptionally dry summer. *Ecology*, 80, 161–174.

Alm, J., Shurpali, N.J., Minkkinen, K. *et al.* (2007) Emission factors and their uncertainty for the exchange of CO_2, CH_4 and N_2O in Finnish managed peatlands. *Boreal Environment Research*, 12, 191–209.

Andersen, R., Grasset, L., Thormann, M.N., Rochefort, L. and Francez, A.-J. (2010) Changes in microbial community structure and function following *Sphagnum* peatland restoration. *Soil Biology and Biochemistry*, 42, 291–301.

Andersen, R., Rochefort, L. and Poulin, M. (2010) Peat, water and plant tissue chemistry monitoring: a seven-year case-study in a restored peatland. *Wetlands*, 30, 159–170.

Andersen, R., Rochefort, L. and Landry, J. (2011) La chimie des tourbières du Québec; une synthèse de 30 années de données. *Le Naturaliste Canadien*, 135, 5–14.

Anderson, A.R., Pyatt, D.G. and White, I.M.S. (1995) Impacts of conifer plantations on blanket bogs and prospects of restoration. In *Restoration of Temperate Wetlands*, ed. B.D. Wheeler, S.C. Shaw, W.J. Fojt and R.A. Robertson. Chichester, UK: John Wiley & Sons, pp. 533–548.

Anderson, J.A.R. (1963) The flora of the peat swamp forests of Sarawak and Brunei, including a catalogue of all recorded species of flowering plants, ferns and fern allies. *Gardens' Bulletin Singapore*, 20, 131–228.

Anderson, J.A.R. (1983) The tropical peat swamps of western Malesia. In *Mires: Swamps, Bogs, Fen and Moor. Ecosystems of the World, 4B*, ed. A.J.P. Gore. Amsterdam: Elsevier, pp. 181–199.

Anderson, P., Buckler, M. and Walker, J. (2009) Moorland restoration: potential and progress. In *Drivers of Change in Environmental Upland*, ed. A. Bonn, T. Allott, K. Hubacek, and J. Stewart. London and New York: Routledge, pp. 432–447.

Anderson, R. (2001) Deforesting and restoring peat bogs: a review. *Forestry Commission Technical Paper 32*. Edinburgh, UK: Forestry Commission.

Anderson, R. (2010) *Restoring afforested peat bogs: results of current research*. Forestry Commission Research Note FCRN006. Edinburgh, UK: Forestry Commission.

Andersson, J.R. (1961) *The Ecology and Forest Types of the Peat Swamp Forests of Sarawak and Brunei in Relation to their Silviculture*. Kuching, Sarawak: Forest Department.

Anielski, M. and Wilson, S. (2001) *The Alberta GPI Environmental Accounts*. Pembina: Institute for Appropriate Development.

Ardron, P. (1999) *Peat cutting in upland Britain with special reference to the Peak District: its impact on landscape, archaeology and ecology*. PhD thesis, University of Sheffield, UK.

Armstrong, A., Holden, J., Kay, P. *et al.* (2010) The impact of peatland drain blocking on organic carbon loss and discoloration of water; results from a national survey. *Journal of Hydrology*, 381, 112–120.

Armstrong, A., Holden, J., Luxton, K. and Quinton, J.N. (2012) Multi-scale relationship between peatland vegetation type and dissolved organic carbon concentration. *Ecological Engineering*, 47, 182–188.

Armstrong, J., Jones R.E. and Armstrong, W. (2006) Rhizome phyllosphere oxygenation in Phragmites and other species in relation to redox potential, convective gas flow, submergence and aeration pathways. *New Phytologist*, 172, 719–731.

Armstrong, K. (2010) *Archaeological geophysical prospection in peatland environments*. PhD thesis. Bournemouth University, UK.

Aronson, J., Blignaut, J.N., Milton, S.J. *et al.* (2010) Are socioeconomic benefits of restoration adequately quantified? A meta-analysis of recent papers (2000–2008) in Restoration Ecology and 12 other scientific journals. *Restoration Ecology*, 18, 143–154.

Arts, K., Fischer, A. and Van der Wal, R. (2011) The promise of wilderness between paradise and hell: a cultural-historical exploration of a Dutch national park. *Landscape Research*, 37, 239–256.

ASEAN (2006) *ASEAN Peatland Management Strategy*. Jakarta: ASEAN Secretariat.

ASEAN Secretariat and Global Environment Centre (2011) Peatlands in Southeast Asia: A Profile. *ASEAN Peatland Forests Project*. Rehabilitation and Sustainable Use of Peatland Forests in Southeast Asia. http://www.aseanpeat.net/index.cfm?andmenuid=38 (accessed 12 Feb 2015).

Augustin, J. and Chojnicki, B. (2008) Austausch von klimarelevanten Spurengasen, Klimawirkung und Kohlenstoffdynamik in den ersten Jahren nach der Wiedervernässung von degradiertem Niedermoorgrünland. *Phosphor- und Kohlenstoff-Dynamik und Vegetationsentwicklung in wiedervernässten Mooren des Peenetals in Mecklenburg-Vorpommern – Status, Steuergrößen und Handlungsmöglichkeiten*, ed. J. Gelbrecht, D. Zak and J. Augustin. Berichte des IGB Heft 26. Berlin: IGB, pp. 50–67.

Azmi, M., Cullen, R., Bigsby, H. and Awang Noor, A. (2009) The existence value of peat swamp forest in Peninsular Malaysia. Paper presented at New Zealand Agriculture and Resource Economics Society Conference, 27–28 August 2009, Tahuna Beach Resort, Nelson, New Zealand.

Baden, W. and Eggelsmann, R. (1963) Zur Durchlässigkeit von Moorböden. *Zeitschrift für Kulturtechnik Flurbereinigung*, 4, 226–254.

Baden, W. and Egglesmann, R. (1970) Hydrological budget of high bogs in the Atlantic region. *Proceedings of the 3rd International Peat Congress 1968*, Québec, Department of Energy, Mines and Resources Ottawa, pp. 260–311.

Baginski, V.F. (ed.) (2007) *Integrated Productivity of Forest Land*. Gomel, Belarus: Forest Research Institute National Academy of Sciences of Belarus. [In Russian]

Bai, J., Ouyang, H., Cui, B., Wang, Q. and Chen, H. (2008) Changes in landscape pattern of alpine wetlands on the Zoige Plateau in the past four decades. *Acta Ecologica Sinica*, 28, 2245–2252.

Bai, J., Lu, Q., Zhao, Q., Wang, J. and Ouyang, H. (2013) Effects of alpine wetland landscapes on regional climate on the Zoige Plateau of China. *Advances in Meteorology*, 2013, Article ID 972430.

Bailey, J.F., Healy, B, Jianlin, H. *et al.* (2002) Genetic variation of mitochondrial DNA within domestic yak populations. *Yak Productions in Central Asian highlands. Proceedings of the Third International congress on Yak in Nairobi, Kenya*, ed. H. Jianlin, C. Richard, O. Hannotte, C. McVeigh and J.E.O. Rege. Nairobi: International Livestock Research Institute (ILRI), pp. 181–189.

Bain, C. (1997) Legislative approach for bogs: does the British approach work?

Conserving Peatlands, ed. L. Parkyn, R. Stoneman and H.A.P. Ingram. Wallingford, UK: CAB International, pp. 343–347.

Bain, C., Bonn, A., Stoneman, R. et al. (2011) IUCN UK Commission of Inquiry on Peatlands. Edinburgh, UK: IUCN UK Peatland Programme.

Baird, A. J., Beckwith, C.W. and Heathwaite, A.L. (1998) Water managment in undamaged blanket peats. In Blanket Mire Degradation: Causes, Consequences and Challenges, ed. J.H. Tallis, R. Meade and P. Hulme. Aberdeen: British Ecological Society, pp. 128–139.

Baird, A.J., Belyea, L.R., Comas, X., Reeve, A.S. and Slate, L.D. (2009) Carbon Cycling in Northern Peatlands. Washington, DC: American Geophysical Union.

Bal, M.-C., Pelachs, A., Perez-Obiol, R. and Cunill, R. (2011) Fire history and human activities during the last 3300 cal year BP in Spain's central Pyrenees: the case of the Estany de Burg. Palaeogeography, Palaeoclimatology, Palaeoecology, 300, 179–190.

Ball, P. (2000) H_2O. A Biography of Water. London: Orion.

Ballard, C., McIntyre, N., Wheater, H., Holden, J. and Wallage, Z. (2011) Hydrological modelling of drained blanket peatland. Journal of Hydrology, 407, 81–93.

Ballhorn, U., Siegert, F., Mason, M. and Limin, S. (2009) Derivation of burn scar depths and estimation of carbon emissions with LIDAR in Indonesian peatlands. Proceedings of the National Academy of Sciences of the United States of America, 106, 21213–21218.

Balshi, M.S., McGuire, A.D., Duffy, P., Flannigan, M., Kicklighter, D.W. and Melillo, J. (2009) Vulnerability of carbon storage in North American boreal forests to wildfires during the 21st century. Global Change Biology, 15, 1491–1510.

BAPPENAS – Government of Indonesia (2009) Reducing carbon emissions from Indonesia's peatlands – Interim Report of a Multi-Disciplinary Study. Jakarta: BAPPENAS.

Barber, K.E. (1981) Peat Stratigraphy and Climatic Change. Rotterdam, The Netherlands: Balkema.

Barber, K.E. (1993) Peatlands as scientific archives of past biodiversity. Biodiversity and Conservation, 2, 474–489.

Barr, C. and Cossalter, C. (2005) Pulp and plantation development in Indonesia. An overview of issues and trends. Centre for International Forestry Research (CIFOR) Seminar for EC Asia Pro Eco Project, Brussels, December, 2005. http://www.cifor.org/publications/pdf_files/research/governance/foresttrade/Brussels/ Attachment46-Barr-Cossalter-BrusselsWshop051205-1535-1615.pdf

Barriopedro, D., Fischer, E.M., Luterbacher, J., Trigo, R.M. and García-Herrera, R. (2011) The hot summer of 2010: redrawing the temperature record map of Europe. Science, 332, 220–224.

Bartoszuk, H. and Kotowski, W. (2009) The large high value wetlands of the Biebrza Valley, Poland. Grasslands of Europe of High Nature Value, ed. P. Veen, R. Jefferson, J. de Smidt, J. v. d. Straaten. Zeist, The Netherlands: KNNV Publishing, pp. 84–93.

Bay, R.R. (1968) The hydrology of several peat deposits in Northern Minnesota, U.S.A. Proceedings of the 3rd International Peat Conference, Québec, Canada, 18–23 August, 212–218.

Behnke, R. (2008) The Socio-Economic Causes and Consequences of Desertification in Central Asia. Dordrecht, The Netherlands: Springer.

Beilman, D.W., MacDonald, G.M., Smith, L.C. and Reimer, P.J. (2009) Carbon accumulation in peatlands of West Siberia over the last 2000 years. Global Biogeochemical Cycles, 23, GB1012.

Bellamy, D.J. (1972) Templates of peat formation. Proceedings 4th International Peat Congress Helsinki, 1, 7–18.

Belyea, L.R. (2004) Beyond ecological filters: feedback networks in the assembly and restoration of community structure. In Assembly rules and Restoration Ecology, ed. V.M. Temperton, R.J. Hobbs, T. Nuttle, M.

Fattorini and S. Halle. Washington, DC: Island Press, pp. 115–131.

Belyea, L.R. and Clymo, R.S. (2001) Feedback control of the rate of peat formation. *Proceedings of the Royal Society of London B: Biological Sciences*, 268, 1315–1321.

Belyea L.R. and Malmer N. (2004) Carbon sequestration in peatland: patterns and mechanisms of response to climate change. *Global Change Biology*, 10, 1043–1052.

Bennett, J.W. (1988) The political ecology and economic development of migratory pastoralist societies in Eastern Africa. In *Power and Poverty: Development Projects in the Third World (Westview Special Studies in Social, Political, and Economic Development)*, ed. D.W. Attwood, T.C. Bruneau and J.G. Galaty Boulder, CO: Westview Press, pp. 31–60.

Berendse, F., van Breeman, N., Rydin, H. et al. (2001) Raised atmospheric CO_2 levels and increased N deposition cause shifts in plant species composition and production in *Sphagnum* bogs. *Global Change Biology*, 7, 591–598.

Berridge, V. and Edwards, G. (1981) *Opium and the People: Opiate Use in Nineteenth-Century England*. London: St Martin's Press.

Bevan, B. (2009) Moors from the past. In *Drivers of Change in Upland Environments*, ed. A. Bonn, T. Allott, K. Hubacek, and J. Stewart. London and New York: Routledge, pp. 261–276.

Biancalani, R. and Avagyan, A. (2014) *Towards Climate-responsible Peatlands Management*. Rome: Food and Agiculture Organization of the United Nations (FAO).

Bieling, C. (2014) Cultural ecosystem services as revealed through short stories from residents of the Swabian Alb (Germany). *Ecosystem Services*, 8, 207–215.

Billett, M.F., Palmer, S.M., Hope, D et al. (2004) Linking land–atmosphere–stream carbon fluxes in a lowland peatland system. *Global Biogeochemical Cycles*, 18, GB1024.

Billett, M.F., Charman, D.J., Clark, J.M. et al. (2010) Carbon balance of UK peatlands: current state of knowledge and future research challenges. *Climate Research*, 45, 13–29.

Bindoff, N.L., Willebrand, J., Artale, V. et al. (2007) Observations: oceanic climate change and sea level. In *Climate Change 2007: The Physical Science Basis. Contribution of Working Group I to the Fourth Assessment Report of the Intergovernmental Panel on Climate Change*, ed. S. Solomon, D. Qin, M. Manning et al. Cambridge, UK and New York, USA: Cambridge University Press, pp. 385–432.

Birkinshaw, S.J., Bathurst, J.C. and Robinson, M. (2014) 45 years of non-stationary hydrology over a forest plantation growth cycle, Coalburn catchment, Northern England. *Journal of Hydrology*, 519, 559–573.

Björk, S. (1993) *The Hongyuan Wetland Research Project. An Ecological and Technical Feasibility Study of Peat Mining in Hongyuan, Sichuan, China*. Lund, Sweden: Bloms Boktryckeri AB.

Blaauw, M., Christen, J.A and Mauquoy, D. 2010. Peatlands as a model system for exploring and reconciling Quaternary chronologies. *PAGES*, 16, 9–10.

Blaauw, M., Christen, J.A., Mauquoy, D., van der Plicht, J. and Bennett, K.D. 2007. Testing the timing of proxy radiocarbon dated events between proxy archives. *The Holocene*, 17, 283–288.

Black, S.E. and Backman, M.V. (1990) *Bunhill Fields: The Great Dissenters' Burial Ground*. Provo, UT: Brigham Young University.

Blackbourn, D. (2011) *The Conquest of Nature: Water, Landscape, and the Making of Modern Germany*. London: W. W. Norton & Company.

Blackford, J.J., Innes, J.B., Hatton, J.J. and Caseldine, C.J. (2006) Mid-Holocene environmental change at Black Ridge Brook, Dartmoor, SW England: a new appraisal based on fungal spore analysis. *Review of Palaeobotany and Palynology*, 141, 189–201.

Blain, D., Murdiyarso, D., Couwenberg, J. et al. (2014) Rewetted organic soils. In *2013 Supplement to the 2006 IPCC Guidelines for National Greenhouse Gas Inventories*, ed. T.

Hiraishi, T. Krug, K. Tanabe *et al.* Geneva: IPCC, Chapter 3.

Blicher-Mathiesen, U. (1994) Borneo Illipe, a fat product from different *Shorea* spp. (Dipterocarpaceae). *Economic Botany*, 48, 231–242.

Blievernicht, A., Irrgang, S., Zander, M. and Ulrichs, C. (2011) Sustainable Sphagnum production to replace peat in commercial horticulture. *Gesunde Pflanzen*, 62, 125–131.

Blievernicht, A., Irrgang, S., Zander, M. and Ulrichs, C. (2013) Sphagnum biomass: the next generation of growing media. *Peatlands International*, 2013/1, 32–35.

Boelter, D.H. (1972) Water table drawdown around an open ditch in organic soils. *Journal of Hydrology*, 15, 329–340.

Boelter, D.H. (1976) Methods for analysing the hydrological characteristics of organic soils in marsh-ridden areas. *Hydrology of Marsh-Ridden Areas. Proceedings of IASH Symposium*, Minsk, 1972, 161–169.

Bonn, A., Allott, T., Hubacek, K. and Stewart, J. (2009) *Drivers of Environmental Change in Uplands*. Abingdon and New York: Routledge.

Bonn, A., Rebane, M. and Reid, C. (2009) Ecosystem services: a new rationale for conservation of upland environments. In *Drivers of Environmental Change in Uplands*, ed. A. Bonn, T. Allott, K. Hubacek and J. Stewart. London and New York: Routledge, pp. 448–475.

Bonn, A., Holden, J., Parnell, M. *et al.* (2010) *Ecosystem services of peat: phase 1*. Report to DEFRA. Project code SP0572. London: DEFRA.

Bonn, A., Reed, M.S., Evans, C.D. *et al.* (2014) Investing in nature: developing ecosystem service markets for peatland restoration. *Ecosystem Services*, 9, 54–65.

Bonn, A., Berghöfer, A., Couwenberg, J. *et al.* (2015) Klimaschutz durch Wiedervernässung von kohlenstoffreichen Böden. In *Naturkapital und Klimapolitik – Synergien und Konflikte. Naturkapital Deutschland TEEB DE report*, ed. V. Hartje, H. Wüstemann and A. Bonn. Berlin, Leipzig: Technische Universität Berlin, Helmholtz-Zentrum für Umweltforschung – UFZ, pp. 124–147.

Booth, R.K., Jackson, S.T., and Notaro, M. (2010) Using peatland archives to test palaeoclimate hypotheses. *PAGES*, 18, 6–8.

Boreham, S., Conneller, C., Milner, N. *et al.* (2011) Geochemical indicators of preservation status and site deterioration at Star Carr. *Journal of Archaeological Science*, 38, 2833–2857

Borger, G.J. (1992) Draining, digging, dredging; the creation of a new landscape in the peat areas of the low countries. In *Fens and Bogs in the Netherlands: Vegetation, History, Nutrient Dynamics and Conservation*, ed. J.T.A. Verhoeven. Dordrecht, The Netherlands: Kluwer Academic Publishers, pp. 131–171.

Bowen, M.R., Bompard, J.M., Anderson, I.P., Guizol P. and Gouyon A. (2001) Anthropogenic fires in Indonesia: a view from Sumatra. In *Forest Fires and Regional Haze in Southeast Asia*, ed. P. Eaton and M. Radojevic. New York: Nova Science Publishers, pp. 41–66.

Bowles, S. (2008) Policies designed for self-interested citizens may undermine 'the moral sentiments': evidence from economic experiments. *Science*, 320, 1605–1609.

Boyer, M.L.H. and Wheeler, B.D. (1989) Vegetation patterns in spring-fed calcareous fens: calcite precipitation and constraints in fertility. *Journal of Ecology*, 77, 597–609.

Bradley, R. (1990) *A Passage of Arms: Archaeological Analysis of Prehistoric Hoards and Votive Deposits*. Oxford, UK: Oxbow.

Bradshaw, A.D. (1996) Underlying principles of restoration. *Canadian Journal of Fisheries and Aquatic Sciences*, 53, 3–9.

Bradshaw, R.H., Hannon, G.E. and Lister, A.M. (2003) A long-term perspective on ungulate–vegetation interactions. *Forest Ecology and Management*, 181, 267–280.

Bragazza, L. (2008) A climatic threshold triggers the die-off of peat mosses during an extreme heat wave. *Global Change Biology*, 14, 2688–2695.

Bragg, O. (2004) The restoration of Kirkconnell Flow: searching for a bog amongst the trees. *International Peat Journal*, 12, 33–40.

Bragg O. and Lindsay R. (2003) *Strategy and Action Plan for Mire and Peatlands Conservation in Europe*. Wageningen, The Netherlands: Wetlands International.

Bragg, O. and Steiner, G.M. (1995) Applying groundwater mound theory to bog management on Puergschachenmoos in Austria. *Gunneria*, 70, 83–96.

Bragg, O.M. (1995) Towards an ecohydrological basis for raised mire restoration. In *Restoration of Temperate Wetlands*, ed. B. Wheeler, S. Shaw, W. Fojt and R.A. Robertson. Chichester, UK: John Wiley, pp. 305–314.

Bragg, O.M. (2002) Hydrology of peat-forming wetlands in Scotland. *Science of the Total Environment*, 294, 111–129.

Brander, L., Florax, R. and Vermaat, J. (2006) The empirics of wetland valuation: a comprehensive summary and a meta-analysis of the literature. *Environmental and Resource Economics*, 33, 223–250.

Brander, L., Ghermandi, A., Kuik, O. et al. (2010) *Scaling up ecosystem services values: methodology, applicability, and a case study*. FEEM Working Paper Series, 9.

Brandyk, T. and Szatyłowicz, J. (2002) The influence of meadow abandonment on physical properties and water conditions of peat soils. In *Restoration of Carbon Sequestrating Capacity and Biodiversity in Abandoned Grassland on Peatland in Poland*, ed P. Ilinicki. Poznań: Akademia Rolnicza, pp. 77–93.

Brantingham, P.J. and Gao, X. (2006) Peopling of the northern Tibetan Plateau. *World Archaeology*, 38, 387–414.

Bräunlich, S. (2014). *Die Bedeutung alternativer Substratausgangsstoffe im Produktionsgartenbau*. Greifswald: Diplomarbeit, Institut für Botanik und Landschaftsökologie.

Bridgham, S.D. and Richardson C.J. (1993) Hydrology and nutrient gradients in North Carolina peatlands. *Wetlands*, 13, 207–218.

Bridgham, S.D., Pastor, J., Janssens, J.A., Chapin, C. and Malterer, T.J. (1996) Multiple limiting gradients in peatlands: a call for a new paradigm. *Wetlands*, 16, 45–65.

Brinson, M.M. (1993) *A hydrogeomorphic classification for wetlands*. Technical Report WRP-DE-4, Vicksburg, MS: U.S. Army Corps of Engineers Engineer Waterways Experiment Station.

British Columbia Wetlands (2010) *A Wetland Action Plan for British Columbia*. Victoria, Canada: Government of British Columbia.

Bronk Ramsey, C. (2008) Deposition models for chronological records. *Quaternary Science Reviews*, 27, 42–60.

Brooks, S. and Stoneman, R. (1997a) *Conserving Bogs: The Management Handbook*. Edinburgh, UK: The Stationery Office.

Brooks, S. and Stoneman, R. (1997b) Tree removal at Langlands Moss. *Conserving Peatlands*, ed. L. Parkyn, R.E. Stoneman and H.A.P. Ingram.. Wallingford, UK: CAB International, pp. 315–322

Brooks, S., Stoneman, R., Hanlon, A. and Thom, T. (2014) *Conserving Bogs: The Management Handbook*. 2nd edn. York: Yorkshire Peat Partnership. http://issuu.com/peat123/docs/conserving_bogs (accessed 27 Feb 2015).

Brown, K.A., (1985) Sulphur distribution and metabolism in waterlogged peat. *Soil Biology and Biochemistry*, 17, 39–45.

Brown, L.E., Johnston, K., Palmer, S.M., Aspray, K.L., and Holden, J. (2013) River ecosystem response to prescribed vegetation burning on blanket peatland. *PloS One*, 8, e81023.

Brown, L.E., Holden, J. and Palmer, S.M. (2014) *Effects of Moorland Burning on the Ecohydrology of River basins, EMBER project executive summary*. Leeds, UK: University of Leeds.

Bruenig, E.F. (1990) Oligotrophic forested wetlands in Borneo. *Forested Wetlands. Ecosystems of the World 15*, ed. A.E.

Lugo, M. Brinson and S. Brown. Amsterdam: Elsevier, pp. 299–334.

Bruenig, E.F. (1996) *Conservation and Management of Tropical Rainforest. An Integrated Approach to Sustainability.* Wallingford, UK: CAB International.

Brunning, R. (2001) *Archaeology and Peat Wastage on the Somerset Moors Spring 2001.* Somerset, UK: Environment Agency and Somerset County Council, England.

Brunning, R. (2007) Monitoring waterlogged sites in peatlands: where, how, why and what next? Archaeology from the wetlands: recent perspectives. *Proceedings of the 11th WARP Conference Society of Antiquaries Scotland*, 191–198.

Brunning, R. (2013) *Somerset's Peatland Archaeology.* Oxford: Oxbow.

Brunning, R. Hogan, D., Jones, J. *et al.* (2000) Saving the Sweet Track: the *in situ* preservation of a Neolithic wooden trackway, Somerset, UK. *Conservation and Management of Archaeological Sites*, 4, 3–20.

Bruno, J., Stachowicz, J. and Bertness, M. (2003) Inclusion of facilitation into ecological theory. *Trends in Ecology and Evolution*, 18, 199–125.

Brzeziński, W. (1992) Recent developments in wetland archaeology in Poland. In *The Wetland Revolution in Prehistory*, ed. B. Coles. WARP Occasional Paper. Exeter, UK: University of Exeter, pp. 73–81.

Buckland, P.C. and Dinnin, M.H. (1997) The rise and fall of a wetland habitat: recent palaeoecological research on Thorne and Hatfield Moors. *Thorne and Hatfield Moors Papers*, 4, 1–18.

Buckles, D. (1999) *Cultivating peace: Conflict and Collaboration in Natural Resource Management.* Ottawa, Canada: International Development Research Centre.

Bugnon, J.-L., Rochefort, L. and Price, J.S. (1997) Field experiments of *Sphagnum* reintroduction on a dry abandoned peatland in Eastern Canada. *Wetlands*, 17, 513–517.

Bullock, A. and Acreman, M. (2003) The role of wetlands in the hydrological cycle. *Hydrology and Earth System Science*, 7, 358–89.

Bullock, C.H. and Collier, M. (2011) When the public good conflicts with an apparent preference for unsustainable behavior. *Ecological Economics*, 70, 971–977.

Bullock, J.M., Aronson, J., Newton, A.C., Pywell, R.F. and Rey-Benayas, J.M. (2011) Restoration of ecosystem services and biodiversity: conflicts and opportunities. *Trends in Ecology and Evolution*, 26, 541–549.

Burke, W. (1972) Aspects of the hydrology of blanket peat in Ireland. *Hydrology of Marsh Ridden Areas: Proceedings of Minsk Symposium*, 171–183.

Burton, R.J.F., Schwarz, G., Brown, K., Convery, I. and Mansfield, L. (2009) The future of public goods provision in upland regions: learning from hefted commons in the Lake District, UK. In *Drivers of Environmental Change in the Uplands*, ed. A. Bonn, T.E. Allott, K. Hubacek and J. Stuart. London and New York: Routledge, pp. 323–338.

Buytaert, W., Celleri, R., De Bièvre, B. *et al.* (2006) Human impact on the hydrology of the Andean paramos. *Earth-Science Reviews*, 79, 53–72.

Byrne, K.A., Chojnicki, B., Christensen, T.R. *et al.* (2004) EU Peatlands: current carbon stocks and trace gas fluxes. *CarboEurope GHG Report*, Specific study 4. Viterbo: Tipo-Lito Recchioni.

Cai, L., Yang, M., Chen, Z.H. *et al.* (1986) Optimization of the age-sex distribution of yak's population and the correlated slaughter programme in Ruoergai County. *Journal of Southwest Nationalities College (Natural Sciences Edition)*, 4, 22–30.

Callaway, R.M., De Lucia, E.H., Moore, D., Nowak, R. and Schlesiger, W.H. (1996) Competition and facilitation: contrasting effects of *Artemisia tridentata* on desert vs. montane pines. *Ecology*, 77, 2130–2141.

Calmé, S., Desrochers, A. and Savard, J.-P. (2002) Regional significance of peatlands for avifaunal diversity in southern Québec. *Biological Conservation*, 107, 273–281.

Campbell, D.R., Rochefort, L. and Lavoie, C. (2003) Determining the immigration potential of plants colonizing disturbed environments: the case of milled peatlands in Québec. *Journal of Applied Ecology*, 40, 78–91.

Canaveira, P. (2013) *Options and elements for an accounting framework for the land sector in the post-2020 climate regime*. Terraprima Report to the Swiss Federal Office for the Environment.

Cannell, M.G., Dewar, R.C. and Pyatt, D.G. (1993) Conifer plantations on drained peatlands in Britain: a net gain or loss of carbon? *Foresty*, 66, 353–369.

Caple, C. (1994) Reburial of waterlogged wood, the problems and potential of this conservation technique. *International Biodeterioration and Biodegradation*, 34, 61–72.

Caple, C. (2004) Towards a benign reburial context: the chemistry of the burial environment. *Conservation and Management of Archaeological Sites*, 6, 155–165.

Cardinale, B.J., Duffy, J.E., Gonzalez, A. et al. (2012) Biodiversity loss and its impact on humanity. *Nature*, 486, 59–67.

Carroll, J., Anderson, P., Caporn, S. et al. (2009) *Sphagnum in the Peak District: Current Status and Potential for Restoration*, Report No. 16. Edale, UK: Moors for the Future Partnership.

Carroll, J.A., Caporn, S.J.M., Cawley, L., Read, D.J. and Lee, J.A. (1999) The effect of increased deposition of atmospheric nitrogen on *Calluna vulgaris* in upland Britain. *New Phytologist*, 141, 423–431.

Carroll, M.J., Dennis, P., Pearce-Higgins, J.W., and Thomas, C.D. (2011). Maintaining northern peatland ecosystems in a changing climate: effects of soil moisture, drainage and drain blocking on craneflies. *Global Change Biology*, 17, 2991–3001.

Caulfield, S. (1978) Neolithic fields: the Irish evidence. In *Early Land Allotment in the British Isles*, ed. H.C. Bowen and P.J. Fowler. Oxford, UK: British Archaeological Reports, pp. 137–143.

Caulfield, S. (1983) The Neolithic settlement of North Connaught. In *Landscape Archaeology In Ireland*, ed. T. Reeves-Smyth and F. Hammond. Oxford, UK: British Archaeological Reports, pp. 195–215.

Caulfield, S., O' Donnell, R.G. and Mitchell, P. I. (1998) 14C dating of a Neolithic field system at Céide fields County Mayo, Ireland. *Proceedings of the Radiocarbon Conference*, 40, 2, 629–640.

CBD (Convention on Biological Diversity) (1992) Article 2. Use of Terms. Montreal, Canada: Convention on Biological Diversity. Online at: http://www.cbd.int/convention/articles/default.shtml?a=cbd-02, (accessed 24 February 2015).

CBD (Convention on Biological Diversity) (2010a) *COP 10 Decision x/33 Biodiversity and Climate Change*. Montreal, Canada: Convention on Biological Diversity.

CBD (Convention on Biological Diversity) (2010b) *COP 10 Decision X/2 – Strategic Plan for Biodiversity 2011–2020*. Montreal, Canada: Convention on Biological Diversity.

Chai, X. and Li, H. (1988) On Ruoergai Plateau peat mire characteristic and its exploitation and conservation. *Proceedings of the VIIIth International Peat Congress Leningrad*, 1, 225–232.

Chambers, F.M and Charman, D.J. (2004) Holocene environmental change: contributions from the peatland archive. *The Holocene*, 14, 1–6.

Chambers, F.M., Daniell, J.R.G. and Brain, S.A. (2007a) Climate Change featuring the ACCROTELM project: dissemination of a European RTD project by film and DVD. In *Information, Communication and Education on Climate Change – European Perspectives*, ed. W.L. Filho, F. Mannke and P. Schmidt-Thome. Frankfurt am Main: Peter Lang, pp. 165–173.

Chambers, F.M., Mauquoy, D., Brain, S.A., Blaauw, M. and Daniell, J.R.G. (2007b) Globally synchronous climate change 2800 years ago: proxy data from peat in

South America. *Earth and Planetary Science Letters*, 253, 439–444.

Chambers, F.M., Mauquoy, D., Gent, A. et al. (2007c) Palaeoecology of degraded blanket mire in south Wales: data to inform conservation management. *Biological Conservation*, 137, 2, 197–209.

Chambers, F.M., Daniell, J.R.G. and ACCROTELM Members. (2010) Peatland archives of late Holocene climate change in northern Europe. *PAGES*, 18, 1, 4–5.

Chan, K.M.A., Shaw, M.R., Cameron, D.R., Underwood, E.C. and Daily, G.C. (2006) Conservation planning for ecosystem services. *Plos Biology*, 4, 2138–2152.

Chan, K.M.A., Satterfield, T. and Goldstein, J. (2012) Rethinking ecosystem services to better address and navigate cultural values. *Ecological Economics*, 74, 8–18.

Chapman, H.C. and Gearey, B.R. (2013) *Modelling Archaeology and Palaeoenvironments in Wetlands: The Hidden Landscape Archaeology of Hatfield and Thorne Moors*. Oxford, UK: Oxbow.

Chapman, H.P. and Cheetham, J.L. (2002) Monitoring and modelling saturation as a proxy indicator for in situ preservation in wetlands: a GIS-based approach. *Journal of Archaeological Science*, 29, 277–289.

Chapman, H.P and Van de Noort, R. (2001) High resolution wetland prospection using GPS and GIS: Landscape studies at Sutton Common (South Yorkshire) and Meare Village (Somerset). *Journal of Archaeological Science*, 28, 365–375.

Chapman, S.B. and Rose, R.J. (1991) Changes in the vegetation at Coom Rigg Moss National Nature Reserve within the period 1958-86. *Journal of Applied Ecology*, 28, 140–153.

Charman, D. (2002) *Peatlands and Environmental Change*. Chichester, UK: John Wiley.

Charman, D.J. (2010) Centennial climate variability in the British Isles during the mid-late Holocene. *Quaternary Science Reviews*, 29, 1539–1554.

Charman, D. J., Hendon, D. and Woodland, W. (2000) *The identification of testate amoebae (Protozoa: Rhizopoda) in peats*. Quaternary Research Association, Technical Guide 9.

Charman, D.J., Booth, R.K., Mäkilä, M. and Sirin, A. (2008) Peatlands and past climate change. In *Assessment on Peatlands, Biodiversity and Climate Change*, ed. F. Parish, A. Sirin, D. Charman, H. Joosten, T. Minayeva, M. Silvius and L. Stringer. Kuala Lumpur and Wageningen, The Netherlands: Global Environment Centre and Wetlands International, pp. 39–59.

Charman, D.J., Beilman, D.W., Blaauw, M. et al. (2012) Climate-related changes in peatland carbon accumulation during the last millennium. *Biogeosciences Discussions*, 9, 14327–14364.

Charman, D.J., Beilman, D.W., Blaauw, M. et al. (2013) Climate-related changes in peatland carbon accumulation during the last millennium. *Biogeosciences*, 10, 929–944.

Chason, D.B. and Siegel, D.I. (1986) Hydraulic conductivity and related physical properties of peat, Lost River Peatland, Northern Minnesota. *Soil Science*, 142, 91–99.

Chatty, D. (2007) *Nomadic Societies in the Middle East and North Africa: Facing the 21st Century*. Leiden, Germany: Brill.

Chen, H., Yang, G., Peng, C. et al. (2014) The carbon stock of alpine peatlands on the Qinghai–Tibetan Plateau during the Holocene and their future fate. *Quaternary Science Reviews*, 95, 151–158.

Chistotin, M.V., Sirin, A.A. and Dulov, L.E. (2006) Seasonal dynamics of carbon dioxide and methane emission from a peatland in Moscow Region drained for peat extraction and agricultural use. *Agrochemistry (Agrokhimija)*, 6, 54–62.

Choi, Y.D. (2007) Restoration ecology to the future: a call for new paradigm. *Restoration Ecology*, 15, 351–353.

Chokkalingam, U., Kurniawan, I. and Ruchiat, Y. (2005) Fire, livelihoods, and environmental change in the Middle Mahakam peatlands, East Kalimantan. *Ecology and Society*, 10, 1–17.

Chokkalingam, U., Suyanto, Permana, R.P. et al. (2007) Community fire use, resource change, and livelihood impacts: The downward spiral in the wetlands of southern Sumatra. *Mitigation and Adaptation Strategies for Global Change*, 12, 75–100.

Christie, M., Hyde, T., Cooper, R. et al. (2011) *Economic Valuation of the Benefits of Ecosystem Services delivered by the UK Biodiversity Action Plan*. Report to DEFRA. Project code SFFSD 0702. London: DEFRA.

Church, A., Burgess, J. and Ravenscroft, N. (2011) Cultural Services. UK National Ecosystem Assessment: Technical Report. Cambridge, UK: UNEP-WCMC, pp. 633–692.

Cicek, N., Lambert, S., Venema, H.D. et al. (2006) Evaluation of a wetland-biopower concept for nutrient removal and value recovery from the Netley-Libau Marsh at Lake Winnipeg. *Biomass and Bioenergy*, 30, 529–536.

Čivić, K. and Jones-Walters, L. (2010) *Peatlands in Ecological Networks in Europe*. Tilburg, The Netherlands: ECNC-European Centre for Nature Conservation.

CKPP (2008) *Provisional Report of the Central Kalimantan Peatland Project. November 2008*. Palangka Raya: CKPP Consortium.

Clark, J., Gallego-Sala, A.V., Allott, T.E.H. et al. (2010) Assessing the vulnerability of blanket peat to climate change using an ensemble of statistical bioclimatic envelope models. *Climate Research*, 45, 131–150.

Clarke, D. and Rieley, J. (eds). (2010) *Strategy for Responsible Peatland Management*. 2nd edn. Jyväskylä, Finland: International Peat Society.

Clarke, G.E. (1987) *China's Reforms of Tibet and their Effects on Pastoralism*. Brighton, UK: University of Sussex.

Cleary, J., Roulet, N. T. and Moore, T.R. (2005) Greenhouse gas emissions from Canadian peat extraction, 1990–2000: a life-cycle analysis. *Ambio*, 34, 456–461.

Climate Action Reserve (2013) *Scoping for a Reserve Peatlands Protocol*. Los Angeles, CA: Climate Action Reserve.

Clutterbuck, B. and Yallop, A.R. (2010) Land management as a factor controlling dissolved organic carbon release from upland peat soils 2: changes in DOC productivity over four decades. *Science of The Total Environment*, 408, 6179–6191.

Clymo, R.S. (1983) Peat. In *Mires: Swamp, Bog, Fen and Moor, Ecosystems of the World 4A General Studies*, ed. A.P.J. Gore. Amsterdam: Elsevier, pp. 159–224.

Clymo, R.S. (1984) The limits to peat bog growth. *Philosophical Transactions of the Royal Society of London B*, 303, 605–654.

Clymo, R.S. (1991) Peat Growth. In *Quaternary Landscapes*, ed. E.J. Cushing and L.C. Shane. Minneapolis, MN: University of Minnesota Press, pp. 76–112.

Clymo, R.S. (1992) Models of peat growth. *Suo*, 43, 127–136.

CMS (Convention on Migratory Species) (2011a) *Appendices I and II of the Convention on the Conservation of Migratory Species of Wild Animals*. Bergen: CMS.

CMS (Convention on Migratory Species) (2011b) *Activities reported by parties on concerted action species*. Tenth meeting of the conference of the parties. Bergen: CMS.

Cobbaert, D., Rochefort, L. and Price, J.S. (2004) Experimental restoration of a fen plant community after peat mining. *Applied Vegetation Science*, 7, 209–220.

Cochard, R., Ranamukhaarachchi, S. L., Shivakoti, G. P. et al. (2008) The 2004 tsunami in Aceh and Southern Thailand: a review on coastal ecosystems, wave hazards and vulnerability. *Perspectives in Plant Ecology, Evolution and Systematics*, 10, 3–40.

Cole, B., McMorrow, J. and Evans M. (2014) Empirical modelling of vegetation abundance from airborne hyperspectral data for upland peatland restoration monitoring. *Remote Sensing*, 6, 716–739.

Coles, B. (1995) Archaeology and wetland restoration. In *Restoration of Temperate Wetlands*, ed. B.D. Wheeler, S.C. Shaw,

W.J. Foit and R.A. Robertson. Chichester, UK: John Wiley, pp. 1–19.

Coles, B. and Coles, J. (1986) *Sweet track to Glastonbury. The Somerset levels in prehistory*. London: Thames and Hudson.

Coles, J. (1984) *The Archaeology of Wetlands*. Edinburgh, UK: Edinburgh University Press.

Coles, J. and Coles, B. (1989) *People of the Wetlands. Bogs, Bodies and Lake-Dwellers*. London: Thames and Hudson.

Coles, J. and Coles, B. (1996) *Enlarging the Past: The Contribution of Wetland Archaeology*. Edinburgh: Society of Antiquaries of Scotland.

Collier, M.J. (2014) Novel ecosystems and the emergence of cultural ecosystem services. *Ecosystem Services*, 9, 166–169.

Collier, M.J. and Scott, M.J. (2008) Industrially harvested peatlands and after-use potential: understanding local stakeholder narratives and landscape preferences. *Landscape Research*, 33, 439–460.

Conaghan, J. (2009) *LIFE Project Number LIFE02 NAT/IRL/8490 Technical Final Report. Appendix 5. Vegetation monitoring report (Reports on the restoration of project sites Nos. 2–20)*. Technical Final Report of LIFE project no.LIFE02 NAT/IRL/8490.

Condliffe, I. (2009) Policy change in the uplands. In *Drivers of Environmental Change in Uplands*, ed. A. Bonn, T. Allott, K. Hubacek and J. Stewart. London and New York: Routledge, pp. 59–90.

Connolly, P. (2011) *The World's Weirdest Sports: Bog Snorkelling, Dwile Flonking, Goat Grabbing and More*. London: Murdoch Books.

Cooper, A. and McCann, T. (1995) Machine peat cutting and land use change on blanket bog in northern Ireland. *Journal of Environmental Management*, 43, 153–170.

Cooper, D. and MacDonald, L. (2000) Restoring the vegetation of mined peatlands in the Southern Rocky Mountains of Colorado, USA. *Restoration Ecology*, 8, 103–111.

Costanza, R., d'Arge, R., de Groot, R. *et al.* (1997) The value of the world's ecosystem services and natural capital. *Nature*, 387, 253–260.

Council of Europe (1979) Convention on the Conservation of European Wildlife and Natural Habitats. http://conventions.coe.int/Treaty/EN/Treaties/Html/104.htm (accessed 6 January 2015).

Couwenberg, J. (2007a) The CO_2 emission factor of peat fuel. *IMCG Newsletter*, 2007/2, 24.

Couwenberg, J. (2007b) Biomass energy crops on peatlands: on emissions and perversions. *IMCG Newsletter*, 2007/3, 12–14.

Couwenberg, J. (2009) *Emission Factors for Managed Peat Soils. An Analysis of IPCC Default Values*. Wageningen, The Netherlands: Wetlands International.

Couwenberg, J. and Fritz, C. (2012) Towards developing IPCC methane 'emission factors' for peatlands (organic soils). *Mires and Peat*, 10, Art. 3, 1–17.

Couwenberg, J. and Joosten, H. (2005) Self organisation in raised bog patterning: the origin of microtope zonation and mesotope diversity. *Journal of Ecology*, 93, 1238–1248.

Couwenberg, J., de Klerk, P., Endtmann, E., Joosten, H. and Michaelis, D. (2001) Hydrogenetische Moortypen in der Zeit – eine Zusammenschau. In *Landschaftsökologische Moorkunde*, 2nd edn, ed. M. Succow and H. Joosten. Stuttgart, Germany: Schweizerbart, pp. 399–403.

Couwenberg, J., Dommain, R. and Joosten, H. (2010) Greenhouse gas fluxes from tropical peatlands in South-East Asia. *Global Change Biology*, 16, 1715–1732.

Couwenberg, J., Thiele, A., Tanneberger, F *et al.* (2011) Assessing greenhouse gas emissions from peatlands using vegetation as a proxy. *Hydrobiologia*, 674, 67–89.

Cowie, N.R., Sutherland, W.J., Ditlhogo, M.K.M. and James, R. (1992) The effects of conservation management of reed beds. I. The flora and litter disappearance. *Journal of Applied Ecology*, 29, 277–284.

Cox, M., Chandler, C., Cox, C., Jones, J and Tinsley, H. (2001) The archaeological significance of patterns of anomalous vegetation on a raised mire in the Solway Estuary and the processes involved in their formation. *Journal of Archaeological Science*, 28, 1–18.

Crawford, R.M.M., Jeffree, C.E. and Rees, W.G. (2003) Paludification and forest retreat in northern oceanic environments. *Annals of Botany*, 91, 213–226.

Crebbin-Bailey, J., Harcup, J. and Harrington, J. (2005) *The Spa Book: The Official Guide to Spa Therapy*. Canada: Thomson.

Cris, R., Buckmaster, S., Bain, C. and Bonn, A. (2011) *UK Peatland Restoration: Demonstrating Success*. Edinburgh, UK: IUCN UK National Committee Peatland Programme.

Cris, R., Buckmaster, S., Bain, C and Reed, M. (eds) (2014) *Global Peatland Restoration Demonstrating SUCCESS*. Edinburgh, UK: IUCN UK National Committee Peatland Programme.

Croes, D.R. (1995) *The Hoko River Archaeological Complex: the wet/dry site (45CA213), 3000–1700 BP*. Pulman, WA: Washington State University Press.

Crowe, S.K., Evans, M.G. and Allott, T.E.H. (2008) Geomorphological controls on the re-vegetation of erosion gullies in blanket peat: implications for bog restoration. *Mires and Peat*, 3, Art. 1, 1–14.

Curry, N. (2009) Leisure in the landscape: rural incomes and public benefits. In *Drivers of Environmental Change in the Uplands*, ed. A. Bonn, T.E. Allott, K. Hubacek and J. Stuart. London and New York: Routledge, pp. 277–290.

Curtis, C. J., Emmett, B. A., Grant, H. *et al.* (2005) Nitrogen saturation in UK moorlands: the critical role of bryophytes and lichens in determining retention of atmospheric N deposition. *Journal of Applied Ecology*, 42, 507–517.

Daily, G. (1997) *Nature's Services: Societal Dependence on Natural Ecosystems*. Washington, DC: Island Press.

Daily, G., Polasky, S., Goldstein, J. *et al.* (2009) Ecosystem services in decision making: time to deliver. *Frontiers in Ecology and the Environment*, 7, 21–28.

Daily, G.C., Kareiva, P., Polasky, S., Ricketts, T.H. and Tallis, H. (2011) Mainstreaming natural capital into decisions. In *Natural Capital. Theory and Practice of Mapping Ecosystem Services*, ed. P. Kareiva, H. Tallis, T.H. Ricketts, G.C. Daily and S. Polasky. Oxford, UK: Oxford University Press, pp. 3–14.

Daniel, T.C., Muhar, A., Arnberger, A. *et al.* (2012) Contributions of cultural services to the ecosystem services agenda. *Proceedings of the National Academy of Sciences of the United States of America*, 109, 8812–8819.

Daniels, S.M., Evans, M.G., Agnew, C.T. and Allott, T.E.H. (2008a) Sulphur leaching from headwater catchments in an eroded peatland. *Science of the Total Environment* 407, 481–496.

Daniels, S.M., Agnew, C.T., Allott, T.E.H. and Evans, M.G. (2008b) Water table variability and runoff generation in an eroded peatland, South Pennines, UK. *Journal of Hydrology*, 361, 214–226.

Dau, J.H.C. (1823) *Neues Handbuch über den Torf, dessen Natur, Entstehung und Wiedererzeugung. Nutzen im Allgemeinen und für den Staat*. Leipzig, Germany: J.C. Hinrichsche Buchhandlung.

Dau, J.H. (1829) *Allerunterthänigster Bericht an die Königliche Dänische Rentekammer über die Torfmoore Seelands nach einer im Herbste 1828 deshalb unternommenen Reise*. Copenhagen: Gyldendahl und Hinrichs.

David, J.S. and Ledger, D.C. (1988) Runoff generation in a plough-drained peat bog in southern Scotland. *Journal of Hydrology*, 99, 187–199.

Davies, A. (2011) Long-term approaches to native woodland restoration: palaeoecological and stakeholder perspectives on Atlantic forests of Northern Europe. *Forest Ecology and Management*, 261, 751–763.

Davies, H. (2012) *Sustainable Management of the Historic Environment Resource in Upland Peat on Exmoor*. PhD thesis. Plymouth, UK: University of Plymouth.

Davies H., Fyfe, R.M. and Charman, D. (2015) Does peatland drainage damage the palaeoecological record? *Review of Palaeobotany and Palynology*, 221, 92–105.

Davies, S. (2006) *Recreation and visitor attitudes in the Peak District moorlands*. Moors for the Future Report no.12. Edale, UK: Moors for the Future Partnership.

Dawson, T.P., Rounsevell, M.D.A., Kluvánková-Oravská, T., Chobotová, V. and Stirling, A. (2010) Dynamic properties of complex adaptive ecosystems: implications for the sustainability of service provision. *Biodiversity Conservation*, 19, 2843–2857.

De Groot, R. (1992) *Functions of nature. Evaluation of Nature in Environmental Planning, Management and Decision Making*. Amsterdam: Wolters-Noordhoff.

De Groot, R., Stuip, M., Finlayson, M. and Davidson, N. (2006) *Valuing wetlands: guidance for valuing the benefits derived from wetland ecosystem services*. Ramsar Technical Report No. 3. Gland, Switzerland: Ramsar Convention Secretariat.

De Groot, R.S., Blignaut, J., Ploeg, S. *et al.* (2013) Benefits of investing in ecosystem restoration. *Conservation Biology*, 27, 1286–1293.

De Vleeschouwer, F., Le Roux, G. and Shotyk, W. (2010) Peat as an archive of atmospheric pollution and environmental change: a case study of lead in Europe. *PAGES*, 18, 20–22.

DECC (Department of Energy and Climate Change) (2008) *Greenhouse Gas Policy Evaluation and Appraisal in Government Departments*. London: Department of Energy and Climate Change.

DEFRA (2002) *Survey of Public Attitudes to Quality of Life and to the Environment: 2001*. London: Department for Environment, Food and Rural Affairs.

DEFRA (2007) *The Heather and Grass Burning Code (2007 Version)*. London: DEFRA.

DEFRA (2010) *Consultation on reducing the horticultural peat in England*. London: DEFRA.

DEFRA (2011) *The Natural Choice: Securing the Value of Nature*. London: DEFRA.

De-Light, D. and Thomas, P. (2005) *The Rough Guide to Trinidad and Tobago*. London: Rough Guides, Ltd.

Dennis, C and Aldhous, P. (2004) A tragedy with many players. *Nature*, 430, 396–398.

Denny, D. (2013) *Tracking peat usage in growing media production. Annual Report*. London: Agriculture and Horticulture Development Board, Horticultural Trades Association and DEFRA. http://www.hdc.org.uk/sites/default/files/research_papers/CP%20100_Report_Annual_July_2013.pdf (accessed 27 February 2014).

Denny, M.W. (1993) *Air and water. The Biology and Physics of Life's Media*. Princeton, NJ: Princeton University Press.

Derwin, J. (2008) Ecological monitoring. End of Project Conference Presentation. Restoring Raised Bog in Ireland. EU LIFE Project No. LIFE04 *NAT/IE/000121*, May 2008. Carrick-on-Shannon, Ireland: EU LIFE. http://www.raisedbogrestoration.ie (accessed 26 November 2015).

Desrochers, A., Rochefort, L. and Savard, J.-P. (1998) Avian recolonization of eastern Canadian bogs after peat mining. *Canadian Journal of Zoology*, 76, 989–997.

Deverel, S.J. and Leighton, D.A. (2010) Historic, recent, and future subsidence, Sacramento-San Joaquin Delta, California, USA. *San Francisco Estuary and Watershed Science*, 8, 1–22.

Devito, K.J., Hill, A.R. and Roulet, N. (1996) Groundwater-surface water interactions in headwater forested wetlands of the Canadian Shield. *Journal of Hydrology*, 181, 127–147.

Dias, A.T.C., Hoorens, B., Van Logtestijn, R.S.P., Vermaat, J.E. and Aerts, R. (2010) Plant species composition can be used as a proxy to predict methane emissions in peatland ecosystems after land-use changes. *Ecosystems*, 13, 526–538.

Dietl, G.P. and Flessa, K.W. (2011) Conservation palaeobiology: Putting the dead to work. *Trends in Ecology and Evolution*, 26, 30–37.

Dinsmore, K., Billett, M.F., Skiba, U.M. *et al.* (2010). Role of the aquatic pathway in the carbon and greenhouse gas budgets of a peatland catchment. *Global Change Biology*, 16, 2750–2762.

Dittrich I. (2009) *Einige hydrologische Bedingungen für die Revitalisierung der Waldmoorflächen, Sebangau, Block A*. Project report. Dr. Dittrich and Partner Hydro-Consult, Bannewitz.

DNPI (2010) *Indonesia's Greenhouse Gas Abatement Cost Curve*. Jakarta, Indonesia: DNPI.

Dohong, A. (2005) Implementation of canal blocking within block a ex-mega rice project: lesson learnt and steps forward. International Symposium and Workshop on Restoration and Wise Use of Tropical Peatland: Problems of Biodiversity, Fire, Poverty and Water Management, Palangka Raya, 21–24 September 2005.

Dommain, R., Couwenberg, J. and Joosten, H. (2010) Hydrological self-regulation of domed peat swamps in south-east Asia and consequences for conservation and restoration. *Mires and Peat*, 6, Art. 5, 1–17.

Dommain, R., Couwenberg, J. and Joosten, H. (2011) Development and carbon sequestration of tropical peat domes in south-east Asia: links to post-glacial sea-level changes and Holocene climate variability. *Quaternary Science Reviews*, 30, 999–1010.

Dommain, R., Barthelmes, A., Tanneberger, F. et al. (2012) Country-wise opportunities. In *Peatlands: Guidance for Climate Change Mitigation by Conservation, Rehabilitation and Sustainable Use, Mitigation of Climate Change in Agriculture Series 5*, ed. H. Joosten, M.-L. Tapio-Biström and S. Tol. Rome: FAO, pp. 45–82.

Dommain, R., Couwenberg, J., Glaser, P.H., Joosten, H. and Suryaputra, I.N.N. (2014) Carbon storage and release in Indonesian peatlands since the last deglaciation. *Quaternary Science reviews*, 97, 1–32.

Dong, Z., Hu, G., Yan, C., Wang, W. and Lu, J. (2010) Aeolian desertification and its causes in the Zoige Plateau of China's Qinghai–Tibetan Plateau. *Environmental Earth Sciences*, 59, 1731–1740.

Dorrepaal, E., Toet, S., van Logtestijn, R.S.P. et al. (2009) Carbon respiration from subsurface peat accelerated by climate warming in the subarctic. *Nature*, 460, 616–619.

Douterelo, I, Goulder, R. and Lillie, M. (2011) Enzyme activities and compositional shifts in the community structure of bacterial groups in English wetland soils associated with preservation of organic remains in archaeological sites. *International Biodeterioration and Biodegradation*, 65, 435–443.

Drösler, M., Verchot, L.V., Freibauer, A. et al. (2014) Drained inland organic soils. In *2013 Supplement to the 2006 IPCC Guidelines for National Greenhouse Gas Inventories*, ed. T. Hiraishi, T. Krug, K. Tanabe et al. Geneva: IPCC, Chapter 2.

Du Rietz, G.E. (1949) Huvudenheter och huvudgränser i Svensk myrvegetation. *Svensk Botanisk Tidskrift*, 43, 274–309.

Du Rietz, G.E. (1954) Die Mineralbodenwasserzeigergrenze als Grundlage einer natürlichen Zweigliederung der nord- und mitteleuropäischen Moore. *Vegetatio, Acta Geobotanica*, 5/6, 571–585.

Dubbe, D.R., Garver, E.G. and Pratt, D.C. (1988) Production of cattail (*Typha* spp.) biomass in Minnesota, USA. *Biomass*, 17, 79–104.

Dudgeon, D. (2000) Riverine biodiversity in Asia: a challenge for conservation biology. *Hydrobiologia*, 418, 1–13.

Dupieux, N. (1998) *La gestion conservatoire des tourbieres de France – premiers elements scientifiqueet techniques*. Orleans, France: Espaces Naturels de France.

Edom, F. (2001) Moorlandschaften aus hydrologischer Sicht. In *Landschaftsökologische Moorkunde*, ed. M. Succow and H. Joosten Stuttgart, Germany: Schweizerbart, pp. 185–228.

Edom, F., Dittrich, I.; Goldacker, S. and Kessler, K. (2007) Die hydromorphologisch begründete Planung der Moorrevitalisierung im Erzgebirge. In *Praktischer Moorschutz im Naturpark*

Erzgebirge/Vogtland und Beispiele aus anderen Gebirgsregionen: Methoden, Probleme, Ausblick. Grillenburg, Germany: Sächsische Landesstiftung Natur und Umwelt, pp. 19–32.

Edwards, D.P., Koh, L.P. and Laurance, W.F. (2012) Indonesia's REDD+ pact: Saving imperilled forests or business as usual? *Biological Conservation*, 151, 41–44.

EEA (2010) *Scaling up ecosystem benefits – Assessing large-scale ecosystem services with primary data.* EEA Technical Report 2010. Copenhagen: European Environment Agency.

eftec (2009) *Economic valuation of uplands ecosystem services.* Report to Natural England NECR029. Peterborough, UK: Natural England.

Ehrenfeld, D. (1988) Why put a value on biodiversity? In *Biodiversity*, ed. E.O. Wilson. Washington, DC: National Academy Press, pp. 212–216.

Ehrenfeld, J.G. (2001) Defining the limit of restoration: the need for realistic goals. *Restoration Ecology*, 8, 2–9.

Ehrenfeld, J.G. and Toth, L.A. (1997) Restoration ecology and the ecosystem perspective. *Restoration Ecology*, 5, 307–317.

Ehrlich, P. and Ehrlich, A. (1981) *Extinction: The causes and consequences of the disappearance of species.* Random House, New York.

Ekstam, B. (1993) *Flora, structure and regeneration of wetland vegetation in Hongyuan, Sichuan, China: A report from the Hongyuan Wetland Research Project prepared for the Sichuan Institute of Natural Resources.* Lund, Sweden: University of Lund.

Ekvall, R. (1968) *Fields on the Hoof: Nexus of Tibetan Nomadic Pastoralism.* New York and London: Holt, Rinehart and Winston.

Eliseev, A.V., Mokhov, I.I., Arzhanov, M.M., Demchenko, P.F. and Denisov, S.N. (2008) Interaction of the methane cycle and processes in wetland ecosystems in a climate model of intermediate complexity. *Izvestiya Atmospheric and Oceanic Physics*, 44, 139–152.

Ellis, C.J. and Tallis, J.H. (2001) Climatic control of peat erosion in a North Wales blanket mire. *New Phytologist*, 152, 313–324.

Emmel, M. (2008) Growing ornamental plants in *Sphagnum* biomass. *Acta Horticulturae*, 779, 173–178.

Engel, S. and Palmer, C. (2008) Payments for environmental services as an alternative to logging under weak property rights: the case of Indonesia. *Ecological Economics*, 65, 799–809.

Engel, S., Pagiola, S. and Wunder, S. (2008) Designing payments for environmental services in theory and practice: an overview of the issues. *Ecological Economics*, 65, 663–674.

English Nature (2003) *Condition Assessment of Sites of Special Scientific Interest.* Peterborough, UK: English Nature.

Engström, J., Nilsson, C. and Jansson, R. (2009) Effects of stream restoration on dispersal of plant propagules. *Journal of Applied Ecology*, 46, 397–405.

Environment Agency (2010) Fisheries statistics report. Bristol, UK: The Environment Agency.

Eppinga, M.B., Rietkerk, M., Wassen, M.J. and De Ruiter, P.C. (2009) Linking habitat modification to catastrophic shifts and vegetation patterns in bogs. *Plant Ecology*, 200, 53–68.

Ernst and Young (2012) *The future of global carbon markets. The prospect of an international agreement and its impact on business.* London: Ernst and Young.

Euroconsult Mott MacDonald, Deltares and Delft Hydraulics, DHV, Wageningen UR, Witteveen+Bos, PT MLD and PT INDEC (2008) *Master plan for the rehabilitation and revitalisation of the ex-Mega Rice Project area in Central Kalimantan. Main Synthesis Report.* Jakarta: Government of Indonesia and Royal Netherlands Embassy.

Euroconsult Mott MacDonald, Deltares and Delft Hydraulics (2009a) *Peatland rehabilitation strategic plan For Block A (North-West) in the ex-Mega Rice Project Area, Central Kalimantan.* Government of Indonesia–Government of

Australia. Project No. IFCI-C0011. Jakarta: Kalimantan Forest and Climate Partnership

Euroconsult Mott MacDonald, Deltares and Delft Hydraulics, DHV, Wageningen UR, Witteveen+Bos, PT MLD and PT INDEC (2009b) *Guideline for the canal blocking design in the ex-Mega Rice Project Area in Central Kalimantan. Technical Guideline Number 4. Master Plan for the Rehabilitation and Revitalisation of the Ex-Mega Rice Project Area in Central Kalimantan.* Jakarta: Government of Indonesia and Royal Netherlands Embassy.

European Commission (1992) Council Directive 92/43/EEC of 21 May 1992 on the conservation of natural habitats and of wild fauna and flora. Brussels: European Commission.

European Commission (2000) Directive 200/60/EC Establishing a Framework for Community Action in the Field of Water Policy. *Official Journal of the European Communities*, L 327 (1).

European Commission (2003a) Directive 2003/30/EC of the European Parliament and of the Council of 8 May 2003 on the promotion of the use of biofuels or other renewable fuels for transport. *Official Journal of the European Union*, L 123, 42–46.

European Commission (2003b) *Horizontal Guidance Document in the Role of Wetlands in the Water Framework Directive.* Brussels: European Commission.

European Commission (2009) Directive 2009/28/EC of the European Parliament and of the Council of 23 April 2009 on the promotion of the use of energy from renewable sources and amending and subsequently repealing Directives 2001/77/EC and 2003/30/EC. *Official Journal*, **L** 140, 16–62.

European Commission (2011) *Our Life Insurance, Our Natural Capital: An EU Biodiversity Strategy to 2020.* Brussels: European Commission.

European Commission (2014) *Mapping and Assessment of Ecosystems and their Services. Indicators for ecosystem assessments under Action 5 of the EU Biodiversity Strategy to 2020.* Brussels: European Commission.

Evans, C.D., Monteith, D.T. and Cooper, D.M. (2005) Long-term increases in surface water dissolved organic carbon: Observations, potential causes and environmental impacts. *Environmental Pollution*, 137, 55–71.

Evans, C., Norris, D. and Rowe, E. (2005) *A regional water and soil quality survey of the North York Moors.* CEH Report C02661 for DEFRA. London: DEFRA.

Evans C.D., Chapman P.J., Clark J.M., Monteith D.T. and Cresser M.S. (2006) Alternative explanations for rising dissolved organic carbon export from organic soils. *Global Change Biology*, 12, 2044–2053.

Evans, C.D., Allott, T., Billettt, M. *et al.* (2013a) *Greenhouse Gas Emissions Associated with Non Gaseous Losses of Carbon from Peatlands – Fate of Particulate and Dissolved Carbon.* Final Report to the Department for Environment, Food and Rural Affairs, Project SP1205. Bangor, UK: Centre for Ecology and Hydrology.

Evans, C.D., Chadwick, T., Norris, D. *et al.* (2013b) Persistent surface water acidification in an organic soil-dominated upland region subject to high atmospheric deposition: The North York Moors, UK. *Ecological Indicators*, 37, 304–316.

Evans, C.D., Bonn, A., Holden, J. *et al.* (2014a) Relationships between anthropogenic pressures and ecosystem functions in UK blanket bogs: Linking process understanding to ecosystem service valuation. *Ecosystem Services*, 9, 5–19.

Evans, C.D., Page, S.E., Jones, T. *et al.* (2014b) Contrasting vulnerability of drained tropical and high-latitude peatlands to fluvial loss of stored carbon. *Global Biogeochemical Cycles*, 28, 1215–1234.

Evans, C.D., Renou-Wilson, F., and Strack, M. (2015) The role of waterborne carbon in the greenhouse gas balance of drained and re-wetted peatlands. *Journal of Aquatic Science*, 1–18.

Evans, M., Allott, T.E.H., Holden, J., Flitcroft, C. and Bonn, A. (2005) *Understanding Gully Blocking in Deep Peat.* Edale, UK: Moors for the Future Partnership.

Evans, M., Warburton, J. and Yang, J. (2006) Sediment budgets for eroding blanket peat catchments: global and local implications of upland organic sediment budgets. *Geomorphology*, 79, 45–57.

Evans, M.G. and Lindsay, J. (2010a) High resolution quantification of gully erosion in upland peatlands at the landscape scale. *Earth Surface Processes and Landforms*, 35 876–886.

Evans, M.G., and Lindsay, J. (2010b) The impact of gully erosion on carbon sequestration in blanket peatlands. *Climate Research*, 45, 31–41.

Evans, M.G., and Warburton, J. (2007) *The Geomorphology of Upland Peat: Pattern, Process, Form*. Oxford, UK: Blackwell.

Evans, M.G., Burt, T.P., Holden, J. and Adamson, J.K. (1999) Runoff generation and water table fluctuations in blanket peat: evidence from UK data spanning the dry summer of 1995. *Journal of Hydrology*, 221, 141–160.

Evans, M.G., Warburton, J. and Yang, J. (2006) Sediment budgets for eroding blanket peat catchments: global and local implications of organic sediment budgets. *Geomorphology*, 79, 45–57.

Evans, M.G., Pawson, R., Daniels, S., Yang, J., and Wilkinson, R. (2009) *Monitoring Carbon Flux from Restoration Sites*. Edale, UK: Moors for the Future Partnership.

Evans, R. (1997) Soil erosion in the UK initiated by grazing animals: a need for a national survey. *Applied Geography*, 17, 127–141.

Evans, R. (1998) The erosional impacts of grazing animals. *Progress in Physical Geography*, 22, 251–268.

Evans, R. (2005a) Curtailing grazing induced erosion in a small catchment and its environs, the Peak District, Central England. *Applied Geography*, 25, 81–95.

Evans, R. (2005b). Monitoring water erosion in lowland England and Wales – a personal view of its history and outcomes. *Catena*, 64, 142–161.

Farber, S., Costanza, R. and Wilson, M. (2002) Economic and ecological concepts for valuing ecosystem services. *Ecological Economics*, 41, 375–392.

Farrick, K.F., and Price, J.S. (2009) Ericaceous shrubs on abandoned block-cut peatlands: Implications for soil water availability and *Sphagnum* restoration. *Ecohydrology*, 2, 530–540.

FAS/USDA (2011) *Oilseeds: World Markets and Trade*. Foreign Agricultural Service, US Department of Agriculture, Circular Series FOP 11–12 December 2011. http://www.fas.usda.gov/psdonline/circulars/oilseeds.pdf (accessed 27 November 2015).

Faubert, P. (2004) *The effect of long-term water level drawdown on the vegetation composition and CO_2 fluxes of a boreal peatland in Central Finland*. MSc thesis. Laval, Canada: University of Laval.

Fay, E. and Lavoie, C. (2009) The impact of birch seedlings on evapotranspiration from a mined peatland: an experimental study in southern Québec, Canada. *Mires and Peat*, 5, Art. 3, 1–7.

Fazey, I., Bunse, L., Msika, J. et al. (2014) Evaluating knowledge exchange in interdisciplinary and multi-stakeholder research. *Global Environmental Change*, 25, 204–220.

Federal Environment Agency (2008) *Economic Valuation of Environmental Damage: Methodological Convention for Estimates of Environmental Externalities*. Dessau, Germany: Federal Environment Agency.

Fell, V. and Williams, J. (2004) Monitoring of archaeological and experimental iron at Fiskerton, England. *Proceedings of the International Conference on Metals Conservation*, 17–27.

Ferland, C. and Rochefort, L. (1997) Restoration techniques for *Sphagnum*-dominated peatlands. *Canadian Journal of Botany*, 75, 1110–1118.

Ferone, J.-M. and Devito K.J. (2004) Shallow groundwater–surface water interactions in pond-peatland complexes along a boreal plains topographic gradient. *Journal of Hydrology*, 292, 75–95.

Field, R.D., van der Werf, G.R. and Shen, S.S.P. (2009) Human amplification of drought-induced biomass burning in Indonesia since 1960. *Nature Geoscience*, 2, 185–188.

Fisher, B., Turner, R.K., Morling, P. (2009) Defining and classifying ecosystem services for decision making. *Ecological Economics*, 68, 643–653.

Fisher, J. and Acreman. M.C. (2004) Wetland nutrient removal: a review of the evidence *Hydrology and Earth System Sciences*, 8, 673–685.

Flanagan, L.B. and Syed, K.H. (2011) Stimulation of both photosynthesis and respiration in response to warmer and drier conditions in a boreal peatland ecosystem. *Global Change Biology*, 17, 2271–2287.

Foggin, J. M. (2000) *Biodiversity protection and the search for sustainability in Tibetan Plateau grasslands (Qinghai, China)*. PhD dissertation. Tempe, Arizona: Arizona State University.

Foggin, J.M. (2008) Depopulating the Tibetan grasslands: national policies and perspectives for the future of Tibetan herders in Qinghai Province, China. *Mountain Research and Development*, 28, 26–31.

Foggin, J.M. (2014) Managing shared natural heritages: towards more participatory models of protected area management in Western China. *Journal of International Wildlife Law and Policy*, 17, 130–151.

Foggin, J.M. and Smith, A.T. (1996) Rangeland utilization and biodiversity on the alpine grasslands of Qinghai Province, People's Republic of China. *Conserving China's Biodiversity (II)*, ed. P.J. Schei, S. Wang and Y Wie. Beijing: China Environmental Science Press, pp. 247–258.

Foggin, J.M. and Torrance-Foggin, M.E. (2011) How can social and environmental services be provided for mobile Tibetan herders? Collaborative examples from Qinghai Province, China. *Pastoralism: Research, Policy and Practice*, 1:21.

Foggin, P.M., Torrance, M.E., Dorje, D. et al. (2006) Assessment of the health status and risk factors of Kham Tibetan pastoralists in the alpine grasslands of the Tibetan Plateau. *Social Sciences and Medicine*, 63, 2512–2532.

Foggin, P.M., Torrance, M.E. and Foggin, J.M. (2009) Accessibility of healthcare for pastoralists in the Tibetan Plateau Region: a case study from southern Qinghai Province, China. In *Ethnic Minorities and Regional Development in Asia: Reality and Challenges*, ed. H. Cao. Amsterdam: Amsterdam University Press, pp. 83–91.

Foley, C. and MacDonagh, M. (1998) Copney stone circles: a County Tyrone enigma. *Archaeology Ireland*, 12, 24–28.

Foley, J.A., DeFries, R., Asner, G.P. et al. (2005) Global consequences of land use. *Science*, 309, 570–574.

Folke, C. (1991) The societal value of wetland life-support. In *Linking the Natural Environment and the Economy: Essays from the Eco-Eco Group*, ed. C. Folke and T. Kaberger. Dordrecht, The Netherlands: Kluwer Academic Publishers, pp. 141–171.

Fontaine, N., Poulin, M. and Rochefort, L. (2007) Plant diversity associated with pools in natural and restored peatlands. *Mires and Peat*, 2, Art. 6, 1–17.

Forster, P., Ramaswamy, V., Artaxo, P. et al. (2007) Changes in atmospheric constituents and in radiative forcing. In *Climate Change 2007: The Physical Science Basis. Contribution of Working Group I to the Fourth Assessment Report of the Intergovernmental Panel on Climate Change*, ed. S. Solomon, D. Qin, M. Manning et al. Cambridge, UK and New York: Cambridge University Press.

Fraga, M.I., Romero-Pedreira, D., Souto, M., Castro, D. and Sahuquillo, E. (2008) Assessing the impact of wind farms on the plant diversity of blanket bogs in the Xistral Mountains (NW Spain). *Mires and Peat*, 4, Art. 6, 1–10.

Francez, A.-J. and Vasander, H. (1995) Peat accumulation and peat decomposition after human disturbance in French and Finnish mires. *Acta oecologica*, 16, 599–608.

Franzén, L.G., Deliang, C. and Klinger, L.F. (1996) Principles for a climate regulation mechanism during the Late Phanerozoic Era, based on carbon fixation in peat-forming wetlands. *Ambio*, 25, 435–442.

Franzén, L.G., Lindberg, F., Viklander, V. and Walther, A. (2012) The potential peatland extent and carbon sink in Sweden, as related to the Peatland/Ice Age Hypothesis. *Mires and Peat*, 10, Art. 8, 1–19.

Fraser, L.H. and Keddy, P. (2005) *The World's Largest Wetlands: Ecology and Conservation*. Cambridge, UK: Cambridge University Press.

Freeman III, A. (2003) *The Measurement of Environmental and Resource Values: Theories and Methods*. Washington, DC: Resources for the Future.

Freeman, C., Evans, C.D., Monteith, D.T., Reynolds, B., and Fenner, N. (2001) Export of organic carbon from peat soils. *Nature*, 412, 785.

Freeman, C., Ostle, N. and Kang, H. (2001) An enzymic 'latch' on a global carbon store – a shortage of oxygen locks up carbon in peatlands by restraining a single enzyme. *Nature*, 409, 149.

Freeman, C., Fenner, N., Ostle, N.J. *et al.* (2004) Export of dissolved organic carbon from peatlands under elevated carbon dioxide levels. *Nature*, 430, 195–198.

French, C.A.I. and Pryor, F. (1993) The south-west Fen Dyke survey project, 1982–1986. *East Anglian Archaeology*, 59.

Friday, E.D. (1997) *Wicken Fen: The Making of a Wetland Nature Reserve*. Colchester, UK: Harley Books.

Friedlingstein, P. and Prentice, I.C. (2010) Carbon-climate feedbacks: a review of model and observation based estimates. *Current Opinion in Environmental Sustainability*, 2, 251–257.

Friedlingstein, P., Cox, P., Betts, R. *et al.* (2006) Climate-carbon cycle feedback analysis: Results from the (CMIP)-M-4 model intercomparison. *Journal of Climate*, 19, 3337–3353.

Fritz, C., Pancotto, V.A., Elzenga, J.T.M. *et al.* (2011) Zero methane emission bogs: extreme rhizosphere oxygenation by cushion plants in Patagonia. *New Phytologist*, 190, 398–408.

Frolking, S. and Roulet, N.T. (2007) Holocene radiative forcing impact of northern peatland carbon accumulation and methane emissions. *Global Change Biology*, 13, 1079–1088.

Frolking, S., Roulet, N.T., Moore, T.R. *et al.* (2001) Modeling northern peatland decomposition and peat accumulation. *Ecosystems*, 4, 479–498.

Frolking, S., Roulet N. and Fuglestvedt, J. (2006) How northern peatlands influence the Earth's radiative budget. Sustained methane emissions versus sustained carbon sequestration. *Journal of Geophysical Research*, 111, G01008.

Frolking, S., Talbot, J., Jones, M.C. *et al.* (2011) Peatlands in the Earth's 21st century climate system. *Environmental Reviews*, 19, 371–396.

Frolking, S., Talbot, J. and Subin, Z.M. (2014) Exploring the relationship between peatland net carbon balance and apparent carbon accumulation rate at century to millennial time scales. *The Holocene*, 24, 1021–1027.

Fronzek, S., Luoto, M. and Carter, T.R. (2006) Potential effect of climate change on the distribution of palsa mires in subarctic Fennoscandia. *Climate Research*, 32, 1–12.

Fyfe, R. and Greeves, T. (2010) The date and context of a stone row: Cut Hill, Dartmoor, south-west England. *Antiquity*, 84, 55–70.

Fyfe R.M., Brück J., Johnston R. *et al.* (2008) Historical context and chronology of Bronze Age enclosure on Dartmoor, UK. *Journal of Archaeological Science*, 35, 2250–2261.

Galaty, J.G. and Johnson, D.L. (1990) *The World of Pastoralism: Herding Systems in Comparative Perspective*. New York: Guilford.

Gallego-Sala, A.V. and Prentice, I.C. (2012) Blanket peat biome endangered by climate change. *Nature Climate Change*, 3, 152–155.

Gallego-Sala, A.V., Clark, J., House, J.I. *et al.* (2011) Bioclimatic envelope model of climate change impacts on blanket peatland distribution in Great Britain. *Climate Research*, 45, 151–162.

Gams, H. and Ruoff, S. (1929) Geschichte, Aufbau und Pflanzendecke des Zehlaubruches. *Schriften der Physikalisch-Ökonomischen Gesellschaft zu Königsberg in Preußen*, 66, 1–192.

Gao, Y., Schumann, M., Chen, H., Wu, N. and Luo, P. (2009) Impacts of grazing intensity on soil carbon and nitrogen in an alpine meadow on the eastern Tibetan Plateau. *Journal of Food, Agriculture and Environment*, 7, 749–754.

Gao, Y., Zeng, X., Schumann, M. and Chen, H. (2011) Effectiveness of exclosures on restoration of degraded alpine meadow in the Eastern Tibetan Plateau. *Arid Land Research and Management*, 25, 164–175.

Garnett, H., Ineson, P. and Stevenson, A.C. (2000) Effects of burning and grazing on carbon sequestration in a Pennine blanket bog, UK. *The Holocene*, 10, 729–736.

Garrity, D.P., Amoroso, V.B., Koffa, S. and Catacutan, D. (2001) Innovations in participatory watershed resource management to conserve tropical biodiversity. In *Seeking Sustainability: Challenges of Agricultural Development and Environmental Management in a Philippine Watershed*, ed. I. Coxhead and G. Buenavista. Manilla: Philippine Council for Agriculture, Forestry and Natural Resources Research and Development, pp. 112–137.

Gaudig, G., Kamermann, D. and Joosten, H. (2008) Growing growing media: promises of *Sphagnum* biomass. *Acta Horticulturae*, 779, 165–172.

Gaudig, G., Fengler, F., Krebs, M. et al. (2014) *Sphagnum* farming in Germany: a review of progress. *Mires and Peat*, 13, Art. 8, 1–11.

Gearey, B.R., Bermingham, N., Moore. C. and Van de Noort, R. (2013) *Review of archeaological survey and mitigation policy relating to Bord Na Móna Peatlands*. Report. Dublin: Department of Arts, Heritage and the Gaeltacht.

Gedney, N., Cox, P.M. and Huntingford, C. (2004) Climate feedback from wetland methane emissions. *Geophysical Research Letters*, 31.

GEF (2001) *Conservation and Sustainable Use of Tropical Peat Swamp Forests and Associated Wetland Ecosystems: Project information*. Washington DC: Global Environment Facility (GEF).

Gellert, P.K. (1998) A brief history and analysis of Indonesia's forest fire crisis. *Indonesia*, 65, 63–85.

Gerrard, P. (2004) *Integrating Wetland Ecosystem Values into Urban Planning: The Case of That Luang Marsh, Vientiane, Lao PDR*. Vientiane, Laos: IUCN, Asia Regional Environmental Economics Programme and WWF Lao Country Office.

Geurts, J.J., Smolders, A.J., Verhoeven, J.T., Roelofs, J.G. and Lamers, L.P. (2008) Sediment Fe: PO_4 ratio as a diagnostic and prognostic tool for the restoration of macrophyte biodiversity in fen waters. *Freshwater Biology*, 53, 2101–2116.

Giesen, W. (2004) *Causes of Peat Swamp Forest Degradation in Berbak NP, Indonesia, and Recommendation for Restoration*. Arnhem, The Netherlands: Arcadis Euroconsult.

Giesen, W. (2009) *Biodiversity and the Ex-Mega Rice Project Area in Central Kalimantan*. Technical Report Number 8. Master Plan for the Rehabilitation and Revitalisation of the Ex-Mega Rice Project Area in Central Kalimantan. Euroconsult Mott MacDonald/Deltares | Delft Hydraulics in association with DHV, Wageningen University and Research, Witteven+Bos Indonesia, PT.MLD and PT.Indec. Jakarta: Government of Indonesia and Royal Netherlands Embassy.

Giesen, W. (2013) *Paludiculture: sustainable alternatives on degraded peat land in Indonesia*. QANS Activity 3.3: Quick Assessment and Nationwide Screening of Peat and Lowland Resources and Action Planning for the Implementation of a National Lowland Strategy. Jakarta: Euroconsult Mott MacDonald, for the Netherlands

Partners for Water Programme, BAPPENAS and the Ministry of Public Works.

Giesen, W. and van der Meer, P. (2009) *Guidelines for the Rehabilitation of Degraded Peat Swamp Forest in Central Kalimantan*. Technical Guideline Number 5. Master Plan for the Rehabilitation and Revitalisation of the Ex-Mega Rice Project Area in Central Kalimantan. Euroconsult Mott MacDonald/Deltares | Delft Hydraulics in association with DHV, Wageningen University and Research, Witteveen+Bos Indonesia, PT.MLD and PT.Indec. Jakarta: Government of Indonesia and Royal Netherlands Embassy.

Gignac, L.D., Nicholson, B.J. and Bayley, S.E. (1998) The utilization of bryophytes in bioclimatic modeling: predicted northward migration of peatlands in the Mackenzie River Basin, Canada, as a result of global warming. *The Bryologist*, 101, 572–587.

Gignac, L.D., Halsey, L.A. and Vitt, D.H. (2000) A bioclimatic model for the distribution of *Sphagnum*-dominated peatlands in North America under present climatic conditions. *Journal of Biogeography*, 27, 1139–1151.

Giller, K.E. and Wheeler, B.D. (1986) Past peat cutting and present vegetation patterns in an undrained fen in Broadland, Norfolk. *Journal of Ecology*, 74, 219–247.

Giller, K.E. and Wheeler, B.D. (1988) Acidification and succession in a flood-plain mire in the Norfolk Broadland, U.K. *Journal of Ecology*, 76, 849–866.

Gill-Robinson, H. (2008) Managing wetland archaeology: environmental degradation at wetland archaeological sites. In *Managing Archaeological Resources*, ed. P. McManamon, A. Stout and J.A. Barnes. Walnut Creek, CA: Left Coast Press, pp. 233–241.

Girard, M., Lavoie, C. and Thériault, M. (2002) The regeneration of a highly disturbed ecosystem: a mined peatland in Southern Québec. *Ecosystems*, 5, 274–288.

Given, D.R. (1994) *Principles and Practice of Plant Conservation*. Portland, OR: Timber Press.

Glaser, P. H. (1999) The distribution and origin of mire pools. In *Patterned Mires and Mire Pools: Origin and Development; Flora and Fauna*, ed. V. Standen, J. Tallis and R. Meade. Durham, UK: British Ecological Society, pp. 4–25.

Glatzel, S., Koebsch, F., Beetz, S. *et al.* (2011) Maßnahmen zur Minderung der Treibhausgase Freisetzung aus Mooren im Mittleren Mecklenburg. *Telma Beiheft*, 4, 85–106.

Glenk, K., Schaafsma, M., Moxey, A., Martin-Ortega, J. and Hanley, N. (2014) A framework for valuing spatially targeted peatland restoration. *Ecosystem Services*, 9, 20–33.

Goetz, R.U. (1997) Land development and pigouvian taxes: the case of peatland. *American Journal of Agricultural Economics*, 79, 227–234.

Goldammer, J.G. (2007) History of equatorial vegetation fires and fire research in Southeast Asia before the 1997/98 episode: a reconstruction of creeping environmental changes. *Mitigation and Adaptation Strategies for Global Change*, 12, 13–32.

Goldstein, M.C. and Beall, C.M. (1990) *Nomads of Western Tibet: The Survival of a Way of Life*. Berkeley, CA: University of California Press.

Gómez-Baggethun, E., de Groot, R., Lomas, P.L. and Montes, C. (2010) The history of ecosystem services in economic theory and practice: from early notions to markets and payment schemes. *Ecological Economics*, 69, 1209–1218.

González, E. and Rochefort, L. (2014) Drivers of success in 53 cutover bogs restored by a moss layer transfer technique. *Ecological Engineering*, 68, 279–290.

Gore, A.J.P. (1983) *Ecosystems of the World, 4A, Mires: Swamp, Bog, Fen and Moor*. Amsterdam: Elsevier.

Gorham, E. (1991) Northern peatlands: role in the carbon-cycle and probable responses to climatic warming. *Ecological Applications*, 1, 182–195.

Gorham, E., Brush, G.S., Graumlich, L.J., Rosenzweig, M.L., and Johnson, A.H. (2001) The value of palaeoecology as an aid to monitoring ecosystems and landscapes, chiefly with reference to North America. *Environmental Reviews*, 9, 99–126.

Gorke, M. (2003) *The Death of our Planet's Species: A Challenge to Ecology and Ethics.* Washington, DC: Island Press.

Gorke, M. (2010) *Eigenwert der Natur: Ethische Begründung und Konsequenzen.* Stuttgart, Germany: Hirzel.

Gormley, S., Donnelley, C., Hartwell, B. and Bell, J. (2009) *Condition and management survey of the archaeological resource in Northern Ireland.* CAMSAR report for the Northern Ireland Environment Agency. Belfast: CAMSAR.

Goulder, L.H. and Parry, I.W.H. (2008) Instrument choice in environmental policy. *Resources for the Future Discussion Paper*, 2, 152–174.

Government of Alberta (2013) Alberta Wetland Policy. http://aep.alberta.ca/water/programs-and-services/wetlands/documents/AlbertaWetlandPolicy-Sep2013.pdf.

Government of Canada (1991) *The Federal Policy on Wetland Conservation.* Ottawa: Ministry of Supply and Services Canada.

Government of Indonesia (2010) *Indonesia Second National Communication Under The United Nations Framework Convention on Climate Change (UNFCCC).* Jakarta: Government of Indonesia.

Government of Nova Scotia (2011) *Nova Scotia Wetlands Conservation Policy.* Halifax, Canada: Government of Nova Scotia.

Government of Saskatchewan (2002) *The Environmental Assessment Act.* Chapter E-10.1 of the Statutes of Saskatchewan 1979–80 (effective August 25, 1980) as amended by the Statutes of Saskatchewan, 1983 c.77; 1988–89 c.42 and c.55; 1996 c.F-19.1; and 2002, c.C-11.1. Regina, Canada: Government of Saskatchewan.

Government of Saskatchewan (2006) *Caring for Natural Environments – A Biodiversity Action Plan for Saskatchewan's Future. 2004–2009. 2004–2006 Progress report.* Regina, Canada: Government of Saskatchewan.

Grace, J.B. and Wetzel, R.G. (1981) Habitat partitioning and competitive displacement in cattails (*Typha*): experimental field studies. *The American Naturalist*, 118, 463–474.

Graf, M.D. and Rochefort, L. (2008) Techniques for restoring fen vegetation on cut-away peatlands of North America. *Applied Vegetation Science*, 11, 521–528.

Graf, M. and Rochefort, L. (2009) Examining the peat-accumulating potential of fen vegetation in the context of fen restoration of harvested peatlands. *Écoscience*, 16, 158–166.

Graf, M.D. and Rochefort, L. (2010) Moss regeneration for fen restoration: Field and greenhouse experiments. *Restoration Ecology*, 18, 121–130.

Graf, M.D., Rochefort, L. and Poulin, M. (2008) Spontaneous revegetation of cutaway peatlands of North America. *Wetlands*, 28, 28–39.

Graf, M.D., Bérubé, V. and Rochefort, L. (2012) Restoration of peatlands after peat extraction: impacts, restoration goals and techniques. In *Restoration and Reclamation of Boreal Ecosystems*, ed. D.H. Vitt and J. Bhatti. Cambridge, UK: Cambridge University Press, pp. 259–280.

Graham, I.D., Logan, J., Harrison, M.B. et al. (2006) Lost in knowledge translation: time for a map? *Journal of Continuing Education in the Health Professions*, 26, 13–24.

Graham, L.L.B. and Page, S.E. (2012) Artificial bird perches for the regeneration of degraded tropical peat swamp forest: a restoration tool with limited potential. *Restoration Ecology*, 20, 631–637.

Granath, G., Strengbom, J. and Rydin, H. (2010) Rapid ecosystem shifts in peatlands: linking plant physiology and succession. *Ecology*, 91, 3047–3056.

Grand-Clement, E., Anderson, K., Smith, D. et al. (2013) Evaluating ecosystem goods and services after restoration of marginal upland peatlands in South-West England. *Journal of Applied Ecology*, 50, 324–334.

Grayson, R., Holden, J. and Rose, R. (2010) Long-term change in storm hydrographs in response to peatland vegetation change. *Journal of Hydrology*, 389, 336–343.

Gregory, D., Helms, A.C. and Henning, M. (2008) The use and deployment of modern wood samples as a proxy indicator for biochemical processes on archaeological sites preserved *in situ* in a variety of environments of differing saturation level. *Conservation and Management of Archaeological Sites*, 10, 3, 204–222.

Gregory, J.M., Huybrechts, P. and Raper, S.C.B. (2004) Climatology: threatened loss of the Greenland ice-sheet. *Nature*, 428, 616.

Gregory, J.M., Jones, C.D., Cadule, P. and Friedlingstein, P. (2009) Quantifying carbon cycle feedbacks. *Journal of Climate*, 22, 5232–5250.

Greider, T. and Garkovich, L. (1994) Landscapes: the social construction of nature and the environment. *Rural Sociology*, 59, 1–24.

Gren, I. (1995) The value of investing in wetlands for nitrogen abatement. *European Review of Agricultural Economics*, 22, 157–172.

Grieve, I., and Gilvear, D. (2008) Effects of wind farm construction on concentrations and fluxes of dissolved organic carbon and suspended sediment from peat catchments at Braes of Doune, Central Scotland. *Mires and Peat*, 4, Art. 3, 1–11.

Grieve, I.C., Davidson, D.A. and Gordon, J.E. (1995) Nature, extent and severity of soil erosion in upland Scotland. *Land Degradation and Rehabilitation*, 6, 41–55.

Grobler, R., Moning, C., Sliva, J., Bredenkamp, G. and Grundling, P-L. (2004) Subsistence farming and conservation constraints in coastal peat swamp forests of the Kosi Bay Lake system, Maputaland, South Africa. *La Conservation des Tourbières*, 79, 317–324.

Groeneveld, E.V.G. and Rochefort, L. (2005) *Polytrichum strictum* as a solution to frost heaving in disturbed ecosystems: a case study with milled peatlands. *Restoration Ecology* 13, 74–82.

Groeneveld, E.V.G., Massé, A. and Rochefort, L. (2007) *Polytrichum strictum* as a nurse-plant in peatland restoration. *Restoration Ecology*, 15, 709–719.

Grootjans, A.P. and Jansen, A.M.J. (2012) An eco-hydrological approach to wetland restoration. In *Calcareous Mires of Slovakia; Landscape Setting, Management and Restoration Prospects*, ed. A.P. Grootjans, A.M.J. Jansen and V. Stanova. Zeist, The Netherlands: KNNV Publishing, pp. 21–28.

Grootjans, A.P. and van Diggelen, R. (1995) Assessing the restoration prospects of degraded fens. In *Restoration of Temperate Wetlands*, ed. B.D. Wheeler, S.C. Shaw, W.J. Fojt and R.A. Robertson. Chichester, UK: Wiley, pp. 73–90.

Grootjans, A. and van Diggelen, R. (eds) (2002) *Selected Restoration Objects in The Netherlands and NW Germany: a Field Guide*. Groningen, The Netherlands: Laboratory of Plant Ecology.

Grootjans, A.P., van Diggelen, R., Joosten, H. and Smolders, A.J.P. (2012) Restoration of mires. In *Restoration Ecology: The New Frontier*, ed. J. van Andel and J. Aronson. Oxford, UK: Blackwell, pp. 203–213.

Grosshans, R.E., Venema, H.D., Cicek, N. and Goldsborough, G. (2011a) Cattail farming for water quality: harvesting cattails for nutrient removal and phosphorous recovery in the watershed. *Proceedings of WEF-IWA Nutrient Recovery and Management 2011*, 1107–1132.

Grosshans, R.E., Zubrycki, K., Hope, A., Roy, D. and Venema, H.D. (2011b) *Netley–Libau Nutrient-Bioenergy Project*. Manitoba, Canada: IISD.

Groves, J., Caitcheon, G., Norris, R. and Williams, D. (2007) Prediction of fluvial seed dispersal and long-term sustainability of riparian vegetation using sediment transport processes. *Proceedings of the 5th Australian Stream Management Conference. Australian Rivers: Making a Difference*, 121–126.

Gulickx, M.M.C., Beecroft, R.C. and Green, A.C. (2007) Introduction of water buffalo *Bubalus bubalis* to recently created wetlands at Kingfisher's Bridge, Cambridgeshire, England. *Conservation Evidence*, 4, 43–44.

Günther, A., Huth, V., Jurasinski, G. and Glatzel, S. (2015) The effect of biomass harvesting on greenhouse gas emissions from a rewetted temperate fen. *GCB Bioenergy*, 7, 1092–1106.

Güsewell, S. and Le Nédic, C. (2004) Effects of winter mowing on vegetation succession in a lakeshore fen. *Applied Vegetation Science*, 7, 41–48.

Gustafsson, L. (1988) Vegetation succession during the establishment of an energy forest on a Sphagnum peat bog in East-Central Sweden. *Scandinavian Journal of Forest Research*, 3, 371–385.

Haapalehto, T.O., Vasander, H., Jauhiainen, S., Tahvanainen, T. and Kotiaho, J.S. (2011). The effects of peatland restoration on water-table depth, elemental concentrations and vegetation: 10 years of changes. *Restoration Ecology*, 19, 587–598.

Haines-Young, R. and Potschin, M. (2013) *Common international classification of ecosystem services. Report prepared following consultation on CICES Version 4*. August–September 2012. EEA Framework Contract No EEA/IEA/09/003. London: European Environment Agency.

Hájkova, P., Grootjans, A.P., Lamentowicz, M. et al. (2012) How a *Sphagnum fuscum* bog changed into a calcareous fen: the remarkable history of a Slovak spring fed mire. *Journal of Quarternary Science*, 27, 233–243.

Häkkinen, J. (2007) Traditional use of reed. In *Read Up on Reed! Part IV, Touch and Thatch*, ed. I. Ikonen. and E. Hagelberg. Turku, Finland: Southwest Finland Regional Environment Centre, pp. 62–72.

Hall, D. (1987) The Fenland Project 2: Cambridgeshire Survey, Peterborough to March. *East Anglian Archaeology*, 35.

Halsey, L.A., Vitt, D.H. and Bauer, I.E. (1998) Peatland initiation during the Holocene in continental western Canada. *Climatic Change*, 40, 315–342.

Hamada, Y., Darung, U., Tho, U., Limin, S.H. and Hatano, R. (2010) Gaseous composition of smoke samples obtained at a tropical peatland fire. *19th World Congress of Soil Science, Soil Solutions for a Changing World*. Brisbane, Australia: World Congress of Soil Science.

Hampicke, U. (1999) The limits of economic valuation of biodiversity. *International Journal of Social Economics*, 26, 158–173.

Hanley, N. and Craig, S. (1991) Wilderness development decisions and the Krutilla-Fisher model: the case of Scotland's 'flow country'. *Ecological Economics*, 4, 145–164.

Hanley, N., Colombo, S., Mason, P. and Johns, H. (2007) The reform of support mechanisms for upland farming: paying for public goods in the severely disadvantaged areas of England. *Journal of Agricultural Economics*, 58, 433–453.

Hanley, N., Ready, R., Colombo, S. et al. (2009) The impacts of knowledge of the past on preferences for future landscape change. *Journal of Environmental Management*, 90, 1404–1412.

Hardin, G. (1968) The tragedy of the commons. *Science*, 162, 1243–1248.

Hargreaves, K.J., Milne, R. and Cannell, M.G.R., (2003) Carbon balance of afforested peatland in Scotland. *Forestry*, 76, 299–317.

Harlow, J., Clarke, S., Phillips, M. and Scott, A. (2012) *Valuing land-use and management changes in the Keighley and Watersheddles catchment*. Natural England Research Reports, Number 44. Peterborough, UK: Natural England.

Harper, J.L. (1977) *Population Biology of Plants*. London: Academic Press.

Harris, J.A., Hobbs, R.J., Higgs, E. and Aronson, J. (2006) Ecological restoration and global climate change. *Restoration Ecology*, 14, 170–176.

Harris, N. and Hooper, A. (2004) Rediscovering the 'spatial' in public policy and planning: an examination of the spatial content of sectoral policy documents. *Planning Theory and Practice*, 5, 147–169.

Harrison, B.M. and Priest, F.G. (2009) Composition of peats used in the preparation of malt for Scotch whisky production – Influence of geographical source and extraction depth. *Journal of Agricultural and Food Chemistry*, 57, 2385–2391.

Harte, J. (1997) Nature conservation: the rule of law in European Community law. *Journal of Environmental Policy*, 9, 139–180.

Hasch, B., Lotsch, H., Luthardt, V., Meier-Uhlherr, R. and Zeitz, J. (2009) DSS-WAMOS: a new web-based planning tool for fen restoration in European temperate forests, *Peatlands International*, 2009/1, 48–51.

Hayen, H. (1987) Peat bog archaeology in Lower Saxony, West Germany. In *European Wetlands in Prehistory*, ed. J.M. Coles and A.J. Lawson. Oxford, UK: Clarendon Press, pp. 117–136.

Heaney, S. (2009) *New Selected Poems 1966–1987*. London: Faber & Faber.

Hedberg, P. and Kotowski W. (2010) New nature by sowing? The current state of species introduction in grassland restoration, and the road ahead. *Journal for Nature Conservation*, 18, 304–308.

Hedberg, P., Kotowski, W., Saetre, P. et al. (2012) Vegetation recovery after multiple-site experimental fen restorations. *Biological Conservation*, 147, 60–67.

Hedberg, P., Saetre, P., Sundberg, S., Rydin, H. and Kotowski, W. (2013) A functional trait approach to fen restoration analysis. *Applied Vegetation Science*, 16, 658–666.

Heijmans, M.M.P.D., Berendse, F., Arp, W.J. et al. (2001) Effects of elevated carbon dioxide and increased nitrogen deposition on bog vegetation in the Netherlands. *Journal of Ecology*, 89, 268–279.

Heikkilä, H. and Lindholm, T. (1995) Mires of Seitseminen: how to make a national park. *Finnish-Karelian Symposium on Mire Conservation and Classification,Vesi-ja Ympäristöhallinnon Julkaisuja – Sarja*, 70–77.

Heil, A., Langmann, B. and Aldrian, E. (2007) Indonesian peat and vegetation fire emissions: study on factors influencing large-scale smoke haze pollution using a regional atmospheric chemistry model. *Mitigation and Adaptation Strategies for Global Change*, 12, 113–133.

Hein, L., van Koppen, C., de Groot, R., van Ierland, E. (2006) Spatial scales, stakeholders and the valuation of ecosystem services. *Ecological Economics*, 57, 209–228.

Helliwell, R.C. Coull, M.C., Davies, J.J.L. et al. (2007) The role of catchment characteristics in determining surface water nitrogen in four upland regions in the UK. *Hydrology and Earth System Sciences*, 11, 356–371.

Henman, J. and Poulter, B. (2008) Inundation of freshwater peatlands by sea level rise: Uncertainty and potential carbon cycle feedbacks. *Journal of Geophysical Research*, 113, G01011.

Henriksen, M. and Sylvester, M. (2007) Boat and human remains from bogs in Central Norway. In *Archaeology from the Wetlands: Recent Perspectives*, ed. J. Barber, J., C. Clark, M. Cressey, A. Crone, A. Hale, J. Henderson, R. H. Sands and A. Sheridan, *Proceedings of the 11th WARP Conference Society of Antiquaries Scotland*, pp. 343–349.

Herzschuh, U., Birks, H.J.B., Ni, J. et al.. (2010a) Holocene land-cover changes on the Tibetan Plateau. *The Holocene*, 20, 91–104.

Herzschuh, U., Birks, H. J. B., Liu, X., Kubatzki, C. and Lohmann, G. (2010b) What caused the mid-Holocene forest decline on the eastern Tibet–Qinghai Plateau? *Global Ecology and Biogeography*, 19, 278–286.

Higgs, E. (2003) *Nature by Design: People, Natural Processes and Ecological Restoration*. Cambridge, MA: MIT Press.

Hiraishi, T., Krug, T., Tanabe, K. et al. (eds.) (2014a) *2013 Revised Supplementary Methods and Good Practice Guidance Arising from the Kyoto Protocol*. Geneva: IPCC.

Hiraishi, T., Krug, T., Tanabe, K. et al. (eds.) (2014b) *2013 Supplement to the 2006 IPCC Guidelines for National Greenhouse Gas Inventories: Wetlands.* Geneva: IPCC.

HM Government (1994a) *Biodiversity: The UK Action Plan.* London: HMSO.

HM Government (1994b) *The Conservation (Natural Habitats, and C) Regulations.* London: HMSO.

Hoag, R. and Price, J.S. (1995) A field scale natural gradient solute transport experiment in peat at a Newfoundland blanket bog. *Journal of Hydrology*, 172, 171–184.

Hobbs, R.J. and Harris, J.A. (2001) Restoration ecology: repairing the Earth's ecosystems in the new millennium. *Restoration Ecology*, 9, 239–246.

Hobbs, R.J., Higgs, E. and Harris, J.A. (2009) Novel ecosystems: implications for conservation and restoration. *Trends in Ecology and Evolution*, 24, 599–605.

Hodder, K.H., Buckland, P.C., Kirby, K.J., and Bullock, J.M. (2009) Can the pre-Neolithic provide suitable models for re-wilding the landscape in Britain? *British Wildlife*, 4–15.

Hodges, J., Foggin, M., Long, R. and Zhaxi, G. (2014) Globalisation and the sustainability of farmers, livestock-keepers, pastoralists and fragile habitats. *Biodiversity*, 15, 109–118.

Hodgson, J.G., Grime, J.P., Wilson P.J., Thompson, K. and Band, R.S. (2005) The impacts of agricultural change (1963–2003) on the grassland flora of Central England: processes and prospects. *Basic and Applied Ecology*, 6, 107–118.

Hoffmann, W.A., Schroeder, W., and Jackson, R.B. (2003) Regional feedbacks among fire, climate, and tropical deforestation. *Journal of Geophysical Research*, 108, 4721.

Hogg, E.H., Lieffers, V.J. and Wein, R.W. (1992) Potential carbon losses from peat profiles: effects of temperature, drought cycles, and fire. *Ecological Applications*, 2, 298–306.

Holden, J. (2005) Peatland hydrology and carbon release: why small-scale process matters. *Philosophical Transactions of the Royal Society A: Mathematical, Physical and Engineering Sciences*, 363, 2891–2913.

Holden, J. and Burt, T.P. (2003) Hydrological studies on blanket peat: the significance of the acrotelm-catotelm model. *Journal of Ecology*, 91, 86–102.

Holden, J., Chapman, P.J. and Labadz, J.C. (2004) Artificial drainage of peatlands: hydrological and hydrochemical processes and wetland restoration. *Progress in Physical Geography*, 28, 95–123.

Holden, J., Chapman, P., Evans, M. et al. (2006a) *Vulnerability of organic soils in England and Wales.* Final technical report to DEFRA, Project SP0532. London: DEFRA.

Holden, J., Evans, M.G., Burt, T.P. and Horton, M. (2006b) Impact of land drainage on peatland hydrology. *Journal of Environmental Quality*, 35, 1764–1778.

Holden, J., Gascoigne, M. and Bosanko, N.R. (2007) Erosion and natural revegetation associated with surface land drains in upland peatlands. *Earth Surface Processes and Landforms*, 32, 1547–1557.

Holden, J., Shotbolt, L., Bonn, A. et al. (2007) Environmental change in moorland landscapes. *Earth Science Reviews*, 82, 75–100.

Holden, J., Kirkby, M.J., Lane, S.N. et al. (2008) Overland flow velocity and roughness properties in peatlands. *Water Resources Research*, 44, W06415.

Holden, J., Wallage, Z.E., Lane, S.N. and McDonald, A.T. (2011) Water table dynamics in drained and restored blanket peat. *Journal of Hydrology*, 402, 103–114.

Holden, J., Chapman, P.C., Palmer, S.M., Kay, P., and Grayson, R. (2012) The impacts of prescribed moorland burning on water colour and dissolved organic carbon: a critical synthesis. *Journal of Environmental Management*, 101, 92–103.

Holden, J., Brown, L., Palmer, S. et al. (2013) Impact of precribed and repeated vegetation burning on blanket peat hydrology. *Geophysical Research Abstracts*, 15, EGU2013-8288.

Holden, J., Wearing, C., Palmer, S. et al. (2014) Fire decreases near surface hydraulic conductivity and macropore flow in blanket peat. *Hydrological Processes*, 28, 2868–2876.

Holzner, W. and Kriechbaum, M. (1998) Man's impact on the vegetation and landscape in the inner Himalaya and Tibet. In *Sediments of Time*, ed. M. Elvin and T. Liu. Cambridge, UK: Cambridge University Press, pp. 53–106.

Holzner, W. and Kriechbaum, M. (2000) Pastures in South and Central Tibet (China): methods for a rapid assessment of pasture conditions. *Die Bodenkultur*, 51, 247–254.

Hooijer, A. (2005) Hydrology of tropical wetland forests: recent research results from Sarawak peat swamps. In *Forest, Water and People in the Humid Tropics*, ed. M. Bonell and L.A. Bruijnzeel. Cambridge, UK: Cambridge University Press, pp. 447–461.

Hooijer, A., van der Vat, M., Prinsen, G. et al. (2008) *Hydrology of the EMRP area: water management implications for peatlands*. Technical Report Number 2. Master Plan for the Rehabilitation and Revitalisation of the Ex-Mega Rice Project Area in Central Kalimantan. Euroconsult Mott MacDonald/Deltares | Delft Hydraulics in association with DHV, Wageningen University and Research, Witteven+Bos Indonesia, PT.MLD and PT.Indec. Jakarta: Government of Indonesia and Royal Netherlands Embassy.

Hooijer, A., Page, S., Canadell, J.G. et al. (2010) Current and future CO_2 emissions from drained peatlands in Southeast Asia. *Biogeosciences*, 7, 1505–1514.

Hooijer, A., Page, S., Jauhiainen, J. et al. (2012) Subsidence and carbon loss in drained tropical peatlands. *Biogeosciences*, 9, 1053–1071.

Hooijer, A., Vernimmen, R., Visser, M. and Mawdsley, N. (2015) Flooding projections from elevation and subsidence models for oil palm plantations in the Rajang Delta peatlands, Sarawak, Malaysia. Deltares report 1207384, 76.

Hoosbeek, M.R., van Breemen, N., Vasander, H., Buttler, A. and Berendse, F. (2002) Potassium limits potential growth of bog vegetation under elevated atmospheric CO_2 and N deposition. *Global Change Biology*, 8, 1130–1138.

Höper, H., Augustin, J., Cagampan, J.P. et al. (2008) Restoration of peatlands and greenhouse gas balances. *Peatlands and Climate Change*, ed. M. Strack. Jyväskylä, Finland: International Peat Society, pp. 182–210.

Houghton, J.T., Jenkins, G.J. and Ephraums, J.J. (eds) (1990) *Climate Change: The IPCC Scientific Assessment, Working Group I*. Cambridge, UK: Cambridge University Press.

Hughes, P.D.M. and Dumayne-Peaty, L. (2002) Testing theories of mire development using multiple successions at Crymlyn Bog, West Glamorgan, South Wales, UK. *Journal of Ecology*, 90, 456–471.

Hughes, P.D.M., Blundell, A., Charman, D.J. et al. (2006) An 8500 cal. year multi-proxy climate record from a bog in eastern Newfoundland: contributions of meltwater discharge and solar forcing. *Quaternary Science Reviews*, 25, 1208–1227.

Hughes, P.D.M., Lomas Clarke, S.H., Schulz, J. and Barber, K.E. (2007) Decline and localised extinction of a major raised bog species across the British Isles: evidence for associated land-use intensification. *The Holocene*, 18, 1033–1043.

Hutchinson, J.N. (1980) The record of peat wastage in the East Anglian fenlands at Holme Post, 1848–1978 AD. *Journal of Ecology*, 68, 229–249.

Huxman, T.E., Wilcox, B.P., Breshears, D.D. et al. (2005) Ecohydrological implications of woody plant encroachment. *Ecology*, 86, 308–319.

Hynninen, A., Fritze, H., Sarkkola, S. et al. (2011) N2O fluxes from peatland buffer areas after high N loadings in five forested catchments in Finland. *Wetlands*, 31, 1067–1077.

Hyvönen, R., Olsson, B.A., Lundkvist, H. and Staaf, H. (2000) Decomposition and nutrient release from *Picea abies* (L.) Karst. and *Pinus sylvestris* (L.) logging residues. *Forest Ecology and Management*, 126, 97–112.

Ikusima, I. (1978) Primary production and population ecology of the aquatic sedge *Lepironia articulata* in a tropical swamp, Tasek Bera, Malaysia. *Aquatic Botany*, 4, 269–280.

Ilnicki, P. and Zeitz, J (2003) Irreversible loss of organic soil functions after reclamation. In *Organic Soils and Peat Materials for Sustainable Agriculture*, ed. L.-E. Parent and P. Ilnicki. Boca Raton, FL: CRC Press, pp. 15–32.

Ingram, H.A.P. (1978) Soil layers in mires: function and terminology. *Journal of Soil Science*, 29, 224–227.

Ingram, H.A.P. (1982) Size and shape in raised mire ecosystems: a geophysical model. *Nature*, 297, 300–303.

Ingram, H.A.P. (1983) Hydrology. In *Ecosystems of the World 4A, Mires: Swamp, Bog, Fen and Moor*, ed. A.J.P. Gore. Amsterdam: Elsevier, pp. 67–158.

Ingram, H.A.P. and Bragg, O.M. (1984) The diplotelmic mire: some hydrological consequences reviewed. *Proceedings 7th International Peat Congress Dublin*, 5, 220–234.

IPCC (2001) *Climate Change 2001: Working Group I: The Scientific Basis*. Cambridge, UK: Cambridge University Press.

IPCC (2006) *2006 IPCC Guidelines for National Greenhouse Gas Inventories, prepared by the National Greenhouse Gas Inventories Programme*, ed. H.S. Eggleston, L. Buendia, K. Miwa, T. Ngara and K. Tanabe. Japan: IGES.

IPCC (2007) Climate Change 2007: The Physical Science Basis. Contribution of Working Group I to the Fourth Assessment Report of the Intergovernmental Panel on Climate Change. Geneva: IPCC.

Isermeyer, F., Otte, A., Christen, O. et al. (2008) *Nutzung von Biomasse zur Energiegewinnung*. Münster-Hiltrup: Landwirtschaftsverlag.

Isselin-Nondedeu, F., Rochefort, L. and Poulin, M. (2007) Long-term vegetation monitoring to assess the restoration success of a vacuum-mined peatland (Québec, Canada). *International Conference Peat and Peatlands 2007. Fédération des conservatoires d'espaces naturels/Pôle relais tourbières*, 23, 153–166.

Ivanov, K.E. (1981) *Water Movement in Mirelands*. London: Academic Press.

Iversen, P., Lee, D. and Rocha, M. (2014) *Understanding land use in the UNFCCC: summary for policymakers*.

Jaenicke, J., Englhart, S. and Siegert F. (2011) Monitoring the effect of restoration measures in Indonesian peatlands by radar satellite imagery. *Journal of Environmental Management*, 92, 630–638.

Jansson, R., Zinko, U., Merritt, D.M. and Nilsson, C. (2005) Hydrochory increases riparian plant species richness: a comparison between a free-flowing and a regulated river. *Journal of Ecology*, 93, 1094–1103.

Jauhiainen, J., Hooijer, A. and Page, S.E. (2012) Carbon dioxide emissions from an Acacia plantation on peatland in Sumatra, Indonesia. *Biogeosciences*, 9, 617–630.

Jauhiainen, S., Laiho, R. and Vasander, H. (2002) Ecohydrological and vegetational changes in a restored bog and fen. *Annales Botanici Fennici*, 39, 185–199.

Jax, K., Barton, D.N., Chan, K.M.A. et al. (2013) Ecosystem services and ethics. *Ecological Economics*, 93, 260–268.

JNCC (2011) *Towards an assessment of the state of UK peatlands*. Joint Nature Conservation Committee report No 445. Peterborough, UK: JNCC.

JNCC and DEFRA (2012) *UK Post-2010 Biodiversity Framework*. Peterborough, UK: JNCC.

Jobbágy, E.G. and Jackson, R.B.M. (2000) The vertical distribution of soil organic carbon and its relation to climate and vegetation. *Ecological Applications*, 10, 423–436.

Jobin, P., Caron, J., and Rochefort, L. (2014) Developing new potting mixes with *Sphagnum* fibers. *Canadian Journal of Soil Science*, 94, 585–593.

Johnston, C. E., Ewing, S. A., Harden, J. W. et al. (2014) Effect of permafrost thaw on CO_2

and CH$_4$ exchange in a western Alaska peatland chronosequence. *Environmental Research Letters*, 9, 085004.

Johnston, E. & Soulsby, C. (2000) Peatland conservation in Buchan, north-east Scotland: The historic context and contemporary issues. *Scottish Geographical Journal*, 116, 283–298.

Johnston, F., Henderson, S., Chen, Y. et al. (2012) Estimated global mortality attributable to smoke from landscape fires. *Environmental Health Perspective*, 120, 695–701.

Johnston, R. and Rosenberger, R. (2010) Methods, trends and controversies in contemporary benefit transfer. *Journal of Economic Surveys*, 24, 479–510.

Jones, J., Tinsley, H.M. and Brunning, R. (2007) Methodologies for assessment of the state of preservation of pollen and plant macrofossil remains in waterlogged deposits. *Environmental Archaeology* 12, 71–86.

Joosten, H. (1993) Denken wie ein Hochmoor: Hydrologische Selbstregulation von Hochmooren und deren Bedeutung für Wiedervernässung und Restauration. *Telma*, 23, 95–115.

Joosten, J.H.J. (1995) Time to regenerate: long-term perspectives of raised bog regeneration with special emphasis on palaeoecological studies. In *Restoration of Temperate Wetlands*, ed. B.D. Wheeler, S.C. Shaw, W.J. Fojt and R.A. Robertson. Chichester, UK: John Wiley, pp. 379–404.

Joosten, H. (2000) The role of peat in Finnish greenhouse gas balances. *IMCG Newsletter*, 2000/3, 2–4.

Joosten, H. (2007) The International Peat Society: fossil or renewable? An analysis of the IPS stand towards peat renewability and climate change. *IMCG Newsletter*, 2007/2, 4–19.

Joosten, H. (2008) What are peatlands? In *Assessment on Peatlands, Biodiversity and Climate Change*, ed. F. Parish, A. Sirin, D. Charman, H. Joosten, T. Minayeva, M. Silvius and L. Stringer. Kuala Lumpur and Wageningen, The Netherlands: Global Environment Centre and Wetlands International, pp. 8–19.

Joosten, H. (2009a) Burning peat or burning fingers? Peatland in the new EU Renewable Energy Directive. *IMCG Newsletter*, 2009/1, 16–21.

Joosten, H. (2009b) Human impacts: Farming, fire, forestry and fuel. In *The Wetlands Handbook*, ed. E. Maltby and T. Barker. Oxford: Blackwell Publishing, pp. 689–718.

Joosten, H. (2009c) *The Global Peatland CO2 Picture. Peatland Status and Drainage Associated Emissions in All Countries of the World*. Wageningen, The Netherlands: Wetlands International.

Joosten, H. (2011a) Selling peatland rewetting on the compliance carbon market. In *Carbon Credits from Peatland Rewetting. Climate – Biodiversity – Land Use. Science, Policy, Implementation and Recommendations of a Pilot Project in Belarus*, ed. F. Tanneberger and W. Wichtmann. Stuttgart, Germany: Schweizerbart, pp. 99–105.

Joosten, H. (2011b) Sensitising global conventions for climate change mitigation by peatlands. In *Carbon Credits from Peatland Rewetting. Climate – Biodiversity – Land Use. Science, Policy, Implementation and Recommendations of a Pilot Project in Belarus*, ed. F. Tanneberger and W. Wichtmann. Stuttgart, Germany: Schweizerbart, pp. 90–94.

Joosten, H. (2012) Zustand und Perspektiven der Moore weltweit. *Natur und Landschaft*, 87, 50–55.

Joosten, H. (2014) Croplands and paludicultures. In *Towards Climate-responsible Peatlands Management, Mitigation of Climate Change in Agriculture Series 9*, ed. R. Biancalani and A. Avagyan. Rome: FAO, pp. 41–43.

Joosten, H. and Clarke, D. (2002) *Wise Use of Mires and Peatlands: Background and Principles Including a Framework for Decision-making*. Saarijarvi: International Mire Conservation Group/International Peat Society.

Joosten, H. and Couwenberg, J. (2008) Peatlands and carbon. In *Assessment on Peatlands, Biodiversity and Climate Change*, ed. F. Parish, A. Sirin, D. Charman, H. Joosten, T. Minayeva, M. Silvius and L. Stringer. Kuala Lumpur and Wageningen, The Netherlands: Global Environment Centre and Wetlands International, pp. 99–117.

Joosten, H. and Schumann, M. (2007) Hydrogenetic aspects of peatland restoration in Tibet and Kalimantan. *Global Environmental Research*, 11, 195–204.

Joosten, H., Haberl, A. and Schumann, M. (2008) Degradation and restoration of peatlands on the Tibetan Plateau. *Peatlands International*, 2008/1, 31–35.

Joosten, H., Tapio-Biström, M.-L. and Tol, S. (2012) Peatlands: guidance for climate change mitigation by conservation, rehabilitation and sustainable use. Mitigation of climate change in agriculture series, No 5. Rome: FAO. (accessed 27 Feb 2014).

Joosten, H., Gaudig, G. and Krebs, M. (2013) Peat-free growing media: *Sphagnum* biomass. *Peatlands International*, 2013/1, 28–31.

Joosten, H., Brust, K., Couwenberg, J. *et al.* (2015a) MoorFutures®. Integration of additional ecosystem services (including biodiversity) into carbon credits: standard, methodology and transferability to other regions. Bonn, Germany: BfN Skripten 407, Bundesamt für Naturschutz.

Joosten, H., Gaudig, G., Krawczynski, R. *et al.* (2015b) Managing soil carbon in Europe: paludicultures as a new perspective for peatlands. In *Soil Carbon: Science, Management and Policy for Multiple Benefits*, ed. S. A. Banwart, E. Noellemeyer and E., Milne. SCOPE Series Vol. 71. Wallingford, UK: CABI, pp. 297–306.

Jordan, W.R., Gilpin, M.E. and Aber, J.D. (1987) *Restoration Ecology: A Synthetic Approach to Ecological Research*. Cambridge, UK: Cambridge University Press.

Jorgenson, M.T. and Osterkamp, T.E. (2005) Response of boreal ecosystems to varying modes of permafrost degradation. *Canadian Journal of Forest Research*, 35, 2100–2111.

Kaakinen, E., Kokko, A., Aapala, K. et al. (2008) Suot. [Mires]. In *Suomen luontotyyppien uhanalaisuus. Osa 1. Tulokset ja arvioinnin perusteet. [Assessment of Threatened Habitat Types in Finland. Part 1: Results and Basis for Assessment]*, ed. A. Raunio, A. Schulman and T. Kontula. Helsinki: Suomen ympäristökeskus. Suomen ympäristö 8/2008, pp. 75–109.

Kaczmarek, Z. (1998) *Human impact on Yellow River water management*. Interim Report IR-98-016/April. Laxenburg, Austria: International Institute for Applied Systems Analysis.

Kadlec, R.H. and Knight, R.L. (1996) *Treatment Wetlands*. Boca Raton, FL: CRC Press.

Kaiser, K., Miehe, G., Schoch, W. H., Zander, A. and Schlütz, F. (2006) Relief, soil and lost forests: Late Holocene environmental changes in Southern Tibet under human impact. *Zeitschrift für Geomorphologie*, 142, 149–173.

Kaiser, K., Schoch, W. H. and Miehe, G. (2007) Holocene paleosols and colluvial sediments in Northeast Tibet (Qinghai Province, China): Properties, dating and paleoenvironmental implications. *Catena*, 69, 91–102.

Kamermann, D. and Blankenburg, J. (2008) Erfahrungen und Ergebnisse eines Feldversuchs im Projekt „Torfmoos als nachwachsender Rohstoff". *Telma*, 38, 121–144.

Kartawinata, K. and Satjapradja, O. (1983) Prospects for agro-forestry and the rehabilitation of degraded forest land in Indonesia. *Mountain Research and Development*, 3, 414–417.

Kaul, F. (1995) The Gundestrup Cauldron reconsidered. *Acta Archaeologica*, 66, 1–38.

Kazoglu, Y. and Papanastasis, V.P. (2001) Effects of water buffalo grazing on the wet plant communities of the littoral zone of Lake Mikri Prespa. In *Neue Modelle* zu Maßnahmen der Landschaftsentwicklung mit großen Pflanzenfressern, ed. B. Gerken and M. Görner. Natur- und Kulturlandschaft 4. Höxter, Germany: Huxaria, pp. 348–351.

Keddy, P. (1999) Wetland restoration: the potential for assembly rules in the service of conservation. *Wetlands*, 19, 716–732.

Kennedy, G.W. and Price, J.S. (2005) A conceptual model of volume-change controls on the hydrology of cutover peats. *Journal of Hydrology*, 302, 13–27.

Kent, D.M. (2000) Evaluating wetland functions and values. In *Applied Wetlands Science and Technology*, ed. D.M. Kent. London: Lewis Publishers, pp. 221–242.

Kerr, A.J. and Bain, C. (1997) Perspectives on current action for biodiversity conservation. In *Biodiversity in Scotland: Status, Trends and Initiatives*, ed. A.C. Newton, J.A. Vickery, M.B. Usher and L.V. Fleming. Edinburgh, UK: HMSO, pp. 273–285.

Ketcheson, S. and Price, J. (2011) The impact of peatland restoration on the site hydrology of an abandoned block-cut bog. *Wetlands*, 31, 1263–1274.

Khazanov, A.M. (1984) *Nomads and the Outside World*. Cambridge, UK: Cambridge University Press.

Kim, J. and Verma, S.B. (1996) Surface exchange of water vapour between an open *Sphagnum* fen and the atmosphere. *Boundary-Layer Meteorology*, 79, 243–264.

Kimmel, K. and Mander, Ü. (2010) Ecosystem services of peatlands: implications for restoration *Progress in Physical Geography*, 34, 491–514.

Kirk, H., Conolly, C. and Freeland, J.R. (2011) Molecular genetic data reveal hybridization between *Typha angustifolia* and *Typha latifolia* across a broad spatial scale in eastern North America. *Aquatic Botany*, 95, 189–193.

Kivimäki, S.K., Yli-petäys, M. and Tuittila, E.S. (2008) Carbon sink function of sedge and *Sphagnum* patches in a restored cut-away peatland: increased functional diversity leads to higher production. *Journal of Applied Ecology*, 45, 921–929.

Klepper, O. (1992) Model study of the Negara River Basin to assess the regulating role of its wetlands. *Regulated Rivers: Research and Management*, 7, 311–325.

Klimanov, V.A. and Sirin, A.A. (1997) The dynamics of peat accumulation by mires of Northern Eurasia during the last three thousand years. In *Northern Forested Wetlands: Ecology and Management*, ed C.C. Trettin. Boca Raton, FL: Lewis Publishers/CRC Press, pp. 319–330.

Klimkowska, A. (2008) *Restoration of several degraded fens: ecological feasibility, opportunities and constraints*. PhD thesis. Antwerp, Belgium: University of Antwerp.

Klimkowska, A., Van Diggelen, R., Bakker, J.P. and Grootjans, A.P. (2007) Wet meadow restoration in Western Europe: a quantitative assessment of the effectiveness of several techniques. *Biological Conservation*, 140, 318–328.

Klimkowska, A., Kotowski, W., Van Diggelen, R. et al. (2010a) Vegetation re-development after fen meadow restoration by topsoil removal and hay transfer. *Restoration Ecology*, 18, 924–933.

Klimkowska, A., Van Diggelen, R, Grootjans, A.P. and Kotowski, W. (2010b) Prospects for fen meadow restoration on severely degraded fens. *Perspectives in Plant Ecology, Evolution and Systematics*, 12, 245–255.

Klimkowska, A., Dzierża, P., Kotowski, W. and Brzezińska, K. (2010c) Methods of limiting willow shrub re-growth after initial removal on fen meadows. *Journal for Nature Conservation*, 18, 12–21.

Klimkowska, A., Dzierża, P., Brzezińska, K., Kotowski, W. and Mędrzycki, P. (2010d) Can we balance the high costs of nature restoration with the method of topsoil removal? Case study from Poland. *Journal for Nature Conservation*, 18, 202–205.

Klimkowska, A., van der Elst, D.J.D. and Grootjans, A. P. (2015) Understanding long-term effects of topsoil removal in peatlands: overcoming thresholds for fen meadows restoration. *Applied Vegetation Science*, 18, 110–120.

Klinge, M. and Lehmkuhl, F. (2005) Untersuchungen zur holozänen Bodenentwicklung und Geomorphodynamik in Tibet – Hinweise auf klimatische und anthropogene Veränderungen. *Berliner Geographische Arbeiten*, 100, 81–91.

Klinger, L.F., Zimmerman, P.R., Greenberg, J.P. et al. (1994) Carbon trace gas fluxes along a successional gradient in the Hudson Bay lowland. *Journal of Geophysical Research*, 99, 1469–1494.

Kloskowski, J. and Krogulec, J. (1999) Habitat selection of aquatic warbler *Acrocephalus paludicola* in Poland: consequences for conservation of the breeding areas. *Vogelwelt*, 120, 113–120.

Knox, S.H., Sturtevant, C., Matthes, J.H. et al. (2015) Agricultural peatland restoration: effects of land-use change on greenhouse gas (CO_2 and CH_4) fluxes in the Sacramento–San Joaquin Delta. *Global Change Biology*, 21, 750–765.

Kobayashi, S. (2000) Initial Phase of Secondary Succession in the Exploited Peat Swamp Forest (*Shorea albida*) at Sungai Damit, Belait in Brunei Darussalam. *Proceedings of the International Symposium on Tropical Peatlands Bogor, Indonesia, 22–23 November 1999*, ed. T. Iwakuma, T. Inoue, T. Kohyama et al. Bogor, Indonesia: Hokkaido University and Indonesian Institute of Sciences, pp. 205–214.

Köbbing, J.F., Thevs, N. and Zerbe, S. (2013) The utilisation of reed (*Phragmites australis*): a review. *Mires and Peat*, 13, Art.1, 1–14.

Koehler, A.-K., Sottocornola, M. and Kiely, G. (2011) How strong is the current carbon sequestration of an Atlantic blanket bog? *Global Change Biology*, 17, 309–319.

Kolomytsev, V.A. (1993) *Bolotoobrazovatelnyj Process v Srednerajezhnyh Landshaftakh Vostochnoy Fennoscandii (The Peatland Formation Process in Middle Taiga Ecosystems of Eastern Fennoscandia)*. Petrozavodsk, Russia: Karelian Research Centre of the Russian Academy of Sciences (in Russian).

Komulainen, V.-M., Nykänen, H., Martikainen, P.J. and Laine, J. (1997) Short-term effect of restoration on vegetation succession and methane emissions from peatlands drained for forestry in southern Finland. *Canadian Journal of Forest Research*, 28, 402–411.

Komulainen, V.-M., Tuittila, E.-S., Vasander, H., Laine, J. (1999) Restoration of drained peatlands in southern Finland: initial effects on vegetation change and CO_2 balance. *Journal of Applied Ecology*, 36, 634–648.

Koontz, T.M. and Bodine, J. (2008) Implementing ecosystem management in public agencies: lessons from the US Bureau of Land Management and the Forest Service. *Conservation Biology*, 22, 60–69.

Korhola, A., Ruppel, M., Seppä, H. et al. (2010) The importance of northern peatland expansion to the late-Holocene rise of atmospheric methane. *Quaternary Science Reviews*, 29, 611–617.

Körner, C. (2003) *Alpine Plant Life: Functional Ecology of High Mountain Ecosystems*, 2nd edn. Heidelberg/New York: Springer Verlag.

Körner, C. (2008) The use of 'altitude' in ecological research. *Trends in Ecology and Evolution*, 22, 569–574.

Kosoy, N. and Corbera, E. (2010) Payments for ecosystem services as commodity fetishism. *Ecological Economics*, 69, 1228–1236.

Kosoy, N., Martinez-Tuna, M., Muradian, R. and Martinez-Alier, J. (2007) Payments for environmental services in watersheds: Insights from a comparative study of three cases in Central America. *Ecological Economics*, 61: 446–455.

Kotowski, W. (2002) *Fen communities. Ecological mechanisms and conservation strategies*. PhD thesis. Groningen, The Netherlands: Groningen University.

Kotowski, W. and Van Diggelen R. (2004) Fen vegetation composition in relation to light availability. *Journal of Vegetation Science*, 15, 583–594.

Kotowski, W., Dzierża, P. Czerwinski, M., Kozub, Ł. and Śnieg, S. (2013) Shrub removal facilitates recovery of wetland species in a rewetted fen. *Journal for Nature Conservation*, 21, 294–308.

Kotowski, W., Jabłońska, E. and Bartoszuk, H. (2013) Conservation management in fens: do large tracked mowers impact functional plant diversity? *Biological Conservation*, 167, 292–297.

Kottelat, M., Britz, R., Hui, T. H., and Witte, K.E. (2006) *Paedocypris*, a new genus of Southeast Asian cyprinid fish with a remarkable sexual dimorphism, comprises the world's smallest vertebrate. *Proceedings of the Royal Society B: Biological Sciences*, 273, 895–899.

Krawczynski, R., Biel, P. and Zeigert, H. (2008) Wasserbüffel als Landschaftspfleger. Erfahrungen zum Einsatz in Feuchtgebieten. *Naturschutz und Landschaftsplanung*, 40, 133–139.

Krutilla, J. (1967): Conservation reconsidered. *The American Economic Review*, 57, 777–786.

Krutilla, J. and Fisher, A. (1975) *The Economics of Natural Environments: Studies in the Valuation of Commodity and Amenity Resources*. Baltimore, MD: Johns Hopkins Press.

Kubacka, J., Oppel, S., Dyrcz, A. et al. (2014) Effect of mowing on productivity in the endangered Aquatic Warbler *Acrocephalus paludicola*. *Bird Conservation International*, 24, 45–58.

Kuhry P., Nicholson B.J., Gignac L.D., Vitt D.H. and Bayley S.E. (1993) Development of *Sphagnum*-dominated peatlands in boreal continental Canada. *Canadian Journal of Botany*, 71, 10–22.

Kulczyński, S. (1949) Torfowiska Polesia. Peat bogs of Polesie. *Memoires de l'Académie Polonaise des Sciences et des Lettres, Classe des Sciences Mathématiques et Naturelles, Sér. B*, 15, 1–359.

Kumaran, S. (2007) *Tasek Bera: Malaysia's First Ramsar site: A Booklet for Ecotourism at Tasek Bera*. Malaysia: Wetlands International.

Kunii, O., Kanagawa, S., Hojo, M. et al. (2000) Assessment of lung health among the inhabitants exposed to haze from the 1997 forest fire in Indonesia. *Respirology*, 5, 167.

Kuntze, H. (1982) Die Anthropogenese nordwestdeutscher Grünlandböden. *Abhandlungen Naturwissenschaftlicher Verein zu Bremen*, 39, 379–395.

Kuuluvainen, T., Aapala, K., Ahlroth, P. et al. (2002) Principles of ecological restoration of boreal forested ecosystems: Finland as an example. *Silva Fennica*, 36, 409–422.

La Vina, A.G.M., Labre, L., Ang, L. and de Leon, A. (2012) *The Road to Doha: The future of REDD-Plus, agriculture, and land-use change in the UNFCCC*. Working paper. London: Foundation for International Environmental Law and Development.

Lachmann, L., Marczakiewicz, P. and Grzywaczewski, G. (2010) Protecting Aquatic Warblers (*Acrocephalus paludicola*) through a landscape-scale solution for the management of fen peat meadows in Poland. *Grassland Science in Europe*, 15, 711–713.

Lafleur, P.M. and Roulet, N.T. (1992) A comparison of evaporation rates from two fens of the Hudson Bay Lowland. *Aquatic Botany*, 44, 59–69.

Lafleur, P.M. and Rouse, W.R. (1988) The influence of surface cover and climate on energy partitioning and evaporation in a subarctic wetland. *Boundary-Layer Meteorology*, 44, 327–347.

Lafleur, P.M., Hember, R. A., Admiral, S. W. and Roulet, N. T., (2005) Annual and seasonal variability in evapotranspiration and water table at a shrub-covered bog in southern Ontario, Canada. *Hydrological Processes*, 19, 3533–3550.

Lähteenoja, O., Reátegu, Y.R., Räsänen, M. et al. (2011) The large Amazonian peatland carbon sink in the subsiding Pastaza Marañón foreland basin, Peru. *Global Change Biology*, 18, 164–178.

Laiho, R. (2006) Decomposition in peatlands: reconciling seemingly contrasting results on the impacts of lowered water levels. *Soil Biology and Biochemistry*, 38, 2011–2024.

Laiho, R. and Finér, L. (1996) Changes in root biomass after water-level drawdown on pine mires in Southern Finland. *Scandinavian Journal of Forest Research*, 11, 251–260.

Laiho, R. and Laine, J. (1997) Tree stand biomass and carbon content in an age sequence of drained pine mires in southern Finland. *Forest Ecology and Management*, 93, 161–169.

Laiho, R., Vasander, H., Penttilä, T. and Laine, J. (2003) Dynamics of plant-mediated organic matter and nutrient cycling following long-term water-level drawdown in boreal peatlands. *Global Biogeochemical Cycles*, 17, 1053.

Laiho, R., Laine, J., Trettin, C. and Finér, L. (2004) Scots pine litter decomposition along soil moisture and nutrient gradients in peatland forests, and the effects of inter-annual weather variation. *Soil Biology and Biochemistry*, 36, 1095–1109.

Laine, A.M., Leppälä, M., Tarvainen, O. *et al.* (2011) Restoration of managed pine fens: effect on hydrology and vegetation. *Applied Vegetation Science*, 14, 340–349.

Laine, J., Vasander, H. and Laiho, R. (1995) Long-term effects of water level drawdown on the vegetation of drained pine mires in southern Finland. *Journal of Applied Ecology*, 32, 785–802.

Laine, J., Vasander, H., and Sallantaus, T. (1995) Ecological effects of peatland drainage for forestry. *Environmental Reviews*, 3, 286–303.

Laine, J., Silvola, J., Tolonen, K. *et al.* (1996) Effect of water-level drawdown on global climatic warming: northern peatlands. *Ambio*, 25, 179–184.

Laine, J., Laiho, R., Minkkinen, K. and Vasander, H. (2006) Forestry and Boreal peatlands. *Boreal Peatland Ecosystems*, ed. R.K. Wieder and D. Vitt. Berlin: Springer, pp. 331–357.

Lamentowicz, M., Van der Knaap, W.O., van Leeuwen, J.F.N. *et al.* (2010) A novel multi-proxy high-resolution approach to reconstructing past environmental change from an Alpine peat archive. *PAGES*, 18, 13–15.

Lamers, L.P.M., Farhoush, C., Van Groenendael, J.M. and Roelofs, J.G.M. (1999) Calcareous groundwater raises bogs: the concept of ombrotrophy revisited. *Journal of Ecology*, 87, 639–648.

Lamers, L.P.M., Smolders A.J.P. and Roelofs, J.G.M. (2002) The restoration of fens in the Netherlands. *Hydrobiologia*, 478, 107–130.

Lamers, L.P.M., Vile, M.A., Grootjans, A.P. *et al.* (2014) Ecological restoration of rich fens in Europe and North America: from trial and error to an evidence-based approach. *Biological Reviews*, 90, 182–203.

Langner, A. and Siegert, F. (2009) Spatiotemporal fire occurrence in Borneo over a period of 10 years. *Global Change Biology*, 15, 48–62.

Lappalainen, E. (1996) *Global Peat Resources*. Jyväskylä, Finland: International Peat Society.

Large, D.J., Spiro, B., Ferrat, M. *et al.* (2009) The influence of climate, hydrology and permafrost on Holocene peat accumulation at 3500 m on the eastern Qinghai–Tibetan Plateau. *Quaternary Science Reviews*, 28, 3303–3314.

LaRose, S., Price, J.S. and Rochefort, L. (1997) Rewetting of a cutover peatland: hydrologic assessment. *Wetlands*, 17, 416–423.

Larsson, L. (2007) Wetlands and major infrastructural programmes: prehistoric wetland sites in excavation projects in Scania, southernmost Sweden. *Archaeology from the Wetlands: Recent Perspectives: Proceedings of the 11th WARP Conference Society of Antiquaries Scotland*, 31–39.

Laurila, T., Lohila, A., Aurela, M. *et al.* (2007) Ecosystem-level carbon sink measurements on forested peatlands. In *Greenhouse Impacts of the Use of Peat and Peatlands in Finland*, ed. S. Sarkkola. Helsinki, Finland: Ministry of Agriculture and Forestry. pp. 38–40.

Lavoie, C. and Rochefort, L. (1996) The natural revegetation of a harvested peatland in southern Québec: a spatial and dendroecological analysis. *Écoscience*, 3, 101–111.

Lavoie, C., Saint-Louis, A. and Lachance, D. (2005) Vegetation dynamics on an abandoned vacuum-mined peatland: five years of monitoring. *Wetlands Ecology and Management*, 13, 621–633.

Lawton, J.H., Brotherton, P.N.M., Brown, V.K. et al. (2010) *Making space for nature: a review of England's wildlife sites and ecological network.* Report to Defra. UK. London: DEFRA.

Le Quéré, C., Moriarty, R., Andrew, R. M. et al. (2014). Global Carbon Budget 2014. *Earth System Science Data Discussions*, 6, 1–90.

Lehmkuhl, F. and Liu, S. (1994) An outline of physical geography including Pleistocene glacial landforms of Eastern Tibet (Provinces Sichuan and Qinghai). *GeoJournal*, 34, 7–29.

Leopold, A. (1949) *A Sand County Almanac, and Sketches Here and There*. Oxford, UK: Oxford University Press.

Li, C. (1989) *Sichuan Yak*. Chengdu, China: Sichuan Nationality Press.

Li, C., Wang, L., Hu, Y. and Wei, Z. (2010) Changes in ecosystem service values in Zoige Plateau, China. *Agriculture Ecosystems and Environment*, 139, 766–770.

Li, W., Dickinson, R.E., Fu, R. et al. (2007) Future precipitation changes and their implications for tropical peatlands. *Geophysical Research Letters*, 34, L01403.

Liew, S. C., Kwoh, L. K., Lim, O. K. and Lim, H. (2001) Remote sensing of fire and haze. In *Forest Fires and Regional Haze in Southeast Asia*, ed. P. Eaton and M. Radojevic) New York: Nova Science Publishers, pp. 67–89.

Lillie, M. and Cheetham, J.L. (2002) *Watertable monitoring at Flag Fen, Peterborough.* Report SAS0FF/02-01. Hull, UK: Wetland Archaeology and Environments Research Centre, University of Hull.

Limin, S.H., Jentha and Ermiasi, Y. (2007) History of the development of tropical peatland in Central Kalimantan, Indonesia. *Tropics*, 16, 291–301.

Limpens, J., Berendse, F., Blodau, C. et al. (2008) Peatlands and the carbon cycle: from local processes to global implications: a synthesis. *Biogeosciences*, 5, 1475–1491.

Lindholm, T. and Heikkilä, R. (eds) (2006) *Finland: Land of Mires, The Finnish Environment 23.* Helsinki: Finnish Environment Institute.

Lindholm, T. and Heikkilä, R. (2012) Mires from pole to pole. *The Finnish Environment*, 38, 1–420.

Lindsay, R. (1993) Peatland conservation – from cinders to Cinderella. *Biodiversity and Conservation*, 2, 528–540.

Lindsay, R. (1995) *Bogs: The Ecology, Classification and Conservation of Ombrotrophic Mires*. Edinburgh, UK: Scottish Natural Heritage.

Lindsay, R. (2010) *Peatbogs and carbon: a critical synthesis to inform policy development in oceanic peat bog conservation and restoration in the context of climate change.* Technical Report. London:University of East London, RSPB, Natural England, SNH, CCW and the Forestry Commission. http://hdl.handle.net/10552/1144 (accessed 27 February 2014).

Lindsay, R., Charman, D.J., Everingham, F. et al. (1988) *The Flow Country: The Peatlands of Caithness and Sutherland.* Peterborough, UK: Nature Conservancy Council.

Litaor, M.I., Reichmann, O. and Shenker, M. (2011) Genesis, classification and human modification of peat and mineral-organic soils, Hula Valley, Israel. *Mires and Peat*, 9, Art. 1, 1–9.

Littleton, C.S. (2005) *Gods, Goddesses, and Mythology*. New York: Marshall Cavendish.

Littlewood, N., Anderson, P., Artz, R. et al. (2010) *Peatland Biodiversity*. Edinburgh, UK: IUCN UK Peatland Programme.

Liu, J., Zhang, Y. and Xin, G. (1980) Relationship between numbers and degree of harmfulness of the plateau pika. *Acta Zoologica Sinica*, 26, 378–385.

Liu, K.B. and Qiu, H.L. (1994) Late-Holocene pollen records of vegetational changes in China: Climate or human disturbance? *TAO*, 5, 393–410.

Locky, D.A. (2011) *Wetlands, Land Use, and Policy: Alberta's Keystone Ecosystem at a Crossroads*. Policy position paper published by the Edmonton, Canada: Alberta Institute of Agrologists.

Lohila, A., Minkkinen, K. Laine, J. *et al.* (2010) Forestation of boreal peatlands: impacts of changing albedo and greenhouse gas fluxes on radiative forcing. *Journal of Geophysical Research*, 115, G04011.

Long, R. and Ma, Y.S. (1997) Qinghai's yak production systems. In *Conservation and Management of Yak Genetic Diversity*, ed. D.J. Miller, S.R. Craig and G.M Rana. Kathmandu: International Centre for Integrated Mountain Development, pp. 105–114.

Lu, T., Wu, N. and Luo, P. (2009) Sedentarization of Tibetan nomads. *Conservation Biology*, 23, 1074.

Lucchese, M., Waddington, J., Poulin, M. *et al.* (2010) Organic matter accumulation in a restored peatland: evaluating restoration success. *Ecological Engineering*, 36, 482–488.

Ludwig, G.X. (2007) *Mechanisms of population declines in boreal forest grouse*. PhD thesis. Jyväskylä, Finland: University of Jyväskylä.

Lunn, A. and Burlton, B. (2010) *The Border Mires: A Conservation History*. Bellingham, UK: Border Mires Committee.

Luoto, M., Fronzek, S. and Zuidhoff, F.S. (2004) Spatial modelling of palsa mires in relation to climate in northern Europe. *Earth Surface Processes and Landforms*, 29, 1373–1387.

Lynch, O. and E. Harwell (2002) *Whose resources? Whose common good? Towards a new paradigm of environmental justice and the national interest in Indonesia*. London: Center for International Environment Law.

Lyon, G. (2010) *Draft Report on the Future of the Common Agricultural Policy After 2013*. Committee on Agriculture and Rural Development. Brussels: European Commission.

MA Millennium Ecosystem Assessment. (2005) *Ecosystems and Human well-being: Synthesis*. Washington, DC: Island Press.

MacDonald, G.M., Beilman, D.W., Kremenetski, K.V. *et al.* (2006) Rapid early development of circumarctic peatlands and atmospheric CH_4 and CO_2 variations. *Science*, 314, 285–288.

Mace, G.M., Norris, K. and Fitter, A.H. (2012) Biodiversity and ecosystem services: a multilayered relationship. *Trends in Ecology and Evolution*, 27, 24–31.

Madaras, M., Grootjans, A.P., Šefferová-Stanová, V., *et al.* (2012) Calcareous spring fen Belianske lúky Meadows; the largest spring fen in North Western Europe. In *Calcareous Mires of Slovakia; Landscape Setting, Management and Restoration Prospects*, ed. A.P. Grootjans, A.M.J. Jansen and V. Stanova. Zeist, The Netherlands: KNNV Publishing, pp. 41–66.

Mäkiranta P., Hytönen J., Aro L. *et al.* (2007) Soil greenhouse gas emissions from afforested organic soil croplands and cutaway peatlands. *Boreal Environment Research*, 12, 159–175.

Mališauskas, A. P. and Kutra, S (2008) Nitrate variation in drainage water under degradation of peat soils. *Ekologija*, 54, 239–244.

Maljanen, M., Sigurdsson, B.D., Guðmundsson, J. *et al.* (2010) Greenhouse gas balances of managed peatlands in the Nordic countries: present knowledge and gaps. *Biogeosciences*, 7, 2711–2738.

Mälson, K. and Rydin, H. (2007) The regeneration capabilities of bryophytes for rich fen restoration. *Biological Conservation*, 135, 435–442.

Mälson, K. and Rydin, H. (2009) Competitive hierarchy, but no competitive exclusions in experiments with rich fen bryophytes. *Journal of Bryology*, 31, 41–45.

Maltby, E. (1997) Peatlands: the science case for conservation and sound management. In *Conserving Peatlands*, ed. L. Parkyn, R.E. Stoneman and H.A.P. Ingram. Wallingford, UK: CAB International, pp. 121–131.

Maltby, E. and Acreman, M.C. (2011) Ecosystem services of wetlands: pathfinder for a new paradigm. *Hydrological Sciences Journal*, 56, 1341–1359.

Maltby, E., Legg, C.J. and Proctor, M.C. (1990) The ecology of severe moorland fire on the North York Moors: effects of the 1976 fires and subsequent surface and vegetation development. *Journal of Ecology*, 78, 490–518.

Manby, T. (2003) The Upper Palaeolithic and Mesolithic periods in Yorkshire. In *The Archaeology of Yorkshire: An Assessment at the Beginning of the 21st Century*, ed. T.G. Manby, S. Moorhouse and P. Ottaway. Occasional Paper No. 3. Leeds: Yorkshire Archaeological Society, pp. 31–44.

Marangon, F., Tempesta, T. and Visintin, F. (2002) Turismo e attività ricreative nelle aree protette italiane: un quadro conoscitivo ancora inadeguato. Paper. II Conferenza Nazionale delle Aree Naturali Protette.

Marlon, J.R., Bartlein, P.J., Carcaillet, C. et al. (2008) Climate and human influences on global biomass burning over the past two millennia. *Nature Geoscience*, 1, 697–702.

Martikainen, P.J., Nykänen, H., Crill, P. and Silvola, J. (1993) Effect of a lowered water table on nitrous oxide fluxes from northern peatlands. *Nature*, 366, 51–53.

Martikainen, P.J., Nykänen, H., Alm, J. and Silvola, J. (1995) Change in fluxes of carbon dioxide, methane and nitrous oxide due to forest drainage of mire sites of different trophy. *Plant and Soil*, 168–169, 571–577.

Martin, P. and Robinson, M. (2003) The lint-holes of Bankhead Moss: Conserving the past to preserve the future? *History Scotland*, January/February, 29–36.

Martin-Ortega, J., Allott, T.E., Glenk, K. and Schaafsma, M. (2014) Valuing water quality improvements from peatland restoration: Evidence and challenges. *Ecosystem Services*, 9, 34–43.

Masing V.V. (1974) Aktualnyje problemy klassifikacii i terminologii v bolovedenii (Some topical questions of classification and terminology in mire science) in: *Tipy bolot SSSR i principy ikh klassifikacii (Mire types of the USSR and principles of their classification)*. Leningrad: Nauka, pp. 6–12.

Matilainen, A., Gjessing, E. T., Lahtinen, T. et al. (2011) An overview of the methods used in the characterization of natural organic matter (NOM) in relation to drinking water treatment. *Chemosphere*, 83, 1431–1442.

Matthews, H.D., Eby, M., Ewen, T., Friedlingstein, P. and Hawkins, B.J. (2007) What determines the magnitude of carbon cycle-climate feedbacks? *Global Biogeochemical Cycles*, 21, GB2012.

Mauquoy, D. and Barber, K. (1999) Evidence for climatic deteriorations associated with the decline of *Sphagnum imbricatum* Hornsch. Ex. Russ. in six ombrotrophic mires from northern England and the Scottish Borders. *The Holocene*, 9, 423–427.

Mauquoy, D. and Yeloff, D. (2008) Raised peat bog development and possible responses to environmental changes during the mid-late-Holocene. Can the palaeoecological record be used to predict the nature and response of raised peat bogs to future climate change? *Biodiversity and Conservation*, 17, 2139–2151.

Mauquoy, D., Engelkes, T., Groot, M.H.M. et al. (2002) High-resolution records of late-Holocene climate change and carbon accumulation in two north-west European ombrotrophic peat bogs. *Palaeogeography, Palaeoclimatology, Palaeoecology*, 186, 275–310.

Mazerolle, M.J., Desrochers, A. and Rochefort, L. (2005) Landscape characteristics influence pond occupancy by frogs after accounting for detectability. *Ecological Applications*, 15, 824–834.

McBride, A., Diack, I. Droy, N. et al. (2010) *The Fen Management Handbook*. Perth: Scottish Natural Heritage.

McCarter, C.P. and Price, J.S. (2013) The hydrology of the Bois-des-Bel bog peatland restoration: 10 years post-restoration. *Ecological Engineering*, 55, 73–81.

McClymont, E.L., Pendall, E. and Nichols, J. (2010) Stable isotopes and organic geochemistry in peat: tools to investigate past hydrology, temperature and biogeochemistry. *PAGES*, 18, 15–18.

McDermott, C. (2007) 'Plain and bog, bog and wood, Wood and bog, bog and plain!': peatland archaeology in Ireland. WARP Occasional Paper 18. *Proceedings of the 11th WARP Conference Society of Antiquaries Scotland*, 17–30.

McGrath, M., and Smith, M. (2006) Sustainable Catchment Management Programme (SCaMP): from hilltop to tap in. *Proceedings of the BHS Ninth National Hydrology Symposium*, 91–96.

McInnes, R., Simpson, M., Wallis, M., Harrison, A. and Deasy, D. (2007) *Wetland Hydrogeomorphic Classification for Scotland*. Final Report on Project WFD66. Edinburgh: SNIFFER.

McMorrow, J., Lindley, S., Aylen, J. *et al.* (2009) Moorland wildfire risk, visitors and climate change: patterns, prevention and policy. In *Drivers of Change in Upland Environments*, ed. A. Bonn, T. Allott, K. Hubacek, and J. Stewart. London and New York: Routledge, pp. 404–431.

Meehl, G.A. and Tebaldi, C. (2004) More intense, more frequent, and longer lasting heat waves in the 21st century. *Science*, 305, 994–997.

Meentemeyer, V. (1984) The geography of organic decomposition rates. *Annals of the Association of American Geographers*, 74, 551–560.

Mellars, P., and Dark, S.P. (1998) *Star Carr in Context: New Archaeological and Palaeoecological Investigations at the Early Mesolithic Site of Star Carr, North Yorkshire*. Cambridge, UK: McDonald Institute Monographs. McDonald Institute for Archaeological Research.

Meredith, D. (1999) Landscape or Mindscape? Seamus Heaney's Bogs. *Irish Geography*, 32, 126–134.

Metsähallitus (1999) *The principles of protected area management in Finland. Guidelines on the aims, function and management of state-owned protected areas*. Metsähallituksen luonnonsuojelujulkaisuja Sarja B No 54 (Nature Protection Publications of the Finnish Forest and Park Service, Series B No. 54). Vantaa, Finland: Metsähallitus (Finnish Forest Park Service).

Michaelis, D. (2002) *Die spät- und nacheiszeitliche Entwicklung der natürlichen Vegetation von Durchströmungsmooren in Mecklenburg-Vorpommern am Beispiel der Recknitz*. PhD thesis. Berlin: Cramer.

Michell, G. (1977) *The Hindu Temple: An Introduction to its Meaning and Forms*. Chicago, IL: University of Chicago Press.

Middleton, B., Van Diggelen, R. and Jensen, K. (2006) Seed dispersal in fens. *Applied Vegetation Science*, 9, 279–284.

Miehe, G., Miehe, S., Schlütz, F., Kaiser, K. and Duo, L. (2006) Palaeoecological and experimental evidence of former forests and woodlands in the treeless desert pastures of Southern Tibet (Lhasa, A.R. Xizang, China). *Palaeogeography, Palaeoclimatology, Palaeoecology*, 242, 54–67.

Miettinen, J. and Liew, S.C. (2010) Degradation and development of peatlands in Peninsular Malaysia and in the islands of Sumatra and Borneo since 1990. *Land Degradation and Development*, 21, 285–296.

Miettinen, J., Shi, C. and Liew, S.C. (2011) Deforestation rates in insular Southeast Asia between 2000 and 2010. *Global Change Biology*, 17, 2261–2270.

Miettinen, J., Hooijer, A., Shi, C. *et al.* (2012a) Extent of industrial plantations on Southeast Asian peatlands in 2010 with analysis of historical expansion and future projections. *GCB Bioenergy*, 4, 908–918.

Miettinen, J., Shi, C. and Liew, S.C. (2012b) Two decades of destruction in Southeast Asia's peat swamp forests. *Frontiers in Ecology and the Environment*, 10, 124–128.

Mighall, T.M., Abrahams, P.W., Grattan, J.P. *et al.* (2002) Geochemical evidence for atmospheric pollution derived from prehistoric copper mining at Copa Hill, Cwmystwyth, mid-Wales. *The Science of the Total Environment*, 292, 69–80.

Minayeva, T., Bragg, O., Cherednichenko, O. et al. (2008) Peatlands and biodiversity. In *Assessment on Peatlands, Biodiversity and Climate Change: Main Report*, ed. F. Parish, A. Sirin, D. Charman et al. Kuala Lumpur, Malaysia and Wageningen, The Netherlands: Global Environment Centre and Wetlands International, pp. 60–98.

Minayeva, T., Sirin, A.A. and Stracher, G.B. (2013) The peat fires of Russia. In *Coal and Peat Fires: A Global Perspective*, ed. G.B. Stracher, A. Prakash and E.V. Sokol. Amsterdam: Elsevier, pp. 376–394.

Minayeva, T. Yu. and Sirin, A.A. (2012) Peatland biodiversity and climate change. *Biology Bulletin Reviews*, 2, 164–175.

Minkkinen, K. and Laine, J. (1998) Long-term effect of forest drainage on the peat carbon stores of pine mires in Finland. *Canadian Journal of Forest Research*, 28, 1267–1275.

Minkkinen, K. and Laine, J. (2006) Vegetation heterogeneity and ditches create spatial variability in methane fluxes from peatlands drained for forestry. *Plant and Soil*, 285, 289–304.

Minkkinen, K., Vasander, H., Jauhiainen, S., Karsisto, M. and Laine, J. (1999) Post-drainage changes in vegetation composition and carbon balance in Lakkasuo mire, Central Finland. *Plant and Soil*, 207, 107–120.

Minkkinen, K., Korhonen, R., Savolainen, I. and Laine, J. (2002) Carbon balance and radiative forcing of Finnish peatlands 1900–2100: the impact of forestry drainage. *Global Change Biology*, 8, 785–799.

Minkkinen, K., Byrne, K.A., and Trettin, C. (2008). Climate impacts of peatland forestry. In *Peatlands and Climate Change*, ed. M. Strack. Jyväskylä, Finland: International Peat Society, pp. 98–122.

Mitchell, F.J.G. (2005) How open were European Primeval forests? Hypothesis testing using palaeoecological data. *Journal of Ecology*, 93, 168–177.

Mitchell, F.J.G. (2011) Exploring vegetation in the fourth dimension. *Trends in Ecology and Evolution*, 26, 45–52.

Mitsch, W.J. and Gosselink, J.G. (2007) *Wetlands*. 4th edn. Chichester, UK: John Wiley.

MLUV MV (2009) *Konzept zum Schutz und zur Nutzung der Moore*. Ministerium für Landwirtschaft, Umwelt und Verbraucherschutz Mecklenburg-Vorpommern, Schwerin.

Moen, A. (1995) Vegetational changes in boreal rich fens induced by haymaking; management plan for the Sølendet Nature Reserve. In *Restoration of Temperate Wetlands*, ed. B.D. Wheeler, S.C. Shaw, W.J. Fojt and R.A. Robertson. Chichester, UK: John Wiley, pp. 167–181.

Moir, J. and Letts, J. (1999) *Thatch, Thatching in England 1790–1940*. English Heritage Research Transactions, Volume 5. London: James and James.

Money, R.P. and Wheeler, B.D. (1999) Some critical questions concerning the restorability of damaged raised bogs. *Applied Vegetation Science*, 2, 107–116.

Monteith, D.T., Stoddard, J.L., Evans, C.D. et al. (2007) Dissolved organic carbon trends resulting from changes in atmospheric deposition chemistry. *Nature* 450, 537–540.

Moore, C. (2000) A wooden vessel from Co. Westmeath, Ireland. *News WARP* 28, 7–8.

Moore, P. (1984) The classification of mires: an introduction. In *European Mires*, ed. P. Moore. London: Academic Press, pp. 1–10.

Moore, P.D. (1989) The ecology of peat-forming processes: a review. *International Journal of Coal Geology*, 12, 89–103.

Moore, P.D. (1993) The origin of blanket mire, revisited. In *Climate Change and Human Impact on the Landscape*, ed. F.M. Chambers. London: Chapman and Hall, pp. 217–224.

Moore, P. D. and Bellamy, D.J. (1974) *Peatlands*. London: Elek.

Moore, T., Blodau, C., Turunen, J., Roulet, N. and Richard, P.J.H. (2005) Patterns of nitrogen and sulfur accumulation and retention in ombrotrophic bogs, eastern Canada. *Global Change Biology*, 11, 356–367.

Moore, T.R., Bubier, J.L., Frolking, S.E., Lafleur, P.M. and Roulet, N.T. (2002) Plant biomass and production and CO_2 exchange in an ombrotrophic bog. *Journal of Ecology*, 90, 25–36.

Morecroft, M.D., Crick, H.Q.P., Duffield, S.J. and Macgregor, N.A. (2012) Resilience to climate change: translating principles into practice. *Journal of Applied Ecology*, 49, 547–551.

Morison, J., Venguelova, E., Broadmeadow, S. et al. (2010) *Understanding the GHG Implications of Forestry on Peat Soils in Scotland*. Roslin, UK: Forest Research.

Morris, J. and Camino, M. *Economic assessment of freshwater, wetland and floodplain ecosystem services*. UK National Ecosystem Assessment Working Paper. Bedford, UK: Cranfield University.

Morris, J., Bailey, A.P., Lawson, C.S. et al. (2008) The economic dimensions of integrating flood management and agri-environment through washland creation: a case from Somerset, England. *Journal of Environmental Management* 88, 372–381.

Morris, P. J., Waddington, J. M., Benscoter, B. W., & Turetsky, M. R. (2011). Conceptual frameworks in peatland ecohydrology: looking beyond the two-layered (acrotelm–catotelm) model. *Ecohydrology*, 4, 1–11.

Morrogh-Bernard, H., Husson, S., Page, S.E. and Rieley, J.O. (2003) Population status of the Bornean orang-utan (*Pongo pygmaeus*) in the Sebangau peat swamp forest, Central Kalimantan, Indonesia. *Biological Conservation*, 110, 141–152.

Moxey, A. and Moran, D. (2014) UK peatland restoration: some economic arithmetic. *Science of the Total Environment*, 484, 114–120.

Müller, J. and Sweers, W. (2016) The production of fodder in paludiculture. In *Paludiculture – Productive use of wet peatlands*, ed. W. Wichtmann, C. Schröder and H. Joosten. Stuttgart, Germany: Schweizerbart, pp. 39–42.

Müller-Wille, M. (1999) *Opferkulte der Germanen und Slawen, Opfer- und Hortfunde in Mooren*. Stuttgart, Germany: Theiss-Verlag.

Musa, S. and Parlan, I. (2002) The 1997/98 forest fire experience in Peninsular Malaysia. In *Proceedings of the Workshop on Prevention and Control of Fire in Peatlands, 19–21 March 2002, Kuala Lumpur*, ed. F. Parish, E. Padmanabhan, C.L. Lee and H. C. Thang. Kuala Lumpur and Wageningen, The Netherlands: Global Environment Centre and Wetlands International, pp. 69–74.

Muster, C., Gaudig, G., Krebs, M. & Joosten, H. (2015) Sphagnum farming: the promised land for peat bog species? *Biodiversity and Conservation*, 24, 1989–2009.

Mutalib, A.A., Lim, J.S., Wong, M.H. and Koonvai, L. (1992). Characterization, distribution and utilization of peat in Malaysia. In *Proceedings of the International Symposium on Tropical Peatland. Malaysia, Kuching, Sarawak, 1991*, ed. S.L. Aminuddin, B. Tan, J. Aziz et al. Kuala Lumpur, Malaysian Agricultural Research and Development Institute, pp. 7–16.

Muuß, U. (1996) Anreicherungspflanzungen im tropischen Feuchtwald Sumatras – eine waldbauliche Herausforderung. *Forstarchiv*, 67, 65–70.

Myers, N., Mittermeier, R.A., Mittermeier, C.G., da Fonseca, G.A.B. and Kent, J. (2000) Biodiversity hotspots for conservation priorities. *Nature*, 403, 853–58.

Myhre, G., Shindell, D., Bréon F.-M. et al. (2013) Anthropogenic and natural radiative forcing. In *Climate Change 2013: The Physical Science Basis. Contribution of Working Group I to the Fifth Assessment Report of the Intergovernmental Panel on Climate Change*, ed. T.F. Stocker, D. Qin, G.-K. Plattner et al. Cambridge, UK: Cambridge University Press, pp. 659–740.

Nash, R.F. (1989) *The Rights of Nature. A History of Environmental Ethics*. Madison, Wisconsin: University of Wisconsin Press.

Natural England (2009) *Experiencing landscapes: capturing the cultural services and experiential qualities of landscape*. Natural England Commissioned Report NECR024. Sheffield, UK: Natural England.

Natural England (2014) *The Restoration of Blanket Bog and the Effects of Managed

Burning on Peatlands. Natural England Uplands Delivery Review Programme Upland Principles –Summary guidance. Peterborough, UK: Natural England.

NAWCA (1989) *North American Wetlands Conservation Act*. www.fws.gov/birdhabitat/Grants/NAWCA/Act.shtm (accessed 25 March 2012).

Nayak, D.R., Miller, D., Nolan, A., Smith, P., and Smith, J.U. (2010) Calculating carbon budgets of wind farms on Scottish peatlands. *Mires and Peat*, 4, Art. 9, 1–12.

NEGTAP (National Expert Group on Transboundary Air Pollution) (2001) *Transboundary Air Pollution: Acidification, Eutrophication and Ground-level Ozone in the UK*. Edinburgh, UK: NEGTAP.

Neugarten, R.A., Wolf, S.A., Stedman, R.C. and Tear, T.H. (2011) Integrating ecological and socioeconomic monitoring of working forests. *Bioscience*, 61, 631–637.

Newberry, J., Chambers, F.M. and Karofeld, E. (2007) Peat multi-proxy data from Männikjärve bog as indicators of Late Holocene climate changes in Estonia. *Boreas*, 36, 20–37.

Ng, P.K.L. (1994) Peat swamp fishes of Southeast Asia: diversity under threat. *Wallaceana*, 73, 1–5.

Nilsson, M., Sagerfors, J., Buffam, I. et al. (2008). Contemporary carbon accumulation in a boreal oligotrophic minerogenic mire: a significant sink after accounting for all C-fluxes. *Global Change Biology*, 14, 2317–2332.

Nordhaus, W. (2007) A review of the Stern review on the economics of climate change. *Journal of Economic Literature*, XLV, 686–702.

Novak, M, Brizova, E., Adamova, M., Erbanova, L. and Bottrell, S.H. (2008) Accumulation of organic carbon over the past 150 years in five freshwater peatlands in western and central Europe. *Science of the Total Environment*, 390, 425–436.

Noyce, G.L., Varner, R.K., Bubier, J.L. and Frolking S. (2014) Effect of *Carex rostrata* on seasonal and interannual variability in peatland methane emissions, *Journal of Geophysical Research*, 119, 24–34.

NPWS (2010) *Ireland 4th National Report to the Convention on Biological Diversity*. https://www.cbd.int/doc/world/ie/ie-nr-04-en.pdf (accessed 27 February 2014).

Nuñez, C., Macelo, A. and Ezcurra, C. (1999) Species associations and nurse plant effects in patches of high-Andean vegetation. *Journal of Vegetation Science*, 10, 357–364.

Nuyim, T. (2000) Whole aspects of nature and management of peat swamp forest in Thailand. *Proceedings of the International Symposium on Tropical Peatlands Bogor, Indonesia, 22–23 November 1999*, ed. T. Iwakuma, T. Inoue, T. Kohyama et al. Bogor: Hokkaido University and Indonesian Institute of Sciences, pp. 109–117.

Nuyim, T. (2005) *Manual on Peat Swamp Forest Rehabilitation and Planting in Thailand*. Kuala Lumpur, Malaysia: Global Environmental Centre and Wetlands International – Thailand Office.

NWWG (1997) *The Canadian Wetland Classification System*, 2nd edn. Waterloo, Canada: University of Waterloo.

Nykänen, H., Vasander, H., Huttunen, J.T. and Martikainen, P.J. (2002) Effect of experimental nitrogen load on methane and nitrous oxide fluxes on ombrotrophic boreal peatland. *Plant and Soil*, 242, 147–155.

O' Connell, M. and Molloy, K. (2001) Farming and woodland dynamics in Ireland during the Neolithic. *Proceedings of the Royal Irish Academy Series B: Biology and Environment*, 101, 99–128.

O'Brien, H.E., Labadz, J.C., Butcher, D.P., Billet, M., and Midgely, N.G. (2008) Impact of catchment management on dissolved organic carbon and stream flows in the Peak District, Derbyshire, UK. *Proceedings of the 10th National Hydrology Symposium*. Exeter, UK: British Hydrological Society.

O'Dea, P. (2008) *LIFE Project Number LIFE02 NAT/IRL/8490 Technical Final Report. Appendix 8 Findings of water monitoring at four demonstration blanket bog sites*. http://www.irishbogrestorationproject.ie/project_promotion/project_reports_appendices.html (accessed 27 November 2015).

Ojanen, P., Minkkinen, K., Alm, J. and Penttilä, T. (2010) Soil-atmosphere CO_2, CH_4 and N_2O fluxes in boreal forestry drained peatlands. *Forest Ecology and Management*, 260, 411–421.

Olde Venterink, H., Kardel, I., Kotowski, W., Peeters, W. and Wassen, M.J. (2009) Long-term effects of drainage and hay-removal on nutrient dynamics and limitation in the Biebrza mires. *Biogeochemistry*, 93, 235–252.

Oleszczuk, R., Regina, K., Szajdak, L, Höper, H. and Maryganova, V. (2008) Impacts of agricultural utilization of peat soils on the greenhouse balance. In *Peatlands and Climate Change*, ed. M. Strack. Helsinki, Finland: IPS, pp. 70–97.

Oliver, T.H., Smithers, R.J., Bailey, S., Walmsley, C.A. and Watts, K. (2012) A decision framework for considering climate change adaptation in biodiversity conservation planning. *Journal of Applied Ecology*, 49, 1247–1255.

Olivier, A. (2004) Great expectations: the English Heritage approach to the management of the historic environment in England's wetlands. *Journal of Wetland Archaeology*, 4, 155–168.

Olivier, A. (2013) International and national wetland management policies. In *The Oxford Handbook of Wetland Archaeology*, ed. F. Menotti and A. O'Sullivan. Oxford, UK: Oxford University Press, pp. 687–703.

OMNR (Ontario Ministry of Natural Resources) (1994) *Ontario Wetland Evaluation System. Southern Manual*, 3rd edn. NEST Technical Manual TM-002. Toronto, Canada: Ontario Ministry of Natural Resources.

Overpeck, J.T., Otto-Bliesner, B.L., Miller, G.H. et al. (2006) Paleoclimatic evidence for future ice-sheet instability and rapid sea-level rise. *Science*, 311, 1747–1750.

Oxbrough, A.G., Gittings, T., O'Halloran, J., Giller, P.S. and Kelly, T.C. (2006) The initial effects of afforestation on the ground-dwelling spider fauna of Irish peatlands and grasslands. *Forest Ecology and Management*, 237, 478–491.

Paavilainen, E. and Päivänen, J. (1995) *Peatland Forestry: Ecology and Principles*. Berlin: Springer.

PACEC (2006) *The economic and environmental impact of sporting shooting. Report on behalf of BASC, CA, and CLA and in association with GCT*. Cambridge, UK: PACEC (Public and Corporate Economic Consultants).

Page, S.E., Siegert, F., Rieley, J.O. et al. (2002) The amount of carbon released from peat and forest fires in Indonesia during 1997. *Nature*, 420, 61–65.

Page, S., Hosciło, A., Wösten, H. et al. (2009) Restoration ecology of lowland tropical peatlands in southeast Asia: current knowledge and future research directions. *Ecosystems*, 12, 888–905.

Page, S.E, Wust, R. and Banks, C. (2010) Past and present carbon accumulation and loss in Southeast Asian peatlands. *PAGES*, 18, 25–26.

Page, S., Rieley, J.O. and Banks, C.J. (2011a) Global and regional importance of the tropical peatland carbon pool. *Global Change Biology*, 17, 798–818.

Page, S.E., Morrison, R., Malins, C., Hooijer, A., Rieley, J.O. and Jauhiainen, J. (2011b) *Review of peat surface greenhouse gas emissions from oil palm plantations in Southeast Asia*. White Paper No. 15. Washington DC: International Committee on Clean Transportation (ICCT).

Päivänen, J. and Hånell, B. (2012) *Peatland Ecology and Forestry: A Sound Approach*. Helsinki: Department of Forest Ecology, University of Helsinki.

Pałczyński, A. (1975) Bagna Jaćwieskie. Pradolina Biebrzy. *Rocznik Nauk. Rolniczych D*, 145, 1–232.

Pałczyński, A. (1985) Succession trends in plant communities of the Biebrza valley. *Polish Ecological Studies*, 11, 5–20.

Palmer, S., Wearing, C., Johnston, K., Holden, J. and Brown, L. (2013) Impact of managed moorland burning on DOC concentrations in soil solutions and stream waters. *Geophysical Research Abstracts*, 15, EGU2013-7326.

Pang, A., Li, C., Wang, X and Hu, J. (2010) Land use/cover change in response to driving forces of Zoige County, China. *Procedia Environmental Sciences*, 2, 1074–1082.

Parish, F. (2002) Overview on peat, biodiversity, climate change and fire. *Proceedings of a Workshop on the Prevention and Control of Fire in Peatlands*, 19–21 March 2002. Kepong, Kuala Lumpur: Forestry Training Unit, pp.11–19.

Parish, F., Sirin, A., Charman, D. *et al.* (eds) (2008) *Assessment on Peatlands, Biodiversity and Climate Change*. Kuala Lumpur and Wageningen, The Netherlands: Global Environment Centre and Wetlands International.

Parish, F., Yiew, C.T. and Yun, C.S. (2012) Status and trends of peat swamp forests in SE Asia. Workshop on Sustainable Management of Peatland Forests in Southeast Asia, 27–28 June 2012, Bogor, Indonesia. www.aseanpeat.net/view_file.cfm?fileid=176 (accessed 12 Feb 2015).

Parker, C., Merger, E., Streck, C. *et al.* (2014) *The land-use sector within the post-2020 climate regime*. TemaNord 2014:520. Copenhagen: Nordic Council of Ministers.

Parry, L.E., Holden, J. and Chapman, P.J. (2014) Restoration of blanket peatlands. *Journal of Environmental Management*, 133, 193–205.

Parviainen, M. and Luoto, M. (2007) Climate envelopes of mire complex types in Fennoscandia. *Geografiska Annaler Series a-Physical Geography*, 89A, 137–151.

Pascual, U. and Muradian, R. (2010) The economics of valuing ecosystem services and biodiversity. In *The Economics of Ecosystems and Biodiversity: Ecological and Economic Foundations*, ed. P. Kumar. London: Earthscan, pp. 183–256.

Patzelt, A., Wild, U. and Pfadenhauer, J. (2001) Restoration of wet fen meadows by topsoil removal: vegetation development and germination biology of fen species. *Restoration Ecology*, 9, 127–136.

Paul, S. and Alewell, C. (2013) *Moorregeneration als Klimaschutzmassnahme: eine Recherche zur neuen Kyoto-Aktivität Wetland Drainage and Rewetting*. Bern: Bundesamt für Umwelt.

Payette, S., Delwaide, A., Caccianiga, M. and Beauchemin, M. (2004) Accelerated thawing of subarctic peatland permafrost over the last 50 years. *Geophysical Research Letters*, 31, L18208.

Pearce, D. (1993) *Economic Values and the Natural World*. London: Earthscan.

Pearce, D. and Nash, C. (1981) *The Social Appraisal of Projects: A Text in Cost–Benefit Analysis*. London: Macmillan.

Pearce-Higgins, J.W. and Grant, M.C. (2006) Relationships between bird abundance and the composition and structure of morrland vegetation. *Bird Study*, 53, 112–125.

Pearce-Higgins, J.W. and Green, R.E. (2014) *Birds and Climate Change. Impacts and Conservation Responses*. Cambridge, UK: Cambridge University Press.

Pearce-Higgins, J.W., Stephen, L., Langston, R.H., Bainbridge, I.P. and Bullman, R. (2009) The distribution of breeding birds around upland wind farms. *Journal of Applied Ecology*, 46, 1323–1331.

Pearce-Higgins, J.W., Dennis, P., Whittingham, M.J. and Yalden, D.W. (2010) Impacts of climate on prey abundance account for fluctuations in a population of a northern wader at the southern edge of its range. *Global Change Biology*, 16, 12–23.

Pearsall, W. (1950) *Mountains and Moorlands*. London: Fontana.

Pearson, R.G. and Dawson, T.P. (2003) Predicting the impacts of climate change on the distribution of species: are bioclimate envelope models useful? *Global Ecology and Biogeography*, 12, 361–371.

Pechony, O. and Shindell, D.T. (2010) Driving forces of global wildfires over the past millennium and the forthcoming century. *Proceedings of the National Academy of Sciences of the United States of America*, 107, 19167–19170.

Pedersen, L, Fischer, A and Aaby, B. (1997) *The Danish Storebaelt since the Ice Age: Man, Sea and Forest*. Copenhagen: A/S Stovebaelt Fixed Link.

Peltoniemi, K., Straková, P., Fritze, H. *et al.* (2012) How water-level drawdown modifies litter decomposing fungal and actinobacterial communities in boreal peatlands. *Soil Biology and Biochemistry*, 51, 20–34.

Peters-Stanley, M. and Gonzalez, G. (2014) *Sharing the stage: state of voluntary carbon markets 2014. Executive summary.* Washington DC: Forest Trends' Ecosystem Marketplace.

Pfadenhauer, J. and Grootjans, A. (1999) Wetland restoration in central Europe: Aims and methods. *Applied Vegetation Science*, 2, 95–106.

Phillipson, J. and Liddon, A. (2010) *Telling stories: Accounting for knowledge exchange.* Rural Economy and Land Use Programme Briefing Series No 10. Newcastle, UK: Newcastle University.

Platteeuw, M. and Kotowski, W. (2006) Floodplain restoration contributes to nature conservation. In *Ecoflood Guidelines: How to Use Floodplains in Flood Risk Prevention*. M.S.A. Blackwell, Maltby, E. and A.L. Gerritsen. Brussels: European Commission, pp. 60–70.

Pleasant, M.M., Gray, S.A., Lepczyk, C. *et al.* (2014) Managing cultural ecosystem services. *Ecosystem Services*, 8, 141–147.

Plunkett, G. (2006) Tephra-linked peat humification records from Irish ombrotrophic bogs question nature of solar forcing at 850 cal. BC. *Journal of Quaternary Science*, 21, 9–16.

Plunkett, G. and Foley, C. (2006) Peatland archaeology in Northern Ireland: an evaluation. *Journal of Wetland Archaeology*, 6, 83–97.

Posa, M.R.C., Wijedasa, L.S. and Corlett, R.T. (2011) Biodiversity and conservation of tropical peat swamp forests. *BioScience*, 61, 49–57.

Poschlod, P., Meindl, C., Sliva, J. *et al.* (2007) Natural revegetation and restoration of drained and cutover raised bogs in southern Germany: a comparative analysis of four long-term monitoring studies. *Global Environmental Research*, 11, 205–216.

Potschin, M.B. and Haines-Young, R.H. (2011) Ecosystem services: Exploring a geographical perspective. *Progress in Physical Geography*, 35, 575–594.

Poulin, M., Rochefort, L. and Desrochers, A. (1999) Conservation of bog plant species assemblages: Assessing the role of natural remnants in mined sites. *Applied Vegetation Science*, 2, 169–180.

Poulin, M., Rochefort, L., Quinty, F. and Lavoie, C. (2005) Spontaneous revegetation of mined peatlands in eastern Canada. *Canadian Journal of Botany*, 83, 539–557.

Poulin, M., Andersen, R. and Rochefort, L. (2012) A new approach for tracking vegetation change after restoration: a case study with peatlands. *Restoration Ecology*, 21, 363–371.

Pouliot, R., Rochefort, L. and Karofeld, E. (2011) Initiation of microtopography in re-vegetated cutover peatlands. *Applied Vegetation Science*, 14, 158–171.

Pouliot, R., Hugron, S. and Rochefort, L. (2014) *Sphagnum* farming: a long-term study on producing peat moss biomass sustainably. *Ecological Engineering*, 74, 135–147.

Poulter, B., Christensen, N.L., Jr. and Halpin, P.N. (2006) Carbon emissions from a temperate peat fire and its relevance to interannual variability of trace atmospheric greenhouse gases. *Journal of Geophysical Research*, 111, D06301.

Powe, N., Garrod, G. and McMahon, P. (2005) Mixing methods within stated preference environmental valuation: choice experiments and post-questionnaire qualitative analysis. *Ecological Economics*, 52, 513–526.

Prager, A., Barthelmes, A. and Joosten, H. (2006) A touch of tropics in temperate mires: on alder carrs and carbon cycles. *Peatlands International*, 2006/2, 26–31.

Prell, C., Hubacek, K., Reed, M.S. *et al.* (2007) If you have a hammer everything looks like a nail: 'traditional' versus participatory model building. *Interdisciplinary Science Reviews*, 32, 1–20.

Price, J. S. (1992) Blanket bog in Newfoundland. Part 2. Hydrological

Price, J. S. (1994) Evapotranspiration from a lakeshore typha marsh on Lake Ontario. *Aquatic Botany*, 48, 261–272.

Price, J.S. (1996) Hydrology and microclimate of a partly restored cutover bog, Québec. *Hydrological Processes*, 10, 1263–1272.

Price, J.S. (1997) Soil moisture, water tension, and water table relationships in a managed cutover bog. *Journal of Hydrology*, 202, 21–32.

Price, J.S. (1998) Methods for restoration of a cutover peatlands, Québec, Canada. In *Proceedings of International Peat Symposium, Peatland Restoration and Reclamation: Techniques and Regulatory Considerations, Duluth, Minnesota*, ed. T.J. Malterer, K. Johnson and J. Steward. Jyväskylä, Finland: International Peat Society, pp. 149–154.

Price, J.S. (2003) The role and character of seasonal peat soil deformation on the hydrology of undisturbed and cutover peatlands. *Water Resources Research*, 39, 1241.

Price, J.S. and Ketcheson, S.J. (2009) Water relations in cutover peatlands. In *Carbon Cycling in Northern Peatlands*, ed. A.J. Baird, L.R. Belyea, X. Comas, A.S. Reeve and L.D. Slater. Washington, DC: American Geophysical Union, pp. 277–287.

Price, J.S. and Maloney, D.A. (1994) Hydrology of a patterned bog-fen complex in south-eastern Labrador, Canada. *Nordic Hydrology*, 25, 313–330.

Price, J.S. and Whitehead, G. (2001) Developing hydrological thresholds for *Sphagnum* recolonization on an abandoned cutover bog. *Wetlands*, 21, 32–42.

Price, J.S. and Whitehead, G.S. (2004) The influence of past and present hydrological conditions on *Sphagnum* recolonization and succession in a block-cut bog, Québec. *Hydrological Processes*, 18, 315–328.

Price, J.S. and Whittington, P.N. (2010) Water flow in *Sphagnum* hummocks: mesocosm measurements and modeling. *Journal of Hydrology*, 381, 333–340.

Price, J.S., Woo, M.K. and Rouse, W.R. (1992) Damming James Bay: II. Impacts on coastal marshes. *Canadian Geographer*, 36, 8–13.

Price, J.S., Rochefort, L. and Quinty, F. (1998) Energy and moisture considerations on cutover peatlands: surface microtopography, mulch cover and *Sphagnum* regeneration. *Ecological Engineering*, 10, 293–312.

Price, J.S., Healthwaite, A.L. and Baird, A.J. (2003) Hydrological processes in abandoned and restored peatlands: an overview of management approaches. *Wetlands Ecology and Management*, 11, 65–83.

Price, J.S., McLaren, R.G. and Rudolph, D.L. (2010) Landscape restoration after oil sands mining: conceptual design and hydrological modelling for fen reconstruction. *International Journal of Mining, Reclamation and Environment*, 24, 109–123.

Putra, E.I., Hayasaka, H., Takahashi, H. and Usup, A. (2008) Recent peat fire activity in the Mega Rice Project Area, Central Kalimantan, Indonesia. *Journal of Disaster Research*, 3, 334–341.

Pyatt, D.G. (1987) Afforestation of blanket peatland: soil effects. *Forestry and British Timber*, March 1987, 15–17.

Pyatt, D.G., John, A.L., Anderson, A.R. and White, I.M.S. (1992) The drying of blanket peatland by 20-year-old conifer plantations at Rumster Forest, Caithness. In *Peatland Ecosystems and Man: An Impact Assessment*, ed. O.M. Bragg, P.D. Hulme, H.A.P. Ingram and R.A. Robertson. Dundee, UK: University of Dundee, pp. 153–158.

Qian, J., Wang, G., Ding, Y. and Liu, S. (2006) The land ecological evolutional patterns in the source areas of the Yangtze and Yellow Rivers in the past 15 years, China. *Environmental Monitoring and Assessment*, 116, 137–156.

Qiu, P., Wu, N., Luo, P., Wang, Z. and Li, M. (2009) Analysis of dynamics and driving factors of wetland landscape in Zoige, Eastern Qinghai-Tibetan Plateau. *Journal of Mountain Science*, 6, 42–55.

Quinton WL and Hayashi M. (2005) The flow and storage of water in the wetland-dominated central Mackenzie river basin: recent advances and future directions. In *Prediction in Ungauged Basins: Approaches for Canada's Cold Regions*, ed. C. Spence, J.W. Pomeroy and A. Pietroniro. Ottawa, Canada: Canadian Water Resources Association, pp. 45–66.

Quinty, F. and Rochefort, L. (2003) *Peatland Restoration Guide*, 2nd edn. Fredericton, Canada: Canadian Sphagnum Peat Moss Association, St. Albert and New Brunswick Department of Natural Resources and Energy.

Rabinowitz, R. and d'Este Hoare, J. (2009) Carbon reduction: a scoping study. *BRE Trust Review* 2009, 70–72.

Raeymaekers, G. (1997) The Habitats Directive: centrepiece of the European Union's nature conservation policy. Its implications for peatland conservation. In *Conserving Peatlands*, ed. L. Parkyn, R. Stoneman and H.A.P. Ingram. Wallingford, UK: CAB International, pp. 357–368.

Raeymaekers, G. (2000) *Conserving mires in the European Union. Actions co-financed by LIFE-Nature*. Ecosystems Ltd. Luxembourg: Office of Official Publications of the European Communities.

Raftery, B. (1996) *Trackway excavations in the Mountdillon Bogs, Co. Longford, 1985-1991*. Transactions of the Irish Archaeological Wetland Unit 3. Dublin: Crannog Publications.

Ramakrishna, S. (2004) *Conservation and Sustainable Use of Peat Swamp Forests by Local Communities in South East Asia*. Selangor, Malaysia Wetland International – Malaysia Office.

Ramchunder, S.J., Brown, L.E. and Holden, J. (2009) Environmental effects of drainage, drain-blocking and prescribed vegetation burning in UK upland peatlands. *Progress in Physical Geography*, 33, 49–79.

Ramchunder, S.J., Brown, L.E. and Holden, J. (2012) Catchment-scale peatland restoration benefits stream ecosystem biodiversity. *Journal of Applied Biology*, 49, 182–191.

Ramchunder, S.J., Brown, L.E. and Holden, J. (2013) Rotational vegetation burning effects on peatland stream ecosystems. *Journal of Applied Ecology*. 50, 636–648.

Ramsar (1971) *Convention of Wetlands of International Importance especially as a Waterfowl Habitat*. Gland, Switzerland: Ramsar Convention Secretariat. Http://www.Ramsar.org (accessed 7 January 2015).

Ramsar (2003) *Guidelines for Global Action on Peatlands*. Gland, Switzerland: Ramsar Bureau.

Ramsar Convention (2008) *The Ramsar Strategic Plan 2009-2015*. Gland, Switzerland: Ramsar Bureau.

Rassi, P., Aapala, K., Suikki, A. et al. (2003) Restoration in protected areas: report by the working group on restoration. *The Finnish Environment*, 618, 1–220 (in Finnish).

Rawes, M. and Hobbs, R. (1979) Management of semi-natural blanket bog in the northern Pennines. *Journal of Ecology*, 67, 789–807.

Reed, M., Evely, A.C., Cundill, G. et al. (2010) What is social learning? *Ecology and Society*, 15, r1.

Reed, M.S. (2008) Stakeholder participation for environmental management: a literature review. *Biological Conservation*, 141, 2417–2431.

Reed, M.S., Arblaster, K., Bullock, C. et al. (2009) Using scenarios to explore UK upland futures. *Futures*, 41, 619–630.

Reed, M.S., Bonn, A., Evans, C. et al. (2013) *Peatland Code Research Project Final Report*. London: DEFRA.

Reed, M.S., Moxey, A., Prager, K. et al. (2014) Improving the link between payments and the provision of ecosystem services in agri-environment schemes. *Ecosystem Services*, 9, 44–53.

Regina, K., Nykänen, H., Maljanen, M., Silvola, J. and Martikainen, P.J. (1998) Emissions of N_2O and NO and net nitrogen mineralization in a boreal forested peatland treated with different nitrogen compounds. *Canadian Journal of Forest Research*, 28, 132–140.

Ren, G. (2000) Decline of the mid- to late Holocene forests in China: climatic change or human impact? *Journal of Quaternary Science*, 15, 273–281.

Rennie, A. (2006) The importance of national parks to nation-building: Support for the National Parks Act (2000) in the Scottish Parliament. *Scottish Geographical Journal*, 122, 223–232.

Renou-Wilson, F., Bolger, T., Bullock, C. et al. (2011) *BOGLAND: Sustainable Management of Peatlands in Ireland*. Dublin: Environmental Protection Agency Ireland.

Retzer, V. (2007) Forage competition between livestock and Mongolian Pika (*Ochotona pallasi*) in Southern Mongolian mountain steppes. *Basic and Applied Ecology*, 8, 147–157.

Rey Benayas, J.M., Newton, A.C., Diaz, A. and Bullock, J.M. (2009) Enhancement of biodiversity and ecosystem services by ecological restoration: a meta-analysis. *Science*, 325, 1121–1124.

Richards, C. (2004) Grouse shooting and its landscape: the management of grouse moors in Britain. *Anthropology Today*, 20, 10–15.

Rijksen, H. D., and Meijaard, E. (1999) *Our Vanishing Relative: The Status of Wild Orang-utans at the Close of the Twentieth Century*. Dordrecht, The Netherlands: Kluwer Academic Publishers.

Rijksen, H.D. and Persoon, G. (1991) Food from Indonesia's swamp forest: ideology or rationality? *Landscape and Urban Planning*, 20, 95–102.

Ringeval, B., Friedlingstein, P., Koven, C. et al. (2011) Climate-CH_4 feedback from wetlands and its interaction with the climate-CO_2 feedback. *Biogeosciences Discussions*, 8, 3203–3251.

Riordan, B., Verbyla, D. and McGuire, A.D. (2006) Shrinking ponds in subarctic Alaska based on 1950–2002 remotely sensed images. *Journal of Geophysical Research*, 111, G04002.

Riutta, T., Laine, J., Aurela, M. et al. (2007) Spatial variation in plant community functions regulates carbon gas dynamics in a boreal fen ecosystem. *Tellus B*, 59, 838–852.

Roach, J., Griffith, B., Verbyla, D. and Jones, J. (2011) Mechanisms influencing changes in lake area in Alaskan boreal forest. *Global Change Biology*, 17, 2567–2583.

Robinson, M. (1990) *Influence on Land Drainage*. Wallingford, UK: Institute of Hydrology.

Robinson, M. (1998) 30 years of forest hydrology changes at Coalburn; water balance and extreme flows. *Hydrology and Earth System Sciences*, 2, 233–238.

Robinson, M. and Armstrong, A. C. (1988) The extent of agricultural field drainage in England and Wales, 1971–1980. *Transactions of the Institute of British Geographers*, 13, 19–28.

Robinson, M., Cognard-Plancq, A.-L., Cosandey, C. et al. (2003) Studies of the impact of forests on peak flows and baseflows: a European perspective. *Forest Ecology and Management*, 186, 85–97.

Rochefort, L. (2000) *Sphagnum*: a keystone genus in habitat restoration. *The Bryologist*, 103, 503–508.

Rochefort, L. and Lode, E. (2006) Restoration of degraded boreal peatlands. In *Boreal Peatland Ecosystems*, ed. R.K. Wieder and D.H. Vitt. Berlin: Springer-Verlag, pp. 381–423.

Rochefort, L., Quinty, F., Campeau, S., Johnson, K.W. and Malterer, T.J. (2003) North American approach to the restoration of *Sphagnum* dominated peatlands. *Wetlands Ecology and Management*, 11, 3–20.

Rodewald-Rudescu, L. (1974) *Das Schilfrohr*. Stuttgart, Germany: Schweizerbart.

Rooney, R., Bayley, S. and Schindler, D. (2012) Oil sands mining and reclamation cause massive loss of peatland and stored carbon. *Proceedings of the National Academy of Sciences of the United States of America*, 109, 4933–4937.

Rosenberger, R. and Stanley, T. (2006) Measurement, generalization, and publication: Sources of error in benefit transfers and their management. *Ecological Economics*, 60, 372–378.

RoTAP (2012) *Review of Transboundary Air Pollution: Acidification, eutrophication, ground level ozone and heavy metals in the UK*. Contract report to the Department for Environment, Food and Rural Affairs. London: Centre for Ecology and Hydrology, UK.

Rotherham, I. (1999) Peat cutters and their landscapes: fundamental change in a fragile environment. *Landscape Archaeology and Ecology*, 4, 28–51.

Rothwell, J.J., Chenery, S.R., Cundy, A.B., Evans, M.G. and Allott, T.E. (2010) Storage and behaviour of As, Pb and Cu in ombrotrophic peat bogs under contrasting water table conditions. *Environmental Science and Technology*, 44, 8497–8502.

Rothwell, R.L., Silins, U. and Hillman, G.R. (1996) The effects of drainage on substrate water content at several forested Alberta peatlands, *Canadian Journal of Forest Research*, 26, 53–62.

Roulet, N., Lafleur, P., Richard, P.J.H. *et al.* (2007) Contemporary carbon balance and late Holocene carbon accumulation in a northern peatland. *Global Change Biology*, 13, 397–411.

Roulet, N.T., Moore, T.R., Bubier, J. and Lafleur, P. (1992) Northern fens: methane flux and climatic change. *Tellus B*, 44, 100–105.

Rouse, W.R., Woo, M.K. and Price, J.S. (1992) Impacts of damming James Bay: I. Climate. *Canadian Geographer*, 36, 2–7.

Roy, V., Bernier, P.Y., Plamondon, A.P. and Ruel, J-C. (1999) Effect of drainage and microtopography in forested wetlands on the microenvironment and growth of planted black spruce seedlings. *Canadian Journal of Forest Research*, 29, 563–574.

Rubec, C. (1994) *Wetland Policy Implementation in Canada. Proceedings of National Workshop*. Ottawa: North American Wetlands Conservation Council.

Rubec, C.D.A. (1996) *Global mire and peatland conservation. Proceedings of an International Workshop*. North American Wetlands Conservation Council (Canada) Report.

Rubec, C.D.A. and Hanson, A.R. (2009) Wetland mitigation and compensation: Canadian experience. *Wetlands Ecology and Management*, 17, 3–14.

Rydin, H. (1993) Mechanisms of interactions among *Sphagnum* species along water-level gradients. *Advances in Bryology*, 5, 153–185.

Rydin, H. and Jeglum, J.K. (2006) *The Biology of Peatlands*. Oxford, UK: Oxford University Press.

Rydin, H. and Jeglum, J.K. (2013) *The Biology of Peatlands*, 2nd edn. Oxford, UK: Oxford University Press.

SAC (2005) *Measuring Public Preferences for the Uplands*. Cumbria, UK: Scottish Agricultural College (SAC), Centre for the Uplands.

Sallantaus, T., Vasander, H. and Laine, J. (1998) Metsätalouden vesistöhaittojen torjuminen ojitetuista soista muodostettujen puskurivyöhykkeiden avulla. (Summary: Prevention of detrimental impacts of forestry operations on water bodies using buffer zones created from drained peatlands). *Suo*, 49, 125–133.

Sanders, G., Jones, K.C., Hamilton, J. and Dorr, H. (1995) PCB and PAH fluxes to a dated UK peat core. *Environmental Pollution*, 89, 17–25.

Sanders, K. (2009) *Bodies in the Bog and the Archaeological Imagination*. Chicago, UK: Chicago University Press.

Sapek, A., Sapek, B., Chrzanowski, S. and Jaszczyński, J. (2007) Mobilization of substances in peat soils and their transfer within the groundwater and into surface water. *Agronomy Research*, 5, 155–163.

Saskatchewan Environment (2005) *Saskatchewan Representative Areas Network. Progress Report*. Regina, Saskatchewan: Saskatchewan Ministry of Environment.

Saskatchewan Watershed Authority (2002) *Your Guide to Saskatchewan Wetland Policy*. Regina, Saskatchewan: SWA.

SBSTA (2013) *Report of the Subsidiary Body for Scientific and Technological Advice on its 39th* session, Warsaw from 11–17 November 2013. FCCC/SBSTA/2013/5. Bonn: UNFCCC. http://unfccc.int/resource/docs/2013/sbsta/eng/05.pdf (accessed 27 November 2015).

SCBD (2014) *Global Biodiversity Outlook 4*. Montreal, Canada: Secretariat of the Convention on Biological Diversity.

Schaefer, K., Lantuit, H., Romanovsky, V. E., Schuur, E. A. G. and Witt, R. (2014) The impact of the permafrost carbon feedback on global climate. *Environmental Research Letters*, 9, 085003.

Schäfer, A. (1999) Schilfrohrkultur auf Niedermoor: Rentabilität des Anbaus und der Ernte von *Phragmites australis*. *Archiv für Naturschutz und Landschaftsforschung*, 38, 193–216.

Schäfer, A. (2004) Umwelt als knappes Gut: Ökonomische Aspekte von Niedermoorrenaturierung und Gewässerschutz. *Archiv für Naturschutz und Landschaftsforschung*, 43, 87–105.

Schäfer, A. (2009) Moore und Euros: die vergessenen Millionen. *Archiv für Forstwesen und Landschaftsökologie*, 43, 156–160.

Schäfer, A. and Joosten, H. (2005) *Erlenaufforstung auf wiedervernässten Niedermooren: ALNUS-Leitfaden*. Greifswald, Germany: DUENE e.V.

Schäfer, J. and Bell, R. (2002) The state and community-based natural resource management: the case of the Moribane Forest Reserve, Mozambique. *Journal of Southern African Studies*, 28, 401–420.

Schaller, G. B. (1998) *Wildlife of the Tibetan Steppe*. Chicago, IL: University of Chicago Press.

Schätzl, R., Schmitt, F., Wild, U. and Hoffmann, H. (2006) Gewässerschutz und Landnutzung durch Rohrkolbenbestände. *WasserWirtschaft*, 11, 24–27.

Schipper, A.M., Zeefat, R., Tanneberger, F. et al. (2007) Vegetation characteristics and eco-hydrological processes in a pristine mire in the Ob River valley (Western Siberia). *Plant Ecology*, 193, 131–145.

Schlotzhauer, S.M. and Price, J.S. (1999) Soil water flow dynamics in a managed cutover peat field, Québec: 1. Field and laboratory investigations. *Water Resources Research*, 35, 3675–3684.

Schmidt, M.H., Lefebvre, G., Poulin, B. and Tscharntke, T. (2005) Reed cutting affects arthropod communities, potentially reducing food for passerine birds. *Biological Conservation*, 121, 157–166.

Schmidt-Vogt, D. (1990) Fire in high altitude forests of the Nepal Himalaya. In *Fire in Ecosystem Dynamics: Mediterranean and Northern Perspectives*, ed. J.G. Goldammer and M.J. Jenkins. The Hague: SPB Academic Publishing, pp. 191–199.

Schmilewski, G. (2008) The role of peat in assuring the quality of growing media. *Mires and Peat*, 3, Art. 2, 1–8.

Scholze, M., Knorr, W., Arnell, N.W. and Prentice, I.C. (2006) A climate-change risk analysis for world ecosystems. *Proceedings of the National Academy of Sciences*, 103, 13116–13120.

Schoomaker, P.K. and Foster, D.R. (1991) Some implications of paleoecology for contemporary ecology. *Botanical Review*, 57, 204–245.

Schot, P.P., Dekker, S.C. and Poot, A. (2004) The dynamic form of rainwater lenses in drained fens. *Journal of Hydrology*, 293, 74–84.

Schothorst C.J. (1977) Subsidence of low moor peat soil in the western Netherlands. *Geoderma*, 17, 265–291.

Schothorst, C.J. (1982) Drainage and behaviour of peat soils. In *Proceedings of the Symposium on Peatlands Below Sea Level*, ed. H. de Bakker and M.W. van den Berg. Wageningen, The Netherlands: Institute of Land Reclamation and Improvement/ ILRI, pp. 130–163.

Schröder, C., Dahms, T., Wichmann, S., Wichtmann, W., and Joosten, H. (2012) Paludikultur – Ein regionales Bioenergiekonzept für Mecklenburg-Vorpommern. *Tagungsband zum 6. Rostocker Bioenergieforum*, ed. M Nelles. Rostock, Germany: Universität Rostock, pp. 69–76.

Schröder, C., Wichtmann, W. and Körner, N. (2013) Paludikultur: Perspektive im Schilf. *Ländlicher Raum*, 03, 16–19.

Schumann, M. and Joosten, H. (2007) *Development, Degradation and Restoration of Peatlands on the Ruoergai Plateau: A First Analysis*. Beijing: Wetlands International China Programme.

Schumann, M. and Joosten, H. (2008a) *Global Peatland Restoration Manual*. Greifswald, Germany: Greifswald University. www.imcg.net/media/download_gallery/books/gprm_01.pdf (accessed 27 February 2014).

Schumann, M. and Joosten, H. (2008b) *Peatland Restoration Assessment: Ruoergai Plateau*. Beijing: Wetlands International China Programme.

Schumann, M., Thevs, N. and Joosten, H. (2008) Extent and degradation of peatlands on the Ruoergai Plateau (Tibet, China) assessed by remote sensing. In *After Wise Use: The Future of Peatlands*, ed. C. Farrell and J. Feehan. Jyväskylä, Finland: International Peat Society, pp. 77–80.

Schwärzel, K., Šimůnek, J., van Genuchten, M. Th. and Wessolek, G. (2006) Measurement modeling of soil-water dynamics evapotranspiration of drained peatland soils. *Journal of Plant Nutrition and Soil Science*, 169, 762–774.

Schweizerische Eidgenossenschaft (2012) Bundesrat will Import und Verwendung von Torf reduzieren (Federal Council of Switzerland wants to reduce import and usage of peat). www.news.admin.ch/message/index.html?lang=deandmsg-id=47174 (accessed 27 Feb 2014).

Secretary of State for Environment, Food and Rural Affairs (2011) *The Natural Choice: Securing the Value of Nature*. Norwich, UK: The Stationery Office (TSO). http://www.officialdocuments.gov.uk/document/cm80/8082/8082.pdf (accessed 27 February 2014).

SEERAD (2008) *The Muirburn Code*. Edinburgh, UK: Scottish Executive Environment and Rural Affairs Department.

Seppälä, M. (1986) The origin of palsas. *Geografiska Annaler A*, 68, 141–147.

SER (2004) *The SER Primer on Ecological Restoration*. Washington DC: Society for Ecological Restoration International, Science and Policy Working Group.

Sernander, R. (1908) On the evidence of postglacial changes of climate furnished by the peat-mosses of northern Europe. *Geologiska Föreningens i Stockholm Förhandlingar*, 30, 467–478.

Setten, G., Stenseke, M. and Moen, J. (2012) Ecosystem services and landscape management: three challenges and one plea. *International Journal of Biodiversity Science, Ecosystem Services and Management*, 8, 305–312.

Shackelford, N., Hobbs, R.J., Burgar, J.M. et al. (2013) Primed for change: developing ecological restoration for the 21st century. *Restoration Ecology*, 21, 297–304.

Shantz, M.A. and Price, J.S. (2006a) Characterization of surface storage and runoff patterns following peatland restoration, Québec, Canada. *Hydrological Processes*, 20, 3799–3814.

Shantz, M. A. and Price, J. S. (2006b). Hydrological changes following restoration of the Bois-des-Bel Peatland, Québec, 1999–2002. *Journal of Hydrology*, 331, 543–553.

Sharitz, R.R. and Gresham, C.A. (1998) Pocosins and Carolina bays. In *Southern Forested Wetlands: Ecology and Management*, ed. M.G. Messina and W.H. Conner. Boca Raton, FL: Lewis Publishers, pp. 343–377.

Shaw, S.C., Wheeler, B.D., Kirby, P., Phillipson, P. and Edmunds, R. (1996) *Literature review of the historical effects of burning and grazing of blanket bog and upland wet heath*. No. 172. English Nature Research Reports. Peterborough, UK: English Nature.

Shen, S. and Chen, Y. (1984) Preliminary research on ecology of the plateau pika at the Dawu area, Guoluo, Qinghai Province. *Acta Theriologica Sinica*, 4, 107–115.

Shepherd, G. (2004) *The Ecosystem Approach. Five Steps to Implementation*.

Ecosystem Management Series. Vernier, Switzerland: Atar Roto Presse SA.

Sheppard, L.J., Leith, I.D., Mizunuma, T. et al. (2011) Dry deposition of ammonia gas drives species change faster than wet deposition of ammonium ions: evidence from a long-term field manipulation. *Global Change Biology*, 17, 3589-2607.

Sheridan, A. (1993) The Rotten Bottom longbow. *PAST*, 14, 6.

Shindell, D.T., Walter, B.P. and Faluvegi, G. (2004) Impacts of climate change on methane emissions from wetlands. *Geophysical Research Letters*, 31, L21202.

Shotbolt, L., Anderson, A.R. and Townend, J. (1998) Changes to blanket bog adjoining forest plots at Bad à Cheo, Rumster Forest, Caithness. *Forestry*, 71, 311-324.

Shotyk, W., Norton, S.A. and Farmer, J.G. (1997) Summary of the workshop on peat bog archives of atmospheric metal deposition. *Water, Air, and Soil Pollution*, 100, 213-219.

Shuttleworth, E.L., Evans, M.G., Hutchinson, S.M. and Rothwell, J.J. (2014) Peatland restoration: controls on sediment productions and reductions in carbon and pollutant export. *Earth Surface Processes and Landforms*, 40, 459-472.

Shvidenko, A., Barber, V., Persson, R. et al. (2005) Forest and Woodland Systems. In *Millenium Ecosystem Assessment. Ecosystems and Human Well-Being: Current State and Trends*, ed. R. Hassan, R. Sholes and N. Ahs. Washington DC: Island Press, pp. 585-621.

Siegel, D.I. and Glaser, P.H. (1987) Groundwater flow in a bog-fen complex, Lost River peatland, northern Minnesota. *Journal of Ecology*, 75, 743-754.

Siegert, F., Ruecker, G., Hinrichs, A. and Hoffmann, A.A. (2001) Increased damage from fires in logged forests during droughts caused by El Niño. *Nature*, 414, 437-440.

Silber, T. (2011) *Conservation and restoration of peatlands in Indonesia: Can the private sector do the job?* MSc thesis, Zurich: Federal Institute of Technology (ETH).

Silvan, N., Regina, K., Kitunen, V., Vasander, H. and Laine, J. (2002) Gaseous nitrogen loss from a restored peatland buffer zone. *Soil Biology and Biochemistry*, 34, 721-728.

Silvan, N., Vasander, H., Karsisto, M. and Laine, J. (2003) Microbial immobilisation of added nitrogen and phosphorus in constructed wetland buffer. *Applied Soil Ecology*, 24, 143-149.

Silvan, N., Vasander, H. and Laine, J. (2004) Vegetation is the main factor in nutrient retention in a constructed wetland buffer. *Plant and Soil*, 258, 179-187.

Silvius, M. (2014) Plantations in Southeast Asia. In *Towards Climate-responsible Peatlands Management*, ed. R. Biancalani and A. Avagyan. Rome: Food and Agiculture Organization of the United Nations (FAO), pp. 53-56.

Silvius, M., Joosten, H. and Opdam, S. (2008) Peatlands and people. In *Assessment on Peatlands, Biodiversity and Climate Change: Main Report*, ed. F. Parish, A. Sirin, D. Charman et al. Kuala Lumpur and Wageningen, The Netherlands: Global Environment Centre and Wetlands International, pp. 47-38.

Silvius, M.J. and Giesen, W. (1996) Towards integrated management of swamp forests: a case study from Sumatra. In *Tropical Lowland Peatlands of Southeast Asia*, ed. E. Maltby, C.P. Immirzi and R.J. Safford. Gland, Switzerland: IUCN, pp. 247-267.

Silvius, M.J., Simons, H.W. and Verheugt, W.J.M. (1984) *Soils, Vegetation, Fauna and Nature Conservation of the Berbak Game Reserve, Sumatra, Indonesia*. RIN Contributions to Research on Management of Natural Resources 1984-3. Arnhem, The Netherlands: Research Institute for Nature Management.

Similä, M., Aapala, K. and Penttinen, J. (2014) *Ecological Restoration in Drained Peatlands: Best Practices from Finland*. Vantaa, Finland: Metsähallitus, Natural Heritage Services, Finnish Environment Institute SYKE.

Simmons, I.G. (1989) Prehistory and planning on the moorlands of England and Wales. *Landscape and Urban Planning*, 17, 251-260.

Simmons, I.G. (2003) *The Moorlands of England and Wales: An Environmental History 8000 BC to AD 2000*. Edinburgh, UK: Edinburgh University Press.

Simmons, I.G and Innes, J.B. (1987) Mid-Holocene adaptations and later Mesolithic forest disturbance in Northern England. *Journal of Archaeological Science*, 14, 385–403.

Simpson, J.R., Cheng, X. and Miyazaki, A. (1994) *China's Livestock and Related Agriculture: Projections to 2025*. Wallingford, UK: CAB International.

Sirin, A. and Laine, J. (2008) Peatlands and greenhouse gases. In *Assessment on Peatlands, Biodiversity and Climate Change*, ed. F. Parish, A. Sirin, D. Charman et al. Kuala Lumpur and Wageningen, The Netherlands: Global Environment Centre and Wetlands International, pp. 118–138.

Sirin A., Köhler, S. and Bishop, K. (1998) Resolving flow pathways in a headwater forested wetland with multiple tracers. *IASH Publications*, No. 248, 337–342.

Sirin, A., T. Minayeva, A. Vozbrannaya, and S. Bartalev. (2011) How to avoid peat fires? *Science in Russia*, 2, 13–21.

Sjörs, H. (1948) Myrvegetation i Bergslagen. (Mire vegetation in Bergslagen, Sweden). *Acta Phytogeographica Suecica*, 21, 1–299.

Sjörs, H. (1950) On the relation between vegetation and electrolytes in North Swedish mire waters. *Oikos*, 2, 241–258.

Sjörs, H. (1990) Divergent successions in mires, a comparative study. *Aquilo, Serie botanica*, 28, 67–77.

Sjörs, H. and Gunnarsson, U. (2002) Calcium and pH in north and central Swedish mire waters. *Journal of Ecology*, 90, 650–657.

Sly, R. (2007) *Fenland Families*. Stroud, UK: The History Press Limited.

Smart, P.J., Wheeler, B.D. and Willis, A.J. (1989) Revegetation of peat excavations in a derelict raised bog. *New Phytologist*, 111, 733–748.

Smith, A.T. and Foggin, J.M. (1999) The plateau pika (*Ochotona curzoniae*) is a keystone species for biodiversity on the Tibetan plateau. *Animal Conservation*, 2, 235–240.

Smith, L.C., MacDonald, G.M., Velichko, A.A. et al. (2004) Siberian peatlands a net carbon sink and global methane source since the Early Holocene. *Science*, 303, 353–356.

Smith, P. (2004) Soils as carbon sinks: the global context. *Soil Use and Management*, 20, 212–218.

Smolders, A.J.P., Lamers, L.P.M., Lucassen, E.C.H.E.T., Van der Velde, G. and Roelofs, J.G.M. (2006) Internal eutrophication: how it works and what to do about it. *Chemistry and Ecology*, 22, 93–111.

SNH (2008) *Public Perceptions of Wild Places and Landscapes in Scotland*. Inverness, UK: Market Research Partners commissioned by Scottish Natural Heritage (SNH).

Soepadmo, E. (1995) Plant diversity of Southeast Asian tropical rain forest and its phytogeographical and economic significance. In *Ecology, Conservation, and Management of Southeast Asian Rainforests*, ed. T. E. Lovejoy and R. B. Primack. New Haven, CT: Yale University Press, pp. 19–40.

Solomeshch, A.I. (2005) The west Siberian lowland. In *The World's Largest Wetlands: Ecology and Conservation*, ed. L.H. Fraser and P. Keddy. Cambridge, UK: Cambridge University Press, pp. 11–62.

Sotherton, N., May, R., Ewald, J., Fletcher, K. and Newborn, D. (2009) Managing uplands for game and sporting interests: an industry perspective. In *Drivers of Change in Upland Environments*, ed. A. Bonn, T. Allott, K. Hubacek, and J. Stewart. London and New York: Routledge, pp. 241–260.

Spahni, R., Joos, F., Stocker, B.D., Steinacher, M. and YU, Z.C. (2012) Transient simulations of the carbon and nitrogen dynamics in northern peatlands: from the Last Glacial Maximum to the 21st century. *Climate of the Past Discussion*, 8, 5633–5685.

Spehn, E.M., Rudmann-Maurer, K., Körner, C. and Maselli, D (2010) *Mountain Biodiversity and Global Change*. Basel, Switzerland: GMBA-DIVERSITAS.

Spikins, P., Conneller, C., Ayestaran, H. and Scaife, B. (2002) GIS based interpolation applied to distinguishing occupation phases of early prehistoric sites. *Journal of Archaeological Science*, 29, 1235–1245.

Statistics Finland (2012) *Greenhouse gas emissions in Finland 1990–2010. National Inventory Report under the UNFCCC and the Kyoto Protocol.* Helsinki: Statistics Finland.

Steiner, G.M. (2005) *Mires from Siberia to Tierra del Fuego.* Stapfia 85. Zugleich Kataloge der Oberösterreichische Landesmuseen. N.S. 35. Linz, Switzerland: Biologiezentrum/Oberösterreichische Landesmuseen.

Stephen, L., England, B., Russell, R. and Malone, K. (2011) *Habitat condition monitoring of the RSPB Forsinard Flows Nature Reserve 2002–2008.* RSPB Scotland Reserves Ecology Report. Edinburgh, UK: RSPB.

Stephenson, T., Holt, A. and Harding, M. (1989) *Forbidden Land: The Struggle for Access to Mountain and Moorland.* Manchester, UK: Manchester University Press.

Stern, N. (2007) *The Economics of Climate Change: The Stern Review.* Cambridge, UK: Cambridge University Press.

Stevens, M. and Hoag, C. (2006) Broad-leaved cattail (*Typha latifolia* L.). Washington DC: USDA NRCS National Plant Data Center.

Stewart, A. J. and Lance, A. N. (1983) Moor-draining: a review of impacts on land use. *Journal of Environmental Management*, 17, 81–99.

St-Hilaire, F., Wu, J., Roulet, N.T. et al. (2008) McGill Wetland Model: evaluation of a peatland carbon simulator developed for global assessments. *Biogeosciences Discussions*, 5, 1689–1725.

Stocks, B., Fromm, M., Goldammer, J., Carr, R. and Sukhinin, A. (2011) Extreme forest fire activity in Western Russia in 2010: fire danger conditions, fire behavior and smoke transport. *Geophysical Research Abstracts*, 13.

Stocks, B.J., Fosberg, M.A., Lynham, T.J. et al. (1998) Climate change and forest fire potential in Russian and Canadian boreal forests. *Climatic Change*, 38, 1–13.

Strack, M. (2008) *Peatlands and Climate Change.* Jyväskylä, Finland: International Peat Society.

Strack, M. and Waddington, J.M. (2007) Response of peatland carbon dioxide and methane fluxes to a water table drawdown experiment. *Global Biogeochemical Cycles*, 21, GB1007.

Strack, M., Waller, M.F. and Waddington, J. M. (2006) Sedge succession and peatland methane dynamics: a potential feedback to climate change, *Ecosystems*, 9, 278–287.

Strack, M., Tóth, K., Bourbonniere, R. and Waddington, J.M. (2011) Dissolved organic carbon and runoff quality following peatland extraction and restoration. *Ecological Engineering*, 37, 1998–2008.

Straková, P., Anttila, J., Spetz, P. et al. (2010) Litter quality and its response to water level drawdown in boreal peatlands at plant species and community level. *Plant and Soil*, 335, 501–520.

Stroud, D.A., Reed, T.M., Pienkowski, M.W. and Lindsay, R.A. (1988) *Birds, Bogs and Forestry: The Peatlands of Caithness and Sutherland.* Peterborough, UK: English Nature.

Stuebing, R.B., Bezuijen, M.R., Auliya, M. and Vorris, H.K. (2006) The current and historic distribution of *Tomistoma schlegelii* (the false gharial) (Müller, 1838) (Crocodylia, Reptilia). *The Raffles Bulletin of Zoology*, 54, 181–197.

Stunell, J. (2010) *Investigating the impacts of windfarm development on peatlands in England.* NECR032. Peterborough, UK: English Nature.

Succow, M. (1988) *Landschaftsökologische Moorkunde.* Jena, Switzerland: VEB Gustav Fischer Verlag.

Succow, M. and Joosten, H. (eds.) (2001) *Landschaftsökologische Moorkunde,* 2nd edn. Stuttgart, Germany: Schweizerbart.

Succow, M. and Lange, E. (1984) The mire types of the German Democratic

Republic. In *European Mires*, ed. P.D. Moore. London: Academic Press, pp. 149–175.

Suckall, N., Fraser, E.D.G., Cooper, T. and Quinn, C. (2009) Visitor perceptions of rural landscapes: a case study in the Peak District National Park, England. *Journal of Environmental Management*, 90, 1195–1203.

Sundberg, S. (2012) Quick target vegetation recovery after restorative shrub removal and mowing in a calcareous fen. *Restoration Ecology*, 20, 331–338.

Sundh, I., Nilsson, M., Mikela, C., Granberg, G. and Svensson, B.H. (2000) Fluxes of methane and carbon dioxide on peat-mining areas in Sweden. *Ambio*, 29, 499–503.

Suryadiputra, I.N.N., Dohong, A., Waspodo, R.S.B. *et al.* (2005) *A Guide to Blocking of Canals and Ditches in Conjunction with the Community. The Climate Change, Forest and Peatlands in Indonesia Project*. Bogor: Wetlands International – Indonesia Programme and Wildlife Habitat Canada.

Suyanto, Khususiyah, N., Sardi, I., Buana, Y. and van Noordwijk, M. (2009) *Analysis of Local Livelihoods from Past to Present in the Central Kalimantan Ex-Mega Rice Project Area*. Bogor: World Agroforestry Centre.

Sweers, W., Horn, S., Grenzdörffer, G. and Müller, J. (2013) Regulation of reed (*Phragmites australis*) by water buffalo grazing: use in coastal conservation. *Mires and Peat*, 13, Art. 3, 1–10.

Sweers, W., Möhring, T. and Müller, J. (2014) The economics of water buffalo (*Bubalus bubalis*) breeding, rearing and direct marketing. *Archiv für Tierzucht*, 57, 1–11.

Swindles, G.T., Blundell, A., Roe, H. and Hall, V.A. (2010) A 4500-year proxy climate record from peatlands in the North of Ireland: the identification of widespread summer 'drought phases'? *Quaternary Science Reviews*, 29, 1577–1589.

Tacconi, L. (2003) *Fires in Indonesia: causes, costs and policy implications*. Occasional Paper No. 38. Bogor: Center for International Forestry Research.

Takakai, F., Morishita, T., Hashidoko, Y. *et al.* (2006) Effects of agricultural land-use change and forest fire on N_2O emission from tropical peatlands, Central Kalimantan, Indonesia. *Soil Science and Plant Nutrition*, 52, 662–674.

Tallis J.H. (1987) Fire and flood at Holme Moss: erosion processes in an upland blanket mire. *Journal of Ecology*, 75, 1099–1129.

Tallis, J. H. (1997) The Southern Pennine Experience: An Overview of Blanket Mire. In *Blanket Mire Degradation: Causes, Consequences and Challenges*, ed. J.H. Tallis, R. Meade and P.D. Hulme. Peterborough, UK: English Nature, pp. 7–15.

Tallis, J.H. (1998) Growth and degradation of British and Irish blanket mires. *Environmental Review*, 6, 81–122.

Tallis, J.H., Meade, R. and Hulme, P.D. (1997) *Blanket Mire Degradation: Causes, Consequences and Challenges*. Aberdeen, UK: Macaulay Land Use Research Institute.

Tang, R., Clark, J.M., Bond, T. *et al.* (2013) Assessment of potential climate change impacts on peatland dissolved organic carbon release and drinking water treatment from laboratory experiments. *Environmental Pollution*, 173, 270–277.

Tanneberger, F. and Wichtmann, W. (2011) *Carbon Credits from Peatland Rewetting: Climate – Biodiversity – Land Use*. Stuttgart: Schweizerbart.

Tanneberger, F., Bellebaum, J., Helmecke, A. *et al.* (2008) Rapid deterioration of aquatic warbler *Acrocephalus paludicola* habitats at the western margin of its breeding range. *Journal of Ornithology*, 149, 105–115.

Tanneberger, F., Tegetmeyer, C., Dylawerski, M., Flade, M. and Joosten, H. (2009) Commercially cut reed as a new and sustainable habitat for the globally threatened aquatic warbler. *Biodiversity and Conservation*, 18, 1475–1489.

Tanovitskaya, N. (2011) Investigation and drainage of peatlands. In *Carbon Credits from Peatland Rewetting: Climate – Biodiversity – Land Use*, ed. F. Tanneberger and W. Wichtmann. Stuttgart: Schweizerbart, pp. 5–7.

Taylor, C.H. and Pierson, D.C. (1985) The effect of a small wetland on runoff response during spring snowmelt. *Atmosphere-Ocean*, 23, 137–154.

TEEB (2008) *The Economics of Ecosystems and Biodiversity: An Interim Report*. Cambridge UK: European Communities.

TEEB (2010a) *The Economics of Ecosystems and Biodiversity. Mainstreaming the Economics of Nature: A synthesis of the Approach, Conclusions and Recommendations of TEEB*, ed. P. Sukhdev, H. Wittmer, C. Schröter-Schlaack *et al.* Malta: Progress Press.

TEEB (2010b) *The Economics of Ecosystems and Biodiversity: Ecological and economic foundations*. ed. P. Kumar, London, Washington: Earthscan.

Temperton, V.M. (2007) The recent double paradigm shift in restoration ecology. *Restoration Ecology*, 15, 344–347.

Temperton, V.M., Hobbs, R.J., Nuttle, T., Fattorini, M. and Halle, S. (2004) Introduction: why assembly rules are important to the field of restoration ecology. In *Assembly Rules and Restoration Ecology*, ed. V.M. Temperton, R.J. Hobbs, T. Nuttle, M. Fattorini and S. Halle. Washington, DC: Island Press, pp. 1–8.

Tengberg, A., Fredholm, S., Eliasson, I. *et al.* (2012) Cultural ecosystem services provided by landscapes: assessment of heritage values and identity. *Ecosystem Services*, 2, 14–26.

Thelaus, M. (1992) Some characteristics of the mire development in Hongyuan County, Eastern Tibetan Plateau. *Proceedings International Peat Congress Uppsala*, 1, 334–351.

Théroux Rancourt, G., Rochefort, L. and Lapointe, L. (2009) Cloudberry cultivation in cutover peatlands: hydrological and soil physical impacts on the growth of different clones and cultivars. *Mires and Peat*, 5, Art. 6, 1–16.

Thesiger, W. (1964) *The Marsh Arabs*. London: Longman.

Theuerkauf, M., Couwenberg, J., Joosten, H., Kreyer, D. and Tanneberger, F. (eds.) (2006) *New Nature in North-Eastern Germany. A Field Guide*. Greifswald, Germany: Institute of Botany and Landscape Ecology.

Theunissen, E.M., Huisman, D.J., Smit, A. and van der Heijden, F. (2006) *Kijkoperatie in het veen van de neolithische van Nieuw Dordrecht*. Amersfoort. Rapportage Archaeologische Monumentenzorg 130.

Thompson, K., Bakker, J.P. and Bekker, R.M. (1996) *Soil Seed Banks of North-West Europe: Methodology, Density and Longevity*. Cambridge, UK: Cambridge University Press.

Thormann, J and Landgraf, L. (2010) Neue Chancen für Basen- und Kalkzwischenmoore. *Naturschutz und Landschaftspflege in Brandenburg*, 19, 132–145.

Timmermann, T., Margoczi, K., Takacs, G. and Vegelin, K. (2006) Restoration of peat-forming vegetation by rewetting species-poor fen grasslands. *Applied Vegetation Science*, 9, 241–250.

Tipping, R., Ashmore, P., Davies, A.L. *et al.* (2008) Prehistoric *Pinus* woodland dynamics in an upland landscape in northern Scotland: the roles of climate change and human activity. *Vegetation History and Archaeobotany*, 17, 251–267.

Tittensor, R. (2009) *From Peat Bog to Conifer Forest: An Oral History of Whitelee, Its Community and Landscape*. Chichester, UK: Packard Publishing.

Tomassen, H.B.M., Smolders, A.J.P., Limpens, J., Lamers, L.P.M. and Roelofs, J.G.M. (2004) Expansion of invasive species on ombrotrophic bogs: desiccation or high N deposition? *Journal of Ecology*, 41, 139–150.

Trenberth, K.E., Jones, P.D., Ambenje, P. *et al.* (2007) Observations: surface and atmospheric climate change. In *Climate Change 2007: The Physical Science Basis. Contribution of Working Group I to the Fourth Assessment Report of the Intergovernmental Panel on Climate Change*, ed. S. Solomon,

D. Qin, M. Manning *et al.* Cambridge, UK: Cambridge University Press, pp. 235–336.

Trepel, M. (2010) Assessing the cost-effectiveness of the water purification function of wetlands for environmental planning. *Ecological Complexity*, 7, 320–326.

Triisberg, T., Karofeld, E. and Paal, J. (2011) Re-vegetation of block-cut and milled peatlands: an Estonian example. *Mires and Peat*, 8, Art. 5, 1–14.

Trimble, S.W. and Mendel, A.C. (1995) The cow as a geomorphic agent: a critical review. *Geomorphology*, 13, 233–253.

Tsuyuzaki, S., Urano, S. I. and Tsujii, T. (1990) Vegetation of alpine marshland and its neighboring areas, Northern Part of Sichuan Province, China. *Plant Ecology*, 88, 79–86.

Tuck, G., Glendining, M.J., Smith, P., House, J.I. and Wattenbach, M. (2006) The potential distribution of bioenergy crops in Europe under present and future climate. *Biomass and Bioenergy*, 30, 183–197.

Tuittila, E.-S., Vasander, H. and Laine, J. (2000) Impact of rewetting on vegetation of a cutaway peatland. *Applied Vegetation Science*, 3, 205–212.

Tuittila, E.S., Komulainen, V-M., Vasander, H. *et al.* (2000) Methane dynamics of a restored cutaway peatland. *Global Change Biology*, 6, 569–581.

Turetsky, M.R. (2010) Peatlands, carbon, and climate: the role of drought, fire, and changing permafrost in northern feedbacks in climate change. 19th World Congress of Soil Science, Soil Solutions for a Changing World, 1–6 August 2010, Brisbane, Australia. Brisbane, Australia: IUSS (published on DVD).

Turetsky, M.R., Wieder, R.K. and Vitt, D.H. (2002) Boreal peatland C fluxes under varying permafrost regimes. *Soil Biology and Biochemistry*, 34, 907–912.

Turetsky, M.R., Bond-Lamberty, B., Euskirchen, E. *et al.* (2012) The resilience and functional role of moss in boreal and arctic ecosystems. *New Phytologist*, 196, 49–67.

Turner, K., Georgiou, S. and Fisher, B. (2008) *Valuing Ecosystem Services. The Case of Multi-Functional Wetlands*. London: Earthscan.

Turunen, J., Tomppo, E., Tolonen, K. and Reinikainen, A. (2002) Estimating carbon accumulation rates of undrained mires in Finland: application to boreal and subarctic regions. *The Holocene*, 12, 69–80.

UKNEA (2011) *UK National Ecosystem Assessment*. Cambridge, UK: DEFRA.

UNDP (2005) *China Human Development Report*. New York, USA: United Nations Development Programme.

UNDP (2010) *Human Development Report 2010: The Real Wealth of Nations: Pathways to Human Development*. New York, USA: United Nations Development Programme.

UNEP (2007) *Peatlands are Quick and Cost-Effective Measure to Reduce 10% of Greenhouse Emissions*. Nairobi: United Nations Environment Programme. http://www.unep.org/Documents.Multilingual/Default.asp?DocumentID=523&ArticleID=5723&l=en (accessed 15 December 2015).

UNESCO (1972) *Convention Concerning the Protection of the World Cultural and Natural Heritage*. Paris: United Nations Educational, Scientific and Cultural Organisation. http://www.refworld.org/docid/4042287a4.html (accessed 6 January 2015).

United Nations (1979) *Protocol to the 1979 Convention on Long-range Transboundary Air Pollution to Abate Acidification, Eutrophication and Ground-level Ozone*. Geneva: UNECE.

United Nations (1992) *Framework Convention on Biological Diversity*. United Nations, New York.

United Nations (1998) *Kyoto Protocol to the United Nations Framework Convention on Climate Change*. New York, USA: United Nations.

Usup, A., Hashimoto, Y., Takahashi, H. and Hayasaka, H. (2004) Combustion and thermal characteristics of peat fire in tropical peatland in Central Kalimantan, Indonesia. *Tropics*, 14, 1–19.

Väänänen, R., Nieminen, M., Vuollekoski, M. *et al.* (2008) Retention of phosphorus in peatland buffer zones at six forested catchments in southern Finland. *Silva Fennica*, 42, 211–231.

Van Andel, J. and Aronson, J. (eds) (2012) *Restoration Ecology: The New Frontier*, 2nd edn. Oxford, UK: Blackwell Science.

Van Beukering, P., Schaafsma, M., Davies, O. and Oskolokaite, I. (2008) *The economic value of peatland resources within the Central Kalimantan Peatland Project in Indonesia: perceptions of local communities*. IVM Project Report. VU University Amsterdam, The Netherlands.

Van de Noort, R., Chapman, H.P. and Cheetham, J.L. (2001a) In situ preservation as a dynamic process: the example of Sutton Common, UK. *Antiquity*, 75, 94–100.

Van de Noort, R., Fletcher, W., Thomas, G., Carstairs, L. and Patrick, D. (2001b) *Monuments at Risk In England's Wetlands*. Report to English Heritage. Exeter, Univesity of Exeter.

Van den Akker, J.J.H. (2010) Introduction to the special issue on degradation and greenhouse gas emissions of agricultural managed peat soils in Europe. *Geoderma*, 154, 171–172.

Van der Sanden, W. (1996) *Through Nature to Eternity: The Bog Bodies of Northwest Europe*. Amsterdam: Batavian Lion International.

Van der Sanden, W. and Capelle, T. (2001) *Immortal Images. Ancient Anthropomorphic Wood Carvings from Northern and Northwest Europe*. Silkeborg, Denmark: Silkeborg Museum.

Van der Schaaf, S. (1999) *Analysis of the hydrology of raised bogs in the Irish Midlands: a case study of Raheenmore Bog and Clara Bog*. Doctoral thesis. Wageningen, The Netherlands: Wageningen Agricultural University.

Van der Valk, A.G., Bremholm, T.L. and Gordon, E. (1999) The restoration of sedge meadows: seed viability, seed germination requirements, and seedling growth of *Carex* species. *Wetlands*, 19, 756–764.

Van der Wal, R., Bonn, A., Monteith, D. et al. (2011) Mountains moorland and heaths. *The UK National Ecosystem Assessment Technical Report*, Cambridge, UK: UNEP-WCMC, pp.105–160.

Van der Werf, G.R., Dempewolf, J., Trigg, S.N. et al. (2008) Climate regulation of fire emissions and deforestation in equatorial Asia. *Proceedings of the National Academy of Sciences*, 105, 20350–20355.

Van der Werf, G.R., Morton, D.C., DeFries, R.S. et al. (2009) CO_2 emissions from forest loss. *Nature Geoscience*, 2, 737–738.

Van Diggelen, R., Grootjans, A.P. and Burkunk, R. (1994) Assessing restoration perspectives of disturbed brook valleys: the Gorecht area, The Netherlands. *Restoration Ecology*, 2, 87–96.

Van Diggelen, R., Molenaar, W.J. and Kooijman, A.M. (1996) Vegetation succession in a floating mire in relation to management and hydrology. *Journal of Vegetation Science*, 7, 809–820.

Van Duren, I.C., Boeye, D. and Grootjans, A.P. (1997) Nutrient limitations in an extant and drained poor fen: implications for restoration. *Plant Ecology*, 133, 91–100.

Van Eijk, P. and Kumar, R. (2009) *Bio-rights in Theory and Practice: A Financing Mechanism for Linking Poverty Alleviation and Environmental conservation*. Wageningen, The Netherlands: Wetlands International.

Van Eijk, P. and Leenman, P.H. (2004) *Regeneration of Fire Degraded Peatswamp Forest in Berbak National Park and Implementation in Replanting Programmes*. Wageningen, The Netherlands: Alterra.

Van Eijk, P., Leenman, P., Wibisono, I. T. C. and Giesen, W. (2009) Regeneration and restoration of degraded peat swamp forest in Berbak National Park, Jambi, Sumatra, Indonesia. *Malayan Nature Journal*, 61, 223–241.

Van Geel, B. and Mauquoy, D. (2010) Peatland records of solar activity. *PAGES news*, 18, 11–21.

Van Heeringen, R.V. and Theunissen, L. (2007) Archaeological monitoring of (palaeo) wetlands in the Netherlands: from best practice to guidelines. WARP Occasional Paper 18.

Van Seters, T.E. and Price, J.S. (2001) The impact of peat harvesting and natural regeneration on the water balance of an abandoned cutover bog, Québec. *Hydrological Processes*, 15, 233–248.

Van Wirdum, G. (1993) An ecosystem approach to base-rich freshwater wetlands, with special reference to fenland. *Hydrobiologia*, 265, 129–153.

Vander Kloet, S.P., Avery, T.S., Vander Kloet, P.J. and Milton, G.R. (2012) Restoration ecology: aiding and abetting secondary succession on abandoned peat mines in Nova Scotia and New Brunswick, Canada. *Mires and Peat*, 10, Art. 9, 1–20.

Vapo Oy (2006) *Local Fuels: Properties, Classifications and Environmental Impacts*. Jyväskylä, Finland: Vapo.

Vasander, H., Laiho, R. and Laine, J. (1997) Changes in species diversity in peatlands drained for forestry. In *Northern Forested Wetlands: Ecology and Management*, ed. C.C. Trettin, M.F. Jurgensen, D.F. Grigal, M.R. Gale and J.K. Jeglum. Boca Raton, FL: CRC Lewis Publishers, pp. 109–119.

VCS (2013) *VCS Version 3 Requirements Document*, 8 October 2013, v3.4. http://www.v-c-s.org/sites/v-c-s.org/files/AFOLU%20Requirements%2C%20v3.4.pdf.

Verhoeven, J.T.A. and Setter, T.L. (2010) Agricultural use of wetlands: opportunities and limitations. *Annals of Botany*, 105, 155–163.

Verrill, L. and Tipping, R. (2010) A palynological and geoarchaeological investigation into Bronze Age farming at Belderg Beg, Co. Mayo, Ireland. *Journal of Archaeological Science*, 37(6), 1214–1225.

Vikman, A., Sarkkola, S., Koivusalo, H. et al. (2010) Nitrogen retention by peatland buffer areas at six forested catchments in southern and central Finland. *Hydrobiologia*, 641, 171–183.

Vileisis, A. (1999) *Discovering the unknown landscape – A history of America's wetlands*. Washington, DC: Island Press.

Vitt, D.H. (2000) Peatlands: ecosystems dominated by bryophytes. In *Bryophyte Biology*, ed. A.J. Shaw and B. Goffinet. Cambridge, UK: Cambridge University Press, pp. 312–343.

Vitt, D.H. (2006) Functional characteristics and indicators of boreal peatlands. In *Boreal Peatland Ecosystems*, ed. R.K. Wieder and D.H. Vitt. Berlin: Spring-Verlag, pp. 9–24.

Vitt, D. and Bhatti, J. (2012) *Restoration and Reclamation of Boreal Ecosystems*. Cambridge, UK: Cambridge University Press.

Vitt, D. H. and Chee, W. L. (1990) The relationships of vegetation to surface water chemistry and peat chemistry in fens of Alberta, Canada. *Vegetatio*, 89, 87–106.

Vitt, D.H., Halsey, L.A. and Zoltai, S.C. (2000) The changing landscape of Canada's western boreal forest: the current dynamics of permafrost. *Canadian Journal of Forest Research*, 30, 283–287.

Vitt, D.H., Wieder, K., Halsey, L.A. and Turetsky, M. (2003) Response of *Sphagnum fuscum* to nitrogen deposition: A case study of ombrogenous peatlands in Alberta, Canada. *Bryologist*, 106, 235–245.

Vompersky, S.E. and Sirin, A.A. (1997) Hydrology of drained forested wetlands. In *Northern Forested Wetlands: Ecology and Management*, ed. C.C. Trettin, M.F. Jurgensen, D.F. Grigal, M.R. Gale and J.R. Jeglum. Boca Raton, FL: Lewis Publishers/CRC Press, pp. 189–211.

Vompersky, S.E., Sirin, A.A., Sal'nikov, A.A., Tsyganova, O.P. and Valyaeva, N.A. (2011) Estimation of forest cover extent over peatlands and paludified shallow-peat lands in Russia. *Contemporary Problems of Ecology*, 4, 734–741. (Original Russian text: *Lesovedenie*, 2011, No. 5, 3–11).

Vompersky, S.E., Sirin, A.A., Tsyganova, O.P., Valyaeva, N.A. and Maykov, D.A. (2005) Bolota i zabolochennyje zemli Rossii: popytka analiza prostranstvennogo raspredelenija i raznoobrazija (Mires and paludified lands of Russia: attempted analyses of spatial distribution and diversity). *Izvestiâ RAN – Seriâ Geografi*, 5, 39–50 (in Russian).

Von Arnold, K., Hånell, B., Stendahl, J. and Klemedtsson, L. (2004) Greenhouse gas fluxes from drained organic forestland in Sweden. *Scandinavian Journal of Forest Research*, 20, 400–411.

Von Arnold, K., Weslien, P., Nilsson, M., Svensson, B. and Klemedtsson, L. (2005) Fluxes of CO_2, CH_4 and N_2O from drained coniferous forests on organic soils. *Forest Ecology and Management*, 210, 239–254.

Von Post, L. (1926) Einige Aufgaben der regionalen Moorforschung. *Sveriges geologiska undersökning: Serie C, Avhandlingar och uppsatser*, 337, 1–41.

Von Post, L. and Granlund, E. (1926) Södra Sveriges torvtillgangar I. *Sveriges geologiska undersökning: Serie C, Avhandlingar och uppsatser*, 335, 1–127.

Von Unger, M., Emmer, I., Joosten, H. and Couwenberg, J. (2015) Carbon market approaches for peatlands: Setting incentives through markets and enhanced accounting. Berlin: German Emissions Trading Authority (DEHSt) at the Federal Environment Agency.

WACLIMAD (2010) Review of legal framework for lowland management. Indonesia: Water Management for Climate Change Mitigation and Adaptive Development in Lowlands.

WACLIMAD (2012a) Institutional framework for the management of tidal lowlands in Indonesia. Working Paper 6. Indonesia: Water Management for Climate Change Mitigation and Adaptive Development in Lowlands.

WACLIMAD (2012b) Population and economic profile of lowland districts in Sumatra and Kalimantan. Technical Paper 6. Indonesia: Water Management for Climate Change Mitigation and Adaptive Development in Lowlands.

WACLIMAD (2012c) Public revenues, expenditure and fiscal policies for peat land use in lowland districts. Thematic Paper 8. Indonesia: Water Management for Climate Change Mitigation and Adaptive Development in Lowlands.

Waddington, J.M. and Day, S.M. (2007) Methane emissions from a peatland following restoration. *Journal of Geophysical Research*, 112, G03018.

Waddington, J.M. and Price, J.S. (2000) Effect of peatland drainage, harvesting, and restoration on atmospheric water and carbon exchange. *Physical Geography*, 21, 443–451.

Waddington, J.M., Warner, K.D. and Kennedy, G.W. (2002) Cutover peatlands: a persistent source of atmospheric CO_2. *Global Biogeochemical Cycles*, 16, 2.1–2.7.

Waddington, J.M., Rochefort, L. and Campeau, S. (2003) *Sphagnum* production and decomposition in a restored cutover peatland. *Wetlands Ecology and Management*, 11, 85–95.

Waddington, J.M., Strack, M. and Greenwood, M.J. (2010) Toward restoring the net carbon sink function of degraded peatlands: short-term response in CO_2 exchange to ecosystem-scale restoration. *Journal of Geophysical Research*, 115, G01008.

Wagner, K.I., Gallagher, S.K., Hayes, M., Lawrence, B.A. and Zedler, J.B. (2008) Wetland restoration in the new millennium: do research efforts match opportunities? *Restoration Ecology*, 16, 369–372.

Wahyunto, Ritung, S. and Subagjo, H. (2003) *Peta Luas Sebaran Lahan Gambut dan Kandungan Karbon di Pulau Sumatera* (Maps of Area of Peatland Distribution and Carbon Content in Sumatera, 1990–2002). Bogor: Wetlands International–Indonesia Programme and Wildlife Habitat Canada (WHC).

Wahyunto, Ritung, S. and Subagjo, H. (2004) *Peta Sebaran Lahan Gambut, Luas dan Kandungan Karbon di Kalimantan* (Map of Peatland Distribution Area and Carbon Content in Kalimantan, 2000–2002). Bogor: Wetlands International–Indonesia Programme and Wildlife Habitat Canada (WHC).

Wallage, Z.E., Holden, J. and McDonald, A.T. (2006) Drain blocking: an effective treatment for reducing dissolved organic carbon loss and water discolouration in a drained peatland. *Science of The Total Environment*, 367, 811–821.

Walton, N. (2009) Water buffalo as a conservation tool. *Conservation Land Management*, 7, 5–7.

Wang, G., Wang, Y. and Kubota, J. (2006) Land-cover changes and its impacts on ecological variables in the headwaters area of the Yangtze River, China. *Environmental Monitoring and Assessment*, 120, 361–385.

Wang, H., Hong, Y., Lin, Q. et al. (2010) Response of humification degree to monsoon climate during the Holocene from the Hongyuan peat bog, eastern Tibetan Plateau. *Palaeogeography, Palaeoclimatology, Palaeoecology*, 286, 171–177.

Wang, Y., Wang, X. and Yang, Z. (2010) Water resources variation in Zoige wetland and causes analysis. In *Conference on Environmental Pollution and Public Heath*, Wuhan, China: Scientific Research Publishing, pp. 1392–1396.

Wania, R., Ross, I. and Prentice, I. C. (2009) Integrating peatlands and permafrost into a dynamic global vegetation model: 1. Evaluation and sensitivity of physical land surface processes. *Global Biogeochemical Cycles*, 23.

Warburton, J., Holden, J., and Mills, A.J. (2004) Hydrological controls of surficial mass movements in peat. *Earth-Science Reviews*, 67, 139–156.

Ward, S.E., Bardgett, R.D., McNamara, N.P., Adamson, J.K. and Ostle, N.J. (2007) Long-term consequences of grazing and burning on northern peatland carbon dynamics. *Ecosystems*, 10, 1069–1083.

Warke, P.A., Curran, J.M., Smith, B.J., Gardiner, M. and Foley, C. (2010) Post-excavation deterioration of the Copney Bronze Age stone circle complex: a geomorphological perspective. *Geoarchaeology*, 25, 541–571.

Wassen, M.J. and Joosten, J.H.J. (1996) In search of a hydrological explanation for vegetation changes along a fen gradient in the Biebrza Upper Basin (Poland). *Vegetatio*, 124, 191–209.

Wassen, M.J., van Diggelen, R., Verhoeven, J.T.A. and Wołejko, L. (1996) A comparison of fens in natural and artificial landscapes. *Vegetatio*, 126, 5–26.

Wassen, M.J., Olde Venterink, H., Lapshina, E.D. and Tanneberger, F. (2005) Endangered plants persist under phosphorus limitation. *Nature*, 437, 547–550.

Water Canada (2010) http://watercanada.net/2010/n-b-developing-guidelines-to-improve-wetlands-protection (accessed 12 Feb 2015).

Watson, A. and Miller, G.R. (1976) *Grouse Management*. Fordingbridge, UK: The Game Conservancy.

Wearing, S. and Neil, J. (2009) *Ecotourism: Impacts, Potentials and Possibilities?* Oxford, UK: Butterworth-Heinemann.

Weber, C.A. (1900) Über die Moore, mit besonderer Berücksichtigung der zwischen Unterweser und Unterelbe liegenden. *Jahres-Bericht der Männer vom Morgenstern*, 3, 3–23.

Weber, C.A. (1930). Grenzhorizont und älterer Sphagnumtorf. *Abhandlungen des Naturwissenschaftlichen Vereins zu Bremen*, 28, 57–65.

Weltzin, J.F., Pastor, J., Harth, C. et al. (2000) Response of bog and fen plant communities to warming and water-table manipulations. *Ecology*, 81, 3464–3478.

Weltzin, J.F., Bridgham, S.D., Pastor, J., Chen, J.Q. and Harth, C. (2003) Potential effects of warming and drying on peatland plant community composition. *Global Change Biology*, 9, 141–151.

Wetlands International (2010) *A Quick Scan of Peatlands in Malaysia*. Petaling Jaya, Malaysia: Wetlands International-Malaysia.

Wetzel, R.G. (1992) Gradient-dominated ecosystems: sources and regulatory functions of dissolved organic matter in freshwater ecosystems. *Hydrobiologia*, 229, 181–198.

Wheeler, B.D. and Proctor, M.C.F. (2000) Ecological gradients, subdivisions and terminology of north-west European mires. *Journal of Ecology*, 88, 187–203.

Wheeler, B.D. and Shaw, S.C. (1991) Above-ground crop mass and species richness of the principal types of herbaceous rich-fen vegetation of lowland England and Wales. *Journal of Ecology*, 79, 285–302.

Wheeler, B.D., Shaw, S.C., Fojt, W.J. and Robertson, R.A. (1995) *Restoration of Temperate Wetlands*. Chichester, UK: John Wiley.

Wheeler W.H. (1896) *A History of the Fens of South Lincolnshire* (2nd edition). Boston: Newcomb.

Whisenant, S.G. (1999) *Repairing Damaged Wildlands: A Process Orientated, Landscape-Scale Approach*. Cambridge, UK: Cambridge University Press.

White, P.S. and Walker, J.L. (1997) Approximating nature's variation: Selecting and using reference information in restoration ecology. *Restoration Ecology*, 5, 338–349.

Whitehouse, N.J., Langdon, P.G., Bustin, R. and Galsworthy, S. (2008) Fossil insects and ecosystem dynamics in wetlands: implications for biodiversity and conservation. *Biodiversity and Conservation*, 17, 2055–2078.

Whiting, G.J., Chanton, J.P. (2001) Greenhouse carbon balance of wetlands: methane emission versus carbon sequestration. *Tellus B*, 53, 521–528.

Whittington, D. (1998) Administering contingent valuation surveys in developing countries. *World Development*, 26, 21–30.

Whittington, P. and Price, J.S. (2006) The effects of water table drawdown (as a surrogate for climate change) on the hydrology of a patterned fen peatland near Québec City, Québec. *Hydrological Processes*, 20, 3589–3600.

Whittington, P. and Price, J.S. (2012) Bioherms: The conduits of connection between the regional (bedrock) and surface (peatland) aquifers in the James Bay Lowlands. Diamond mining and the fate of peatlands. *Hydrological Processes*, 26, 1818–1826.

Wibisono, H.T. and Pusparini, W. (2010) Sumatran tiger (*Panthera tigris sumatrae*): a review of conservation status. *Integrative Zoology*, 5, 313–323.

Wibisono, I.T.C., Labueni, S. and Suryadiputra, I.N.N. (2005) *Panduan Rehabilitasi dan Teknik Silvikultur di Lahan Gambut. Proyek Climate Change, Forest and Peatlands in Indonesia*. Bogor: Wetlands International–Indonesia Programme and Wildlife Habitat Canada (WHC).

Wibisono, I., Silber, T., Lubis, I. R. et al. (2011) *Peatlands in Indonesia's National REDD+ Strategy*. Bogor, Indonesia, and Ede, The Netherlands: Wetlands International–Indonesia Programme and Wildlife Habitat Canada (WHC).

Wichmann, S. (2016) Economic aspects of paludiculture on the farm level. In *Paludiculture – Productive use of wet peatlands*, ed. W.Wichtmann, C. Schröder and H. Joosten. Stuttgart, Germany: Schweizerbart, pp. 109–116.

Wichmann, S. and Wichtmann, W. (2009) Bericht zum Forschungs- und Entwicklungsprojekt Energiebiomasse aus Niedermooren (ENIM). Greifswald, Germany: Institut für Botanik und Landschaftsökologie,.

Wichmann, S. and Köbbing, J.F. (2015) Common reed for thatching: A first review of the European market. *Industrial Crops and Products*, 77, 1063–1073.

Wichmann, S., Gaudig, G., Krebs, M. and Joosten, H. (2012) Paludiculture – ecosystem services of Sphagnum farming on rewetted bogs in NW Germany. *Proceedings 14th International Peat Congress* in Stockholm, Sweden.

Wichtmann, W. and Couwenberg, J. (2013) Reed as a renewable resource and other aspects of paludiculture. Foreword. *Mires and Peat*, 13, Art. 0, 1–2.

Wichtmann, W. and Joosten, H. (2007) Paludiculture: peat formation and renewable resources from rewetted peatlands. *IMCG Newsletter*, 2007/3, 24–28.

Wichtmann, W. and Schäfer, A. (2007) Alternative management options for degraded fens: utilization of biomass from rewetted peatlands. In *Wetlands: Monitoring, Modelling and Management*, ed. T. Okruszko, E. Maltby, J. Szatylowics, D. Miroslaw-Swiatek and W. Kotowski. Boca Raton, FL: CRC Press, pp. 273–279.

Wichtmann, W. and Wichmann, S. (2011a) Environmental, social and economic aspects of a sustainable biomass production. *Journal of Sustainable Energy and Environment* Special Issue, 77–83.

Wichtmann, W. and Wichmann, S. (2011b) Paludikultur: Standortgerechte Bewirtschaftung wiedervernässter Moore (Paludiculture: site adapted management of re-wetted peatlands). *Telma Beiheft*, 4, 215–234.

Wichtmann, W., Couwenberg J. and Kowatsch, A. (2009) Standortgerechte Landnutzung auf wiedervernässten Niedermooren - Klimaschutz durch Schilfanbau. *Ökologisches Wirtschaften*, 1, 25–27.

Wichtmann, W., Tanneberger, F., Wichmann, S. and Joosten, H. (2010) Paludiculture is paludifuture. *Peatlands International*, 2010/1, 48–51.

Wichtmann, W., Wichmann, S. and Tanneberger, F. (2010) Paludikultur – Nutzung nasser Moore: Perspektiven der energetischen Verwertung von Niedermoorbiomasse. *Naturschutz und Landschaftspflege in Brandenburg*, 19, 211–218.

Wichtmann, W., Oehmke, C., Bärisch, S. et al. (2014) Combustibility of biomass from wet fens in Belarus and its potential as a substitute for peat in fuel briquettes. *Mires and Peat*, 13, Art. 6, 1–10.

Wichtmann, W., Schröder, C. and Joosten, H. (2016) *Paludiculture – Productive use of wet peatlands*. Stuttgart, Germany: Schweizerbart.

Wieder, R.K. and Vitt, D.H. (2006) *Boreal Peatland Ecosystems*. Berlin: Springer.

Wiegleb, G. and Krawczynski, R. (2010) Biodiversity management by Water Buffalos in restored wetlands. *Waldökologie, Landschaftsforschung und Naturschutz*, 10, 17–22.

Wiener, G., Jianlin, H. and Ruijun, L. (2003) *The Yak*. Bangkok: Food and Agriculture Organization (FAO), Regional Office for Asia and the Pacific.

Wild, U., Kamp, T., Lenz, A., Heinz, S. and Pfadenhauer, J. (2001) Cultivation of *Typha* spp. in constructed wetlands for peatland restoration. *Ecological engineering*, 17, 49–54.

Willems, W. (1998) *The Future of European Archaeology*. Oxbow Lecture Series 3. Oxford, UK: Oxbow.

Williams, D.R. and Stewart, S.I. (1998) Sense of place: an elusive concept that is finding a home in ecosystem management. *Journal of Forestry*, 96, 18–23.

Williams, K., Ewel, K.C., Stumpf, R.P., Putz, F.E. and Workman, T.W. (1999) Sea-level rise and coastal forest retreat on the west coast of Florida, USA. *Ecology*, 80, 2045–2063.

Willis, K.J., Gilson, L., Brnic, T.M. and Figueroa-Rangel, B.L. (2005) Providing base-lines for biodiversity measurements. *Trends in Ecology and Evolution*, 20, 107–108.

Wilson, L., Wilson, J., Holden, J. et al. (2010) Recovery of water tables in Welsh blanket bog after drain blocking: discharge rates, time scales and the influence of local conditions. *Journal of Hydrology*, 391, 377–386.

Wilson, L., Wilson, J., Holden, J. et al. (2011) Ditch blocking, water chemistry and organic carbon flux: evidence that blanket bog restoration reduces erosion and fluvial carbon loss. *Science of the Total Environment*, 409, 2010–2018.

Wilson, M.C. and Smith, A.T. (2015) The pika and the watershed: the impact of small mammal poisoning on the ecohydrology of the Qinghai-Tibetan Plateau. *Ambio*, 44, 16–22.

Wind-Mulder, H.L., Rochefort, L. and Vitt, D.H. (1996) Water and peat chemistry comparisons of natural and post-harvested peatlands across Canada and their relevance to peatland restoration. *Ecological Engineering*, 7, 161–181.

Winkler, D. (2000) Patterns of forest distribution and the impact of fire and pastoralism in the forest region of the Tibetan Plateau. *Marburger Geographische Schriften*, 135, 201–227.

Wołejko, L., Aggenbach, C., van Diggelen, R. and Grootjans, A.P. (1994) Vegetation and hydrology in a spring mire complex in western Pomerania, Poland. *Proceedings Royal Netherlands Academy of Science*, 97, 219–245.

Woodland, W.A., Charman, D.J. and Sims, P.C. (1998) Quantitative estimates of water tables and soil moisture in Holocene peatlands from testate amoebae. *The Holocene* 8, 261–273.

World Bank (2014) *State and Trends of Carbon Pricing 2014*. Washington DC: World Bank.

Worrall, F. and Evans, M. (2009) Carbon budgets in upland peatlands. *Drivers of Environmental Change in Uplands*, ed. A. Bonn, T. Allott, K. Hubacek and J. Stewart. London and New York: Routledge, pp. 59–90.

Worrall, F., Armstrong, A. and Holden, J. (2007) Short-term impact of peat drain-blocking on water colour, dissolved organic carbon concentration, and water table depth. *Journal of Hydrology*, 337, 315–325.

Worrall, F., Evans, M., Bonn, A. *et al.* (2009) Can carbon offsetting pay for ecological restoration in uplands? *Science of the Total Environment*, 408, 26–36.

Worrall, F., Bell, M.J. and Bhogal, A. (2010) Assessing the probability of carbon and greenhouse gas benefit from the management of peat soils. *Science of the Total Environment*, 408, 2657–2666.

Worrall, F., Holden, J., Evans, C. *et al.* (2010) *Peatlands and Climate Change*. Edinburgh, UK: IUCN UK Peatland Programme.

Worrall, F., Chapman, P., Holden, J. *et al.* (2011a) A review of current evidence on carbon fluxes and greenhouse gas emissions from UK peatlands, No 442. JNCC Report. Peterborough, UK: IUCN.

Worrall, F., Rowson, J.G., Evans, M.G. *et al.* (2011b) Carbon fluxes from eroding peatlands – the carbon benefit of re-vegetation following wildfire. *Earth Surface Process and Landforms*, 36, 1487–1498.

Wösten, J.H.M., van den Berg, J, van Eijk, P. *et al.* (2006) Interrelationships between hydrology and ecology in fire degraded tropical peat swamp forests. *Water Resources Development* 22: 157–174.

Wu, N. (1997) Indigenous knowledge and sustainable approaches for the maintenance of biodiversity in nomadic society: experience from Eastern Tibetan Plateau. *Die Erde*, 128, 67–80.

Wu, N. (2000) Vegetation pattern in Western Sichuan, China and humankinds impact on its dynamics. *Marburger Geographische Schriften*, 135, 188–200.

Wunder, S. (2005) Payments for environmental services: some nuts and bolts. Occasional Paper No. 42. Bogor: CIFOR.

Wyss, P. (2004) A pilot facility for stormwater retention and cattail production in Geuensee, Switzerland. First experiences with harvesting and use of cattail seeds. *EcoEng Newsletter*, 9.

Xiang, S.A., Guo, R.Q., Wu, N. and Sun, S.C. (2009) Current status and future prospects of Zoige Marsh in Eastern Qinghai-Tibet Plateau. *Ecological Engineering*, 35, 553–562.

Yallop, A.R., Thacker, J.I., Thomas, G. *et al.* (2006) The extent and intensity of management burning in the English uplands. *Journal of Applied Ecology*, 43, 1138–1148.

Yallop, A.R., Clutterbuck, B. and Thacker, J. I. (2010) Increases in humic dissolved carbon export from upland peat catchments: the role of temparature, declining sulfur deposition and changes in land management. *Climate Research*, 45, 43–56.

Yan, G., Wang, F.B., Shi, G.R. and Li, S.F. (1999) Palynological and stable isotopic study of palaeo-environmental changes on the Northeastern Tibetan plateau in the last 30,000 years. *Palaeogeography,*

Palaeoclimatology, Palaeoecology, 153, 147–159.

Yan, Z. and Wu, N. (2005) Rangeland privatization and its impacts on the Zoige Wetlands on the Eastern Tibetan Plateau. *Journal of Mountain Science*, 2, 105–115.

Yang, H., Rose, N.L., and Battarbee, R.W. (2001) The dating of recent catchment peats using spheroidal carbonaceous particle (SCP) concentration profiles with particular reference to Lochnagar, Scotland. *The Holocene*, 11, 593–597.

Yang, X., Rost, K.T., Lehmkuhl, F., Zhenda, Z. and Dodson, J. (2004) The evolution of dry lands in northern China and in the Republic of Mongolia since the Last Glacial Maximum. *Quaternary International*, 118–119, 69–85.

Yang, Y. (2000) Mire conservation in China – the latest research progress and current viewpoints. *Millennium Wetland Event: Programme with Abstracts*, ed. A. Crowe, A.S. Campeau and C. Rubec. Québec, Canada: Millenium Wetland Event, pp. 219.

Yeloff, D., Charman, D., van Geel, B. and Mauquoy, D. (2007) Reconstruction of hydrology, vegetation and past climate change in bogs using fungal microfossils. *Review of Palaeobotany and Palynology*, 146, 102–145.

Yeloff, D.E., Labadz, J.C., Hunt, C.O., Higgitt, D.L. and Foster, I.D.L. (2005) Blanket peat erosion and sediment yield in an upland reservoir catchment in the southern pennines, UK. *Earth Surface Processes and Landforms*, 30, 717–733.

Yu, Z., Beilman, D.W. and Jones, M.C. (2009) Sensitivity of northern peatland carbon dynamics to Holocene climate change. In *Carbon Cycling in Northern Peatlands*, ed. A.J. Baird, L.R. Belyea, X. Comas, A.S. Reeve and L.D. Slater. Washington, DC: American Geophysical Union, pp. 55–69.

Yu, Z., Beilman, D.W., Frolking, S. *et al.* (2011) Peatlands and their role in the global carbon cycle. *EOS*, 92, 97–108.

Yu, Z., Loisel, J., Brosseau, D.P., Beilman, D.W. and Hunt, S.J. (2010) Global peatland dynamics since the Last Glacial Maximum. *Geophysical Research Letters*, 37, L13402.

Yu, Z., Loisel, J., Turetsky, M.R. *et al.* (2013) Evidence for elevated emissions from high-latitude wetlands contributing to high atmospheric CH_4 concentration in the early Holocene. *Global Biogeochemical Cycles*, 27, 131–140.

Yu, Z.C. (2012) Northern peatland carbon stocks and dynamics: a review. *Biogeosciences*, 9, 4071–4085.

Yule, C.M. (2010) Loss of biodiversity and ecosystem functioning in Indo-Malayan peatswamp forests. *Biodiversity and Conservation*, 19, 393–409.

Zaccone, C., Coccosa, C., Cheburkin, A.K, Shotyk, W. and Miano, T.M. (2007) Highly organic soils as 'witnesses' of anthropogenic Pb, Cu, Zn, and ^{137}Cs inputs during centuries. *Water Air and Soil Pollution*, 186, 263–271.

Zafariou, O.C., Joussot-Dubien, J., Zepp, R.G. and Zika, R.G. (1984) Photochemistry of natural waters. *Environmental Science and Technology*, 18, 358–371.

Zak, D., Wagner, C., Payer, B., Augustin, J. and Gelbrecht, J. (2010) Phosphorus mobilization in rewetted fens: the effect of altered peat properties and implications for their restoration. *Ecological Applications*, 20, 1336–49.

Zeitz, J. and Velty, S. (2002) Soil properties of drained and rewetted fen soils. *Journal of Plant Nutrition and Soil Science*, 165, 618–626.

Zhang, M., Zha, K., Wang, Q. and Gu, H. (2010) Qualitative evaluation on filling operations for drains of Ruoergai Arctic-alpine wetland. *Sichuan Forestry Exploration and Design*, 4, 15–19.

Zhang, T., Barry, R.G. and Haeberli, W. (2001) Numerical simulations of the influence of the seasonal snow cover on the occurrence of permafrost at high latitudes. *Norsk Geografisk Tidsskrift – Norwegian Journal of Geography*, 55, 261–266.

Zhang, X., Liu, H. and Xing, Z. (2011) Challenges and solutions for sustainable land use in Ruoergai-the highest altitude peatland in Qinhai-Tibetan Plateau, China. *Energy Procedia*, 5, 1019–1025.

Zhang, X., Liu, H., Baker, C. and Graham, S. (2012) Restoration approaches used for degraded peatlands in Ruoergai (Zoige), Tibetan Plateau, China, for sustainable land management. *Ecological Engineering*, 38, 86–92.

Zhang, Y., Zhang, Z. and Liu, J. (2003) Burrowing rodents as ecosystem engineers: the ecology and management of plateau zokors *Myospalax fontanierii* in alpine meadow ecosystems on the Tibetan Plateau. *Mammal Review*, 33, 284–294.

Zhilin M.G. (2007) Mesolithic wetland sites in Central Russia. In *Wetland Archaeology and Environments. Regional Issues, Global Perspectives*, ed. M. Lillie and S. Ellis. Oxford, UK: Oxbow, pp. 65–78.

Zhong, H., Zhou, Q. and Sun, C. (1985) The basic characteristics of the rodent pests on the pasture in Inner Mongolia and the ecological strategies of controlling. *Acta Theriologica Sinica*, 5, 241–249.

Zhou, W., Yu, S.-Y., Burr, G.S. *et al.* (2010) Postglacial changes in the Asian summer monsoon system: a pollen record from the eastern margin of the Tibetan Plateau. *Boreas*, 39, 528–539.

Zoltai, S.C. and Vitt, D.H. (1995) Canadian wetlands: environmental gradients and classification. *Plant Ecology*, 118, 131–137.

Zoltai, S.C., Morrissey, L.A., Livingston, G.P. and De Groot, W.J. (1998) Effects of fires on carbon cycling in North American boreal peatlands. *Environmental Reviews*, 6, 13–24.

Index

aapa mire 29, 232
abandonment 144, 341
absorbent material 72
Acacia 35, 259, 260, 285
Acacia plantations 35, 260
acidification 39, 80, 82, 91, 155, 176, 200, 220
acrotelm 40, 57, 78, 79, 84, 86, 206, 208
acrotelm mire 39, 40
adaptive management 211, 355, 370, 410
aerenchymous plants 67, 74
aerial seeding 91
aerobic conditions 58, 65, 68, 175
aesthetic values 118, 119, 123, 125, 127, 162
afforestation 39, 52, 59, 153, 159, 160, 161, 213, 214, 215, 219, 221, 224, 231, 298, 378, 400
Africa 48
agricultural emissions 306
agriculture 31, 33, 50, 52, 68, 85, 86, 88, 147, 154, 157, 174, 180, 187, 260, 262, 304, 329, 341, 385, 389
agri-environmental schemes 333, 334, 355, 381
agroforestry 283, 284, 336
air pollution 71, 82, 162, 220, 262, 263
Alaska 29, 38, 146
albedo 71, 139
alder *Alnus glutinosa* 174, 329
Amazon Basin 24, 101, 133, 403
anaerobic conditions 65, 98, 174
Andes 377
anoxia 67, 129, 175, 178, 179
aquatic warbler *Acrocephalus paludicola* 56, 188, 349, 354, 377
arable farming 50, 122, 175, 177
archaeology 95, 97, 98, 101, 107, 109, 111, 123, 180
archive value, 95, 101, 104, 105, 109, 110, 113, 123, 340, 406, 416, *see also* palaeo-environmental record
Arctic 48, 132

Argentina 103
art 121, 123
assembly rules 193, 194, 203, 210, 212
Association of Southeast Asian Nations (ASEAN) 306, 384, 385, 386, 388, 389, 399, 413, 414
atmospheric CO_2 64, 131, 135, 137, 141, 262
atmospheric deposition 85, 155, 157, 158, 160, 220
atmospheric pollution 153
Austria 52
bare peat 58, 74, 84, 86, 91, 153, 156, 160, 161, 163, 165, 166, 186, 205, 206
base flow 84, 87, 239, 241, 280
base saturation 172
bedding material 72
Belarus 34, 35, 36, 56, 179, 343, 344, 349, 377, 403
Belgium 176, 214, 215
Berbak National Park, Sumatra, Indonesia 35, 256, 262
Biebrza 39, 177, 188, 349
bioclimatic envelope 130, 131, 132, 138, 139, 143, 148, 158, 410
biodiversity *51*, 2, 9, 42, 43, 44, 45, 46, 47, 48, 49, 50, 51, 53, 54, 55, 57, 58, 59, 60, 61, 62, 77, 122, 124, 144, 160, 164, 172, 173, 175, 179, 180, 188, 191, 201, 202, 213, 215, 216, 226, 233, *236*, 241, 242, 247, 258, 285, 286, 321, 333, 334, 335, 340, 349, 352, 353, 361, 362, 367, 369, 371, 372, 376, 382, 383, 384, 390, 403, 404, 406
biodiversity loss 50, 176, 218, 336, 340
bioenergy 38, 72, 144, 283, 284, 305, 329, 342, 347, 348, 351, 354, 377, 403, 412
biogas 347, 355
biomass 42, 57, 58, 65, 71, 121, 179, 248, 342, 343, 347, 348, 349, 351, 352, 353, 354, 355
biomass carbon stock 70, 291, 301

Bio-rights approach 286
birch *Betula* spp. 195, 200, 225
birds 45, 48, 55, 56, 57, 60, 146, 179, 180, 181, 354
blanket bog 38, 40, 78, 79, 80, 84, 85, 86, 87, 89, 91, 93, 105, 106, 133, 139, 140, 153, 154, 155, 156, 158, 159, 162, 163, 166, 168, 221, 232, 330, 372, 382, 384, 400, 406
bog 40, 56, 59, 60, 77, 78, 79, 80, 103, 106, 132, 139, 197, 201, 203, 205, 208, 214, 222, 224, 232, 344, 352
bog bodies 99, 117
bog snorkelling 125
boreal zone 42, 63, 70, 131, 132, 138, 144, 195, 214, 226, 228, 343, 406
Borneo 35, 36, 73, 132, 253, 255, 258, 263, 264, 376
Bourtanger Moor 110
Brazil 38
Bronze Age 100, 109, 117
Brunei 35, 254, 255, 258, 287, 389, 399

Cameroon 38
Canada 3, 24, 29, 36, 37, 38, 39, 59, 60, 67, 72, 83, 88, 132, 136, 142, 146, 186, 192, 206, 214, 351, 352, 392, 396, 397, 403, 412
capillary flow 87, 88, 89
carbon credits 300, 309, 310, 311, 354
carbon cycle 6, 68, 136, 141, 142, 149, 150, 405, 406, 410
carbon dioxide (CO_2) 64, 69, 80, 141, 145, 147, 148, 155
carbon dioxide (CO_2) emissions *181, 271,* 2, 19, 35, 67, 68, 70, 71, 73, 137, 143, 144, 145, 159, 189, 206, 208, 264, 265, 329, 341, 385, 403, 406
carbon loss 65, 67, 70, 71, 72, 73, 85, 138, 139, 143, 144, 149, 158, 159, 200, 206, 218, 219, 231, 254, 265, 328, 348, 407
carbon markets 5, 76, 167, 291, 292, 300, 305, 308, 311, 312, 334, 362, 400, 411, 414
carbon policies 291
carbon sequestration, 40, 64, 65, 66, 71, 73, 129, 133, 135, 137, 140, 146, 149, 155, 158, 159, 161, 162, 166, 167, 173, 175, 179, 206, 210, 214, 218, 219, 228, 229, 264, 265, 286, 298, 328, 333, 353, 362, 398, 406
carbon stock 57, 63, 64, 65, 70, 76, 129, 134, 141, 147, 155, 214, 218, 219, 241, 264, 285, 301, 328, 333, 340, 362, 398, 400, 405, 407
catchment 2, 24, 84, 86, 92

catotelm 65, 70, 78, 79, 83, 208
cattail *Typha* spp. 79, 186, 350
charcoal 104, 105, 144, 236
China 35, 39, 40, 177, 235, 241, 249, 250, 252, 353
climate change 6, 42, 47, 49, 54, 56, 62, 65, 76, 85, 104, 106, 107, 129, 135, 137, 138, 139, 141, 145, 148, 158, 168, 173, 180, 232, 375, 404, 405
climate change adaption 42, 129, 353, 404
climate change effects 62, 131, 230
climate change mitigation 4, 149, 213, 214, 291, 312, 328, 335, 348, 354, 356, 405, 415
climate regulation 76, 131, 134, 138, 146, 155, 177, 213, 214, 216, 218, 241, 254, 261, 264, 265, 285, 321, 362, 371, 402
climate space 132
coastal land loss 42, 400, 403
coastal peatlands 147, 148, 255, 264, 287, 341
commodification 334
Common International Standard for Ecosystem Services (CICES) 9, 10, 114
common reed *Phragmites australis* 57, 174, 187, 329, 348
compaction of peat 50, 87, 178, 188, 237
compensation 335, 336
Congo Basin 24, 403
conservation 43, 47, 48, 95, 105, 110, 149, 156, 283, 286, 307, 320, 337, 355, 361, 362, 365, 367, 404, 414
Convention concerning the Protection of the World Cultural and Natural Heritage 107
Convention on Biological Diversity (CBD) 4, 44, 307, 376, 381, 382, 384, 392, 397, 403, 404, 413
Convention on International Trade in Endangered Species of Wild Fauna and Flora (CITES) 376
Convention on the Conservation of European Wildlife and Natural Habitats (Bern Convention) 7, 107
Convention on the Conservation of Migratory Species of Wild Animals (Bonn Convention) 56, 377
cooling effect 66
cost–benefit analysis 191, 329, 359, 384
cottongrass, 159, *see Eriophorum vaginatum*
cranberry 229, 344
cranberry *Vaccinium oxycoccos* 229, 344
cross-compliance 306
cultural ecosystem services 7, 9, 42, 44, 96, 114, 115, 116, 120, 121, 122, 123, 124,

126, 127, 173, 227, 261, 314, 320, 324, 331, 340, 356, 402
cultural heritage 120, 121, 123, 174, 240
cultural value 43, 111, 122, 232, 416
cutover peatlands 15, 88, 89, 205, 211, 224, 352, 412

dam building 73, 242, 243, 245, *276*, 277, 280, 281
dating 137
decomposition 31, 58, 64, 65, 66, 68, 77, 103, 129, 133, 138, 141, 147, 158, 175, 178, 200, 220, 280
decomposition gradient 130
deforestation 144, 164, 236, 254, 259, 280, 301, 399
degradation 40, 58, 85, 175, 177, 189, 241, 252, 261, 265, 314, 321, 352, 409
degradation of Ruoergai peatlands 235, 238, 239
degradation stages 40
degraded peatland 57, 330, 334, 343, 403
denitrification 80, 174
Denmark 34, 98, 99
desertification 238, 241
desiccation 161, 341
direct payments 306, 328, 334, 347, 413
dispersal 60, 61, 204, 208
dissolved organic carbon (DOC) 67, 68, 80, 82, 143, 144, 145, 155, 158, 159, 161, 162, 165, 220, 331, 383
disturbance 52, 54, 130
drain blocking 56, 57, 88, 91, 94, 143, 163, 165, 209, 210, 228, 229, 274
drainage 31, 33, 35, 39, 42, 50, 52, 58, 60, 67, 68, 69, 70, 72, 81, 82, 83, 84, 85, 86, 87, 88, 119, 122, 143, 144, 147, 153, 157, 159, 175, 177, 180, 183, 187, 196, 197, 214, 217, 218, 219, 226, 231, 238, 261, 265, 274, 301, 339, 341, 347, 352, 355, 357, 378
drinking water 2, 42, 80, 82, 177, 219, 220, 241, 248, 384
drought 46, 144, 149, 158, 180

ecological restoration 7, 53, 55
economic benefits 191, 230, 321, 329
economic value 126, 143, 213, 241, 263, 315, 321, 328, 359, 384, 385, 408
ecosystem function 51, 55, 58, 61, 94, 130, 168, 175, 194, 210, 239, 264, 367, 406, 407
ecosystem service approach 359, 370, 372
ecosystem services *182*, 2, 8, 9, 13, 39, 40, 43, 44, 51, 57, 61, 62, 76, 94, 112, 115, 127, 129, 130, 131, 135, 143, 148, 159, 173, 180, 197, 254, 286, 310, 315, 320, 343, 352, 356, 362, 363, 365, 372, 376, 377, 384, 400, 402, 406, 407, 408, 410, 411, 412, 415
ecotourism 126
education 123, 124, 230, 231
El Niño 144, 254, 255, 259, 262, 263, 287
emission factors *69*, 74
emission reduction 75, 291, 306, 309, 311, 348
emission trading, 312, 333, *see also* carbon markets
energy crops, 347, 348, *see also* bioenergy
England 59, 72, 97, 99, 100, 105, 106, 107, 109, 110, 119, 121, 124, 126, 157, 158, 160, 161, 163, 164, 165, 167, 183, 380
environmentally harmful subsidies 328, 329, 334
ericaceous shrubs 208
Eriophorum vaginatum 159, 160, 166, 209, 222, 225
Estonia 101
ethical considerations 337
EU Biodiversity Strategy to 2020 305, 328, 404
EU Common Agricultural Policy (CAP) 4, 306, 378, 413
EU Directive on Bioenergy 305
EU Emissions Trading Scheme 382
EU Habitats Directive 7, 37, 107, 156, 305, 362, 380, 381, 400
EU LIFE programme 5, 56, 215, 305–306, 333, 372
EU LULUCF Accounting Decision 292, 301, 304, 312
EU Water Framework Directive (WFD) 4, 157, 383, 384
European Union 177, 305, 347, 378, 397
eutrophication 80, 91, 155, 176, 179, 183, 187, 350
evaporation 58, 88, 92
evapotranspiration 77, 79, 87, 88, 132, 146, 188, 220

feedback loop 149, 370
fen 32, 46, 77, 78, 79, 80, 83, 84, 132, 170, 171, 173, 175, 183, 188, 189, 191, 197, 203, 204, 222, 229, 340, 348, 349, 350
fen degradation 174, 175, 176
fen meadow 55, 171, 173, 180, 183, 340
fen restoration 170, 177, 189, 203
fencing 247
fertilisation 59, 70, 176, 178, 204, 210, 220, 277
filling-in of drainage ditches 187

Finland 33, 34, 35, 36, 214, 215, 218, 221, 222, 226, 230, 403, 414
fire 67, 72, 85, 104, 124, 131, 138, 143, 144, 149, 160, 259, 262, 263, 279, 280, 285, 287, 334, 341, 385, 388, 390, 400, 403
fish ponds 277
fishing 124
floating fen 173
flood control 2, 92, 131, 156, 164, 165, 167, 173, 174, 180, 229, 340, 341, 400
flooding 49, 50, 66, 85, 143, 239, 256, 400, 403
floodplain peatland 48, 60, 177, 181
Flow Country 34
food 343
Food and Agricultural Organization of the United Nations (FAO) 4, 415
forested peatland 70, 230, 261, 304, 390
forestry 33, 68, 70, 85, 86, 149, 159, 174, 217, 224, 254, 261, 406
forestry-drained peatlands 214, 221
France 214, 215
frost heave 89, 200, 209
fuel 35, 159, 173, 175, 412
fuel briquettes/pellets 349
funding 54, 231, 286, 363, 371, 384, 407, 411
future climate change 113, 129

Georgia 38
Germany 33, 97, 98, 110, 214, 215, 299, 310, 328, 329, 341, 347, 348, 349, 352, 353, 354, 403, 405, 412
global peatland area 67
global peatland models 142
global warming potential 66, 74, 265, 329, 408
Gothenburg Protocol 380
grassland 69, 177, 340, 347
grazing 33, 40, 55, 58, 60, 70, 105, 106, 122, 123, 147, 149, 154, 157, 159, 164, 238, 247, 248, 249, 354, 400
Greenhouse gas Emission Site Types (GEST) approach 329
greenhouse gas emissions *302*, 31, 42, 66, 67, 68, 69, 71, 73, 74, 76, 80, 135, 138, 143, 149, 158, 173, 177, 179, 183, 215, 220, 228, 254, 287, 291, 292, 298, 301, 304, 306, 311, 329, 343, 347, 348, 351, 377, 385, 389, 402, 403, 405, 410, 412
groundwater 77, 79, 178, 179
groundwater abstraction 175
groundwater discharge 60, 66, 145, 178
groundwater flow 177
groundwater level 177
grouse 71 *see* red grouse
gully blocking 89, 163, 166, 383

gully erosion 58, 86, 89, 153, 160, 161, 166, *241*, 242
gully re-profiling 163

habitat 221
habitat conditions 45, 46, 47, 57, 61, 62, 214, 334, 362, 402
habitat loss 162, 216, 258, 340, 403
habitat restoration 55, 221
handicrafts 121, 123
hay transfer 122, 181, 182, 184, 186, 204
haze 143, 254, 262, 263, 385
health conditions 42, 143, 149, 180, 181, 230, 263, 334, 335, 385
heather *Calluna vulgaris* 158, 160, 165, 166, 378
heavy metals, 155, 158, *see also* lead
heritage 110, 123, 125, 416
heritage crafts 121, 123
high-altitude mires 39, 235, 238, 242, 252
Holocene 64, 104, 105, 106, 113, 136, 137, 235, 264
horticultural peat 35, 37, 72, 175, 192, 196, 198, 205, 352, 382, 412
Hudson Bay Lowlands 24, 149, 374
human activities 49, 50, 52, 54, 61, 98, 104, 138
human impact 67, 85, 95, 102, 123, 124, 135, 189, 252, 274, 403
hunting 71, 122, 124, 125, 174, 232, 343
hydraulic conductivity 78, 79, 83, 84, 86, 87, 145, 178
hydraulic properties 66, 88, 252
hydro-energy 38, 85, 403
hydrologic conditions 40, 49, 50, 58, 60, 62, 67, 77, 86, 94, 105, 129, 131, 142, 172, 177, 189, 204, 209, 256, 276, 280, 371, 381, 390, 405
hydrological restoration 88, 187, 277, 281, 369, 373
hydrophobic peat 88, 178, 341

Iceland 38, 403
identity 120, 125, 240
incentives 382, 400, 413
indigenous people 120, 146, 258, 281, 282
Indonesia 1, 3, 33, 35, 73, 117, 143, 144, 145, 147, 255, 258, 261, 262, 264, 277, 280, 284, 286, 287, 301, 341, 384, 389, 390, 399, 400, 403, 413
industrial heritage 120
industrial peatlands 195
Industrial Revolution 85, 157
infrastructure development 38, 73, 98, 242
insects 49, 57, 107
inspiration 121, 156
intellectual benefits 123

Intergovernmental Panel on Climate Change (IPCC) 74, 138, 299
Intergovernmental Platform on Biodiversity and Ecosystem Services (IPBES) 9, 315, 415
international policies *379*, 378
intrinsic value 13, 126, 323
inundation 73, 85, 147
investment 377, 401, 415
Iraq 353
Ireland 34, 35, 38, 52, 97, 98, 99, 100, 105, 120, 121, 153, 214, 215, 224, 403, 412
Iron Age 97, 99, 117

Japan 300

Kalimantan 3, 143, 147, 254, 255, 258, 261, 262, 263, 277, 280, 284, 334
knowledge exchange 364, 365, 372, 374, 401, 409, 415
Kyoto Protocol 3, 4, 76, 292, 293, 294, 298, 299, 300, 310, 348, 377, 382, 392, 397, 413

lagg 84, 201
land acquisition 187
land loss, 42, *see also* coastal land loss
land use 68, 81, 109, 138, 176, 196, 254, 261, 298, 299, 375, 403
land-use change 72, 104, 105, 194, 254, 375, 377, 378
land-use planning 381, 390
land use policy 157, 375, 382
Land Use, Land-Use Change and Forestry (LULUCF) 4, 292, 300, 377, 397
landscape connectivity 48, 49
Latvia 34
lead 104, 158
legislation. 107, 378, 380, 413
Liechtenstein 34
livelihood 119, 248, 249, 277, 282, 286, 355, 389, 403
logging 261, 262, 286, 385, 390, 400
long-term monitoring 149, 195, 205, 209, 232, 350, 407

macrofossil analysis 105
macrofossils 103, 105
macropores 83, 86, 160
Malaysia 33, 35, 38, 120, 121, 253, 254, 255, 260, 263, 264, 277, 287, 341, 343, 384, 389, 412
management 55, 56, 62, 82, 104, 117, 119, 123, 127, 130, 144, 176, 192, 231, 252, 335, 356, 358, 360, 374, 388, 405
mangroves 255
market failure 321, 399, 413

market-based instruments, 292, 333, 408, 414, *see also* carbon markets
mass failure 161
medicinal plants 283, 343
medicine 72, 241
Mega Rice Project 259
mesoclimate regulation 173
Mesolithic 100, 109
meso-trophic fens 176
methane (CH_4) 64, 66, 67, 135, 142, 143, 145, 161
methane (CH_4) emission *181*, 65, 66, 67, 68, 69, 70, 71, 73, 74, 135, 136, 141, 142, 145, 147, 159, 173, 179, 181, 184, 229, 262, 264, 406
methanogenesis 67, 74
microclimate 45, 58, 199
microtopography 55, 58, 59, 101
milled peat 59, 89
Millennium Ecosystem Assessment 8, 9, 315
mineral oil 35, 38
minerotrophic 60, 77, 132, 170, 203
mining, 49, 85, 149, *see also* peat extraction
mire 19, 45, 48, 52
mire breathing, 83, *see also* oscillation
mire characteristics 45
mire classification 61, 78
mire margin 52
mire massif 46, 50, 52, 54, 55, 57, 58, 60, 61
mire patterns *342*, 29, 46
mire species 45, 46, 50, 221, 355, 384
mire typology *28*, *30*, 24, 26, 130, 132, 139, 214, 237, 364
mitigation costs 328, 329
monetisation of ecosystem services 126, 320, 323, 337, 408
monitoring 94, 123, 184, 187, 209, 229, 258, 298, 370, 371, 372, 382, 401, 406, 407
monitoring programme 54, 82, 210, 374
MoorFutures® 310, 312
moss establishment 201, 205, 210
mowing 39, 55, 58, 74, 184, 188, 349, 350, 355
mulching 186, 209

Natura 2000, 48, 187, 226, 229, 380, *see also* EU Habitats Directive
natural capital 2, 9, 15, 403, 414
natural peatlands 45, 46, 65, 73, 172, 175, 177, 189, 202, 402, 403
naturally forested peatlands 214, 215, 226, 255, 384
nature conservation 340, 348, 355, 356
Neolithic 97, 98, 100
net primary production *131*,
New Zealand 133, 300

Nigeria 38
nitrogen (N) 79, 85, 105, 155, 158
nitrogen availability 175
nitrogen deposition 71, 176
nitrogen losses 82, 160, 179
nitrogen oxides 73
nitrogen retention 82, 230
nitrous oxide (N_2O) 69, 71, 135, 143, 145
nitrous oxide (N_2O) emissions 65, 68, 69, 70, 71, 73, 230, 264
non-material benefits, 114, *see also* cultural ecosystem services
non-use values 331
North America 34, 64, 78, 80, 83, 104, 119, 206, 209, 343, 406
Northern Ireland 98, 100, 106, 380
Northern peatlands 136, 137, 141, 149
Norway 34, 99, 214, 389
novel ecosystems 411
nurse crop 92, 163, 199, 209, 210
nutrient availability 58, 80, 176, 178, 179, 182, 232
nutrient limitation 175
nutrient retention 82, 183, 198
nutrient-rich peatlands 32, 135, 214
nutrients 79, 80, 174, 355

oceanic mires 139
Oil palm *Elaeis guineensis* 3, 35, 144, 254, 258, 259, 260, 264, 287, 347, 390, 400, 403
oil sands 39, 49, 398
oligo- to mesotrophic fens 176
ombrotrophic peatlands 103, 132, 139, 203, 264
orang-utan *Pongo* spp. 254, 257, 258, 376
organic material 64, 65, 98
organic remains 95
oscillation 87, 237, 240
overgrazing 33, 40, 50, 70, 81, 85, 237, 242, 252
overland flow 85, 87, 159

palaeoclimate 103, 104, 105, 113, 124
palaeo-environmental record 2, 42, 54, 95, 96, 98, 99, 100, 101, 103, 104, 105, 106, 107, 109, 110, 113, 123, 130, 135, 137, 176, 352, 366, 405, 406
palm oil 35, 347, 377, 389, 390
palsa mire 29, 46, 132, 146
paludiculture 57, 76, 149, 282, 284, 285, 304, 306, 328, 334, 340, 342, 343, 345, 348, 353, 354, 355, 356, 390, 411
paludification 26
particulate organic carbon (POC) 82, 160, 161, 162, 165
pastoralism 235, 237, 248, 347
Patagonia 133

payments for ecosystem services 333, 334, 335, 337, 363, 378, 400
peak flow 156, 167, 219, 239, 241
peat 20
peat accumulation 21, 46, 65, 72, 77, 79, 106, 129, 137, 141, 143, 146, 178, 204, 206, 210, 241, 264, 342, 405
peat alternatives 38
peat bunds 88
peat composition 21
peat decomposition 265
peat degradation 168, 187
peat dome 52, 224, 255, 256, 258, 273, 274, 279, 280, 285, 385, 389
peat erosion 40, 58, 68, 70, 72, 82, 91, 94, 106, 130, 138, 139, 143, 158, 159, 160, 161, 166, 178, 241, 243, 247, 334, 371
peat extraction 35, 36, 37, 40, 50, 52, 59, 60, 67, 68, 72, 85, 86, 89, 98, 106, 120, 121, 122, 144, 159, 175, 180, 183, 192, 197, 198, 199, 201, 205, 206, 208, 224, 241, 352, 378, 403
peat fire 1, 2, 67, 254, 263 *see also* fire and wildfires
peat formation 19, 40, 45, 65, 85, 135, 174, 175, 177, 227, 282, 284
peat fuel 35, 37, 85, 263
peat litter 159
peat mineralisation 68, 70, 172, 175, 179
peat oxidation 40, 67, 70, 72, 87, 88, 145, 161, 175, 200, 254, 280, 305, 329, 341, 405, 412
peat plateau mires 29, 132
peat properties 198
peat swamp forest 33, 35, 121, 126, 253, 255, 256, 257, 258, 260, 261, 263, 265, 273, 274, 276, 277, 282, 283, 285, 288, 334, 376, 384
peat swamp forest degradation 253, 254, 257, 260, 261, 262, 282, 286, 377, 385, 399, 412
peat swamp forest restoration 279, 280, 284, 313
peatland archive, 42, 95, 405, 406, *see also* palaeo-environmental record
peatland classification, *133*, 77, 78 *see also* mire typology
peatland conservation 104, 306, 329, 358, 366, 378, 389, 400, 404
peatland degradation *81*, 3, 39, 43, 76, 80, 196, 242, 254, 327, 404, 411, 413
peatland distribution *24*, *136*, 7, 19, 23, 129, 130, 131, 136
peatland fires, 145, 388, *see also* fire, peat fire and wildfires
peatland forestry 214, 341

peatland functions 46, 62, 204, 206, 405
peatland loss 339, 398, 403, 412
peatland regeneration 54, 106
peatland restoration 4, 5, 6, 7, 39, 57, 60, 62, 76, 91, 123, 162, 167, 168, 193, 195, 201, 209, 215, 248, 274, 305, 334, 337, 349, 359, 363, 377, 382, 384, 400, 405, 406, 407, 410, 412, 415
peatland rewetting 299, 304, 307, 308, 309, 311, 312, 404
peatmoss 37 *see Sphagnum*
Pennines *92, 166*, 83, 84, 106
percolation mire 32, 39, 40, 83, 132, 173, 187, 235, 239, 240, 241, 244, 252
permafrost 42, 46, 49, 131, 132, 138, 142, 145, 146, 148
permafrost degradation 146
pH 70, 166, 172, 175
phosphate 175, 179, 220, 228, 350
phosphate fertilisation 209
phosphate limitation 176
phosphate mobilisation 179
phosphate removal 230, 351
physical properties 46, 50, 88, 94, 175, 195, 196
pioneer species 184, 199, 225
plant productivity 141, 147, 175
plantations 3, 254, 258, 259, 260, 264, 265, 280, 283, 284, 287
poetry 122
Poland 34, 39, 56, 98, 101, 177, 188, 349, 354
policy 3, 4, 157, 162, 189, 291, 337, 365, 375, 376, 381, 382, 389, 392, 400, 413, 414, 415
policy drivers 360, 361, 376
policy goals *404*, 382
policy instruments 381, 382, 400, 413
pollen 100, 101, 104, 105, 107
pollution 80, 85, 104, 105, 157, 189, 194, 220, 371, 375, 378
polygon mires 29, 46
Polytrichum strictum 200, 209, 210
pools 59, 201, 202
potassium (K) 175, 176, 178, 179, 220
precipitation 58, 66, 132, 138, 145, 219, 235, 255, 256
primary production 129, 206, 219
pristine peatland 65, 69, 70, 71, 76, 173, 214, 220, 223, 227, 255, 261, 265, 273, 403, 406
productivity 129, 133, 149, 171, 172, 179, 204, 240, 241, 344
propagules 59, 60
provisioning services *345*, 7, 9, 42, 43, 44, 120, 124, 145, 173, 174, 177, 189, 230, 240, 241, 258, 261, 263, 265, 282, 314, 320, 324, 331, 340, 343, 344, 355, 375, 403
public goods 115, 320, 333
pulp wood 3, 33, 35, 259, 260, 264, 390, 403
purple moorgrass *Molinia caerulea* 105, 122, 159, 195, 223

radiative forcing 66, 69, 76, 142
radiocarbon dating 100, 102, 105
raised bog 34, 37, 39, 40, 46, 52, 83, 84, 224, 344
Ramsar Convention 4, 7, 44, 107, 242, 307, 361, 376, 392, 397, 403, 413
rare species 39, 126
reclamation 119
recolonisation 55, 59, 198, 199, 200
recreation 2, 72, 123, 173, 180, 221, 231
recreational shooting 400
red grouse *Lagopus lagopus* 71, 125, 156, 160, 161, 165, 169, 378
Reducing Emissions from Deforestation and forest Degradation (REDD+) 76, 287, 291, 301, 312, 333, 377, 400, 413
reed canary grass *Phalaris arundinacea* 348
reference site 174, 195
reforestation *274, 278*, 276, 277, 279, 282, 283, 285, 298, 336
regeneration of peat swamp forests 284, 287
regional carbon standards, 311, *see also* carbon markets
regional standards 310
regulating ecosystem services 9, 42, 82, 124, 173, 177, 189, 230, 241, 248, 314, 320, 324, 340, 356
rehabilitation 57, 171
reintroduction 59, 62, 163, 186, 187, 197, 201, 204, 205, 209
relaxation 125
relict plant species 47
religious and spiritual values 115, 117, 120
remote sensing 101, 371, 372
remoteness 117
renewable energy, 377, 378, 400, *see also* bioenergy
reservoirs 49
resettlement *252*,
resilience 54, 57, 106, 135, 139, 143, 148, 158, 172, 176, 178, 189, 191, 320, 405, 406, 407
restoration goals 204, 229, 372, 373, 404, 406
restoration measures 55, 110, 187, 204, 208, 222, 265, 359

restoration of hydrology 89, 187, 265, 274, 276, 285
restoration of peatland vegetation 57, 58
restoration programme 157, 405
restoration techniques 163
re-vegetation 59, 60, 73, 88, 89, 92, 162, 163, 164, 165, 166, 167, 183, 186, 204, 205, 223, 231, 330, 350, 352, 383
rewetting *246, 247, 297,* 73, 76, 88, 162, 164, 165, 178, 189, 209, 210, 225, 228, 229, 232, 242, 243, 244, 245, 280, 299, 328, 333, 340, 342, 347, 348, 353, 354, 355, 356, 405, 410
rice cultivation 259
rich fen 176, 185, 186, 187
ritual practices 99, 117
ritual significance 117
roof thatching 122, 174
rotational burning 71, 105, 160, 169
runoff 52, 58, 79, 83, 84, 86, 87, 88, 92, 156, 160, 161, 167, 219, 229, 235, 256, 258, 274, 277
Ruoergai Plateau *236,* 39, 235, 242
Russia 1, 5, 33, 34, 35, 36, 46, 48, 59, 67, 73, 143, 144, 214, 300, 333, 334, 343, 360

salt water intrusion 147, 341
Sarawak 253
Scandinavia 38, 52, 122, 214, 403
scientific challenges 401, 405, 409
scientific value 230
Scotland 34, 38, 48, 52, 55, 84, 99, 118, 119, 120, 154, 159, 160, 161, 225, 378, 380, 403
sea level rise 42, 124, 131, 147, 148, 403
Seamus Heaney 121
Sebangau National Park, Kalimantan, Indonesia 35, 256, 262, 277, 279
sediment retention 80, 89
seed and propagule sources 60
seed bank 60, 89, 182, 184
seed dispersal 60, 186
self-organization 29
self-perpetuation 46
semi-natural 173
sense of place 116, 416
sheep 57, 70, 154, 159
Shorea albida 257, 261
shoreline erosion 147
shrinkage of peat 50, 87
shrub encroachment 173, 188, 340
Siberia 24, 29, 38, 137, 149, 360
site designation 380
Sites of Special Scientific Interest (SSSI) 231, 361, 380
sloping mire 153

smog, 2, 143, 263, *see also* haze
snow cover 146
social capital 121
socio-cultural value 315
soil improver 159
soil respiration 206, 229
soil water storage 280
solitude 156
South East Asia 3, 24, 33, 34, 35, 43, 67, 73, 101, 133, 145, 254, 255, 262, 265, 278, 280, 282, 283, 285, 287, 347, 397, 399, 414
Spain 38
spatial planning 384, 389
Special Areas for Conservation (SAC) 156, 380, 381
Special Protection Areas (SPAs under the Birds Directive) 380
specific yield 78, 88
Sphagnum 37, 55, 81, 89, 107, 148, 156, 158, 159, 161, 176, 198, 199, 200, 204, 205, 206, 208, 210, 225, 229, 231, 352
Sphagnum austinii 105, 156
Sphagnum farming 57, 208, 352, 354
Sphagnum layer transfer method 205
spiritual values, 126, *see also* religious and spiritual values
sports 125
spring fen 178, 187
steppe 48
storage coefficient 145 *see also* specific yield
stormflow 84, 86, 87, 156, 160, 167
sub-fossil remains 101, 107
subarctic peatlands 146
subsidence 31, 52, 86, 87, 94, 143, 144, 145, 147, 149, 175, 280, 281, 287, 341, 400, 403
subsidies 181, 378, 400, 413
success criteria 370, 373, 406
succession 123, 139, 172, 217, 223, 229, 232
sulfate 80, 82, 85, 147, 155, 157, 221, 380
Sumatra 3, 73, 147, 254, 257, 258, 260, 262, 263, 376
Sundaland 255, 257, 263, 264
supporting services 9, 173, 189, 226, 227, 232, 264
surface flow 77
surface flow mire 40, 237, 239, 240, 252
surface water 79
surface water storage 84, 276
sustainable peatland management, 50, 121, 128, 282, 364, 376, 388, *see also* paludiculture
swamp 78
Sweden 33, 34, 35, 36, 214, 219
Switzerland 354, 414

synergies 180

target species 55, 183, 195, 209, 210
temperate zone 42, 43, 137, 214, 340, 342, 357, 403, 406
tephra 103
terrestrialisation 26, 146, 185
testate amoebae 101, 103
Thailand 255, 399
The Economics of Ecosystems and Biodiversity (TEEB) 315
The Netherlands 34, 60, 97, 98, 110, 147, 176, 185, 341, 405, 413
Tibet 153, 403
timber 33, 57, 157, 216, 221, 261, 285, 384, 389, 390
Tollund Man 99,
topography 84, 131, 132, 141, 220, 255
topsoil removal *183*, *184*, 58, 89, 182, 183, 186, 189
tourism 119, 126, 221, 242, 400
trackway 97, 98, 110, 180
tramping 159
transfer of plant material, 186, *see also* hay transfer
tree removal *223*, 164, 187, 225, 229, 231
tropical peatlands 133, 137, 144, 255, 264, 285, 334, 342, 384, 385, 403, 406
tufa deposition 171
turbary 120 *see* peat extraction
Turkey 353
Typha spp. 79, 186, 350

UK Habitat Action Plans 382
UK Peatland Carbon Code 310
UK peatland strategy 169
UK policy 378
Ukraine 34, 333
undisturbed peatland, 195, *see also* pristine peatland
United Kingdom (UK) 33, 56, 57, 71, 80, 82, 83, 85, 91, 98, 106, 126, 145, 153, 154, 155, 157, 159, 214, 215, 219, 310, 354, 360, 365, 372, 378, 381, 384, 400, 405, 412, 414
United Nations Framework Convention on Climate Change (UNFCCC) 4, 44, 76, 291, 292, 293, 294, 299, 302, 377, 413
United States of America (USA) 334, 149, 179, 215, 214
urban development 85

Valletta Treaty 110
valley mires 132, 237
valuation 315, 320, 324, 333, 335, 337, 408

vegetation 39, 49, 50, 52, 67, 87, 129, 140, 201, 248
vegetation change 52, 82, 85, 102, 104, 105, 148, 158, 159, 175, 222, 228
vegetation die-off 147
vegetation loss 143
vegetation management 59, 172, 349
vegetation recovery 89, 164
vegetation removal 72, 187, 197
vegetation restoration 89, 231
Verified Carbon Standard (VCS) 309, 310
volunteering 125

Wales 72, 105, 106, 158
water balance *273*, 45, 52, 87, 88, 129, 149, 405
water buffalo *Bubalus bubalis* 347, 354, 355
water chemistry 66
water colour, 82, 160, 220, 331, *see also* dissolved organic carbon (DOC)
water deficit 85, 280
water deterioration 164
water erosion, 67, 69, 247, *see also* peat erosion
water flow regulation 353
water level 45, *see also* water table
water management 89, 264
water movement 46, 66
water pollution 71
water purification 215, 230, 340
water quality 50, 52, 58, 60, 79, 80, 81, 82, 94, 109, 143, 155, 157, 160, 164, 165, 167, 215, 331, 333, 348, 351, 353, 400
water quantity 94, 160, 215
water regime 39, 40, 52, 58, 66, 78
water regulation 129, 138, 173, 177, 209, 219, 228, 237, 239, 241, 254, 261, 352, 402
water retention 78, 87, 88, 198, 328
water storage 83, 84, 87, 88, 177, 180, 256, 274, 280
water table *224*, *226*, 21, 45, 50, 56, 58, 66, 83, 109, 137, 145, 181, 189, 200, 201, 210, 226, 229, 280, 352, 356
water table drawdown 70, 83, 84, 86, 145, 217, 220
water table fluctuations 39, 66, 83, 155, 178, 341
water treatment 145, 155
water yield 220
waterlogging 64, 98, 101, 109
watershed management 333
weirs 187, 244
Western Pomerania 56
wet agriculture 149 *see* paludiculture
wetland 20, 61, 204

Wetland Drainage and Rewetting 304
Wetlands Restoration and Conservation (WRC) 309
whisky 120
white peat 37, 352
wilderness 117, 118, 119, 156, 242, 416
wildfires 73, 85, 143, 144, 158, 160, 334
wildlife appreciation 126
willingness to pay (WTP) 335, 344
wind erosion 67, 69
wind farms 38, 85, 119, 161, 403, 412